Deirdre Madden and
Mary Ann Halton

BETTER
HOMEMAKING

Gill and Macmillan

Published in Ireland by
Gill and Macmillan Ltd
Goldenbridge
Dublin 8
with associated companies throughout the world
© Deirdre Madden and Mary Ann Halton, 1984
© Artwork, Gill and Macmillan, 1984
0 7171 1354 X
Print origination in Ireland by
Keywrite Limited Dublin

Contents

PART I

1. Nutrition and You   1
2. Meal Planning   23
3. Managing our Money   33
4. Consumer Education   44
5. A Home of Your Own   52
6. Water: A Basic Necessity   60
7. Heating a Home   69
8. Air and Ventilation   80
9. Lighting and Electricity   84
10. Floor Coverings and Their Care   92
11. Furnishing Your Home   102
12. Interior Decorating   118
13. The Reception Rooms   131
14. Bedrooms and Bedsitters   140
15. Bathrooms   150
16. The Kitchen   157
17. Kitchen Utensils   166
18. Appliances and Equipment   174
19. Small Appliances   189
20. Home Laundry   196
21. The Family Wash   201
22. Washing Equipment   209
23. Hygiene in the Home   217
24. Running a Home   221
25. Household Work Routines   225

PART II

26. The World of Fibres and Fabrics   231
27. Simple Tests to Identify Fabrics   246
28. Before You Sew   248
29. Basic Sewing Equipment   254
30. Choosing and Using Paper Patterns   261
31. Pattern Layouts   269
32. Stitches   276
33. Seams   286
34. Fitting and Shaping Garments   291
35. Pressing   301
36. Underlining and Lining   305
37. Interfacing   309
38. Openings   311

39. Facings   314
40. Collars   318
41. Sleeves   324
42. Cuffs   335
43. Fastenings   339
44. Finishing Touches   355
45. Waist Finishes   361
46. Pockets   364
47. Hems   372
48. Belts   376
49. Simple Tailoring   378
50. Repairing Garments   380

1.
Nutrition and You

A good diet is our most basic human need. All living things need food in order to keep alive and to keep their body processes in working order.

The kind of Sunday dinner enjoyed by many west European families (Camera Press)

FOOD IS NECESSARY

1. for growth and to repair worn out body cells;
2. to produce heat and energy;
3. to regulate the health of the body and prevent disease.

A food is any substance, solid or liquid, which performs one or more of these functions. A food which is nutritious such as milk will have several important nutrients present; a less nutritious food may have only one, e.g. sugar contains only *carbohydrate.*

A balanced diet is a way of eating which gives **all the essential nutrients in the correct proportions.** A varied diet containing plenty of raw fruit and vegetables, whole cereals, together with some meat, fish, eggs, milk and/or cheese should provide the correct balance of nutrients.

Food *constituents* can be classified under these headings:

protein   vitamins
carbohydrate   mineral elements
lipids   water

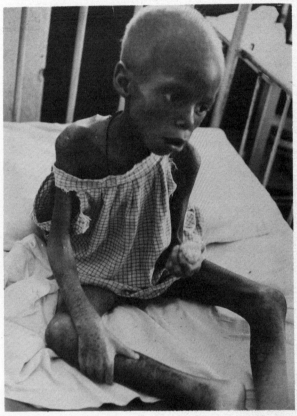

One of many Nigerian children dying of protein starvation (Camera Press)

THE ENERGY VALUE OF FOOD

The dictionary tells us that *energy* is our ability to do work. We need plenty of energy if we have to dig a garden or scrub a floor, less if we sit in an office, typing. It is clear that if we are involved in strenuous activities, our muscles need a good supply of energy.

We also need energy to power the *muscles* inside our bodies — our heart, lungs and digestive organs. This is why we use up energy even when we are asleep. Many of the chemical reactions which take place in the body use up energy, and energy is also needed to keep the body warm.

The energy your body needs comes from the food

you eat. You can compare your body to a car: this burns up petrol to fire the engine and make the car go — your body burns up food to make your muscles work and to keep you warm.

You need *oxygen* in order to burn up the food you eat. This is taken from the air by the lungs when we breathe, and it is carried to every cell in the body by the blood. In each cell, food is burned up, i.e. the *carbon* in the food combines with the oxygen in the blood to produce energy. This special kind of burning up in the cells is called oxidation or respiration. It produces waste in the form of carbon dioxide (which we breathe out) and urea (a residue from protein).

The only **nutrients** which supply energy are proteins, carbohydrates and lipids. Alcohol, which is not a nutrient, also supplies energy.

Running is an energetic activity (John Topham Picture Library)

FUNCTIONS OF ENERGY

Energy is needed by the body
1. **For all activity:** (a) the working of internal organs, e.g. the heart; (b) normal day-to-day living, e.g. walking, cycling, working machinery, doing housework. Extra will be needed for very strenuous activity, e.g. jogging, team games, weight lifting, etc.

2. **To maintain body temperature:** the body functions best at a temperature of 37°C.
3. **For cell and nerve activity** and the manufacture of new cells. Although this uses very little energy when compared with physical activity, it is still essential if the body is to continue functioning normally.

MEASURING ENERGY

Energy can be measured in many ways. Celsius and Fahrenheit are two methods of measuring heat, for example. The heat and energy we get from food is measured in **kilocalories.**

A kilocalorie is the amount of heat needed to raise the temperature of 1 litre (1000 g) water by 1°C.

KILOCALORIES OR KILO JOULES?

Many people use the term *calorie* when referring to the energy value of food. Strictly speaking, the calorie (used in physics) is one thousand times smaller than the kilocalorie we use in nutrition. In order to distinguish between the two, the calorie used in nutrition, which is one thousand times greater, must be written with a capital C; but to avoid confusion it is safer to keep to the more modern term kilocalorie.

An internationally used measurement of energy has now been introduced which is approximately 4.2 times greater than a calorie; this is known as a joule. In nutrition, as with calories, a unit one thousand times greater is used, called a kilojoule.

1 kilocalorie (kc) = 4.184 kilojoules (kj)
(This is usually rounded up to 4.2)

To convert kilocalories to kilojoules, multiply by 4.2, e.g. 20 kilocalories × 4.2 = 84 kilojoules.

THE ENERGY VALUE OF FOOD

The amount of energy we get from food varies quite a lot. If we want to find out how much energy we get from our diet, we need to know the amount of kilocalories in each food we eat.

The energy value of pure protein =
    4 kilocalories per gram.

The energy value of carbohydrate =
    4 kilocalories per gram.

The energy value of fat = 9 kilocalories per gram.

It follows that foods containing a high percentage of fat are a good source of energy, and those containing a large amount of water, e.g. fruit and vegetables, contain relatively few kilocalories.

It is interesting to note that *alcohol,* although not considered to be a nutrient, contains 7 kilocalories per gram.

Of course, few foods contain just one nutrient; most foods are a mixture of two or more. In order to find out the energy value of food, it would be necessary to know the amount of each nutrient present and multiply by the number of kilocalories produced by that nutrient. As this would be a complicated exercise, we usually rely on *food tables* or *calorie charts* to tell us the nutritional value of foods.

Eating too much leads to malnutrition in those who are very fat (John Topham Picture Library)

ENERGY INTAKE AND WEIGHT

If we balance our energy intake, i.e. the food we eat, with the amount of energy we use up in day-to-day living, we will neither gain nor lose weight. If on the other hand we consume more energy foods than the body needs, it will be stored by the body as fat. Obesity (being greatly overweight) is usually caused by eating too many high energy or fattening foods combined with lack of exercise.

Weight loss occurs only when energy intake (food) is less than energy output (activity) see page 30).

BASAL METABOLISM

We have already seen that the amount of energy we use is related to activity. People who are active use up far more energy than those who lead an easy-going life-style. Yet we all need a basic amount of energy just to stay alive — to keep our heart beating, our lungs breathing and to power the millions of chemical reactions which take place in the body. This basic, minimum amount of energy which keeps our body functioning is called the *basal metabolic rate.*

The basal metabolism of individuals varies widely; this is why some people can eat huge amounts of food and not get fat, while others of similar size put on weight very easily, even though they eat less. The reason for this is the subject of much research; it seems that fat-type people burn up food slowly and tend to store it as fat more readily, while thin, wiry types tend to burn it up quickly.

Any activity increases the amount of energy we need.

Activity	*Kilocalories per hour*
sleeping	70
sitting	85
standing	90
writing	115
walking slowly	185
light housework	200
scrubbing floors	315
cycling	400
dancing	450
squash	400
swimming	575
walking upstairs	1000

DAILY ENERGY REQUIREMENT

This varies according to
1. *activity:* as just mentioned;
2. *body size and type:* long, lean figures require more energy foods than short, plump figure types;

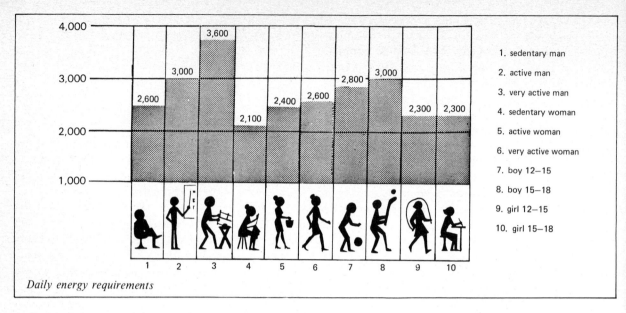

Daily energy requirements

1. sedentary man
2. active man
3. very active man
4. sedentary woman
5. active woman
6. very active woman
7. boy 12–15
8. boy 15–18
9. girl 12–15
10. girl 15–18

3. *age:* while this may relate to size, e.g. a ten-year old will have greater energy requirements than a four-year old, it also covers the fact that during periods of rapid growth, e.g. childhood and puberty, energy requirements are greater per kilo than at any other time. During old age, energy requirements are less;
4. *pregnancy and lactation:* during pregnancy and breastfeeding, the metabolic rate tends to increase. However care must be taken to avoid gaining too much weight during pregnancy;
5. *male/female:* males require a higher kilocalorie intake than females of similar age, size and activity;
6. *climate:* more kilocalories are required in cold countries than in the tropics in order to help maintain body heat.

DAILY KILOCALORIE REQUIREMENT

Age	Kilo calories
children 0-1	800
children 5-7	1800
girls 9-18	2300
boys 12-15	2800
boys 15-18	3000
men (sedentary)	2700
men (active)	3500
men (elderly)	2250
women (sedentary)	2100
women (active)	2500
women (pregnant)	2400
women (breast-feeding)	2700
women (elderly)	2000

CARBOHYDRATES

Carbohydrates are the cheapest and most plentiful nutrients in the world. They are produced by the action of sunlight on plants (called photosynthesis) and are stored mainly in the roots and fruits of plants. Their main function is to produce heat and energy.

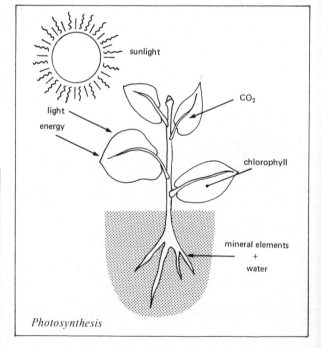

Photosynthesis

ENERGY VALUE

1 gram carbohydrate when oxidised produces 4 kilocalories.

4

ELEMENTAL COMPOSITION

Carbohydrates are composed of carbon, hydrogen and oxygen in the ratio 1:2:1, e.g. glucose = $C_6H_{12}O_6$

CLASSIFICATION

Carbohydrates are classified according to their structure:
1. monosaccharides ⎫
2. disaccharides ⎭ sugars
3. polysaccharides, e.g. starch, cellulose
1. All carbohydrates are based on a single sugar unit called a *monosaccharide,* e.g. glucose, fructose (in fruit).
2. When two single sugar units join together, they form a *disaccharide.* Sucrose is a disaccharide present in sugar cane and sugar beet, and therefore in table sugar which is made from these. Lactose is a disaccharide present in milk, and maltose is present in barley.
3. *Polysaccharides*
These consist of many monosaccharide units linked together in complicated chains.

EXAMPLES

Starch is the best known polysaccharide, consisting of many glucose units linked together. Cereals, bread and potatoes contain starch.

Glycogen (animal starch): this polysaccharide is found in the liver and muscle. It is converted from glucose in order that it can be easily stored as an energy reserve by the body.

Dextrin: is a polysaccharide formed by the action of heat on starchy foods. When starch is subjected to heat, the molecules nearest the surface are converted into simpler substances (dextrins) which brown easily, e.g. the crust on the surface of bread, the browning of toast.

Pectin: a polysaccharide in plentiful supply in many fruits and some vegetables. It consists of an arrangement of very complicated molecules linked together. While it has little nutritional importance, it is essential for the setting of jams.

Cellulose: this is another polysaccharide arranged in complicated linked chains. It forms the structural framework of the plant and is present in all plant foods, generally forming the skin and cell framework of fruit and vegetables and the outer bran layers of cereals. It cannot be digested by humans but is vitally important in our diet as it stimulates the muscles of the intestine to move food quickly through (peristalsis) and, as a result, it helps prevent constipation and other bowel disorders.

SOURCES OF CARBOHYDRATE

1. *sugar:* table sugar and sugars and syrups used in cooking, e.g. treacle; cakes; sweets; biscuits; jam; icecream. More nourishing sources are milk, fruit, honey and certain vegetables such as onions and sweet-corn.
2. *starch:* cereals and cereal products, e.g. wheat, oats, barley, rice, flour, bread, cakes, pasta, breakfast cereals, many vegetables, particularly potatoes and other roots and pulses.
3. *pectin:* just-ripe fruits, commercially-prepared pectin.
4. *cellulose:* fruit, vegetables, cereals especially the outer skins and husks, e.g. bran. It is lacking in processed cereals.

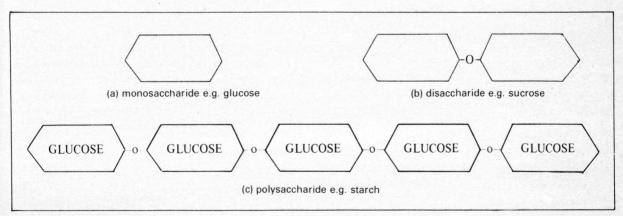

(a) monosaccharide e.g. glucose

(b) disaccharide e.g. sucrose

GLUCOSE —o— GLUCOSE —o— GLUCOSE —o— GLUCOSE —o— GLUCOSE

(c) polysaccharide e.g. starch

Classification of carbohydrates

PROCESSING OF CARBOHYDRATE FOODS

Many of today's carbohydrate foods are processed in such a way that much of the cellulose is removed from them; white bread and rice are typical examples. Due to consumer demand, the more nourishing parts of the cereals are removed, resulting in soft, tasteless foods which lack fibre. In western countries there are increasing numbers of cases of constipation, diverticular disease (a painful bowel disorder) and cancer of the colon (bowel), whereas in more primitive countries where whole cereals are eaten regularly these disorders are rare.

BIOLOGICAL FUNCTIONS OF CARBOHYDRATES

1. Carbohydrates provide the body with heat and energy.
2. Excess carbohydrate is converted into fat. This is stored as adipose tissue, beneath the skin; it has the advantage of reducing heat loss but too much causes obesity.
3. Cellulose stimulates the peristaltic action of the bowel.

CARBOHYDRATES REQUIREMENTS

While there is no recommended intake of carbohydrates, it is usual for about two-thirds of an average diet to consist of this nutrient. In wealthy western countries, carbohydrates may form less than half the average diet; in poor countries, over 80 per cent of the diet consists of carbohydrates.

The only recommendation from nutritionists is to eat fewer refined carbohydrates and more of the unprocessed variety. Hence the swing back to wholemeal flour, brown rice and other whole cereals.

PROPERTIES OF CARBOHYDRATE

1. *Solubility*
● Starch is insoluble in cold water but will dissolve in warm water.

● Sugar will dissolve in warm or cold water — more easily in warm water than cold.

● The resulting syrup can be reduced by boiling, when it will gradually change to a caramel, and eventually burn.

● Cellulose is insoluble in water and as a result it is not affected by our digestive juices.

2. *Thickening*
● Starch is capable of thickening liquids; starch grains absorb water and swell, e.g. in white sauce. When rice is cooked, about three times its volume of liquid is absorbed.

● Pectin is capable of thickening and setting liquids by forming a gel.

3. *Formation of dextrin*
● Dry heat breaks down starch molecules changing them to dextrin, a simpler polysaccharide.

LIPIDS

The fats and oils found in food are called lipids. Lipids are a very concentrated source of energy, supplying twice as much energy as other nutrients. It follows that foods with a large percentage of fat/oil, e.g. butter, cooking oil and cheese, are high in kilocalories and tend to be fattening if eaten in large amounts.

ENERGY VALUE

Lipids, whether fats or oils, supply 9 kilocalories per gram.

ELEMENTAL COMPOSITION

Lipids are composed of carbon, hydrogen and oxygen. It is because they have a high proportion of carbon (fuel) that they supply large amounts of heat and energy.

CLASSIFICATION/SOURCES

Lipids can be grouped into animal and vegetable sources.
1. *animal sources:* meat, suet, lard, dripping, butter, cream, cheese, milk, egg yolk; oily fish and fish liver oils.
2. *plant sources:* nuts and nut oils, e.g. ground nut oil (which is the oil in most cheap cooking oils); vegetable oils, e.g. olive oil, corn oil; margarine and cooking fats (usually made from vegetable oils); whole cereals, e.g. oatmeal, wholemeal, wheat germ.

SATURATED/UNSATURATED FATS OR OILS

Another way of grouping fats is according to whether they are 'saturated' or 'unsaturated'. This term refers to differences in their chemical structure. Saturated fats are found in greater proportions in animal foods such as meat fat, suet, butter, cheese and cream, and unsaturated fats in oily fish and vegetable foods, e.g. nuts and cooking oils.

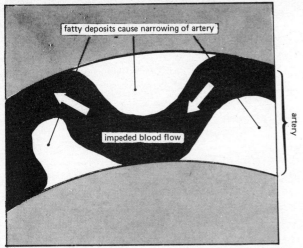

Fats – 'heart specialists'

Heart specialists have found out that a diet high in animal fats tends to increase the level of cholesterol in the blood. This is a substance which narrows the arteries of the heart causing a serious heart disease, atherosclerosis. It has also been noticed that a diet high in polyunsaturated fats tends to lower the blood cholesterol level. For this reason adults are now encouraged to reduce their intake of animal fats and to use in their place marine and vegetable oils. This is likely to reduce the chances of heart disease and early death.

FUNCTIONS OF LIPIDS

1. They supply large amounts of heat and energy.
2. They protect delicate organs, e.g. kidneys.
3. They insulate the body (excess fat is stored beneath the skin as adipose tissue).
4. Fat-soluble vitamins A, D, E and K are often found in foods containing lipids.
5. Because they are digested slowly, they delay the feeling of hunger.

PROPERTIES OF LIPIDS

1. *Solubility:* lipids are insoluble in water but soluble in grease solvents, e.g. benzine, ether.
2. *Emulsion:* lipids can be forced to combine with water (or a water-based substance) as an *emulsion.* In this case it does not dissolve but disperses in minute droplets. A *temporary emulsion* can be formed by

shaking both liquids vigorously together. If an emulsifier is added it draws the two liquids together to form a more *permanent emulsion.* Lecithin (in egg yolk) is a frequently used emulsifier; in mayonnaise, for example, it causes the oil and vinegar to combine successfully as an emulsion.

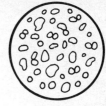

Emulsions

3. *Hydrogenation:* this is a chemical process used in the manufacture of margarine and other fats, whereby liquid oils are converted into solid fats. It is done by forcing hydrogen through the oil which causes it to become solid.
4. *Rancidity:* oils and fats do not keep well. This is because of a chemical change in the lipid structure which causes the lipid to become rancid, i.e. develop an unpleasant odour and flavour. One type of rancidity is caused by oxygen in the air reacting with the lipid. This is slowed down by storing fats and oils in a cool dark place, by keeping them well wrapped up (e.g. foil-wrapped butter), or sealed in containers.

Note. Antioxidants: These are added to oils and fats, and to foods containing these, in order to slow down the oxidation and subsequent rancidity of foods. Ascorbic acid (Vitamin C) is an antioxidant occurring naturally in food. Other synthetic antioxidants, e.g. BHT, BHA, are frequently used in convenience foods and snack foods, e.g. potato crisps, in order to delay rancidity.

Animal protein in chops, kidneys and sausages (Deegan Photo Ltd.)

PROTEINS

Protein is a vital part of body cells. It is essential in the diet; without it, growth and repair of cells could not take place and we would waste away and die.

ENERGY VALUE

Proteins supply 4 kilocalories per gram.

ELEMENTAL COMPOSITION

Like carbohydrates and fats, proteins contain carbon, hydrogen and oxygen. But they also contain *nitrogen,* an element essential for cell formation. They may also contain small amounts of sulphur and phosphorus.

STRUCTURE

Proteins are made up of chains of units called amino acids. There are over 20 amino acids from which proteins are made up. They can be arranged in various ways to form different proteins, just as the 26 letters of the alphabet can be arranged to form thousands of words. When a protein food is eaten, it is broken down into its constituent amino acids by enzymes in the digestive system. These are then carried by the blood to the liver, and then all over the body to where they are needed, e.g. to repair a damaged cell or to increase the cells of a growing child.

Essential amino acids: some amino acids can be made by the body, but a small number must be eaten 'ready made', so to speak. These are called the 'essential' amino acids; 8 are essential for adults, and another 2 for children, making 10 in all.

CLASSIFICATION

The value or quality of a protein is decided by the number of essential amino acids it supplies.

(i) *Animal proteins*

The foods which contain all the essential amino acids in the correct proportions for our requirements are grouped together and called animal proteins or first class proteins, (a) because they come from animal sources and (b) because most of the protein present is utilised by the body, leaving little waste.

Exception: gelatine is an animal protein of which none is made available to the body.

(ii) *Vegetable proteins*

Proteins which do not contain all the essential amino acids are called vegetable proteins or second-class proteins, (a) because most come from plant sources e.g. nuts, cereals, and (b) because at least 25 per cent waste occurs in these proteins, i.e. not all of them are made available to the body, e.g. for growth and repair. For example, only 40 per cent of the protein in maize is made available to the body.

SOURCES OF PROTEIN

(i) *Animal proteins*

Meat, fish, eggs, milk and cheese (including processed foods, e.g. tinned fish, frozen meat, dried milk)

(ii) *Vegetable proteins*

Nuts, pulse vegetables, e.g. peas, beans; whole cereals, bread. Potatoes, mushrooms and other vegetables contain small amounts.

COMPLEMENTARY OR SUPPLEMENTARY VALUE OF PROTEINS

While many vegetable proteins lack one or more of the essential amino acids, it is possible for some proteins to make up for this lack in other proteins if they are eaten together. This is known as the supplementary or complementary value of proteins.

This is useful in vegetarian diets, where if a wide variety of vegetable proteins is eaten, the body will obtain all the essential amino acids.

For the average diet it is usually recommended that half our protein intake should be from animal sources and half from plant sources.

In either case we should bear in mind that our protein intake should come from a wide range of foods rather than from one or two.

FUNCTIONS OF PROTEIN

1. It is essential for growth and repair (particularly important in the diet of babies, children, pregnant and nursing mothers).
2. It is a secondary source of energy (see *Note* below).
3. It is essential for the formation of important body chemicals such as enzymes, hormones and antibodies.

Note: When the amount of protein needed for growth and repair has been used, the remaining protein is converted into energy which will be stored as fat if it is not needed by the body. This is known as *deamination.*

REQUIREMENTS

The recommended daily intake of protein is 1 gram for each kilogram of body weight, e.g. a person weighing 70 kilos will require 70 g protein per day. Growing children, babies, teenagers as well as pregnant and nursing mothers will require more. In adulthood and old age, protein requirements are proportionately less, as it is needed only for cell repair.

DENATURATION

In cooking many proteins are altered, i.e. are broken down so that they lose their chain-like structure. This process is generally irreversible, i.e. the protein cannot return to its original form.

Denaturation, as this is called, is caused by
1. heat, e.g. eggs coagulating, curdling;
2. whipping, e.g. egg white for meringues;
3. adding strong chemicals, e.g. acid or alcohol.

PROPERTIES OF PROTEINS

1. *Solubility:* Many proteins are insoluble in water; some, e.g. egg white and gelatine, are water soluble.
2. *Coagulation:* can be caused by heat, e.g. an egg sets when cooked, or by enzymes, e.g. rennin clots milk proteins in the stomach.
3. *Elasticity:* some proteins resemble a coiled spring, which makes them elastic, e.g. gluten in wheat, meat muscle.

VITAMINS

Most vitamins were discovered only in the early twentieth century, and new facts about them are still being uncovered. While many vitamins can be identified by a letter, all vitamins also have a chemical name.

Vitamins are complex substances, usually (but not always) obtained from food, and required by the body for its normal functioning. Each vitamin has a specific function and if it is not included in the diet will cause a disease of deficiency, e.g. scurvy from lack of vitamin C.

Only minute amounts of any vitamin are required by the body. With the exception of small amounts of vitamins B and K, the body cannot manufacture its own vitamins.

It is rarely necessary to supplement the diet with vitamin tonics and pills if care is taken to eat a good mixed diet containing raw fruit and/or vegetables. There is no proof that extra vitamins improve health.

CLASSIFICATION OF VITAMINS

Vitamins can be divided into two groups:
1. fat-soluble, A, D, E, K
2. water-soluble, B group, C

Vitamins do not need to be digested before being absorbed into the blood stream. Water-soluble vitamins are absorbed in the stomach. Fat-soluble vitamins are absorbed in the small intestine at the same time as lipids. While fat-soluble vitamins can be stored by the body, water-soluble vitamins cannot and must therefore be taken regularly, ideally every day.

FAT-SOLUBLE VITAMINS

VITAMIN A (RETINOL) CAROTENE

Vitamin A is a fat-soluble vitamin and is therefore found in foods containing fats/oils. A secondary source of this vitamin is a substance called **carotene** (also called pro-vitamin A) which is converted to vitamin A in the intestine. Most carotene comes from vegetable sources, e.g. carrots.

Note: As carotene is not as easily absorbed as vitamin A, only about one-third of the carotene we eat is converted into vitamin A for body use.

Sources (listed in order of importance)

Vitamin A	Carotene
halibut liver oil	carrots
cod liver oil	spinach
liver	watercress
butter	dried apricots
margarine	tomatoes
cheese	prunes
eggs	cabbage
herrings	peas
milk and cream (in summer)	lettuce

Functions of vitamin A
1. Necessary for healthy skin and lining membranes, e.g. those of bronchial tubes and cornea of the eye.
2. Regulates growth, especially of children.
3. Necessary for healthy eyes, essential in the formation of the pigment in the retina which is sensitive to dim light.

Effects of deficiency
1. Dryness of skin and lining membranes. In severe cases, e.g. in the Third World, this leads to xeropthalmia, a disease which causes blindness.
2. Retarded growth in children.
3. Night blindness (inability to see in dim light).
4. Lowered resistance to infection.

Recommended daily allowance
The World Health Organisation recommends:
Children 300-700 μg (see page 26)
Adults 750 μg
Pregnant and nursing mothers 1200 μg

9

Properties/stability
1. Little affected by heat;
2. Some loss on drying, e.g. raisins dried in the sun;
3. Almost insoluble in water, therefore little affected by moist cooking methods, e.g. boiling, stewing.
4. Some loss of carotene, due to oxidation if vegetables are grated or chopped.

VITAMIN D (CALCIFEROLS)

Vitamin D can be obtained by the body in two ways: (a) from food containing fat, and (b) from sunlight, when the ultra-violet rays are absorbed by the skin.

Sources
1. Sunlight acting on the skin;
2. Dietary sources (listed below in order of importance)

	µg cholecalceferol per 100 g
halibut liver oil	up to 10,000
cod liver oil	200-750
oily fish, e.g. herrings	
salmon	5-40
margarine	2-9
eggs	1-1, 5
dairy produce in summer	0.1-2.0

Functions
1. Essential in formation of bones and teeth. Vitamin D in conjunction with calcium and phosphorus helps to build up bones, particularly those of children and pregnant women.
2. Assists absorption of calcium in the body.

Effects of deficiency
1. *Rickets,* a disease which causes malformation of bones in children. Because this is directly due to lack of vitamin D, it is sometimes called the anti-rachitic vitamin. Rickets are rare in developed countries.
2. *Osteomalacia,* a disease similar to rickets which occurs in adults. The bones gradually lose calcium. It is found most often in elderly people and in women after repeated pregnancies.
3. Dental decay.

Note: Vitamin D deficiency is more common in industrial cities where fog and pollution prevent absorption of sun-light. It is rare in tropical countries.

Recommended daily allowance

This relates to the amount of sunlight to which a person is subjected. In summer it is not necessary to obtain any vitamin D from food, if one spends a reasonable length of time out of doors. Elderly people, hospitalised patients and other housebound people will need to make sure of a reasonable amount in their diet.

The recommended daily intake of this vitamin is measured in micrograms (µg) of cholecalciferol (the form of vitamin D found in food and manufactured in our skin from sunlight):

Children and adults   2.5 µg cholecalciferol
Pregnant and nursing mothers
                         10 µg cholecalciferol

Properties/stability
1. Insoluble in water, unaffected by steeping or moist cooking
2. Unaffected by heat
3. Unaffected by oxidation, acids, alkalis. This is probably the most stable vitamin; there is little or no loss in cooking or preserving.

VITAMIN E (TOCOPHEROLS)

While this vitamin is found in many foods, particularly plant foods containing oils, e.g. cereals, it is considered to be far more important in the diet of animals than in the diet of humans. No deficiency disease has been found in humans as a result of lack of vitamin E.

Sources
Cereals, wheat germ
soya beans
vegetable oils
pulse vegetables
liver, eggs, milk

Functions
(Some of these are not entirely proved.)
1. Thought to be essential for normal metabolism.
2. Although associated with fertility in animals, e.g. rats, it is not thought to have any effect on human fertility.
3. Its antioxidant properties (see below) are thought to delay oxidation of polyunsaturated fats in the body which may reduce the chances of heart disease.

Effects of deficiency
None known.

Properties
1. Fat soluble;
2. Insoluble in water;
3. Antioxidant: the only useful function of vitamin E which is known for certain is its antioxidant property, i.e. it delays rancidity in vegetable fats. It is used commercially as an antioxidant in many foods.

VITAMIN K

This is another vitamin about which a lot still has to be learned. It is more important in the diet of animals and is thought to be essential in the process of blood clotting in humans.

Sources
1. Liver, green vegetables, fish and fish liver oils, eggs;
2. Also manufactured by bacteria in the intestine

Function
Necessary for normal blood clotting.

Effect of deficiency
Failure of blood to clot, which could cause prolonged bleeding.

VITAMIN B GROUP

This is a group of vitamins which share certain functions and are present in similar foods. Vitamin B group as a whole is involved in the release and utilisation of energy in the body. It includes the following vitamins:

Thiamine (B_1)
Riboflavin (B_2)
Niacin (nicotinic acid)
Pyridoxine (B_6)
Folic acid
Cyanocobalamin (B_{12})

THIAMINE (B_1)

Sources
cereals (including fortified breakfast cereals and flour);
wheat germ and oatmeal, particularly good sources;
meat, particularly pork, bacon, beef;
yeast

Functions
1. Concerned with the release of energy from nutrients.
2. Essential for nerves, preventing the nervous disease beri-beri.
3. Necessary for growth, appetite and general health.

Effects of deficiency
1. In mild cases, a feeling of being 'run down', tiredness, loss of appetite, depression.
2. Nervous complaints: In severe cases *beri-beri,* a disease found among people whose staple diet consists of polished rice. It affects the transmission of impulses along the nerves, eventually causing paralysis and even death.
3. Alcoholics, who often fail to eat properly, may suffer a similar disease, alcoholic neuritis.

Recommended daily allowance of thiamine
This is related to kilocalorie intake, which in turn is generally related to body size and activity: a sound average would be 1 mg per day.

Properties/stability
Thiamine is a very unstable vitamin.
1. It is extremely water-soluble, and preparation and cooking methods using water must be avoided (page 13).
2. It is easily affected by heat. The thiamine content of food is destroyed by intense heat, over cooking, reheating or keeping foods warm for a long time.
3. Food processing and milling almost totally destroy thiamine.
4. It is affected by alkalis, e.g. bread soda and preservatives such as sulphur dioxide.

RIBOFLAVIN (B_2)

Sources
beef, liver, kidney;
yeast, meat extract, e.g. Bovril;
eggs, milk, cheese;
green vegetables;
beer

Function
Involved in energy release.

Effects of deficiency
Cracks around mouth, tongue and eyes. No major deficiency disease.

Recommended daily allowance
Related to total kilocalorie intake, a sound average would be 1.5 mg for adults

Properties/stability
1. Water soluble; avoid steeping and moist cooking methods.

11

2. Avoid, if possible, very high temperatures, e.g. when pressure cooking, keep the heat as low as possible.
3. Riboflavin is destroyed by normal cooking temperatures when alkalis are present.
4. It is affected by light, therefore avoid leaving milk bottles standing in sunlight.

NIACIN (ALSO CALLED NICOTINIC ACID)

Sources
meat, especially liver, kidney;
meat extracts, e.g. Bovril;
whole cereals, wheat germ;
pulse vegetables;
yeast;
fish;
is also manufactured in the intestine in small amounts.

Functions
It is involved in energy release from food.

Effects of deficiency
Deficiency is rare in western countries. *Pellagra* is a disease common in countries where the staple diet is maize. Its symptoms include a raw rash on face and neck, diarrhoea and nervous symptoms such as depression, irritability and in severe cases dementia (madness).

Recommended daily allowance
It is related to total energy expenditure and the amount of the amino acid tryptophan in the diet. (This is lacking in maize). The recommended average intake is 15-20 mg daily.

Properties/stability
1. Soluble in water; it is lost by moist cooking methods.
2. It is unaffected by heat or acids.
3. There is slight loss in food processing.
4. Milling, e.g. cereals into flour, causes severe loss, often up to 80 per cent.

Summary of most other B-group vitamins

	Source	Function	Deficiency	Daily requirement
Pyridoxine (B_6)	wheat germ, liver	releases energy	convulsions	2 mg
Folic acid	offal, cereals, greens	helps make red blood cells	anaemia	200 μg
Cyanocobalamin (B_{12})*	protein goods especially offal, meat	helps make red blood cells	pernicious anaemia (while not always caused by B_{12} deficiency can be treated by giving this vitamin)	1 μg

Other B vitamins include biotin, pantothenic acid.

*NB B_{12} is likely to be lacking in vegetarian diets.

VITAMIN C (ASCORBIC ACID)

Sources*
Most fresh fruit and vegetables:

Best fruit sources	*Best vegetable sources*
rose hip syrup	peppers
blackcurrants	parsley
citrus fruits	broccoli

Less vitamin C in	
strawberries	spinach
raspberries	watercress
gooseberries	cabbage
	tomatoes
	lettuce
	new potatoes

*lacking in animal foods

Functions
1. Necessary for healthy tissue; gums, skin, bones and teeth.
2. Strengthens blood vessels, helps to heal wounds and prevent bruising.
3. Prevents *scurvy,* a disease with symptoms of sore, bleeding gums, loose teeth, tiredness and pains in the limbs.
4. Helps fight infection. Some say large amounts of vitamin C prevent or lessen the effects of colds, flu, etc. This is not proved.
5. Necessary for absorption of iron.
6. Necessary for metabolism (energy release).
7. Used as an antioxidant.

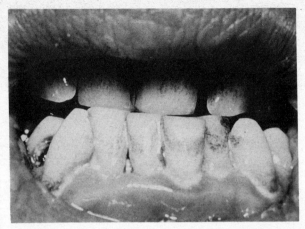

The effects of vitamin C deficiency (C. James Webb)

Effects of deficiency
1. diseases of skin, gums, teeth;
2. delayed healing of wounds, e.g. after operations; bruising;
3. general ill health, leading in severe cases to scurvy;
4. susceptibility to infection;
5. incomplete absorption of iron, leading to anaemia;
6. tiredness, irritability, a feeling of being 'run down'.

Recommended daily allowance
adults and children	30 mg
teenagers	40-50 mg
pregnant women	80 mg
nursing mothers	100 mg

Note: Allow for 50-90 per cent loss of vitamin C in cooked foods.

Properties/stability
Vitamin C is the most unstable of all vitamins.
1. It is very soluble in water; avoid steeping foods or cooking by moist methods.
2. It is easily affected by heat which destroys it. (There is less lost when acid is present.)
3. It is readily oxidised; oxygen in the air destroys this vitamin.
4. When chopped or shredded, an oxidising enzyme (oxidase) present in the cell walls of plants, destroys vitamin C. To avoid loss, eat soon after preparation.
5. It is destroyed by alkalis; avoid adding alkalis, e.g. bread soda, to cooking water.
6. Processing: freezing has little effect on vitamin C as the damaging enzymes are destroyed in the blanching process. There is some loss on canning and considerable loss when food is dried.
7. This vitamin is also reduced by storage; the longer it is kept, the less vitamin C remains.

Special points for retaining vitamins C (and B to a lesser extent) in food:
- eat raw where possible;
- avoid steeping;
- when cooking, cook for the shortest possible time;
- avoid keeping food warm for a long time; avoid reheating;
- when cooking in liquid, use the minimum possible amount of liquid and keep the lid on the saucepan to reduce oxidation;
- use as soon as possible after chopping or shredding;
- shred vegetables with a stainless steel knife; do not tear;
- never use bread soda when cooking greens.

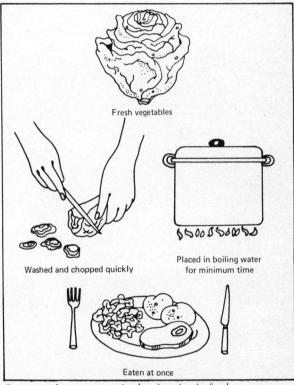

Fresh vegetables

Washed and chopped quickly

Placed in boiling water for minimum time

Eaten at once

Some good ways to retain the vitamins in food

General points about vitamins and minerals
1. As the amount of vitamins and minerals required by the body is extremely small, they are usually measured in milligrams (mg) — 1/1,000 of a gram, or in micrograms (μg) — 1/1,000,000 of a gram.
2. It must be remembered that the food with the largest amount of a vitamin or mineral is not necessarily the best source. Parsley, for example is one of the best sources of vitamin C, but as it is not eaten in great amounts, a food which contains less of the vitamin but which is eaten in larger amounts, e.g. potatoes, is a better source of the vitamin in our diet.

Some of the sources of vitamin C (John Topham Picture Library)

3. Minerals, and vitamins B and C are water soluble and are therefore likely to dissolve in any water used in their preparation or cooking, therefore avoid steeping such foods and when cooking in liquid use the minimum amount. Use the liquid left after cooking, as stock for soups or sauces.
4. Several vitamins and minerals are affected by heat. Keep cooking processes to a minimum. Do not keep food warm for prolonged periods; avoid using reheated food too often and where possible serve foods, e.g. fruit and vegetables, raw.
5. Vitamins B and C are lost readily from the body so must be replaced regularly, if possible daily, as they cannot be stored by the body.
6. Processing reduces the vitamin content of many foods, sometimes destroying it totally. Milling removes many of the B vitamins from cereals.
7. Many modern foods such as breakfast cereals, flour and convenience foods are 'fortified' with added vitamins and minerals to make good the loss in processing.

MINERAL ELEMENTS

The human body requires about 20 mineral elements in order to keep all organs and systems working efficiently.

These are the minerals required in the greatest amounts (bearing in mind that few foods have a mineral content of more than 1-2 per cent):

calcium	phosphorus	chlorine
sodium	iron	sulphur
iodine	potassium	magnesium

Others are required in minute amounts; these include copper, zinc, cobalt and fluorine and are called trace elements.

Each mineral salt has a specific function and is found in certain foods, so it is difficult to generalise about the functions of minerals as a whole. All help to protect the body from disease; many are involved in the upkeep of body cells, others with metabolism and some with bone or blood formation.

As with all nutrients, a good mixed diet should supply all the necessary minerals in sufficient amounts. The two minerals most commonly deficient in the diet are calcium and iron.

CALCIUM

There is more calcium than any other mineral in the body. Most of it is in the bones, with small amounts in muscle and the blood. Calcium and phosphorus work together in bone formation. For maximum absorption, they must be in the ratio of 1:1.5 calcium to phosphorus. Vitamin D is essential for the utilisation of calcium and phosphorus as it controls absorption of calcium and the way it is laid down in the bones. Vitamin C is also important in calcium absorption.

Sources of calcium
milk
cheese
tinned fish (of which the bones are eaten, e.g. sardines)
green vegetables
hard water
flour (when fortified)

Functions
1. necessary for development of strong bones and teeth;
2. necessary for normal clotting of blood;
3. necessary for normal working of muscles.

Effects of deficiency
1. rickets and osteomalacia often occur in severe cases;
2. bad quality teeth, dental decay
3. irritability and muscular spasm.

Recommended daily allowance

adults	500-800 mg
children	1,000 mg
pregnant and nursing mothers	up to 2,000 mg

A mother expecting another baby needs calcium (Camera Press)

The importance of calcium in the diet of children and pregnant and nursing mothers cannot be over stressed. If extra calcium is not taken during pregnancy, it will be drawn from the mother's bones to supply the foetus, thus endangering the health of the mother, particularly in the case of repeated pregnancies.

PHOSPHORUS
This element is present in many proteins and, like calcium, is stored in the bones.

Sources
Phosphorus is found in all natural foodstuffs. Good sources are

meat	dairy products
fish	green vegetables

Functions
1. bone and tooth formation;
2. necessary for normal metabolism;
3. essential component of many enzymes and hormones.

Effects of deficiency
Because phosphorus is present in all foods, deficiency is unknown. There is no recommended allowance for the same reason.

IRON

Most of the iron in the body is found in the blood. Iron is also present in the liver, spleen and bone marrow. Small amounts of iron are lost through wear and tear of the body; large amounts are only lost through haemorrhaging and menstruation.

Sources of iron
liver, kidney and other meats, e.g. corned beef,
whole cereals, brown and white bread, wheatgerm, nuts,
treacle, dried fruit, curry powder, cocoa.

Functions
Necessary for the formation of haemoglobin in the red blood cells. This carries oxygen from the lungs to the tissues for respiration.

Absorption of iron
Only 10 per cent of all the iron we eat is absorbed by the body. Both vitamins C and E help its absorption.

While spinach contains a good proportion of iron, chemicals also present in spinach (oxalates) prevent its being absorbed, so as a dietary source of iron it is useless. (So much for Popeye!)

Teenagers need iron for activities such as climbing (John Topham Picture Library)

Effects of deficiency
The main effects of iron deficiency are tiredness and feeling run down. In severe cases, anaemia results. This is common during growth spurts in children and teenagers.

Many women, particularly those who have heavy or prolonged menstrual periods, suffer from varying degrees of anaemia. Pregnancy, particularly repeated pregnancies, increases the risk of anaemia. Severe anaemia can contribute to congenital abnormalities and can threaten the life of the mother at birth.

Normal babies are born with enough iron to last them six months, but iron-rich foods such as egg yolk and minced liver should then be introduced. Remember, milk is a poor source of iron.

Recommended daily allowance
adult men	10 mg
adult women	12 mg
pregnant women	15 mg

SODIUM

This element is present in all body fluids and is essential for life. Its main source is common salt. It is excreted by the kidneys and lost through the skin in perspiration. In hot climates or occupations where physical exertion causes excessive perspiration, extra salt must be taken.

Sources of sodium
salt added in cooking or at the table;
bacon, smoked fish, cheese, bread and butter.

Functions
1. Necessary for correct water balance of body.
2. Keeps blood and body fluids alkaline.

Effects of deficiency
Muscular cramps

Effects of excess salt in diet
1. Dehydration, particularly in babies. Avoid adding salt to a baby's diet.
2. Blood pressure: excess salt in the diet is known to increase blood pressure.

Sodium is lost through perspiration during extreme physical exertion (John Topham Picture Library)

IODINE

Sources
1. Plentiful in seafood (fish) and seaweed.
2. Most vegetables grown in soil reasonably near the sea contain iodine. In countries with large land masses such as Africa, goitre (see below) is very common, and salt containing iodine is used at table and for cooking to compensate.

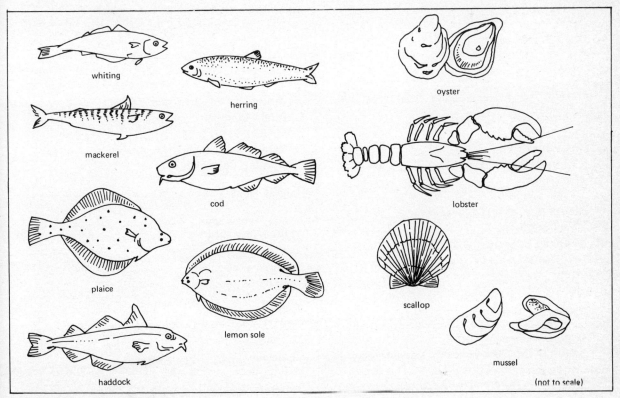

whiting

herring

oyster

mackerel

cod

lobster

plaice

scallop

lemon sole

mussel

haddock

(not to scale)

Fish are a good source of iodine

Function

Essential for proper functioning of the thyroid gland which controls the metabolic rate.

Effects of deficiency

1. Enlargement of the thyroid gland in the neck causing goitre.
2. Lack of energy, obesity and mental backwardness.

Recommended daily allowance.

For adults, 150 μg.

Functions of other elements

Potassium: necessary for body cells. Sources: mixed diet.

Copper: necessary for absorption of iron. Sources: liver, kidney.

Chlorine: necessary for manufacture of hydrochloric acid. Sources: as for sodium.

Fluorine: prevents dental decay. Sources: added to water.

SUMMARY

Recommended daily allowance of nutrients (for adults)

Protein	1 g per kilogram weight
Carbohydrate	related to individual metabolism and physical activity
Lipid	as for carbohydrate (half from animal, half from vegetable sources)

Vitamin A	750 μg
Vitamin D	2.5 μg
Vitamin B$_1$	
(Thiamine)	1 mg
Riboflavin	1.5 mg
Nicotinic acid	15.20 mg
Vitamin C	30 mg
Calcium	600 mg
Iron	12 mg
Iodine	150 μg
Water	
(liquid)	1.5 litres
(food sources)	.8 litre

Note: In the past, vitamins A and D were measured in International Units. This form of measurement is now obsolete.

WATER

While not classified as a nutrient, water is essential for life. It makes up two-thirds of the body weight. It forms the main part of the cell liquid, extra cellular fluid and blood. Body secretions, lymph and digestive fluids are also largely composed of water.

ELEMENTAL COMPOSITION

Water is composed of hydrogen and oxygen in the proportion of 2:1 (H_2O).

Sources

1. All beverages, alcoholic drinks, milk, drinking water. The average person drinks 1.5 litres of fluid each day.
2. Many foods also contain water, particularly fruit and vegetables. Green vegetables and citrus fruits contain 90 per cent water. Dried foods and foods containing large proportions of lipids contain little water. About .8 litre of water per day is obtained from food sources.

Functions

1. Transport: water (in the form of blood) transports nutrients, oxygen, CO_2, blood cells, hormones and enzymes around the body.
2. Helps control body temperature by evaporation of perspiration from skin.
3. Distributes heat generated by metabolism.
4. Dissolves food, forms secretions and aids digestion and absorption.
5. Assists in removal of waste from the body, e.g. urea from kidneys.
6. Is an essential ingredient of all body cells.
7. Water is frequently a source of minerals, e.g. calcium, fluorine.

Energy value

None.

Daily requirement

As 2-2.5 litres of water are excreted daily by the kidneys, skin, lungs etc., an equal amount is required by the body to avoid dehydration.

Properties of water

1. Pure water has no colour, taste or smell.
2. The pH value of water is neutral; it is neither acid nor alkaline.
3. It is very solvent and thus capable of dissolving many substances.
4. It readily absorbs and retains heat.

5. It freezes at 0°C and boils at 100°C.
6. It evaporates easily — more quickly at high temperatures.

DIGESTION

The main nutrients we eat — proteins, lipids, carbohydrates — are made up of large molecules which must be broken down into simpler substances before they can be absorbed by the blood and eventually used by our cells.

The digestive process breaks down food *physically,* i.e. by churning it about and *chemically* by the action of enzymes.

Enzymes are organic chemicals which cause chemical changes (e.g. in food) without changing themselves. Each enzyme will work only on a particular substance and no other. Enzymes in humans work best at normal body temperature (37°C). Each enzyme favours a particular environment; some work best in an acid pH, others in alkaline conditions.

During digestion, each nutrient must be broken down into its components:

proteins into amino acids;

fats into fatty acids and glycerine;

carbohydrates into monosaccharides, e.g. glucose

Before learning the processes of digestion, it is necessary first to study the organs of digestion.

The digestive system includes the mouth, oesophagus, stomach, liver, pancreas, small and large intestine.

The alimentary canal consists of the passage the food passes through from the time it is eaten until the waste is expelled from the body, i.e. the mouth, oesophagus, stomach, small and large intestine.

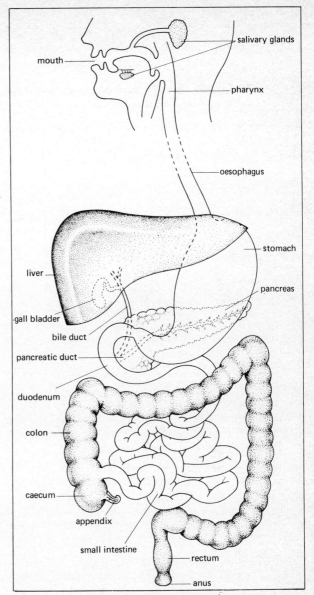

How digestion works: the alimentary canal

THE MOUTH

Food is broken down by the teeth while the saliva softens the food to prepare it for digestion. Saliva is produced by three pairs of glands in the mouth, two under the tongue, two under the jaw and two at the back of the cheeks. Saliva contains an enzyme, *ptyalin,* which acts on cooked starch, breaking it down into *dextrin,* a simpler molecule, and *maltose,* a disaccharide.

THE OESOPHAGUS

When food has been sufficiently masticated (chewed), the tongue forms it into a ball and passes it into the throat; this is the act of swallowing.

The oesophagus (or gullet) lies behind the trachea running parallel with it. During swallowing, the epiglottis (a kind of lid) closes over the trachea to prevent food passing down the 'wrong way'.

The oesophagus is a straight muscular tube about 25 cm long which extends from the pharynx (the back of the throat) to the stomach. As the food passes down, the muscles of the oesophagus contract rythmically, first in front of the food, then behind it, pushing the food gradually towards the stomach. This wave-like muscular movement known as *peristalsis* continues throughout the length of the alimentary canal. No digestion takes place in the oesophagus.

THE STOMACH

The stomach is situated on the left of the abdomen, immediately below the diaphragm. It lies beside the liver and in front of the pancreas. It is a large, hollow pouch-shaped organ.

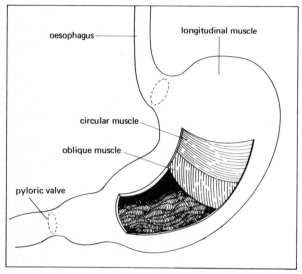

How digestion works: the stomach

In common with other digestive organs, it consists of three layers: an outer coat of peritoneum, a thick layer of muscle tissue and an inner lining of mucus membrane. This inner coat is deeply folded when the stomach is empty, and scattered between the folds are huge numbers of gastric glands which secrete gastric juice. The entrance and exit point of the stomach are guarded by strong sphincter muscles.

When food enters the stomach, the muscular walls contract and expand, churning the food about in order to mix it with the gastric juice. Food remains in the stomach between two and five hours depending on the type of food; proteins and fats remain longer than carbohydrates. Before it leaves, it has reached a thick creamy consistency known as *chyme*.

DIGESTION IN THE STOMACH

● Gastric glands secrete hydrochloric acid, mucus and gastric juice into the stomach.
● Gastric juice contains the enzymes pepsin and rennin.
● Pepsin acts on proteins, breaking them into smaller chains called *peptones*.
● Rennin causes milk to clot, because in this way it is more easily digested.

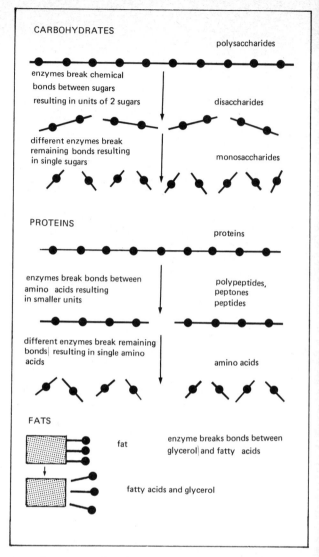

How digestion works: chemical changes

● Hydrochloric acid is necessary to create the degree of acidity needed for the gastric enzymes to work. It also destroys many bacteria present on the food we eat. Nervous tension increases secretion of hydrochloric acid which may cause indigestion and heartburn, or, in more severe cases, stomach ulcers.
● The heat of the stomach melts fats and releases them from any proteins to which they may be attached.
● The stomach helps to break down the cellulose covering on many plant foods, releasing their contents to the action of enzymes.
● Absorption: a little absorption takes place in the stomach, mainly water and soluble foods, such as glucose, salt, alcohol, water-soluble vitamins and drugs.

When the chyme leaves the stomach it enters the first section of the small intestine called the *duodenum*. Into this area pour the secretions of two important glands: the *pancreas* and the *liver*.

The *pancreas* produces pancreatic juice which contains three enzymes: trypsin, lipase and amylase. The *liver* produces bile, an emulsifier which has an important part to play in the digestion of lipids.

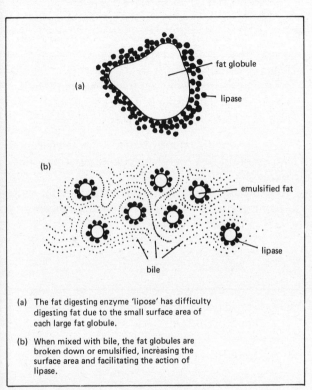

(a) The fat digesting enzyme 'lipose' has difficulty digesting fat due to the small surface area of each large fat globule.

(b) When mixed with bile, the fat globules are broken down or emulsified, increasing the surface area and facilitating the action of lipase.

How digestion works: emulsifying of bile

THE SMALL INTESTINE

This is a narrow tube about 6 m long which is coiled about the abdomen and is held in place by a thin membrane. The walls contain the same three layers as those of the stomach:

1. an outer covering of peritoneum;
2. a middle muscular/elastic layer;
3. an inner lining of mucous membrane which is also deeply folded, with glands scattered between the folds.

The inner surface of the mucous membrane is covered by thousands of tiny hair-like projections which give it a velvet-like appearance: these are known as *villi*, and it is through these that most food is absorbed.

DIGESTION IN THE INTESTINE

1. The duodenum
The pancreatic enzymes
trypsin — breaks protein into smaller chains called peptides;
lipase — combines with bile to create an emulsion and splits fats into their components, fatty acids and glycerine;
amylase — breaks down carbohydrate, particularly starch, into maltose.

2. The ileum
Glands in the walls of the small intestine secrete intestinal juice which contains the following enzymes:
(a) Eripsin, which finishes off the digestion of proteins, converting partially-digested proteins into absorbable amino acids.
(b) Carbohydrate-splitting enzymes convert partially digested carbohydrates such as disaccharides into monosaccharides, e.g. glucose:
maltase converts maltose to glucose;
lactase converts lactose (milk sugar) to glucose;
invertase or sucrase converts sucrose to glucose and fructose.
(c) Any remaining fats are converted by intestinal lipase into fatty acids and glycerine.

Digestion is now completed — all nutrients which have to be digested have been broken down into soluble substances.

ABSORPTION

Each villus of the small intestine contains a lacteal (a lymph vessel) and a network of tiny capillaries. Both the folds of the mucous membrane and the huge number of villi increase enormously the surface area of the intestine. This means that nutrients can be more easily absorbed. As the walls of the intestinal lining are extremely thin, fluids and small molecules can easily pass through them.

Monosaccharides and amino acids pass through these walls into the capillaries and are carried from the intestine to the liver by the portal vein.

Glycerides and fatty acids pass into the lacteals which combine to form large lymph vessels, pass upwards through the thoracic duct and empty into the bloodstream at the left jugular vein.

After four or five hours in the small intestine, most nutrients have been absorbed. Substances which have not been absorbed pass through the ileocaecal valve into the large intestine or bowel.

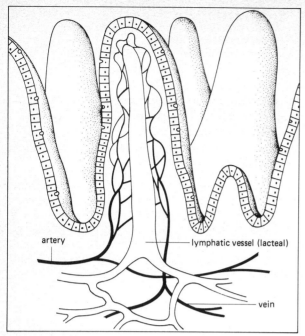

artery

lymphatic vessel (lacteal)

vein

How digestion works: structure of villi

The *large intestine* reabsorbs liquids from undigested food and also manufactures some vitamin K and B group. Bacteria present in the intestine break down undigested substances such as cellulose before eliminating them from the body as faeces.

QUESTIONS/CHAPTER 1

1. Classify carbohydrates according to their structure, giving two examples of each.
Name the unit of energy used in nutrition. List the energy nutrients, giving the energy value of each.
Discuss the relationship between energy intake and obesity.

2. Write a note on carbohydrates. Refer to elemental composition, biological functions, calorific value, sources.
List three factors which affect energy requirements.
Define pectin, cellulose, dextrin and glycogen.

SUMMARY OF DIGESTION

Digestive gland	Secretion	Enzymes and other Substances	Substances acted upon (Substrate)	Product
Salivary glands (Mouth)	Saliva (alkaline)	Ptyalin or salivary amylase	Cooked starch	Destrin Maltose
Gastric glands (Stomach)	Gastric juice (acid)	Pepsin Rennin Gastric lipase Hydrochloric acid (not an enzyme)	Protein Caseinogen (milk protein) Fats	Peptones Casein Fatty acids, glycerol
Liver	Bile (alkaline)	Bile salts (not an enzyme)	Fats	Emulsified fat
Pancreas	Pancreatic juice (alkaline)	Trypsin Amylase Lipase	Protein Starch Fats	Polypeptides Maltose Fatty acids, glycerol
Ileum	Succus entericus (alkaline)	Peptidase (eripsin) Lipase Maltase Sucrase (invertase) Lactase	Peptides Fats Maltose Sucrose Lactose (milk sugar)	Amino acids Fatty acids, glycerol Glucose Glucose, fructose Glucose, galactose

3. Discuss proteins or fats under the following headings: classification, biological functions, energy value, properties.
What is the importance of a *mixture* of protein foods in the diet?

4. Differentiate between saturated and unsaturated fats. Give examples of each.
State the relevance of the above in the diet.
Describe the digestion and absorption of fats.

5. Explain the term basal metabolic rate.
What physiological factors influence total metabolism. State how each factor modifies the basal metabolic rate.
Write a note on the nutrient needs of adolescents.

6. Discuss the importance of ascorbic acid in the diet. List its main sources, functions and symptoms of deficiency.
Write a note on the effects of cooking on this vitamin.

7. Write a note on four of the following: carotene, thiamine, gluten, fluorine, retinol.
What is the function of salt in the diet?
What are the results of (a) excess salt and (b) a deficiency of salt in the diet?

8. Discuss the fat-soluble vitamins. Refer to biological functions, important sources, deficiency symptoms, stability, approximate daily requirement.
Explain the following terms: micrograms (μg), joules.

2.
Meal Planning

A BALANCED DIET

● A well-balanced diet should contain all the necessary nutrients in the correct proportion for the needs of the individual (see below). The easiest way of doing this is by eating a good mixture of fresh foods.
● It is important to eat fruit and vegetables raw, and in season, where possible, and when cooked make sure they get the minimum cooking time necessary in order to retain vitamins.
● Avoid too many modern over-processed foods; make sure to include lots of fibre in the diet.
● Convenience foods should be kept to a minimum. Many are over-processed and contain additives which could be dangerous if eaten in large quantities.

DAILY FOOD REQUIREMENTS

Every day, make sure you eat food from each of the following groups:

PROTEIN GROUP

● 2 portions (100 g) of animal protein in the form of meat, fish, eggs, cheese;
● 2 portions (100 g) vegetable protein, e.g. pulses, cereals, nuts, bread.

DAIRY GROUP

● milk — adults 300 ml, children 500 ml daily;
● cheese, yoghurt etc.

PROTECTIVE GROUP

vitamins — minerals — roughage*
● 2-3 portions of vegetables, one at least raw
● 1 portion of fruit

CARBOHYDRATE GROUP

Fill out the diet from this group after other essential needs have been met.
● bread, breakfast cereals, rice;
● choose whole, unrefined cereals rather than the less nutritious refined foods.

ROUGHAGE*

Many nutritionists now recommend an increase in the intake of fibre. This is because tests indicate that the faster food passes through the intestine, the lower the risk of cancers forming in the bowel. Fibre, even though it cannot be digested, stimulates the peristaltic action of the intestinal muscles and pushes the food along more quickly.

MEAL PLANNING FOR ADULTS

A normal, well-balanced diet as explained above is essential for adults. Certain groups of adults, though, need to take special precautions, e.g. the elderly or those with an illness or disability which might influence diet.

Sedentary workers: those whose jobs are not very active, e.g. office workers, need to be careful of kilocalorie intake if they are to avoid gaining too much weight. Cellulose is important to prevent constipation. Avoid rushed lunches; choose salads, low-fat cheese and high-fibre lunch meals rather than high-calorie snacks such as cream buns and chips. Eat fresh fruit rather than biscuits and cake.

Manual workers: these can afford a higher than normal kilo calorie intake as they will work off the energy produced by such foods. Packed lunches should contain protein, fat and carbohydrate (preferably high-fibre) — meat or cheese sandwiches are ideal. The high energy foods many of us have to restrict, such as fat meat, fried and starchy foods, are acceptable in the diet of a manual worker.

Adolescents: teenage boys and girls require a good supply of protein for growth and repair. As energy needs are usually high, particularly of boys, foods with a fairly high kilocalorie content may be eaten, if the diet also supplies enough vitamins and minerals. Milk and cheese are good sources of protein and calcium. Liver, meat and green vegetables are good sources of iron, a mineral which may be deficient in girls due to menstruation. Avoid too many fried or greasy foods which might aggravate acne and lead to obesity.

DAY'S MENU FOR AN ACTIVE MAN

Breakfast	*Packed lunch*	*Dinner*
Orange juice	Cheese sandwiches	Roast lamb
Porridge	Fruit cake	Boiled potatoes
Milk, sugar	Apple	Boiled cabbage
Grilled bacon	Flask of tea	
and tomato		Apple tart
Toast, butter		Custard
Tea		

SAMPLE DAY'S MENU FOR AN ACTIVE MAN

	Amount	kcal	Protein	Fat	Carbohy.	Vitamins	Minerals	Roughage
Breakfast								
Orange juice	50 g	20	0	0	5.0	A,C	Calcium	trace
Grilled bacon	50 g	225	12.5	20.0	0	B	Cal. Iron	—
Grilled tomato	50 g	6	0.4	0	1.2	A,C	Cal.	medium
Oatmeal	25 g	100	3.0	2.2	18.0	B	Cal. Iron	high
Sugar	25 g	100	0	0	25.0	0	0	—
Milk (⅓ pt)	50 ml	65	3.3	3.8	4.8	A,B	Cal.	—
Tea	0	0	0	0	0	B	0	—
Toast (2 slices)	75 g	190	6.0	1.0	40.0	B	Cal. Iron	low
Butter	50 g	365	0.2	40.0	0	A,D	Cal.	—
Packed Lunch								
Chedder cheese	50g	206	13.0	17.0	0	A,B,D	Cal.	—
Bread (4 slices)	150 g	375	12.0	2.25	82.0	B	Cal. Iron	low
Margarine (Flora)	50 g	367	0	40.0	0	A,D	Cal.	—
Fruit cake	50 g	184	2.3	8.0	28.0	A,B	Cal. Iron	medium
Apple	100 g	46	0	0	12.0	A,C	Cal.	medium
Tea, milk, sugar		25	0	1.0	4.0	—	—	—
Dinner								
Roast lamb	100 g	290	23.0	22.0	0	B	Cal. Iron	—
Boiled potatoes	200 g	160	2.5	0	39.0	B,C	Cal.	medium
Cabbage	100 g	15	1.5	0	2.3	A,C	Cal.	high
Apple tart	100 g	281	3.0	14.4	40.4	A,C	Cal.	low
Custard	50 g	46	1.5	1.75	6.5	A,B	Cal.	—
		3,066	84.2	173.4	308.2			

Working with cattle needs plenty of energy (Camera Press)

Comments

1. The energy content of this menu is correct for an active man. If this man were to have a morning or afternoon snack or a couple of pints of beer after work on a regular basis, he would exceed his daily quota of kilocalories and probably put on weight.
2. The protein content is higher than necessary. A mixed salad could be eaten instead of sandwiches, or tomatoes and lettuce substituted for the cheese. These would have a lower protein content.
3. Reducing the protein in this way would also reduce the animal fats in this menu. Vegetable fats should be substituted for animal fats, e.g. polyunsaturated margarine instead of butter.
4. It would be advisable to increase the amount of fibre in this diet. This could be done by eating wholemeal bread instead of white bread. This would also add valuable iron and vitamin B to the diet.

Alterations in above diet for moderately active woman

1. Reduce intake of sugar, bread and potatoes a little.
2. Substitute brown bread for white.
3. For breakfast, eat a boiled egg or porridge — not both.
4. A nourishing salad at lunchtime is better than sandwiches and would increase vitamin and mineral intake.

Further modifications for a low-calorie diet

A low-calorie diet would involve further reductions in carbohydrate. Sugar would be eliminated and bread and potatoes and fats reduced drastically. Cakes and biscuits should be cut out and an orange or natural yoghurt substituted for a high-calorie pudding. Throughout, menu portions could be reduced slightly.

MEAL PLANNING FOR CHILDREN

BABIES

Ideally, small babies should be breast-fed. Breast milk provides all the nutrients a baby needs, in the correct proportions and at the right temperature. Breast-feeding is more hygienic than bottle-feeding, therefore gastroenteritis is less likely as are other diseases, owing to the fact that the mother's immunity is passed to the child.

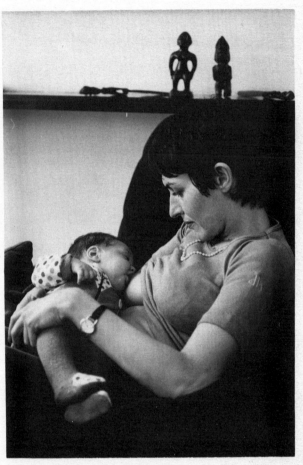

Breast-feeding baby (Camera Press)

BOTTLE-FEEDING

● Sterilise bottles and teats thoroughly.
● Cow's milk must be sweetened and diluted with boiled water (for young babies).
● Keep feeds cool, if made in advance.
● Follow instructions on dried formula milk exactly. Never add an extra scoop or the feed will be too concentrated. This will cause dehydration and may have serious consequences.

Bottle-feeding baby (Camera Press)

● Bottle-fed babies must have their diet supplemented with
   (a) vitamin C (orange juice or rose hip syrup);
   (b) iron (strained green vegetables, egg yolk);
   (c) vitamins A and D (cod liver oil or vitamin drops).

MIXED FEEDING

● Solids can be introduced at about three to four months.
● These should consist of puréed protein and protective foods, e.g. strained liver, greens, carrots or pulse vegetables rather than high-carbohydrate foods such as baby rice.
● Home-made adult dishes, strained or puréed, are cheaper and more nourishing than canned baby foods.

FEEDING CHILDREN

1. All foods should be concentrated sources of nutrients. Children should be encouraged to eat a varied selection of foods if they are to develop a nourishing and sensible eating pattern.

2. Fresh air and exercise before meals help to develop a good appetite.
3. Children should not be over-tired or too hungry at mealtimes or they may be cross and lose interest in their food.
4. Serve meals at regular times each day.
5. Avoid too many refined carbohydrate foods, particularly sweets and biscuits.
6. Avoid between-meal snacks; they take the edge off the appetite and can unbalance the diet.
7. Serve food attractively, in small portions. Remove bone, fat and gristle from meat, which should be chopped or minced.
8. Introduce new foods gradually. Adults should set a good example by eating all foods. Children quickly pick up bad habits.
9. The atmosphere at mealtimes should be relaxed and enjoyable. If children make a scene about refusing food, it is often better to ignore them rather than make an issue of the matter.

SUITABLE FOODS

Protein: plenty of animal and vegetable protein for growth.

A good mixture of vegetables, and at least one portion of raw fruit, for vitamins A and C, as well as iron.

Bread, butter, potatoes, etc. will provide plenty of energy, needed because children are very active.

Milk and cheese: they supply calcium for bones and teeth. Milk is preferable to coffee, tea or fizzy drinks.

Oily fish or cod liver oil, to supply vitamins A and D. Liver, meat and dark green vegetables will supply iron.

Brown bread, rice and porridge are preferable to refined carbohydrates.

PREGNANT AND NURSING MOTHERS

The diet should be well balanced with an emphasis on foods for growth and protection. The idea of eating for two is not correct although an expectant mother may need an increase in particular nutrients, such as the following:

1. protein, both animal and vegetable, for growth;
2. vitamins A and D for growth of the baby's bones and teeth;
3. vitamin B group for maximum utilisation of energy;
4. vitamin C for absorption of iron, healthy blood vessels and general health;
5. calcium/phosphorus for bones and teeth;

6. iron for blood of both mother and baby. Many pregnant women are found to be anaemic. They are often prescribed iron and folic acid for this reason.
7. energy: energy needs increase slightly during pregnancy and the appetite increases to meet these needs. But it is essential that the mother does not gain too much weight; a weight gain of approximately 22 lb (10 kilos) is normal. An over-weight mother may experience difficulties during pregnancy and birth, such as varicose veins, haemorrhoids and toxaemia.

A nursing mother should keep up her pregnancy diet. As adipose tissue is used up during milk production, a mother who breast-feeds will regain her figure more quickly.

THE ELDERLY

Most elderly people can continue to follow a normal well-balanced diet, but kilocalorie intake should be reduced slightly because basal metabolism decreases in old age and also because old people tend to be less active.

1. Protein is still essential for repair of tissues. Meat or cheese should be taken once a day; white fish is ideal for those with digestive problems. Eggs — 3-4 a week (too many would raise cholesterol level).
2. Protective foods: 3 portions daily of vegetables and/or fruit for vitamins A and C and minerals such as iron.
3. Milk: 300-500 ml daily to supply calcium and protein.
4. Carbohydrate: emphasis should be on carbohydrate foods which also supply roughage, e.g. porridge, brown bread.

Some problems encountered in diets of old people
● Some suffer from poor digestion and must eat easily-digested foods such as milk, white fish, chicken etc.
● Disabilities such as loss of teeth or arthritis can interfere with eating and cooking.

Eating and drinking can be a social occasion, especially for the elderly (Camera Press)

27

● Many nutritious foods such as meat, fish, fruit and vegetables are also expensive; many old people therefore avoid these in favour of less nourishing foods such as bread, jam and tea.

● Many elderly people make little effort to cook themselves a nourishing main meal. They may have failing sight or be handicapped in some other way. Meals-on-wheels is a community effort which helps to overcome this problem.

INVALIDS

Food for the invalid and convalescent should provide the maximum amount of nourishment with the minimum amount of bulk. The following are essential in an invalid diet:

1. protein to repair diseased and wasted tissue;
2. vitamin C, which helps heal tissues, wounds and blood vessels and helps prevent bed sores;
3. vitamin A helps prevent infection and creates healthy membranes;
4. vitamin B group for nervous tissue, vitality and energy release;
5. iron to prevent anaemia, which is common in illness;
6. roughage to prevent constipation, a common complaint in bed-ridden patients;
7. energy foods should be restricted and used only to satisfy the appetite after the more essential nutrients have been eaten.

During illness, digestion is often upset; avoid indigestible foods such as pastry, oily fish, fat meat, fried foods, cheese and highly-seasoned foods.

Rules for feeding invalids
1. Follow doctor's orders.
2. Use best-quality fresh food. Avoid using left-overs or convenience foods which are less nutritious.
3. Observe strict hygiene in the preparation, cooking and serving of meals.
4. Choose light, easily-digested foods. Steaming, stewing and poaching are suitable methods of cooking.
5. Trim food where appropriate, removing bone, gristle and excess fat. Foods should be cut up or minced if necessary to make them easier to eat.
6. Serve meals at regular times. Several small meals are better than two large meals.
7. Meals are an important feature of the day for an invalid. Have everything as clean and attractive as possible. The tray should be neatly laid and cloth, glasses, cutlery and napkin should be spotless. Food should be served attractively in small portions in clean individual dishes.

8. The tray should be large enough and comfortable to hold. A tray with legs or an invalid table such as those used in hospitals would be ideal for long-term patients.
9. Hot meals should be served hot on heated dishes and covered to keep them so. Cold food and drinks should be well chilled.
10. Remove all food from the sick-room when the meal is finished.

INVALID DIETS

(a) During fever, e.g. influenza or measles
Much water is lost from the body through perspiration when the temperature is high. The diet should consist of plenty of liquids to replace this, but need not exclude solid food. Drinks and light meals should be given alternatively every two hours.
Proteins should be supplied in meat broths, milky drinks and eggs, e.g. egg flip.
Carbohydrates can be given in milk puddings, breakfast cereals, barley drinks, toast and sugar or glucose in food and drinks. Vitamins are obtained from strained citrus juices, blackcurrant juice or rose hip syrup.
Minerals will be present in many of these foods.

(b) After fever
Follow a light diet. All foods should be lightly cooked and easy to digest. Continue to serve plenty of liquids.
Suitable foods
Eggs — poached or scrambled.
Chicken breast, white fish, sweetbreads — poached or steamed.
Fruit, vegetables — stewed or puréed.
Jellies, icecream, milk puddings, milky drinks.
Raw fruit, vitamin C drinks.

(c) During convalesence
The patient should be able to eat small portions of most foods apart from particularly indigestible ones, such as fries, pastry and suet. Kilocalorie intake will still be reduced through lack of activity, but make sure main body-building and protective nutrients are present.

Other diet restrictions and recommendations
Diabetes — low carbohydrate
Anaemia — foods rich in iron, e.g. offal, lean meat, green vegetables
Ulcers — bland foods; avoid fatty and high-fibre foods and alcohol
Gastroenteritis — liquids only for 12-24 hours; thereafter eat bland foods, skim milk. Avoid fatty and high-fibre foods.

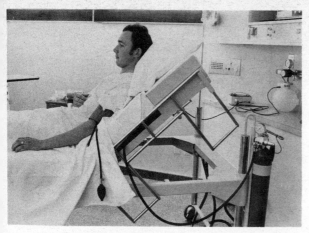
A hospital patient availing of modern equipment (Camera Press)

LOW CHOLESTEROL DIET

Cholesterol is a type of fat found in the body. When too much builds up in the blood it is deposited on the walls of the arteries, particularly those of the heart, causing them to become narrow. This is called atherosclerosis and is a major cause of heart attack.

Research points to a connection between the amount of animal fats in the diet and this cholesterol build up, particularly if the patient leads an inactive life. Foods high in polyunsaturated fats are thought to reduce the cholesterol level, and for this reason those with a high cholesterol level in the blood are put on a diet low in animal fats, and foods high in polyunsaturates are substituted for them.

FOODS HIGH IN CHOLESTEROL

Egg yolk, butter, full-fat cheese, cream, milk, meat fat, suet, lard, dripping, offal, shellfish.

FOODS HIGH IN POLYUNSATURATES

Polyunsaturated margarines, e.g. Flora (most margarines are not polyunsaturated); polyunsaturated oils, e.g. sunflower seed oil, corn oil, oily fish.

FACTORS WHICH CONTRIBUTE TO HEART DISEASE

diet — a diet high in animal fats
lack of exercise
obesity
cigarette smoking
emotional stress
heredity

Rules for reducing cholesterol

1. Reduce intake of foods rich in saturated fat and cholesterol.
2. Increase intake of polyunsaturates. Use oil for cooking.
3. Avoid over-eating. Lose weight if necessary.
4. Take regular exercise.
5. Give up smoking.
6. Avoid worry and stress.

Eat plenty of these:
fruit, vegetables, white and oily fish
skim milk rather than whole milk
cottage cheese rather than full-milk cheese
vegetable proteins, e.g. cereals and pulses
chicken

Cut down on these:
egg yolk (no more than 3 weekly)
shellfish
offal (not more than once a week)
fried foods, sugar
butter, cream, cheese
fat meat, e.g. bacon

HIGH-FIBRE DIET

Nutritionists today encourage a major increase in the amount of fibre eaten. This is because it has been discovered that our modern highly-refined foods have led to an increase in bowel disorders such as constipation, diverticulosis and even cancer of the bowel (large intestine). In countries where the diet consists largely of unrefined cereals and other plant foods, such diseases are rare.

Most of us would benefit from an increase in the fibre content of our diet, particularly those who suffer from constipation or other complications of the bowel.

Eat plenty of these:
wholemeal bread, bran, porridge
foods containing oats, whole cereals, wheatgerm
brown rice, nuts, vegetables, fruit, (preferably raw and unpeeled)

Cut down on these:
white bread
white rice
white sugar
convenience foods

LOW KILOCALORIE DIETS

A slimming or low-kilocalorie diet is one in which the amount of energy foods eaten is less than that which the body requires for energy production. The body then begins to use up its own store of energy, i.e. adipose tissue, so that weight is lost.

A good knowledge of nutrition is necessary before planning a low-kilocalorie diet — or any other.

1. Check with a doctor before starting any diet, particularly if you are a teenager or expecting a baby.
2. The only way to reduce weight is to reduce the intake of kilocalories or increase activity (or preferably both).

Fat people are often very anxious about their weight

3. A small steady weight loss is preferable to a drastic (and possibly dangerous) diet which promises a miracle reduction.
4. Remember, no food is slimming. All foods and liquids with the exception of water, tea and coffee contain kilocalories or potential energy and therefore potential fat.
5. *No* food helps burn up kilocalories.

6. Although exercise alone will not result in marked weight loss, it tones up flabby muscles and improves the figure.
7. It is easier to reduce food consumption slightly before too much weight is gained than to wait until a major diet is necessary.

DIETING

● The diet must be well balanced, with all necessary nutrients in a concentrated form.
● The purpose of a diet, apart from losing weight, is to retrain the appetite into a good eating pattern.
● It is dangerous to plan a diet on kilocalorie values alone. One could obtain sufficient calories by eating chips for breakfast, lunch and dinner! The overall value of each food must be considered. This is why cheese and oily fish, while high in kilocalories, are still included in many diets.
● Restrict carbohydrate intake, especially sugar, sweets and alcohol. These contain no nourishment, just pure kilocalories.
● Do not leave out fat entirely; it often contains vitamins A and D.
● Protein intake should be unchanged or slightly higher.
● Eat plenty of fruit and green vegetables; these are rich in vitamins, minerals and roughage.
● Never eat between meals.

Low energy menus

Breakfast: Include a protein food; as this is sustaining, you will be less tempted by mid morning snacks.

Main courses: Two portions daily from the following: lean meat, poultry, fish, eggs, low-fat cheese e.g. Edam. Eat offal e.g. liver once a week for iron. Trim visible fat from meat. Grill, boil, steam or bake — avoid frying. Vegetables and fruit: raw vegetables or fruit should be eaten daily, as well as one or two portions of cooked vegetables.

Milk and milk products: 250 ml distributed between food and drink. In strict diets, use skimmed milk. Do not exceed 15 g butter/margarine daily. Cottage cheese has the lowest energy value of any cheese.

Carbohydrate: 1 slice of bread or 1 small roll daily, plus 1 small portion of rice of 1 small potato; on strict diets, reduce these quantities or cut them out altogether.

Drinks: Unsweetened tea or coffee with very little milk; artificial sweeteners may be used.

	Breakfast	Lunch or Tea	Dinner
Sun.	Whole orange Muesli	Grilled mackerel Roll	Roast lamb Casserole of root vegetables or ratatouille Apple snow
Mon.	Boiled egg Brown bread and butter	Cheese salad Roll and butter	Shepherd's pie Carrots Pear
Tues.	Grapefruit half Porridge, half slice toast	Cauliflower cheese Fresh fruit	Grilled white fish Broccoli, small potato
Wed.	Poached egg on half slice toast Raw tomato	Rollmop herring Green salad Half slice brown bread	Baked chicken Peas Yoghurt
Thurs.	Orange juice Grilled rasher and mushroom Half slice toast	Coleslaw Hard-boiled egg	Beef curry Small portion rice Fruit salad
Fri.	Grapefruit juice Scrambled egg on toast	Savoury rice with mushrooms, peas	Liver casserole Fresh fruit
Sat.	Grilled kipper Raw tomato	Cheese omelette small roll	Consommée Mixed salad

Alternative main courses: Grilled steak or hamburger, Kebabs or baked fish, Corned beef.

A Japanese family enjoying an oriental dish of snakes (Orion Press)

Avoid these	*Restrict these*
fried foods	butter, margarine
tinned foods	starchy vegetables
cream	pulse vegetables
sugar, jam	fat meats
biscuits, sweets	certain fruits, e.g.
cakes, pastry	grapes and bananas
mayonnaise	bread, toast
nuts	breakfast cereals
convenience foods	rice, pasta
alcohol, soft drinks	cocoa

Eat plenty of these	
lettuce and salad vegetables	white fish
mushrooms (not fried)	fresh fruit juice
green vegetables	low-fat natural yoghurt
liver	cottage cheese
	lean meat

VEGETARIAN DIETS

Vegetarianism is the practice of living on vegetable foods. Animal flesh, fowl and fish are not eaten. A large proportion of the world's population survives on a vegetarian diet, usually through poverty and the unavailability of animal foods, rather than from choice.

Many vegetarians have religious reasons for not eating animal flesh; others consider it inhumane to kill animals for food. There is a growing swing towards vegetarianism in the western world, helped no doubt by the increasing cost of animal foods, but also influenced by other cultures, by travel and the media.

Health-food shops and delicatessens now sell many foods which in the past were difficult to find, enabling those who wish to follow this alternative eating pattern to do so without difficulty.

There are two types of vegetarian:

(a) the lacto-vegetarian, who refuses to eat animal flesh and fish but will eat animal products such as milk, cheese and eggs;

(b) the vegan — a strict vegetarian who eats no animal produce whatsoever — no milk, cheese, eggs, cream, butter. It is this diet which creates difficulties for the cook and which may produce nutritional deficiencies unless it is carefully planned.

NUTRITION

As the diet of the lacto-vegetarian is usually well balanced, we will deal from here on with the vegan diet. We have learned that vegetable proteins contain fewer essential amino acids than animal proteins contain. In order to obtain all these amino acids, the vegan must eat a very wide range of plant foods to include cereals, pulses and other vegetables in order to compensate for the lower quality of protein in them. Textured vegetable protein, a synthetic meat substitute made from soya beans, is a useful ingredient in a vegan diet as it contains all the essential amino acids and can be used in many ways.

If a wide range of plant foods is eaten, it is unlikely that any deficiencies will occur, with the exception of vitamin B_{12}. Most vegans now take supplements of this vitamin. Vitamin A deficiency may be found in those eating mainly rice, and niacin is sometimes deficient in diets where the staple food is maize.

ADVANTAGES OF VEGETARIANISM

1. Obesity is rare among vegetarians.
2. Blood cholesterol is lower.
3. Owing to the large amount of fibre eaten, diverticulosis and other bowel disorders are rare.
4. Many claim a feeling of well-being, a reduction of allergies etc. on a meat-free diet, but these claims have not been scientifically proven.
5. Social and economic advantages in using land for producing plant foods, rather than rearing animals which is wasteful.

PLANNING A VEGETARIAN DIET

1. A sound knowledge of nutrition is necessary to ensure that the diet is well balanced and not lacking any essential nutrient.
2. More ingenuity and skill is necessary if one is to avoid a dull and monotonous diet than when meat is included in the menu.
3. Many vegetarian meals are served eastern-style, either with several small courses or with an assortment of dishes on the table at one time — in Indian or Chinese style. This may be followed by tea or coffee.
4. Vegetable soups are useful as first courses, but meat stock or stock cubes may not be used.
5. Pasta dishes, e.g. spaghetti and noodles, and cereal dishes based on wheat, oats, rice or millet are substantial and nourishing, e.g. risotto, pilaf, muesli, fried rice.
6. Pulse vegetables should be included for their high protein content. A wide range of dried pulses is available in health stores and delicatessens, e.g. lentils, split peas, haricot and red kidney beans.
7. Nuts are a good source of protein and fat. They may be used in main dishes such as nut roasts and rissoles, sprinkled over dishes or in stuffings and cakes.
8. Whole cereals or ground whole cereals, e.g. wholemeal, are preferable to processed or milled cereals because of the roughage and B vitamins they provide. Use wholemeal flour and bread instead of white, brown rice instead of polished white rice.
9. Cheese, milk and eggs, if taken, should be included regularly as they are a good source of animal protein.
10. Use herbs, spices, sauces etc. to give extra flavour to bland foods. Sauces add moisture, flavour and colour to dishes.
11. Use vegetable fats and oils only.

Suggested dishes

(a) Lacto-vegetarian

Omelettes, quiches and savoury flans, curried eggs or vegetables, pizza, macaroni cheese, milk puddings, cakes etc. plus dishes used by

(b) Vegans

Vegetable casseroles and pies, salads, vegetable soups, fried rice, nut roasts and cutlets, TVP dishes (e.g. spaghetti bolognese) stuffed vegetables, pilaf, risotto, Indian and other eastern dishes.

MACROBIOTIC DIET

This is quite similar to a vegetarian diet, although meat is permitted on rare occasions. Only 'natural' foods, organically grown, are allowed. Refined foods, preservatives and chemicals are avoided. Fruits and vegetables are eaten in season or dried naturally. Grain is the main food eaten. Certain foods may not be eaten together. Like all vegetarian-type diets, this has a high fibre content.

QUESTIONS/CHAPTER 2

1. List the special points which must be remembered when planning meals for (a) old people, (b) children. Plan a menu for one day for either of these groups, giving reasons for your choice of food.

2. Discuss vegetarianism. Refer to
   (a) reasons,
   (b) advantages and disadvantages,
   (c) planning menus.
   Write a day's menu for a vegan and give reasons for your choice of each dish.

3. Write a menu for three days for a female office worker who wishes to lose weight. Refer to the approximate kilocalorie value of each food mentioned and give the total energy intake for one day.

4. What is a balanced diet? List the daily requirements for an average adult, giving examples of suitable foods in each case.
   Write a paragraph on the importance of fibre in the diet.

5. List the nutritional needs of pregnant women. Plan a menu for one day which would meet these needs. Discuss briefly the pros and cons of breast-feeding.

6. What is cholesterol? List the main ways by which the level of cholesterol could be lowered.
   Plan a two-day menu for a 50-year-old man on a low-cholesterol diet.
   What factors other than diet contribute to heart disease?

3.
Managing our money

We hear a lot of talk today about the 'cost of living'. People complain about high prices and inflation. Each young wage-earner soon discovers that large chunks of a weekly wage packet are quickly swallowed up. There are government deductions such as income tax and social insurance, as well as essential spending such as food, clothes and transport.

EARNING

Most of us are paid regularly, either weekly or monthly.

Gross income is the total amount of money we earn each week, month or year.

Net income is the amount of money left after compulsory deductions have been made; in other words, the amount we have to spend.

Deductions to expect from income include:
(1) *income tax,* pay as you earn (PAYE);
(2) pay-related *social insurance* (PRSI);
(3) *superannuation,* i.e. payment towards a pension;
(4) *health insurance;* and many others.

SPENDING

Bills tend to arrive very irregularly. Some come once a year, others twice a year, or every two or three months. We buy items such as food and newspapers every day, while seasonal spending such as summer clothes, school books, Christmas presents and unexpected items like house repairs or doctor's or chemist's bills crop up only now and then.

Because spending is so irregular, we need to put aside much of our money each pay-day so that it is there when we need it for essentials. A plan for spending is called a **budget.**

Lots of people find it hard to make ends meet, yet few go to the trouble of planning how to spend their money. We should sit down and list our **needs** — what we **must** have (food, shelter) — separately from **wants** (what we would like). Then we can allocate the amount of money needed for essentials and feel safe in the knowledge that what is left over can be spent on entertainment or other personal use without worrying about the next major bill.

Budgeting therefore gives us control over our money and, as a result, over our lives.

Trying to keep a balance between earning and spending

HOW TO PLAN A BUDGET

1. Divide a large sheet of paper into two columns (use a pencil as you may have to do some erasing!).

2. At the top of one column, write *Income* (money coming in). Under this you will list your weekly wage (after deductions). Married couples should write down both incomes, if both are working, plus children's allowances or any other extra income. It is better not to be too optimistic: for example don't allow for overtime unless you are certain that it will continue all year.

3. At the top of the second column, write *Expenditure,* and list firstly all important bills and expenses that must be paid, and then the less essential expenses.

4. Allow a sum for savings and emergencies, if possible.

5. After all these essentials have been met, plan a sum for entertainment and personal spending.

Income	£	Expenditure	£
1. Husband's earnings		1. Rent/mortgage	
2. Wife's earnings		Food	
3. Children's allowances		Electricity	
4. Interest on savings (if any)		Other fuels	
		Household expenses	
		Education/health	
		2. Clothes	
		Telephone	
		Insurance	
		Travel (car/fares)	
		Furniture	
		3. Savings	
		4. Personal	
		Entertainment	
		Holidays	

Having worked out a **yearly budget,** make sure you check it each month against expenditure. It may be necessary to alter it to suit changing circumstances, such as a new baby, or retirement. You may find you are over-spending in one area and leaving yourself short in a more essential area. It is impossible to work out a budget to suit everyone. Each family will have different priorities depending on (a) *income,* (b) the *stage of the family,* for example newly-weds, those with school-going children or pensioners, (c) the *number in the family,* and so on. For example a single girl will have less essential spending than a young family, which has mortgage commitments, baby requisities, children's clothes and furniture to buy.

Money worries

Remember: a **family budget** should be a joint venture; both husband and wife should be involved in planning how family income should be spent.

ALLOCATING YOUR INCOME

This gives an idea of how family income should be spent.

25% Housing
Rent or mortgage repayments; house insurance; house and garden maintenance

20-25% Food
It is important to feed the family a well-balanced diet, otherwise you will have higher doctor's and chemist's bills. Economise by shopping carefully; cut down on meat consumption and use the cheaper cuts; buy fruit and vegetables in season, and avoid too many convenience foods.

20% Household
This includes fuel for cooking, heating and lighting; furniture and equipment; household linen; cleaning materials; telephone. Keep fuel bills down by insulating the house well. Economise on heating and cooking fuels.

7-10% Clothing
Clothes, shoes and dry-cleaning come under this heading. Economise by shopping in chain stores or during sales. Better still, make your own clothes.

5% Car/Fares
Lots of money can be saved here if you live near work or use a bicycle.

5% Education/Health
School books, sports gear, extra classes, for example music, are included here, as well as doctor's, dentist's and chemist's bills. Pay Voluntary Health Insurance from here also.

5% Savings
Always set aside a regular sum towards emergencies. Life assurance may also come from this area.

Buying new clothes (Camera Press)

5% Entertainment
Cinema, theatre, discos, baby-sitters. Don't forget, many hobbies cost little or nothing: walking, jogging, football, joining a library. Certain hobbies such as gardening, woodwork and dress-making can *save* money.

5% Personal
Cosmetics, hairdresser, gifts, hobbies, books, stationery, sports and pets come from here.

HERE IS HOW A TYPICAL FAMILY'S INCOME WAS SPENT IN 1980:

Housing	7.2%	
Fuel and light	6.1%	20.7%
Household durables	5.5%	
Household non-durables	1.9%	
Food	27.7%	
Alcoholic drink	4.4%	
Clothing, footwear	8.9%	
Transport	14.9%	
Services and other expenditure	16.8%	
Tobacco	2.8%	
Miscellaneous goods	3.8%	
	100.0%	

BUDGET FOR THOSE ON A LOW INCOME

Many families have to make ends meet on extremely low incomes, for example those on unemployment benefit, elderly couples on retirement or old-age pensions. These people must spend all their money on necessities and it is unlikely that they will have sufficient left over to put some by in savings. Here is a sample budget for those with very little cash:

Food	35%
Rent	20%
Fuel (heat, light, cooking)	20%
Clothes (particularly for children)	10%
Fares	10%
Extras	10%
Total	100%

SAMPLE BUDGET FOR A YOUNG SINGLE PERSON

Keep	up to 35%
Fares	10%
Lunches/Snacks	10%
Clothes	15%
Entertainment	15%
Savings/Insurance	10%
Miscellaneous including hobbies	5-10%

POCKET MONEY AND EARLY EARNINGS

It is never too early to start budgeting. It teaches children to handle money sensibly, makes them independent and prepares them for life after school. They should be taught to put some money by from their pocket money for future purchases. The amount of pocket money given will depend on the family income. Extra money can often be earned by doing jobs such as baby-sitting.

Older children may benefit from a clothes allowance, for example a quarterly sum from which all clothes must be bought. This teaches youngsters the value of money and the importance of buying good quality clothes.

Budgeting for clothes
1. Keep money for clothes in a separate account.
2. Save to buy goods, classic clothes rather than the latest fashions which soon go out of date. Avoid impulse buying.
3. Plan your wardrobe around one or two basic colours which co-ordinate.
4. Each year, extra items can be added to this core of basic clothes.
5. Buy good quality accessories, for example leather bags, belts and shoes, in neutral colours which will suit most items in your wardrobe and which won't date.

KEEPING ACCOUNTS

It is a good idea to keep a simple account of what you spend each week. By doing this you will know exactly where the money is going and how much you have left to spend. Each evening, jot down your daily spending and before long it will be obvious, if you are running into debt, where you are being extravagant, and where you can cut back.

Here is a sample account.

Date	Goods or Services paid for	Cash
4 Oct.	Coal	£50.00
	Milk	5.50
	Supermarket	30.00
	Newspapers	.80

Don't forget to list every single item of spending.

It is possible to buy cash notebooks that are suitable for keeping accounts. Larger account books, often with household spending itemised to make it easier, are also available.

PAYING THE BILLS

When you buy an item or avail of a service, there are several ways of paying for it.

1. Cash: This is the easiest, quickest and cheapest way of paying. It is used for most small transactions and is accepted everywhere. A disadvantage is that it can be lost or stolen. It is very risky to carry large amounts.
2. Cheque: This is a safer way of paying for large purchases. One usually needs to have a current account in a bank (see p. 39). A cheque card is almost always necessary. This means that the bank guarantees to pay the sum on the cheque up to a certain limit, its purpose being to protect the public from fraud.
3. Credit card: (see p. 41). This is useful when paying fairly large sums of money.
4. Credit transfer (Giro): This is useful for those who have not got a bank account as well as those who have. By this method one can transfer sums of money to other banks anywhere in the country. One can pay several bills in one transaction. Fill in a giro form for each payment you wish to make (electricity bill, phone bill, etc.) and pay cash or write a cheque to cover the total amount. The bank will then transfer the money to the bank account of each of the companies. This method saves trouble and each payment made costs a fraction less than sending a cheque by post.
5. Postal orders: These are bought in a post office for a nominal charge. They are useful for paying bills by post.
6. Some companies make it easier for us to pay their large bills by allowing us to buy regular 'stamps' which can be used to offset the bills when they arrive. Examples are electricity bills and television licences.

SAVINGS

From the start, children should be taught to put aside a little of their pocket money each week. A young person should start saving from the moment s/he starts earning. The important thing about saving is to get into the habit of it as soon as possible. You can start saving for a particular object, such as a coat or a holiday, or just save so that you have money there whenever you should need it.

A family will also want to save for specific items such as a house or a car but they should also have an emergency fund which is kept separate and is drawn from only in a genuine emergency. It is hard for those on low incomes to save but it is important to set aside even a small sum for emergencies. For those with unstable jobs, it is essential.

Once you decide to save, the next question is where to invest your money. Under the mattress is not such a good idea: it earns no interest, it may be stolen or the house may go on fire!

The three main things to consider are: (a) Rates of interest; (b) Ease of withdrawal; (c) Safety and reliability.

Rates of interest

These vary a lot. Banks, building societies, etc. always charge the borrower a higher rate of interest than they pay to the investor. These companies run their offices and pay their staff on the difference between these rates of interest. Most rates of interest are based on the bank rate. When this rises, most other financial institutions raise their rates.

Ease of withdrawal

With some accounts, notice must be given before withdrawing large sums of money. It is handier to save

---

ADVANTAGES OF BUDGETING

The only *disadvantage* of budgeting is the bother of keeping accounts but this is more than made up for by its *advantages:*

1. Greater sense of security and comfort.
2. A budget usually allows for major bills and seasonal spending and makes sure something is set aside for emergencies.
3. Without a plan, there is a danger of overspending on luxuries and not having enough for necessities.
4. A budget cuts down on impulse buying and irresponsible spending.
5. By writing down expenditure, it is easy to see where overspending occurs and where to cut down, if necessary.
6. It gives children a good example in the handling of money and makes them responsible.
7. Failure to plan spending can lead to serious financial problems.

The wrong way to save

with a group that has many branches, e.g. post offices and banks, as withdrawals and deposits can usually be made at any branch in the country.

Safety

Most well-known institutions (banks, large building societies and government sponsored savings) are very safe places to save. Investing in the stock market or in new unproven financial investments is not reliable. Keeping large sums of money at home is not only risky — it is just plain silly.

WHERE TO PUT YOUR MONEY

Government sponsored saving

Post office savings bank: A post office account can be opened with as little as 50p. A savings book is issued which should be produced each time a deposit or withdrawal is made. One can withdraw small amounts without notice; for larger amounts, a few days' notice in writing must be given. The main advantage of a post office account is conveneince, as one can deposit or withdraw at any post office in the country.

National instalment savings (post office)

Under this scheme a person agrees to save a certain amount each month for one year. This is left on account for at least two more years, when a bonus related to the consumer price index is paid. This ensures that the amount repaid will never be less in real terms than the amount saved. There is an extra bonus if savings are left for five years.

Savings certificates

Usually bought in post offices in units of £1, £5, £10, £20, £50 or £100, up to a certain limit. Interest, which is tax free, is averaged over five years.

Investment bonds

Bought in multiples of £10, these gain a high rate of interest (but this is liable for income tax) as well as a bonus on maturity after five years.

Savings stamps

Bought in a post office, these cost a few pence each. They are usually used by children to save money. The stamps are put into a savings book until one page (or the book) is filled. They may be cashed in at any time.

Prize bonds

These cost £5 each and are available at banks and post offices. No interest is paid, but each bond goes into a draw which takes place weekly and monthly, for a large top prize and several smaller prizes.

Trustee savings banks

These are non-profit-making organisations, which are state guaranteed, e.g. Trustee Savings Bank. They offer similar facilities to the post office for savers,

although they sometimes provide chequebooks and various types of loans.

Commercial banks

These are large financial institutions with subsidiaries in other financial areas, for example Bank of Ireland and Allied Irish Banks. There are two types of account.

Current account

This is useful for keeping everyday money safe. A *chequebook* is used with this type of account, which saves carrying around large sums of money. Regular bills can be paid by *'standing order'* — so long as the amount does not change — this saves remembering them every month. Two or more people, e.g. a husband and wife, can have a *joint account,* and either can draw

cheques. A *cheque card* or *bank card* is available to facilitate the cashing of cheques. There is no interest paid on money in a current account. In fact there is an annual charge which increases according to the number of transactions you make. Each month or quarter a *statement* is issued showing the present balance. One may also get permission to overdraw an account (spend more than one has) if one has a kindly bank manager.

Deposit account

This is quite different from a current account. Its main purpose is for saving money and interest is paid on money in the account. Cash can be withdrawn on production of the deposit book.

Many banks now enable customers to withdraw cash and avail of other services outside banking hours

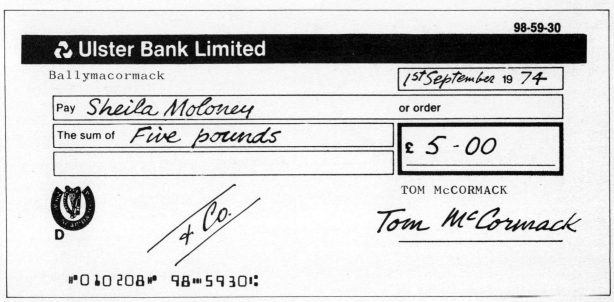

A cheque all ready to be used

by means of a computer card which can be inserted in machines outside certain branches, and linked up to a central computer. Banks also offer safety deposit facilities, loans for personal and commercial use, financial advice and many other services.

Building societies

These are a good place to save, especially if one is thinking of buying a house in the future. Those who have saved with a building society will get a preference when it comes to getting a loan. Interest is free of standard rate tax. There are two types of account:

(a) *Deposit account:* This is the more usual. You have a deposit book and can deposit or withdraw (up to a certain limit) when you like.

(b) *Shares account:* One saves a set amount monthly. It is necessary to give advance notice of withdrawal. There is a slightly higher rate of interest with this type of account.

Insurance companies

Most insurance companies have various schemes for saving money. These include pension plans and unit trusts (collective long-term investment in property or shares run by experts in these matters). There is usually tax relief if you invest with Irish insurance companies, such as Irish Life.

Piggybanks will encourage small children to save

Credit unions

These are ideal for small savers. Although the rate of interest is low for savers, it is also low if one wants to borrow money. The credit union is run by local members, often on a voluntary basis, which cuts down on overheads. Members' savings are insured while invested and provide loans to other members at low interest. Credit unions encourage people on low incomes to save and therefore perform an important service for the community.

ADVANTAGES OF SAVING

1. One *earns* interest, instead of paying it.
2. The money saved can be spent on something worthwhile instead of being wasted.
3. Savings give the individual and the family a sense of security.

CREDIT BUYING

'Neither a borrower nor a lender be', Shakespeare (*Hamlet*). Attitudes to credit have changed since Shakespeare's time. Although it used to be regarded with distrust, there is no doubt that credit can be very useful if used wisely. It is foolish to say that credit itself should be avoided, but it is essential to be cautious where any form of credit is concerned.

Note: Credit is more easily obtained by reliable people, those with a steady job and a good credit rating.

Credit comes in many forms: mortgages, overdrafts, budget accounts, credit cards, hire purchase (HP), but

Take care when buying on credit

they all amount to the same thing: buy now, pay later. Most people use at least one form of credit during their lifetime.

When you borrow money, you must expect to pay (often dearly) for the privilege. Companies and banks make large profits from lending money. When the price they charge for borrowing money (called interest) is added to the original loan, it is considerably increased.

ARE YOU A GOOD RISK

Credit is based on trust. Before any bank or finance company lends money to an applicant, it is necessary for it to find out whether s/he is trustworthy. The applicant must fill out a form giving personal details about job, expenses and whether s/he has used credit before. Names of individuals who will give references will be requested so that the company can check whether previous debts have been promptly paid. If so, the applicant will be considered a good credit risk; if not, s/he may be turned down.

There are several forms of credit:

HIRE PURCHASE

Hire purchase is based on the principle that the buyer hires the goods and pays for them in regular instalments over a certain period of time. During this time the buyer has the use of the goods but does not *own* them until the final instalment has been paid.

The buyer pays the normal cash price of the goods plus interest. A deposit may be required. A person under eighteen needs a guarantor. A hire purchase agreement should state clearly in writing:
1. the cash price of the goods;
2. the amount of each instalment;
3. the full hire purchase price, inclusive of interest;
4. the date on which instalments fall due;
5. a clear description of the goods;
6. details of your rights should you wish to return the goods.
Note: Beware of signing any agreement which is not fully understood. Read the contract carefully, including the small print, and do not sign a blank form. Once signed, the agreement is binding.

It is important to know your rights should you be unable to continue paying. If one-third of the price of the goods has been paid, the finance company cannot just walk into your house and take the goods. They must first take out a court order to repossess the goods. On the other hand, if after paying a couple of instalments you decide you don't want to continue

paying, and ask them to take the goods back, they can insist that you pay half the full hire purchase price and pay for any damage to the goods.

CREDIT SALES

The most usual way that we avail of this form of credit is to run up a bill in a shop or department store which we pay at the end of the month. Our milk and bread deliveries are paid for in this way also. Sometimes small purchases such as clothes or soft furnishings can be paid for in instalments over a short period, say six months or a year. As the rights of the seller are not as well protected as in hire purchase, it is a less common form of credit today. The main difference is that the goods become the property of the buyer at the time of sale, and if s/he defaults in paying, the shop will have to sue for the balance.

BUDGET ACCOUNTS

A budget account is a form of revolving credit which is frequently offered by department stores or clothes shops. Here is how it works.

An agreement is made to pay a fixed sum to a shop every month, £10 for example. After the first payment, goods up to ten times that value — £100 in this instance — can be purchased. When some of that has been paid off by the monthly instalments, more goods can be purchased, as long as the credit limit is not exceeded. Interest with this type of account varies considerably, so carefully check the annual interest before signing.

CREDIT CARDS

A credit card enables one to buy an item in a shop or avail of a service in a hotel or garage which displays an appropriate symbol, without using cash. Some well-known credit cards are Access, Visa and American Express. They are not to be confused with bankers' cards, which guarantee cheques. One doesn't need to have a bank account to own a credit card, but one must have a good credit rating.

A credit card allows its owner to buy goods or pay for services up to a pre-arranged limit, e.g. £400. A monthly account is issued which itemises purchases. If the whole bill is paid promptly, some companies charge no interest. Otherwise a percentage of the balance must be paid off and interest is charged on the remainder. It is conveneint to be able to pay for many of your monthly purchases with one cheque, but there is a very real danger of overspending and getting deeply into debt, particularly if one is a compulsive buyer.

Advantages of credit
1. The buyer has the use of the goods long before s/he could afford to buy them for cash.
2. Large items such as cars or houses would be almost impossible to buy without credit.
3. Today prices increase very rapidly. If you were to save first, it might be difficult to keep up with price increases. With credit sales, one is not affected by price increases, indeed the interest charges are often offset by price increases.
4. Goods may be serviced or repaired during the repayment period.
5. It avoids the risk of carrying large sums of money.
6. It encourages a flow of cash and goods, thereby increasing employment.
7. It can sometimes save money, e.g. buying a sewing machine, you can make your clothes more cheaply, while you are still paying for the machine.

Disadvantages of credit
1. Interest rates are high. It might be better to save first.
2. There is a danger of taking on too many credit commitments and not being able to keep up the repayments.
3. Credit is too tempting for weak-willed or compulsive buyers.
4. Many door-to-door salesmen take advantage of housewives at home on their own by persuading them to sign agreements for items they don't need.

MORTGAGE LOANS

This is one of the most frequently used forms of credit. Few of us would be able to buy a house if we had to pay cash for it. Instead we borrow the money from a building society or bank and pay them back over 20-25 years (see p. 55-6).

CREDIT AND THE LAW

The consumer who wishes to buy on credit is protected by the Hire Purchase Acts 1946 and 1960 which laid down certain conditions for hire purchase agreements. More recently, the Sale of Goods and Supply of Services Act 1980 has tightened up certain areas of the law to further protect the consumer.

INSURANCE

The purpose of insurance is to share risks. Those insured pay into a central fund from which the losses of the unlucky (e.g. those who crash their cars) are paid. All money paid in is used by the company or paid out to claimants; it is not paid back if you do not have a claim.

Insurance can be compulsory, e.g. social insurance or car insurance, or voluntary, e.g. life assurance.

The sum of money paid to the insurance company is called a *premium*. This can be paid directly to the company or through an *insurance broker*. If you have a

claim e.g. if you are burgled or your house goes on fire, you fill out a claims form and after investigation the insurance company will pay out a sum of money to compensate you.

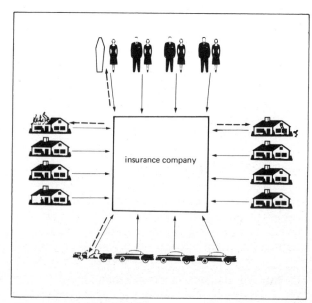

Insurance means sharing risks

Types of insurance
1. *Life assurance*

This is a form of insurance taken out on the life of a person. If the person dies, a sum of money will be paid to the person named (usually a husband or wife). There are basically two forms of life assurance:

(a) Term (temporary) — a basic life cover which insures a person's life for a fixed number of years (usually while the family is young). If s/he dies during this time, a sum of money is paid to the spouse by the insurance company.

(b) Endowment assurance — by this method a sum of money is paid either if the policy-holder dies during a fixed period, e.g. before the age of 60, or if s/he survives the period s/he receives a capital sum at 60. In other words, it is a combination of saving and life assurance and for this reason the premiums are more expensive than for term assurance.

(The word *assurance* is used when the event is certain to happen, e.g. death; *insurance* is used when it might happen, e.g. fire or accident.)

2. *House insurance*

All houses should be insured against **fire, storms and damage.** It is also wise to take out a policy (mortgage protection policy) to cover the repayment of a mortgage loan if the mortgagor dies.

Contents: quite a small annual premium will cover the contents of an average house against fire, theft and damage. No household should be without it.

All risks: this is an extra policy to cover any valuables (furs, jewellery, stereo). They will be covered whether in or out of the house.

3. *Social insurance*

This is a compulsory insurance scheme implemented by the state to which all employees over sixteen must contribute. The employer pays part of the contribution for each employee, while the remainder is deducted from each employee's weekly pay-packet. As this is in proportion to one's earnings, it is known as pay-related social insurance (PRSI).

Social insurance benefits are generally paid weekly and are also pay-related. They include
Unemployment benefit: payment to those who are unemployed.
Disability benefit: paid to those unable to work due to illness or disability.
Maternity benefit: paid to mothers for six weeks before and six weeks after confinement.
Invalidity pension: paid to those permanently unable to work.
Contributory widow's pension: paid on either wife's or husband's insurance.
Deserted wife's benefit: paid on either wife's or husband's insurance.

Contributory old age pension: paid to those aged 66 and over.

Other benefits include treatment benefit for *dental* and *optical treatment, death grant* and *maternity grant.*

Note: certain conditions must be fulfilled before payment will be made, particularly relating to the number of contributions made (usually 26 — in the *previous* insurance year).

4. *Permanent health insurance*

For those not covered by social insurance, e.g. certain state employees and the self-employed, this ensures payment of a percentage of salary during temporary or permanent disability.

5. *Voluntary Health Insurance* (VHI)

Most people are entitled to free accommodation and treatment in the public wards of any hospital. Voluntary health insurance covers the cost of private accommodation, specialists' fees for those (above a certain income) who must pay their own, as well as the cost of basic medical expenses: doctors' fees, prescriptions not covered by Health Board entitlement, X-rays, pathology tests. The annual premium varies with the size of the family and the amount of cover required. It is important to have sufficient cover with this and all types of insurance.

6. *Superannuation or pension plans*

Individuals or companies can pay a percentage of salary into a *pension scheme*. After working the required number of years, often forty, the employee receives a pension. Schemes vary between companies.

Other common types of insurance
7. Car insurance: third party or comprehensive
8. Insurance against educational expenses
9. Travel insurance

Advantages of insurance
1. Most people, particularly families, feel happier and more secure in the knowledge that the breadwinner is insured so that they will be provided for should s/he die.
2. Insurance protects you against the shocks of life — robbery, fire, accident and attempts to make up for them.
3. Insurance can be used as a form of saving or as a pension for old age.
4. Tax relief can be claimed on life, health and medical insurance.

---

1. List the major areas of expenditure to be accounted for when planning a family budget. How are these apportioned: (a) on an income of £100 per week, (b) on an income of £150 per week? Describe two ways by which a family might reduce its expenditure in order to keep within its budget.
2. Name the deductions to be expected from a gross weekly pay packet. List the current rates of

    (a) basic social insurance contributions;

    (b) basic and upper rate of income tax;

    (c) current rate of interest for savers in the post office savings bank;

    (d) current rate of unemployment benefit for a single person.

3. Explain the difference between 'wants' and 'needs'. List ten 'wants' and ten 'needs' a teenager might have. Plan a weekly budget for a young first-time wage earner, assuming s/he is still living at home.
4. What basic factors should be considered, and why, when deciding where to invest regular savings? Name three government-sponsored savings schemes and describe one in detail, together with its advantages and disadvantages.
5. Explain the term 'credit buying'. Name three forms of buying on credit and describe one in detail. List the general advantages and disadvantages of credit purchase.
6. Name three forms of voluntary insurance which you would consider necessary for a breadwinner and family. Describe one in detail. List the main benefits one is entitled to under PRSI.

4.
Consumer education

SHOPPING AND YOU

One of the most basic lessons each consumer must learn is how to shop wisely. Much consumer information can be picked up from articles in newspapers and magazines, but the vast majority of us learn the hard way: through trial and error.

'Never judge a book by its cover'! Even the most sensible people can make very silly decisions when it comes to shopping. We are often tempted to buy because of an attractive wrapper on a product or a catchy TV jingle.

How many times have we been disappointed when the product didn't live up to the description the advertisers gave it?

Manufacturers spend lots of time and money finding out our weaknesses: our favourite colours, foods and TV ads, things we like and dislike. They use this knowledge to help them design packets, advertisements and even supermarkets, in order that we will buy as much as possible. We must be just as smart as they are, and refuse to allow such unimportant outward appearances rather than quality to influence what we buy.

QUALITY AND VALUE

For those who have lots of money, it's easy (but nonetheless wasteful) to shop carelessly. When money is scarce it is extremely important to shop with care, paying close attention to what we are buying and how much it costs. Most of us like to get good value when we shop, so much so that we often forget about quality in our eagerness to save money. It is essential that each item we buy is suitable for its purpose and that when meant to do so, it should last a reasonable time.

What you buy should be
1. good quality;
2. good value for money;
3. suitable for its purpose;
4. well designed and made;
5. suited to your needs;
6. capable of withstanding normal wear and tear (except for items used at once e.g. food).

COMPARING SHOPS

INDIVIDUAL SHOPS

Most are privately owned and give personal attention and service. There is often a more friendly atmosphere in this type of store, which includes butchers, greengrocers, delicatessens and other small food shops, clothes boutiques, and newsagents. Although often more expensive than large stores, many people prefer the small shop where the customer is known and the service friendly.

ADVANTAGES

1. Many stay open at weekends and late at night for the convenience of their customers, particularly in city 'flatland' areas.
2. Housewives use them for daily supplies of perishables such as milk or fruit, or for items forgotten in the weekly visit to the supermarket.
3. Old people like them because many shopkeepers will stop for a chat, give them advice on purchases, and sell them items such as eggs and sausages in small amounts.
4. It is possible to send a child for a message to this type of shop, as he will probably be known to the shopkeeper and the shop is likely to be nearby.
5. Credit is often allowed, the customer paying his bill at the end of the week or once a month. Whether this is an advantage is arguable.
6. Some small grocery shops deliver goods.

SUPERMARKETS AND SELF-SERVICE STORES

The principal difference between a supermarket and a self-service store is in its size: any self-service store with a floor area of over 374 sq. metres is considered a supermarket. A hypermarket or superstore is an exceptionally large supermarket, often ten to twenty times greater in size. It is usually situated in an out-of-town location where it can attract many customers. Apart from a huge supermarket area, they have many full-sized shops under one roof, selling as varied a selection of goods as one would find in any town or city.

Supermarkets are probably the cheapest food shops of all. This is due to the fact that they buy in huge quantities directly from the manufacturer at competitive prices. The self-service system cuts down on the number of staff required, lowering costs still further.

A great deal of thought and money goes into the planning of supermarkets. They are designed partly for the comfort and convenience of the customer, but also to encourage him to spend as much money as possible. The warmth, attractive surroundings and piped music tend to hypnotise the shopper so that s/he does not notice how much he is buying. Many shoppers fail to notice that many tempting goods are placed at eye level, or that essentials are displayed towards the back of the shop, ensuring that 'special offers', biscuits, soft drinks, and other luxuries must be passed before the shopper reaches the more important items. The customer is unable to resist the temptation to slip one or two into the trolley and is dismayed at the checkout to find that the bill is far larger than expected. Another well-known trick is the display of sweets at the checkout at just the right height for small children. Many mothers faced with this dilemma either give in and buy sweets or suffer the possible embarrassment of a screaming child.

SIGNS OF A GOOD SUPERMARKET

1. The shop should be clean and hygienic. Perishables should be covered and chilled if necessary.
2. Assistants should be clean, wear fresh overalls and have hair which is neat. Hands and fingernails should be spotless. Cuts should be covered in waterproof dressings. They should not smoke, handle face or hair, or cough or sneeze over food.
3. The assistants should be helpful, the manager efficient.
4. Goods should be well displayed, with prices clearly marked.
5. All food stores should display clearly a list of basic food prices.
6. There should be a good turnover, with plenty of variety. New stock should not be packed in front of old stock on the shelves.
7. Aisles should be wide enough to enable two trolleys to pass easily.
8. There should be sufficient checkout points to avoid queues, particularly at rush hours.
9. Good car parking space should be provided as well as a convenient bus stop.
10. Toilets, an indoor pram parking area and a crèche are useful extras.

HYGIENE

A good shopper should insist on cleanliness wherever s/he shops. Complain when you come across dirty conditions.

Avoid any food shop with these faults:
1. A dirty, unswept shop where flies are plentiful and shelves and equipment unwashed.
2. No restriction on dogs.
3. Perishables such as meat, fish and cakes not covered or refrigerated.
4. Raw and cooked meats displayed and sold together.
5. Frozen food not stored at correct temperatures.
6. Food for sale after its expiry date.
7. Packages which look as though they have been bitten through; this may indicate infestation by mice.

8. Dirty, unkempt staff with dirty hands or soiled overalls.
9. Staff who handle both food and money.

ADVANTAGES OF SUPERMARKETS

1. Supermarket prices are generally the cheapest.
2. A wide range of goods is available with many sizes and brands.
3. Many supermarkets sell cheap 'own brand' products.
4. The shopper can spend time comparing prices.
5. Goods are easily identified and clearly marked.
6. Unit pricing in some supermarkets makes it easier to compare sizes, brands and prices.
7. The trolleys provided enable a shopper to make a large number of purchases and to stock up for a week for two. Large bags are provided to hold the purchases. Trolleys are also convenient for a mother with a young child.
8. Shopping in a supermarket is quick and convenient if there are enough checkouts in operation.
9. Most supermarkets maintain a high standard of service and hygiene.
10. All household shopping can be done under one roof.

DISADVANTAGES

1. Shopping in a supermarket can be impersonal and cold. Assistants are often too busy and unhelpful to assist a customer.
2. Self-service stores encourage the buyer to overspend on non-essentials.
3. Long queues tend to form at checkout points.
4. Old people find this system confusing and have difficulty coping with baskets and trolleys.
5. As most food is prepacked, it is difficult to buy a small amount. This is inconvenient for old-age pensioners and others living alone. (Note: Some supermarkets now sell dry goods loosely, e.g. rice, cereals. This works out cheaper, but care must be taken that the food bins and the area around them are kept very clean, otherwise there might be a danger of contamination by vermin and micro-organisms.)
6. It is difficult to check the prices when they are rung up on the register, especially if one is trying to pack goods into bags at the same time.
7. Prepacked meat and vegetables are often a bad buy: inferior fatty parts of meat are turned to the inside of the pack; soft vegetables are often included in the pack.

8. There is a danger of shoplifting, especially by children, as the goods are so easily accessible.
9. Supermarkets with an off-licence enable under-age drinkers to buy alcohol quite easily.
10. No credit or delivery facilities are available.

COMPLAINTS

If a customer buys inferior goods or there is a genuine mistake in the checkout bill, most supermarkets will readily rectify the matter in order to maintain good relations with their customers. If, on the other hand, one buys food which is mouldy, sold after the date on its packet, or gnawed at the corners, it is more advisable in the interest of all consumers to take the complaint to the local health department. A health inspector will investigate the complaint and make sure that the shop is storing food in hygienic conditions. This will ensure that the fault does not occur again.

TEN SHOPPING TIPS

1. Make a shopping list and keep to it.
2. Shop once a week to help cut down impulse buys.
3. Get to know the price of basics. Shop around for the best value if there is time.
4. Leave children at home if possible, as they can be distracting.
5. Avoid shopping when tired or hungry. People tend to buy more at these times.
6. Only bulk buy if you are sure it is better value.
7. When buying perishables, do not stock up with large amounts. Little and often is the best policy.
8. Avoid buying a lot of convenience foods which are more expensive than the fresh variety.
9. Shop locally to avoid travel costs.
10. Look out for 'hidden' price rises, where the weight or size of an item is reduced instead of increasing the price.

SHOPPING TERMS

Retail shops offer many inducements to customers in order to encourage them to buy.

SPECIAL OFFERS

Regardless of the publicity given by the shopkeeper, an offer is only special if it is an item which the customer will use and if it is being sold more cheaply than its normal price. A special offer can take the form of a price reduction or a free 'gift', such as a sample pack of face cream attached to a bottle of shampoo. Some supermarkets reduce the price of ten or twenty items every week, selling them as special offers. A clever consumer can make the most of these offers by visiting different supermarkets in the area and stocking up on the offers which are good value. On the other hand, there are many who cannot resist a bargain in any store. People like this should make a shopping list and stick to it.

LOSS LEADER

This is an extra-special offer where a shop sells one or two items either at cost price or at a loss, hence the name. The shop offsets the loss on the special offer against the profit on other goods. The Restrictive Practices Act 1970 prohibits the advertising of grocery goods at less than the invoice price. This is to protect the smaller retailer.

TRADING STAMPS

Stamps are a form of discount on purchases made in certain garages and supermarkets. Stamps are given in proportion to the amount spent in the shop. The stamps are collected in saver books which can be exchanged when full for cash, gifts or against the cost of goods.

The stamp companies and shop owners who use them claim that trading stamps attract customers and encourage competition. It is the consumer who pays in the long run. Most shops pay the trading stamp company a percentage of their annual turnover. It would obviously be better to reduce the prices in the shop by this amount instead.

SALES

Most shops other than food stores hold a *sale* at least twice a year, usually when there is a slump in business in January and mid-summer. The purpose of a sale is to get rid of old stock and soiled or damaged goods to make way for the new stock coming in. Many stores also buy large consignments of *seconds* from manu-

facturers. Many are only slightly flawed or faded and if carefully examined can be a good buy. Other good sales buys are usually bed linen, towels, china, carpets and furniture.

SPECIAL OFFER

BRAND AND OWN BRAND GOODS

A *brand* is a name or trademark used on the products of a manufacturer so that they are instantly recognisable.

Own brand goods are items which have been specially manufactured or packed for a supermarket or store and are printed with the name of the store. They are usually cheaper than the regular product due to practical packaging and lack of advertising. Many supermarkets sell own brand soups, tinned beans, washing-up liquid and many other products. Extra cheap own brand goods are sometimes sold, e.g. Yellow Pack.

BULK BUYING

Bulk buying sounds like an easy way of saving money and in certain cases it is — but not always. It does save time, as shopping trips are less frequent. The customer can bulk buy from *cash-and-carry* warehouses and *freezer* centres, wholesale fish and vegetable *markets* in the city, or from a *market gardener*.

Before deciding to bulk buy, the customer should consider the following:

1. Is there enough storage space in the house to accommodate large quantities of food and household goods?
2. Is the family large enough to make bulk buying worthwhile? As many goods deteriorate on storage, it makes little sense to bulk buy for two or three.
3. Is there enough money available to pay the periodic bills which bulk buying entails? People on low weekly incomes would find it difficult to save enough money to pay these bills.
4. Will the family be extravagant in the use of goods if there is a large reserve supply?
5. Will the family be bored with one variety of a product such as soup? Make sure to buy varieties which are very popular at home.

DATE-STAMPING

This is a system of stamping perishable goods with the date by which the product should be sold. It takes into account one or two days' storage at home before the product is eaten. Foods commonly date-stamped are vacuum-packed meats such as cooked ham, sausages and bacon, while yoghurt, cream, cheese, meat pies and some cakes may also be date-stamped.

Note: Vacuum-packed foods, long-life cream, many dried foods, especially dried milk, and tinned and frozen food keep for a long time unopened and in the right conditions. Once opened they must be treated as fresh foods and used up quickly.

UNIT PRICING

With the exception of tea, sugar, flour and a few other products, food can be sold in packets of any weight. This makes it difficult to compare prices, unless a calculator is used. Can you work out quickly which is cheaper: 546 g at 35p or 625 g at 38½p? The incomplete change over from the imperial to the metric system has confused things even further. Eventually it is hoped that all goods will be sold in standard sizes, such as 50 g, 100 g, 1 kilo. This should make it easier to compare prices. It will also prevent hidden price rises, when the price remains static, but the amount in the packet is reduced.

The unit system of pricing shows the price per unit (per gram or ml) on the supermarket shelf. If one compares tins of different sizes, it is easy to see which is the better value.

Example

50 g jar of coffee at 61p = 1.22p per g
100 g jar of coffee at 115p = 1.15 per g
200 g jar of coffee at 225p = 1.13p per g

Clearly the largest size is the cheapest, but the 100 g jar is almost as good value. It is generally assumed that the larger tin or packet is better value — but this is not always true.

Unit pricing is worked out by the retailer, which makes it economic only for the bigger supermarket chains to use it. It would take too much time and cost too much for a small shopkeeper. Butchers are required by law to display the price of each cut of meat per lb or kg; this is another example of unit pricing.

PRICES

The subject of food prices is one which affects everyone. Many increases in prices are due to world market conditions over which we have no control. This is little consolation to the housewife who has to pay more each week for her groceries.

Among the causes of food price increases are inflation, fuel cost increases, scarcities, weather, the EEC and wage increases. There are also the hidden costs of packaging and advertising. Inflation, and the consequent lowering of the buying power of money, has been a major cause of increasing prices. The high price of oil has increased the cost of many manufactured goods, of transport, and of food production (consider tomatoes grown in heated greenhouses). World scarcity of certain commodities such as coffee or wheat can put up the price of these foods. Such scarcity is often due to bad weather. The Common Agricultural Policy of the EEC ensures that all Europe's farmers are paid a minimum price for their produce. This is fine for the farmer, but again the consumer bears the cost and rarely benefits by any lowering of prices when a good growing season produces a glut. Probably the only cause of increased food prices over which there can be control is increases in wages. Workers in food production and manufacturing get wage increases to keep up with the cost of living. This puts up the cost of food, and so the price spiral continues.

CONSUMER INFORMATION

There is now such a wide variety of consumer goods available that it is becoming extremely difficult for a shopper to know how to get value for money. Household equipment is becoming more complex every year, synthetic textiles, food additives and a vast selection of products to clean our houses make it so confusing that it is vital for the consumer to be well informed and alert. Shopping has become an art which requires ingenuity, will-power and effort.

EXAMPLES OF CONSUMER INFORMATION

In the past few years, due to pressure from *consumer organisations,* manufacturers have increased the amount of information they supply to their customers.

FOOD LABELLING

Many countries have laws regulating the grading and labelling of foods. The EEC, for example, stipulates that eggs, fruit and vegetables should be graded according to size and quality. The contents of packets and tins should be accurately described. The ingredients should be listed in decreasing order, by weight. (The ingredient that weighs most comes first in the list). Additives must be listed. The net weight must be clearly visible, that is — the weight without tin or packet. The weight of a food e.g. tinned strawberries without liquid is called the drained weight. The name and address of manufacturer or producer are also required as are clear cooking/heating instructions.

STAR MARKING (page 182)

This is a system which indicates the standard temperatures of refrigerators and deep freezers. It also provides a guide as to how long frozen foods will keep.

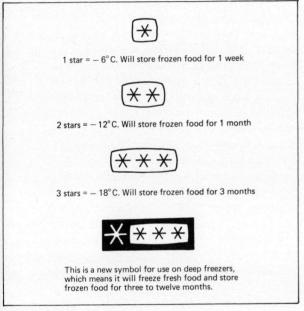

Star-marking

CARE LABELLING (page 201)

Standardised labels which are sewn onto garments and linen indicating washing and drying instructions.

SEALS OF APPROVAL/QUALITY MARKS

Many manufacturers of good quality products submit their goods to be independently tested for safety, design or quality. On passing these tests they are permitted to use various symbols or seals on their product. These seals indicate reliability and high quality. Examples are the British Standards 'kite' mark and its Irish equivalent Caighdean Eireannach; Design Centre; Woolmark; Real Leather; British Carpet Centre; and Guaranteed Irish.

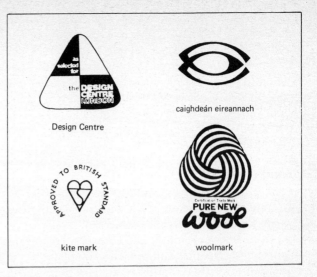

INSTRUCTIONS

When buying large and complicated equipment and many other modern products, it is essential that full instructions for the assembly, use, care and cleaning of the product are supplied. Most well-known manufacturers provide instruction booklets with such household equipment as washing machines, cookers, refrigerators and sewing machines. Check that foreign pieces of equipment have instructions in English. If the instructions are not clear, ask the retailer to demonstrate the product or explain how to use it.

Many people do not make full use of equipment because they fail to read or understand the instructions. The various attachments or programmes should be used from the beginning to make sure one gets full value for money. It is bad economics to pay more money for a complicated machine if the different processes are not used, especially if this is due to ignorance. Instructions on packets of food, cleaning agents and other products are often ignored. It makes sense to follow the advice given with these products as it has been worked out by experts after months of testing to give the best possible results.

Note: It is a good idea to keep all instruction books, leaflets and care or cleaning information slips together in a file or large envelope in the kitchen so that they are easy to find when needed.

GUARANTEES

A guarantee is a contract, usually between the manufacturer and the consumer, in which the manufacturer accepts responsibility for any faults which occur in a product within a reasonable time. The usual

49

period of a guarantee is one year, but such items as shoes have a shorter guarantee, while furniture and bed linen are sometimes guaranteed for five years. The consumer is usually required to fill in and return the guarantee form to the manufacturer or else keep it at home in a safe place. Most manufacturers of good quality articles give a guarantee.

A good guarantee can help the shopper to get satisfaction quickly if the product proves faulty or inferior. However, it is important to remember that the contract of sale is between the buyer and the shopkeeper, not the manufacturer. Regardless of guarantees, the shopkeeper is legally obliged (Sale of Goods Act 1893) to sell goods of merchantable quality, and he is responsible for the goods he sells. This means that the customer may still bring his complaint to the shopkeeper, who in turn will have to settle the problem with the manufacturer.

The Sale of Goods and Supply of Services Act 1980 stipulates that a guarantee should be clearly legible, refer to specific goods or one category of goods, state the name and address of the person to whom claims should be directed, state the duration of the guarantee from the date of purchase, state clearly the procedure (which should be reasonably straightforward) for claiming under the guarantee, and state clearly what the manufacturer/supplier undertakes to do and what extra charges (such as carriage) may be incurred by the buyer.

Note: Neither the manufacturer nor the shopkeeper is responsible if the article is misused. If an article shrinks through being washed incorrectly or a washing machine breaks down because of overloading, they will not be covered under any guarantee.

ADVERTISING

Advertising is a system whereby the manufacturer makes us aware of a product, and in certain cases helps us to understand how to use it. Forms of advertising include newspaper and magazine advertisements, radio, TV and cinema advertising, sports sponsorship, store promotions and door-to-door leaflets and/or free samples.

Advertisements can be very misleading and can encourage us to buy products we do not really want or need. They often take advantage of our weaknesses and play on pride, fear, sex, greed to make us buy their products. Manufacturers of items such as alcohol and cigarettes spend vast amounts encouraging us to use products which are known to be bad for us.

While advertising has become part of modern economics, a wise consumer will refuse to allow him/herself to be unduly influenced by its persuasive techniques.

CONSUMER PROTECTION

A. THE CONSUMER AND THE LAW

There are many laws to protect the consumer when s/he buys a product or avails of a service. The law cannot protect a consumer from his own ignorance and mistakes, but consumer information and consumer protection can. The expression *caveat emptor* — let the buyer beware — is a useful guide for all shoppers.

One of the first laws introduced to protect the consumer was the Sale of Goods Act 1893. This stipulates that an item sold should be of merchantable quality, fit for the purpose for which it is sold, and must live up to its description: leather shoes must be made from real leather. Under this Act, if an item doesn't work when first used or food is found to be mouldy, the goods are not of merchantable quality and the purchaser is entitled to a new item or his money back. It is important to keep the receipt and to return the offending article quickly in order to be legally entitled to an exchange or a refund. If the shopper does not bother to return the item for three or four months, the shopkeeper can reasonably claim that it was misused or broken by the customer. When inferior goods are returned, the shopkeeper often suggests repairing the article or offers a credit note, but the consumer can legally insist on a cash refund or a new article.

Note: Shops are not obliged to return money or even exchange goods if a customer changes his mind about a colour or size, although many shops will exchange as a gesture of good will.

Many other laws exist which control the quality of our food and drink. They restrict the use of additives in food, ensure that premises where food is manufactured or sold, e.g. restaurants, supermarkets, are kept in a hygienic condition. Laws govern the use of weighing and measuring equipment e.g. shop scales. Inspectors investigate premises for breaches of such laws and those found guilty are fined.

Other laws control hire purchase, labelling of goods, advertising and consumer information.

Improving consumer legislation

Consumers today have far greater protection than in the past, but a lot more could be done. Pressure from consumers and consumer organisations can encourage government representatives to work towards more effective consumer legislation. It is also up to shoppers to force manufacturers and retailers to sell good quality articles by being particular about what they buy and by complaining about inferior quality or service when necessary.

Making a complaint

Although many consumers are loth to make a complaint, most people at one time or another will be right to complain about a bad product or service. The shopper will only get redress if he knows his rights. Many retailers are quite willing to exchange goods or refund money where appropriate, but others have a tough policy on complaints and many try to dodge their responsibility.

This is the correct procedure for making a complaint:
1. Return to the shop as soon as possible.
2. Ask to see the manager or buyer. Assistants are often not interested or knowledgeable enough.
3. Be polite and keep to the facts. Be firm without being aggressive. It is unwise to lose your temper.
4. Let the shopkeeper suggest a remedy. If he does not, ask for a replacement or refund.
5. If this is not forthcoming, write to the manufacturer enclosing copies (not originals which may be needed as evidence) of receipts and any other documents relating to the purchase. The letter should be brief, accurate and courteous.
6. If the manufacturer is uncooperative, it may be helpful to consult a solicitor who can advise whether it is worthwhile going to court. This is rarely necessary.
7. A letter to the newspapers or consumer programmes on the radio, or complaining through a consumer organisation are other methods of bringing the problem to a speedy conclusion.

B. GOVERNMENT AGENCIES

Apart from basic laws dealing with consumer affairs, the government has initiated several schemes to protect the consumer.

National Prices Commission

This is an advisory body which makes recommendations to the Minister for Industry and Commerce on the price of manufactured goods, basic foodstuffs, and most services. Before a manufacturer may increase the price of his product, he must apply to the Minister for Industry and Commerce, giving reasons for the proposed increase. The application is investigated by the National Prices Commission. On their recommendation, the Minister decides whether to grant the full increase or a partial increase, or to reject the application. Increases are usually due to increased costs of labour, overheads or raw materials. The Commission also makes monthly reports on consumer issues as well as issuing a monthly list of price increases. The maximum retail price of basic food-stuffs is strictly controlled.

Institute of Industrial Research and Standards

The Irish national standards body has its own standard mark — Caighdeán Éireannach. Goods which have passed various tests for reliability and quality may use this standard mark. The Institute provides technical services to industry and is concerned with research, development, pollution control and technology.

Safety

The government implements various regulations which maintain high standards of safety in many products, particularly those relating to electricity and children. These ensure that the consumer is protected by law for his own safety. All children's nightdresses must comply with a regulation ensuring that they are non-flammable. There are other standards relating to the toxicity and safety of toys. Anoraks and other outer clothing for children must not have drawcords. There are several regulations involving electrical safety, and electrical equipment must satisfy stringent tests. All flexes of new appliances must carry a label explaining the colour code of the new wiring system.

C. VOLUNTARY ORGANISATIONS

Local Community Information Centres

These are places where advice is given on consumer issues, as well as social, health and legal problems. They are staffed by those knowledgeable in one or other of these fields who give their help on a voluntary basis.

Consumer organisations

The establishment of a number of voluntary organisations in Ireland has helped to improve the life of the Irish consumer. Organisations which are directly or indirectly concerned with consumer issues include: the Irish Countrywomen's Association, the Irish Housewives' Association, residents' associations, the

Association of Combined Residents' Associations, and the Consumers' Association.

The Consumers' Association of Ireland has two functions: to protect the interests of the consumer and to maintain a high standard of goods and services. It publishes a monthly booklet, *Inform,* which reports on Irish consumer problems, and distributes *Which,* an excellent monthly magazine published by the British consumers' association. This reports on tests and surveys carried out by the association on items of equipment, food, services and so on. The association also publishes books on consumer topics such as buying a house, central heating and retirement, as well as articles in newspapers and magazines. The association may advise the government when consumer regulations are being drafted.

Housewives' Associations are also concerned with consumers and shopping. From time to time they have organised boycotts to draw attention to inferior or over-priced goods. Consumer groups in Japan and the US succeeded in lowering prices considerably when they launched major boycotts of certain consumer goods.

D. THE MEDIA

As interest in consumer affairs has grown, there has been a corresponding increase in the amount of coverage given by the media to consumer topics. Daily papers publish a market report which gives a good indication of which fruit, vegetables and fish are cheap and plentiful. Most papers have a consumer column which publishes complaints and gives advice. Newspapers and many magazines run articles of interest to shoppers. Many radio programmes now devote a lot of time to consumer affairs and there are even television programmes which deal solely with such subjects.

QUESTIONS/CHAPTER 4

1. Explain what is meant by consumer protection. Describe two forms of consumer protection currently available to the shopper.
   Describe the procedure for (a) making a complaint, or (b) claiming under guarantee.
2. Write a note on the following:
   (a) trading stamps;   (c) date stamping;
   (b) bulk buying;   (d) unit pricing.
   benefits the consumer or not. Give reasons for your answer.
3. The consumer gets the goods and services s/he deserves. Discuss.
4. List some areas of law by which a government can help protect the consumer.
   Name two government agencies and two voluntary organisations which help protect the consumer and state the function of each.
5. Compare shopping in a supermarket with shopping in smaller specialist food shops. Use the following headings to guide you:
   (a) comfort and   (c) quality of goods;
       convenience;   (d) variety;
   (b) value for money;   (e) hygiene.

5.
A home of your own

'The sparrow even finds a home at last, the swallow a nest for its young ...;'

Ps. 83.4

Most young people have to set up home on their own when they leave their family. Your first experience of living on your own might be in 'digs' where you have a room in somebody else's house. Or you might choose to share with a friend. Sharing a flat or bedsitter is cheaper; for example, two people use the same amount of heat and light as one person. It is also less lonely.

SHARING

Be sure to work out a budget from the start. Both should agree to pay a set amount into a 'kitty' towards household expenses. Chores should also be shared equally; either one person does all the work one week and nothing the next week, or else work out a rota dividing the daily chores between the two. Sometimes a whole house will be shared by three or four young people. In such a case, it is more important than ever to make proper arrangements to share the housework and shopping in a spirit of give and take.

Sharing a flat can mean problems

Example of a work routine for two sharing a flat

Week 1
Pat cooks and shops; Jo cleans and does household laundry e.g. sheets, towels.

Week 2
Jo cooks and shops; Pat cleans and launders.
Each person does his/her own personal laundry.

Week 1
Morning:
Pat cooks breakfast, sets table.
Jo tidies bedroom and bathroom.
Both wash, dry and tidy up after breakfast.
Lunchtime:
Pat shops for food.
Evening:
Pat prepares meal, sets table.
Jo tidies flat, sees to fire, does ironing.
Both wash and dry dishes and tidy up after meal.
Jo tidies living-room before going to bed.
Saturday:
Pat prepares lunch, bakes if desired.
Jo shops, goes to launderette, gives flat thorough cleaning.

Week 2
Reverse jobs.

Points to check when looking for a furnished flat

1. Position: Is it in an area you like, near work or public transport? Are there amenities nearby such as a park, beach, pool, church etc. and facilities for sport and entertainment?

2. The flat: Is it self-contained, with its own front door, kitchen and bathroom? Sharing these rooms is not to be recommended. Check
   (a) for signs of dampness and for draughts;
   (b) is it clean and well maintained?
   (c) what are the kitchen facilities — cooker, fridge, storage?
   (d) comfortable bed, table, chairs;
   (e) electricity — is it safe, with sufficient power points and your own meter?
   (f) what form of heating is there? How do you pay for it? If there is central heating, do you control it? If not, when does it turn on and off?
   (g) facilities for waste disposal; parking space for pram, bicycle, car;
   (h) last but not least, security: good locks on doors and windows.

3. Rent: How much? Is it paid weekly or monthly? By cash or cheque? If it is by cash, make sure you get a rent book into which each payment is recorded by the landlord. Is it paid in advance (this is usual)? Does it include heating/electricity? Are there extras such as charges for maintenance of public areas, e.g. stairs? Can rent be increased? If so, how often and how much notice must be given?

4. Is a deposit needed? The landlord may be entitled to keep this when you leave the flat, to pay for any damage or breakages. Is there an inventory (a list of contents of the flat)? Check this when you take possession.

5. How much notice is required on either side when vacating the flat? (Make sure it's at least two weeks to allow you time to find another.)

6. Who is responsible for maintenance? The landlord is usually responsible for outdoor and structural maintenance; you may be responsible for indoor maintenance.

7. Insurance: The landlord should have the building and his own contents insured. It is up to you to take out a policy to cover your property against burglary, fire or accident.

8. Restrictions: Are there restrictions on pets, visitors, parties etc.? May you use the garden? Clothes line? Remember if children are not allowed, a couple may have to leave if the wife gets pregnant.
   Note: Many of the above points will apply also if you are renting a house.

UNFURNISHED FLATS

These flats are usually to be found in modern, purpose-built blocks, although some are still to be found in large, older houses. They are usually rented on a long-term basis, e.g. between one and five years. They are ideal for single people or retired couples, as they are smaller and easier to maintain than houses. Also, they are often nearer to the city centre than the average suburban house.

A lease

When renting an unfurnished flat, and sometimes in the case of furnished accommodation, it is necessary to sign a lease. A lease is simply a legal document or agreement between the landlord and tenant stating the rights and responsibilities of each. It will be drawn up for a specific length of time, e.g. one year, and after that either party is free to renew it or not, as they wish. As long as both keep to the terms of the lease, there is no problem and the tenant cannot be thrown out. Most of the terms in the previous list will be mentioned in the lease, in legal terms, and it is advisable to have a solicitor check it over before you sign.

Never sign any legal document without reading it very carefully.

BUYING A HOUSE

A dream house

Advantages

1. It is a good investment. It will almost certainly go up in value.
2. It provides security. In your old age, you won't have to worry where the rent money is to come from.
3. You have more personal interest and satisfaction in decorating and maintaining your own house and garden than a rented house and garden.
4. In renting, the money you pay for accommodation is lost; in buying by mortgage, it is buying you a good investment.

5. Tax relief is allowed on the interest you pay on your mortgage. Also, inflation causes the repayments to drop in real terms over the years so that they don't take such a large slice of your income, whereas rents continue to rise.

Disadvantages

1. Buying a house is a very expensive undertaking, particularly for young couples.
2. It is difficult to save enough money for a deposit.
3. It may be difficult to get a loan, particularly on a low salary. (You may be entitled to a cheap Local Authority loan in this case).
4. A lot of time is spent looking for houses and arranging loans and conveyancing (legal work).

ANNUAL OUTGOINGS

Buying a house
(a) Mortgage repayments
(b) Possible repayments on bank loan
(c) Local Authority charges (e.g. water)
(e) Insurance of house
(f) Insurance of contents
(g) Mortgage protection policy, p.00.
(h) Repairs and maintenance costs (about 1% of house price each year)
(i) Fuel for heating etc.
(j) Furniture

Renting a house
(a) Rent
(b) Insurance of personal contents
(c) Most repairs and maintenance costs are the responsibility of the landlord
(d) Fuel
(e) Furniture
(f) Saving (towards a house)

CHOOSING A HOUSE

1. Neighbourhood

Do you prefer a small or large estate? It should be well laid out, whether a newly-built or mature area. Is it near work, shops, schools, public transport, amenities such as parks and play-grounds? Avoid busy roads, densely built-up areas, derelict buildings, rubbish dumps, large industries which might be noisy or give off unpleasant fumes. Be suspicious of open spaces: they may be built on in the future. Check plans in the Local Authority office for zoning (commercial, residential, industrial or open spaces). Check any proposed development e.g. road widening. A pleasant aspect e.g. a sea or mountain view is nice but you will pay more for it.

2. Type of house

Do you prefer a bungalow, detached, semi-detached or terraced house? Old or modern house? Garage or not? Is the garden attractive and well maintained? Is it too large for you to maintain if you have little time for gardening?

3. Layout of house

Does the house suit your family and the type of life you lead? Are there sufficient bedrooms? A room for children to play or study in? A well-planned kitchen is important. Good ventilation? A modern bathroom and downstairs lavatory would be considered essential today. Do not be over-influenced by the taste of the previous owner. It is relatively easy to redecorate a house, if in every other respect it is a good buy.

4. Structural features

Have a *surveyor* check these, if possible. Roof, chimney, gutters and drainpipes; no missing slates, or leaks; sound foundations; check existence of *damp-proof course; walls* — look for cracks, dampness, crumbling plaster or pointing; *floor and woodwork* — look for damp rot, dry rot and woodworm; *doors and windows* — should be sound and well fitting; *plumbing* — pipework, drainage, tank in attic, lagging on pipes; *heating* — what type of system, fuel; insulation, especially in attic; immersion heater; back boiler *electricity* — is it safe; plenty of power points with modern 3-pin sockets?

COSTS INVOLVED IN HOUSE PURCHASE

Buying a house is probably the most expensive purchase you will ever make. Because of this it is essential to save as much as you can beforehand in order that you will have enough cash to pay for the many expenses involved. These include:
(a) deposit: up to 25% of the cost of the house;
(b) stamp duty: a government tax (most new houses are exempt);
(c) your solicitor's fees: charged in ratio to the cost of the house (average, 2% of house price). To his bill is added
(d) legal fees for stamp duties and searches;

(e) lender's solicitor's fees: the company who is giving you a loan will also hire a solicitor to check the title, but you must pay his fees!
(f) lender's surveyor's fees: the lending company wants to make sure the house you are buying is a good investment for them. They hire a surveyor to check this and you pay when you apply for the loan. If the loan is refused, your money is not refunded.
(g) if it is an old house, it would be wise to have your own surveyor look over it; his bill also must of course be paid by you.

The total cost of the deposit and these fees comes to several thousand pounds, but the largest sum involved is the bulk cash for the house. This you will probably have to borrow.

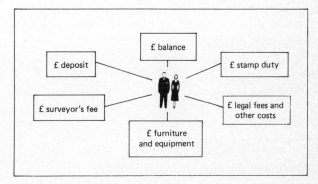

Costs to be met in buying a house

BORROWING THE HOUSE PRICE

When you borrow money, putting up the house as security, it is known as a mortgage loan. The lender (mortgagor) holds the title deeds (papers proving ownership(until the loan is repaid in full.

Money for house-purchase can be borrowed from:
building societies,
banks,
insurance companies,
local authorities.

The following restrictions are made on most loans:
1. Amount lent: the prospective borrower may only borrow two-and-a-half to three times his/her annual salary, excluding overtime. If a wife has a professional occupation (a well-paid, secure and pensionable job), her salary will be considered by some societies. This restriction ensures that monthly repayments will not be too great a burden, especially if the wife leaves work to have a family.
2. Period of repayment: this is usually twenty to thirty years. Banks lend for twenty years, building

societies for twenty to twenty-five years, and local authorities will allow thirty years. A borrower over fifty may have difficulty obtaining a loan and have to repay the loan in a shorter time (ten to fifteen years).

3. Good record and deposit: the borrower is expected to have a fairly steady job and have a good financial record, with no bad debts. He is expected to have saved the deposit for the house.

4. Old houses, especially if they are in a bad state of repair or on a short lease, are a bad investment for the lending company. They often refuse to give loans on such properties. It is easier to get a loan for a new house, especially for first-time borrowers.

Borrowing from a building society.

Building societies normally lend money only to people who have been saving with them for a time. For this reason it is a good idea, when you are saving for a house, to save with a building society.

(a) Rates of interest fluctuate with the economy.

(b) Income tax relief is allowed on interest paid.

(c) Loans are usually repaid in monthly instalments over twenty to twenty-five years.

(d) Conditions vary slightly between one society and another.

Borrowing from an assurance company

A small percentage of house loans are arranged through life assurance companies. The loan is tied up with an endowment policy. When this matures, in twenty or twenty-five years, depending on the arrangement, or if you die before that, your loan is paid off.

Borrowing from a bank

Banks also lend money for house purchase but on a very small scale. The repayments are usually spread over twenty years; mortgage interest varies according to the current bank rate.

Banks are also useful for supplying bridging loans. These are short-term loans which 'bridge' the gap between getting loan approval from a building society and actually receiving the cheque, or between buying a new house and selling your existing one.

Remember, the interest rate on bridging loans is very high.

Local authorities

To qualify for a local authority loan, the borrower must be on a fairly low income. Up to 95% of the house price may be borrowed, up to a certain limit. The amount of loan is usually limited to two-and-a-half to three times the borrower's salary, repayable over thirty years. The borrower must intend to live in the house, not to rent it.

There are facilities to enable local authority tenants who so wish, to buy their house, either outright or by weekly instalments over a period of up to thirty years.

The low-rise mortgage scheme caters for people who wish to purchase reasonably priced houses, but who cannot afford normal repayments. Mortgage repayments are subsidised over the first nine years of the loan. There are some restrictions with this scheme such as repaying the subsidy if you sell the house within fourteen years.

There may be minor variations on some of the above conditions as situations vary between one local authority and another. Find out the rules which govern local authority loans in your district. These can be found in local county council offices.

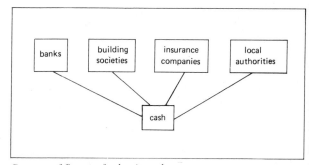

Sources of finance for buying a house

House purchase terms you may need to know:

Auctioneer or estate agent: a person who auctions, sells or arranges rental of houses, land, flats etc. For this service he charges the seller a fee based on the price of the house. Advertising costs are extra.

Auction: at an auction, the house is sold to the highest bidder. Because of this, it is important to have your solicitor study the details well beforehand. When the auction is over, the buyer must pay one-quarter of the house price at once, and the remainder within a month.

Certificate of reasonable value: this is granted by the Department of the Environment to builders whose houses have reached a certain minimum standard. If a cerfiticate is not issued, the buyer may lose benefits such as grants and stamp duty exemption.

Contract: this is the written agreement between buyer and seller which states the terms on which the house is bought. The terms 'subject to contract' and 'subject to loan' should be written into any agreement or deposit so that if the loan is rejected or there is some problem over the sale, you will get your deposit back.

Conveyancing: transferring the legal ownership of property from one person/company to another.

Freehold: this means that the house and land on which a house is built belongs to the owner forever and no ground rent has to be paid. All houses built since 1978 are freehold.

Leasehold: this means that title to the land is held by a person or company other than the owner. If this is the case, you will have to pay ground rent. It is now possible to pay a sum of money (roughly nine times the ground rent) in order to obtain the freehold of a property.

Maisonette: a self-contained flat, usually on more than one floor.

Planning permission: when building a house or making any alteration which changes the appearance of a house or increases its size by more than 18 sq.m, you need to get planning permission from the local authority. *Outline planning permission* gives a general agreement to the structure being built. *Full planning permission* requires detailed inspection of the house plans by the local authority. If rejected, it is possible to appeal the decision.

Property: a building or a piece of land, or both together.

Registration of houses: most new houses are registered in the Land Registry Office. Each change of ownership is also recorded. When a house is being sold, the buyer's solicitor can check that each change of ownership was legal and correct. Older, unregistered houses are more complicated to deal with.

Solicitor: a person specialised in the legal procedures of house purchase. He prepares the contracts and checks the title at the Land Registry Office. Both buyer and seller must each employ a separate solicitor.

Stamp duty: this is a form of tax on house purchase. New houses under 125 sq.m (this includes an average three or four-bedroom house) are exempt from stamp duty. If you buy a previously-occupied house or a house larger than 125 sq.m you will have to pay stamp duty on a sliding scale, i.e. the dearer the house, the higher percentage you pay to the government.

Surveyor: a survey of a house can be carried out by a surveyor, an architect or an engineer. A survey is particularly necessary if the house you are considering is an old one. A survey should describe in writing the condition of foundations, walls, roof, plumbing and wiring, and whether any faults can be put right and if so, the approximate cost of the work. Note: the building society's surveyor will only report the results of his survey to the society, not to you, even though you pay his fees!

Title deeds: legal documents proving ownership.

BUYING A HOUSE — STEP BY STEP

Step 1
When you decide to buy a house, first find out how much you can afford. This usually depends on your job, because the amount of money you can borrow will be in proportion to your annual income.

Step 2
Look through the property pages of the newspapers to see what is available. Visit the areas you would like to live in — there may be 'for sale' signs. Visit new housing estates to see houses within your price range.

Step 3
During this time you should visit a building society or other lending company to find out the position on loans (you will get preference if you have saved with that company for a time). You must also hire a solicitor.

Step 4
When you see a few houses you like, within your price range, arrange with the owner or builder to view them. If you are serious about one or two, have a surveyor look them over but have a full survey done on your final choice, particularly if it is an old house.

Step 5
You must now apply quickly for a loan. You will probably be required to put down a small deposit to 'hold' the house. This should be 'subject to contract and loan approval' so that you will get your money back should the deal fall through.

Step 6

Your solicitor will now be doing most of the work. S/he will check out legal details and study the contract prepared by the seller's solicitor.

Step 8

Your solicitor will be busy for the next couple of weeks checking the title, registration and so on.

Step 7

You will now be asked to sign the contract. This is the point of no return, so make sure your loan has been approved before you sign. You must now pay the main deposit (usually 25%).

Step 9

When all the legal details have been worked out, you will be asked to sign the document transferring the house to you. The building society will hand over the cheque for the balance of the house price and the house is yours — or at least it will be when you finish paying off the mortgage in twenty-five years!

BUYING FROM A BUILDER

Most people buy their first house in a new housing estate. When buying from a builder, check the following.

1. The *price* of the house, amount of deposit and when the balance must be paid. He may require you to pay instalments, as each stage of the building is completed.
2. Watch out for a *price variation clause*. This allows the builder to increase the price of a house after you pay the deposit. In other words, although you agree to a price in January, when you put your deposit on the house, in July, when the house is finished and you come to pay the balance, it may be £2,000 dearer due to a cost increase in materials or labour. Avoid this clause, if possible.
3. Has the builder got a *certificate of reasonable value* for the house, and is the price you are being charged the same as that on the certificate? If it is higher, you will lose your right to grants and stamp duty exemption.
4. Has the builder got full *planning permission* for the house?
5. Is he on the Register of Housebuilders so that you will be covered by their six-year guarantee against serious structural faults?
6. Does his contract provide for a *maintenance period* (1-2 years) during which the builder will be responsible for repairing other faults?
7. How much is allowed in the price towards wallpaper, bathroom fittings etc.? Putting in your own choice may be expensive.
8. Decide on any changes or extras and put them in writing together with the costs, signed by both parties.
9. Check that the builder's planning permission ensures that he 'completes' the estate — that is, finishes off roads and footpaths etc. If he does not, the local authority will refuse to take over the estate (for sweeping and dustbin collection, for example) and you may be refused a loan.
10. Does your contract specify a completion date? There are often long delays, due to strikes etc. Make sure the builder gives you possession of the house on time or you may have to waste a lot of money renting accommodation or paying a bridging loan.

Don't forget: immediately the sale is completed, your house must be insured against fire and damage: do not wait until you move in. As soon as you have it furnished, insure the contents with a householder's comprehensive policy.

A modern housing estate (John Topham Picture Library)

SUGGESTED READING

The Department of the Environment, *A home of your own.*

QUESTIONS/CHAPTER 5

1. Discuss briefly the points which should be considered by young couples choosing their first home. Describe the procedure for
   (a) buying a new house
   (b) taking out a mortgage
   Name three sources of house purchase finance and outline the basic conditions under which such loans are granted.
2. Explain the following terms:
   (a) conveyancing
   (b) price variation clause
   (c) freehold
   (d) stamp duty
   (e) certificate of reasonable value
   Describe the procedure for buying a house at an auction.
3. What advice would you give to a friend who was looking for a rented apartment in the city?
   Name the points to be looked for
   (a) on viewing the apartment
   (b) before signing the lease
   Discuss the pros and cons of furnished and unfurnished flats.
4. Find out the following:
   (a) the current mortgage interest rate charged by a building society
   (b) current rate of stamp duty
   (c) the cost of renting a single bedsitter in your area
   (d) the cost of renting a low-priced three bedroom semi-detached house in your locality

6.
Water — a basic necessity

Every living creature must have water to survive. We need pure water for drinking and for preparing our food and we also need a good supply for washing, cleaning and drainage if we hope to have a reasonable standard of hygiene in our homes.

In the past, people spent much time and labour each day collecting water from springs and wells. In modern homes water is available at the turn of a tap, so that we often take it for granted. It is not until our water is cut off that we appreciate its importance.

COMPOSITION OF WATER

Water is made up of two gases, hydrogen and oxygen. It contains twice as much hydrogen as oxygen and can be written briefly as H_2O.

WHERE DOES IT COME FROM?

Our water supply begins as rain. When it falls to earth, some of it flows over the earth's surface to form streams. The rest seeps through the soil until it reaches hard, non-porous rock where it collects underground and eventually finds its way to the surface as a spring. Both springs and streams form rivers and lakes, and eventually the water flows back to the sea. The heat from the sun evaporates water from the sea, rivers and lakes. This rises to form clouds, then falls to the ground as rain, and the cycle begins once again.

Rural water supply

Most rural homes have their water pumped from the nearest well. These are made by boring a hole in the ground until ground water is reached, then drawing the water to the surface using pumps. *Shallow wells* are liable to contamination by fertilisers, animal excreta and sewage from leaking pipes. *Deep wells* which penetrate to a second non-porous layer of clay, are less likely to be polluted. They usually contain pure water, although it may be hard due to absorption of minerals from the soil.

Urban water supply

The local authorities store water for large towns and cities in **reservoirs.** These are natural or man-made lakes which are situated on high ground, so that there is enough pressure for the water to flow to the town which they supply. Low-lying areas may need a water tower to create a 'head of water' — that is, sufficient gravity to feed water into every building in the area.

Water is carried to towns in large pipes called *mains.* There are openings here and there on each main, called *hydrants,* marked with a large H. These are fitted with nozzles to which pipes may be attached for fire-fighting etc.

A *service pipe* leads from the mains and runs underground into each house. Outside the house is a *stopcock* (valve) so that the water can be cut off when repairs are being carried out.

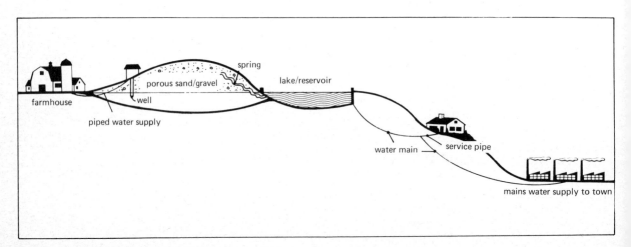

Water supplied to town and country areas

60

THE HOUSEHOLD WATER SUPPLY

When the service pipe enters the house, it rises directly to the *storage tank or cistern* which is usually placed in the attic. A branch from this main pipe feeds the cold water tap in the kitchen sink to provide pure fresh drinking water. The stopcock is placed near the entry point of the service pipe which controls the water entering the house.

The storage tank, usually made from galvanised iron or polythene, is large enough to store over 200 litres of water. From it, cold water flows to all the cold-water taps except the kitchen tap. This storage tank also supplies the lavatory and the water-heating system. Because it may be contaminated with dust, water from the cistern should not be used for drinking. The cistern should be covered to keep the water as clean as possible, and insulated to prevent it freezing up in winter.

A *ballcock* (a valve controlled by a floating ball) controls the entry of water and shuts it off when the cistern is full. Just in case the ballcock is faulty, tanks are fitted with an *overflow pipe* which leads to the outside of the house to prevent flooding.

Water pipes in modern houses are made from copper or plastic. Copper is strong and can be used for hot and cold water, but is is very expensive. Plastic is cheaper but it is only suitable for cold water. Pipes should be lagged to prevent freezing and to prevent heat loss from hot-water pipes.

Daily water requirements

Each person in a household requires about 140 litres of water each day, for cooking, personal washing, bathing, flushing the lavatory, laundry, cleaning and washing dishes. Conserve water when scarce by
1. checking taps for dripping,
2. not leaving water running,
3. not using garden sprinklers,
4. re-using 'clean' water (e.g. washing-up or bath water) for watering garden or washing car,
5. using showers instead of baths.

Impurities in water

Pollution is a major problem today. Water is easily contaminated by animals, sewage and general dirt and dust. On farms, fertilisers and other chemicals can enter the water supply if great care is not taken.

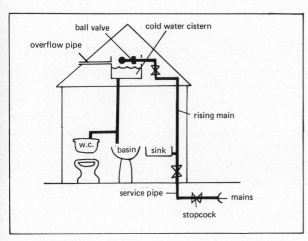

Cold water supply

Water pollution

	Cause	Origin	Effect	How to prevent or reduce effect
A	*Suspended solids* e.g. dust, sand, grit, pollen	Soil, air, domestic and industrial waste	Clogs up pipes. May be toxic or irritant	Filtering and 'settling' during storage
B.	*Bacteria and organic waste*	Human and animal waste e.g. sewage and slurry, soil, vermin	Dysentery, typhoid, cholera, food-poisoning e.g. gastro-enteritis	Correct sewage disposal and treatment. Water purification. Immunisation
C.	*Dissolved minerals* e.g. calcium and magnesium, bicarbonates and sulphates.	Soil	Hard water	Boiling or adding chemicals e.g. lime, borax
	Lead	Old pipes, cisterns	Accumulation in body is fatal	Replace lead plumbing. Modern plumbing is non-toxic
D.	*Toxic chemicals,* e.g. in pesticides and weed killers	Farming and gardening procedures	Many are directly poisonous, often fatal	Avoid use, e.g. practise organic farming. Use with extreme caution. difficult to remove from water.

PURIFYING OUR WATER SUPPLY

The local authorities are responsible for keeping our water pure. They make by-laws in an attempt to prevent individuals and companies polluting the water supply. Water is tested regularly and 'treated' in various ways to make it fit for drinking. Here are some of the treatments water undergoes before it is piped to our homes.

1. Storage: while the water lies in the reservoir, solids settle at the bottom. Bacteria and other micro-organisms are destroyed by the fresh air and sunlight, while tiny oxygen-producing plants which live in the water help to keep it fresh.
2. Filtering: as the water leaves the reservoir, it passes through filter-beds, seeping slowly through layers of sand and gravel which remove many of the suspended impurities.

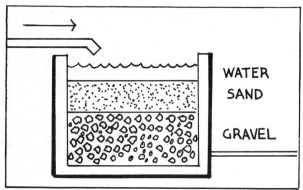

WATER
SAND
GRAVEL

A filter bed

3. Adding chlorine: this is sometimes added to water supplies to destroy bacteria. The amount permitted in the water is carefully controlled, so that it kills bacteria without leaving a 'swimming-pool' taste in the water.
4. Softening: chloride of lime is added in hard water areas in order to soften the water (see page 198).
5. Adding fluoride: because it was found that people living in areas where the water contained a natural supply of fluoride had much stronger teeth, it is now added to water supplies lacking in fluoride in order to reduce tooth decay.

Other methods of obtaining pure water

6. Boiling: boiling water for five minutes will destroy dangerous bacteria. This method of purifying is obviously suitable only for fairly small amounts of water. This is the method you would use if you were camping, for instance, and suspected the water might be contaminated.

7. Distillation: this is a scientific method of obtaining pure H_2O. Water is boiled and the steam passes through coils of tubing which cool and condense it back into water. Distilled water is used for medical and scientific purposes and for filling steam irons and car batteries.

CHARACTERISTICS OF GOOD DRINKING WATER

Drinking water must be pure without any harmful substances dissolved in it. It should be
1. colourless (bluish in large amounts)
2. odourless
3. tasteless but palatable (a salty taste may indicate pollution by sewage)
4. sparkling and well aerated
5. neither acid nor alkaline
6. free from harmful impurities

Water for laundry

You may have noticed in some parts of the country that kettles are lined with a hard greyish substance and that baths and handbasins have a 'tidemark' of scum after you wash. This is a sign that the water in the area is *hard,* that is, not good for washing due to the dissolved minerals it contains.

How does water become hard?

Water is a very solvent substance. When rain forms in the clouds, it is very pure and soft, but as it falls it collects gases, particularly carbon dioxide and other impurities from the air. While it seeps through the ground it dissolves several minerals, depending on the type of soil it passes through.

Most of these are harmless, indeed many are considered to be good for us. Areas where the water contains large proportions of minerals have in the past developed into 'spas' such as Bath in England, where people used to go to drink and bathe in the waters.

Certain minerals though, make it difficult for soap to make a lather, causing scum instead. This is known as *hardness* in water. The minerals which cause hardness are
1. bicarbonate of lime (or magnesium),
2. sulphates of lime (or magnesium).

Softening water

Bicarbonate of lime causes temporary hardness, i.e. it can be removed by boiling. The boiling expels the carbon dioxide which was holding the bicarbonates in solution so that they are deposited on the sides of the kettle or boiler.

Sulphates of lime and magnesium cause permanent hardness which can be removed by adding lime to the water at water-treatment plants, or at home by adding borax to the washing water. Boiling has no effect on permanent hardness.

Water softeners

These contain chemicals such as sodium chloride (in common salt) which are exchanged for the chemical elements that cause the hardness. They can be attached to the household water system. Now and then they must be recharged by running a salt solution through them. Water softeners remove both temporary and permanent hardness.

Heating water

Water may be heated by
1. individual heaters, e.g. an immersion heater,
2. a direct system,
3. an indirect system

THE WORKING PRINCIPLE OF WATER-HEATING SYSTEMS

Most systems are based on the principle of convection, i.e. that water expands when heated and rises from the heat source: as it cools, it falls, due to gravity. As over-heating may produce steam, it is essential for safety that cylinders and systems containing hot water should have an expansion pipe which empties into the tank in the attic.

INDIVIDUAL WATER HEATERS

While it is possible to boil small amounts of water in a kettle, larger heaters are required to meet the needs of a family.

1. INSTANTANEOUS HEATERS

These may be heated by gas or electricity. They are sometimes called geysers. They are installed beside or under a sink. Most models are suitable only for heating water for one outlet. Multi-point heaters are available, which heat sufficient water for a number of outlets. Water passes from the cold supply, through a narrow coil of pipes (gas) or over a heated plate (electricity),

which heat the water to warm, hot or boiling, depending on the thermostat setting. A pilot light ignites the gas jets as soon as water is turned on.

Note: gas heaters of this type must have a flue to expel carbon monoxide, otherwise they could cause asphyxiation.

Instant hot water for the kitchen by gas (Ascot)

Advantages.
1. Really hot water is always on tap, even boiling water.
2. As only the amount of water required is heated, there is no waste. This is especially convenient in flats and bedsitters, where it would be wasteful to have a system which heated large amounts of water all day.

Disadvantages
1. Gas heaters may produce unpleasant fumes.
2. There is an element of danger in gas water heaters, should the flue become blocked.
3. This is an expensive form of water heating, if constantly in use.
4. Some large appliances on the wall look unsightly.

2. ELECTRIC IMMERSION HEATER

An immersion heater consists of a long electric element in a metal sheath. It is thermostatically controlled, i.e. when heating the cylinder from cold, it stays on until the water reaches correct temperature. When this temperature is reached it switches off, and only comes on now and then to maintain that temperature. The immersion heater is fitted inside the hot-water cylinder. A dual immersion heater is more economical. It consists of two elements: one short, which heats the

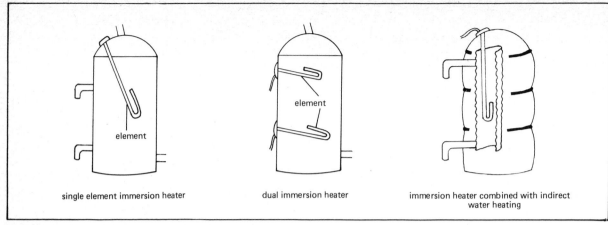

| single element immersion heater | dual immersion heater | immersion heater combined with indirect water heating |

Different types of immersion water heaters

upper half of the cylinder; and the one long, which is turned on when large amounts of water are required. Immersion heaters may be horizontal or vertical — the latter heat the water more quickly. A 3 kW heater is usually the best size, as it heats the water quickly and economically.

Advantages
1. quick, efficient and clean,
2. hot water always available — if it is kept on constantly,
3. useful in summer when alternative forms of water heating (fires, solid fuel cookers, central heating) are not used,
4. thermostatically controlled.

Disadvantages
1. quite expensive to run,
2. installation costs fairly high — must be fitted by electrician,
3. rather slow to heat up from cold,
4. possibility of power cuts.

3. STORAGE WATER HEATERS

These are insulated water storage tanks which are heated by a thermostatically controlled gas or electric circulator. They may be large or small. They keep an amount of water warm and ready for use. Gas storage heaters should be connected to an outside flue.

4. COOKER BOILERS AND BACK BOILERS

These have a boiler (usually copper) fixed at the back of the cooker or fire. The heat from the fire heats the water in the boiler, from which it rises to the hot-water cylinder where it is stored. Many boilers are large enough to heat two or more radiators as well.

Advantage
1. economical — as the fire is also used to heat the room, water heating by this method is virtually free.

Disadvantages
1. involves setting, cleaning and stoking fires,
2. not suitable for use in summer — needs to be supplemented with an immersion or other form of heating.

5. THE DIRECT SYSTEM OF WATER HEATING

This is used in houses where there is no central heating or where 'dry' forms of heating such as warm-air heating are used.
1. Water is heated at a single source of heat: a boiler grate behind a fire, solid fuel cooker, or gas or electric boiler.
2. The hot water rises and is stored in an insulated storage cylinder, usually in the hot press.
3. Cooled water flows from the base of the storage cylinder to the boiler, where it is heated and begins the cycle once again.
4. An expansion pipe from the top of the cylinder allows steam and overheated water to escape into the storage tank in the attic.
5. As hot water is drawn, it leaves the top of the cylinder and flows through a number of pipes until it reaches the sink or bath.
6. Cold water from the attic tank flows into the base of the cylinder to take its place.

The disadvantage of the direct system is that the constant stream of fresh water through the system may cause scaling of pipes in hard-water areas.

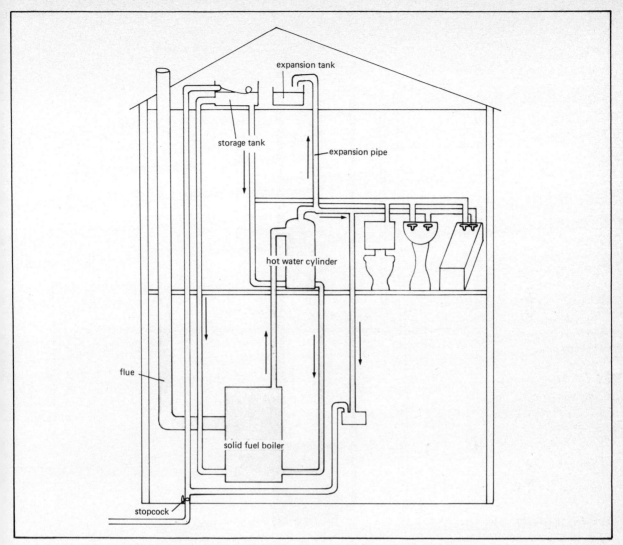

Hot water system – direct

6. INDIRECT SYSTEM

This method of heating is usually part of a central heating system. It is also used in hard-water regions to prevent scaling of pipes.

1. Water for the central heating system is heated in a boiler.
2. A pipe brings the hot water upwards to the storage cylinder by natural convection or pumps (x).
3. Instead of flowing directly into the cylinder as in the direct system, the water flows through a coil of pipes within the cylinder, called a heat exchanger. Heat from these pipes indirectly heats the cylinderful of water.
4. The central heating pipe (a) leaves the cylinder and returns to the boiler to be heated once again.

5. A separate pipe (b) leaves the cylinder, and branches off bringing hot water to taps all over the house.
6. As hot water is used up, water from the main storage tank in the attic flows downwards and into the cylinder to replace it.

Note: at no time does the water in the central heating system mix with the household supply of hot water. They are entirely separate. The central heating system is entirely enclosed, with the same water circulating continuously and the system is never drained except for repairs.

A separate storage tank and an expansion pipe (in case the water overheats) are required for an indirect system such as this

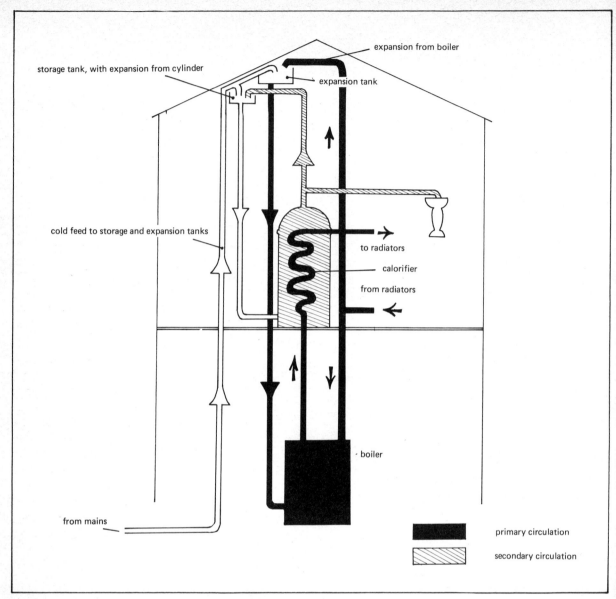

expansion from boiler

storage tank, with expansion from cylinder

expansion tank

cold feed to storage and expansion tanks

to radiators

calorifier

from radiators

boiler

from mains

primary circulation

secondary circulation

Hot water system – indirect

SAVING FUEL ON WATER HEATING

1. The main storage cylinder and all hot water pipes should be well lagged.
2. The distance between the storage cylinder and the taps which provide hot water should be as short as possible.
3. Showers are more economical than baths, as they use less water.
4. Avoid washing items under running water. Wait until there are enough items, then wash together.
5. Use a plastic basin to wash small amounts of clothes or delph; it uses less water than filling the sink.
6. Avoid switching storage and immersion heaters on and off. It is cheaper to leave them on all the time, if they are well lagged and thermostatically controlled.

THE HOUSEHOLD DRAINAGE SYSTEM

One of the main reasons for the huge reduction in disease and death over the last century has been the introduction of a water-based system of removing human excreta from homes and other buildings. Drains are a system of pipes which remove effluent from baths, sinks and lavatories. They also dispose of rainwater.

A good drainage system
1. should not pass under a house,
2. should be laid in straight lines, where possible, (to avoid blockages),
3. should rest on concrete,
4. should have inspection covers at intervals, especially on bends and corners where blockages are likely to occur,
5. should be constructed of glazed stoneware or cast-iron pipes, 150 mm in diameter,
6. should have well-sealed joints,
7. should have a fall away from the house, so that effluent will pass easily through,
8. should have gullies or traps between drains and the house,
9. should be well ventilated.

TRAPS

These are deep U-shaped bends which are permanently filled with water, to prevent smells and germs getting back into the house. Every lavatory, sink and basin has a U- or S-shaped trap. The water in the trap is replaced automatically when the appliance is flushed or emptied.

DRAINAGE SYSTEMS

Urban areas

Houses have a double system of drainage. A ventilated soil pipe, leading from the lavatory, empties directly into an underground drain. Other appliances discharge into a hopper or gully and from there into the main drain. A system of underground drains and sewers brings effluent to the *sewage treatment plant*. Here the sewage is treated in various ways.
1. It may be broken up, filtered and then released into the sea.
2. It may be filtered and waste allowed to settle in huge septic tanks. The solids settle to the bottom, and the liquid is subjected to bacterial action which renders

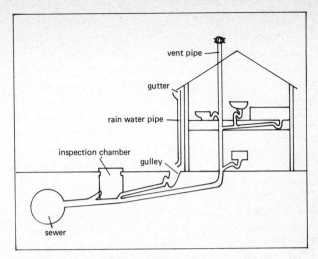

Common house drainage system

it harmless. It is then discharged into rivers or sea. The solids are either loaded onto boats and discharged far out at sea or sometimes dried and used as fertilisers.

Rural areas

In isolated houses, sewage is discharged into *septic tanks*. It first lies in a soak pit. Here the solids sink to the bottom and the bacteria over a period of time decompose the sewage into harmless compounds. The liquid waste is filtered out through a fan of underground drainage pipes. It is essential to avoid using large amounts of disinfectants, antiseptics, bleaches and other cleaning agents with septic tanks as these destroy the bacteria which work on the sewage. Septic tanks need to be drained now and then.

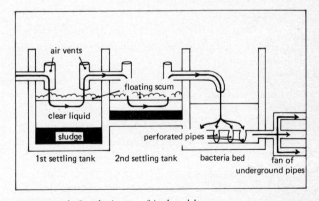

Septic tank for drainage of isolated houses

Cesspools are also used in rural areas. The waste is drained into brick lined pits from which it is removed by special tankers to the sewage works.

LOCAL AUTHORITIES AND POLLUTION

The local authorities are responsible for providing a wholesome water supply and for the collection and purification of sewage in towns and cities. Building regulations which concern drainage are very strict, as they are necessary to ensure the health and hygiene of the community at large. No major alteration to a drainage system is permitted without planning permission. When house plans are submitted to the local authority, the drainage and plumbing systems are carefully checked, e.g. fresh-water pipes and drains must not be laid side to side.

It is illegal to discharge untreated sewage into rivers or sea. Factory effluent such as detergents or chemicals can harm animal and vegetable life. Detergents and other chemicals should be biodegradable, i.e. easily broken down by bacteria. If not, they will cause foaming at sewage works and may damage plant and marine life.

ILL EFFECTS OF BAD DRAINAGE

1. can cause serious diseases such as cholera, dysentery, typhoid, gastro-enteritis and other food-poisoning diseases,
2. unpleasant smell,
3. attracts flies,
4. may contaminate pure-water supply if not laid in separate trenches.

Maintenance of drains

1. Flush sink and overflow regularly with cold clean water.
2. Avoid emptying food, tea leaves, fat and such things as plaster filler and adhesives into drains: they cause blockages.
3. Keep sink, overflow, pipes and drains free from germs as possible by regular use of boiling water and disinfectants.
4. Clean lavatories every day, paying particular attention to flushing rim, handle and seat — top and bottom.
5. Pour washing soda and boiling water down sink and bath drains now and then to prevent accumulation of fat and soap.
6. Clean gullies (the visible grating on top of an outside drain) regularly, by pouring boiling water with Jeyes Fluid dissolved in it into and around gully. Remove leaves regularly in autumn.
7. Once or twice a year, scrub the inside of the gully, using hot water and washing soda (use an old lavatory brush and wear rubber gloves).

Blocked drains

1. Use a plunger (block the overflow first), *or*
2. Loosen the obstruction with a long piece of wire, then flush with boiling water, *or*
3. Use a commercial caustic waste-pipe cleaner, *or*
4. If none of these work, place a basin under the S-trap, remove screw and loosen the obstruction with wire. Clean pipe with an old brush and flush with water. Replace screw and flush with cold water to fill S-trap again.

Frozen pipes

1. Turn on taps.
2. Wrap pipes with hot cloths, starting at the tap and working backwards. Replace cloths now and then until ice melts.

Burst pipes

1. Turn off water mains at stopcock and also turn off all sources of water heating.
2. Turn on taps.
3. Wrap a rag and polythene bag tightly around leak.
4. Ring plumber quickly. Meanwhile remove furniture and lift carpets if necessary.

CLEANING AGENTS USED ON DRAINS

(a) Disinfectants: these destroy pathogenic bacteria, but have little effect on viruses. They can be divided into two groups: natural and chemical disinfectants.

Natural disinfectants

1. heat — fire, steam, boiling water,
2. ultra-violet radiation — sunlight,
3. fresh air — germs dislike oxygen.

Chemical disinfectants

1. soap and soap powders,
2. hydrogen peroxide,
3. chlorine,
4. carbolic acid,
5. phenols (found in heavy-duty disinfectants, like Jeyes fluid, made from coal tar),
Commercial products: Dettol, Jeypine, Lifeguard.

(b) Bleaches: these destroy organisms by chemical oxidation of the cells. They destroy most bacteria, viruses and fungi. They remove colour and odours. Many household bleaches contain sodium hypochlorite and have a strong smell. Other bleaches are chlorine, sodium perborate, hydrogen peroxide. Most bleaches are poisonous. Use them carefully.
Commercial products: Harpic, Sanilav

(c) Waste pipe cleaners: most contain sodium hydroxide which melts any grease in the waste pipe. Some contain strong abrasives which wear away the blockage by friction. They may be used regularly to keep drains clear, and are also used to free blocked drains. Most also have a disinfectant effect on the drain. Commercial product: Clearway.

(d) Washing soda: this is a strong alkaline crystal of sodium carbonate, which removes grease.

Note: Many cleaning agents are poisonous — keep them locked away out of reach of children.

QUESTIONS/CHAPTER 6

1. Write a note on the distribution of water to homes in urban areas.
   Describe with the aid of a diagram the circulation of cold water in the house.
   How may water be conserved during water shortages?

2. Name three types of water pollutant. In the case of each, state its origin and how it may be removed or rendered harmless.
   How would you identify pure drinking water?

3. Explain the causes of hardness in water. What are its effects?
   Describe in detail how hardness may be removed from water.

4. List the scientific principle which underlies household water heating systems.
   Name two methods of heating large amounts of water for household use and in the case of one, describe it in detail with the aid of diagrams.

5. Describe how household effluent may be removed (a) in urban areas, or (b) in rural areas. Use diagrams to illustrate your answer.
   State the effects of bad drainage.
   List the points to be observed in order to keep drains functional and hygienic.

7.
Heating a home

A warm home is important for the comfort, health and well-being of the family. The method of heating used in a home will depend on the season, climate, type of house and life-style of the family. In one family a parent may be at home all day with small children; in this case all day heating will be required, perhaps a boiler grate with radiators. In a family where everyone is out all day, individual heaters which heat up quickly when they come home would be more practical.
   Central heating is probably the ideal. It provides heat automatically when and where you want it: but it is expensive to instal and run.

HOW MUCH HEAT

   The average winter temperature in this climate is about 6°C. In order to provide a comfortable temperature in our homes we would need an average of 15°C or more. Children and old people need a higher temperature than average.

HEAT TRANSFER

Heat can travel in three ways: conduction, convection and radiation.

CONDUCTION

   By this method, heat travels from one molecule of a liquid or solid to the next. Example: put a metal spoon in a saucepan of boiling water. Heat travels along the spoon until the handle is so hot that it cannot be touched.
   Metals conduct heat well; wood, rubber and plastic are bad conductors. These are often used to insulate buildings as they are slow to let the heat out.
   Conduction is rarely used as a method of heating a house. Most methods of heating are based on *convection* and *radiation.*

CONVECTION

   When gas or liquid is heated, the molecules expand, become less dense, and subsequently rise. More cold gas/liquid flows in underneath to replace it. This sets up convection currents. Some forms of central heating and many of the heating appliances used in the home are based on this principle. Ovens are also heated in this way. Fans or pumps are often used in heating systems to assist or speed up the convection of hot air or liquid.

RADIATION

By this method heat passes in straight waves or rays from the heat source to an object without warming the air through which it passes. Convection currents of air rise from the heated object, causing the surrounding area to be heated. Open fires, radiant electric and gas fires, and radiators work on this principle. As bright shining surfaces radiate heat well, they are used on **radiant** fires to reflect the heat more efficiently.

A home can be heated by
1. Individual heaters in each room — either fixed or portable.
2. Background heating which provides a low level of heat, e.g. storage heaters,
3. Full or partial central heating.

A cheerful fire in the hearth (Barnaby's Picture Library)

FUEL

The four most common sources of heat in this country are solid fuel, oil, coal gas and electricity. Other sources of heat include solar energy, natural gas, and nuclear energy. It is difficult to determine which fuel is the most economical: prices are constantly fluctuating; fuels which seem the least expensive are less efficient; others become scarce at times, or are subject to strikes. Try if possible not to be dependent on one type of fuel. The important point is that all fuels should be used economically, and insulation should be extensively used to reduce heat loss and wastage.

SOLID FUEL

The term includes coal, turf, wood, charcoal (carbonised wood), and smokeless fuels such as coke and anthracite. Solid fuels contain carbon, hydrogen and oxygen. The higher the carbon content, the greater will be the amount of heat and energy produced. Wood contains 50% carbon; the remaining 50% produces smoke, soot, ash and waste gas. Turf contains 60% carbon; coal 88% carbon; and anthracite 94% carbon. If solid fuel is burned in an open grate, its efficiency decreases because much of the heat goes up the chimney. If it is burned in an enclosed stove or cooker, less heat is lost.

Smokeless fuels

There is an increased emphasis on the use of smokeless fuels, because they cause less smoke and air pollution than coal and other solid fuels; they produce little ash; and they have a high carbon content, making them burn more slowly and produce more heat. Smokeless fuels are usually burned in closed stoves.

Manufactured smokeless fuels are oval-shaped. They are sold under brand names, such as Phurnacite.

Advantages of solid fuel
1. Solid fuel systems are relatively cheap to run.
2. An open fire is a focal point in a room — it is cheerful and homely to sit by.
3. Home heating can be combined with water heating by using boiler grates.
4. Open grates assist ventilation and do not dry the air.

Disadvantages
1. Solid fuel systems are less efficient than most other forms of heating.
2. The fuel is awkward and heavy to deliver, and requires a large storage area.
3. Solid fuel is time-consuming, with the fuelling, cleaning and setting of fires.
4. Solid fuel is dirty: it involves carrying fuel, stoking, emptying ashes. The disposal of ashes is inconvenient and troublesome.

Solid fuel burning appliances include open fires, convector fires, stoves, boiler grates, cookers and boilers.

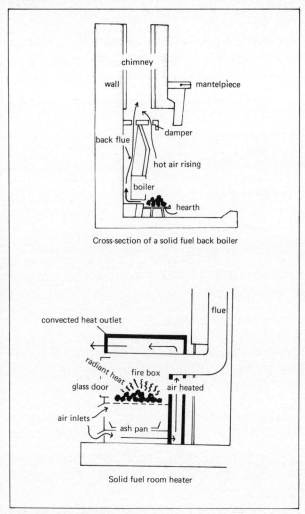

Cross-section of a solid fuel back boiler

Solid fuel room heater

Solid fuel appliances

Open fires: these provide a cheerful form of radiant heat. Modern grates are well designed and incorporate efficient draught controls, restricted throat in chimney, and sealed grates. These improvements over the old-fashioned grate reduce draughts and heat loss up the chimney, and increase the amount of heat radiated into the room.

Convector fires: these have a space behind the fire, containing air which is warmed and passes out into the room through an outlet *grille* near the top of the fireplace. Cold air enters through grilles near the base of the fireplace. The advantage of this type of fire is that it produces continual convection currents as well as the normal radiant heat of an open fire.

Boiler grates or back boilers: these fireplaces are specially designed to hold a metal cylinder behind the fire. The cylinder is fed with cold water from the storage cistern in the attic, and the water heated in the boiler is stored in the storage cylinder in the hot press. The fire is used in the normal way. In summer, of course, this system needs to be substituted by some other form of water heating, e.g. an immersion heater.

Stoves or solid-fuel room heaters: because of the increased cost of fuel, stoves are becoming more popular as they are less wasteful of fuel and heat. There are two basic types: stoves that can be opened, and closed stoves. Both are sealed metal boxes which fit into an existing fireplace. A flue connects the heater with the chimney. They heat by convection and radiation. Some types have a door which may be opened during use. Closed stoves are more effecient than those that open: they are more economical as less heat is lost. They usually burn smokeless fuels and often incorporate a back boiler. High output boilers are designed to heat up to ten radiators as well as providing hot water for the kitchen and bathroom.

Advantages of room heaters
1. Economical: they use less fuel than an open fire.
2. Greater heat output provides an even warmth throughout the room.
3. Rate of combustion is controlled.
4. Less fuelling and cleaning are required than for an open fire.
5. The heaters burn continuously and are very safe if installed properly (see below).
6. Many will burn various forms of solid fuel, but they work most efficiently with smokeless fuels.

Disadvantages
1. Ventilation is reduced, as these fires are sealed.
2. The stove is less attractive than an open fire.
3. More attention is required than for gas, oil or electric heaters.

Solid fuel central-heating boilers: the modern solid-fuel boiler burns smokeless fuels. it is fuelled only once a day, and as these fuels produce little ash the ashbox is emptied once or twice a week. It is possible to feed the anthracite from a hopper above the boiler, thus reducing the frequency of fuelling. This is called an automatic or hopper-fed boiler.

Solid fuel cookers: see chapter 18.

Economising on solid fuel
1. Fires and stoves should be installed so that air may enter only through the regulator.
2. Once the fire is burning well, reduce air inlet.
3. Use dampened slack on open fires to slow down the rate of burning.
4. Don't let the fire burn down too low before refuelling.
5. Empty the ash pan regularly.
6. Buy solid fuel in bulk. Buying by the bag is very expensive.

OIL

Petroleum is the source of all fuel oils. Petroleum consists of the remains of tiny shellfish. Over millions of years they have been subjected to the pressure of layers of rock and sand and converted into crude oil (or petroleum).

The oils most commonly used for domestic heating are paraffin and fuel oil. Paraffin oil is used in paraffin heaters, stoves and lamps. Fuel oil is used in vaporising burners, such as those in central heating boilers and oil-fired cookers.

Advantages
1. Oil is easy to deliver and store.
2. Oil is an efficient fuel; there is little waste of heat.
3. Portable oil heaters can be moved from room to room *when unlit*.
4. Oil-fired central heating requires the minimum of attention.

Disadvantages
1. Fire is a great risk with all oil heaters. Ensure they conform to safety standards, are sturdy and difficult to overturn, and cut out if overturned. Do not use in areas of draught, heavy traffic, or where children are playing. Do not move when lit.
2. Unpleasant fumes are given off, especially if not kept clean.
3. Oxygen in the air is used up, requiring a good system of ventilation.

Oil heaters
Drip-feed heater: the paraffin drips onto a piece of gauze which burns when lit, giving off both radiant and convected heat.

Wick-feed heater: cotton wicks are suspended in the paraffin, which is soaked up by capillary action and burned at the surface of the wick.

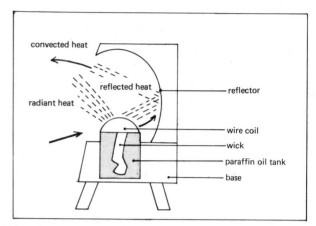

Paraffin wick-feed radiant heater

Pressure or vapour heater: the vapour from the paraffin burns. This type is very economical, light, portable and suitable for camping.

Convector heater: these are usually wick-feed heaters which heat air with the appliance. The warmed air rises and leaves the heater through a grille on the top. Cold air is drawn in underneath.

Oil-fired boilers
Two types of oil may be used: vaporising oil and domestic fuel oil (pressure-jet). The type of oil will depend on the burner in the boiler. Boilers must be serviced once or twice a year. Each house has an individual oil storage tank holding approximately 1,300 litres. A communal tank may be used in housing estates. In this case supply into each house is recorded on a meter.

GAS

Some large cities have a piped gas supply. Gas mains carry gas underground and a service pipe enters each house. Within the house is a control tap, which can cut off the gas supply if necessary, and a meter which records consumption in cubic metres. The gas may be coal gas or natural gas.

Reading a gas meter

Read dials from left to right.

EXAMPLE: When the pointer is between two numbers always write down the lesser number as on the dial reading 4 above. But if the pointer is between 0 and 9 write 9. Thus the above reading is 3496. Subtract from it your reading for the previous week. The difference is your consumption in 100 cu. ft.

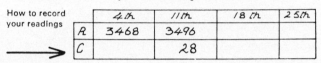

How to record your readings		4th	11th	18th	25th
→	R	3468	3496		
	C		28		

Bottled gas

This is useful where piped gas is not available, and also for camping and on boats and caravans. Very small containers are available for single gas burners. A small double burner and cylinder are useful as a standby when electric power cuts occur. There are cookers, refrigerators, roomheaters and water heaters which can be connected to bottled gas cylinders. One of the most popular and efficient gas heaters now available is a radiant heater which holds the cylinder within the heater body (Super Ser). This has three settings and is an attractively designed, powerful heater.

Care of bottled gas containers

1. Avoid storing them horizontally.
2. Store them away from heat and direct sunlight. Strong heat could cause an increase in pressure when full.
3. Keep appliances and metal connections clean.
4. Ensure adequate ventilation and avoid using them in bedrooms.
5. On suspicion of a leak, call the supplier. Never use a match to search for leaks.
6. When purchasing, get clear directions for using and changing the cylinder.

Advantages of mains gas

1. Storage is not required as it is piped directly.
2. An efficient form of fuel, it is clean and easy to control.

3. Gas may be used for central heating, individual heaters, cooking and water heating.

Disadvantages

1. Gas is fairly expensive
2. An efficient flue is usually required to remove the carbon dioxide and vapour produced through an outside wall.
3. Some heat is lost through the flue.
4. Appliances must be installed, serviced and repaired by a qualified fitter.
5. Flueless heaters may only be used in large, well-ventilated areas.
6. There is a danger of leaks.
7. Gas tends to have an unpleasant odour.

Gas appliances include radiant/convector heaters, convector heaters, gas cookers and gas boilers.

Radiant convector heaters have gas jets which heat a fire-clay grille until it is white hot. This throws out radiant heat. Air is also drawn in at the base, heated and expelled through a grille at the top of the heater. Large heaters may use a fan to assist the circulation.

Convector heaters are slim heaters usually fitted to a wall. Inside the heater gas jets heat the air, which rises and passes out through the top of the heater. Large heaters will require a balanced flue for ventilation (see below). Small models may be used without a flue but only in a hallway or well-ventilated room — never in a confined space. Flueless convector heaters dry the air.

Gas convector heater (Studio Briggs)

The importance of ventilation

Gas when burning produces carbon dioxide and water vapour; these must be removed through some form of outlet. Most gas radiant and convector heaters are fitted into an existing fireplace, and use the chimney as a flue. If not, they require a *balanced flue* which must be fitted (by an expert) onto an outside wall. This lets stale air out, and warms the fresh air which enters to replace it.

ELECTRICITY

Electricity provides many forms of heating.

Advantages
1. Electric heating is the most efficient form of heating. There is no waste, no ash, no fumes.
2. It is available, literally, at the flick of a switch.
3. There are no delivery or storage problems.
4. It is a very clean form of heat.
5. It lends itself to modern features such as time switches, fans, thermostats etc.

Disadvantages
1. Electricity is one of the most expensive forms of heating.
2. It tends to dry the air.
3. ESB power cuts occur more often than interruptions in supply of other fuels.

Electric heating appliances include radiant and convector heaters, fan heaters, oil-filled and storage heaters, cookers and central-heating systems.

Fuel-effect electric fire (Dimplex)

Radiant heaters vary from a simple, single-bar, portable heater to a three-bar, coal-effect fire. A portable radiant heater consists of a thin element wire, wound tightly round a fireclay rod. There may be one to three bars on this type of fire. The back of the fire is made of polished metal, which reflects the heat outwards. A safety guard should always be fitted on this type of fire. It needs a 13 amp fused plug.

Infra-red heaters consist of a rod element, encased in silica (a glass-like material), backed by a reflector. As it is light, it is more suitable for mounting on walls. It is the safest form of electric heating for a bathroom, as long as it is installed by a good electrician, with a pull cord instead of a switch.

Convector heaters consist of a metal box with electric elements near the base. Cold air is drawn in through the base, and heated as it passes over the elements; then it rises and leaves the heater through an outlet grille near the top of the heater. An electric convector heater can be free-standing or mounted on a wall. Most have a thermostat and a selection of heat settings.

Fan heaters: a fan draws cold air in over a heating element and out through a grille. It heats a room quickly and evenly but it is inclined to be expensive to run and noisy. Most have more than one heat setting, two speeds, and some have a thermostat which switches the heater on and off as the temperature rises and falls.

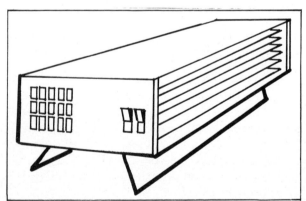

Electric fan heater

Oil-filled radiators (e.g. Dimplex): although these look like radiators used in central heating systems, they are free-standing and they plug in. They consist of an element situated at the base of the heater, which heats by convection the oil which is present in the radiator. They generally incorporate a thermostat, are fairly expensive to buy and very expensive to run.

Storage heaters consist of heating elements embedded in blocks of fireclay or concrete. These are covered with insulating material such as glass fibre or asbestos, and the whole is encased in a streamlined metal casing. The elements heat up the fireclay at night on cheap off-peak electricity. The insulating material prevents immediate heat loss: this occurs slowly during the day, giving out an even background heat. The heat is sometimes boosted during the afternoon. New models may have a fan to provide heat quickly when necessary. Storage heaters have a separate meter and wiring circuit and they are wired directly to the system, i.e. sockets are not used.

Slimline electric storage heater (Dimplex)

Advantages of storage heaters
1. They are cheaper and less troublesome to install than conventional central heating.
2. They provide an even background heat.
3. Fan-assisted heaters are more efficient but more expensive to run.

Disadvantages
1. Heating needs to be supplemented except on mild days.
2. Running costs are fairly high.
3. Heaters are heavy and bulky.
4. They are not easy to control: the heaters are slow to heat up and cool down.

USING HEATERS SAFELY

1. Only heaters of a reliable make, which conform to accepted safety standards, should be used.
2. Do not place heaters too near furniture or curtains.
3. Open fires and radiant electric fires should be protected by a securely fixed fireguard.
4. Never leave clothes to dry over any heater, as it may overheat and cause a fire.
5. Never move oil heaters once lit.
6. Gas heaters, except the bottled gas kind, should have some form of flue, except in a very well ventilated area.
7. Keep heaters clean and serviced.
8. Children: extra care should be taken when children are about. Small children should not be left unsupervised in the same room as any heater within their reach. Keep them away from hot radiators and other heaters. Only non-flammable nightwear should be used. Guards are available which clip onto cookers and fires to prevent accidents.

CENTRAL HEATING

So far we have discussed ways of heating individual areas of the house.

The term central heating means that the whole house is warmed from a central source, usually a boiler. The advantage of central heating is that it enables the whole house to be used at one time, makes the house comfortable, and prevents the danger of chill when moving from a hot to a cold room. It is also both convenient and labour saving.

There are three types of Central Heating

1. Full central heating, which should be fully or semi-automatic, should heat every room, including the hall, to a comfortable temperature.
2. Background heating warms the whole house a little but needs to be supplemented with individual heaters.
3. Partial or selective heating may heat part of the house, e.g. two or three radiators at a time.

There are many combinations of heating systems which can be used successfully in the modern house. These are three of the most common:
1. the small bore system, using radiators — a wet system,
2. warm air central heating — a dry system,
3. electric storage and under-floor heating — a dry system.

SMALL BORE SYSTEM: A WET SYSTEM

This involves heating water in a boiler, which may be fuelled by solid fuel, oil or gas. The hot water is pumped through narrow diameter (small bore) pipes which feed each radiator, and returns to the boiler to be heated again. This system usually incorporates a water-heating system, whereby the pipes pass through a heat exchanger within the hot-water storage cylinder to heat the domestic hot-water supply. A separate attic cistern is required to feed cold water into the system as necessary, and an overflow pipe emptying into this cistern is a safeguard against overheating.

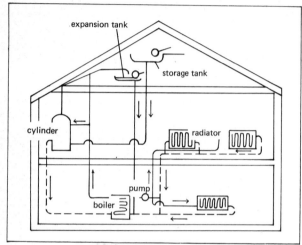

Small bore central heating system

INSTALLATION OF SMALL BORE SYSTEMS

1. Discuss the type of system required and get estimates from several reliable heating engineers. These should stipulate the minimum guaranteed temperature in each room:

Livingroom	18°-20°C
Bedrooms, kitchen and bathroom	15°-18°C
Hall	14°-16°C

2. The system should include a sufficiently powerful boiler and circulating pump. The more noisy and less streamlined boilers are often more efficient and may be situated in a garage or separate boilerhouse. Relatively noiseless, enamelled boilers are available for kitchen use.
3. Radiators: these provide 80% convected heat and 20% radiated heat, so are inappropriately named. Usually made from pressed steel, they vary in size and finish. They may be single or double panelled or designed to look like a skirting board. Radiators work more efficiently under a window, as they warm the cold air entering the room to prevent draughts.

4. Thermostats: most systems include two thermostats, one on the boiler and another within the house, usually in the livingroom. When the temperature in the room becomes too hot, the thermostat cuts off the boiler.

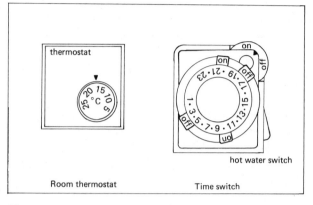

Thermostats

5. Automatic controls: these usually include an on/off switch for boiler and pump; a time switch on a 24 hour clock — it can be set to switch the heating on and then off twice a day, usually morning and evening; and a switch which can change the system over to water heating alone in summer.
6. Humidity: most central heating systems dry the air. To avoid this a humidifier should be used to replace the moisture lost. This may take the form of a small container of water left near or clipped onto a radiator, or an electric humidifier which releases steam or water vapour into the air.
7. Make sure each room is ventilated.
8. Make sure the whole house is well insulated.

Advantages
1. This form of heating is fully automatic, quick and efficient.
2. The system can be installed in older houses.
3. It is easily controlled and adjusted and can be turned on/off in any room as required.
4. Water heating is usually included.
5. A dual boiler can be installed which can be changed from oil to solid fuel when wished.

Disadvantages
1. Radiators may interfere with the layout of a room.
2. Necessity for a pump makes the system dependent on electricity whatever the fuel used.
3. It is expensive to install.

WARM AIR CENTRAL HEATING: A DRY SYSTEM

Principle: air is heated in a warm air unit, a type of heater which may be run on gas, oil or electricity. The air is blown over the heat source by a powerful electrically-driven fan. It travels through ducts, concealed in the floor and roof space, and passes into each room through controllable grilles placed at floor level. The stale air leaves through outlet grilles at ceiling height. Most warm air units incorporate an air filter and humidifier. Thermostats placed in the heating unit and in one or more rooms control the temperature. Oil and gas fired warm air units must have an outlet flue. Electric warm air heating works on the same principle as an electric storage heater. Its heat storage unit uses off-peak electricity.

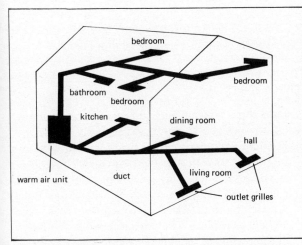

Warm air central heating

The household hot water supply is not usually heated by warm air systems, although some indirect systems use hot water pipes as the source of heat in the warm air unit

Advantages
1. It heats up very quickly.
2. It usually includes an air filter and humidifier.
3. It is easy to control — can be shut off in one or two rooms as required.
4. The inlet grilles are unobtrusive, leaving more scope for decorating.

Disadvantages
1. It needs large ducts: unsuitable for installation in ready-built houses.
2. A flue is required, unless an electric system is used.
3. Noise, dust and odours are likely to pass from one room to another through the grilles.

4. Water heating is not usually included.
5. Heat is likely to escape from ducts and grilles, even when closed.

UNDER-FLOOR HEATING: A DRY SYSTEM

Under-floor heating works on the same principle as the storage heater (see p. 75). Cheaper off-peak electricity is used to heat elements, which are embedded in concrete or other heat-storing material in the floor of the house. This retained heat is gradually released to provide background heat for some hours afterwards. An afternoon boost of heat is usually required to provide heat into the evening.

Disadvantages
1. This method is suitable for bungalows, not for upper floors of houses, although it is sometimes used in office blocks, which have cement floors.
2. It must be installed during the building (or reflooring) of a house.
3. If the system needs repair, it may be necessary to take up the floor.
4. Some find the warmth makes feet uncomfortable.
5. Separate water heating is required.

Comparing costs
When installing any central heating system, consider:

1. installation costs — i.e. cost of boiler, heaters and labour;
2. running costs — fuel bills and maintenance, although these are very difficult to compare as the price of fuel is constantly changing;
3. heat efficiency — are you getting enough heat for your money?
4. insulation, which will increase heat efficiency and will repay its cost quickly;
5. convenience — a fully automatic system may be marginally more expensive but saves much time and labour

Economising on central heating
1. Instal good insulation throughout the house.
2. Switch off radiators or grilles in rooms not in use.
3. Do not set thermostats too high.
4. Keep doors closed to avoid loss of heat.
5. Use time switches sensibly, reducing heating time and thermostats as weather gets warmer.
6. Have central heating system/boiler serviced regularly.
7. Some fuels are cheaper when bought in bulk.

INSULATION

An uninsulated house can lose 75% of all heat produced. Insulation is an essential part of any heating system; by reducing heat loss, it lowers running costs. The cost of installing many forms of insulation is offset by the saving on fuel bills which follows. The least expensive way to insulate any house is to do so at the time of construction.

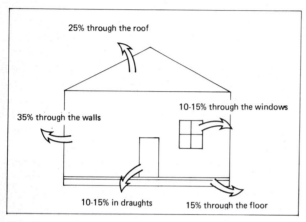

How heat escapes from a house without insulation

Most forms of insulation use bad conductors of heat (air, polystyrene, fibreglass) to reduce the convection of warm air into the atmosphere outside the house. They work on the principle of trapping air (a very poor conductor of heat) between their layers, thus reducing heat loss. As insulating materials tend to absorb noise, they also help to make a house soundproof.

Insulating the roof is probably the most successful form of insulation . Twenty-five per cent of heat loss occurs as hot air rises through ceilings. This can be greatly reduced by insulating the floors of the attic with one of the following insulating materials. They are relatively cheap and easy for the home handyman (or waman) to lay.

1. Glass fibre blanket is laid across or between the joists. The rolls are 10 cm deep, 41 cm wide, 6.5 m long. Eighteen to twenty rolls are required for the average house.
2. Loosefill pellets of polystyrene are poured between the joists.

Roof insulation should be fitted well into the eaves, and it is also important to insulate the trap door. As the attic will now become very cold in winter, the area beneath the storage cistern must not be insulated, but the cistern should be wrapped in glass fibre. The warmth escaping up underneath the tank will prevent it from freezing. Any visible pipes in the attic should be lagged with foam or other insulating material.

DRAUGHTS

Draughts which may occur through doors, windows, floors and chimneys are easily corrected.

1. Draught excluders: fitted on doors and windows, these may be temporary or permanent. Temporary excluders are self-adhesive foam strips. Although cheap, these tend to peel off. Permanent excluders are metal and plastic strips of various types. which are tacked in place. They are more expensive, but are durable and can be painted over.
2. Curtains: heavy, lined and interlined curtains when drawn across windows and doors can reduce heat loss considerably at night.

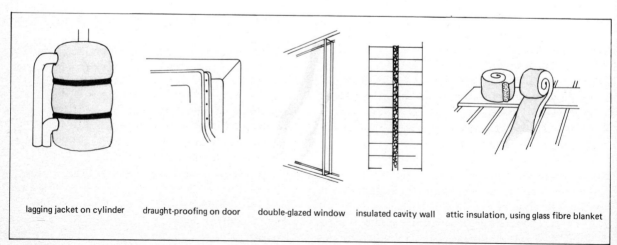

lagging jacket on cylinder   draught-proofing on door   double-glazed window   insulated cavity wall   attic insulation, using glass fibre blanket

Insulation to conserve heat

3. Floors: fitted carpets with a thick underlay will help to reduce heat loss through floors. Corrugated foil can be tacked to the joists if it is possible to get underneath the floor. Hardboard, laid under vinyl floors, improves insulation.
4. Cracks in floorboards, skirting, around windows and doors should be filled with an appropriate wood or plaster filler before painting. Large cracks in the floor can be filled cheaply with papier-maché or a mixture of sawdust and wallpaper adhesive.
5. Chimneys: if the fireplace is never used, brick it up leaving a small ventilating grille. If the fireplace is sometimes used, a fitted firescreen will prevent draughts when not in use.

WALLS

Most houses built since 1930 have cavity walls. The 5 cm air space between these provides some insulation. Modern houses may have polystyrene sheeting between the layers to further improve insulation.

It is possible to fill the air space in existing cavity walls by using plastic foam or mineral wool. These are pumped into the cavity through a number of holes drilled through the outer wall. When the filling has entirely filled the space, the holes are filled in. It is an expensive operation and must be carried out by a reliable firm specialising in this type of work. It eventually pays for itself in a few years of fuel saving.

DOUBLE-GLAZING

This is the most expensive form of insulation. It reduces heat loss through windows by 50%. As a relatively small percentage of heat is lost through windows (15%), it is unlikely to be economic unless the windows are in a bad state of repair and need to be replaced anyway.

The principle of double-glazing is to use air (a bad heat conductor) to reduce heat loss. Two panes of glass have a sealed layer of still air between them. This pocket of air reduces outward convection of heat. Cheaper forms of double-glazing, such as a second sheet of glass or plastic, may be fixed to existing windows. Many do-it-yourself double glazing kits are available.

HOT WATER CYLINDERS AND PIPES

These should be insulated to prevent loss of heat and reduce fuel costs. Fitted cylinder jackets of various thicknesses are available: the thicker the better. All hot water pipes should be lagged with rags, fibreglass or foam tubes.

QUESTIONS/CHAPTER 7

1. Suggest an efficient and economical heating plan for a small house in a rural or urban area. Draw a diagram of the plan. State the ideal temperature (a) in the living-rooms, (b) in the bedrooms, during winter months.
2. Describe a project you worked on relating to home heating or insulation. Describe the aim of the project, sources of information and results.
3. Compare solid fuel with electricity as energy sources for home central heating, under the following headings:
   (a) efficiency;
   (b) convenience;
   (c) temperature;
   (d) cost;
   (e) safety.
   Write a note on smokeless fuels.
4. Explain the basic principle of insulation. Discuss the importance of insulating a modern home. Describe in detail one method of insulating each of the following:
   (a) the roof;
   (b) windows;
   (c) walls;
   (d) doors.
5. Discuss gas heaters under the following headings:
   (a) types;
   (b) efficiency;
   (c) ease of use;
   (d) cost of buying and running.
6. What is the current cost of these fuels:
   (a) coal;
   (b) electricity;
   (c) oil.

8.
Air and ventilation

AIR

Air is a mixture of three gases: oxygen, nitrogen and carbon dioxide. When we breathe, we take in oxygen and breathe out carbon dioxide, a poisonous waste gas. More than 0.06% carbon dioxide in the air is considered harmful.

AVERAGE COMPOSITION OF AIR		
	Fresh air	Stale air
Nitrogen	79%	79%
Oxygen	20.96%	16.96%
Carbon dioxide	0.04%	4.04%
Temperature	varies	37°C
Humidity	varies	very high level
Impurities	vary	contains large numbers of bacteria and micro-organisms

Air pollution in dockland (Barnaby's Picture Library)

AIR POLLUTION

Pollution is now a major health problem. The air around us, particularly in cities, is contaminated with impurities; some are suspended or floating in the air, e.g. dust, pollen; others such as carbon dioxide and carbon monoxide are dissolved in the air.

Pollutant	Origin	Damage caused	Methods of Prevention
Carbon dioxide	All forms of combustion including breathing	People more likely to get chest infections; poisonous in large amounts	Improve ventilation. Use solar and wind energy instead of solid fuels
Carbon monoxide	Incomplete combustion in industrial and domestic furnaces, car exhausts	Reduces oxygen level in blood eventually causing unconsciousness and death	Improve ventilation. Restrict cars in built-up areas. Modify engines and exhausts
Sulphur dioxide	Industrial combustion e.g. oil refineries etc.	Lung damage, chest infections. Damage to plant and animal life and buildings	Remove sulphur from fuels. Decentralise industry
Pathogens e.g. bacteria and viruses	Unhygienic habits e.g. careless coughing, sneezing, which cause droplet infection	Chest infections, TB, various infectious diseases	Improve ventilation. Vaccination, more fresh air and exercise
Tar, smoke, nicotine	Cigarette smoking	Heart disease, lung cancer, bronchitis and other chest infections	Do not smoke. Protest against smoking in public places or avoid such places
Suspended particles e.g. dust, soot, ash	Domestic and industrial combustion, mining, certain industrial occupations	Respiratory infections. Damage to lungs e.g. emphysema etc.	Use smokeless fuels. Use solar/wind energy

VENTILATION

The purpose of ventilation is to remove stale air containing impurities and replace it with fresh air, without producing a draught or suddenly lowering the room temperature. The room should remain comfortably warm and moist — neither humid nor too dry. A good system of ventilation will introduce convection currents to change the air in the room at least once every hour.

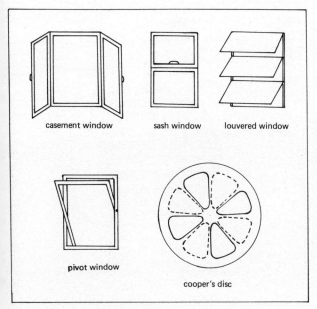

casement window   sash window   louvered window

pivot window

cooper's disc

Ventilation by different means

A well-ventilated house is essential for good health and comfort. With the emphasis on good insulation, there is a danger of creating stuffy, unhealthy rooms by insulating so thoroughly that fresh air is unable to enter the house.

Humidity

This is the amount of water vapour in the air. There is a natural humidity in air outside, due to the evaporation taking place after rainfall and from lakes, rivers and the sea.

The sources of humidity in the home are cooking, washing and bathing, laundering, breathing, perspiration, combustion from some heating appliances.

Kitchens, bathrooms and laundry areas have the highest humidity levels in the home. Good ventilation (and care during cooking and laundry) can reduce humidity to a comfortable level. A high level of humidity causes condensation, drowsiness and discomfort, and can aggravate sinus trouble and laryngitis. Electric heating has a tendency to cause over-dry air. Humidifiers are natural and mechanical methods of adding water vapour to dried-out air.

Condensation

This is the process whereby water vapour in the air changes to water droplets. It occurs when warm air, saturated with moisture, comes in contact with a cold surface. The air becomes colder, less able to hold water vapour, and the vapour then condenses to water. Common examples of this are the steamy kitchen or bathroom, where the cold surfaces cloud over and eventually rivulets of water run down the walls and windows, and the centrally-heated house in winter with the warm, humid air condensing on cold windows.

Severe condensation leads to the growth of moulds and fungi; damages walls, wallcoverings and paintwork; and causes extensive rusting of metals.

To prevent condensation

1. Improve the system of ventilation by adding an extractor fan.
2. Improve insulation: double-glazed windows are not cold on the inside, so water vapour will be unlikely to condense on them.
3. Do not have cold and glossy surfaces which increase condensation. Polystyrene tiles and matt-finished walls reduce condensation.
4. Skirting heaters warm the walls, making them less prone to condensation.
5. Use hygroscopic (water-absorbing) materials, such as wool and cotton, for carpets and furnishings.

METHODS OF VENTILATION

Good ventilation creates a balance between fresh air, warmth and humidity — a combination not easily achieved.

Natural methods
1. *Doors*

Open doors ventilate the room efficiently but cause draughts and cool the room too quickly.

2. *Windows*

Casement windows are similar to a door. The main window can be opened in summer; in winter it is usual to open only the small top window, to facilitate the removal of stale air.

Sash: the top can be lowered to allow hot air to escape; fresh air enters between the frames.

Louvre: three or four panes of glass on a hinged frame are operated by a lever. The louvred panes direct the incoming air in an upward direction to encourage convection.

Pivot: these allow stale air to leave through the top; fresh air enters through the lower opening in an upward direction. Pivot windows can be reversed for easy cleaning.

Note: if weather permits, windows in each room should be opened wide for a couple of hours every morning to air and ventilate the house.

3. *Fireplaces*

These ventilate the room by allowing the stale warm air to escape up the chimney. Wind blowing overhead can improve this method of ventilation by creating suction up the chimney. This method is most efficient when the fire is lit, as the fire warms the air in front of it, causing the air to expand and rise quickly up the chimney.

4. *Cooper's discs*

These are two circular glass or metal discs, one placed in front of the other, each with the same number of holes, fixed in a window or wall. If one disc is turned so that the holes lie over one another, fresh air can enter. To close, the disc is turned so that the holes do not correspond.

5. *Ventilator bricks*

These are bricks with cone-shaped holes, which are built into a house below floor level to ventilate the underfloor area and prevent wet and dry-rot. They are protected by a metal grating on the outside.

Most of these methods provide for the removal of stale air only. Fresh air usually finds a way in around doors and windows to fill the vacuum created. Inlet openings should be directed upwards so that the fresh air will be circulated around the room, creating convection currents. Outlets should be near the top of the room: as stale air is warm and lighter, it rises to the ceiling.

ARTIFICIAL OR MECHANICAL METHODS

Kitchens and bathrooms usually require more than a natural ventilating method to remove condensation and fumes. The warm humid conditions which exist in badly-ventilated kitchens encourage the multiplication of germs. A good mechanical ventilator will remove hot, grease-filled air and reduce the necessity for frequent redecoration. Kitchens need a complete air change ten to twenty times an hour.

1. *Extractor fans:* these are electrically-driven fans which suck air out of the room. They usually have two speeds, and some can be reversed to blow in cool air in summer. They operate by a switch or pull cord, which automatically opens the shutters of the fan and starts the motor. The rotating blades create suction which draws the stale air from the room. The fan, made of strong plastic and light in weight, can be fitted into a window or wall. Extractor fans are available in various sizes (15 cm, 25 cm, 30 cm diameter) which should relate to the size of the room in order to provide the required ten to twenty air changes per hour.

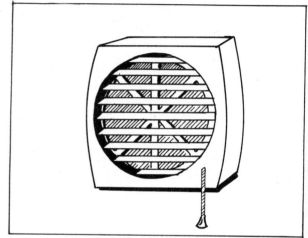

An extractor fan

Installation: the positioning of the fan is important if it is to work properly. A hole must be cut in the window or wall, fairly high up in the room. The fan should be between the cooker and the sink in order to catch steam from both. It should be placed as far as possible from the door into the house, in order to draw fumes away from this area and prevent odours escaping into the rest of the house. The fan needs a 13 amp socket, which should be earthed to avoid risk of shock due to condensation.

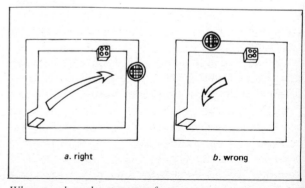

a. right   b. wrong

Where to place the extractor fan

2. *Cooker hoods:* these may be ducted or ductless. Both should be placed 60 to 90 cm above the hob or 40 to 60 cm above an eye-level grill.

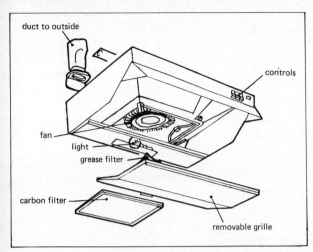

Cooker hood

A ducted hood is a fireproof canopy made from stainless steel, copper or aluminium. It contains a filter to remove grease and a fan which sucks the air through a duct to the outside of the house. This type is more efficient than the ductless hood.

A ductless hood consists of a metal filter and an activated charcoal filter, encased in an enamelled steel canopy. Stale air is drawn into the hood by a fan. Grease and odours are filtered from the air, which is then recirculated into the kitchen. The metal filter becomes very greasy and should be washed regularly in hot, soapy water. Failure to do this could cause a fire. The charcoal filter which absorbs odours is replaced in nine to eighteen months, depending on use. The ductless hood is simple to install if there is a 13 amp earthed socket nearby. Most hoods run at two speeds, and also have a light.

3. *Air conditioning* combines heating and ventilation. The air conditioning unit draws in fresh air, warms or cools it (depending on the time of year), and them humidifies it, adding or removing moisture as necessary. The average temperature provided is 20° to 22°C and the humidity 30 to 70%. The air is blown around the building through ducts by a powerful electric fan. Many warm air heating systems incorporate an air conditioning unit. Most large buildings, shops and offices use air conditioning to keep the atmosphere comfortable and healthy. The unit should be serviced annually and the filter cleaned six times a year.

SMOKING

Cigarette smoke is one of the main polluters of air in homes and places of entertainment. The nicotine and tar from cigarettes irritate the lungs, not just of the smoker, but also of people who regularly inhale air from a smoke-filled room. The smoke contributes to lung cancer, heart disease, bronchitis and other respiratory complaints. When pregnant women smoke, they cause stress to the foetus, which will be smaller and less resistant to infection when born than the baby of a non-smoker. Cigarettes also produce dirt and ash. They give the smoker and his house an unpleasant smell.

THE EFFECTS OF BAD VENTILATION

1. drowsiness and lack of concentration,
2. headache, weakness, even fainting,
3. clamminess, increased perspiration,
4. condensation,
5. increased risk of colds and infection due to high concentration of bacteria,
6. long-term effects for those constantly in badly-ventilated dwellings: chest infections, bronchitis, TB.

QUESTIONS/CHAPTER 8

1. What is the purpose of ventilation?
   Describe the basic principle on which most ventilating systems are based.
   Describe how to ventilate a bathroom (a) by natural means, (b) using mechanical ventilation.
2. List the effects of inadequate ventilation in a home.
   Describe one method of ventilating a living-room in summer, and another which is suitable for winter.
   Explain the term humidity in relation to ventilation.
3. Describe the structure of a cooker hood.
   Refer to
   (a) types; (d) efficiency;
   (b) position; (e) cleaning.
   (c) installation;
      What are the ill effects of condensation?
   List some methods of reducing condensation in the home.
4. Discuss (a) the causes and (b) the ill effects of air pollution in cities.
   List some methods by which air pollution may be reduced.
   Write a note on the hazards of cigarette smoking.

9.
Lighting and electricity

Good lighting makes a home more attractive and pleasant to live in. Proper lighting
1. helps us see what we are doing,
2. prevents eye-strain,
3. helps prevent accidents,
4. cleverly used, it can create interesting decorative effects, providing atmosphere in a room.

When light rays fall on a surface, they can be
1. *reflected:* the rays of light bounce off a shiny surface;
2. *refracted:* bent, as they pass through thick or ridged glass;
3. *diffused:* scattered on an opaque, non-reflecting surface, preventing too much glare;
4. *absorbed:* no light is reflected, as by a dark or matt-finished surface;
5. *dispersed:* each ray broken down into its component colours by a crystal or prism. The spectrum is the name of the colours which form light: red, orange, yellow, green, blue, indigo, violet.

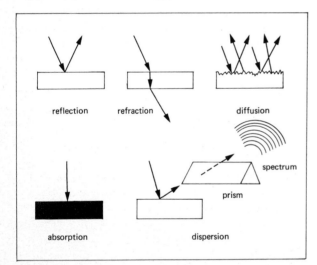

Properties of light

NATURAL LIGHTING

This is to allow the rays of the sun to illuminate the rooms of a house. It is the most suitable light for working and recreation, it does not cause eye-strain and it costs nothing.

Natural light is introduced by use of
1. windows — see chapter 8
2. glass doors — French or patio doors;

3. glass bricks used in building;
4. Perspex and other plastics — these are sometimes used in roofs; they may be a fire hazard as they melt and ignite at high temperatures;
5. mirrors — used to reflect light into or around a room;
6. white paint — used on window frames, recesses, sills — helps to reflect the daylight into the room.

Natural light is suitable only for daylight hours. At night or in rooms which receive insufficient natural light, the alternative is some form of artificial lighting.

ARTIFICIAL LIGHTING

Lighting should be considered early in the planning of rooms, as the wiring needs to be installed before much decoration is done and before carpets are fitted. Although rooms can be lit by gas, oil or candles, these are generally used only in emergencies or in isolated areas. The most common, versatile and safe form of light is the electric light.

ELECTRIC LIGHTING

There are two basic types of electric lamp: filament lamps and fluorescent lamps.

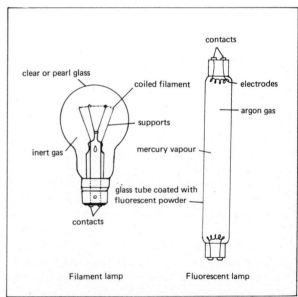

Two kinds of electric lighting

The *filament* lamp consists of a glass bulb, filled with an inert gas such as argon. Passing into the centre of the bulb is a thin filament of coiled tungsten wire. When the light is switched on, the tungsten wire glows white with heat (tungsten can withstand very high temperatures). Filament lamps should last about one thousand hours. The strength of a lamp is measured in watts: 25 W, 40 W, 60 W, 75 W, 150 W, 200 W. Bulbs can be made from

1. clear glass, which gives a strong, harsh light and must be used with a shade;

2. pearl or silica-coated glass, which gives a softer, more diffused light;

3. coloured glass, for various effects;

4. silvered glass, used in spotlights. Part of the bulb is silvered, directing the light inwards or outwards.

Fluorescent lamps consist of a narrow glass tube, coated on the inside with a fluorescent chemical. There is a small coil or electrode at each end of the tube, which also contains argon gas and a small amount of mercury. When the current is switched on, the electrodes cause the mercury to vaporise, producing ultra-violet light which makes the fluorescent lining of the tube glow with light. The starting device (which often gives off a slight hum) and the controls are housed in the fitting, not the lamp. The tubes are available in lengths from 30 cm to 2.5 m; the wattage increases with the length. You will know when a tube needs replacing, because it will take longer to light up, give less light, and blacken slightly at each end.

Advantages of fluorescent lamps
1. They give three to four times as much light as a filament lamp of the same wattage.
2. They last about three times as long, but should not be turned on and off frequently as this shortens their life and wastes electricity.
3. They give a bright, shadowless light very like daylight. Many people find this harsh and cold, so warmer shades have been developed.
4. They are cool in operation, and thus suitable for pelmet lights.

Disadvantages
1. They are much more expensive than filament lamps.
2. They may cause glare, but can be fitted with shades to reduce it.
3. Some people find the hum disturbing over time.

RULES FOR GOOD LIGHTING

1. There should be enough light to enable people to work or read without eye-strain.
2. The light should not cause glare. This is caused when bright light or too much reflection from shiny surfaces dazzles the eyes.
3. Close work — reading, writing, sewing — needs direct light shining down onto the work from 75 to 85 cm above.
4. Lamps used in open fittings should be pearlised to reduce glare.
5. All other shades should cover the bulb sufficiently so that it is not visible in use.
6. Hazardous places — stairs, steps, porches, should be very well lit.
7. Colour affects light: dark colours absorb light, so more light fittings are required in a dark room. Fewer fittings (or a lower wattage) are required in a bright room.
8. The shape and size of the room affect requirements: a long room may require a minimum of two fittings, while in a square room of the same area one may suffice.
9. Lights can be fitted to ceilings or walls. Movable or portable fittings, standard and table lamps, add versatility to lighting arrangements.

LIGHTING SAFETY AND ECONOMY

1. Appliances other than lamps should never be connected to lamp fittings, as they may overheat.
2. Switches should be placed at a convenient height, just inside the door, so that the light may be turned on upon entering the room.
3. Avoid turning lights on and off: this wears out the bulb, especially in the case of fluorescent lamps.
4. Bulbs of the correct size and wattage should always be used.
5. Avoid placing bulbs too near the shade; this could cause over-heating and fire.
6. Allow sufficient sockets in each room for portable lights — adaptors can be hazardous.

LIGHT FITTINGS

The fitting and shade used with a lamp can do much to improve (or detract from) the lighting of a room. The shade controls the spread of light from the lamp.

Shades should be heat resistant. The hot air produced by the light should have room to escape. Clean lamps, shades and fittings regularly for maximum efficiency.

Shades can
1. reflect light — downwards or upwards;
2. diffuse light — fluorescent tubes, opaque glass and paper shades all do this;
3. light directly — spotlights throw light in one direction in a narrow beam;
4. light indirectly — reflecting 90 per cent of light onto a white ceiling, which in turn reflects light all over the room.

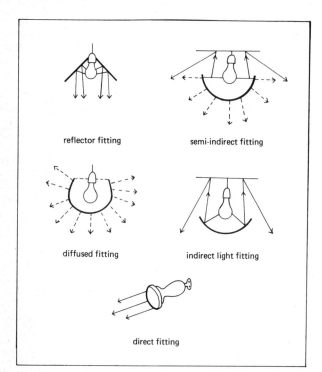

How light fittings affect light

MODERN FITTINGS

1. Dimmer switch: this is a special switch containing an electronic device, which controls the amount of light put out by a ceiling or wall fitting or a portable lamp. It can lower the light level, for example in a child's bedroom at night, and may provide a relaxing background light in a livingroom. Dimmer switches are easy to install in place of usual on/off switches, but cannot be used for fluorescent fixtures.

2. Track lighting: this is a metal and plastic channel carrying continuous live, neutral and earth conductor strips. Spotlights are mounted onto special adaptors

which plug into the track. Light tracks can be ceiling or wall mounted. Track lighting lends itself to unusual and striking arrangements. The lighting scheme can be changed by moving the lights along the track.

3. Spotlights: these give directional light — a powerful beam lights up a small area, e.g. a desk or an ornament.

4. Flexible lamps: these have pivoted joints or a pliable stem which enable the lamp to turn in almost any direction. Others can be moved up and down on a vertical stem. They are ideal for desk work. The lamp fitting is usually a spotlight which directs light onto the required area.

5. Recessed ceiling lighting: this consists of a spotlight set into a recess in the ceiling. It usually requires a false ceiling to provide a recess of sufficient depth to house the fitting and to hide the wiring. It is sometimes possible to install recessed lights in normal ceilings if the space between the ceiling and the floor above is sufficiently deep.

6. Display lighting: light fittings (often short fluorescent tubes) are hidden behind shelving, throwing light upwards or down to illuminate glass, ornaments and other bric-a-brac.

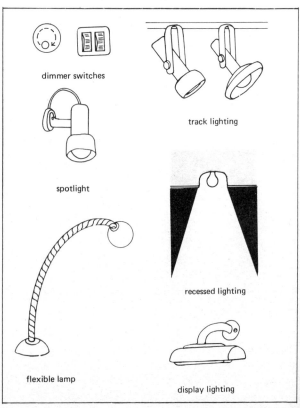

Modern light fixtures

LIGHTING THE HOME

As well as providing visual comfort and safety in the home, good lighting can be used to add atmosphere and warmth to a basic decor. Rooms must be planned to make the best use of both daylight and artificial light. One ceiling fitting and one socket are no longer acceptable. An adequate number of sockets will ensure that a variety of light fittings — table, standard and spotlights — can be plugged in without danger from trailing flexes.

PLANNING THE LIGHTING SYSTEM

Consider

1. the *purpose* of the room: many rooms in modern homes are multi-purpose. A central ceiling fitting is rarely sufficient. Two to four lights are often required, e.g.
(a) background or central lighting,
(b) light for desk or study,
(c) reading light,
(d) dining light;

2 the *function of each area:* the light fitting should be of sufficiently high wattage to give the correct light for each particular activity. Functional lighting, i.e. for reading or handwork, must be positioned to allow the light to fall where it is needed. The lamp should be high enough to do this, i.e. slightly behind the reader at shoulder level. Older people may need stronger lights as eyes weaken with age;

3. *safety:* any electrical work should be done by a competent electrician. Many lamps are plugged into three-pin sockets. These should be fitted with a low amp fuse (3 or 5 amp), not the 13 amp fuse which comes with the plug, as the socket circuit is too high for lighting and any fault may overheat the lamp. Follow rules for safety already mentioned. Buy good quality, reliable lamps and fittings with a steady base;

4. *appearance and decor:* the base and shade should be in proportion to one another and tone in with the colour scheme of the room. They should also harmonise with the style (period or modern) of the room. Correct placement of lamps is necessary for maximum effect. Clever use of light and shade gives an interesting dimension to the room, e.g. light shining at an angle can emphasise the texture of wallpaper and paintings; clever lighting can highlight good architectural features or help camouflage less attractive features;

5. *cleaning:* light fittings should be easy to clean, ideally with a removable shade which can be washed. Dusty shades reduce the efficiency of the light.

LIGHTING ROOM BY ROOM

Once the light you have chosen is safe and adequate, lighting a room is very much a matter of individual taste. Here are some brief suggestions; for more detail, see relevant chapters.

LIVINGROOM

Central diffused (100 W) fitting, switch at door. Two table lamps for reading or close work.

Living-room with well-placed lighting

DINING-ROOM OR EATING AREA

'Rise and fall' fitting (100 W) over dining-table.
Background wall lights (60 W) and/or
Spotlight or wall light over serving area.

HALL, STAIRS, LANDING

Hall: attractive ceiling fitting (75 W).
Stairs: one fitting shining on stairs (100 W) with two-way switch.

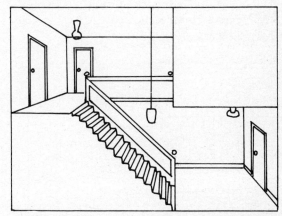

Hall and stair lights should switch on and off both upstairs and down

Landing: if necessary another fitting on ceiling (the stair light might suffice). All lights in these areas should match or tone with one another.

BEDROOMS

Central diffused light (75/100 W).
Bedside light for each occupant (75 W).

A bedroom needs good lights for reading and applying make-up

Strip light at dressing-table.
Childrens' room: emphasis on safe secure fittings, a dimmer switch is a good idea.

BATHROOM

Central diffused light (100 W).
Fluorescent filament light over mirror, with pull cord.
All other switches outside bathroom.

KITCHEN

One or two 1 m fluorescent fittings on ceiling, depending on size and shape of room.
Strip lighting (under wall cupboards) or spotlights to highlight work areas.

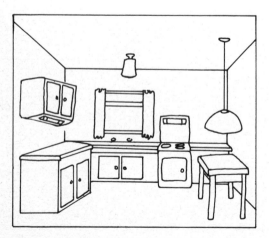

Good lighting in the kitchen is essential

MORE ABOUT ELECTRICITY

When electricity enters the house, it passes through the meter, which records the consumption of electricity, and then into the main fuse box. Consumption of electricity is measured in units.

READING THE METER

Most modern installations have a digital meter, which works like the milometer in a car. It records consumption automatically. A meter reader calls to each dwelling periodically to read the meter. The figures indicating consumption are subtracted from the previous reading: the result is the number of units used in that time.

Present reading	104,306
Previous reading	102,782
Consumption	1,524 units
Current cost per unit	000
Total cost of electricity used	000

If the meter reader cannot gain access to read the meter, an estimate of consumption is worked out based on previous consumption. Due to this difficulty, meters in most new houses are installed in sealed cupboards accessible from outside, so that the meter can be read without inconveniencing the consumer.

PAYING FOR ELECTRICITY

Electricity bills are issued every two months. They show the present and previous reading, the cost of the unit, including a variable charge according to the current cost of fuel, and the cost of units used at the cheap, off-peak rate. A small standing charge is also made, which varies according to the number of rooms in the house. Bills must be paid promptly or electricity may be cut off.

THE FUSE BOX

This is the central distribution point for household electricity. There is generally one fuse for each circuit, rated according to the load it has to carry. For example there may be a fuse for
1. upstairs lighting
2. upstairs power points
3. cooker
4. downstairs lighting
5. downstairs power points
6. immersion heater.

Lighting circuits will use low amp fuses (5 amp) whereas the cooker and immersion heater will need more powerful fuses: 16 amp (immersion heater) and 35 to 63 amp (small to large cooker). The fuse box also carries a main fuse or a main switch which should be removed or switched off when any repairs are being carried out.

FUSES

A fuse is a deliberate weak link in an electric circuit. It is a bakelite or porcelain container through which a wire, thinner than the rest of the circuit, passes. If too much current flows into a circuit, the wires in an appliance could become dangerously hot. This could happen if (a) there were a short circuit, i.e. if positive and negative wires touch, for example due to loosening of wires in a plug or a frayed flex; (b) when an appliance overheats, e.g. if the thermostat was faulty; (c) if the circuit is overloaded due to too many appliances being used. When this happens, the fuse wire becomes very hot and melts, cutting off elelctric current to the faulty area. Before replacing the blown fuse, check flexes, plugs and appliances. Switch off overloading appliances.

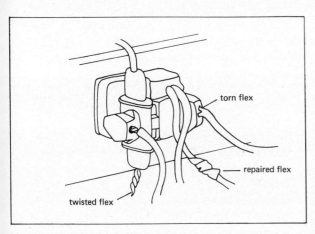

Overloaded electric socket and dangerously worn flex

To replace a fuse: cartridge fuses are used in most fuse boxes. These should not be rewired, and never use foil as a temporary connection. Always keep at least one spare fuse of each amperage used in the fuse box for emergencies. First gently unscrew the main fuse. The coloured disc at the end of the spent fuse is usually loose, indicating which fuse must be replaced. Unscrew this fuse and discard; replace with new fuse, making sure that it is of the correct amperage. Replace cover.

Switch on mains or replace main fuse. These are the fuses available:
Small (DZ 2):
  5 amp, 10 amp, 16 amp, 20 amp, 25 amp.
Large (DZ 3):
  35 amp, 63 amp.

WIRING

Electric wiring is usually made of copper, an excellent conductor. Most cables and flexes contain three wires which are insulated with different coloured plastics.

1. A **live** wire carrying electric current from the power station generator, coloured brown;

2. A **neutral** wire carrying the current back to the generator, coloured blue;

3. An **earth** or safety wire, which leads leaking or faulty current to earth, coloured green/yellow.

In old installations: live = red; neutral = black; earth = green.

Some non-metal appliances, e.g. hair driers, electric razors, are very well insulated and they do not require the safety earth wire. Flexes used for lighting (two core flexes) do not have an earth wire.

EARTH

This is a safety device which connects all earthed appliances through their wiring system to the ground. It ensures that if a fault occurs, e.g. a short circuit, which makes the appliance 'live' i.e. capable of shock or fire, the current is conveyed safely to earth.

A well-lit living-room (John Topham Picture Library)

SOCKETS, PLUGS AND SWITCHES

All modern electrical installations use three-pin flat fused plugs (13 amp). The *sockets* contain three rectangular holes which are usually shuttered so that children cannot poke objects into them. A socket with a switch is safer than one without. Double sockets cost little more than single ones, and this also reduces the necessity for adaptors. *Switches* break or connect the electric circuit. Bathroom switches should be out of reach of the person using the bath/shower; therefore they are usually outside the door. A pull-cord switch is safer to use in kitchens and bathrooms; there is less danger of shock if hands are wet when it is switched on.

Wiring a plug

1. Unscrew the large central screw. Remove cover.
2. Loosen cord grip and remove cartridge fuse.
3. Loosen the screws of the three terminals.
4. Strip back sufficient outer flex covering so that it finishes just inside the cord grip.
5. Measure the length of each wire to its appropriate terminal, allowing at least 15 mm for insertion.
6. Trim frayed or thin wires and pare insulation from wires to about 20-25 mm (use a penknife or pliers). Be careful not to cut any of the tiny wires.

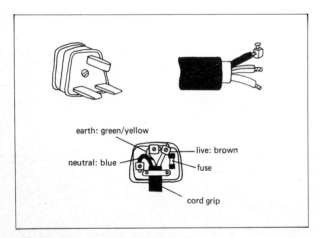

earth: green/yellow
neutral: blue
live: brown
fuse
cord grip

Wiring a plug

7. Fix wires firmly in position, inserting into holes if necessary, and screw down firmly. No loose wires should protrude. Tighten cord grip.
   Positions:
   Live (brown) wire to the L (fused) pin — right-hand side. Neutral (blue) wire to the N pin — left-hand side. Earth (green/yellow) wire to the E pin — top of plug.

8. Replace cartridge fuse — check first that it is the correct amperage. Three amp fuses are sufficient for lights and small appliances (less than 720 watts) and 13 amps for all other items. If a high amp fuse is used on a low watt appliance, there is a danger that the appliance could overheat and catch fire.
9. Replace cover and test.

HOW MUCH ENERGY DO THEY USE?

One unit of electricity gives the following use:

Electric blanket: 12 hours
Boiling ring: 1-2 hours
Clothes dryer: $\frac{1}{2}$ hour
Cooker: averages 1 unit per person per day
Dishwasher: 1 hour per unit (Full load 2-2$\frac{1}{2}$ units)
Extractor fan: 20-40 hours
Fan heater (2 kW): $\frac{1}{2}$ hour
Fire: 1 hour heating by a 1 kW fire
Freezer: chest 1-1$\frac{1}{2}$ units per 28 litres per week
    upright 1$\frac{1}{2}$-2 units per 28 litres pe r week
Hair dryer: 1$\frac{1}{2}$ hours
Heater (radiator or convector): $\frac{1}{2}$ hour's heating; more if thermostat used
Immersion heater: 19 litres hot water (average family uses 50 units per week)
Iron: 2$\frac{1}{2}$ hours (one week's average ironing)
Kettle: 10 litres boiling water
Lighting: 100 watt lamp for 10 hours, or 60 watt lamp for 16 hours, or 1.5 m 80 watt fluorescent tube for 10 hours
Refrigerator: 1 day
Storage heater: 120 to 150 units per week, during winter
Toaster: 2 hours
Razor: 5 years (one shave a day)
Radio: 100 hours
Television: black and white — 8-10 hours, colour — 5-7 hours
Washing machine (twin tub): 3 units per wash
Washing machine (automatic): 2-2$\frac{1}{2}$ units per wash
Vacuum cleaner: 2-3 hours
Sewing machine: makes 11 children's dresses
Spin-dryer: 60 loads of washing spun
Tumble dryer: $\frac{1}{2}$ hour
Record player/tape recorder: 30 hours

Electric toaster for economically made breakfast (Russell Hobbs)

SAFETY

1. Never touch an electric appliance with wet hands.
2. Never overload electric sockets.
3. Never have electric sockets or switches in a bathroom.
4. Use a pull cord for bathroom heaters. Light switches should be outside.
5. Never bring portable electric appliances — especially heaters — into a bathroom.
6. Keep electric equipment in good condition: replace frayed flexes, and wires, cracked sockets and plugs.
7. Avoid long trailing flexes.
8. Never run flexes or wiring under rugs or carpets. They will wear more quickly and may cause a fire.
9. Switch off appliances before cleaning or repairing. Switch off kettles and irons before filling.
10 Switch off equipment when not in use, particularly televisions at night.
11. Use a qualified electrician for all wiring and installation.
12. Only attempt minor repairs — wiring a plug, changing a fuse — if you understand how to do them.
13. Use earthed equipment only.
14. Use three-pin flat plugs and shuttered sockets.
15. Use the correct fuse for the appliance.
16 Never dry clothes over electric heaters.
17. Switch off electric under-blankets before going to bed. Have electric blankets serviced regularly.
18 Never join a flex.
19. Wiring has a limited life. Most houses need to be rewired after twenty-five to thirty years.

QUESTIONS/CHAPTER 9

1. List the features of a good lighting system. Describe a method of lighting a family room using both direct and diffused light sources. Explain the following terms, relating to light rays:
   (a) refraction:
   (b) reflection:
   (c) dispersion.

2. Write a note on the importance of safety when planning the lighting of a home.
   Using diagrams, describe briefly the construction of (a) a filament lamp and (b) a fluorescent lamp.
   List some safety rules to be remembered when buying light fittings.

3. Explain how lighting can be used with effect to improve the appearance of a room.
   Describe in detail three modern light fittings or systems suitable for a family home. State the cost of each item mentioned.

4. Explain the following terms relating to electricity:
   (a) fuse;
   (b) earth;
   (c) unit.
   Describe (i) how to replace a fuse, or (ii) how to wire a three-pin plug.
   What is the current cost of electricity (a) at the normal rate and (b) at the off-peak rate?

5. Write an essay on the importance of safety in the home.

10.
Floor coverings and their care

Floor coverings are an expensive part of home decorating and one where it is not always possible to economise. The constant wear and tear of people walking over them means that you must buy good-quality, durable floor coverings if they are to last. Cheap floor coverings are false economy as they wear badly. Always buy the best you can possibly afford.

Floor coverings should be

tough	comfortable
durable	stain resistant
quiet	heat resistant
hygienic	water resistant
easy to lay	non-slip when wet or dry
warm	easy to clean and maintain
attractive	resilient, i.e. flexible and resistant to indentation.

The type of room will influence the choice of floor covering. For example,

1. In a *kitchen*, emphasis is placed on hygiene, ease of cleaning and resistance to stains such as grease, acids, alkalis, water and heat.
2. In a *hall, stairs and landing*, the emphasis is on durability and practicality.
3. In a *bedroom*, the main emphasis is on appearance, as there is not so much wear and tear.
4. In a *bathroom*, hygiene, water resistance and non-slip finishes are most important.

Other factors which influence choice are amount of traffic, decor and style of room, structure of floor and money available.

PREPARATION

Before laying any floor covering, make sure that the floor underneath is dry, smooth and in good condition. If floorboards are sound and reasonably smooth, it is possible to sand the boards with a sanding machine (which can be hired) and then seal them with polyurethane seal.

A. WOODEN FLOOR COVERINGS

1. *Strip flooring* is uniform lengths of planed soft or hardwood, fixed side by side with no spaces between the boards. They are sanded and sealed.
2. Wood block floors (parquet) are made of

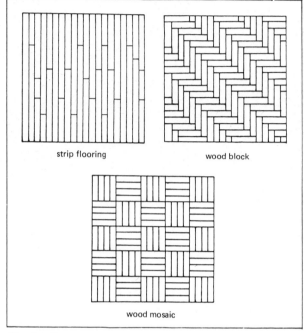

strip flooring   wood block

wood mosaic

Wooden floors

rectangular blocks of hardwood, laid in herringbone or basket-weave pattern over a wooden or concrete sub-floor.
3. Wood mosaic consists of thin strips of hardwood, arranged in decorative panels and attached to a plywood base 45 cm square. These panels are glued or pinned to the sub-floor, stained if desired and sealed with polyurethane or shellac. This produced a high gloss, easily-maintained finish.

Advantages of wooden floors
1. attractive,
2. hard wearing,
3. reasonably warm and resilient.

Disadvantages
1. wood block and wood mosaic are expensive,
2. noisy,
3. need careful maintenance.

Care
1. Avoid soaking with water. Mop up spills at once.
2. Sweep daily to remove harmful grit.
3. Clean regularly, polishing unsealed floors with wax

polish. Avoid over-polishing, which makes the surface sticky and slippery.

Wooden floors are most suitable in hallways, living and dining-rooms.

B. CARPETS

With the wide range of carpets available, it is essential to have some knowledge of the construction of carpets, in order to choose one that is suitable for its purpose.

Construction

Most carpets are woven, tufted or bonded

1. **Woven carpets:** these are made by weaving a thread in and out through a jute or canvas backing. The pile should be tightly packed and firmly caught into the backing, if the carpet is to give good wear.

Wilton carpets are particularly hard wearing. The threads are woven into the backing, providing a thicker carpet. This limits the number of colours used: most Wiltons are plain or the designs are limited to not more than five colours. Wiltons are closely woven, and the pile is cut to give a tufted pile. Wiltons with an uncut or looped pile are known as Brussels carpets.

Axminster carpets are made by a method of weaving which involves catching tufts of yarn into the backing as it is woven. Any number of colours can be used, so there is a greater variety of colour and design. Most patterned carpets are manufactured in this way. The pile is always cut.

Note: Axminster and Wilton are names given to the method of construction. They are not brand names or indications of quality. It is possible to buy a top quality or inferior Axminster or Wilton carpet. Good quality Wiltons and Axminsters are hard-wearing and durable.

Cord carpets are woven by the Wilton method but the pile is not cut. It is tightly woven in and out of the backing, producing no definite pile.

2. **Tufted carpets** are made by inserting tufts of yarn into a ready-woven backing. Tufts are held in place by adhesive and then secured by a backing of latex or foam rubber. These carpets are cheaper, as they are quicker to make, and they are reasonably hard wearing. Colour is introduced by using different coloured yarns or by printing. Length of pile varies — many long pile carpets are tufted. Pile may be cut or uncut.

3. **Bonded or non-woven carpets:** fibres are glued or fixed in position on the PVC backing by fine needles which compress the fibres into a flat surface. These carpets have very little pile. Many carpet tiles are made by this method.

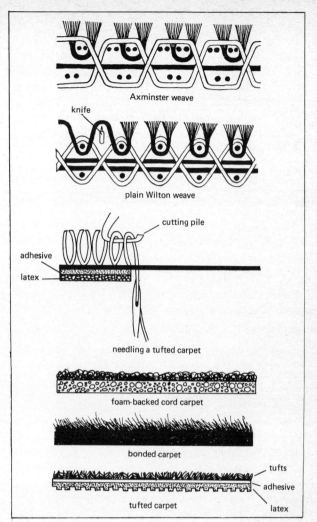

Carpet construction

Carpet fibres

natural		synthetic	
wool	sisal	acrylic	polypropylene
cotton	jute	nylon	rayon
silk	hair	polyester	

Wool is used for Wiltons, Axminsters, tufted and hand-made carpets. A good blend of wools makes the best possible carpet. Wool is warm, resilient, durable, has a natural resistance to liquids, dyes well, is springy and does not flatten easily. It is also expensive. As wool carpets are susceptible to attack, it is wise to buy mothproofed carpets.

Cotton is suitable for bathroom carpets. It is easy to clean and cheap, but it crushes easily.

Hair, sisal and jute are hardwearing but rough and slippery. They are difficult to vacuum, as dirt passes through the carpets onto the floor, and they also stain easily. These fibres are fairly cheap.

Acrylics (Acrilan, Courtelle, Orlon, Teklan) are used for Wilton and Axminster carpets. They are hard wearing, do not flatten easily, but tend to show the dirt. However acrylics are easy to clean and flame resistant. They have a natural silicone-like aversion to liquid and resist liquid stains. Acrylic carpets are in the medium price range.

Nylon (Bri-nylon, Celon, Enkalon) wears well, but tends to soil easily. It is easy to clean and fairly cheap. Cigarette burns can leave permanent marks on most synthetics.

Polypropylene is often used in kitchen and bathroom carpets as it is resistant to water. It is also used for carpet backings. It is fairly cheap.

Rayon is used for cheap carpets. It does not wear well, flattens easily and soils quickly.

Blends are a combination of two or more fibres. These can combine the best qualities of the two fibres. For example an 80% wool, 20% nylon blend will combine the wearing qualities of nylon with the warmth, springiness and resilience of wool.

Pile
This can be long (shaggy pile), short (velvet pile), cut or looped. It can be twisted to resist footmarks. Cord carpets have a hard-wearing, ribbed finish. Bonded carpets have little or no pile. Sculptured, carved or embossed pile involves a combination of cut and uncut pile, or pile of different height — creating a patterned effect.

Carpet terms
Backing — the fabric which holds the pile in position.
Body carpet — carpet sold in narrow widths, usually 69 cm or 91 cm. Fitted carpets are made from lengths of body carpet stitched together.
Broadloom — wide carpet which is woven on a broad loom, usually 183 cm to 549 cm in width.
Fitted carpets — carpets which cover the floor from wall to wall.
Indian carpets — heavy, colourful carpets with a hand knotted, looped pile.
Carpet tiles — squares of carpet, usually non-woven.
Static — many synthetic fibres build up static electricity which attracts dirt.
Chinese carpets — luxury, sculptured, velvet pile carpets in pastel shades, often using silk yarn.
Mothproofing — essential in wool carpets, this is a finish which resists moth damage.

Choosing a carpet
Consider
1. the amount of money available;
2. the amount of traffic in the room;
3. the proposed (or present) colour scheme (a carpet is an important factor in planning a colour scheme as it will last long after the room has been redecorated);
4. design — whether patterned or plain carpet is required (plain colours and pastels show up dirt and need to be cleaned often; patterned carpets don't show up dirt and stains as easily, but a strong pattern can dominate a room);
5. whether a carpet square, fitted carpet or carpet tiles are required.

Visit a carpet showroom to study carpets and get advice without pressure to buy.

Check
1. The density and height of the pile: a dense or tightly packed pile means that the wear is on the ends, rather than the sides, of the fibres. A close pile will therefore wear better. To check pile:
   (a) bend the carpet back: the easier it is to see the backing from the front, the less dense the pile;
   (b) look at the backing: is it firm and closely woven?
   (c) tug at a tuft: it should not come out easily.
2. The carpet label: this will indicate the quality and usually the fibre. The 'Woolmark' will be present on wool carpets. Carpets are usually classified as
   (a) light domestic use (bedroom);
   (b) medium domestic (dining-room);
   (c) general domestic (living-room);
   (d) heavy domestic (living-room, hall, stairs);
   (e) luxury domestic/heavy contract (living-room, hall, stairs).
3. Ask the advice of the salesman.
4. Allow plenty of time and shop around for good value.
5. Get a written estimate to include carpet, felt, fitting and laying.

Underlays
Almost all carpets benefit from the use of a good underlay, although an underlay is not essential under foam-backed carpets.

Advantages
1. It makes the carpet feel thicker and more comfortable.
2. It provides insulation.
3. It reduces noise.

4. It improves and makes even the wear of the carpet by reducing friction.

Types of underlay
1. Felt — available in different thicknesses, cheap, but tends to flatten in use.
2. Foam (polyurethane, latex or rubber) — thicker and softer than felt, cannot be used with underfloor heating, expensive.
3. Layered (a layer of rubber and felt) — harder wearing than foam, softer than felt; expensive.

FITTING A CARPET

This can be a do-it-yourself job but special tools are required to stretch the carpet. The carpet is attached by
1. tacking: the edges are turned in and tacked at intervals:
2. carpet grippers: metal or wooden strips set with pins are nailed around the perimeter of the floor; the carpet is stretched over these and anchored in position;

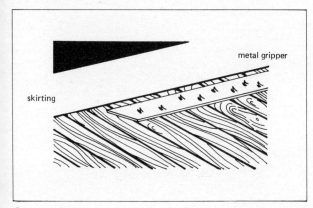

Carpet grippers

3. sticking with adhesive: carpet tiles may be fixed in this way.
   Note: floor must be clean and even with no projecting nails or loose boards.

   Fitted carpets look luxurious and attractive and help insulate and soundproof a room. They leave no wooden border to clean and dust. They are expensive.
   Carpet squares are cheaper, can be turned around to give even wear, and fit many rooms; they can be transferred to another room or house.
   Carpet tiles are tough and durable and ensure little waste. They can be loose laid and moved around to give even wear. They can be easily lifted when moving house, or for use in another room.

CARE OF CARPETS
1. Carpets should be cleaned regularly to remove dirt and grit as these damage the carpet fibres. Vacuum cleaning is the most convenient method of cleaning.
2. Avoid dragging heavy furniture over carpets. Use castors where possible.
3. Wipe up spills at once.
4. Shampoo occasionally, according to composition.
5. Hand sweep new carpets to avoid removing too much fluff.
6. Protect from fading on sunny days by drawing curtains or blinds.
7. Turn non-fitted carpets and move stair carpets regularly to prevent uneven wear.

To shampoo a carpet
Choose a warm, sunny day. Remove as much furniture as possible. Vacuum carpet very thoroughly. Follow instructions for using detergent exactly, testing first if necessary. Apply evenly and gently, using a sponge or carpet shampooer. Do not overwet the carpet. Rinse in the same way. Sponge as dry as possible and leave to dry with windows open. Do not walk on the damp carpet. When absolutely dry, vacuum thoroughly.

C. PLASTIC FLOORING

Many new materials have been developed to provide easily cleaned, hard-wearing surfaces for kitchens and bathrooms. Some are attractive enough to be used in other rooms also. Most of these plastic type floor coverings consist of
1. binder: PVC (polyvinylchloride),
2. filler: asbestos, which helps to fill it out, thus reducing costs,
3. pigments.

Types of vinyl
   1. *Vinyl asbestos* or PVA consists of asbestos and other fillers mixed with vinyl (vinyl content is 25 per cent). Sold in tile form, it wears well and is stain resistant. It is easy to lay and maintain and comes in many colours. It is resistant to damp and therefore useful for laying in old houses which do not have a damp course.
   Its disadvantages are that PVA is less flexible than other vinyls and is not suitable for use with underfloor heating.
   2. *Plain vinyl or PVC* consists of 35-70 per cent vinyl. This is available in sheet or tile form. The design, which

may be plain or elaborate, can be printed on the surface or form part of the material. Printed designs may eventually wear away.

3. *Cushioned vinyl* is backed with a layer of foam. This makes it more comfortable, quiet and warm than plain vinyl. It is only available in sheet form, but is easy to lay, as it does not have to be stuck down onto the floor. It resists most kitchen stains and is easy to clean. It is unsuitable for houses using underfloor heating.
Cork-backed vinyl: as for cushioned vinyl.

4. *Thermoplastic* floor coverings contain a large percentage of asbestos and only a small amount of vinyl, so they are less flexible than the other vinyl coverings. They are cheap and easy to lay.

Advantages of plastic floor coverings
1. hardwearing and easy to clean;
2. flexible and resilient;
3. resist indentation, e.g. heel or furniture marks;
4. resistant to acids, alkalis, water and grease;
5. soft, comfortable, reasonably warm and quiet;
6. not very slippery;
7. available in sheet (3 m wide) or tile form (30 cm square);
8. available in a wide range of colours and designs, many with a veined, tiled, embossed or marbled effect;
9. easy to lay, tiles may be self-adhesive or need a special adhesive;
10. cheap and hygienic.

Care of vinyl
1. Some vinyls have a transparent film on the surface, which only requires a rub of a damp mop to keep it clean.
2. Others should be washed regularly with warm water containing a little detergent, e.g. Flash.
3. Many manufacturers supply their own cleaner and polish.
4. Avoid using abrasives, which may damage the surface.
5. Avoid wax polishes: these soften the surface and make it prone to scratching. Water-based emulsion polishes are more suitable.
6. If self-shine polishes (like Seel) are used continuously, they cause a build-up which must be removed every six months or so. Solvents to remove this build-up are available in most hardware shops.

D. CORK

Cork is obtained from the bark of the cork oak tree. The cork is broken into chips and heat treated under pressure. The natural resins present in cork enable it to be formed into sheets and tiles without the use of any adhesive.

Cork is available in various shades of brown and beige. A variety of designs and textures is available, according to the size of the chips in the mixture. Cork comes in small sheets and tiles of various sizes and thicknesses. The thicker (3-5 mm) tiles are used for flooring, place mats and bathmats. The thinner tiles are used as a wall covering. Some modern cork tiles have a transparent vinyl layer on the surface.

1. Cork must be laid on an absolutely flat surface, such as hardboard.
2. It should be sealed with at least two coats of polyurethane varnish.
3. Most adhesives can be used to stick cork to walls or floor.
4. Do not use cork over underfloor heating, which would melt the adhesive.
5. Cork is suitable for all rooms, especially bathrooms.

Advantages
1. attractive and natural looking;
2. water resistant, although it does watermark;
3. resists most stains except oils;
4. warm, quiet and resilient underfoot;
5. light, but reasonably hard wearing: use of a good seal increases its wearability;
6. acts as an insulator of heat and sound;
7. flame resistant;
8. easy to lay.

Care of cork
1. Sweep often to remove damaging grit.
2. Use wax polish on unsealed tiles. An emulsion polish can be used now and then on sealed tiles.
3. Sharp heels and heavy furniture can damage cork. Use castors on furniture.
4. Wipe over sealed floors with a damp cloth.

E. STONE, QUARRY TILES AND CERAMIC TILES

These are all very hard-wearing floor coverings. They are not resilient so are unsuitable for such areas as kitchens, where one is standing for long periods. They are used in porches, patios and sun rooms. As they are particularly heavy, it is essential to check that the sub-floor is strong enough to bear the weight of stone or tiled floors.

Stone or slate floors

These are available in square or rectangular blocks or tiles. They are found in many old houses; they are cold, hard and often damp. They can withstand hard wear and are easy to clean. They are very expensive to install.

Quarry tiles or clay tiles

Fired tiles, 15 cm square, made from clay and other materials, usually unglazed, are cold, hard, noisy and tiring underfoot. However they are easy to keep, with excellent resistance to stains. They are usually available in brick colours and blue-grey. These tiles are often used in kitchens to give a country-style look. In this case, an area of vinyl sheeting or rubber matting should be laid around the main work areas, to reduce the likelihood of tired feet.

Ceramic tiles

These are made from fired clay. They are available in many designs, some with a textured finish and most are finished in a high gloss vitreous glaze. The tiles are smooth and easy to clean, but also hard, cold, noisy and very tiring underfoot. Breakages are likely, if crockery is dropped on them.

Tiles used for floors come in different shapes, sizes and thicknesses. Thinner tiles are available for use as wall coverings. Floor tiles are difficult for the amateur to lay, as they must be fixed in cement mortar.

CLEANING FLOORS

Correct maintenance can add years to the life of a floor covering. The use of modern polishes and equipment can reduce much of the work involved in caring for the floors of a modern house.

ELECTRIC VACUUM CLEANERS

How they work: an electric motor drives a high speed fan, which draws out dust, dirt and grit from the floor covering by suction. The dirt is sucked in through the hose or base of the cleaner and is collected in a dust bag. Upright cleaners have revolving brushes or beaters which assist in cleaning the floor by loosening and sweeping up the dust.

Always buy a reliable model which conforms to accepted safety standards. Make sure it is guaranteed, with spare parts readily available. There are two basic types of vacuum cleaner: the upright type and the cylindrical or spherical type.

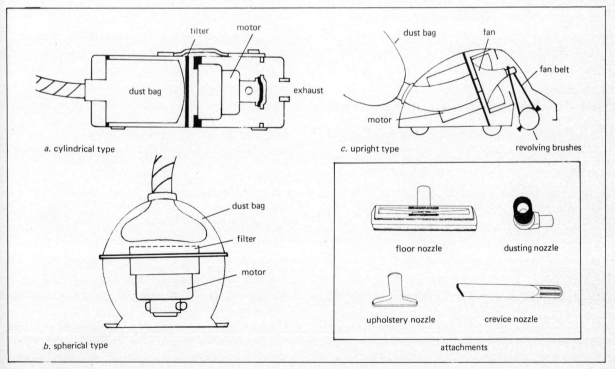

a. cylindrical type

b. spherical type

c. upright type

floor nozzle

dusting nozzle

upholstery nozzle

crevice nozzle

attachments

Vacuum cleaners

The upright type

1. As these work by both suction and friction, they are thought to do a more thorough cleaning job.
2. They are less tiring to use and easier to handle. They move with just the slightest push.
3. They are ideal for houses with a large expanse of carpet.
4. As the brushes assist in the cleaning action, a less powerful motor is required to provide suction (200-500 W). This makes them cheaper to run.
5. The cleaner can be adjusted to different heights to suit long, medium and short pile carpets.

Disadvantages

1. not particularly stable on stairs, heavy to carry;
2. hose must be attached for corners, skirtings and stairs as the upright cleaner cannot get right into corners;
3. unsuitable for use on hard floors, wood and vinyl;
4. tends to wear out the carpet more quickly due to the double action of beating and suction;
5. inclined to be noisy.

The cylindrical type

1. This type is ideal for homes with a combination of carpets and hard floor coverings.
2. It is lightweight, safe and easy to use on stairs.
3. It is also more suitable for long piled carpets.
4. A small hand-held model is available — ideal for vacuuming cars, caravans etc.

Disadvantages

1. uses slightly more electricity due to more powerful motor (400-750 W);
2. more awkward and cumbersome to pull along on flat surfaces;
3. longer and more tiring to vacuum a room.

The spherical or canister type is much the same as the cylindrical model. It is heavier, but it is easy to move about as it floats on a cushion of expelled air. There is a wide range of attachments.

CONSTRUCTION

Most vacuum cleaners are made of tough, lightweight plastic and metal. Both types have a large selection of attachments which can be fitted to the hose and used for cleaning and dusting curtains, upholstery etc. They should have an extra long flex and should be connected to a 13-amp fused socket.

The *upright cleaner* has a long hinged handle which gives flexibility of movement. To this is attached a dust bag, within which is fixed a disposable bag. The air which is drawn into the machine is filtered through the porous dust bag to be released into the room. The rotating brush is attached to the suction fan by a rubber fan belt, which has to be replaced now and then. A flexible hose is attached to the cleaner for various jobs; to this is fixed one of several attachments. The cleaner is made mobile by four small wheels on the base. The on/off switch is foot operated and some models have a small light, which is useful when cleaning dark corners.

The cylindrical model has a dust container within the machine, which may be used with disposable bags. Most have a flex rewind button, variable suction strength, reverse blowing action — useful for drying shampooed carpets and for spraying paint. Some also have a carpet shampooing attachment.

Latest features include an indicator to show when the bag is full; variable suction control; hinged flex holder for quick release; flat perforated nozzle for cleaning radiators and crevices; side opening on base for easy cleaning of carpet edges.

Use

1. Read instruction book and follow manufacturer's instructions.
2. Guide both types of cleaners gently. Do not force them or bang them against woodwork (although most cleaners have rubber bumpers to prevent damage to furniture.)
3. Empty bag before it becomes too full. A full bag reduces the cleaning power of the machine. Disposable bags can be used two or three times.
4. Rewind the flex loosely to avoid damage to its plastic casing.
5. Wipe over now and then, using a little silicone polish.
6. Avoid picking up metal objects, such as pins and nails, and objects too large for the machine, e.g. polythene bags.
7. If an object gets stuck in the machine, stop the machine at once, unplug, and carefully attempt to dislodge it. If unsuccessful, bring it to a service engineer.
8. Have the machine serviced regularly. Spare parts are usually available from the supplier.
9. Never wash the bag, as it is treated with a special finish to prevent dust escaping.

ELECTRIC FLOOR POLISHERS

In homes which have a lot of hard floor coverings such as wood or vinyl, an electric floor polisher will save hours of hard work.

How it works: an electric motor rotates two or three circular brushes. The sheer weight of the cleaner exerts sufficient pressure to remove the dirt. The polisher can be used for both washing and polishing a floor. Certain models can be used to shampoo carpets.

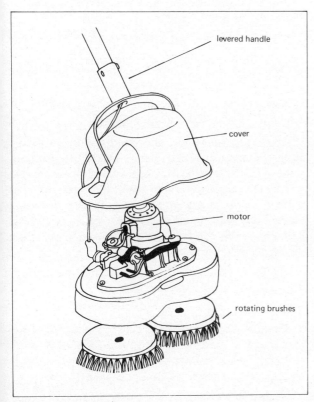

Electric floor polisher

CONSTRUCTION

Most models are similar in appearance to an upright vacuum cleaner, with a long vertical handle onto which the flex is wound when not in use. Controls are generally situated on the handle. Three sets of polishers are usually supplied: a set of stiff brushes for scrubbing, a set of soft brushes for polishing, and a set of felt pads for buffing. Some models have an automatic polish or shampoo dispenser.

Use

1. To wash floors: sweep thoroughly to remove dust and grit. Use a suitable floor cleaner and spread over the floor area to be cleaned. Direct the machine (fitted with scrubbing brushes) over the floor, rinsing and drying one area by hand or mop before proceeding to the next.

2. To polish floors: spread polish over cleaned floor, either by hand or using the polisher with polishing brushes attached. Allow to dry thoroughly, then use the buffers to achieve a good shine.

Care

1. Follow instructions supplied. Use a recommended polish.
2. Wash brushes and buffers regularly and replace when necessary.
3. Polisher should be serviced regularly.
4. Allow to dry before storing and if possible store by hanging from a hook, to avoid standing polisher on its brushes.

CARPET SWEEPERS

These are not worked by electricity but are pushed by hand. Two stiff revolving brushes brush the dirt and dust into a dust box within the cleaner. This is emptied regularly by pulling a release lever. Carpet sweepers are available in various sizes

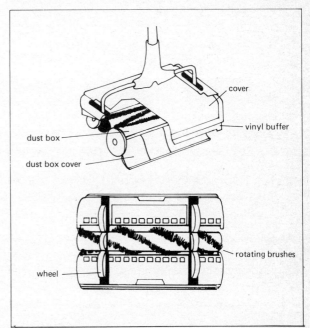

Carpet sweeper

Use

1. Carpet sweepers are quick and handy to use.
2. They are ideal for small carpet-sweeping jobs, but do not clean as thoroughly as a vacuum cleaner.

3. They cause less wear and tear on carpets.
4. They may need to be serviced once or twice during their lifetime; otherwise, regular emptying, cleaning of brushes and occasional oiling are sufficient.

FLOOR POLISHES

1. *Solid wax polish* is a mixture of waxes dissolved in spirit-based solvents, such as white spirit. The spirit evaporates after application, leaving a layer of wax on the floor. Silicones are often added to make the polish easier to apply and to give a water-resistant, high gloss. Many have perfumes added and some, for use on quarry tiles, have colouring added. *Examples:* Mansion Guardshine, lavender wax.

Use
(a) Apply sparingly: too much will make the floor sticky and dangerously slippery.
(b) As this type of polish needs to be rubbed in very thoroughly, an electric floor polisher is useful.
(c) Never use on vinyl or rubber floorings, as the spirit content damages the surface.
(d) This polish is suitable for wood, cork and linoleum covered floors.

2. *Liquid wax polish* contains a much higher proportion of spirit — often up to 90 per cent — resulting in an easy to use liquid polish. *Example:* Johnson's Beautiflor.

Use
(a) Apply sparingly.
(b) These polishes clean as well as polish, i.e. they remove scuff marks from the floor with a little rubbing.
(c) Less elbow grease is required to get a good shine.
(d) They are less slippery than solid wax polishes, as they lack silicone.

3. *Emulsion polishes* consist of a blend of waxes and resins emulsified in water. The water evaporates after application, leaving a hard, shiny surface. They spread easily without streaking, and give a high gloss upon drying, with no need to buff the floor. *Examples:* Glocoat, Seel, Kleer.

Use
(a) The floor must be thoroughly cleaned before application, as they do not clean the floor.
(b) Spread evenly with a soft cloth or damp mop and leave to dry for about 20 minutes.

(c) The shine can be buffed up between applications.
(d) The build-up of a sticky coating should be removed occasionally with a proprietary cleaner or steel wool.
(e) This polish is suitable for vinyl type floors, rubber, lino, sealed wood and cork, quarry tiles.

4. *Combined cleaners and polishes* are an emulsion-type polish with cleaning agents added, only suitable for slightly soiled floors. Apply sparingly — otherwise use in the same way as emulsion polish. *Examples:* Dual, Mansion One-Two.

5. *Floor cleaners:* these contain strong detergents with low foaming qualities and often additives such as disinfectants, ammonia and perfume. These help to remove the build-up of old polish and should be rinsed thoroughly and allowed to dry before polish is applied. *Examples:* Flash, Clean-o-Pine, Safeshine.

6. *Carpet shampoos:* the composition varies — usually a mixture of detergent, alkalis and sometimes ammonia. *Example:* 1001. Carpet dry-cleaners are also available. These contain an absorbent substance (e.g. fuller's earth) and a grease solvent. The cleaner is shaken on and brushed lightly. When dry, it is vacuumed off. This is not as thorough as carpet shampoo.

Simple tests to establish the composition of floor coverings

1. Wool carpet: remove a tuft and burn it. It should produce the characteristic protein odour of burnt feathers.
2. Nylon carpet: remove a tuft and burn it. It is difficult to burn, gives off a celery-like smell, and leaves a hard residue.
3. PVC: a sliver when set alight will burn with a greenish tinge. PVC softens at 80°C.
4. Acrylic fibre will burn rapidly. Residue consists of a rough black bead.

QUESTIONS/CHAPTER 10

1. Describe the type of floor covering you would consider most appropriate for a hall and stairs. Refer to
(a) composition
(b) appearance
(c) durability
(d) care
(e) current cost.
Compare carpet tiles with fitted carpets for use in the home.

A good looking carpet (John Topham Picture Library)

2. Assuming you have taken part in a project on carpets, set out points of information relating to each of the following:
   (a) types available   (c) suitability for purpose
   (b) composition   (d) care and cleaning.
   Discuss the need for an underlay when laying a carpet.

3. List the properties required of a kitchen floor covering. Name three floor coverings which satisfy most of these requirements.
   In the case of one, describe how it should be cared for and cleaned, in order to keep it in good condition.

4. Compare hard and soft floor coverings suitable for use in a bathroom. Refer to
   (a) properties   (d) maintenance
   (b) selection and quality (e) cost.
   (c) suitability for purpose

5. What points should be considered when choosing a vacuum cleaner or an electric polisher for use in a large, old house with polished, wooden floors? In the case of the vacuum cleaner, explain
   (a) the working principle   (c) use.
   (b) the basic structure
   List 4 cleaning agents suitable for use on wood floors.

11.
Furnishing your home

Good-quality furniture will last many years, if not a lifetime. Because furniture is so expensive, we cannot afford to throw it out when we grow tired of it. For this reason it is wise to choose fairly standard styles and shapes which are well designed, attractive and functional.

When the time comes to furnish your home, take your time and think carefully about the style of furniture which will suit rooms of your house and the lifestyle you lead.

STYLES

Furniture is available in several styles.

1. *Antique:* furniture made before 1830. As few can afford antiques, many people are turning to reproduction furniture which copies the lines of antique furniture, using expensive woods or wood veneers. Reproduction furniture is also very expensive.

2. *Victorian:* although several styles of furniture were in vogue during the long reign of Queen Victoria, much Victorian furniture is large and heavy and unsuited to our smaller modern homes.

3. ***Between the wars***, 1918-39: much of the furniture made during this period is not considered fashionable today, and can therefore be picked up cheaply at auctions. Art Nouveau, a futuristic style at the time, is now more popular and therefore more expensive.

4. *Scandinavian:* popular during the late 1950s and 1960s, lines are long and low, unfussy and streamlined. Much is made in teak or teak veneer with upholstery in tweed.

Pieces of antique furniture make this an attractive room (John Topham Picture Library)

102

5. **Modern:** glass, plastic and metals such as chrome are used extensively. Upholstery has a fuller, softer appearance. Modular unit furniture which can be added to over the years is practical and useful. A wave of nostalgia has brought back cottage-style furniture — Windsor chairs, pine dressers, stained softwoods and soft furnishings in chintz and 'granny' prints.

A fine dining-room (Irish Times)

Modern furnishings and decor can also look good

ARRANGING THE FURNITURE

See page 119-20.

BUYING FURNITURE

As furniture is such an expensive purchase, a great deal of thought and planning should be done before buying. Buy essential large pieces first. keep the whole house in mind so that design, size and style will harmonise. Remember it is better to buy a few good pieces of basic furniture at first and save for the rest, than to buy a lot of cheap, shoddy items in a rush to get the house furnished. Choose from standard ranges of furniture which are not likely to be discontinued. Extra items may be purchased over the years.

Consider
1. The cost: cheap furniture is usually not worth buying.
2. The shop: visit many shops if time allows, but concentrate on those which stock a large range of good quality, guaranteed furniture at competitive prices.
3. Style: the furniture chosen should suit the decor of the room for which it is intended. It should blend in size, colour and style with existing furniture and furnishings. This does not mean that modern and period furniture cannot be mixed — such an arrangement can in fact create a very pleasant effect.

   Modern furniture is smaller in scale than old-fashioned styles, so it blends well in appearance and size with small modern houses and flats. Its low, smooth lines create a feeling of spaciousness in a room. Modern finishes and absence of ornate decoration make it easy to clean and maintain. Modern storage furniture is particularly well designed and adaptable.
4. The design: the furniture should look attractive, well proportioned, and be suitable for its purpose. A chair or bed should be comfortable; a table should be strong and steady.
5. Quality: this is usually, but not always, related to the cost. Good quality furniture is well made from seasoned wood, rust-resistant metal, and durable fabrics. It should, given reasonable wear, last ten or twenty years.

   Quality marks — for example the Design Centre label — ensure that the article is well made and durable.
6. Durability: all furniture should be reasonably durable, but this is a particularly important factor with articles which get rough treatment — a kitchen cupboard, living-room settee or child's bed.
7. Maintenance: avoid furniture which will be difficult to clean or easily stained. This includes pale shades, plain fabrics, ornate woodwork, non-washable fabrics, loosely-woven chair covers.

8. Mobility: most items of furniture should be easy to move for cleaning; add castors if necessary.
9. Construction: examine each piece of furniture carefully in a good light. It should be steady. Joints should fit well: they may be dovetailed or glued, not stapled. Screws fasten furniture more securely than nails do. Drawers should slide in and out easily. The finish should be smooth and evenly applied. The inside should be smooth, without protruding nails or roughly chipped wood — these are signs of bad workmanship. Doors should fit well, hang squarely and close properly. Hinges and catches should be unobtrusive but secure. Handles and other fittings should be comfortable and of good quality. Cheap fittings can detract from an otherwise well-designed article. Check whether furniture is of solid wood or a veneer.
10. Ask the salesman: about delivery, guarantees and repairs; and also find out about the materials and finishes used, to know how to clean and care for the furniture properly. Most manufacturers of good quality furniture supply an explanatory leaflet.

SPECIAL POINTS ABOUT TABLES

1. A table should be strong and steady.
2. A round table takes up more space than a rectangular one, but seats more people. Allow at least 60 cm width for each person.
3. The table should be a comfortable height, usually 76 cm from the floor, but this really depends on the height of the chair seat. Allow about 18 cm knee space between the chair seat and the table for diners to sit comfortably.
4. The top should be easily cleaned and reasonably heat and stain resistant. Laminated plastic makes a splendid table-top for a kitchen. For dining tables, a polyurethane varnish is more heat resistant than most other finishes.
5. Drop-leaf or extendable tables are useful if numbers dining vary. Most modern drop-leaf tables are well designed and fold to a very small size when not in use.

SPECIAL POINTS ABOUT CHAIRS

1. Chairs should be strong, steady and comfortable.
2. They should support the back.
3. Easy chairs should also support the shoulders, and if possible, the head.

4. Easy chairs should not be too deep. Fifty to 60 cm is usual; more will mean the occupant's feet will not touch the floor.
5. The seat of a dining chair should be 40-45 cm from the floor.
6. Arms should be a comfortable height.
7. Legs should be sturdy, preferably with the wood grain running vertically for strength.

SPECIAL POINTS ABOUT UPHOLSTERED FURNITURE

1. It is difficult to judge upholstered furniture on outward appearances, as the entire construction of the upholstered area is hidden from view by the outer covering.
2. Look for a reliable make which carries an informative label stating details of construction and materials used.
3. The frame should be of sound construction. Test the back and arms of chairs to see if they are securely fixed.
4. Wooden arms are most practical for chairs which are to be in continuous use.
5. Look underneath the chair. Webbing or canvas covering should be taut, neatly and firmly secured. Staples, which are often used, are not as secure as tacks. Springs, if used, should be plentiful and firmly attached.
6. Chairs should be well padded with hair, latex foam or synthetic wadding.
7. Outer fabric should be closely woven and fairly thick, durable, easily cleaned and stain resistant. Modern upholstery fabrics are impregnated with silicones which delay the absorption of stains — allowing time to mop them up. Good upholstery fabrics should be colourfast, shrink resistant and mothproofed (if wool). *Examples:* leather or artificial leather (PVC), dralon velvet or corduroy, tweed, moquette, wood mixtures, cotton cretonne, chintz, tapestry, linen repp or union, synthetics — rayon, nylon, brocade.

SPECIAL POINTS ABOUT CABINET FURNITURE

1. Cupboards, wardrobes and chests of drawers should be solid and steady, standing firmly on the floor.
2. Doors and drawers should fit well.
3. Drawers should be the right size for their purpose, i.e. shallow for gloves and scarves, large for sweaters, deep for large, tall containers.

4. Wardrobes should be divided into shelving areas for hats, bags and shoes, and hanging areas for long, short and medium length clothes. They should be sufficiently wide for clothes on hangers to fit comfortably. If the wardrobe is too small, the clothes will not be sufficiently ventilated, and they will also become creased.
5. Sideboards and other storage cupboards should have the storage area designed to suit articles being stored.
6. If there is a possibility that the back of the unit may be exposed, it should be presentable.

SECOND-HAND FURNITURE

Although most people cannot afford to buy genuine antiques, second-hand furniture can be a very good buy. It can be bought at auction or in second-hand salerooms.

Advantages

1. Construction of old furniture is often superior to that of modern pieces.
2. Good workmanship and attention to detail are more likely.
3. Materials are usually solid and hard wearing, having survived the test of time.
4. Fittings are generally better quality.
5. Styles usually blend in with most interiors and are unlikely to go out of date.
6. Second-hand furniture is often cheaper than its modern equivalent. Many bargains can be found at auctions.

Disadvantages

1. There is a danger of woodworm and other infestations. If there is any sign of woodworm, furniture must be treated before it is brought into the house.
2. Pieces are often heavy and cumbersome.
3. Many pieces are too large for modern homes.
4. Certain styles, such as Victoriana, Art Nouveau, become expensive and difficult to find as they become fashionable and popular.
5. The furniture may need to be cleaned and/or renovated. Renovating may include the following processes: stripping, bleaching, sanding, staining, sealing, varnishing, waxing, painting, and re-upholstering.

STORAGE

In the average family home, storage space is required for a large number of items:
 food — staples and perishables
 crockery, china, cutlery
 kitchen utensils
 cleaning equipment
 clothes and shoes
 bed and table linen
 books
 luggage
 stationery and household records
 precious objects
 material for hobbies
 toys and games
 seasonal equipment
 sports equipment
 gardening tools and materials

When the house is being built, provision should be made for storing normal household items. Some new houses have many built-in features: wardrobes and dressing tables in bedrooms, vanity units in bathrooms, a plentiful supply of kitchen units, and cupboards or shelving in living areas. These add to the overall cost of a new house, but are actually a way to save money later, because less furniture is needed in a house with good storage facilities.

Built-in storage

1. This is usually a permanent structure attached to the walls.
2. It is usually neat and streamlined. Cupboards are generally built to ceiling height, providing maximum storage on the minimum of floor space.
3. It saves space, as it cuts down the amount of furniture required.
4. It can utilise waste space: alcoves on either side of the fireplace, drawers under beds, window seats which lift up.
5. Employ a skilled carpenter to build in the fitments. Costs vary according to materials used: cupboards made from chipboard or whitewood will be cheaper than those made from teak or mahogany.

Unit storage

Modular unit systems are ready-made arrangements of furniture which can be built up to form one complete unit. They can take the form of light shelving or more substantial cupboards and desks, which can house books, equipment and other items, and display ornaments, photographs and pot plants. They are not cheap, but they have an advantage in that they can be bought bit by bit over a period, and can be taken down when moving home.

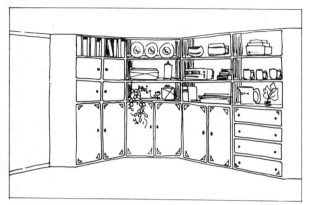

Unit storage: ready-made modular unit furniture

The structure: may take the form of
1. a ladder-type fitting onto which the units hang;
2. steel strips attached to a wall into which brackets are slotted; shelves then rest on the brackets;
3. more substantial wooden units which are complete in themselves, but which can be placed side by side to form one large area of cupboards and shelves.

In each case furniture and accessories are designed in standard widths to fit onto the basic structure.

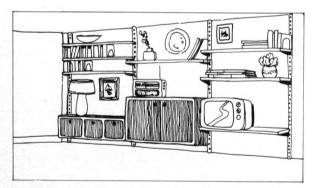

Unit storage: steel uprights with adjustable brackets for shelves

Fitments for unit storage
1. shelves — wood, veneered chipboard, glass or fibreglass and plastic;
2. desks;
3. television cupboards, which can be closed when not in use;
4. cocktail cabinets, with space for bottles and glasses and a laminated plastic surface for pouring drinks;

5. general purpose storage cupboards;
6. wardrobes and dressing table units (see Chapter 12);
7. kitchen units (see Chapter 13).

Summary on storage
1. It should be functional but form an integral part of the furnishings of the room.
2. Each room should have sufficient storage for the items used in that room.
3. Storage should be planned to suit the items being stored, e.g. wardrobes wide enough for hangers to fit comfortably, small drawers for small items such as gloves and jewellery.
4. Units should be large and strong enough to house any heavy items, such as books or TV.
5. To save space in small rooms, keep storage on walls rather than on floors.
6. Be generous when planning storage. Make allowance for increases in the amount to be stored.
7. Keeps items in constant use near to hand and easily accessible.
8. Store seasonal items (Christmas decorations, sports equipment) out of the way, e.g. in high cupboards.
9. Remember open shelves are not suitable for untidy people — and they need constant dusting.

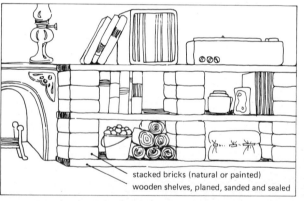

stacked bricks (natural or painted)
wooden shelves, planed, sanded and sealed

Cheap do-it-yourself shelving

SEVEN IDEAS FOR CHEAP STORAGE

1. Orange boxes and tea chests can be trimmed, painted or papered, and stacked together.
2. Stacked bricks and wooden planks provide cheap book shelving; these can also be painted.
3. Cheap plastic kitchen buckets and basins provide colourful storage for children's toys, and can be used for play.
4. Fit out the understair area with lots of shelving and coat hanging space and use as a cloakroom.

5. Hang baskets on the back of cupboard doors to house small items. Plastic-coated wire baskets are available for this purpose.
6. Nail the lids of screwtop jars to the underside of shelves or dupboards. The filled jars can be screwed into the lids.
7. Junk-shop finds of cheap ugly furniture can be given a new lease of life by sanding down and varnishing or repainting.

MATERIALS USED IN FURNISHING

wood	glass
plastic	textiles
metal	

A. WOOD

Wood is classified as follows:

Hardwood:		*Soft-wood:*
ash	oak	cedar
beech	poplar	fir
birch	rosewood	parana pine
elm	sycamore	redwood
mahogany	teak	spruce (whitewood)
maple	walnut	

Soft-woods come from fast-growing, coniferous trees which produce wood which is relatively cheap. The term soft-wood does not refer to the lightness or strength of the wood. Soft-woods are used for carpentry, flooring, doors, windows and other building work, and also for cheap or veneered furniture. Deal, one of the cheapest woods, is a collective name for timber from fir, pine and spruce trees.

Hardwoods come from slow-growing, deciduous trees. The long, slow growth makes them tough and strong and produces finer graining than soft-wood. This beautiful graining makes them ideal for making into good quality furniture. Each hardwood has a particular colour and grain.

Ash, beech and elm, which are used for strong, plain utility furniture, vary from grey to yellow in colour.

Oak, a pale-coloured wood, is hard wearing and durable, but expensive. It can be used for furniture and outdoor woodwork.

Maple, used for best quality flooring, is golden to warm brown.

Walnut, with its ornate grain, varies from golden to dark brown in colour.

Teak, with a straight, even grain and a warm to dark brown colour, is strong, hard and durable, and can be used on the outside of a house. Much modern Scandinavian furniture is teak veneered.

Mahogany and rosewood are a dark reddish-brown colour and clearly grained, strong, hard-wearing and attractive; used in good-quality furniture.

In spite of its beauty and usefulness, wood has some disadvantages.
1. It is expensive.
2. There is much waste in its production, e.g. ends and offcuts.
3. The grain can split, and knots can weaken it.
4. Wood can shrink, warp and swell.

Man-made boards

Many alternatives to wood are now used in furniture manufacture. Most are available in sheets 244 cm × 122 cm or less.

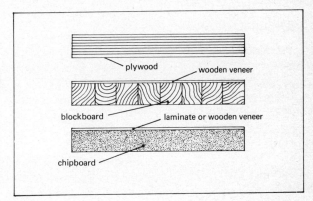

Man-made boards

1. **Hardboard** consists of sheets of compressed wood pulp. It is about 3 mm thick, usually dark brown in colour, with a smooth surface on one side and a rough absorbent underside.

   Special finishes are available such as perforated peg board and laminated hardboard.

2. **Plywood** is made of thin sheets of wood glued together, with the grain of the sheets running alternatively lengthwise and crosswise to give it strength. It is available in different thicknesses and different qualities.

   Special finishes are available, such as decorative veneers, e.g. covered with thin sheets of teak, oak or mahogany.

3. **Blockboard** is a layer of wood strips sandwiched with adhesive between veneers. The veneers run at right angles to the wood strips for strength.

4. **_Chipboard_** is made of chips of wood glued together under heat and pressure. It is graded according to quality and strength.

Special finishes include laminated chipboard, sealed chipboard (which absorbs less paint), and wood-veneered chipboard, popular for making cheap shelving units and cupboards.

Advantages of man-made boards
1. cheapness;
2. less likely to warp;
3. lightweight;
4. available in very large sizes (244 × 122 cm).

They are quicker to work with as there are fewer joints.

Disadvantages
1. less durable;
2. unsuitable for exterior use;
3. badly damaged by water.

VENEERS

As hardwood is so expensive, very little modern furniture is made from solid hardwood. Instead much furniture is made in soft-wood, chipboard or blockboard, and a very thin sheet of hardwood is fixed to the surface with adhesive. This is known as a _veneer_. The edges are finished with beading of the same wood.

Advantages
1. cheaper than solid hardwood;
2. less likely to warp or shrink;
3. often lighter.

Disadvantages
1. veneer may chip off with rough handling;
2. adhesive may dissolve with over-wetting or heating, causing the veneer to lift off.

WOOD FINISHES

Wooden furniture is usually treated
1. to preserve it;
2. to improve the colour;
3. to bring out the grain;
4. to make it easier to maintain;
5. to protect it from rot and insects;
6. to make it moisture and stain resistant.

STAIN

This is a transparent wood colouring, which may be oil or water based. Oil-based and spirit-based stains contain a solvent such as turpentine or methylated spirits — therefore not all varnishes or other finishes may be used over them. Water-based stains are cheap and easy to use; they can be applied with a brush or cloth. Any type of varnish may be used over them.

Stains are available in light and dark wood shades as well as in some colours, such as red, yellow, green and blue. The darker the shade required, the more coats of stain are used. Stains are often incorporated into French polishes and varnishes.

VARNISH

This is a transparent finish consisting of a mixture of resins and solvent. The usual solvent is methylated spirits; the most durable and hard-wearing resin is polyurethane.

Polyurethane is ideal for floors and furniture which get a lot of wear. It is heat and moisture resistant, and available in gloss or matt finish. Maintenance is easy: just rub with a damp cloth.

To apply varnish:
1. The surface should be smooth and free of dust.
2. Using a paintbrush, apply two or three coats of varnish.
3. Allow each coat to dry completely, then sand down lightly with fine sandpaper and dust or vacuum thoroughly before applying the next coat.
4. After application, ventilate the room to remove fumes as the solvent evaporates.

FRENCH POLISH

This is made from a mixture of resin (shellac) and solvent (methylated spirits); it generally has colour added. It produces a very glossy sheen and is ideal for fine grained hardwoods such as mahogany, walnut and rosewood. The application of French polish, which is rubbed in by hand, is a specialised job.

French polish is easily affected by heat and moisture, especially alcohol. Wipe up spills at once. Spilt perfume will ruin a French-polished dressing table. Use mats under hot dishes. To shine, rub with a soft cloth. Polish is not necessary.

OTHER MODERN WOOD FINISHES

1. Cellulose: a transparent gloss or matt finish; easy to maintain; used on TV sets, and much modern furniture.
2. Paint: gloss or matt finish can be used to hide cheap woods completely.

3. Lacquer or enamel: names given to a particularly high gloss pigmented varnish. True lacquer is an oriental resin used to produce the high gloss finish often seen in Eastern furniture and trinkets.
4. Wood preservatives: products which are used to preserve wood and prevent damage by insects and rot include creosote, anti-woodworm treatments and outdoor wood preservative, to protect against weathering.
5. Wax polish: made in much the same way as wax floor polishes, it usually contains beeswax and a solvent. It brings out the colour and the grain of the wood and produces a rich sheen. It protects the wood against moisture and some stains but is easily affected by heat. It should be used sparingly and rubbed well in to avoid stickiness.
6. Furniture oil: linseed or teak oil are rubbed into the wood and allowed to dry. Furniture oil is suitable for woods such as teak and mahogany. It nourishes and protects the wood against moisture but is not heat resistant. It gives a glowing natural finish, where shine is not required. It is unsuitable for chairs, as it may stain clothes.
7. Furniture cream: is a liquid wax containing a mixture of wax, an emulsifying agent and water. Some contain silicone which resists dirt and water. It is easy to apply. Many modern floor and furniture polishes, creams and sprays contain silicones, as do certain fabrics and floor coverings.

B. PLASTICS

Since World War II, the use of plastics has increased enormously. Many items of furniture, toys, utensils, machinery and building materials are now composed largely of plastic. Plastics used in furniture include perspex, polystyrene, PVC and laminated plastics.

Plastic as a furnishing material

The long-held view that plastics were a poor imitation of the real thing is finally changing. Plastics are now accepted in their own right as a versatile and attractive material with almost limitless uses within the home, the factory and in commercial fields.

Advantages
1. lightweight but strong;
2. quiet;
3. many forms and uses;
4. cheap;
5. comfortable to handle;
6. available in a wide variety of colours and textures;
7. does not rust or scratch;
8. resilient and pliable; often unbreakable;
9. hygienic;
10. good insulator — ideal for electrical equipment.

Uses
Kitchen utensils: buckets, basins, dustbins, brushes, cups and saucers, laundry baskets, dustbins, trays, containers, handles of saucepans
Bathroom fittings: splashbacks, towel rails, toilet roll holders, baths, flooring
Furniture: chairs, laminated table tops, light fittings and shades, vinyl wallpaper, perspex windows
Electrical goods: hair dryers, vacuum cleaner casings, electric shavers, mixers and liquidisers, handles of irons, plugs and sockets

Care of plastic in the home
1. Do not let it come in contact with high temperatures — it will melt or char.
2. Avoid use of strong chemicals such as bleaches.
3. Never use abrasives.
4. Wash in fairly hot soapy water, using a soft cloth or brush.
5. Many plastics should not be washed in a dishwasher.
6. Never allow plastic to become too soiled before washing.
7. Avoid handling too roughly — thermosetting (hard) plastics may break.

Kitchen showing use of laminated plastic (John Topham Picture Library)

Laminated plastics
A laminate is made by compressing several sheets of paper including a decorative or coloured surface paper, and using thermosetting (very hard) plastic to

bond them under heated pressure. The resulting thin sheet can then be attached to chipboard of blockboard with strong adhesive. It is used for kitchen worktops, cupboards doors and linings, sink and bath splashbacks, table tops and as a veneer on cheap furniture e.g. sideboards and coffee tables.

Laminated plastics are
1. easy to clean;
2. heat resistant (except for intense dry heat);
3. waterproof;
4. stain resistant;
5. durable and hard-wearing.

But they may be damaged by
1. dry heat such as very hot saucepans, cigarettes and dyes;
2. certain chemicals;
3. sharp knives;
4. harsh abrasives.

Care of laminated plastics
1. Wash with warm soapy water, rinse and dry.
2. Never chop food directly on work top — use a chopping board.
3. Never use abrasives, steelwool or scouring powders.
4. Stubborn stains can be softened and removed by placing a damp cloth over the stain for a short time, then wiping off.

C. METAL

Metals used in furnishing include brass, aluminium, steel and chromium. Metals may take the form of sheet metal, tubes (used in tubular steel kitchen tables) as frames and bases for pictures and lamps and as decorative edgings, knobs, handles etc. on cabinet furniture.

D. GLASS

Glass can be used in furnishing for table tops (particularly popular for occasional tables), room dividers, shelving and mirrors. Think twice about using glass where children are about. It can cause horrifying accidents.

CARE AND CLEANING OF FURNITURE

1. *Wood*

Buff up regularly with a soft cloth. Polish occasionally using a little furniture cream and rubbing well in. Most people over-polish furniture. Finger marks can be removed from polished wood with a little polish or with a cloth wrung out of warm soapy water. Rinse and dry well. Avoid wetting wood — use coasters to protect tables from glasses. Use thick insulating mats under hot dishes.

2. *Cane and wicker*

Vacuum thoroughly. Wash occasionally with warm soapy water using a soft brush. Avoid over-wetting. Rinse well and dry with an absorbent cloth. Apply a little spray-on silicone polish when fully dry.

3. *Paint*

Wash in warm water containing suitable detergent, e.g. Ajax liquid. Rinse and dry quickly with a soft cloth.

4. *Upholstery*

Vacuum thoroughly with appropriate attachments or brush lightly. Clean by sponging with the lather from warm water containing detergent. Rinse with a wrung out sponge. Do not over-wet. Allow to dry out of doors in the shade or in a warm, well-ventilated room. Always test on an inconspicuous area first.

5. *Laminated plastic*

See page 161.

To remove marks
(Test first on the underside of the furniture.)
1. Wax build-up: rinse with a mild vinegar and warm water solution.
2. Heat marks: rub firmly but gently with linseed or camphorated oil.
3. Water marks: rub gently with fine steel wool, then polish with tinted polish or patent scratch remover.
4. Scratches: use scratch remover or a little turpentine.
5. Scuff marks: use fine steel wool dipped in paraffin.

SOFT FURNISHINGS

Soft furnishings, which include curtains, bedspreads, chair covers and cushions, can do much to improve the overall appearance of a room. The choice of fabric is most important when deciding on the soft furnishing requirements of a home.

FABRICS

Desirable qualities in fabrics

Curtain fabrics	Upholstery fabrics
reasonably durable	tough and durable
hang and drape well	resistant to abrasion
preshrunk	preshrunk
easy to clean — preferably washable	easy to clean—spongeable
dirt resistant	stain resistant
resistant to fading and sunlight	resistant to fading
colourfast	colourfast
flame resistant	closely woven to prevent sagging

Net curtains

These give privacy, especially if the room is overlooked. They can be made from several fabrics.

1. *Cotton* is available in plain or lacy weaves. It is inclined to shrink and ironing is necessary.
2. *Terylene* has almost replaced cotton for making net curtains. It is hard wearing, easy to wash, drip-dry, and only requires ironing if it is creased during washing.
3. *Dralon* is a thicker, softer fabric which may be used either as net curtains or as main drapes. It is available in many colours and weaves, but is most popular in shades of cream and beige. It is easy to wash and drip-dries.

Note: remember white is difficult to keep: it yellows with age. Dylon Superwhite is useful for whitening yellowed net curtains.

Fabrics for curtains, upholstery and cushions

1. *Cotton:* 100% cotton is reasonably expensive. Chintz is a heavily glazed printed cotton; cretonne a heavier printed cotton. Both are also suitable for making loose chair covers. Cotton blends are also available and are less expensive, e.g. cotton/rayon. Cottons look fresh and crisp — they launder well, but are inclined to shrink.
2. *Linen:* pure linen is expensive and creases readily. Blends, such as Moygashel and repp, are more suitable. As these fabrics shrink considerably, allowance should be made for this.
3. *Linen union* is a mixture of cotton and linen, popular in large floral prints, ideal for loose covers.
4. *Velvet* is a pile fabric, made in much the same way as a carpet. Originally made from silk, then cotton, most furnishing velvets are now made from dacron or dralon. These are reasonably hard wearing, they drape well, and are washable. Velvet is very expensive and it looks best in a large expanse of curtaining, rather than small curtains.
5. *Wool:* expensive, it is more usually available as part of a blend or mixture. (*A mixture* is a fabric in which two different yarns are woven or knitted together, e.g. terylene warp and cotton weft. *A blend* is a fabric made from a yarn which contains a blend of threads from two or more different fibres, e.g. rayon and polyester.) Tweed is the most popular furnishing fabric made from wool. Wool drapes well, has good insulating properties, but is liable to attack by moths, and may shrink and felt if washed. For these reasons, it should be moth-proofed and dry-cleaned only.
6. *Man-made fibres:* these may be regenerated or cellulose fibres (rayon, tricel or acrylics) or synthetic fibres produced from chemicals (nylon, polyester, terylene, trevira, dralon, fibreglass). As they are controlled at each stage of their manufacture, furnishing fabrics made from man-made fibres can be given properties suited to their function, e.g. draping qualities, stain resistant finishes and so on. Most man-made fibres have the following properties: they are durable, stain resistant, moth-proof, rot resistant, easy to wash and drip-dry.
7. *Glass fibre:* only suitable for curtains, this is easy to wash, drip-dry, non-flammable, resistant to sunlight. It tends to split after some time.

Upholstery fabrics

Heavier weights of many of the fabrics mentioned above may be used: cretonne, repp, linen union, dralon velvet, tweed and man-made fibres. Other fabrics suitable for upholstery are

1. *moquette:* a looped pile fabric made from cotton and wool;
2. *brocade* and *tapestry:* rich intricate weaves;
3. *leather* and *leather-look plastics:* easy to clean, but danger of tears which are difficult to mend.

CURTAINS

The choice of curtains will depend on the following factors:

1. type of window;
2. style of room;
3. amount of wear expected;
4. purpose of the curtains;
5. money available.

Type of window

Windows vary a lot in shape and style. They may be

1. long and narrow;
2. large picture windows;
3. French windows;
4. small dormer or attic-type windows;
5. bay or bow windows.

Curtains must suit the type of windows, but they can do much to alter and improve a badly proportioned window. Examples:

1. Long narrow windows can be made to look wider by carrying the curtain 50 to 100 cm past the window. The curtains when open come just to the edge of the window.
2. Large picture windows or French windows are expensive to curtain: the curtains may cover the whole window wall.
3. Small dormer windows are usually given a cottage-style look by using Liberty prints or checks — often with matching wallpaper.
4. Bay windows need careful fitting, and they require a lot of fabric. It may be possible to use short curtains.
5. Recessed windows: the curtain may hang in front of the recess, but this will reduce floor space.

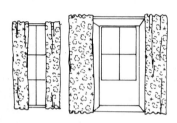

Tall, narrow windows can be made to look wider by extending the track beyond window at each side.

Make a small window appear larger by extending curtains at each side and hanging mock café curtains below.

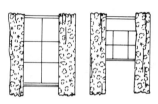

Matching curtains can create a unified look when windows differ in size.

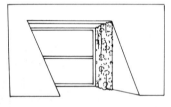

Short curtains in a dormer window should clear the window by day.

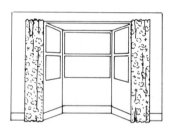

Curtain track placed outside the bay window saves fabric, but floor space is lost when drawn at night.

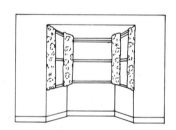

Curtains arranged within the bay.

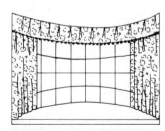

Short curtains and pinch-pleated pelmet on a bow window.

Curtains can change the look of windows

Style of room

1. Velvet or brocade curtains suit an old house with a formal setting. Chintzes, cretonnes and gingham will look well in a room with a lived-in look.
2. Large prints and designs are only suitable for large rooms and large windows. Choose plain fabric or small patterns for small rooms and small windows.
3. The curtains should blend with the overall design of the room. Curtains can match the bedspread or chair covers; however, in a small room it is best to have curtains which are the same colour as the walls. As this does not break up the wall area, it makes the room look bigger.
4. Modern designs look well in modern rooms.

Amount of wear

Delicate fabrics such as velvet and satin brocades are unsuitable for a room which gets a lot of wear. Be practical. If children are using the room, choose patterned fabrics in easy-care, stain resistant materials. Avoid pastels, plain fabrics, and those which need dry cleaning.

Purpose of curtains

Curtains are used for several reasons: to decorate, to ensure privacy, to insulate, to shut out light. If the room is cold or facing north, heavy, interlined curtains will improve insulation. If windows are double-glazed, less emphasis need be placed on insulating qualities. Long curtains will provide better insulation than short curtains. On the other hand, if there are radiators under a window, short curtains must be used. Most people consider long curtains more attractive. This must be weighed against the fact that they are also far more expensive. Net curtains give privacy by day, but not at night when lights are on. If blinds are use, mock curtains may suffice.

Money available

Obviously, if money is no object, one has unlimited choice of fabrics and styles. If it is necessary to economise, consider the following points.

1. Avoid skimping on fullness: it is better to buy a cheap fabric and allow plenty of fullness, than to have skimpy curtains in expensive fabric.
2. Kitchen, bathroom and some bedroom curtains can be made from cheap furnishing remnants or dress fabrics, such as gingham, and left unlined.
3. Cafe curtains which come halfway up a window provide some privacy for less cost.

Other points

1. Consider the outside appearance of the windows — all the curtains on one side of the house should be lined in the same colour to provide uniformity from the outside.
2. Lined curtains hang better, provide better insulation, keep out more light and protect the curtain fabric from the sunlight.
3. *Shrinkage:* most furnishing fabrics shrink a great deal — often up to 10 per cent. Allow four centimetres per metre extra when calculating curtain materials, to allow for shrinkage. If possible, wash fabric before making up. Even so, allow an extra deep temporary hem at first, and only attach lining at the heading, in case lining and fabric shrink unequally.
4. *Fading:* most good quality curtain materials are resistant to fading, but they will fade in time. Fading is not so obvious when pastels are used, and linings also help prevent fading.
5. *Washability:* when buying, check whether fabric may be washed. Velvets and heavy fabrics usually need to be dry cleaned. If in doubt, dry cleaning is safer.
6. Look at the fabric in both daylight and electric light when deciding on colour.
7. Extra material is required if a large pattern has to be matched.

Curtain tracks and fittings

A wide range of curtain tracks is available, depending on the style of curtain heading required. Most are sold with a set of runners and end stops. Hooks and heading tape are sold separately. Tracks may be made from metal or some form of plastic or nylon. Plastic tracks are cleaner, do not rust or jam, are more pliable and quiet.

Types of tracks

1. simple T shaped exposed track — suitable for fitting to wall or ceiling;
2. 'no pelmet' track — suitable for deep headings;
3. tracks equipped to take a pelmet rail;
4. overlapping tracks and cord drawn tracks;
5. wooden, brass and nylon rods and rings.

Type of heading

1. gathering heading, using 2 cm wide cotton or terylene tape;
2. pencil pleats, using a stiff deep tape which pulls curtains into pleats;

3. pinch pleats, using a deep tape together with special three-pronged hooks;
4. scalloped heading, used with poles and rings.

Pelmets

These are less common now. They help to hide old-fashioned fittings. There are several types of pelmet.
1. wooden constructed pelmet;
2. gathered frill;
3. covered buckram;
4. draped heading.

Lining

The chief lining fabric is cotton sateen, available in many colours. It is safer to stick to neutral colours so that all linings will match. White lining must be used with white curtains. Insulated lining is backed with a metallic finish.

Linings are usually sewn into the curtain tape. Special tapes allow linings to be attached separately and removed for easy washing.

Interlining is a thick flannelette-type fabric which gives the curtain extra body and improves the draping and insulating properties of the curtain.

Measuring for curtains

1. Fix the track according to manufacturer's instructions.
2. Measure the length of the track — not the window.
3. The width of the curtaining should be two to two-and-a-half times the width of the track, plus extra for side turnings and seams. If the window is two metres wide, curtaining must be at least four metres wide — preferably more.
4. Measure the fall of the curtain, i.e. distance from track to 25 mm from the floor or to the sill. Add 150 mm-200 mm for heading and hem, and extra for matching and shrinkage.
5. To calculate amount of fabric, divide required width by width of fabric. Most furnishing fabrics are 122 cm wide. The answer is the number of lengths required. Multiply this by the fall of the curtain plus extras for hem etc. The answer is the number of metres required.

Making curtains

1. Cut material to individual lengths.
2. Sew seams, matching pattern carefully if necessary.
3. Turn in side hems and slip stitch in place. Press.
4. Machine sew lining seams and press.
5. Place curtain flat on table or floor.

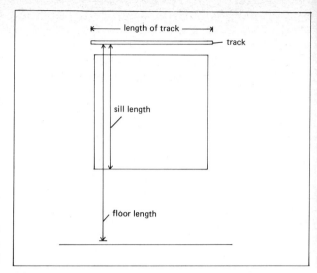

Measuring a window for curtains

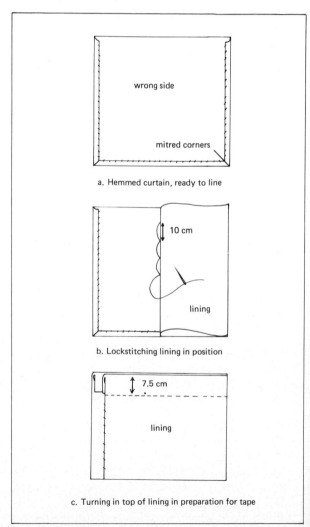

a. Hemmed curtain, ready to line

b. Lockstitching lining in position

c. Turning in top of lining in preparation for tape

Making curtains

114

6. Lay lining over it, wrong sides together, lining lying 1 cm below top of curtain.
7. Press down a 2 cm turning on top of curtain.
8. Cut tape to fit curtain, allowing 3 cm turnings. Lay curtain tape over the turning 1 cm from top. Turn back the ends.
9. Tack and machine sew top and bottom edges of tape, and ends. (Lining is included in machining.)
10. Lock stitch lining in place if curtains are large.
11. Insert hooks, pull gathering threads, and test hang for a few days to allow curtain to drop.
12. Pin up hem, mitre corners, turn under or neaten, and slip stitch.
13. Slip stitch lining to sides of curtain.
14. Machine stitch lining hem.

Note: Press seams and hems at each stage of making.

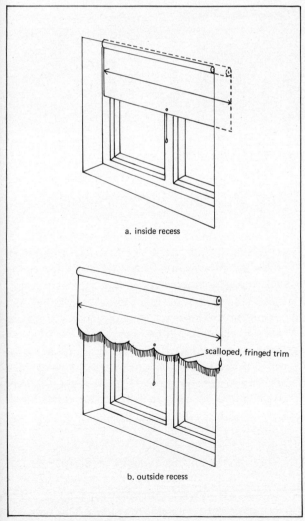

a. inside recess

b. outside recess

scalloped, fringed trim

Placing a blind correctly

BLINDS

Blinds may be used as an alternative to curtains or for windows in recesses which are difficult to curtain. They can also be used to block off storage areas, instead of doors.

1. Roller blinds are usually made-to-measure. They can also be made at home with special kits. They are made from these fabrics: *holland* — a specially stiffened type of linen; *vinyl* — in various patterns and designs; *fabric* — specially treated and often part of a co-ordinating range of soft furnishings, wallpapers and blinds. Care of roller blinds is simple: just wipe with a damp cloth. Trimming may need to be washed.
2. Venetian blinds are made from enamelled aluminium slats; various colours are available. They can be adjusted to allow large or small amounts of light to enter: this is useful in sunny rooms, where they protect furnishings and prevent glare.
   Care: dust regularly — avoid letting them get too dirty. Clean with a damp cloth, wrung out of warm water and detergent. Oil moving parts occasionally. These blinds are difficult and time-consuming to clean. Special gadgets are available to simplify cleaning.
3. Vertical blinds are made from textured plastic.

LOOSE COVERS

These protect upholstery from wear and damage. They may be used when upholstered furniture has become shabby, to give it a new lease of life.

Loose covers should be attractive, dirt resistant and washable. Cotton, linen type fabrics, and synthetics are all used for making loose covers. Cretonne and linen union are used to make traditional, floral chair covers. Tailored covers are usually made from linens and repps. Ready-made covers are available in knitted stretch-nylon. They can fit a wide variety of standard chairs and settees.

Loose covers can be made to measure — an expensive job. The making often costs more than the cost of the large amount of the fabric needed to make them. They can also be made at home. If so, great care should be taken to measure carefully and fit covers at each stage. Whether it's a professional or do-it-yourself job, it is a wise precaution to wash the length of fabric before cutting it out, to eliminate excessive shrinkage.

Good furniture set against a plain but pleasing decor (Barnaby's Picture Library)

CUSHIONS

Cushions can add much to the comfort and style of a room. They vary enormously in size, from dainty smocked cushions, through tie-on chair cushions, scatter cushions, to giant floor cushions and sag-bags, which are used mainly by young people instead of more conventional seating.

Almost any fabric can be used to cover a cushion, provided it is closely woven and washable. Inner covers should also be made from a washable fabric, unless down or feathers are used for filling, in which case down-proof cambric must be used.

Fillings for cushions

1. down or feathers;
2. kapok — a cotton wool type filling;
3. synthetics: terylene fibre filling — soft and washable; foam — in sheet form in varying sizes and thicknesses, or in foam pieces which are slightly lumpy;
4. chopped up tights or rags make a satisfactory and economical filling: make sure they are clean and dry.

Care of Soft Furnishings

1. Never allow them to become too dirty before cleaning.
2. Vacuum curtains and upholstery regularly to remove dust and grit. Use the special upholstery nozzle on the vacuum cleaner. Do not forget the tuck-in edges and crevices of upholstered furniture.
3. Clean regularly. It is essential to know the composition of fabrics, so that the most appropriate care and cleaning will be used.
4. Washables should be washed gently in lukewarm water, rinsed at least twice and only squeezed if they are meant to be ironed. Iron slightly damp, stretching fabric and seams to reduce shrinkage.
5. Drip-dry fabrics should not be squeezed. Only iron if necessary.
6. Have curtains dry cleaned when necessary.
7. Upholstery should be sponged lightly, rinsed and allowed to dry — never rub, and do not over-wet.
8. Curtain rails should be dusted now and then with a cloth dampened with silicone polish. This prevents rusting.

116

The plants give character to this modern lounge (Barnaby's Picture Library)

QUESTIONS/CHAPTER 11

1. Discuss the importance of design in modern furniture. What points should influence your choice when buying the following:
   (a) a dining-room suite;
   (b) a living-room suite.
   State the advantages and disadvantages of second-hand furniture.

2. Discuss soft furnishings under the following headings:
   (a) choice;
   (b) suitability for purpose;
   (c) resistance to fading;
   (d) care and cleaning;
   (e) durability.
   What is meant by linen union?

3. Compare the use of wood and plastics in the manufacture of furniture. Refer to:
   (a) appearance;   (d) ease of cleaning;
   (b) durability;   (e) cost.
   (c) function;
   Explain the term laminated plastic.

4. Write a note on modular 'unit' furniture systems for use in bedrooms or living-rooms. Refer to:
   (a) types;   (d) cost;
   (b) structure;   (e) materials used.
   (c) use
   Describe how to care for and clean a wood-veneered unit storage system.

5. Discuss the use of curtains in the interior decoration of a home.
   Compare curtains with blinds as a method of window covering.
   List the types of curtain tracks and headings available today.

12.
Interior decorating

One of the nicest stages in planning your home and the one in which you can most enjoy using your imagination, is that of planning the design and colour scheme of each room.

A home should reflect the personality of its owner, it should be comfortable, attractive and easy to keep clean. You can achieve this expensively by buying luxury items of furniture and soft furnishings, or economically, by keeping an eye open for bargains in shops and furniture auctions; but particularly when it comes to painting and decorating, you can learn how to do it yourself.

Do remember that your house is first of all a home. Many house-proud people can manage to make their guests ill at ease by placing undue emphasis on appearance and not enough on a friendly atmosphere.

ROOM PLANNING

Before you rush out to buy furniture or wallpaper, think first about the use and purpose of each room.

1. *Use of space*

As houses become more compact, there is a greater emphasis on using the available space to the best possible advantage. The layout of a home must be flexible to allow for the many activities which take place in it — eating, cooking, sleeping, studying, relaxing, hobbies etc. A large house will probably have space for these activities. If space is limited, as in smaller houses, problems may arise. Open-plan arrangements are rarely practical: they allow little privacy and are difficult to heat efficiently.

An airy room in a country cottage (Barnaby's Picture Library)

2. *Size of rooms*

The size of each room has a bearing on how it will be furnished and decorated. Small rooms will need smaller pieces of furniture, small patterns, less heavy texture so that they do not look cluttered. A large room allows more scope in decorating but will be costly to heat.

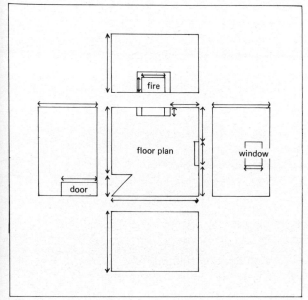

Scale plan of a room

3. *The function of each room*

Many rooms in today's homes are used for several activities. A living-room might be used for reading, sewing, studying, watching TV or playing games. If necessary, most rooms can be used for several purposes. A bedroom could double as a study or sewing room; a bathroom and laundry could be combined; or a dining.room could be used as a playroom.

4. *Changing family lifestyles*

The lifestyle and needs of a family will change from time to time. A young family will need practical, childproof finishes in most rooms, and one room where children can play in safety without worrying about whether they damage furniture or floors. Older or childless couples won't have this problem. Teenagers will need somewhere quiet for study e.g. a desk in a corner of their bedroom. A family which entertains a lot will require ample living-room and dining space. If you frequently put up friends and relations you will need an extra bedroom, or else the living-room will have to double as a spare guest room, using a convertible sofa.

A well-planned room should
1. be comfortable and visually attractive;
2. take advantage of the architectural features of the room;
3. be planned to make full use of all available space;
4. have a reliable source of heating;
5. have an efficient system of lighting and ventilation;
6. have adequate storage space;
7. have sufficient furniture for the purpose of the room but not so much that it appears cluttered;
8. be arranged to allow ease of access to each area in the room;
9. be easy to keep clean and tidy.

ARRANGING THE FURNITURE

● *Existing fixtures and fittings,* such as doors, windows and fireplace, must be taken into account when planning the arrangement of the futniture. These and wall-mounted radiators may restrict greatly the amount of wall space against which you may place furniture.

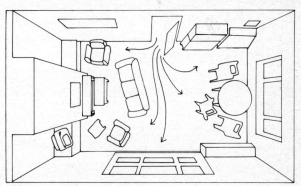

Traffic flow in a living-room

● *Traffic patterns* must also be considered. It should be possible to walk to every part of the room without difficulty. You will find that regular journeys are made between doors and windows, doors and fireplace, and so on. These must be left free of furniture, lamps and trailing flexes which might otherwise get in the way and cause accidents.
● *If a room is small,* keep furniture around the walls as far as possible; this leaves a greater expanse of floor and makes the room appear larger.
● Group *furniture and fitments* according to the activities which take place in the room. Large rooms can be divided into 'areas'; for example in a living-

room you might have a dining area, a play corner, a hi-fi centre and a conversation area, e.g. comfortable chairs often grouped around a fireplace. In bedrooms there is usually a sleeping area (bed and bedside tables), dressing area (wardrobe, mirrors and possibly a shower or washbasin), and a make-up area (dressing-table and mirror) — this may also be situated in a bathroom *en suite*.

● Consider *style and proportion.* The furniture and furnishings of a room should complement each other and suit the style or period of the room. Pieces should be in proportion so that a balance of size, width and height is achieved. For example one enormous piece of furniture in a room filled with small delicate items might look out of place.

A symmetrical arrangement of furniture and accessories is easier on the eye and produces a balance of size, width and height. Pictures and other accessories, carefully placed, can do much to correct an unbalanced arrangement in a room.

A symmetrically arranged room

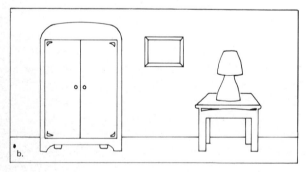

Obvious lack of proportion and balance

● *Emphasis:* many rooms can look dull and uninteresting, particularly if they are decorated in neutral colours. The introduction of a strongly contrasting colour, for example in a lamp, cushion or other accessory, can create much-needed emphasis which 'lifts' the room. Clever use of lighting creating pools of light and shade can have the same effect and give another dimension and greater depth to the arrangement.

A PLANNING FILE

A planning file saves you time measuring and re-measuring room and fittings and can be carried to the shops whenever you wish to match up colour schemes etc.

Buy a ring binder or keep a file which contains all the details and samples relating to each room. It would usually contain:

1. squared paper for drawing out room plans;
2. steel tape measure for measuring room, windows, etc.;
3. ruler and coloured pencils;
4. paint charts;
5. wallpaper samples;
6. soft furnishing samples;
7. carpet samples;
8. furniture pamphlets;
9. price lists;
10. paint and wallpaper calculations (amount of paint/paper required for each room).

A scale plan of each room should be drawn to include alcoves, doors, windows, radiators, plumbing fixtures, power points and electrical fixtures, fireplace and any existing built-in units or cupboards. List the length, breadth and height of the room and measurements of fixtures such as windows and doors. As well as drawing a floor plan of the room, a scale plan (elevation) of each of the four walls should be made, showing the position of doors, windows, etc., and their measurements. Small blocks can be cut to scale to represent furniture; these can be moved about on the plan until the best arrangement is reached.

INTERIOR DECORATION

Doing up a room or a home is an expensive operation which should be carefully planned. The furnishings and materials used in decorating are not cheap, and as it is likely they will be expected to last for years, they should be durable, easy to clean and well designed. As money is often limited, it is worth while shopping around for good value. It makes sense to do up a house or flat in stages to a high standard, rather than attempt the whole lot at once, and end up with a second-class result.

COLOUR

Colour plays a major part in creating the mood of a room. A good sense of colour is an important asset to the home decorator. Many people lack this sense — for these it is safer to keep to pale or neutral shades, with slight touches of colour here and there.

The colour wheel

Twelve colours make up the colour wheel. The basic or primary colours are red, yellow and blue. These form a triangle on the colour wheel. The secondary colours are a mixture of equal parts of two primaries, e.g. yellow and red = orange; blue and yellow = green; red and blue = violet.

When each primary colour is mixed with one of the secondary colours beside it, six intermediate or tertiary colours are produced, e.g. yellow-green, blue-green and so on.

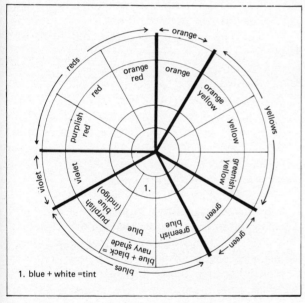

1. blue + white = tint

The colour wheel

Several schemes can be worked out using this wheel.

1. **Triad scheme:** using three colours which divide the wheel into three sections, e.g. green, orange and violet or green-yellow, blue-violet and red-orange. This scheme tends to be bright and gaudy. One colour should dominate; the others should be toned down and used in small amounts.

2. **Complementary scheme:** using a pair of colours exactly opposite each other on the wheel, e.g. yellow and violet, red and green. One should dominate, the other be used as an accent. Remember, opposite colours produce a very bright effect.

3. **Analogous or adjacent scheme:** based on two or more colours side by side on the wheel, e.g. orange, orange-yellow, and yellow. Textures and intensities of colour should vary.

4. **Monochromatic scheme:** various tones of a single hue (colour) can be very effective if different textures and patterns are used. A little accent colour may be needed. *Example:* pale cream walls and curtains; honey carpet; beige furniture; accent — orange/yellow lamps.

Other colour terms

Cool colours: those on the blue/green side of the colour wheel, e.g. blue, green, blue-purple and grey. Use in sunny room on the south side of a house.

Warm colours: those on the red/orange side of the colour wheel, e.g. red, orange, yellow, also brown, beige, warm pinks and purples. Use in cold rooms, e.g. on the north side of a house. Warm colours give a homely, welcoming feel to a room, but used over a large area can be tiring on the eyes.

Neutral colours: these provide a good background on which to use other colours, e.g. cream, grey, beige, brown. Black and white, although not considered colours, can be used as a background or accent for most other colours.

Pastels: very pale, soft shades of blue, green, pink, lilac and yellow; popular in nurseries and bedrooms where a feminine atmosphere is required.

Hue: a basic colour, e.g. red, yellow, blue.

Tone: a basic colour which has been lightened (by mixing with white) or darkened (by mixing with black).

Intensity: a measure of the brightness or dullness of a colour — mixing in other colours, especially grey, will lower the intensity of a colour.

Harmony: when colours go well together (i.e. they do not clash) they are said to harmonise. *Examples:* a group of warm colours; a group of cool colours; various tones of one colour, e.g. shades of brown; neutral colours.

THE EFFECT OF COLOUR

Colour can appear to alter the shape or size of a room. This factor can be used to advantage in rooms which are badly proportioned. It can also increase the sense of space.

1. Bright colours and dark shades of various colours advance: they make a wall seem nearer, a ceiling seem lower, a room smaller.

2. Pale colours or colours of low intensity retreat: they sink into the background, making a room seem larger or a ceiling higher.

3. Pale colours also reflect light, especially white and cream. Too much white may create glare; so off-white in a matt finish is preferable to pure white, especially white gloss.
4. Strong dark colours, e.g. brown and navy, absorb light, making an area darker.
5. Strong bright colours, e.g. red and orange, are stimulating and tiring on the eyes; they should be used sparingly.
6. Greens, blues and pastels are restful colours and ideal for bedrooms.

A small room or house can appear to be larger if pale colours are used throughout, say white, cream or pale grey on walls, ceiling, woodwork with a slightly darker shade of carpet and furniture. Accent colours can be introduced to brighten up each area.

Colour schemes
Consider the house as a whole when planning a colour scheme. Each room should blend with the next without any violent contrasts. The different areas should relate to one another. This can be achieved by using the same background colour throughout: carpet the house throughout with a neutral carpet, or paint the complete interior of a house beige or off-white. Each room should have a dominant colour — other colours should provide an accent or contrast.

Experiment with swatches of colour before deciding on a permanent scheme. It is safer and more economical to keep carpets and furniture in fairly *neutral shades*, so that it is possible to change the colour scheme later without having to replace these expensive furnishings. Many colours look different in artificial light. When selecting carpets, paint or fabrics, look at them in both natural and various forms of artificial light, under fluorescent and filament lamps.

When choosing wall colours, consider *the size and the mood* of the room — small rooms look best painted in pale or neutral shades. It is possible to be more adventurous with colour in a large room. A study needs a calm, unobtrusive colour scheme, such as a brown monochromatic scheme. A playroom can afford to have bright, vibrant colours. A bedroom should have restful colours — pastels, blues, greens, neutrals.

Ugly features, such as radiators, badly proportioned doors and other fixtures, can be disguised by painting them the same colour as their background. *Good features,* decorative cornices and windows can be highlighted by painting in a contrasting colour. See sample colour schemes, p. 000.

The *aspect* of each room, i.e. whether it faces north or south, has an important bearing on its colour scheme. North-facing rooms get little sun and need to be 'cheered up' with bright warm colours e.g. peach, yellow, pink. Sunny south-facing rooms can use cool colours e.g. green. Rooms with little light are best decorated in white or pastels.

PATTERN

A pattern is a decorative design which may form part of a fabric or a surface — e.g. woven cloth, stonework or wooden floors — or be superimposed upon it. Pattern, which may be found in wallcoverings, curtains, upholstery and floor coverings, varies in size from tiny, almost invisible designs to large, floral or abstract patterns.

Pattern is important when planning interior decoration. The type and amount varies according to the style of the room and current trends. Exercise great care when buying patterned fabrics, carpets and wall-coverings. They can create a fussy, untidy effect if badly used.

Guide to using pattern
1. Avoid using too much pattern.
2. Pattern, like colour, can appear to change the shape of a room. Horizontal designs widen a room; vertical designs increase the apparent height of the room.
3. Large, bold patterns are more suitable for large rooms. Many are tiring on the eye and should be used sparingly, on one wall or in an alcove.
4. Small patterns, e.g. Liberty prints, look well in small rooms. The design may be lost in a large room.
5. In a room with many doors and windows, patterned wallcovering may make the room look cluttered.
6. Avoid using more than two patterns, as they are difficult to match successfully. Matching and coordinating wall-covering, fabric and blinds are now available to make the job easier.
7. Use of pattern can do much to create an atmosphere in a room. Chintz, linen union, and Liberty prints, give a room a traditional, 'country cottage' style; glass and chrome, with abstract designs, create a modern look.

TEXTURE

This is the thickness, roughness or feel of an object. Rooms may combine many different textures; for example, thick, textured tweeds and carpets with smooth walls, paintwork and glass. Textures provide an interesting third dimension to a room.

Smooth finishes include glass, mirrors, gloss paint, marble, vinyl and other plastics, leather, metal, wood, and ceramics (tiles and vases).

Textured finishes include carpets (particularly with long pile), rugs, tweeds and other upholstery fabrics, most curtain fabrics (velvet, slubbed silk, linen, hessian), flocked wallcoverings, brick and stonework, carved furniture, rough ceramics, woven or macramé hangings.

Guide to using texture

1. Never use all smooth or all textured finishes in one area: half and half is usual.
2. Smooth surfaces usually reflect sound and light. Too many smooth surfaces make a room cold and uninviting, as well as producing glare and noise.
3. Textured surfaces absorb sound and light. Many textured surfaces in a room will make it quiet and possibly cosy, but will also darken the room, giving it a crowded or perhaps a claustrophobic atmosphere.
4. Textured surfaces are often difficult to clean. Smooth surfaces are used extensively in kitchens and bathrooms, as they are easy to keep clean and hygienic.
5. Textured surfaces appear to make a room smaller.

CONCLUSION

Colour, pattern and texture should never be used in equal proportions. Use a main colour (background) and a subsidiary (accent); a main texture (shaggy carpet) and a subsidiary (upholstered furniture); a main pattern (curtains) and a subsidiary (cushions).

The clever use of accessories can add colour, pattern and texture to the most basic room. The accessories can range from family photographs, cushions and flowers to books, paintings and light fittings.

Pleasant decor in a modern front hall (Barnaby's Picture Library)

REDECORATING

PAINT

Paint is necessary to protect surfaces and to improve their appearance. Wood and metal must be painted regularly to prevent damage by rotting or rust. Paint is a thick, liquid substance, which may be oil or water based. It is chiefly composed of:

pigment		binder		solvent
or	+	or	+	or
powder		medium		thinner

1. *Pigment:* both natural and synthetic pigments are used. These give the paint its colour and ability to cover. Lead, which was used commonly in the past, is not contained in most paints now, because of its toxicity. Beware of using old toys and furniture, which may be painted with lead paint, if you have a baby or young child who is likely to put these things into his mouth.
2. *Binder* may be linseed oil or resin, and often contains added plastic substances.
3. *Solvent:* in gloss and oil paints, the solvent is white spirit or turpentine; in emulsions, it is water. The purpose of the solvent is to help spread the paint. After application, the solvent evaporates quickly.
4. Many paints now include a *drier* which speeds up the drying of the paint.

In the *manufacture* of paint, the pigment and binder are mixed together by a process known as grinding. This ensures that they will not separate again. The other ingredients are then blended in.

Paint is usually sold in tins of the following sizes: 250 ml, 500 ml, one litre, 2½ litre, 5 litre.

WATER BASED PAINTS

1. *Distemper* is a cheap paint, often used for ceilings and walls. It is rarely used now and has been almost completely replaced by emulsion paints. It had several *disadvantages*: it was non-washable, had a tendency to flake, and had to be completely washed off before repainting.
2. *Emulsion paint* consists of a plastic type binder and colour pigments dissolved in water. Emulsion paint is only used for interiors. Available in matt, silk or gloss finishes, it is mainly used for walls and ceilings. Emulsion gloss is ideal for radiators, as it has no odour. Two coats will usually obliterate previous paintwork. Emulsion can be washed with care, but it will become shiny with repeated washing. *Advantages:* easily applied, little smell, quick drying, brushes easily cleaned in water.
3. *Acrylic and vinyl emulsions* contain acrylic or vinyl binders which give them a particularly hard-wearing finish. They are available, in lustre or eggshell finish (neither glossy nor matt — more like satin in appearance) and in floss finish. These emulsions can be washed successfully. *Advantages:* easy to apply, easy to clean, hard wearing.
4. *Stone paints* are a form of emulsion paint containing powdered stone or cement. They may also include colour pigments, plastics (for durability) and silicones (to give a waterproof finish to walls). Stone paint helps to mask cracks in walls. It is used on the exterior, or brick and masonry. Many stone paints have a textured finish. Although this paint is expensive, it is long lasting. Depending on quality, the finish should last from five to fifteen years.

OIL BASED PAINTS

A. *Gloss paints* contain colour pigments, a binder such as linseed oil, and a solvent — usually turpentine or white spirit. Drying occurs when the solvent evaporates and the other ingredients harden to form a protective skin on the surface. Gloss paint is suitable for woodwork, metal, and small areas of wall. It is useful in kitchens and bathrooms, as it resists moisture.

Advantages
1. extremely tough and hard wearing;
2. very easy to clean;
3. can be used indoors or outdoors.

Disadvantages
1. more expensive;
2. gloss enamels need an undercoat (gloss lacquers do not);
3. more difficult to apply smoothly than emulsion;
4. not suitable for large areas, as it tends to produce glare;
5. can aggravate condensation;
6. leaves a strong smell after painting;
7. it is essential that surfaces are absolutely dry before using gloss paint as it forms an impervious layer when it hardens, through which evaporation cannot take place — the result is flaking and blistering.

B. *Eggshell or lustre finish:* some manufacturers produce an oil based paint with a less glossy appearance. This is also hard wearing and ideal for kitchens, woodwork, walls and painted furniture, where a high gloss is not required.

C. **_Polyurethane paint_** (containing polyuirethane binder) is a particularly durable paint which dries very quickly. Like all paints which dry quickly, it is difficult to apply and needs practice. It is available in gloss and eggshell finishes. It is not usually necessary to use an undercoat. Polyurethane paint is ideal for anywhere subjected to continuous hard wear: skirtings, radiators, doors, kitchen cupboards, shelves, children's playrooms, furniture, and toys.

D. **_Lacquer_** is a very glossy, heat resistant paint.

E. **_Floor and furniture stains:_** see chapter 11.

Paint systems

It is usual to paint metal and woodwork in three stages:
1. primer
2. undercoat
3. top coat

The instructions on the can of top coat will indicate whether one or both base coats are necessary. It is preferable to use the recommended primer and undercoat, i.e. one specially designed for use with the particular gloss paint.

A Primer is necessary when the material to be painted is bare, i.e. it has not been covered before or has been stripped to the original surface. A primer adheres well to a bare surface and provides a 'key' for subsequent coats. It also helps to seal wood and prevents rusting in metals. Primers are usually designed either for wood or for metal surfaces. All-purpose primers are also available: these are suitable for both wood and metal.

An **_undercoat_** should be close to the colour of the final coat. It helps obliterate previous colour and also provides a key for the final coat. If the previous colour contrasts strongly, two undercoats may be needed.

NEW PAINTS AND FINISHES

A. **_Thixotropic or non-drip paints_** are available in gloss, emulsion or eggshell.

Advantages
1. They do not drip or splash when applied — ideal for ceilings.
2. They are thick, and therefore rarely need an undercoat.
3. The paint does not separate in the can.
4. The paint is simple to apply: the friction used when painting melts the jelly and it spreads easily.

Disadvantages
1. Colours cannot be mixed — as this paint should not be stirred.
2. They do not go as far an non-thixotropic paints.

B. **_Heat resisting paints_** containing silicones are ideal for radiators

C. **_Textured paints_** contain plastic or synthetic fibres which give a textured finish.

D. **_Aerosols_** are hard-wearing enamel and lacquer-finish paints available in aerosol form. They are ideal for small areas; for awkward items like chairs, carved furniture and cane-work; and for touching up shabby kitchen equipment.

When using, prepare surface in usual way, dust down well, protect surrounding area with newspapers. Any parts of the object which are not to be sprayed should be covered in masking tape. Cover nose and mouth to avoid inhaling paint or fumes.

EQUIPMENT FOR PAINTING

Depending on the job, you will need all or some of these: brushes, rollers, bucket, masking tape, cloths, paint, primer, sandpaper, paint stripper, brush cleaner, ladder, scraper (2.5-7.5 cm), blow torch, filler (Polyfilla).

Brushes: use good quality bristle brushes — these are easier to use than man-made fibres. They should have an even tapered edge with no stray hairs. It is false economy to use cheap brushes — the bristles are short and thin, and they wear out quickly. A set of four brushes should suffice for most painting jobs: 2.5 cm; 5 cm; 7.5 cm; and 13 cm.

Cleaning brushes
1. Wipe brushes over a newspaper several times until surplus paint is removed.
2. Immerse brushes used for oil-based paints in white spirit, turpentine or brush cleaner. Clean thoroughly.
3. Wash brushes used for water-based paints in warm soapy water.
4. Both should be rinsed well in warm water and hung up to dry completely.
5. Apply vaseline to metal ferrule (holder) for longterm storage.
6. Wrap brush carefully in newspaper, so that bristles are lying straight.

How to store a paintbrush overnight

sandpaper

1. Prepare surfaces
primer
2. Apply primer
3. Undercoat
4. Sand down to create key
5. Top coat

Painting a wooden surface

7. If a brush is required again in one or two days, it can be left suspended in a jar of water, making sure the bristles are not resting on the bottom.
8. A brush which is well cleaned after use and handled carefully will last a long time.
9. Badly hardened paint brushes may be restored by steeping in paint stripper.

Rollers: these are ideal for painting large surfaces (e.g. walls) quickly. They are available in lambswool, foam and mohair. The latter is most suitable for gloss paint and flat surfaces. Worn out roller sleeves may be replaced. A matching paint tray is usually sold with each roller. Clean as above — points 1, 2, 3 and 4.

PAINTING A ROOM

For a professional finish, do not skimp on preparation.

1. *Prepare room:* remove curtains, blinds, and as much furniture as possible. Take up carpets or cover them with polythene, old sheets or newspaper. Cover large furniture with dust sheets.
2. *Wear suitable protective clothing.* Use old clothes and protect hair with an old cap.
3. *Prepare surfaces:*
   a. *Fill* cracks and holes in wood (wood filler); and in walls (general filler)
      or use an all-purpose filler, e.g. Polyfilla.
   b. When dry *sand down* with sandpaper. Brush down.
   c. *Wash* ceiling, walls and woodwork with warm water and detergent. Rinse and allow to dry. The room should be free of dust during painting.

   d. *Sand down gloss paint* to provide a key. Badly *flaking* paint should be removed with a *chemical stripper* (Polystrippa) or a blowtorch and a scraper. Use carefully, as both stripper and blowtorch can be dangerous.
   e. *Apply suitable primer* to new wood or metal and size newly plastered walls. Take care: most primers are poisonous.

4. *Paint in this order:* ceiling, walls woodwork.

How to Paint

1. Read instructions on tin for information on whether to stir or dilute.
2. Apply primer if necessary. Allow to dry.
3. Apply one or two undercoats as required.
4. When dry, apply final coat. Dip brush or roller in paint (not too much) and start painting in up and down strokes, then paint across in strokes and finally lay off paint in light up and down strokes to wipe out brush marks. When a roller is used, a small 5 cm brush is used to paint the edges, as the roller cannot paint into corners.
5. Using a stepladder, roller paint ceiling or wall in 50 cm squares, starting in top right hand corner (if right handed). If possible, work away from the window and work down in 50 cm squares.
6. Continue to paint in sections of 50 cm, blending joins well until the whole wall is covered.

7. Doors: paint frame the day before, if possible. Flush doors — open door and paint as for walls. Panelled doors — paint edges first, then mouldings, then four panels, finally working from top to bottom the area around the panels.
8. Windows: paint frame the day before. Leave window open when painting and drying. Use masking tape to avoid getting paint on the glass. Work from top to bottom, starting with sections nearest the glass and finishing with the wider edges.

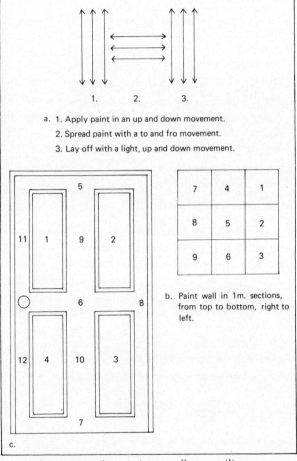

a. 1. Apply paint in an up and down movement.
   2. Spread paint with a to and fro movement.
   3. Lay off with a light, up and down movement.

b. Paint wall in 1m. sections, from top to bottom, right to left.

c.

(a) Applying paint: (b) painting a wall or a ceiling: (c) painting sequence for a panelled door

Economy
1. Use paint sparingly to avoid 'sagging' and dribbles.
2. Transfer left-over paint into a container just large enough for it, e.g. a screw-top jar or tin.
3. Turn container upside down to form a seal at the lid.
4. Strain through a fine mesh, e.g. nylon tights, before re-use.
5. All paint should be stored in a cool, dry place. Remember many paints are highly inflammable.

WALLCOVERINGS

As walls make up the largest surface area in a room, the choice of wallcovering will influence the entire character of the room. Before buying wallcoverings consider the area in which they are to be used. Wallcoverings should be attractive, reasonably durable, and easy to clean. Wallcoverings introduce pattern and texture as well as colour. It is important to remember that the wallcovering should act as a background — not predominate. Wallcoverings are available in many colours, designs and finishes. Most papers are a standard length and width: 10.04 metres long and 524 mm wide. Some continental and hand printed wallcoverings come in different sizes. Check carefully before buying.

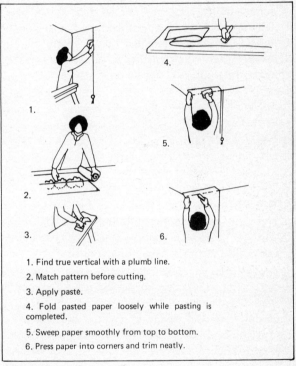

1. Find true vertical with a plumb line.
2. Match pattern before cutting.
3. Apply paste.
4. Fold pasted paper loosely while pasting is completed.
5. Sweep paper smoothly from top to bottom.
6. Press paper into corners and trim neatly.

Papering a wall

Manufacture
1. Strengthened paper is cut and covered with a base coat of pigment.
2. It is dried quickly.
3. Printing machines transfer the design onto the paper. Expensive papers may be block printed or silk screen printed, often by hand.
4. The paper may them be embossed by passing it through moulding rollers.
5. Washable papers may have a coating of resin applied.

Papers

1. **Lining paper** is thin white paper, used under wallpaper to improve the surface. It may be hung horizontally or vertically. The seams of the lining paper and the wallpaper should not lie on top of one another. It is possible to paint over lining paper, but a heavier paper, such as woodchip, is more suitable.

2. **General purpose papers** come in various thicknesses, colours and designs. Thin papers are difficult to hang, as they tear easily when moistened with paste. Very thick papers may also be difficult to use. If the design in a paper must be matched, extra paper will be required.

3. **Embossed papers** are printed papers into which the design is pressed, so that it stands out in relief. They provide an attractive textured effect and disguise minor wall blemishes. Care must be taken when hanging that they are not rubbed too heavily, which might flatten the design. They usually require matching. As they are heavy papers, a thick or heavy-duty paste should be used.

4. **Washable papers** have a surface coating of resin or silicone which gives some water resistance. In spite of their name they should not be washed — just gently wiped with a damp cloth. Too much water will damage the surface coating and printed design. They are less popular now, due to the availability of more practical vinyl wallcoverings.

5. **Woodchip paper** is an inexpensive paper made from high grade wood pulp and containing tiny wood chips. It provides a textured finish which disguises uneven walls and is usually painted over.

6. **Anaglypta** is a thick, embossed paper containing cotton fibres. It is durable and hard wearing and is available in high and low relief versions. It looks like plaster when applied and can be painted over. Ceilings lend themselves to decoration with this paper. When papering, the walls should be well prepared, sized and preferably lined. A heavy-duty paste should be allowed to soak into the paper for a few minutes before hanging.

7. **Flock** is a heavy quality paper with a design which resembles the pile of velvet. Some flock wallcoverings are made from good quality heavy paper with a design made from wool or cotton fibres. Modern flock coverings are made from vinyl with a nylon pile. These are easier to handle, are more durable, and can be washed. As most flock wallcoverings are of a traditional and rather large design, they look best in rooms decorated in 'period' style.

Vinyl wallcoverings

1. **Vinyl papers** are available in a wide variety of colours and designs. They are more expensive than wallpaper. They consist of a paper backing covered with a thin coat of PVC (polyvinyl chloride). They are durable, grease and waterproof, and easy to clean. They are easy to hang and are not as easily damaged when wet as wallpapers. They are ideal for heavy wear areas, e.g. bathrooms, stairs, kitchens, children's rooms. They withstand frequent washing — even scrubbing. An anti-fungicidal paste should be used when hanging vinyl.

2. **Ready-pasted vinyls** have a dried coating of paste on the paper. They are very easy to use. Instead of making up and brushing on paste (a messy job), the cut lengths of vinyl are immersed paste side out in a trough of water, steeped for a short time, drained and then hung.

3. **Nova mura** is a thick, but light, easy to handle wallcovering made of foamed polyethylene. The wall is pasted, and the wallcovering applied to it.

4. **Metallic finished vinyls** have an unusual reflective surface. As they are particularly striking, their use is best restricted to small areas.

Note: all wallcoverings with an impervious surface, such as vinyls, other plastics, and washable papers, should be applied using an antifungicidal heavy-duty paste.

To remove heavy-duty wallcoverings, score with a sharp instrument before wetting, to allow the moisture to penetrate through to the paper backing. Most vinyl papers can be peeled off without soaking, leaving the backing paper on the wall as a lining paper.

WALLCOVERINGS

Equipment

large pasting table	sharp scissors or
two stepladders	handyman's knife
bucket (for paste)	wallpaper brush
pasting brush	plumb line and pencil
steel ruler and T square	wallpaper
(for measuring and cutting)	suitable paste
	clean rags

Work in this order:
1. paint ceiling;
2. paint woodwork;
3. apply wallcovering.

Preparation

1. Wear old clothes.
2. Remove small furniture. Lift carpet or fold into centre of room. Move large furniture to centre of room and cover with dust sheet. Lay polythene or newspapers on floor.
3. Prepare wall. Soak old wallpaper well with warm water or a solution of wallpaper stripper. Scrape off carefully using stripping knife.
4. Wash down walls, and allow to dry.
5. Fill any cracks or holes with filler — allow to dry.
6. Sand down walls to remove bumps and pieces of paper.
7. Porous walls and newly plastered walls should be sized. *Size* is a watered-down solution of paste, i.e., 50% prepared paste, 50% water. Paint it over walls and allow to dry. It seals the wall and allows paper to move about more easily during hanging.
8. Light switches and other fittings should be removed before papering.
9. Paint ceiling and woodwork.

Adhesives

Standard — for light and medium weight papers.

Plus — for heavy papers.

Heavy-duty — for vinyls and other impervious papers (this contains a fungicide).

PVA — for sticking any overlaps of vinyl, and for sticking paperbacked fabrics. This is available in tubes.

Follow making up instructions exactly to avoid lumps.

Hanging the paper

1. Start papering either at the centre of a chimney breast or to the right of the window, working away from the light source. Halfway through, start from other side of window, to the left. This ensures that joins are in shadow.
2. Pattern matching: arrange pattern so that the top of the design starts at the ceiling, i.e. do not cut a large flower or medallion in two. Measure wall carefully. Measure paper, allowing 50 mm top and bottom for triming. Using set square, pencil and scissors, mark and cut the first length of paper. Lay on table, right side up. Match a second length of paper (there may be some waste). Measure and cut as above.
3. Place first length face down on table, with one edge overlapping the edge of the table. Paste liberally. Make sure the entire length is pasted, especially the edges. Paste from the centre of the paper to the edges. When the entire table length of paper is pasted, fold one end over to the centre, pull up the remaining paper, paste and fold in to meet in the centre.
4. Using a plumb line, make a vertical line about 50 cm from the window. Pencil a line 2 m long.
5. Fold paper over one arm, unfold top half and place edge of paper to pencil line, leaving 50 mm sticking up at top. Press in gently.
6. Brush paper from centre outwards to remove air bubbles.
7. Unfold lower fold, line up to pencil line and brush in. Avoid creases.
8. Press paper in close to skirting. Score with back of scissors, lift slightly and cut with scissors.
9. Trim top of paper.
10. Match and measure next strip, cut out, paste and hang. Continue until finished. Edges should meet in a *butt join,* not an overlap.
11. Use plumb line at corners — as they are rarely 'true'.
12. Paper neatly around doors, windows and light switches, making diagonal cuts to ensure a close fit on corners.

Buying wallcoverings

1. Make sure to buy a sufficient amount (see below).
2. All rolls should have the same batch number to ensure that the dyes match exactly.
3. Modern wallpapers are sold ready trimmed, i.e. with no 'selvedge' edge.

To calculate amount of wallpaper

Measure room from floor to ceiling to see how many lengths can be got from one roll. If it is 2.4 metres or under, four lengths can be cut from a roll, when there is no matching.

Find the perimeter of the room, i.e. measure all around the room. Four lengths x 524 mm wide = 2.096 m. Divide this figure into perimeter to find number of rolls or use this chart.

Remember to allow extra for matching patterns.

WALLPAPER CALCULATION CHART

Height
from skirting   Measurement round walls, including doors and windows — Number of rolls required

metres	8.53m	9.75m	10.97m	12.19m	13.41m	14.63m	15.85m	17.07m	18.29m	19.51m	20.73m	21.95m	23.16m
2.13 to 2.29	4	4	5	5	6	6	7	7	8	8	9	9	9
2.30 to 2.44	4	4	5	5	6	6	7	8	8	9	9	10	10
2.45 to 2.59	4	5	5	6	6	7	7	8	8	9	9	10	10
2.60 to 2.74	4	5	5	6	6	7	8	8	9	9	10	11	11
2.75 to 2.90	4	5	6	6	7	7	8	9	9	10	10	11	12
2.91 to 3.05	5	5	6	7	7	8	9	9	10	10	11	12	12
3.06 to 3.20	5	5	6	7	8	8	9	10	10	11	12	12	13

QUESTIONS/CHAPTER 12

1. Describe how to plan the layout of a living room. Describe the correct use of space and storage in room planning.
2. Write a brief note on the manufacture and composition of paint.
   List the steps to be followed when painting a room. Refer to:
   (a) preparation
   (b) method of painting
   (c) cleaning brushes
   List five modern paint finishes available to the home decorator and state suitable uses for each.
3. Describe how pattern and texture can be used with effect in the interior design of a room.
   List some textured wall finishes. Describe how one type is applied to a new wall.
4. Colour plays an important part in creating the mood of a room. Comment on this statement, making reference to:
   (a) effect of colour
   (b) suitable colour schemes
   Define the following terms relating to interior decor:
   (a) monochromatic scheme
   (b) primary colours
   (c) complementary scheme
   (d) neutrals
5. Name the essential equipment required for wallpapering a room.
   Describe briefly how to calculate the amount of wallpaper required for a room.
   List the precautions to be observed when applying a vinyl wallcovering.

13.
The reception rooms

THE HALL

Halls vary a lot in shape and size. A large hall looks well, but when space is limited it may be better to include the space in a larger living-room instead. As the hall is the first impression visitors will get of your home, make sure it is warm and welcoming. As it is subjected to lots of wear and tear, it should be decorated with hard-wearing, easy to clean furnishings.

Hall with hardwearing tiles (Topham)

TO MAKE A SMALL HALL SEEM BIGGER

1. Use pale colours, particularly white or cream.
2. Paint all the doors the same colour as the walls.
3. Mirrors on each side of the wall will make it seem wider.
4. Use a carpet with a small design.
5. Keep furniture to a minimum.

FLOOR

In the hall and stairs, use a hard-wearing, practical floor covering, as it gets the most punishing treatment of all the floors in the house. Avoid plain floor coverings and pale colours, as these show up dirt and stains and need constant cleaning. Choose a basic shade which will blend with the other rooms leading from it.

1. Carpets: use best quality Wilton or Axminster, often called 'contract quality'.
2. Parquet flooring looks well in a hall, with an open.tread stairs. It should be covered with several layers of polyurethane seal for ease of maintenance. It is expensive, but cheaper if you lay it yourself — and it lasts a lifetime.
3. Vinyl or quarry tiles are suitable for hallways where there is particularly hard wear, for example guesthouses. Vinyl is available in a wide range of colours.

WALLS

These should be hard-wearing and easy to clean.
1. Vinyl wall covering is ideal. Choose plain if you have a patterned carpet; you may like to use a pattern if the carpet is plain. A large design can safely be used if the hall is large.
2. Vinyl emulsion is a cheaper way of decorating a hall; pale colours in a small hall, using matching gloss on doors. A large hall might look well with a dark colour on walls and white paintwork to provide a contrast.

Colour scheme

If you use a neutral colour in a hall, it will be less likely to clash with colours in all the rooms opening from it. Beige and cream are practical but smart colours. Consider the colour scheme of the house as a whole and if possible have toning colours in all the rooms.

FURNITURE

Very little is needed.
1. If you do not have a cloakroom opening from the hall, a coat stand will be necessary.
2. A decorative mirror will provide a focal point.

3. A telephone table and seat will be required if the telephone is wired into the hall.
4. Storage: under the stairs the cloakroom, if it is large enough, can be fitted with shelves, cupboards and hangers for coats. It can also house the vacuum cleaner and similar pieces of equipment.
5. Optional: a traditional or modern umbrella stand; a small antique table on which to place a floral arrangement.

DOORS

Glazed doors introduce light to the hallway. Curtains or frosted glass give privacy. Invest in good quality lacquered door fittings, e.g. handle, letterbox. Cheap chrome fitments weather badly. Invest in a good mortice lock and door chain for security. Fit draught proofing around and underneath the door. A heavy lined curtain provides extra insulation in exposed areas.

Heating
Central heating, storage heaters or a gas or electric convector heater are all suitable. A cold hall will draw warm air from the heated rooms of a house.

Lighting
Invest in an attractive light fitting for the hall. The stairs should be well lit for safety. A landing light correctly placed will light the stairway also; if not, a third light will be needed to light the treads of the stairs. The light fittings in the hall, stairs and landing should tone with or match one another. A two-way switch is required for stair-lighting so that it can be switched on from upstairs or downstairs.

A strong weatherproof porch light will guide visitors safely to the door and deter burglars.

LIVING-ROOM

Before planning the arrangement of the living-room, consider the lifestyle of the family and the demands which will be made upon the room. The terms living-room or sitting room can have many different meanings. In some homes, the living-room is kept for entertaining and special occasions; while in others it is the centre of family activity. This latter kind of family room has many functions. It may be used for reading, listening to music, radio and TV, for quiet conversation, games and hobbies, study, needlework or other handcrafts. This type of all-purpose room will require careful planning, ample storage, and easily maintained surfaces. If the room is kept for 'best', it will not get quite such hard wear and more attention can be paid to appearance than to durability.

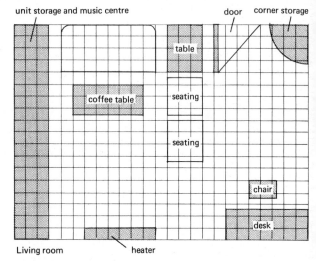

Plan for a livingroom

PLANNING

1. A living-room should be large and well-proportioned.
2. Windows should be large enough to provide plenty of natural light. Ideally they should overlook a garden.
3. If possible, avoid having the front door opening into the living-room — this allows little privacy.
4. The dining area, if any, should be near the door to the kitchen.
5. If the room is sufficiently large it can be divided into areas or centres for
   (a) conversation — a group of chairs arranged around a focal point, usually a fireplace or window with a view;
   (b) reading and sewing — a single comfortable chair, near a bookshelf, with a suitable light placed behind the chair;
   (c) games and hobbies — equipment for these could be stored in a cupboard, and a small table (or the dining table if a dining area is included) should be available;
   (d) music centre — a hi-fi and radio arrangement may take the form of a radiogram or be incorporated into a shelving unit; a piano provides homemade entertainment;
   (e) desk — for letter writing and dealing with household accounts.

Arrangement of furniture should lend itself to the function of the room. Small tables are desirable near each group of chairs to hold ashtrays and glasses. Chairs should be arranged so that they do not have to be moved for watching television.

FLOOR

The floor covering should be durable, warm, comfortable, attractive, and unobtrusive. It should not stain easily or show up dirt.

SUITABLE COVERINGS

1. Carpet or carpet tiles in a patterned design are practical. Avoid pale colours. Plain dark colours also show up dirt easily. Choose a heavy domestic quality, preferably a wool or wool mixture carpet with a twist pile for appearance and durability. Consider a carpet square; it can be turned to equalise wear. Wall-to-wall carpeting is more luxurious, absorbs noise, and acts as an insulator.
2. Wooden floors should be sanded and sealed. Parquet or block flooring is expensive but wears well. This also can be sealed.

Texture can be introduced by the use of scatter rugs which blend with the general decor.

WALLS

1. A hard-wearing vinyl wallpaper is ideal: it is durable and easy to clean.
2. Wood panelling looks well but is very expensive.
3. If money is scarce, walls can be painted in emulsion paint. A warm, dark colour will not show the dirt and extra paint can be kept for touching up now and then. Vinyl emulsion paints can withstand frequent washing.
4. Doors and windows should be painted with gloss paint — either white or the same shade as the walls.

Colour scheme

This is a very personal choice: it should be tasteful but practical. Restful colours, e.g. greens, blues, beige, are preferable. Traditional designs are homely and unlikely to date, whereas modern geometric designs can be unsettling. As it is likely there will be lots of detail from accessories such as pictures and ornaments, choose an unobtrusive design which will

A living-room to relax in (Barnaby's Picture Library)

Some colour schemes for a living-room

Basic colour	Walls	Curtains	Carpet	Settee	Chairs	Cushions
beige	pale beige	pale beige	dark brown	milk chocolate	yellow	white
Brown	white	chestnut	dark brown	beige	dark brown	dark brown
red	off white	scarlet	scarlet/wine	cream	cream	scarlet/cream
white	pale grey	white	mid grey	grey/white	grey/white	lemon
green	ice green	ice green	dark blue/green	olive	olive	white
blue	pale aquamarine	white	moss green	turquoise	blue/green	saffron
pink	pale pink	pale pink	raspberry	moss green	moss green	shocking pink
grey	dark grey	pale grey	grey/black	black and white	scarlet	scarlet

provide a background for these objects. Coordinated or mix and match wallpaper provides interest in an otherwise rather simple room. This has a plain design, which can be used on two or three walls, and a more elaborate version, incorporating the plain design, to be used on the remaining wall, or in alcoves.

FURNITURE

Furniture should be arranged to suit the purpose of the room (see Planning). Personal preferences will influence the type of furniture used. Provision should be made for comfortable seating, occasional tables, storage, entertainment, and dining if necessary.

1. Seating: this is probably the main priority. It should be arranged to encourage relaxed conversation. It should be comfortable and visually attractive. The conventional three piece suite is less common now. Alternatives include:
   one sofa and two or three toning chairs;
   two sofas placed opposite or at right angles to each other;
   two different pairs of upholstered chairs;
   a selection of different chairs, all blending with the colour scheme;
   unit seating: free-standing upholstered chairs which can be arranged as a settee or individually, as the occasion demands.
   In a small room or flat, fold-away chairs or larger floor cushions may be useful. Consider a convertible sofa, which can be used as a spare bed if required.
2. Occasional tables: each seating area should have a small table or other suitable surface nearby for coffee cups and ashtrays. Ideally these should be the same height as the arm of the chair to give a good visual line. They should have easy to clean, spill-resistant surfaces. Nests of tables are a good choice as they can be stacked when not in use; a table which

doubles as a trolley is also useful. Some tables are fitted with shelves, record racks or drinks cupboards, providing useful extra storage.

3. Storage: a wall unit system is a good choice — this can house books, drinks, ornaments, and sometimes even the television set. Alternatively, a bookshelf, one or two cupboards and perhaps a desk will be required. These should blend with one another in colour and style. It is possible to mix modern furniture with old, but this needs careful planning and a certain flair.

Furnishing pointers
1. Furniture and upholstery should be stain resistant and easily maintained.
2. Furniture should be easy to move.
3. Avoid overcrowding a room — allow space to walk between pieces of furniture.
4. Avoid placing furniture across corners, which wastes space.
5. Arrange furniture in suitable groupings.
6. Avoid cluttering the top of furniture with too many objects.
7. Built-in furniture will allow more space in a small room.
8. A TV on a table fitted with wheels can be removed from the room easily if wished.

Soft furnishings
Curtains play an important part in the overall furnishing scheme of a living room. They help to soften the overall look by providing texture. They ensure privacy and help to insulate the room against draughts and heat loss. They protect the furnishings against excessive sunlight.
1. Choose an attractive and durable cloth.
2. Both curtain and lining fabric should be easily cleaned and preshrunk.

134

3. In a small room, curtains should match the walls. A strong contrast in colour or pattern will 'break up' a wall.
4. Consider matching wallpaper and curtains, e.g. Sanderson 'Triad'.
5. Suitable fabrics include dralon velvet, tweed, tapestry, linen repp, heavy cotton (chintz), linen union.
6. Net curtains provide added privacy.
7. Holland or venetian blinds may be useful if the room is subjected to strong sunlight.
8. Loose covers on upholstered chairs protect the furniture and are easily laundered.

More detail about soft furnishing will be found in chapter 14.

Heating

The ideal form of heating for comfort, ease and efficiency is some form of central heating. Whether or not central heating is available, an open fireplace is desirable in a living-room. It provides visual warmth and appeal and is a natural focal point for seating and conversation.

Lighting

Lighting should allow for the many possible uses of this room. Some form of background lighting is required, such as a set of wall lights or a ceiling fixture, preferably connected to a dimmer switch which lowers the intensity of the light — giving a more intimate atmosphere for talking or watching TV. A standard lamp and one or two table lamps will provide essential local lighting. At least one should have a sufficiently high wattage for reading or sewing. Light fittings and shades should be chosen to blend with and enhance the general decor of the room. At least three, preferably four, sockets are required — possibly two double sockets. Two are required for portable lamps and one each for TV and stereo unit.

Accessories

One or two paintings carefully chosen will enhance the decor of a living room. Pot plants or an arrangement of fresh or dried flowers will give the room a lived-in look. Photographs, souvenirs and ornaments provide a personal touch.

A welcoming room (Barnaby's Picture Library)

DINING ROOM

The dining area may be a separate room or form part of a kitchen or living-room. If it is situated at one end of another room, it must obviously blend with the decor in that room. A dining room may have to cater for family meals, children's parties or more formal entertaining. Many are also required to serve as a study, playroom or sewing room.

An attractive dining-room (Barnaby's Picture Library)

PLANNING

1. It should be as near the kitchen as possible, to facilitate serving and tidying up.
2. A serving hatch or a two-way cupboard between kitchen and eating area saves unnecessary walking.
3. A large picture window looking over a garden will provide sufficient natural light and a pleasant view for day-time eating.
4. A sliding door or double door can be used to cut off the dining from the living area, or provide plenty of space for entertaining when required.
5. In a small house where space is limited, it is wasteful to use a dining room exclusively for eating. Small areas can be set aside for study, sewing, etc. Example: the alcoves on either side of the fireplace could house a built-in system, to include bookshelves and a desk for study and paperwork and/or cupboards for sewing equipment or toys. Portable screens or more permanent partitions can be used to separate one area from another.

FLOOR

Dining room floor coverings should be easily cleaned, as spills of food and drink are likely. They should be stain-resistant, hard-wearing and not cause much noise.

1. Vinyl, in sheet or tile form, is ideal if there are children. Choose an attractive design rather than a plain vinyl, which will show up every mark.
2. Wood.block flooring looks well and is easy to maintain if sealed.
3. Cork tiles, which should be sealed, are quite and warm looking.
4. Carpet: in formal settings many people still prefer carpet in spite of its impracticality. Avoid deep pile carpets, as food is difficult to remove. A carpet containing a percentage of synthetic fibres will be fairly easy to clean. Carpets with a pattern are preferable to plain carpets, which will show up every crumb.

WALLS

If the room is used solely for eating, a hard-wearing washable wall finish is not as essential as in other rooms. Suitable materials are emulsion paint or wallpaper, with gloss paint on woodwork. Calm, restful colours should be used, so that they will not distract the diners.

FURNITURE

The furniture should harmonise with the general colour and style of the room. Keep furniture to a minimum. Basic requirements are a dining table, four to eight dining chairs, a sideboard or serving area. An occasional table or desk is optional.

1. Dining table: a solid, steady table is required — preferably one which can be expanded by adding a central leaf. It can be placed in the centre of the room or to one end — perhaps on a raised platform. It should be of a comfortable height.

   Suitable materials for the dining table are *wood,* either solid or veneered (popular modern table woods include teak and rosewood veneers and solid pine; good wooden tables can be picked up fairly reasonably at auctions — often made from oak or mahogany); *laminated plastic,* available in wood finishes (suitable for homes with lots of children or where the dining table is used for hobbies, such as dressmaking); *chrome* and *glass,* with an ultra-modern appearance, can look well — but glass is easily scratched.
2. Dining chairs can match the dining table as part of a suite, or contrast with the table. Sets of six chairs are most popular: traditional sets consist of four armless

136

chairs and two 'carvers', i.e. with arms. Chairs should be sturdy but comfortable. Benches can be used where space is limited — but these do not provide support for the back.

3. Sideboard or dresser: this is a useful item of furniture, as it can be used for storing glass, china and cutlery, as well as providing a surface for serving.
4. Other furniture: an occasional table is both decorative and functional — a table lamp or a floral arrangement can be placed on it. A trolley is useful for serving food and for clearing the table quickly. A hostess trolley is a heated trolley, useful for keeping food warm. A cocktail cabinet may also be kept in the dining room.

Heating

The room should be comfortably warm before starting a meal. Central heating is ideal — it provides evenly distributed heat. Alternatives are a fan heater, a gas or electric convector heater, an open fire or a coal-effect fire. The table should not be too near a radiant heat source or some diners may get uncomfortably warm.

Lighting

A central rise-and-fall fitting over the table is ideal. Make sure the height is such that it shines on the table but does not dazzle diners. A diffused light will provide a soft light without glare. Candle light is flattering and provides atmosphere for special occasions. A wall lamp or a standard lamp near the serving area is necessary to provide light for serving food. Two electric sockets should be sufficient — one for a portable light and one for a heated trolley or coffee percolator. If the dining area is part of a kitchen or living-room, use lighting to accentuate it as a separate area. Other lights may be switched off while eating, to conceal the working area.

TABLE SETTINGS

China, pottery and other table accessories help create the required atmosphere for a meal. If possible, they should blend with the decor of the room in colour and style. Rush mats, chunky pottery and wooden utensils create an informal country-type setting, while linen cloths, crystal glass, china and traditional silverware is best kept for formal meals. The centrepiece, a candle, flower or fruit arrangement should be low enough to allow people to talk over them.

TABLE LINEN

1. Tablecloths should be large enough to cover the table with a drop of about 25 cm. Check table size before buying.
2. They should be easy to launder and drip-dry if possible.

A table setting suitable for a dinner party

3. Colours should blend with the colour scheme of the room and any tableware used.
4. Fabrics: damask (white self-patterned linen) is used on formal occasions, but is tedious to launder. Floral prints, gingham and open-weaves in cotton or rayon are easier to wash. Plastic is useful for children's meals and paper is handy for children's parties. Matching napkins are often available.
5. Table mats, used more often for informal meals, are cheap to buy and can be made at home. Cork-backed heat-resistant mats are available. Table mats can be made from cork, plastic, tweed, linen, cotton, rushwork or raffia. For formal meals, white Irish crochet mats can look very effective over a dark coloured tablecloth, e.g. green or red.

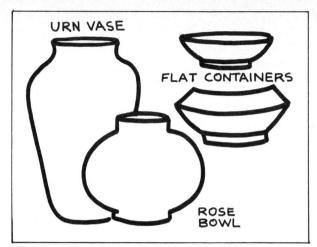

Containers for flowers

FLOWER ARRANGING

Fresh flowers are probably the most attractive accessory you can use in your home. As well as providing a display of colour, many release a pleasant perfume. Flowers add beauty and charm to a house, giving it a cared-for, homely atmosphere.

Equipment

While it is not essential to have every one of the following items, they help make flower arranging easier.
1. Flower holders, to hold flowers steady in the vase. They include spiky pin-holders, crumpled-up chicken wire, and floral pack or oasis (a green spongy material which is soaked before the flowers are inserted in it).

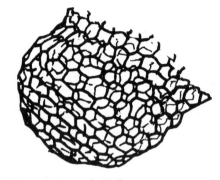

Crumpled lettuce wire to hold flowers

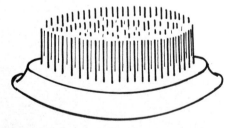

A pin holder for flower arranging

2. Scissors or florists' shears.
3. Containers: a well-chosen container should complement the flowers. Homely flowers like daisies look best in pottery or copper containers; glass and silver suit more formal arrangements. Containers must be kept spotlessly clean to prevent growth of bacteria. Many types of vases are available and everyday objects such as mugs, bowls, old kettles etc. can also be put to good use as containers.

Florists' shears

Preparation of flowers
1. Cut (never pull) flowers late in the evening. Never cut flowers when wet with rain.
2. Strip off all lower leaves as they rot under water.
3. Stand flowers up to their necks in a deep container of water for at least an hour or preferably overnight, before arranging. They should be left in a cool dark place.
4. Bruise woody-stemmed plants, e.g. roses, before soaking.

Arranging

1. Place a flower-holder in position and fill the vase with water, preferably lukewarm, before you start the arrangement, or
2. Soak an oasis until thoroughly moistened.
3. Colours of the arrangement should complement one another and blend with the decor of the room. Avoid using too much colour in one arrangement.
4. Let the form and shape of the flowers influence how you arrange them. Remember, flowers should appear to be growing from a central point, as they do in nature.
5. For a simple arrangement, try to have a fan-like shape with the flowers high in the centre, spreading out over the vase as they come down. The tallest flowers should be $1\frac{1}{2}$ times the height of the vase.
6. Never put too many flowers in a vase. Strip off some foliage if the arrangement seems too heavy.
7. Use foliage to fill out the arrangement and add contrast of colour, shape and texture. Foliage is particularly useful at times of the year when flowers are expensive.
8. Remember the position of the finished arrangement, e.g. on a dining table; flowers should be low enough for diners to have a clear view of each other. Arrangements should look good from every angle, unless they are in a position where they will be seen only from one side, e.g. on a hall table.

Aftercare

1. Keep arrangements out of direct sunlight.
2. Make sure the water in the container remains clean and fresh; top up daily and change only if necessary.
3. Some arrangements benefit from a slight spraying occasionally.
4. Place the arrangement in a cool place at night.

Dried arrangements

These are useful for winter months when fresh flowers are scarce and expensive. Many garden flowers are simply dried by hanging upside down in a warm place. Special oases are available for dried flower arrangements.

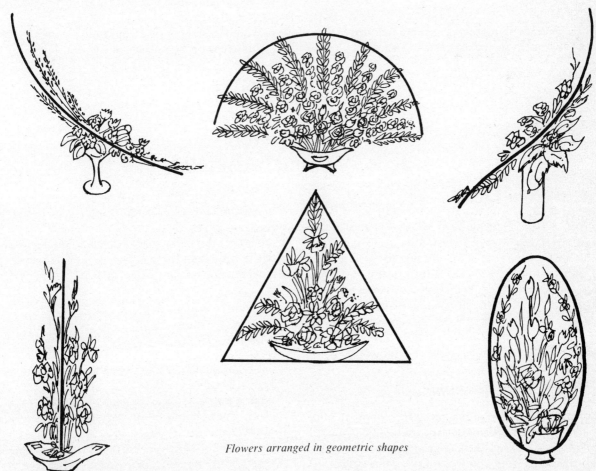

Flowers arranged in geometric shapes

PLANTS IN POTS

1. Grow flowers e.g. azaleas and chrysanthemums in pots, e.g. hyacinths, daffodils and crocuses. These effort.
2. Many spring bulbs can be grown indoors in bowls or pots, e.g. hyacinths, daffodils and crocuses. These flower soon after Christmas, long before the same flowers appear in the garden.
3. House plants provide lots of greenery. A wide variety is available, and many of them are easy to propagate, so that without much trouble or extra expense it is possible to grow a large number from scratch.

QUESTIONS/CHAPTER 13

1. Plan the interior decoration of a dark, narrow hall in an old house. Refer to:
   (a) wall and floor covering;
   (b) paintwork;
   (c) furniture;
   (d) heating;
   (e) lighting;
   (f) methods of improving appearance/proportions.
   Give reasons for your choice in each case.

2. Sketch and describe the arrangement of furniture and fittings in a modern living/dining-room.
   Describe in detail the soft furnishings used and their approximate cost to make at home.
   Write a note on the colour scheme of the above room.

3. The quality and design of modern table linen and table ware need careful consideration before purchasing. Discuss this statement, with particular reference to:
   (a) variety available;
   (b) materials used;
   (c) finishes;
   (d) sizes;
   (e) cost and value for money.

4. Sketch a table setting suitable for a formal dinner for six people. Describe the china/delph and table linen used, with reference to materials, colour, design and cost.

5. List the points to remember when choosing (a) wallpaper and (b) floor coverings for a regularly-used family room.
   What form of heating would you recommend for the above room; give reasons for your answer.

14.
Bedrooms and bedsitters

The development of central heating and other efficient forms of room heating have led to a change in the traditional use to which bedrooms were put. It is wasteful to keep rooms for sleeping only, so today's bedrooms have become multi-purpose rooms. Teenagers use their bedrooms for studying and recreation, children's bedrooms are also playrooms and even the so-called master bedroom is now furnished in such a way that it can be used for quiet reading, hobbies and even is some cases as a miniature gym!

PLANNING

Bedrooms should be at the back of the house in busy areas, to avoid traffic noise. The traditional layout of bedrooms is to place the bed-head against one wall, a dressing table under the window and a wardrobe and/or cupboard against another wall. As bedrooms in modern houses are small, careful planning is necessary to make the most of the space available. Ample storage space is necessary for clothing as well as personal belongings, and in many cases bed linen.

BEDS

1. Avoid placing the bed in a draught, beside a door or window.
2. The bed should be positioned so that it is easy to make up.
3. Single beds can be placed parallel with the wall to save space. They should be on castors to roll out for making.
4. Consider bunk beds when two children have to share a room. They take up half the space of twin beds.

FLOOR

Floor covering should be comfortable, quiet, practical and easy to maintain. A fitted carpet is ideal, as it is luxurious and easy to clean. It is not necessary to use top quality carpeting, as the bedroom gets light wear. A plain carpet may show up spills from make-up or perfume. A sanded floor with scatter rugs is a cheaper alternative, but less comfortable. Vinyl or linoleum are practical and easy to clean, but cold on the feet.

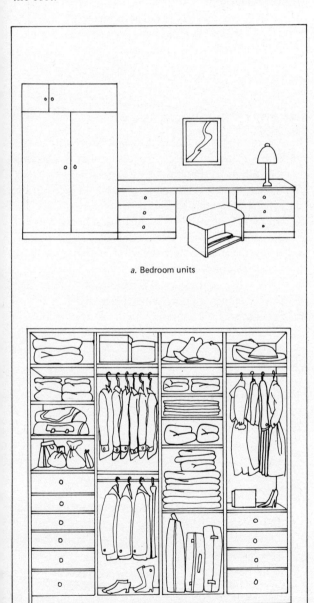

a. Bedroom units

b. Bedroom clothes storage

Bedroom units

WALLS

As there is not much wear and tear in an adult's bedroom, it is possible to indulge in delicate finishes. Examples are wallpaper in pale colours and pastels, hessian or other fabric wallcovering, and emulsion paint. Teenagers' and children's bedrooms may require a more durable finish, such as vinyl wallcovering or vinyl emulsion paint.

Colour scheme
1. Choose quiet, restful colours, neutrals or pastels.
2. Startling colours may interfere with sleep and rest, and would be particularly tiring during a long illness.
3. It is better not to decorate the master bedroom in flowers, pastels or frills. Most husbands dislike such an obviously feminine room. Compromise with neutral colours and unfussy furniture.

FURNITURE

1. Bed — see below.
2. *Clothes storage;* a traditional suite — a wardrobe, chest of drawers, and a dressing table — is popular. Separate items of furniture may also be used. Remember, free-standing pieces of furniture take up a lot of space.
3. *Bedroom units* are available, sold in single units which fit together. These include wardrobe, chest of drawers, dressing table, and luggage cupboard to fit over wardrobe. They are available in a wide range of sizes and finishes, including painted whitewood, teak veneer, melamine. Louvred or mirrored doors are optional. Many useful fittings are included: shoe racks, sets of small drawers, as well as open shelves and hanging space. Wardrobes may have hinged or sliding doors (hinged doors take up more space). Hanging space should be able to take clothes of different lengths and be wide enough to allow clothes to hang freely: fifty to sixty centimetres is a minimum width. Dressing table units are available with mirror and lights.
4. A *dressing table* should be comfortable to sit at, with sufficient space for the knees. It should be well lit by day and night. It should have washable surfaces and a fitted drawer for cosmetics. An adjustable mirror is useful.
5. *Seating:* a comfortable easy chair in a bedroom will help to make it a quiet spot for relaxing or reading. A stool will be necessary for the dressing table.

6. *Plumbing;* it is worth while going to the expense of having a hand basin and vanity unit fitted in the bedroom. This is very convenient and takes the pressure off the bathroom. A small bathroom and lavatory 'en suite' is an even better arrangement.
7. *Bedside tables* or lockers are useful for holding cups and glasses, books and magazines. Reading lights can be placed on top.
8. A full-length *mirror* is essential.

SOFT FURNISHINGS

1. Curtains in a bedroom provide privacy and insulation, and generally improve the appearance of the room.
2. They should be lined to improve the hang of the curtains, to protect them against sunlight, and to increase opacity — keeping the room dark on summer mornings.
3. Unless the room is large, curtains look better if they match or tone with the walls. Matching or coordinating wallpaper and curtains are ideal for bedrooms.
4. Suitable fabrics for bedrooms are cotton, dralon and rayon.
5. Alternatives to curtains: *Holland blinds* are smart but difficult to clean. They do not provide the same furnished feeling as curtains. *Net curtains* give privacy during the day and are useful if the room is overlooked.
6. *Bedspreads* can match curtains or provide a good contrast.

Heating

It is important that any form of heating used in a bedroom can be switched off when not in use during the day. For this reason storage heaters would be a bad idea; better would be central heating or fan or convector heaters.

Lighting

1. For background or general lighting, a central fitting which provides soft, diffused light is ideal.
2. Specific lighting at the dressing table area could include a fluorescent fitting at either side of the mirror, or a filament fitting, with a shade which throws the light onto the face and gives better results when making up.
3. Bedside lights: strong, directional fittings, e.g. angled spotlights, are suitable if arranged so that they do not shine into the eyes of the person in bed.

4. A wardrobe light is useful, particularly if the wardrobe is deep or situated in a dark corner. It turns on as the wardrobe is opened and off when the door is closed.
5. Lamp shades can be pretty and delicate, as there is little dirt or wear and tear in a bedroom.
6. Two or three power points are required for lighting, hairdryers, heaters and so on.

Ventilation

Every bedroom should be well ventilated. It should be possible to leave a small window open at night. Otherwise a small ventilator — such as a cooper's disc or a ventilating brick high on the wall — would be necessary.

CHILDREN'S BEDROOMS

1. Avoid expensive scaled-down furniture with teddy-bear transfers, etc: it will quickly become redundant as the child grows up.
2. Simple whitewood furniture is ideal: it is cheap and can be repainted easily.
3. Buy only essential baby furniture: carry-cot, cot, playpen and adjustable baby seat.
4. A low table top is necessary for changing the baby.
5. Lots of cupboard and drawer space is needed for baby's belongings: clothes, nappies, cream, talc, towels, nappy bucket, baby bath, etc.
6. A comfortable nursing chair is important for feeding the baby. It should support the back, preferably be without arms, and be situated out of a draught.
7. Keep all furniture against walls, leaving lots of floor space free for playing.
8. Older children require a well-lit desk for study.
9. Heating should be safe: central heating or storage heaters are ideal. If these are not available, use a wall-mounted, electric convector or infra-red heater.
10. Lighting: a central fitting is usually sufficient in a child's room, preferably with a dimmer switch so that it can provide dim light at night. Portable lights are easy to break and can be dangerous. Switches and sockets should be out of reach. All plugs should be of the shuttered, three pin type. Older children will require a bedside light and an adjustable desk light.
11. Windows: a blind is ideal. A black-out blind is useful as it keeps the room dark on bright mornings, so that the child does not wake early.

Mock curtains in gingham or cotton print are cheap, practical and pretty. Bedspreads or cot covers can be made to match. Keep curtains short: long curtains are impractical for a child's room.

12. Walls: use a vinyl paper, or paint walls with vinyl emulsion. This can be washed and then touched up with paint when necessary. Bright, gay colours are suitable for children's rooms.

13. Floor: vinyl flooring is most practical at first, as it is hard wearing and washable. A carpet square or large rug could be laid over the vinyl when the child is older, as it is warmer and more comfortable when playing on the floor. If the room is carpeted, a small vinyl-covered area could be left for messy play such as plasticine and painting. In the long run it is probably safer to let children use such materials under supervision in the kitchen or living-room.

BUYING A BED

1. As one spends a large part of one's life in bed, it is essential that the bed should be comfortable, yet provide sufficient support.

2. A good bed should have a strong, well-sprung base and a reasonably firm mattress with well-padded sides.

3. Heavy people need a firm mattress. A mattress of medium firmness is more suitable for light people.

4. As the only sure way to test a mattress is to lie on it for a few minutes, it is wise to shop for a bed early in the day — before too many customers are about!

5. To test a mattress, lie on your back, then on your side. Turn over and back a couple of times and try sitting up.

6. Couples who differ greatly in weight can buy two separate beds which zip up the centre, rather than a double bed which does not suit one partner. This type of bed helps to prevent the lighter partner rolling into the valley created by the heavier one.

7. Price is usually an indication of quality. A cheap bed is usually false economy, as it may give too little support, be uncomfortable, and probably have a short life.

8. Do not be impressed by glamorous bedheads and decorative mattress covers — it is the inside construction that counts.

9. Invalids and elderly people should avoid low beds as they are difficult to get in and out of. Standard height from floor is fifty centimetres.

10. Beds should have castors on the legs to make them easier to make, and to be moved for cleaning.

Sizes

New metric sizes are now available:

standard single	100 cm x 200 cm
standard double	150 cm x 200 cm
king size	180 cm x 200 cm

A bed should be at least fifteen centimetres longer than the occupant. Wide beds are more comfortable than narrow beds, so these should be used unless space is restricted. Very large, king.size beds require extra-large bedding which is expensive.

Cost

This varies according to the structure of matress and base. The best and most expensive beds have a large number of pocketed springs, a thick layer of padding above and below the springs and a deep mattress.

Structure

Beds consist of a base and a mattress. Most good quality beds have either a spring-edged base or a box-edged base.

Spring-edged base: this is the most expensive type. Coiled springs come right out to the edge of the base. This makes the bed more comfortable and springy at the sides, but beds which are often sat upon — such as divans — will be damaged easily.

Box-edged base: the springs of the base are boxed in. This bed is less comfortable to sit on or to lie near the edge of, but will wear better. It is ideal for divans in bedsitters which are used regularly as seats.

Other bases:

1. *Solid wood:* often used in children's built-in beds — a thick foam mattress is placed on a wooden base. It is not particularly comfortable. It should be drilled to allow ventilation of the mattress.

2. *Wire base:* used to be found on many beds — now used mainly on bunk beds and children's cots. This base tends to tear the mattress, is less comfortable than a sprung base, and is inclined to squeak.

3. *Webbed base:* rubber webbing stretched across a metal or wooden frame is used on bunk beds.

Sprung mattress consists of an arrangement of springs which are well padded above and below with layers of upholstery. The usual types of sprung mattress are:

1. *Individual springs* connected to the mattress top and bottom. When one spring is pressed down, those surrounding it also bend inwards.

2. *Continuous wire:* a method of springing using a mesh of springs. This allows one person to move in a bed

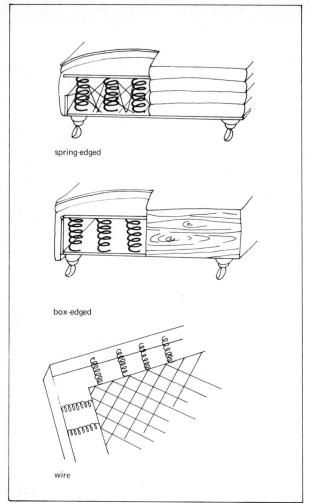

spring-edged

box-edged

wire

Bed bases

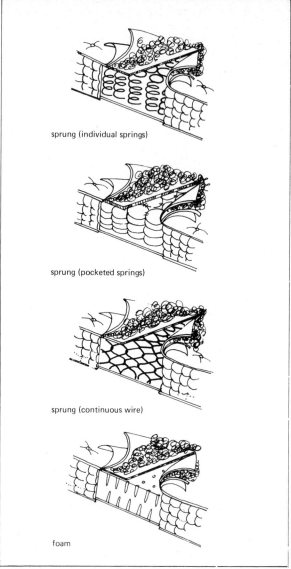

sprung (individual springs)

sprung (pocketed springs)

sprung (continuous wire)

foam

Mattresses

without the movement of the springs being felt by the other.

3. ***Pocketed springs:*** the most expensive type, but also the most comfortable and hard-wearing. Each spring is enclosed in a fabric pocket, and therefore works independently of the others.

The upholstery covering the springs may consist of wool, felt, animal hair or foam. The thickness of this layer depends on the quality and cost of the mattress. The whole mattress is enclosed in ticking and finally covered. This covering may be held in place by quilting.

Foam mattresses usually consist of a solid block of latex or polyether foam with air spaces throughout. The more expensive foam mattress may have dense foam in the centre to give added firmness, or at the edge to strengthen the sides against damage by sitting

on them. Foam mattresses are available in varying thicknesses.

Advantages
1. soft, comfortable, yet firm;
2. useful for those suffering from asthma and other allergies, as they do not produce dust;
3. some types do not require turning.

Upholstered mattresses have no springs, but are firmly packed with wool, hair, kapok or feathers. They become uncomfortable with continued use and eventually become lumpy and hard. They are rare nowadays.

Care

A good bed should last twenty to twenty-five years. To prolong its life:
1. Use a mattress cover to keep it clean.
2. Turn regularly — handles are fixed to mattresses for this purpose.
3. Air well each morning before making.
4. Vacuum now and then.
5. Avoid sitting on the edges.
6. Use an underblanket to protect against perspiration.
7. Children's mattresses should be protected with a water-proof sheet.

SPACE SAVING BEDS

1. *Convertible beds* are folding beds which look like a settee by day and can be opened out to form a single or double bed at night. They are ideal where space in limited e.g. in flats and bedsitters, and are very useful for accommodating extra guests. They are not always as comfortable as a real bed.
2. *Bunk beds* are generally made of wood or metal, with wire or webbed bases, and foam mattresses about ten centimetres deep. They can be free-standing or built-in. They should be sturdy to withstand the activity of normal children.

   Advantages
   (a) useful in small rooms, as they save space;
   (b) make more floor space available for play;
   (c) most children like bunk beds as they can be used for playing and climbing.

   Disadvantages
   (a) Many are shorter and narrower than a normal single bed. Minimum size should be 1.90 m x 90 cm.
   (b) They are difficult to make — this problem can be overcome by using duvets and fitted sheets.
   (c) Bunk beds are unsuitable for very young children. Only children over five should be allowed to sleep on the top bunk.
   (d) They are dangerous unless the top bunk is fitted with a strong, well-designed safety rail and ladder.
   (e) As children tend to grow out of them, be sure to buy bunk beds which can be separated into twin beds later on.

3. *Raised beds* are useful for children's rooms, especially where space is limited. The bed is built on a raised frame, at about the same height as an upper bunk bed. The space underneath is used as a wardrobe, desk or dressing table.

4. *Slide-away twin beds* are a pair of beds, one lower than the other. The lower bed rolls under the higher bed when not in use.

Headboards

The purpose of a headboard is to prevent the wall surface behind the bed from becoming soiled. It is more comfortable to sit up in bed if there is a headboard to provide support and prevent pillows from slipping behind the bed. The headboard should be at least the same width as the bed. It can be simple or elaborate and can do much to improve the appearance of the bed.

Materials:
1. wood, varnished or painted;
2. quilted with fabric or vinyl;
3. cane or wrought iron;
4. traditional brass bedstead;
5. veneered chipboard;
6. fitted bedhead units containing cupboards and/or shelves at the sides;
7. do-it-yourself bedheads can be made from a rectangle of chipboard, covered in thin foam, and finally with plain, patterned or quilted fabric to match or tone with other soft furnishings in the room.

BEDDING

PILLOWS

Pillows should be lightweight but durable. When buying, squeeze pillow tightly, then release. A good pillow will bounce back into shape. When shaken, loose fillings should not fall to one end — this is a sign that they will flatten easily in use.

Fillings

1. Down is obtained from the soft breast feathers of ducks and geese. It is expensive, but is very comfortable, durable and resilient.
2. Down and feathers (duck or goose) is durable and resilient, but not as comfortable or as expensive as pure down
3. Poultry feathers are cheap, but the pillow becomes flat fairly quickly as the feathers loose their curl.
4. Latex foam (Dunlopillo) is solid foam, light and comfortable, yet firm. There is a slight smell of rubber when new. Foam is expensive, long lasting, and does not need plumping up. It does not aggravate asthma and other allergies, as it does not produce dust.

5. Polyester/terylene is light and warm; some consider it too warm. It lacks resilience.
6. Foam pieces are very cheap, but lack resilience and are slightly bumpy.

Care

1. Pillows should be sponged down now and then with hot, soapy water.
2. Most pillows can be dry-cleaned, although many cleaners refuse to take them.
3. Avoid washing down and/or feather pillows unless absolutely necessary. An inner pillow slip will help to keep the pillow clean.
4. Artificial fillings can be washed gently in warm, soapy water. Rinse three or four times in warm water. Spin dry for one to two minutes, then line dry.
5. Drying pillows takes a few days. A tumble dryer at a low heat setting will speed up drying time. Do not put polyester or latex pillows in the tumble dryer. Be careful that the capacity of the drier is large enough.

Pillowcases

The standard size is 50 cm x 75 cm. Most pillowcases are 'housewife style', i.e. with a tuck-in flap at the open end. Fabrics and patterns — see Sheets.

SHEETS

1. Make sure the sheets are large enough. They should be 85 to 90 cm longer than the bed, to allow for shrinkage and a generous tuck-in top and bottom. Nothing is more frustrating than sheets which are too small.
2. Single sheets should be 85 to 90 cm wider than the bed, and double sheets one metre wider, to allow for tucking in.
3. As synthetics only shrink very slightly, when buying sheets made from nylon or polyester a slightly smaller (10 cm less) allowance can be made.
4. The terms single or double can cover a large number of sizes. Check all measurements.
5. Fitted sheets are sold by the dimensions of the bed. A bed 90 x 190 cm requires a fitted sheet 90 x 190 cm. The undersheets are mitred or elasticised on each corner. The top sheets are fitted at one end only. They prevent sheets crumpling at night and make bed-making easier, but it is not possible to change top sheets around to equalise wear.
6. Sales: some sales produce genuine bargains in bed linen — guaranteed linen of well-known brands. Unfortunately many shops buy large stocks of factory seconds. Some of these are satisfactory but in many cases the sheets are too short or too narrow, or have major flaws in the weave. Any sale purchase should be opened out and carefully examined and the measurements checked, before buying.
7. Some cheap cotton sheets have a starch-like filler added to give them the appearance of better quality. Rub between fingers: if a white powder is released, they have been treated in this way.

Bed size		Flat sheets
standard single	100 x 200 cm	180 x 260 cm
standard double	150 x 200 cm	275 x 275 cm
king-size	180 x 200 cm	275 x 275 cm

(some firms make slightly larger king-size sheets)

Number of sheets required:
two pairs of nylon sheets per bed; or
three pairs of cotton, linen or polyester sheets per bed;
three pillowcases per pillow.

Fabrics

Linen is very expensive and rarely used nowadays for bed 'linen'. It is strong, cool and durable, but needs thorough laundering and ironing.

Cotton: good quality cotton is expensive but cool, hard wearing and absorbent. **Cotton percale** is a very fine quality cotton. Cheap, loosely woven cottons do not wear well. **Flannelette** is a brushed soft cotton, often used for cot sheets. It is not very hard wearing.

Nylon is hard wearing, fairly cheap, and easy to launder. It dries quickly and requires no ironing. It is nonabsorbent and feels slippery, clammy and uncomfortable in bed. When used with synthetic nightwear sparks may fly, as it causes a build-up of static electricity. Brushed nylon is less slippery, but still feels uncomfortably hot in use.

Polyester is hard wearing and easy to launder, requiring minimum or no ironing. It is not as absorbent as natural fibres.

Mixtures are usually 50% cotton/50% polyester. They combine the best qualities of each fibre. They are strong, cool and absorbent, due to the cotton content, and easy to launder and drip-dry, due to the polyester content. They are expensive, but are available in a wide range of colours and patterns.

Colours and design

Most sheets and pillowcases are manufactured in a wide range of colours and patterns. Embroidery, frills, patterned fabric or unusual colours generally add to the cost of the bed linen. Many manufacturers design a co-ordinated range of sheets, pillowcases, duvet covers and valances, curtains and towels.

Repairing

When sheets become worn, they can be joined sides-to-middle. Cut down the centre. Join the former sides with a flat, machine-fell seam. Machine a double hem on the new sides.

BLANKETS

The warmth of a blanket depends on the amount of air trapped among the fibres. A loosely woven, light blanket can provide more warmth than a thick, heavy one.

Construction

1. Plain *woven:* a simple warp and weft weave, constructed like most fabrics. Most blankets are made in this way and finished with a satin or blanket.stitched trim.
2. *Cellular:* this may be woven or knitted in such a way as to leave large air holes, like a honeycomb. If the cellular blanket is surrounded by closely woven fabric (such as a quilt above and a sheet underneath), the air spaces form a layer of insulation and keep the bed warm.

Fibres

1. *Wool* is warm, soft and fluffy, but expensive and easily damaged by moths. It must be washed with great care, using a cool wash, several rinses, and a short spin. Wool tends to matt, pill and shrink when carelessly washed. Wool blankets can be washed or dry-cleaned professionally, if a washing machine is not available.
2. *Wool mixtures:* wool and cotton; wool and rayon; wool and man-made fibres; these are cheaper and easier to wash but less warm.
3. *Synthetics:* nylon, Acrilan, Courtelle; short, fluffy fibres are available in plain and cellular weaves. They are soft and warm, easy to wash, and dry quickly. These fibres are cheap, but also prone to static electricity, and may harden with wear, particularly if carelessly washed.

Blanket size

standard single	180 x 250 cm
standard double	250 x 280 cm
king-size	250 x 300 cm

CONTINENTAL QUILTS

An alternative to layers of sheets and blankets is the continental quilt or duvet. This consists of a large fabric envelope filled with down, down and feathers, or terylene wadding, with fabric channels stitched down the length of the quilt to keep the filling in place. Unlike the eiderdown, which had thin areas where the top was stitched through to the bottom, the duvet has an even thickness of down throughout. Because of this, it can be used alone to provide the same amount of heat as several blankets.

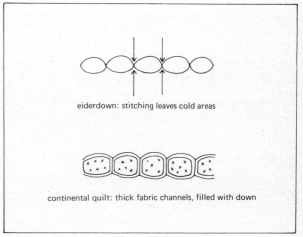

eiderdown: stitching leaves cold areas

continental quilt: thick fabric channels, filled with down

Eiderdown and duvet construction

A good duvet will

1. be large enough to hang at least 23 cm over the edge of the bed on each side and at the end;
2. have a light, easy to wash, non-slip cover: cotton seersucker, terylene lawn, or cotton/polyester are suitable;
3. have a downproof inner cover and casings;
4. be filled with pure down and/or feathers; terylene wadding is a cheaper alternative filling.

Advantages of a continental quilt

1. warm, light and cosy;
2. simplifies bed-making — ideal for bunk beds;
3. eliminates much laundering of bed clothes;
4. co-ordinating sets of duvet cover, pillowcase, sheet and valance are available;
5. Terylene-filled quilts are non-allergenic and are more easily washed.

Disadvantage

1. They may seem expensive but are no more so than buying two or three blankets.

BED COVERS

Called quilts, bedspreads or counterpanes, these have one basic function: to hide the bedclothes and give an attractive finish to a bed. They should be large enough to almost touch the floor. Fabrics should match or tone with other soft furnishings and should be washable.

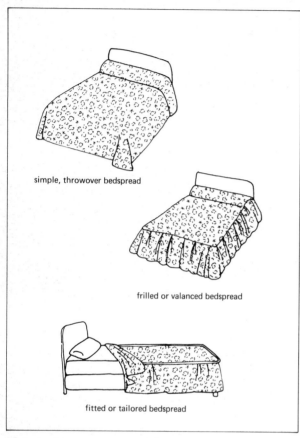

Bedspreads

Types
1. simple, throw-over bedspread;
2. fitted or tailored bedspread;
3. frilled or valanced bedspread.

Fabrics
1. candlewick: tufted cotton, easy to launder and crease resistant;
2. tapestry weave: with an intricate design;
3. linen/cotton: in many colours, patterns and designs;
4. lace or crochet: requires careful laundering;
5. nylon or polyester: easy to launder, drip-dry;
6. patchwork;
7. fake fur.

ELECTRIC BLANKETS

There are two types of electric blanket: underblankets and overblankets. Both consist of a low voltage heating element, enclosed in a wool or rayon/cotton blanket. Single and double blankets are available, with one to three heat settings, and an indicator light to show when the element is on. Dual controls are available on many double blankets.

Underblankets are used to pre-heat the bed and should be turned off before getting into bed.

Overblankets are used instead of conventional blankets, and should be used with a sheet beneath them and a good insulating cover, such as another blanket, over them to keep the heat in. They are more expensive to run. They do not last as long as underblankets, as daily handling during bed-making tends to weaken and damage them.

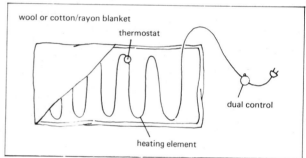

Electric blanket

Use
1. Avoid folding or creasing sharply; this may damage the wires.
2. Some models may be machine-washed.
3. All electric blankets should be cleaned and serviced every few years by the manufacturer.
4. Always buy a reliable make, electrically approved (BEAB), which has cleaning and repair facilities available.

CARE AND CLEANING OF BEDROOMS

Care
1. Keep bedroom well ventilated and air well each morning.
2. Vacuum regularly; don't forget under the bed, otherwise dust accumulates and moths may have time to damage the carpet.
3. Vacuum mattress once a month and turn the mattress three or four times a year, from side to side and top to bottom, for even wear. A second person is needed to turn a double or king-sized mattress.

A pleasant bedroom (Barnaby's Picture Library)

Cleaning — daily

1. Turn back bedclothes on rising, to air the bed and open the windows to air the room.
2. Tidy the room; hang up clothes, put away books, toys etc.
3. Collect soiled clothes for washing.
4. Make the bed. Each member of the family should make his/her bed.
5. Sweep or vacuum the floor, according to type.
6. Dust over surfaces and wipe over the handbasin if there is one.

Cleaning — weekly or periodically

1 — 5 As above.
2. Clean windows if necessary.
3. Wash paintwork, using warm, soapy water and a cream cleanser for stubborn stains. Rinse and dry.
4. Give the handbasin and surrounds a thorough clean.
5. Polish the furniture, mirrors etc.
6. Change the bed linen once a week.
7. Tidy the wardrobe, cupboards and drawers regularly in rotation.

8. In summer, shake out blankets and air well. Wash according to type when necessary.
9. Wash curtains and bedspread when necessary, according to type.
10. Dust tops of cupboards, pelmet or curtains rails periodically.
11. Dust and wash down walls now and then.

BEDSITTERS

When many young people leave home, their first experience of independence is living in a bedsitter. A bedsitter is a room in which one sleeps, cooks, eats and relaxes. Studying may also be done there. Many bedsitters are found in old converted houses, large rooms which have been furnished by the landlord to his taste; others are purpose-built in modern blocks. Very often landlords divide large rooms with partition walls, into small pokey 'flatlets'. A better alternative if more space is required would be to divide the room horizontally, i.e. build a platform across a portion of the room using the upstairs as a sleeping area and the downstairs for living and cooking. This type of conversion is only possible in rooms with high ceilings and can be rather expensive.

Because a bedsitting-room has so many functions, it is important that it be well planned. The room should be separated into three or four different areas.

1. *Cooking area:* bedsitter 'kitchens' generally consist of a cooker, small sink, some cupboards and possibly a small refrigerator. It is a good idea to separate this area from the rest of the room, by using a divider unit with cupboards underneath. The counter top can then be used for eating. Alternatively the kitchen can be fitted into an alcove with a folding or sliding door which shuts it off when it is not in use. Make every effort to avoid having cooker and sink in separate parts of the room, or the bedsitter will look too much like a kitchen. The cooking area must be well ventilated so will almost certainly have to be situated against an outside wall so that a window or extractor fan can remove the cooking fumes, otherwise there will be a permanent smell of cooking in the room.

2. *Dining area:* you will need a table and two or more chairs around it. As this area might also be used as a study or work area, good lighting is essential and book shelves nearby would be convenient.

3. *Sleeping:* as you will not want the room to look like a bedroom by day, try to have the sleeping arrangements as discreet as possible. A divan, while satisfactory, is not ideal as the edges are easily damaged by being constantly sat upon. A bed which folds up or lifts into a cupboard is useful, although the best arrangement is probably a studio couch, i.e. a convertible bed which looks like a settee by day and can be opened out into a bed at night. Many studio couches have space for storing bedclothes underneath. Fitted sheets and a duvet are the most practical bed-clothes with this arrangement.

4. *Living area:* a comfortable chair or two and lots of storage space are required here. Large cupboards and wardrobes can be fitted into a fireside alcove, or alternatively place bedroom unit furniture e.g. wardrobes along one wall if space allows. Open shelving for ornaments and plants is also desirable and could house a stereo or portable TV.

Flooring

A fitted carpet is practical, comfortable and cosy. Buy a good-quality patterned carpet, as it will get lots of wear. If you cannot afford to carpet the room — a couple of rugs will help to cover and cheer up a dull or worn looking carpet. The floor of the kitchen area should be a vinyl floor covering as this is more hygienic and easy to clean.

Heating

If central heating is not installed, a gas or electric convector heater would heat the room quickly when you return home. Open fires are often blocked up when converting old houses yet they provide a cheap homely source of heat. Of course you must take into account the extra work involved in keeping a fire and whether there is somewhere to store the fuel.

Lighting

A central fitting is rarely enough. Spotlights on a central track would be more efficient or else place individual lights in each area: a fluorescent strip in the cooking area, a reading lamp beside the bed, an angled desk lamp or rise-and-fall fitting over the table for study and writing.

QUESTIONS/CHAPTER 14

1. Plan and sketch a bedroom suitable for a teenager. Refer to:
   (a) wall covering;
   (b) floor covering;
   (c) soft furnishings;
   (d) study area;
   (e) storage;
   (f) recreation facilities.
   Describe the colour scheme of the room of your choice.
2. Describe the points to consider when buying a double bed. Refer to structure, size and cost.
3. Write a note on modern bedlinen and bedclothes, under the following headings:
   (a) sheets;
   (b) pillow cases;
   (c) blankets;
   (d) bed covers;
   (e) duvets.
4. Plan and sketch a bedsitter suitable for a male student. Refer to:
   (a) wall covering;
   (b) floor covering;
   (c) soft furnishings;
   (d) lighting;
   (e) heating;
   (f) kitchen facilities.
   Describe the colour scheme of the above room.

15.
Bathrooms

Many bathrooms tend to be cold and uninviting. This is usually due to the obvious need for washable, water-resistant surfaces. A bathroom today neither has to look nor to feel cold. Ceramic tiles and vinyl wallpapers which are suitable for bathroom use come in a wide variety of colours and designs. More pattern and texture can be introduced by clever use of accessories, curtains and towels.

Most bathrooms can be brought up to date with careful planning and the minimum of major alterations. The amount of improvement possible in a bathroom depends largely on the amount of money available.

FLOOR

The ideal bathroom floor should be soft, warm, waterproof, washable, non-slip and hard wearing. Unfortunately such a floor covering is not easy to come by, so one must compromise by opting for either the luxury and warmth of carpet or the easily cleaned, but cold, linoleum or vinyl. Most people choose the latter, but use a warm fluffy bath-mat to provide comfort and absorbency. When laying a floor covering, consider bringing it up the side of the bath — this looks very attractive.

1. *Cork tiles* should be sealed with polyurethane to make them waterproof.
2. *Vinyl* in sheet or tile form is washable and durable. Cushioned vinyl is more comfortable.
3. *Carpet* is comfortable and warm. Care must be taken to avoid overwetting a carpet or it may rot: a synthetic fibre carpet will be less affected by water. Machine washable bathroom carpets are now available: some are made from 100% cotton, others from nylon. Carpet tiles are handy as they can be moved around to equalise wear and are washable. Avoid carpeting the area around the lavatory: a matching vinyl should be used there.

WALLS

All surfaces in a bathroom should be easy to clean as well as attractive.
1. *Vinyl wallpaper* is available in so many patterns and finishes that almost any decorative effect may be achieved. Vinyl wallpaper only should be used in a bathroom: it is hard wearing, washable and can

withstand constant steam and splashing. It is essential to use the special fungicidal paste recommended for vinyls, otherwise mould may develop beneath the wallpaper. Areas which are constantly wet, around the bath and behind the handbasin, should preferably be covered with a more durable material, such as ceramic tiles or laminated plastic.

2. *Ceramic tiles* may be plain, marbled, patterned or textured. They are available in several colours and designs. The sizes most easily available are 11 cm and 15 cm. More unusual tiles are available from builder's merchants. Ceramic tiles are easily fixed by the amateur. They are very hard wearing, washable and waterproof. Their only disadvantage is that due to their high gloss, they encourage condensation. They are quite expensive initially, but last a lifetime.

A bathroom with practical, pretty fittings (Barnaby's Picture Library)

3. *Paint:* both gloss and emulsion may be used on bathroom walls. Gloss is easier to clean, but tends to produce glare if used over a large area of wall. It is generally only used on doors and windows and small areas of wall, as it is prone to condensation. Emulsion, although not as easily maintained, is softer on the eye and does not produce as much condensation.

4. Other suggestions:
   (a) **Cork tiles** are warm to look at and to touch. They must be sealed with polyurethane seal.
   (b) **Laminated plastic** (Formica) may be used to box in a bath, to protect the wall around the bath, and on the surface of vanity units and cupboards. It is very durable and easy to clean.
   (c) **Mirror:** a well-lit mirror is an essential feature of a bathroom. A good quality mirror is required, sealed at the edges to prevent deterioration due to condensation. Mirror tiles are also available.

Colour scheme

Avoid cold colours such as grey, blue and green. If used, strong, dark shades of these colours should be chosen. Avoid bathroom wallpaper patterned with fish and seagulls — one tires of these very quickly. Try a small floral print with plain curtains/blinds, or a plain wall with patterned curtains/blinds. Matching vinyl wallpaper and curtains/blinds can be very effective.

Coloured suites: remember that a coloured bathroom suite will restrict the colour scheme each time a bathroom is redecorated. A white or off-white suite will allow unlimited scope for using colours, and is usually cheaper. Colour can be introduced by use of towels, wallpaper, etc.

PLANNING

The planning of a bathroom is usually restricted by the position of the plumbing fitments. If these are very badly arranged, it is possible but expensive to have them moved. Many bathrooms are too small: these can often be improved by boxing-in fitments such as sink and bath, and using the boxed-in area for storage. One bathroom is not enough for a large family. In two storey houses, a downstairs bathroom, or at least a cloakroom (lavatory and washbasin) is almost a necessity. If a bathroom is large enough, it could be divided in two: one half containing a bath, hand basin and lavatory, the other containing a shower, another handbasin, and perhaps a second lavatory. It is sometimes possible in a large bathroom to have all plumbing fixtures attached to a false wall. Ugly features, such as piping and cisterns, are hidden away — but not so that they cannot be exposed for repairs. All pipes should be reasonably accessible for repair work.

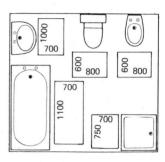

Space (in mm) required when using bathroom equipment

Every bathroom should have a window to let in light and fresh air. If possible avoid placing a bath under a window as this may cause draughts. It is also more difficult to clean and to open and close the window.

There are **building regulations** which control the positioning of drainage and plumbing. As these are to ensure safety and public hygiene, they should be obeyed. Likewise, certain rules govern any electric installations in a bathroom, and the installation of gas water heaters.

It is worth noting that there are **grants** from local authorities and the Department of the Environment towards the cost of installing a water supply, bathroom and/or lavatory in a house without such facilities.

BATHROOM FITTINGS

Bathroom fittings are sold in **suites:** this means that a complete set — bath, wash basin, lavatory, bidet and shower — can be bought in matching colour and design. Although the colours are identical, the materials used vary considerably.

BATHS

Baths should be made from a material which is hard wearing, easily cleaned, scratch resistant and attractive. Usual materials are:
1. vitreous-enamelled cast-iron: strong, heavy, durable, reasonably expensive;
2. vitreous-enamelled pressed steel: less durable, lighter and cheaper;
3. acrylic plastics, such as perspex;
4. glass-reinforced polyester (GRP) or glass fibre.

Moulded acrylic and GRP come in a wide range of unusual colours and designs. They are expensive, less slippery, less cold, and do not chip. These need specialised installation in a strong supporting frame. Dry heat, e.g. cigarettes, can burn these materials, which also need specialised cleaning.
Note: old baths which are sound can be reenamelled professionally.

Standard bath *size* is 170 x 75 cm and 50 to 60 cm in height. Smaller baths are available, even a bath small enough for sitting in only. These are suitable where space is restricted; they save water and therefore fuel; and they are ideal for the elderly and for children. Most baths are rectangular: round, oval or even double baths are available but they tend to be expensive. The inside of most baths is curved to facilitate cleaning and most have one sloping end for comfort. Almost all modern baths are boxed-in, using a material which matches the bath. Many colours are available, but be careful when taking delivery of a suite that colours of each piece match exactly.

Design features to look out for

1. *Grab-bars:* chrome grips placed at the centre of the sides of a bath. They make it easier to get in and out of the bath and are an important safety feature for children, the elderly and infirm.
2. *Drop side:* the centre of the outside of the bath slopes downward for ease of access. It also makes bathing children more comfortable.
3. *Moulded soap dishes* may be incorporated in the top or side of a bath.
4. *Non-slip base:* if this is not available, a rubber mat or plastic self-adhesive strips can be used.

Taps

The position of taps is usually determined by the arrangement of the pipes. Taps may be situated at the top, the side or the corner of a bath.

1. Taps may be made from stainless steel, chrome plated brass, acrylic covered metal, or even gold plated brass!
2. Most baths are fitted with a mixer tap, which makes it easier to check that the water filling the bath is of the correct temperature.
3. Many mixer taps include a shower fitting, which may be handheld or clipped high up on the wall to make a fixed shower.
4. Remember the price of a plumbing fitment such as a sink, bath or hand basin does not include the cost of the taps. These are extra — and often a very expensive extra.

HAND BASINS

Hand basins can be made from vitreous china, glazed fireclay or earthenware, or acrylic or glass fibre. Sizes and shapes vary. They include rectangular, round, lotus shape, and corner basins. They may be wall mounted, mounted on a pedestal, or enclosed in a counter top as part of a vanity unit.

This last has many *advantages:*
1. it provides a useful counter top for make-up, etc;
2. it provides storage space;
3. it hides ugly pipework;
4. it looks neat and streamlined.

A good bath and basin should

1. be easy to clean with no sharp corners;
2. have an efficient overflow;
3. have a well-fitting plug fixed to a chain;
4. have a grooved, sloping soap tray which allows water to drain off;
5. allow waste water to flow out without too much noise;
6. have comfortable taps, mounted far enough from the wall so that they do not catch the fingers, which are easy to turn even when hands are wet.

THE LAVATORY

The lavatory consists of two parts: the cistern and the bowl or pan. Both cistern and pan are usually made of vitreous china or glazed earthenware. These materials are fired at a very high temperature making them strong, hard, non-porous, resistant to stains and acids, and easy to clean. Cheaper cisterns may be made from plastic materials.

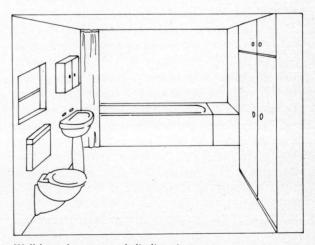

Well-hung lavatory and slimline cistern

The cistern may be situated high above or behind the lavatory. Water supply to the cistern is controlled by a ball valve (see Drainage p. 67) and an overflow pipe is fitted to prevent flooding. The cistern holds about four litres of water which is released when the handle, chain or foot pedal are used. A foot pedal, which prevents the spread of bacteria, is ideal for public lavatories. The water flushes into the pan by either **siphonic action,** which empties the pan thoroughly and quietly, or by the **washdown principle:** this involves a powerful flow of water, but is not as effective.

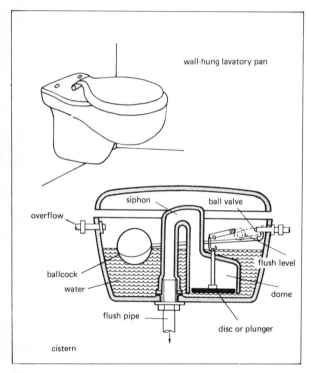

The constituent parts of a lavatory cistern

The lavatory bowl or **pan** is normally 41 cm from the floor. It has a flushing rim and a curved interior and exterior to facilitate cleaning. Many modern lavatories have a rimless flush, which is more hygienic and efficient. All lavatories have a water trap, which prevents waste gases and germs returning from the soil pipe. Modern traps are smoothly moulded to form part of the lavatory bowl. The toilet seat and cover can be made from bakelite, PVC or acrylic material, available in a selection of colours to match lavatories. The lavatory should be situated on an external wall to facilitate plumbing and to allow sufficient light and ventilation. Wall-hung lavatories are neat and easy to clean — the cistern and plumbing are sometimes concealed behind a false wall. A lavatory should be

installed as far as possible from the washing area of the bathroom, ideally in a separate room. If this is not possible, it may be possible to have a screen or divider between the lavatory and the rest of the room.

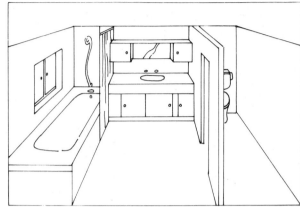

Bathroom and separate lavatory

BIDETS

These provide a hygienic method for cleansing the genital area. Because of this they should be connected to the sewage drain, rather than the drains collecting basin and bath water. They are also handy for sluicing soiled babies' napkins and indeed for cleansing soiled babies. They are made from the same material as lavatories (glazed earthenware), but are more expensive.

SHOWERS

These are quicker, more convenient, and more economical to use than baths. They use less than one-third of the water required for a bath. They also save space in a small bathroom or bedroom.

1. Modern showers are either enclosed units made from acrylic plastic or a walled-in corner of a room (not necessarily the bathroom), which is lined with ceramic tiles. The base of the shower, or shower tray, is usually made from enamelled fireclay, pressed steel, or acrylic plastic.
2. A grip handle on the wall is an important safety feature.
3. Modern showers have a thermostatic mixing valve, which mixes hot and cold water and releases it through small holes in the shower head. Instantaneous showers are now available — heated by electricity.

4. The cold water tank in the attic must be a minimum height (usually one metre) above the shower to provide sufficient water pressure for the shower to work efficiently.
5. Manufacturer's instructions must be followed.
6. Shower curtains or doors should be waterproof and sufficiently long to prevent water escaping onto the bathroom floor.

ACCESSORIES

A wide range of matching bathroom accessories is now available: soap dishes, lavatory paper holders, toothbrush racks, towel rails and so on. Some form of shelf beside the bath is essential to hold bathing toiletries.

Moulded splashbacks are available to fit behind standard wash basins and baths. They are made of moulded acrylic and usually incorporate fitments such as soap trays, toothbrush holders and mirrors.

A wastepaper bin and a laundry basket are useful extras.

Storage

If space permits, a built-in cupboard should be fitted to store bathroom necessities. A vanity unit, incorporating one or two hand basins, can also act as a dressing table with shelves or cupboards underneath. Open bathroom shelves, often illustrated in magazines displaying neatly folded towels and other accessories, will require constant cleaning, dusting and tidying. As the stored items will be subjected to a frequently steamy atmosphere, open shelves are not ideal.

The first-aid and medicine cupboard, if kept in the bathroom, should be locked and out of the reach of children. Ideally it should be kept in the kitchen, where most accidents occur.

Soft furnishings

1. A washable *blind* is most practical.
2. *Curtains,* if used, should be washable and drip-dry: cotton, towelling and fibreglass are good; plastic curtains are practical, but seldom look as attractive.
3. Bath and lavatory *mats* should be washable and blend with the colours in the bathroom.
4. *Towels:* the colours of towels can brighten up an otherwise dull bathroom. They should harmonise with the colour scheme. A wide range of colours and patterns is available to suit every type of bathroom and every colour scheme. Towels come in plain *terry weave,* with even loops, and *jacquard weave,* with some raised and some smooth areas. Cost is usually a good indication of quality, although good quality towels are often reduced at sale time.
Hand towels measure approximately 55 x 99 cm.
Bath towels measure approximately 75 x 150 cm.
Turkish towels should have a thick, absorbent pile, a firm selvedge, and a double hem.

VENTILATION AND CONDENSATION

As condensation is a major problem in bathrooms, steps should be taken to keep it to a minimum. This is discussed fully in chapter 8.
1. A small window will help to remove steam. The glass should be opaque for privacy.
2. An efficient extractor fan is even better.
3. Have the room well heated. Skirting board heaters help to warm the walls, reducing condensation.
4. Thin polystyrene sheeting under wallpaper or polystyrene ceiling tiles raise the temperature of these surfaces to reduce condensation.
5. Avoid the use of many impervious or high gloss surfaces, such as ceramic tiles, mirrors, gloss paint.

HEATING

1. Radiator or warm-air central heating is ideal.
2. A wall-mounted, infra-red heater with a pull cord is a safe form of electrical heating.
3. A heated towel rail warms both towels and bathroom.
4. Gas room or water heaters *must* have a balanced flue i.e. an opening to the outside air.

LIGHTING

A central fitting with a glass or plastic globe diffuser is easy to clean. Fluorescent strips over the mirror or vanity unit, with a pull cord, provide a good light for shaving or make-up.

SAFETY

The bathroom can be the scene of any number of accidents — falls, cuts, poisonings, and electric shocks. The housewife must be vigilant to prevent these.
1. All electrical work must be carried out with the utmost care. It must comply with certain safety rules. These are found in chapter 9. Never install power points or electric light switches in a bathroom. Any electrical fittings should have a pull cord. Specially earthed, safety razor sockets are available.

2. No heater should be within reach of the bath. If a fault occurred, the electricity would pass through the bath to get to earth, causing severe shock and probable death.
3. Safety locks are available for the door, which in an emergency can be opened from outside.
4. Razor blades, lavatory bowl cleansers, medicines and other poisons should be locked away out of reach of small children.
5. Wet, soapy, slippery surfaces in a bathroom are the cause of many falls. Use non-skid rubber mats or strips in the bath and shower. Bath mats used on tiled floors should have a non-slip rubber backing.

CLEANING A BATHROOM

1. Open windows to air room.
2. Wipe over bath and hand basin, using cream cleanser if necessary.
3. Tidy soaps, flannels etc. Straighten towels.
4. Wipe over lavatory seat and pan. Brush lavatory bowl and flush to rinse. (Keep special cloth for cleaning lavatory and disinfect it often.)
5. Dust paintwork and mop over floor. Wipe with damp cloth if necessary.
6. Check soap, lavatory paper, toothpaste and replace these when necessary.

CLEANING THE FITTINGS

Most bathroom fittings can be cleaned with a paste cleaner, such as Gumption or Jif, or a crystalline all-purpose cleaner, such as Flash.

Acrylic fitments require special treatment.
1. Never use scouring pads, powder or pastes, as the surface is easily scratched.
2. Use liquid detergent to remove stains, rinse and dry off with a damp cloth.
3. Never use dry cloths to dust or clean, as these build up static in the plastic, attracting dirt and often causing scratches.
4. Special anti-static polishes are available: if these are hard to find, use an impregnated cloth such as those for cleaning records.

WEEKLY

1. Wash hand basin, bath and tiled surrounds thoroughly using a non-scratch cream. (If bath is washed out directly after use every time, harsh cleaning should not be necessary.)

2. Rinse, then polish up taps and tiles with soft cloth.
3. Brush lavatory pan thoroughly, pay particular attention to the part under the rim. Flush and apply lavatory cleaner, e.g. Harpic or bleach, e.g. Domestos.
   Note: Never use both together.
4. Wash outside of lavatory with hot soapy water, starting at the cistern and working down. Wash the lavatory seat and lid (don't forget the back of each). Rinse, using disinfectant in the water, and polish up lid and seat with a dry cloth.
5. Wash over paintwork, shelves etc. with a clean cloth, wrung out of hot soapy water. Rinse and dry.
6. Sweep or vacuum floor and/or wash according to type. Rinse, using a little disinfectant in the water.
7. Shake mats etc. outside and replace them. Wash and disinfect bath and lavatory mats regularly. Cistern and lavatory seat covers are unhygienic and unnecessary.

QUESTIONS/CHAPTER 15

1. Plan the redecoration of a small bathroom in a modern house, assuming that the bath and sanitary fittings are white. Refer to:
(a) wall and ceiling finish;
(b) floor covering;
(c) lighting;
(d) ventilation;
(e) heating;
(f) storage.
   Give an itemised estimate of the total cost of the project.
2. Write a note on bathroom fittings and sanitary ware (bath, washbasin, lavatory etc.). Refer to:
(a) materials used;
(b) colours;
(c) design;
(d) care/cleaning;
(e) cost.
3. Explain the working principle of a shower unit or lavatory.
   Describe briefly some recent developments in the design of these items.
   How should a lavatory be cared for and cleaned in order to keep it as hygienic as possible?
4. List the materials most suitable for covering bathroom walls. Refer to the advantages and disadvantages of each.
   Describe some ways of reducing the level of condensation in a bathroom.

16.
The kitchen

Because most of the work done in a house takes place in the kitchen, it is important that it should be carefully planned. Not many people, however, have a say in how the kitchen in their new home is arranged — this is left to the architect who designs the house. However, changes *can* be made, particularly when an old kitchen is being modernised or refitted, which can make kitchen chores easier and more efficient. Even in existing kitchens, just rearranging the contents of your cupboards so that they are near where you need them, can do much to simplify kitchen jobs and reduce the amount of time spent working there.

Kitchen planning is not difficult if you follow a few basic guidelines and work out a scale plan on paper before you start. Measure accurately the room and existing appliances, bearing in mind fixtures such as doors and sink which must stay where they are.

Where you have drawn a plan on squared paper, cut out, to scale, cardboard squares to represent the units and equipment. Move them around on the plan until you find an arrangement which suits you. Remember, if you think that this is going to too much trouble, that it is far easier to move bits of cardboard around now, rather than heavy pieces of equipment later. A good kitchen should be

safe;	well ventilated;
well planned;	attractive;
easy to clean;	with heating which is easy
well lit;	to control.

THE WORK TRIANGLE

A housewife can walk for miles each week, in her own kitchen! As she goes about preparing meals, tidying and cleaning, she walks regularly between fridge, cooker and sink, so that if these pieces of equipment are placed near one another she can save literally miles of walking.

WORK AREAS

Most kitchen work areas fall into one of the following categories: galley or corridor, L shape, or U shape.

The galley shape is suitable for a narrow kitchen. The work units are placed against two opposite walls with little space between. This reduces walking and working

movements to a minimum, unless the room is wide. It has two *disadvantages:* one may feel restricted in the small space; and if there is a door at either end (as there usually is), it tends to be a corridor with people passing through from the house to the garden.

The L shape has equipment and storage units placed against two walls at right angles to each other. This method saves a lot of walking if the the room is not too large, and leaves the opposite corner free for a dining table or play area. On the other hand less storage is possible than in a U shaped kitchen. This shape suits rectangular rooms.

The U shape is probably the most useful arrangement for a square kitchen. The units and equipment are arranged along three walls, forming a U. In a large kitchen, a peninsular unit can form one side of the U, to separate the room into work area and dining or play area.

PLANNING

1. Decide on the amount of money that can be spent on the kitchen and plan accordingly. It may be worth borrowing from the bank in order to buy really good quality equipment.
2. Decide whether the kitchen will be basically a food preparation area or whether it must include one or more of the following: laundry equipment; dining area; play area for children; living area; office corner — containing bookshelves, desk, files and phone.

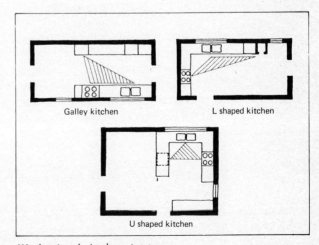

Galley kitchen

L shaped kitchen

U shaped kitchen

Work triangle in three kitchens

3. Make allowance for fixtures which cannot easily be moved: doors, sink, radiator and boiler. These often create the greatest problem in a kitchen as the whole plan must be arranged with these in mind. If badly positioned, they can make a good kitchen arrangement impossible. It is possible to change them, e.g. block up one door and open up another in a more suitable position, but at a cost.

4. Preparing meals follows a natural sequence: food storage; food preparation; cooking; serving. Units should be arranged if possible in that order.

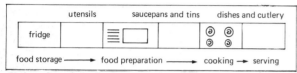

Order of work in food preparation

(a) Food storage — vegetable rack, fridge/freezer, food cupboards, bread bin.

(b) Worktop — for food preparation. Cupboards underneath contain kitchen cutlery, gadgets, chopping board and refuse bin.

(c) Sink — for washing food and delph, with washing-up equipment underneath.

(d) Worktop — for preparation before cooking, with tins, pots and pans underneath.

(e) Cooker — with a heat-proof surface and cooking tools alongside.

(f) Worktop — for serving food, with dishes underneath.

(g) Dining area, door or serving hatch to dining room.

Note: there should be a work surface on either side of major appliances where possible. Store utensils and ingredients near the area where they are needed.

5. Laundry equipment (the washing machine and dryer) is often situated in the kitchen. If so, the washing machine should be near the sink, perhaps under the draining board, for ease of plumbing. The dryer is better placed outside the kitchen, because of the amount of moisture it releases into the air. A dishwasher may also be placed near the sink, or, if plumbing permits, at the end of the units under the serving area. Ironing equipment should be away from the main work area.

6. Size of room: ideally a kitchen should neither be too large nor too small. A large kitchen will mean unnecessary walking: a small kitchen is claustrophobic and frustrating to work in. The ideal size for a working kitchen would probably be 4 m x 4 m (L shaped) or 4 m x 3 m (U shaped).

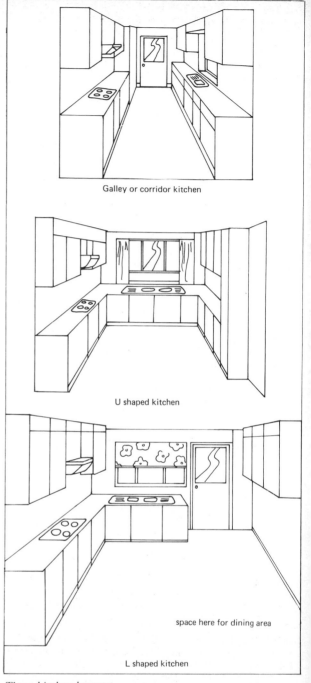

Galley or corridor kitchen

U shaped kitchen

space here for dining area

L shaped kitchen

Three kitchen layouts

If the room is too large, divide it into a work area and a dining or play area, using a divider or peninsular unit with doors which open from both sides. If the kitchen is too small, it may be possible to extend it or to convert an adjoining room (e.g. breakfast room) into a kitchen, turning the former kitchen into a utility room or laundry.

158

7. Alternatively, if the kitchen is too small consider rearranging it. If space is limited, consider
   (a) a stacking washing machine and dryer;
   (b) a fridge/freezer instead of one of each;
   (c) sliding doors on units instead of hinged doors;
   (d) laminated peg board on the wall at the back of the units for hanging small equipment and kitchen tools;
   (e) wall-mounted items such as weighing scales, can openers, spice racks and open shelves;
   (f) use of a breakfast bar and stools, which take up less space than a table and chairs.

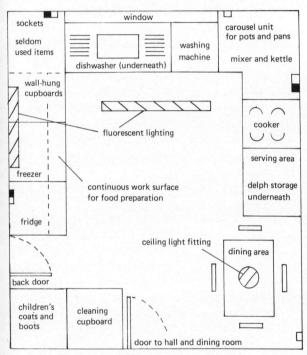

A kitchen that shows good planning

8. When planning a kitchen, allow space for subsequent additions of labour-saving equipment. Most newly-weds are lucky if they are able to afford a cooker and a fridge. Later on they may wish to install a washing machine, dryer, dishwasher and deep freeze. Space for a washing machine and dishwasher could be left under a sink, which could in the meantime house a dustbin, stools or kitchen stepladder. Alternatively leave space at the end of the units between the last cupboard and the door or wall.
9. The kitchen should be in easy reach of front and back doors and near the children's play area. These should be easy access to all parts of the house, especially the dining room.

10. The sink should be placed against an outside wall for ease of plumbing, and under a window for light to illuminate food and clothes during washing, and for a pleasant outlook. If the window faces south, the sun will shine directly into the kitchen for most of the day: this will be uncomfortable unless venetian blinds are used.
11. All surfaces should be washable, stain resistant, as well as resistant to heat, acids and alkalis.
12. Long continuous worktops are efficient and hygienic. Place as much large equipment as possible beneath worktops.
13. As the housewife spends much of her time in the kitchen, it is important that both the kitchen and the outlook should be as bright and cheerful as possible. Ideally a kitchen should look out on a garden. If this in impossible, a colourful window box is an attractive alternative.

A spacious kitchen with room for meals (Topham)

STORAGE

1. The kitchen is expected to store a greater number and selection of items than any other room in the house. Make sure that there are sufficient cupboards for present and future needs.
2. Kitchen cupboards or units should be well designed and their position carefully planned, so that the minimum of walking, bending and stretching is necessary when using them.
3. Items which are used regularly should be stored in the shelves just over or under the worktop, between 45 and 180 cm from the floor. Items used less often can be stored above or below this level. Storage over two metres from the floor should be limited to items rarely used as you will need kitchen steps to reach them.

wide shelves for bulky items

carousel unit

vegetable racks

cleaning cupboard

Storage in the kitchen

4. The **standard floor unit** is 915 mm from the floor. This matches the height of standard kitchen equipment such as cookers, refrigerators and washing machines, and provides continuity of line in a fitted kitchen. Standard floor units are generally 60 cm deep and 50 cm wide; multiples of 50 are used for double or treble units, e.g. 100, 150 cm. These measurements replace the old standard 21 x 21 inch units.

Most floor units consist of a shelved cupboard with a drawer on top. A recessed plinth at the base, 15 cm high, provides toe space, making it easier to stand close to the unit. It should be covered in dark, laminated plastic to prevent scuffmarks. Cupboards and drawers are lined with a thin laminate, while the work surface and unit fronts are protected by a heavier laminate such as Formica or Warerite. Unit fronts are also available in various wood veneers.

5. **Wall-hung units** are approximately 35 cm deep, 55 cm high, and are available in the same widths as floor units. They have laminated doors to match the floor units although some wall units are available with glass fronts. Wall units should not be fixed too high above the level of the work top, or it will be difficult to see into or reach items stored in them. If they are too low, they are likely to cause bumped heads. The correct height is between 33 and 45 cm from the worktop, depending on the height of the worker.

6. **Doors:** kitchen units are available with hinged or sliding doors. Hinged doors give greater visibility and easier access to contents of cupboards, but need plenty of space to open. Sliding doors are more suitable where space is restricted. They are safer on wall cupboards, as there is less chance of bumping one's head.

Handles may be the full width of the door, made of grooved aluminium or they may be knobs.

Shelves, particularly on wall units, should not be too deep — to avoid rummaging about to find items.

Drawers should be sturdy, but light. They should slide in and out easily. Some drawers are fitted with cutlery trays. Awkwardly shaped utensils and tins can be stored in deep drawers near the cooker.

7. **Food storage:** perishables should be stored in a refrigerator. All other food can be kept in dry, ventilated presses — preferable not at ground level, to avoid attracting insects or rodents

8. **Modern features** which maximise usable space:
   (a) fitted larder and cleaning cupboards;
   (b) narrow vertical cupboards to hold trays and pastryboards; they may also be fitted with telescopic towel rails;
   (c) adjustable shelves and upright shelves for tins and trays;
   (d) carousel corner units, with revolving shelves;
   (e) racks and baskets of various sizes, which fit inside shelves and hang from doors;
   (f) cantilevered shelf for an electric mixer — it lifts up and out and folds away after use;
   (g) fitted rubbish bins which open when the supboard door is opened;
   (h) units designed to house built-in ovens, refrigerators, etc;
   (i) peninsular floor and wall units, which act as room dividers, accessible from either side;
   (j) rounded edges at the fronts and backs of worktops — these eliminate ugly joins and are more hygienic, leaving no corners for dust or germs;
   (k) self-assembly units to save money, sold in flat boxes, containing everything necessary for assembling the units, plus full instructions;
   (l) concealed hinges, magnetic catches, nylon tracks for non-stick sliding doors;
   (m) slide-out trolleys and work flaps.

Work heights

Most kitchen equipment and work units are manufactured to a standard height of 915 mm or slightly less. This is considered too high for many

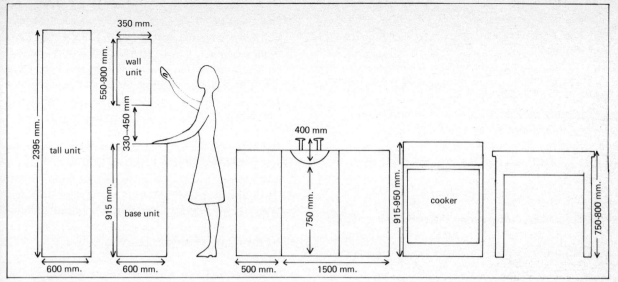

Work heights

cooking operations and for use by small people, too low for tall people. It is possible but expensive to have individually built units made by a craftsman, but it is rarely possible to have mass-produced units altered. Some manufacturers will vary the height of the plinth to suit individual customers. A kitchen table at a lower level will provide a lower work surface for those who require it, or a high stool could be used beside the work-top. To test for the correct height stand in comfortable shoes with legs about 15 cm apart. Raise arms from elbows, so that they are at right angles to the body. The height where the palms rest is the correct working height.

Work surfaces

Kitchen work surfaces should be easy to clean; resistant to stains, especially acids and alkalis; unaffected by water; heat resistant.

1. *Laminated plastic* (Formica or Wareite) is the ideal kitchen work surface. It is washable and resists water and most other stains. It has some heat resistance but cannot withstand extreme heat, e.g. very hot saucepans such as chip pans. It is *not* a suitable chopping surface as it is slippery, blunts knives, and eventually shows knife marks. Laminates are available in many colours and some patterns, usually a marbled or wood finish. A patterned surface is less inclined to show fingermarks, and eventual wear, and should be used for worktops.

2. *Wood* is ideal for chopping, as it is non-slip and does not blunt knives. The knife can sink into the wood and cut through food efficiently. Its use is now mainly restricted to wooden chopping boards. Wood needs regular scrubbing. Avoid pastry and chopping boards with joins, as these harbour bacteria and dirt. Wood is reasonably heat resistant, and not too expensive.

3. *Stainless steel* is an expensive but particularly hard wearing surface. It is completely heat resistant, easy to clean, but tends to water mark — in spite of its name. If cleaned with hot soapy water, rinsed and dried off immediately, this should not occur. It comes in one colour only, but is available in a matt or gloss finish, in sheet or tile form. Most catering establishments use stainless steel almost exclusively, because of its durability and hygienic qualities.

4. *Marble* is very expensive and heavy. Because it is so cold, it is an excellent surface on which to make and roll pastry.

5. Other surfaces, such as *slate, quarry tiles, ceramic tiles* are heavy and lack resilience: most objects will smash if dropped on them. They are heat resistant, hard wearing, and washable — but joints between tiles may harbour dirt and germs.

THINGS TO AVOID

1. a low ceiling;
2. a kitchen which is tob small;
3. placing a table in the middle of the kitchen — you will constantly have to walk around it;
4. impractical surfaces, e.g. delicate wallpaper, carpet;

5. placing fridge or deep freeze too near a heat source, e.g. cooker, radiator;
6. two doors facing each other — these create a draught;
7. too many open shelves and unnecessary accessories — these look pretty in magazines, but get in the way, and have to be cleaned regularly;
8. placing wall units where there is no base unit below — risk of bumping one's head walking into them;
9. rugs or mats on the floor;
10. trailing flexes, portable heaters or lights.

THE SINK

This often takes priority in kitchen planning because it is best positioned on an outside wall near drains for ease of plumbing.

POSITION

It should be placed under a window to give an interesting outlook, and provide light for washing and cleaning. The standard height for the sink top is 915 mm from the floor. It should not be too deep, or it may cause backache.

The wall area behind the sink should be protected with a durable, waterproof finish such as ceramic tiles, laminated plastic or stainless steel. Modern sinks are designed to fit over standard 100 cm or 150 cm units. Ideally there should be worktops on either side of the sink and a draining board to stack dishes before washing and after drying.

MATERIALS

1. **Stainless steel** (see previous column): moulded all-in-one with draining board. Many sizes and shapes are available, from double sinks with double drainers, through single sinks with one drainer, to bowl-shaped sinks which are inset into laminated worktops.
   Note: inset sinks should be carefully installed and sealed at the edges. If water seeps under the lip of the sink, it will soak into the chipboard under the laminate, causing it to swell and eventually disintegrate.
2. **Vitreous enamel** is cheaper and heavier than stainless steel. It is easily cleaned, but has no resilience: objects dropped onto it are likely to break and cause the enamel to chip off.
3. **Fibreglass and acrylic** materials are lightweight, attractive and quiet. They are available in a range of colours. They are very resilient, so no breakages are likely, but scratch easily, so abrasives must never be used. They are not as durable as other sink materials, and can be damaged by intense heat, such as hot fat or hot pans.
4. **Glazed fireclay** was the only type of sink available for years. It had a wooden draining board and tended to mark easily, was heavy and non-resilient. It is rarely used nowadays as this arrangement is unhygienic and difficult to keep clean.

Taps may be made from stainless steel or chrome plated metals, sometimes with a decorative acrylic top. Kitchen taps should be high enough (at least 35 to 40 cm from the base of the sink) to allow large items like buckets to be filled and removed without spilling. Mixer taps, often with a swivel arm and a rinsing spray attachment, are expensive but very convenient.

Draining rack: a plastic-covered wire tray for stacking washed delph is handy and reduces breakages. Dishes can be left to dry on this rack, eliminating the need for tea towels.

Waste pipes have a standard opening 4 cm in diameter. If a waste disposal unit is required, a 9 cm opening is necessary.

Waste disposal units

A waste disposer is an electrically powered grinding machine, fitted to the base of the sink. It pulverises waste, which is washed away by a continuous flow of

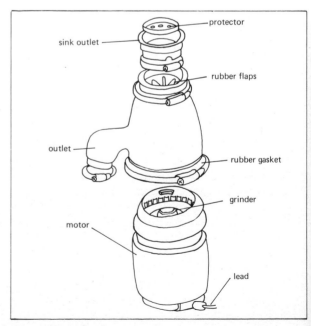

protector
sink outlet
rubber flaps
outlet
rubber gasket
grinder
motor
lead

Waste disposal unit

cold water, into the waste pipe and finally into the main drains.

When the machine is turned on, rotating blades grind the waste into a pulp sufficiently fine to be washed away. Most food waste, including bones, skins and pips, can be pulverised in this way. Any sort of fibrous matter, such as cloth, twine, polythene or rubber, should not be put into the waste disposer.

There are two types: the batch feed and the continuous feed. Both types may have an automatic cut-out which stops the machine if unsuitable waste falls in; or a reverse action to allow the machine to free itself when jammed.

The **batch feed** is filled up with waste, covered, and then switched on. This is safer in a house with children, as they cannot put anything down it while it is on.

The **continuous feed** accepts scraps dropped into the chamber while the machine is running. It is faster and handier than the batch feed.

Advantages
1. It is a convenient, labour-saving, and hygienic method of waste disposal.
2. It eliminates the need for waste bins in the kitchen.

THE FLOOR

Kitchen flooring should be non-slip when wet or dry, well fitted, quiet, easy to clean, resilient, impervious to water, stain and grease resistant, heat resistant, durable, and attractive. The following floors are most suitable (see also chapter 10).
1. **Vinyl** is the ideal floor covering. In tile or sheet form, fixed to the sub-floor with adhesive, it conforms to most of the specifications above. Cushioned vinyl is more comfortable. Thermoplastic and vinyl asbestos are also suitable for kitchen use.
2. Good quality **linoleum** and **sealed cork** are also suitable.
3. **Quarry or ceramic tiles** are very easy to keep, resistant to stains, water and heat *but* anything dropped on them would probably break, and they are very hard and tiring underfoot.
4. **Carpets,** even so-called kitchen carpets made from polypropylene, are unhygienic as they harbour germs and stain easily.

THE WALLS

Kitchen wall finishes should be durable, washable, stain and water resistant, and warm — to reduce condensation.

1. **Paint:** vinyl emulsion is hard wearing, stain resistant and washable. Small areas which become very soiled can be touched up. Avoid gloss paint for large areas of wall, because it aggravates condensation. Paint doors, woodwork and window frames with tough, polyurethane gloss.
2. **Vinyl wallcovering** is washable. A patterned paper is very practical as it does not show the dirt. Remember to use a fungicidal paste. Other washable papers are unlikely to stand up to the large amounts of grease, steam and heat in a kitchen.
3. **Ceramic tiles** are excellent for areas frequently subjected to steam, heat and water. They are ideal for use behind sinks, cookers and worktops. They are not suitable for the whole kitchen, as the high gloss would increase condensation. They look very effective when filling the entire area between worktop and wall unit, with the rest of the kitchen finished in vinyl emulsion.

COLOUR SCHEME

The colours of the kitchen depend very much on the personal taste of the individuals who work in it. The amount of natural light will influence the choice of colours.
1. Plain walls in white or pastels are bright, but show up dirt and stains and may look cold.
2. Warmer colours and patterns are more practical and enjoyable to live with. Warm orange, yellow, red brick, brown earthy shades are popular and homely looking, and they counteract the clinical look of many modern kitchens.
3. Textured finishes are impractical in a kitchen. Keep them to a minimum. Smooth surfaces are more hygienic.

FURNITURE

Apart from storage units and appliances, the kitchen does not require much furniture.
1. The table and chairs should have practical, easily cleaned surfaces. Tables covered in laminated plastic are ideal: they can be used as a work surface for baking as well as for meals.
2. A high stool is a good investment. It allows one to sit down while working; some stools incorporate kitchen steps.
3. A trolley which fits under a work surface saves a lot of carrying and walking to and fro. It can be used for storage if necessary.

WINDOWS

A kitchen needs one or two large windows to admit plenty of day light and to assist ventilation. In a bright kitchen it is easy to see dirt and stains. Good lighting also prevents many accidents. If the window is too small, consider enlarging it.

Curtains are impractical in a kitchen. They are a fire hazard if they are too near the cooker. A roller blind in spongeable vinyl is a better choice. Venetian blinds are useful if the sun shines into the kitchen for most of the day. In a kitchen they will become greasy quickly, requiring frequent cleaning. Washing them is slow and tedious.

HEATING

The kitchen temperature should be 15° to 18°C. If central heating is not installed, consider the following.
1. A **solid fuel cooker** or **boiler** will help to keep the kitchen warm, probably too warm in summer.
2. An **open fire** with a boiler grate behind it will give the kitchen a very homely atmosphere and will assist ventilation, but needs a lot of maintenance. It is not ideal, as work surfaces and food will be soiled by soot and dust.
3. A gas or electric wall-mounted **convector heater** is safe. A gas heater will need a balanced flue.
4. **An infra-red wall heater** provides instant heat when required, and the pull cord eliminates danger of handling plug with wet hands.
5. **Avoid** portable heaters: all heaters should be wall-mounted or fixed.

LIGHTING

The kitchen requires strong lighting for maximum visibility and safety. Lighting should be arranged so that the worker is not in shadow. One or two central fluorescent tubes are efficient and economical to run, but cold and clinical. Spotlights on a track are an alternative. Tube fittings under wall-hung cupboards are ideal for illuminating the worktop. Portable lamps are unsuitable for kitchen use.

VENTILATION

The kitchen needs the most efficient ventilation of all rooms in the house. Good kitchen ventilation is necessary to remove cooking odours and steam, and reduce the risk of condensation. Windows provide some natural ventilation but a cooker hood and/or extractor fan keeps condensation to a minimum and removes grease-filled air quickly and efficiently (see chapter 8).

A badly ventilated kitchen results in
1. an unpleasant atmosphere to work in, constant steam, and stale odours about the house;
2. condensation;
3. more frequent cleaning;
4. more frequent redecorating;
5. possible rusting of metal appliances.

SOCKETS

These should be installed just above worktop level, not too near the sink. Make sure that there are enough sockets: three double sockets would be the **minimum**. Some equipment (fridge, freezer) will be permanently plugged in. Many kitchens have six to ten electrical appliances, many of which are needed at one time: kettle, washing machine, dishwasher, toaster, mixer, iron. Only three-pin earthed sockets should be used: some large appliances (dishwasher, washing machine) may need a more powerful, 16 amp, round-pinned socket. Check with the electrician.

REFUSE DISPOSAL

1. Refuse should be disposed of quickly and hygienically.
2. A kitchen bin should be placed near the food preparation area.
3. It should be covered at all times and emptied daily. The bin should not be too large, as there is a temptation not to empty it until full, which could take three or four days.
4. A pedal bin, flip-top bin, or disposal bag fitment is ideal for the kitchen.
5. Use polythene or paper bags to line bin, and wrap wet food in newspaper before disposing.
6. If bin liners are used, a weekly wash in warm, soapy water, followed by a rinse with warm water containing disinfectant, should be sufficient to keep the refuse bin clean and fresh. Wipe the outside with a damp cloth two or three times a week.
7. Waste disposal units are convenient and hygienic.

SAFETY IN THE KITCHEN

The kitchen can be the most dangerous room in the house. Most household accidents occur there. At each stage of kitchen planning, safety should be considered.
1. Use a non-slip floor covering.

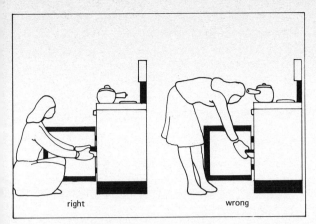

The correct position at the oven

2. Avoid having cooker and sink on opposite walls. One often goes from one to the other with a pan of boiling water: a child could be standing behind when one turns.
3. Avoid placing an electric cooker and the sink beside each other: this provides the dangerous combination of water and electricity.
4. Never place a cooker at the end of a line of units, especially not behind a door, which might knock off saucepans when opened.
5. Do not leave saucepan handles sticking out, especially where children are about. Use a cooker guard.
6. Avoid curtains on windows.
7. Gas appliances should only be used in well-ventilated rooms
8. Metal strips on the base of wall-unit doors can cause head injuries.
9. Fix a gate or safety barrier to keep children out of the working area of the kitchen.
10. Keep knives and other sharp implements safely out of the way of small fingers.
11. Keep a fire extinguisher or fire blanket near the cooker.
12. All areas in a kitchen should be well lit by day and by night when in use, to avoid accidents.
13. Avoid trailing flexes.

SAFETY IN THE HOME

ELECTRICITY

1. All electrical (and gas) installations should be carried out by experienced and qualified tradesmen.
2. Water and electricity do not mix. Never touch an electrical appliance with wet hands. Unplug electric appliances before repairing, handling or filling e.g. kettles, washing machines, dish-washers.
3. Electrical appliances **should** never be taken into a bathroom. Bathroom light switches should be outside the room — or else use a pull cord.
4. Make sure electrical appliances are properly earthed — use modern three-pin shuttered sockets.
5. Do not buy cheap, shoddy electrical equipment; it is likely to be dangerous.
6. Never use faulty appliances; have fraying wires and flexes seen to.
7. Unplug TV and other appliances before going to bed.

FIRES

1. Place a fire-guard around all fires. Buy flame-proof nightwear only.
2. Never place a mirror over a fire; it's easy for clothes to catch fire while you admire yourself!
3. Be extra careful if you smoke; do not leave lit cigarettes lying about, and **never** smoke in bed.
4. Have a fire extinguisher in an easy-to-reach spot, e.g. in the hallway, and keep it in working order.
5. Close all doors at night to prevent spread of fire.
6. Have chimneys cleaned regularly.

POISONING

1. Store weedkillers and other dangerous chemicals in a safe place locked away from children. Never put poisons in harmless bottles, e.g. lemonade bottles. Keep them in their original containers, clearly marked 'Poison'.
2. Rooms containing gas appliances e.g. water-heaters in bathrooms, must be well ventilated.
3. If a gas leak is suspected, call the gas company; do not use a match to search for it yourself!

FALLS

1. Avoid polishing under rugs; do not over-polish floors.
2. Make sure worn carpets are mended at once, particularly on the stairs.
3. Avoid leaving objects e.g. toys lying about the floor or stairs. Train children to put away their things.
4. Use non-slip floor coverings in kitchen and bathroom.
5. Use proper steps or a step-ladder to reach things in high places and for do-it-yourself work.
6. Light steps and stairs well, with a light-switch upstairs and downstairs.

CHILDREN

1. Fix children securely into prams, buggies etc. with a safety harness.
2. Keep a firm hold of small children when walking on busy roads. They are likely to dart out unexpectedly.
3. Never allow small children to play unsupervised, especially near water. A child can drown in a few centimetres of water. Teach all children to swim at an early age.
4. Store dangerous objects out of reach of small children: matches, lighters, plastic bags, knives, pins, beads.
5. Store medicines, dangerous cleaning agents, e.g. bleach, garden chemicals, cosmetics etc., out of reach of children, preferably in a locked press.

QUESTIONS/CHAPTER 16

1. What points must be taken into consideration when planning a kitchen? With these in mind, sketch and describe a kitchen suitable for a medium-priced modern house. (Do not use the plan illustrated in this chapter). Show the position of cupboards, cooker, sink, lighting and power points.
2. Adequate storage is essential in a working kitchen. Write a detailed description of modern kitchen storage units. Make reference to:
   (a) size and suitable measurements;
   (b) finishes, e.g. surfaces;
   (c) various types;
   (d) modern features.
3. Describe how you would redecorate the kitchen of a post-war bungalow. The storage units, coloured cream, are to be retained. Make reference to:
   (a) wall covering;
   (b) floor covering;
   (c) ventilation;
   (d) heating;
   (e) window covering.
4. Write a detailed note on safety in the home, in relation to each of the following:
   (a) care and maintenance of electrical equipment;
   (b) care in use and storage of poisonous chemicals;
   (d) care and maintenance of floors and furniture.

17.
Kitchen utensils

Well-designed equipment and utensils should
1. serve their purpose efficiently;
2. be reasonably strong and durable, unbreakable if possible;
3. be of sound construction and well balanced;
4. be comfortable and easy to handle;
5. be safe;
6. be easy to clean and stain resistant.

POTS AND PANS

1. A good cooking pan should conduct heat well and evenly — this saves fuel.
2. The pan should be strong, durable and heavy for its size.
3. It should have a thick flat base (minimum 2 mm). It is essential that saucepans used on electric and solid-fuel cookers have a thick, machine-ground base, to provide complete contact with the hot plate. Poor contact produces uneven cooking, wastes fuel and slows down cooking time.
4. Lids should fit snugly, but not too tightly. Avoid very thin lids, as these buckle easily if dropped.
5. Handles should be securely fixed, heat resistant and designed so that the fingers can grasp them without getting burned.
6. Large and very heavy saucepans require two handles.
7. Materials used should not rust.
8. Curved interiors are easier to clean than those with sharp corners.
9. Consider size of hot plates when choosing saucepans for an electric cooker. The diameter of the base of the pan should be the same as the hot plate. If the pan is larger, the contents will take longer to boil; if it is smaller, fuel is wasted.
10. Requirements:
    two small saucepans (one with pouring lip).
    one or two medium saucepans;
    one large saucepan;
    one frying pan and separate omelette pan if possible;
    one deep-fat frying pan (optional).

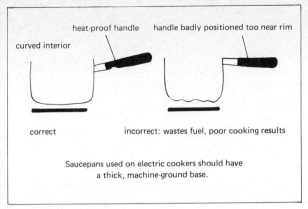

Well-designed saucepan

MATERIALS

Aluminium, made from bauxite, is a relatively cheap, light-weight metal used for saucepans and other kitchen equipment. It is available in several gauges or thicknesses. The best and most expensive saucepans are made from heavy gauge, cast aluminium. Lighter gauge, pressed aluminium is cheap and can work well enough on gas burners, but tends to burn food, buckle easily, become unbalanced and is generally bad value for money.

Non-stick fry-pan (Teflon Silverstone, Castle Brand)

Whistling kettle (Castle Brand)

Care
1. Wash, rinse and dry cooking pans in warm soapy water, using abrasives for stubborn stains.
2. Avoid leaving food or liquid in aluminium — it may cause staining.
3. Never use washing soda or fabric detergents in aluminium containers: these cause pitting and dis-colouration of the aluminium.

Cast iron is made from iron ore. It is possible to buy saucepans, casseroles and dishes made from cast iron, usually with an enamelled finish both inside and outside. It is also possible to get non-stick interiors. Cast iron utensils are very heavy and liable to break if dropped on a hard floor. They are ideal for long, slow cooking, such as stews and casseroles.

Advantages
1. Cast iron is an excellent conductor of heat. As it also retains heat well, the hot plate or burner can be kept at a low temperature throughout cooking, thus saving fuel.
2. Cast iron is durable, unless it is dropped.
3. Cast iron is very suitable for electric and solid fuel cookers — its weight together with its flat base maintains maximum contact with hot plate.
4. It is available in colourful and attractive designs and finishes, ideal for oven-to-table ware.
5. Cast iron can be used as a casserole, if handles are of a heat resistant material.

Disadvantages
1. The metal is brittle and will break if dropped on a hard surface.
2. Cast iron is expensive.
3. Utensils are very heavy, especially when full.
4. The enamel may chip.

Care of enamelled cast iron
1. Use wooden spoons to avoid scratching enamel.
2. Handle and wash carefully to avoid chipping.
3. Never heat an empty pan — this can cause chipping.
4. Avoid using high temperatures. They are not necessary as these vessels retain heat exceptionally well.
5. Use oven gloves — handles become extremely hot.
6. Cleaning: wash in warm soapy water. Rinse and dry thoroughly. The non-enamelled base will rust if left damp. Never use abrasives. If stained, steep overnight in biological detergent.

Enamelled aluminium or stainless steel: enamelling is a method of applying a glass-like coating to a metal, usually to prevent corrosion. The metal utensil is spray-washed, etched to enable the enamel to adhere well, and finally sprayed with molten enamel or dipped in it. A thin enamel coating is more resistant to damage and chipping than a thick one. After the enamel is applied the vessel passes through a furnace which fuses the enamel to the base metal. Various colours can be achieved by adding pigments to the enamel. Good quality enamelled ware carries a 'Vitramel' standard label. *Care* as for enamelled cast iron.

Advantages
1. It has an attractive and easily cleaned finish.
2. Food, acids and alkalis have no effect on it.
3. Some enamelled saucepans have a stainless steel rim to reduce chipping.

Disadvantages
1. Enamel has a tendency to chip: better quality utensils are resistant to chipping.
2. Toxicity: cadmium, used as a primer on the vessel and pigment of the enamel can have a cumulative toxic effect. For this reason a maximum level of cadmium is enforced in most countries. For absolute safety, it is wise to place a sheet of tin foil between the lid and top of older casseroles during cooking. White enamel does not contain this substance.

Stainless steel is made from iron ore. Nickel is added to harden it and make it rust resistant, and chromium is added to give it strength and durability. As stainless steel is a poor conductor of heat, saucepans and other cooking vessels are treated either by soldering a copper or aluminium disc onto the base of the pan or sandwiching a core of plain steel (which conducts heat well) between two stainless steel layers.

Advantages
1. non-toxic;
2. stain resistant and easily cleaned, can be washed in a dishwasher;
3. does not chip or break;
4. strong and durable, yet light in weight.

Disadvantages
1. expensive;
2. poor conductor of heat unless constructed as described above;
3. can be damaged and discoloured by over-heating.

Care of stainless steel
1. Never leave an empty pan on the heat — it discolours badly.
2. Use oven gloves.
3. Avoid using abrasives.
4. Wash in hot soapy water, rinse and dry quickly to prevent water marking.

Copper is an excellent conductor of heat. Copper must be lined with tin, as untinned copper is toxic. Although it looks attractive, copper is less frequently used nowadays as it is expensive, needs frequent cleaning, and the tin lining tends to wear off. Some stainless steel pans have a copper-plated base to provide even heat.

Advantages
1. good, even conductor of heat;
2. reasonably strong and durable;
3. attractive and warm in appearance.

Disadvantages
1. Unlined copper is poisonous.
2. It can reduce the vitamin C content of foods.
3. It stains easily and requires regular cleaning.
4. It is expensive.

Care of copper utensils
1. Wash thoroughly after use in hot soapy water, rinse and dry.
2. Polish the outside regularly with proprietary cleaner.
3. Avoid using metal utensils or abrasives. These damage the tin lining.
4. If lining is damaged, the pan must not be used as it is toxic. It is possible to have copper pans relined with tin, but this may prove more expensive than it is worth.

Tin is rarely used in the manufacture of pots and pans, except as a lining for copper utensils. However, it is still used extensively for making baking tins as well as utensils such as moulds, whisks, sieves, cutters, graters and so on. Most of these are made from steel coated with tin and tend to rust, especially when the tinning wears off.

Advantages
1. cheap;
2. easily moulded in various shapes;
3. cutting utensils take a sharp edge;
4. acids and alkalis have little effect on tin.

Disadvantages

1. tendency to rust;
2. can be damaged by intense heat, i.e. temperatures higher than 230°C.

Care of tin

1. Tin should be handled carefully, as it is easily damaged.
2. Never place onto direct heat, e.g. hot plate.
3. Wash in hot, soapy water, rinse well and dry thoroughly — to avoid rusting.
4. Avoid using harsh detergents or abrasives. If the article is badly burned, steep for a long time in hot soapy water. This loosens dirt and eliminates the need for scouring agents.
5. Avoid washing in a dishwasher.
6. Grease well before use.

Non-stick finishes are applied to the interior of pans, casseroles, baking tins, utensils and ovens. Most consist of a layer of polytetra-fluoroethylene (PTFE). This was originally designed as a protective coating for spacecraft. Its non-stick qualities make it ideal for use in the kitchen and it is highly resistant to chemicals. A non-stick finish can be applied to many metals, aluminium, cast iron and tin being the most usual. Brand names (Teflon, Fluon) are only used on best quality non-stick ware.

Manufacture

1. The non-stick substance can be applied either before or after the pan or utensil is pressed or shaped.
2. Firstly the alumium (or other metal) is roughened by a sanding process — this provides a grip for the subsequent layers.
3. The next step is called fritting: it is similar to enamelling — a ceramic or glass-like mixture is sprayed onto it.
4. A primer coat of PTFE is sprayed over the frit. This is fired at 240°C.
5. The final coat of PTFE is applied and fired at 440°C. This fuses the layers together, providing a smooth surface.
Note: Non-stick bakeware is sprayed directly with PTFE without the hard frit layer. This is because it is not subjected to the same wear and tear as saucepans.

Advantages

1. Food does not stick.
2. The surface is easy to clean.

Disadvantages

1. Great care must be taken to avoid scratching.
2. Coating, especially on cheaper saucepans, eventually wears off.

Care

1. Never use metal utensils for lifting or stirring food. Use special PTFE-coated utensils, or wooden or plastic spatulas.
2. Never use abrasives.
3. Avoid stacking pans.
4. Grease non-stick bakeware lightly.
5. Over-heating, or heating empty pans, damages the surface.
6. Cleaning: wash in hot soapy water, rinse well and dry. Wiping with a damp cloth is not sufficient — this causes a build-up of staining which reduces the efficiency of the pan.
7. Staining: should this occur put one cup of water, one-half cup of domestic bleach, and 2 tbsp. bicarbonate of soda into the pan. Boil for five to ten minutes. Wash, rinse and dry.
8. Expensive pans can be recoated with PTFE. Aerosol sprays are available for those who wish to do it at home. The surface provided is temporary.
9. Check whether utensil can be washed in a dish-washing machine: some can, some cannot.

Ceramic and Glass Cookware

Cooking pots have been made from ceramic materials from the earliest times.

1. ***Stoneware*** is made from clays which can be fired at a very high temperature. This makes it almost completely vitreous (non-porous) and when glazed it does not absorb food flavours, it is stain resistant, and easy to clean.
2. ***Earthenware*** as the name implies, is made from earth — or red clay. As it is fired at a relatively low temperature, it does not vitrify. It is therefore porous and absorbs odours and flavours easily. Unless glazed it will stain easily, and once stained it is difficult to clean. It chips and breaks very easily — but it is quite cheap. Earthenware and stoneware conduct heat slowly and evenly. Decoration may be under or over the glaze. Overglaze decoration is likely to wear off more quickly.
3. ***Glassware:*** normal glass made from sand, borax, silica and other ingredients has the major disadvantage that it cannot withstand thermal shock (sudden changes of temperature). By varying the basic ingredients of the glass and by tempering it, successively heating and cooling it, a certain amount

169

Pyrexware – practical and heat-resistant

(e) Any type of glassware will smash if dropped on a hard surface.
(f) Wash in hot, soapy water. Avoid abrasives unless absolutely necessary.
(g) Never place heat resistant glass directly under a grill or on a hot plate.

Advantages
(a) impervious to cooking flavours and smells;
(b) inexpensive;
(c) does not rust or bend;
(d) conducts and retains heat well.

Disadvantages
(a) breaks easily;
(b) can be scratched, e.g. by whisks and beaters;
(c) care must be taken to avoid changes in temperature — except for pyroceramic ware.

of heat resistance can be achieved. Heat resistant ovenware, e.g. Pyrex, is made from borosilicate glass and is used for casseroles, bowls, jugs and dishes of many shapes and sizes. Pyrex is heat resistant but not flameproof,i.e. it can be placed in a hot oven without breaking, but it must not be placed directly on a hot plate or gas flame. Heat resistant glassware is now available in an attractive smoked glass finish. **Pyroceram** is an exceptionally tough ceramic glass, first developed for the nose cones of rockets, to withstand the sudden change in temperature from the cold of outer space to the friction of re-entry into the earth's atmosphere. It can therefore be taken from the freezer and placed into a hot oven or hob without damage. Its attractive appearance enables it to be taken directly from the oven and used as a serving dish. Clip-on handles are available which are removed when cooking in the oven, or when freezing. Brand names: Pyroflam, Corningware (formerly known as Pyrosyl).

Care
(a) Avoid sudden changes in temperature: pyroceramic ware can withstand them, other glassware cannot.
(b) Never use a wet cloth to remove Pyrex dishes from a hot oven.
(c) Never place a hot dish on a cold surface or in cold water.
(d) Steep, after cooling, to soften stains and facilitate cleaning.

Tableware
Attractive table settings can do much to improve the appearance of food and add to the enjoyment of a meal. Table settings should be considered as a whole. Table-cloth, place mats, napkins, tableware and cutlery should blend together to form a pleasant and tasteful background to the food.

Consider the style in which the room is furnished, the type of meal for which the items are required, and keep these in mind when buying. Bone china, sterling silver and damask suit formal rooms and occasions; whereas sturdy pottery, easy-to-clean stainless steel cutlery, and gingham placemats provide a homely atmosphere and are more practical for everyday living.

Choosing tableware
1. It should be well designed, stable and attractive.
2. Handles and stems should be securely fixed. Handles of cups should allow room to be held comfortably.
3. Choose a design unlikely to be discontinued, for which single piece replacements are available.
4. Consider proportion, design, colour and patterns — these have an important bearing on the overall table setting.
5. Tableware should be easy to clean, without unnecessary ridges and crevices. Check whether it may be washed by machine.

Ceramic ware
This includes bone china, porcelain, earthenware, stoneware, pottery and delph.

Bone china, also known as soft-paste porcelain, is made from 50 per cent calcined animal bone, mixed with various clays — including china clay. It is fired at 1300°C, which causes the china to vitrify or become glass-like. Bone china is thin, translucent and delicate looking, but is stronger and more resistant to chipping than other ceramics. It is used for fine dinner and tea services, ornaments and serving dishes.

Hard-paste porcelain is a mixture of china clay, felspathic stone and quartz. It is fired at a high temperature and is reasonably resistant to heat. It may be thin and translucent like china, or thicker and more like pottery in appearance.

Earthenware, whose manufacture has been described, is used for most household delph, mugs, bowls, jugs and so on. It may be glazed or unglazed. Glazed pottery is easier to clean. Earthenware is the cheapest tableware available.

Stoneware is used for chunky dishes and casseroles. As it contains a high porportion of flint, it is rather heavy.

Glass is basically made from sand (silica), soda (sodium carbonate), and lime (calcium carbonate). It may contain other ingredients such as potash, lead or borax — depending on the type of glass required. All ingredients are melted in a furnace until they liquify. This molten glass may then be blown, pressed (moulded), or rolled. Containers, such as bowls, glasses and bottles, are made from blown or pressed glass; sheets of glass, such as window glass, are rolled into shape. Lead crystal glass is usually blown and decorated by cutting, engraving or carving.

Advantages
1. inorganic and incombustible;
2. non-absorbent — does not absorb flavours;
3. hygienic;
4. cheap;
5. can be tempered to make it heat resistant;
6. transparent — useful for containers, you can see what is in them.

Disadvantages
1. very brittle;
2. little heat resistance.

Choice
1. Look for well-designed glasses, made from clear, smooth flawless glass.
2. Avoid very narrow stems — they are easy to break or overturn.

3. Wine glasses should have a tulip shape, with a medium stem and wide base.
4. Lead crystal glass is sparkling and attractive, but also expensive and heavy.

Wood: whitewood (deal) is used for chopping boards and many kitchen utensils, such as spatulas, wooden spoons, rolling pins. Teak is used for salad bowls, knife handles, condiment sets. Teak is an ideal kitchen wood, as it has a high resistance to moisture.

Care
1. Avoid soaking wood in water.
2. Wash quickly in warm soapy water, rinse and dry thoroughly.
3. Salad bowls, contrary to some opinions, should be washed after use — otherwise the oil from dressing remaining in the bowl can go rancid. Wash and rinse quickly in warm water. Dry thoroughly.
4. The wood of salad bowls can be oiled occasionally.

Plastic

Thermoplastics, such as polythene and PVC, are soft plastics used for many kitchen utensils and containers, buckets, basins; polypropylene bowls are used for steaming puddings.

Thermosetting resins (bakelite, which are rigid, are mainly used for handles and knobs on saucepans, kettles, irons. Melamine is used for tableware, such as cups and saucers, and laminated plastic worktops are also made from thermosetting resins.

A modern double oven cooker among assorted well-designed kitchen equipment (Creda)

Advantages

1. cheap, plentiful;
2. colourful and attractive;
3. resistant to breaking;
4. washable;
5. lightweight.

Disadvantages

1. most are damaged or destroyed by heat;
2. hard plastics can break;
3. tendency to scratch and peel;
4. damaged by sharp utensils;
5. some impart a taste to food.

Care

1. Follow manufacturer's instructions; composition and therefore the care of plastics can vary considerably.
2. Avoid abrasives, strong detergents and bleaches.
3. Check the heat resistance before subjecting article to heat. All are damaged by intense dry heat, e.g. placing on a hot plate. Some are damaged by boiling water. Some are not suitable for use in dishwashers.

Cutlery

Good cutlery should be durable, comfortable to hold, efficient to use, stain resistant, easy to clean, and attractive. Expensive cutlery fulfils most, if not all, of the above conditions. Cheap cutlery is usually not worth the money: it rusts, stains and often becomes inefficient or breaks.

Choosing cutlery

1. Consider cost: buy the best you can afford, within reason.

A drawerful of good-looking cutlery

2. Type should suit place settings and style of home.
3. Amount: be sure to buy enough, especially if a dishwasher is used. It is easy to run out of cutlery.
4. Handle each item of cutlery before buying to feel if it is comfortable and efficient. It should balance well in the hand and on the table.
5. Handles, unless moulded all-in-one with the rest of the cutlery, should be firmly fixed and washable. Handle materials include bone, horn, plastic, wood. Separate handles usually involve special care, and are rarely suitable for a dishwasher.
6. Bad design features: blades which do not cut efficiently; forks which do not hold food; spoons which are too shallow to lift food; sharp handles which cut into the palm of the hand.

Materials

1. *Solid silver.* or sterling silver, has a beautiful appearance and is available in traditional designs. Solid sterling silver, like all precious metals, is hallmarked to guarantee its authenticity, and its price is prohibitive.
2. *Electroplated nickel silver* (EPNS), also called silver plate, consists of a base, made from iron or other strong metal, which is coated with a nickel silver alloy.*

   The thickness of the coating varies: a thick, good quality coating should last for twenty-five years. Like silver, EPNS tarnishes easily, but this may be removed with a proprietary cleaner. The design of much silver cutlery is traditional and unlikely to date.

   *An *alloy* is a mixture of different metals. Examples:

   brass is an alloy ...   of copper and zinc;
   bronze is an alloy ...   of copper and tin;
   stainless steel is an alloy ... of iron, chromium and nickel.

3. *Stainless steel:* the quality of stainless steel varies. Cutlery should have a good proportion of carbon steel, to enable it to take a sharp edge. The main advantage of stainless steel is that it is stain resistant (not really stain*less*) and is easy to care for. It can be made in modern or traditional patterns and shapes.

Dishwashers

Both stainless steel and modern silver or silver plate may usually be washed in a dishwasher. Check with the manufacturer. Some manufacturers suggest that these metals should be kept in separate containers in the dishwasher to avoid *electrolytic action,* i.e. the metals reacting upon one another and causing staining. Remove cutlery from the dishwasher immediately the cycle has ended, to prevent water marks.

Cutlery requirements

Most items of cutlery can now be bought individually. Not long ago, they had to be bought in sets of six or twelve place settings. The minimum requirement would be two place settings for each member of a household. A family with a dishwasher, or one which entertains a lot, would require extra cutlery.

A *place setting* includes
one dinner knife and fork;
one dessert knife, fork and spoon;
one teaspoon;
one soupspoon.

Tablespoons and extra teaspoons are also required.
Other essential cutlery includes a carving knife and fork, a bread knife, and salad servers. Optional cutlery includes jam and grapefruit spoons, fish knives and forks, a cake server or knife, and steak knives.

Kitchen knives

One of the most essential pieces of equipment in a kitchen is a good sharp knife, or preferably a set of cook's knives. These are usually made from carbon steel or stainless steel. Carbon steel takes a very fine edge, but is inclined to blacken and rust. Stainless steel is easier to care for, but does not take such a sharp edge. A sharp knife is less dangerous than a blunt one, as it is less likely to slip. The handle, which is usually wooden, should be firmly riveted onto the blade.

Basic requirements:

1. cook's knife or chopping knife (blade 17 to 18 cm long), used for chopping, dicing, cutting meat;
2. filleting knife (blade 13 to 14 cm long) for filleting and boning;
3. paring knife (blade 8 cm long) for peeling, scraping, coring, and fine chopping;
4. bread knife;
5. palette knife (with flexible blade), used as a spatula;
6. carving knife and fork, with protective guard;
7. cleaver, for butchering meat (optional);
8. freezer knife if required (optional);
9. grapefruit knife (optional);
10. knife sharpener, either electric, hand-operated, or a steel.

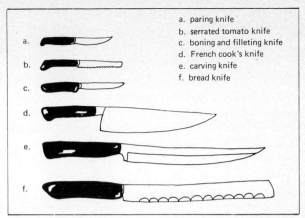

a. paring knife
b. serrated tomato knife
c. boning and filleting knife
d. French cook's knife
e. carving knife
f. bread knife

Kitchen knives

Note: With the vast array of kitchen equipment. utensils and tableware available today, it is obvious that the use, care and cleaning of many items will vary considerably. It is essential to read the instructions supplied with each product and to follow the directions for use, before working with a new piece of equipment.

QUESTIONS/CHAPTER 17

1. Imagine you have completed a project on saucepans and casseroles. Discuss the following;
   (a) types available;
   (b) materials used;
   (c) efficiency and durability;
   (d) ease of handling and cleaning.
   Explain the effects which two different foods have on metals
2. Discuss a project in which you have taken part relating to one of the following subjects:
   (a) cutlery for table and kitchen use;
   (b) glass — its uses in cooking and storage;
   (c) ceramic ware from oven to table.
   Explain the term polytetrafluoroethylene. Give examples of its use.
3. Compare cast iron and stainless steel as materials for kitchen saucepans and casseroles. List the sources of
   (a) aluminium;
   (b) copper;
   (c) tin.
   Write an informative note on non-stick finishes, explaining briefly how the finish is applied.
4. Write a paragraph on each of the following:
   (a) choosing kitchen knives and gadgets;
   (b) choosing cutlery for everyday table use;
   (c) choosing china for special occasions.
   Refer to composition, design, cost, care and cleaning.

18.
Appliances and Equipment

The increased influence of technology and automation has found its way into the modern home, as it has also done in so many other places. If they can afford it, a young couple setting up home have a wide choice of gadgets and machines. These can cut physical labour by half and thus increase the time available for leisure pursuits.

Before buying a large appliance, check these points:

1. Can you afford it? Would a hire purchase agreement be worthwhile? Consider also the cost of installing and running it.
2. Is it really necessary? Will it save time and/or labour? Or are you just keeping up with the Joneses? Many freezer owners make little use of their freezers, for example.
3. Will the number of times it is used justify the cost?
4. Is there space for it in the kitchen or a nearby utility room?
5. Ask friends and neighbours: find out their experiences; benefit from their mistakes. Find out the pros and cons of each item of equipment.
6. Read *Which* reports (indexed yearly volumes are available in the public library).

CHOOSING A LARGE APPLIANCE

1. Make sure it is good value for money.
2. Buy from a reliable dealer who carries a wide selection of goods, offers unbiased advice, and provides after-sales service. Use only well-established electrical and gas shops and showrooms.
3. Buy a well-recommended, reliable make which carries a service guarantee and a British or Irish Standards mark, and if electric is guaranteed electrically safe.
4. Make sure reliable servicing is easily available, preferably locally.
5. Consider the size of the family, and the amount of use the equipment will get. Consider the future: do not necessarily buy the smallest size. When in doubt, go for larger sizes.
6. Measure the area into which the appliance must fit. Bring measurements when shopping. Most illustrated brochures give dimensions of each appliance.

7. Consider height: will it fit under or alongside work-tops?
8. Consider childproof safety features, if children live in the house.
9. The appliance should be well-designed for its purpose, sturdy, and easily cleaned. Do not be too much influenced by flashy gadgets and trimmings.
10. It should be easy to operate, with a selection of operations or programmes.
11. Consider proximity to plumbing and power points. The further away it is situated, the more installation will cost. Get an estimate for installation.
12. Arrange a demonstration and make sure you get an instruction book, with clear instructions in English.
13. Read and keep safely the instructions which come with an appliance. Machines work more economically, break down less often, and last longer when properly used.

COOKERS

The cooker is the most important piece of equipment in the kitchen.

Choosing a cooker

1. It should be good value for money and within your price range.
2. Decide whether a gas, electric, solid fuel or oil-fired cooker is most suitable, and browse around the appropriate showroom.
3. Size of cooker will depend on the amount of cooking done. A person with a large family who does a lot of baking and/or entertaining will require a larger than average cooker.
4. Most families require the standard cooker, with three of four hot plates, reasonably large oven, and full width grill. Only those who do very little cooking and little or no baking (those in flats or bedsitters perhaps) should buy anything smaller.
5. Oven interior and hob should be easy to clean.
6. Consider dimensions of cooker. Will it fit into kitchen plan? Most cookers are about 915 mm high, 460 to 600 mm wide and 600 mm deep — much the same size as a base kitchen unit.

Electric cooker with eye-level grill (Creda)

THE FOUR BASIC TYPES OF COOKER

1. The **table cooker,** consisting of two boiling rings and a grill or small oven is operated from a 13 amp plug. It is useful in flats and bedsitters.

2. **Floor-standing cooker** (the standard cooker) has three or four hot plates, a grill, and a large or medium-sized oven. It may be fired by gas or electricity.

3. **Double width or range cooker** is a large cooker, fired by solid fuel, oil or gas. It has two or three ovens, a large hob, and often a griddle. Electric versions may incorporate a grill and a rotisserie.

4. **Split-level cooker** is a built-in cooker, fired by gas or electricity. The oven and grill are fitted into a wall unit at waist level. A separate hob is recessed into a suitable section of the worktop.

Advantages
(a) Oven and hob can be fitted at the most convenient height and position for the worker.
(b) It makes kitchen lay-outs more flexible.
(c) A waist-level oven is easier to clean and eliminates stooping.
(d) Controls are safer — usually at the side of the hob and the top of the oven units.
(e) It is possible to have one part fuelled by gas, the other by electricity.

Disadvantages
(a) The hob reduces the worktop area considerably.
(b) The oven unit breaks the sweep of worktop, making the kitchen look smaller (this may be acceptable in a large kitchen).
(c) It is doubtful if the convenience justifies the expense: at least one-and-a-half times the cost of an equivalent floor-standing cooker, with fitting about twice the cost of fitting a standard cooker.
(d) Special housing cabinets may be required.
(e) Ovens with drop-down doors are difficult to reach into and to clean.

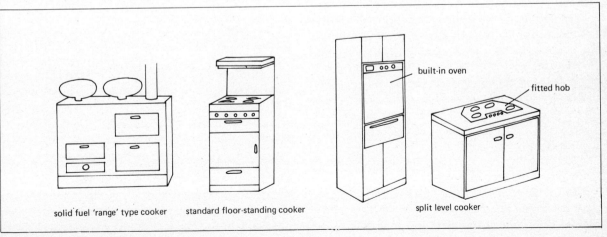

solid fuel 'range' type cooker   standard floor-standing cooker   built-in oven   fitted hob   split level cooker

Different types of cookers

Cooker construction

A standard cooker consists of a hob, with two to four rings or burners, a grill and an oven. Some have a plate-warming cabinet. Most cookers are made from enamelled steel, insulated with asbestos or fibreglass. Alternative finishes include brushed chrome and heat resistant glass (sometimes used on doors). Cookers should be mounted on castors or rollers to facilitate cleaning behind them.

Hobs are usually made from enamelled steel, brushed chrome, or stainless steel. The latter two are stain resistant. The hob should have sealed hot plates which lift up, or a removable drip tray, which makes it easy to wipe up spills as they occur. Saucepans should be able to sit steadily on the hob without wobbling or scratching it. Draw-off space for saucepans on the hob is convenient.

Hot plates: eighty per cent of cooking is done on hot plates. They should be quick to heat up, with variable controls. Cooking rings may consist of gas burners, radiant coils, or solid discs.

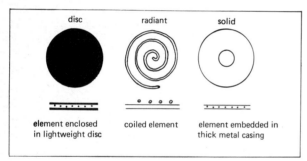

Grills

Duplex or dual-control hot plates consist of two elements: the inner one is used for small pans, the two together for full-sized pans. This is economical on fuel.

Simmerstats are hot plates with a special thermostat in the centre of the ring. This senses the temperature of the pan and keeps it at simmering point, preventing boiling over.

Ceramic hob: the hob surface is one continuous sheet of heat-resistant opaque glass. Four circular patterns on the glass indicate the position of heating elements underneath. The controls and elements work in much the same way as normal hot plates. The main advantage is the smooth, streamlined appearance of the hob and the ease of cleaning.

Grills may be at eye level, in a separate compartment, or within the oven.

Eye level grills are convenient and prevent stooping: *but* they are unpleasantly hot on the face; always on

view; tend to dirty the wall behind them; lifting the grill pan can be awkward.

Enclosed grill is cleaner and neater; grill compartment can be used as a second oven (often with its own thermostat) or for plate warming; drop-down door is handy for resting dishes and grill pan when turning food; *but* grill pan must be pulled out regularly to check cooking.

A grill in the **main oven** is a very bad arrangement; the oven cannot be used when grill is on and vice versa.

Dual element grill is very economical: half the grill can be switched on when cooking small amounts of food.

Heat resistant handle is essential to prevent burning the hands.

Rotisserie is a rotating spit under a high-level grill.

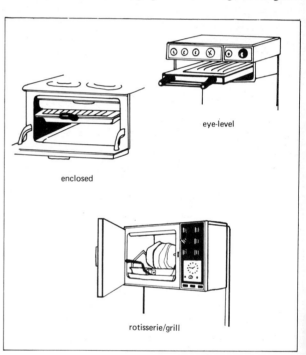

Convection currents cook food in gas oven

Controls should be out of reach of children, firmly fixed, easy to manipulate, with a non-ridged surface. They should be variable from low to high temperatures, with a clear indicator to show when they are on.

Oven should be big enough to take a large turkey. The capacity of an oven is measured in litres: the standard oven is approximately 60 litres. Most cookers are sold with two shelves; electric cookers can have an interior light and an inner glass door. Electric elements (2 to 3 kW) may be on the sides or the base of the oven.

176

Gas burners are usually at the base of the oven. Both are thermostatically controlled.

Check the following:

Is oven door a drop-door or hinged? If hinged, does the door open on the most suitable side for the kitchen design? Does it open within the width of the oven or is extra space needed?

Does oven have removable linings for easier cleaning or an easily cleaned surface?

MODERN FEATURES

Fan ovens have a circular element at the back of the oven, with a fan which blows heated air into and around the oven. The temperature throughout the oven is even — giving better results when the oven is full than cookers which have elements at the sides or base of the oven. Food can be placed on any shelf to cook and brown evenly. Fan ovens are ideal for those who do large amounts of baking, e.g. batch cooking for a freezer, as the oven can be filled without restricting circulation of heat. They are more expensive to buy than standard cookers, but more economical to run. They also tend to be easier to clean. For those who use an oven to cook meals which may require different temperatures between top and bottom shelves, a standard cooker is preferable.

Autotimers have become a feature of most electric and some gas cookers. They consist of an electric or battery-operated clock which can be set by operating one or two dials. These switch on the oven at a pre-set time and turn it off when the dish has cooked. The normal oven switch is set to the required cooking temperature. Some models include a separate timing device which can be used to time cakes, etc. — this rings when the time is up. The autotimer is fairly difficult to understand. It is advisable to get a demonstration of its use before buying. Read instructions carefully and use the same temperature, cooking time, and position in oven as in normal cooking. It is a good idea to have a practice run, when one is there to check it.

The oven switches automatically on and off by a pre-arranged setting in the absence of the cook. This is suitable for casseroles, braised dishes, some puddings and many other items, but not for foods which need a high temperature at the start of cooking, e.g. pastry, sponges and many other cakes. Dry foods (meat and fish) should be brushed with oil before putting in oven. Vegetables should be covered with water to prevent discoloration.

Note: Avoid leaving food in oven for long periods in hot weather: the warmth may activate bacteria and cause food poisoning.

Cleaning

There are several kinds of oven which are especially easy to clean. Solid fuel ovens clean themselves by burning off spills and splashes. Many ovens have enamelled sides, top and base which can be removed for cleaning. Some have a coating of *PTFE* (see non-stick pans), which reduces the amount of dirt that adheres to the sides of the oven. If wiped down with a soft cloth, wrung out of soapy water, *every* time the oven is used, they will continue to work efficiently for a considerable time. If stains are allowed to bake on, it will be impossible to remove them without using an abrasive, which in turn will damage the lining.

Catalytic linings are found in 'stay-clean' ovens: oven walls are coated with a matt-finished enamel, containing a catalyst which oxidises splashes and spills while the oven is hot. This leaves the oven clean after cooking. The walls should be wiped with a damp cloth after use. It is possible to replace the linings after a few years — when they become inefficient. In many cookers, the roof and floor of the cooker are finished in normal enamel, which should be cleaned in the normal way.

Pyrolytic ovens are self-cleaning ovens found in some expensive cookers. They work in the following way: the oven is set to the cleaning temperature — usually about 482°C — for between two and six hours, then allowed to cool. During the cleaning programme the door is automatically locked. The dirt carbonises (burns off), leaving a little ash on the base. Because of the high temperature used, these ovens must be very well insulated. A cleaning cycle will use three or four units of electricity.

A rotisserie is a revolving spit which is rotated by an electric motor — usually situated behind the rear wall of the oven. Electric rotisseries are usually within the oven, those in gas cookers are often placed under the grill and are sometimes battery operated. A rotisserie may be used to spit-roast poultry, joints of meat or (in some models) kebabs. Grill or oven should be preheated for five to fifteen minutes before use.

Advantages

1. Roasts need less attention as they are self-basting.
2. The meat is more evenly cooked, and more moist and tender than oven-roasted meat.

Double ovens are available in more expensive cookers. They are worth while for large families or those who cook a lot. They may take the form of a thermostatically-controlled grill compartment or two overs side-by-side, as in a range.

A built-in *meat thermometer* is available in some cookers. A buzzer sounds when meat is ready.

Lights: most electric cookers have an oven light; some have a hob light which illuminates the cooking area.

Coloured enamelled finishes are available in some expensive cookers.

Hinged lid over hob is neat and hides the cooker hob from view when not in use.

COMPARING COOKING FUELS

ELECTRICITY

1. Electricity produces heat without combustion, fumes or soot: this makes it the cleanest form of cooking. The kitchen surrounds stay relatively clean.
2. It is efficient, easy to control, noiseless and odourless.
3. Electric cookers are more up-to-date, with many of the modern features mentioned above available in different models.
4. Heavy, machine-ground saucepans must be used.
5. Electric cookers retain heat for longer: oven may be switched off before cooking is finished.
6. Most electric cookers have the control panel on the splash-back: this is safer for children but can cause nasty scalds from steaming saucepans.
7. Solid hot plates are slow to heat up; coiled elements heat more quickly.
8. Both eye-level and under-hob grills are available.
9. Dual element grills and hot plates are available: half the grill or hot plate can be turned on.
10. Plate-warming space is available.
Note: electric cookers must be connected to a powerful fuse, usually 30 amp.

GAS

1. Gas cooks quickly and evenly, faster than electricity.
2. Gas flame is easy to see and control, giving excellent cooking results.

3. Piped gas is only available in certain large towns and cities, although butane gas is now available throughout Ireland.
4. Gas fumes tend to soil kitchen paint-work, saucepans and utensils.
5. Gas ovens heat up more quickly than electric ovens.
6. Most gas cookers have either a pilot light, push button or spark ignition.

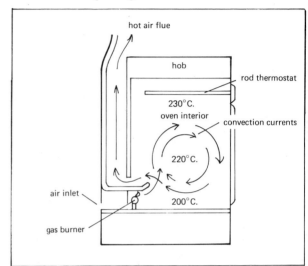

Gas cooker with eye-level grill

7. Most gas cookers have controls at the front of the cooker — handy for the housewife, but dangerous where children are about.
8. Fewer gas cookers have modern features, e.g. auto-timers, dual grills. This should change with the introduction of natural gas.
9. Most grills on gas cookers are at eye level.
10. Safety feature — most have a flame failure device which cuts off gas if flame goes out.

Conclusion

There is little to choose between a gas or electric cooker in use, initial or running costs.

SOLID FUEL

The solid fuel cooker consists of a well-insulated, cast-iron fire-box, with flues which carry the heat to two or more ovens and two large cast-iron hot plates, and a balanced flue to carry away smoke and soot. Because the cooker is so well insulated, very little heat is lost to the surrounding area — unlike older range-type cookers. Large solid fuel cookers may have a large or small *boiler,* which heats radiators in other rooms and/or the household hot water supply. The hot plates — one hot, one cooler — are covered when not in use with large, hinged, insulated lids. The oven nearest to the source of heat is very hot and used for roasting and baking. The cooler oven is used for simmering. Special equipment is available for grilling and toasting. Modern solid fuel cookers are fitted with adjustable flues and a thermostat which indicates the oven temperature. This type of cooker has proved so successful that it has now been adapted to use *oil or gas.*

Advantages

1. The modern solid fuel cooker is a far cry from the smoky old-fashioned range which had to be black-leaded regularly.
2. It provides hot water and sometimes selective central heating.
3. It is constantly ready for use.
4. It is cheap to run. Gas and oil models are less economical.
5. It cleans itself: burnt food carbonises on hot plate and oven.
6. A large amount of cooking can be done at one time: six or seven saucepans can fit on hot plates, with plenty of draw-off space. This is ideal for the housewife who has a large family, cooks a lot, or runs a guest house.

Disadvantages

1. This type of cooker is very expensive and must be installed by an expert.
2. It is quite large and cumbersome, not suitable for a small kitchen.
3. A flue is required.
4. Fuel storage facilities are required, for oil and solid fuel models.
5. Solid fuel needs regular attention — fuelling, stoking, etc.
6. Flues must be cleaned periodically.
7. Solid fuel is difficult to regulate. More practice is required to get used to a solid fuel cooker than a gas or electric cooker.
8. The cooker can make the kitchen very hot in warm weather. It is useful to have an alternative form of cooking for hot summer days.

Note: Take care to have cooker installed correctly. Use recommended fuel for maximum efficiency. Use saucepans with a machine-ground base for direct contact with the hot plate.

MICROWAVE OVENS

Transference of heat

Heat is caused by the motion of molecules. In normal cooking, the flame *(radiant heat)* touches the saucepan causing the metal molecules to oscillate (move about) rapidly and become hot; the water in turn heats up by the same method; and finally the food in the water becomes hot — on the outside first and gradually inwards until the entire food has been cooked by *conduction.*

If the molecules can be made to move at very high speeds, more friction occurs within the substance, heating it very quickly. It is on this principle that microwave cooking is based.

Principle of microwave cooking

Microwave ovens emit electromagnetic waves of very high frequency, which penetrate the food and produce a rapidly alternating magnetic field. This changes the position of the molecules within the food continuously and rapidly. The resulting friction heats the food in all parts simultaneously, instead of the usual, more gradual, heating process from the outside in.

Structure of microwave ovens

Most microwave ovens consist of three parts: the magnetron, the oven cabinet, and the supply unit.

The *magnetron* is the core of the microwave oven. It

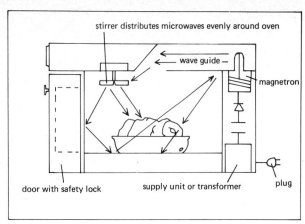

Microwave oven

generates high frequency electromagnetic waves, of a higher frequency than radio waves. The waves/rays pass into the oven cabinet through a specially constructed tube or **wave guide**.

The **oven cabinet** is lined with stainless steel or aluminium. The rays pass into the oven, where they are reflected in a continuously changing pattern, so that all parts of the oven are evenly heated. The door is made of safety glass, with a fine steel mesh which prevents the passage of rays outside. The door should have a good seal and safety lock to prevent radiation leakage when the cooker is turned on. Controls include a timing dial marked in seconds, heat control, one or two starting buttons, and sometimes an indicator light or buzzer — to show when time is up.

The **supply unit** is a transformer which boosts the mains voltage (220) to the very high voltage required by the oven.

Properties of microwaves

Microwaves can be absorbed, reflected or transmitted, depending on the materials used.

Absorption: organic materials such as food absorb microwave energy and are therefore capable of being heated and cooked by microwaves.

Reflection: metals reflect microwave energy and are used in the walls of the oven, but must not be used for food containers.

Transmission: materials such as glass, ceramics and some plastics neither absorb nor reflect microwave energy, but allow it to pass through. They are very suitable food containers for use in microwave ovens. Plastics must be able to withstand the temperature of boiling liquid (100°C). Certain plastics — such as polystyrene and melamine — are therefore unsuitable for use in microwave ovens.

Use of microwave ovens

1. The thicker and larger the item to be heated, the more time will be necessary to heat it: small pieces of meat are more suitable than large joints; four small dishes of stew will reheat quicker than one large casserole.
2. Food of a dense structure will take longer to cook than a similarly sized piece of food with a loose structure: a sponge pudding will be heated faster than a steak and **kidney** pudding.
3. It is wasteful to use the cooker for one item.
4. The lower the temperature of the food to be cooked, the longer it will take: a frozen beefburger will take longer than a fresh one. Most cookers have a thawing setting on the dial.
5. Precooked food obviously requires less time in the oven.
6. A small thin dish allows rays to pass through more easily; therefore avoid using thick, heavy containers for food.

Microwave cooker (Tricity)

Care

1. Avoid rough handling: a microwave oven is a delicate piece of equipment.
2. Never use metal containers, which may damage the magnetron.
3. Do not attempt to repair any faults: contact the service engineer.
4. To clean, unplug and wipe with a damp cloth after use.

Advantages

1. Speed and economy: foods cook three to five times more quickly than in conventional ovens.
2. The microwave oven can be used to heat or cook raw, precooked or frozen food.

3. Nutritive value remains unchanged, due to speed of cooking.
4. It is absolutely safe; microwaves are cut off if door is opened.
5. It is ideal for those in a hurry. Hotel and catering establishments, working wives, and flat dwellers would find them particularly useful.
6. Cooking dishes remain cool enough to handle.
7. It can be used from a normal 13 amp socket.

Disadvantages
1. The microwave oven is expensive to buy.
2. It is unsuitable for slow cooking, e.g. stewing.
3. It only browns food with a large mass, i.e. which needs longer cooking. A browning element is incorporated in some cookers, to enable smaller items to brown successfully.
4. As this is a completely different type of cooking, it takes a while to get used to.
5. It is only suitable as a supplementary method of cooking. A normal cooker would usually be required as well for baking, large scale cooking, and processes which require the hob.

REFRIGERATORS

A refrigerator is an extremely cold, well-insulated cupboard, designed to keep perishable food at a temperature sufficiently low to retard the growth of microorganisms.

Principle

During *evaporation,* heat is absorbed from the surrounding area: this occurs, for example, during perspiration. Refrigeration is worked on the principle that if a liquid is evaporated, heat will be drawn from the surrounding area (the refrigerator cabinet), causing it to drop in temperature. Suitable liquids (called *refrigerants*), which convert readily from liquid to gas and vice versa, are used in the working unit of the refrigerator. Examples of such refrigerants are liquid ammonia and Freon 12.

There are two types of refrigerator: the compressor type and the absorption type. The compressor is the most common type — used in most family fridges.

The compressor refrigerator
1. A *compressor,* driven by a small electric motor, forces the relatively warm gaseous refrigerant into a condenser, where it loses its heat and reverts to a liquid form. This heat is released outside the refrigerator, usually at the back.

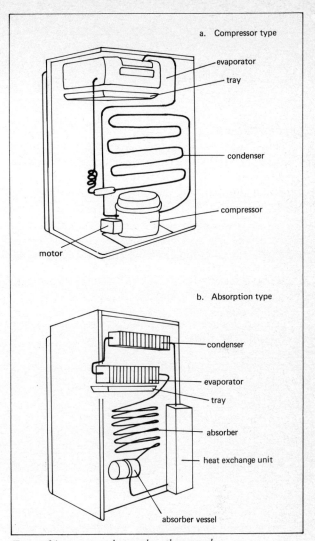

Two refrigerators: what makes them work

2. The liquefied refrigerant passes into the *evaporator* (or frozen food compartment) where it evaporates, drawing heat from the inside of the refrigerator cabinet, which now becomes cool.
3. The gaseous refrigerant is drawn into the compressor and the cycle begins again.

A thermostat disconnects electricity to the compressor when the temperature is falling and reconnects it to start the motor again as the temperature within the refrigerator rises. This causes the intermittent hum common to all compressor refrigerators. The compressor method of refrigeration is the one most often used for electric fridges and deep freeze cabinets.

Absorption refrigerators are usually run on gas or oil, although they may be run on mains electricity or batteries. They are ideal for use on boats and caravans, where mains electricity is not available.

Refrigerator temperatures

The temperature within the refrigerator cabinet varies between 2°C and 7°C. It should never rise above 7°C. Below this temperature, the activity of micro-organisms and enzymes — which cause deterioration of food — is greatly reduced.

Star markings

With the growth in consumption of frozen foods, it became necessary to increase the size of the ice-box, or evaporator, formerly used only to make ice cubes, so that a reasonable amount of frozen food could be stored in the refrigerator. This compartment, now known as the frozen food storate compartment, is marked with star symbols to indicate the degree of coldness or the length of time frozen food may be stored in it.

One star*
indicates a temperature of —6°C or below, where food may be stored for up to one week.
Two stars**
indicates a temperature of —12°C or below, where food may be stored for up to one month.
Three stars***
indicates a temperature of —18°C or below, where food may be stored for up to three months.
Note: None of the above markings indicate a deep freeze temperature; therefore, these frozen food compartments should not be used for freezing fresh or raw foods.

Deep-freeze cabinets have a storage temperature of —18°C but can be reduced to —25°C for freezing fresh food. They have four-star marking****

Construction

Modern refrigerators are made from enamelled pressed steel. They are lined with polystyrene, the door having moulded plastic fitments for eggs, butter, cheese and bottles. Between the outer and inner casing is a layer of insulating material. The frozen food storage compartment may be inside the refrigerator, with a drop-down door. Larger models have a separate frozen compartment over the refrigerator with its own door. Magnetic catches, plastic-coated removable wire shelves, a plastic vegetable drawer, interior light, and laminated worktop are standard features. A drip tray/chiller is usual in most models. Expensive models may have coloured or wood finished doors. Doors should open within the width of the cabinet, and are available to open from left or right.

Dimensions: fridges come in various sizes. The standard model, to fit alongside or under worktops, is usually similar to standard base kitchen units, i.e. 500 mm wide, 600 mm deep and 850 or 915 mm high (worktop height). Larger models, either slimline or double width with two doors, and fridge freezers (with two separate compressor units and doors) are a good deal higher and should be placed at the end of a line of floor units, to avoid breaking the continuity of the worktop. There are also small tabletop models for flats and bedsitters.

The *capacity* of a fridge is the amount of space inside the cabinet. This used to be measured in cubic feet, but is now measured in litres. Sizes vary from 28 to 350 litres: the average household size is 115 litres.

The arrangement of this internal space is important if the maximum use is to be made of the refrigerator. Adjustable shelves, a place for tall bottles, and a frozen food compartment are regarded as essential features.

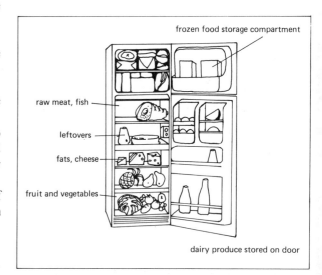

Correct food storage in a refrigerator

Controls: electric refrigerators are connected to a three-pin earthed socket. A thermostatically controlled dial controls the temperature within the cabinet. The freezer may have an independent thermostat in fridge/freezer models.

Defrosting

Defrosting is necessary to remove the build-up of ice around the evaporator. If this is not removed, the refrigerator will work less efficiently and waste electricity or gas. Methods of defrosting vary from one refrigerator to another.

1. *Manual defrosting:* controls are set to 'off' or 'defrost' until all ice has melted. Frozen food should be removed and wrapped in insulating material (newspaper) to prevent thawing. Defrosting can be accelerated by placing a bowl of very hot water inside the evaporator unit. When defrosting is over, the dial is re-set and food returned to the refrigerator.

2. *Push-button defrosting:* when defrost button is pressed, the refrigerator stops working until all ice is melted. It then commences once again, without resetting. Frozen food must be removed. Some models have accelerated defrosting — hot liquid is piped through the evaporator to speed up defrosting.

3. *Automatic defrosting:* this takes place continuously at regular intervals. Every few hours the compressor stops for about fifteen minutes, to allow the frost to melt. It restarts automatically. There is no build-up of ice and no need to remove frozen food.

Note: Defrosting is required when the thickness of ice on the evaporator is over 7 mm.

Position

A refrigerator should be placed on a level surface. Adjustable feet are available on many models. Make sure there is free circulation of air above and behind it — particularly if it is built-in under a worktop. Avoid placing near a source of heat. Make sure that the door can open wide enough to remove drip tray and shelves.

CHOOSING A REFRIGERATOR

Consider

1. the size of the household — allow 30 litres per person;
2. the amount of cooking and entertaining done;
3. convenience of shops — those far from shops may need extra refrigerator space;
4. amount of kitchen space available;
5. fuel available — gas or electricity;
6. amount of money to spend.

Compare

1. design and finish — look for a durable, reliable make;
2. well-designed interior which makes full use of space, with strong, adjustable shelves;
3. direction in which the door opens — does it suit the kitchen lay-out?
4. type of defrosting — preferably automatic.
5. guarantee — one year minimum; the sealed unit at the back may be guaranteed for three or four years.

Running costs

These depend on several factors:
1. size and type of refrigerator;
2. temperature of room;
3. how much food is put in;
4. how often the door is opened.

Average running cost of an electric refrigerator is that of one to two units per day.

Advantages of refrigeration

1. Hygiene: protects food from contamination by dust and flies.
2. Preservation: delays decay by retarding bacterial action.
3. Economy: reduces waste caused by decayed food; enables left-overs to be kept for another day.
4. Convenience: cuts down on shopping trips — a weekly trip may suffice.
5. Time-saving: meals can be prepared in advance and kept until required.
6. Cooking: useful for cold cookery, cold souffles, jellies and salads.
7. Taste: certain foods taste nicer when chilled — fruit juices, milk, white wine, beer, salads and cold sweets.
8. Frozen food: a supply of frozen food, ice cream and ice cubes is readily available.

Use

1. Wrap or cover foods before storing, because refrigeration has a drying effect on food, and to avoid strong-smelling foods contaminating others.
2. Never put warm or hot food in the refrigerator: this causes excessive build-up of ice on the evaporator.
3. Check over contents daily and use up left-overs.
4. Avoid overcrowding foods; allow free circulation of air.
5. Storage: The evaporator is the coldest part of the refrigerator. The door and base of the refrigerator are less cold. Store food accordingly.
   Frozen food compartment: frozen foods, ice cream, ice cubes.
   Top of cabinet: raw meat, fish, offal, sausages.
   Centre of cabinet: left-overs, fats, cheese, bacon.
   Vegetable drawer or hydrator: lettuce, vegetables, fruit.
   Door: eggs, butter, milk and other drinks.
6. Wipe shelves daily; mop up spills at once.
7. Clean and defrost regularly — usually once a week.
8. Clean interior with warm water containing bread soda, rinse and dry thoroughly. Never use a detergent or abrasives.

9. Dust coils behind refrigerator once a year, and polish outside now and then with a silicone polish.

Economy — to save fuel
1. Read instruction book and follow instructions.
2. Never place near a source of heat, e.g. cooker or heater.
3. Avoid unnecessary opening of door: make sure door closes properly.
4. Never place hot or even warm foods in refrigerator.
5. Allow space for circulation of air behind and inside refrigerator.
6. Defrost regularly to make the most efficient use of evaporator.
7. Do not set thermostat too low. Adjust according to conditions: low during warm spells, normal during cold weather.

FOOD FREEZERS

Food freezers are cooled by the same method as compressor refrigerators. The type of **condenser** used varies.
1. External condensers, visible at back of freezer, collect dust.
2. Fan-cooled condensers, within the freezer body, are fairly noisy.
3. Skin condensers, embedded in the outside walls of the freezer, are quiet, do not require cleaning and are resistant to damp.

The deep freeze **cabinet** consists of two steel layers, with a 10 cm space between them. Within this space the refrigerant flows through coils placed against the inner casing. The rest of the space is packed tightly with insulating material, such as fibreglass.

Controls consist of a thermostatically controlled dial, including a fast freeze position, and two or three lights:
1. an on/off light;
2. a fast freeze indicator;
3. a warning light if the temperature rises too high.

There are three types of freezer available: chest freezers, upright freezers and fridge/freezers.

Chest freezers
1. Usually large, they are more economical to run as less cold air is lost when freezer is opened.
2. They need to be defrosted less often — usually once a year.
3. They take up more floor space than upright freezers.
4. It is more difficult to find items. Small people will find it difficult to reach the bottom.

5. All shapes and sizes of food packets will fit.
6. Most have removable baskets.
7. They should have counter-balanced lids, which prevent them shutting accidentally.

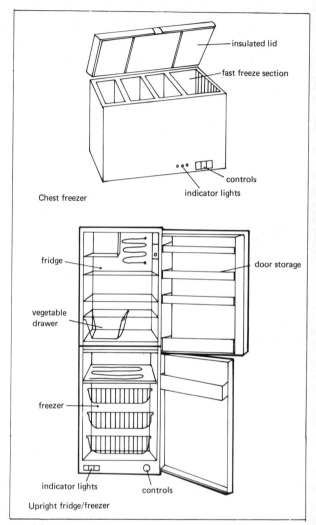

Food freezers

Upright freezers
1. They need defrosting more often.
2. They take up less floor space.
3. Contents are more accessible due to shelving system.
4. Large items (turkeys) may be difficult to fit unless shelving is flexible.
5. Small models may be fitted under a worktop.
6. They are slightly more expensive to buy and run.

Fridge/Freezers

It is possible to buy a combined fridge/freezer: an upright model with two compartments, two compressor units, and separate doors. These are convenient and economical, as they take up little floor space and are cheaper to run than a separate refrigerator and freezer.

Fridge-freezer (Tricity)

Other frozen food units

Display cabinets in shops for storing food operate at —18°C. Like the frozen food compartments in most refrigerators, they are not sufficiently cold to deep-freeze fresh food. All deep-freeze appliances, as already mentioned, must display a four star symbol ****. If deep freezing is attempted in other frozen food storage compartments, the food will freeze too slowly, resulting in loss of moisture, nutrients, colour and flavour.

CHOOSING A FREEZER

The capacity of a freezer is measured in cubic litres. Sizes available range from 100 to 510 litres. The choice of size depends on:
1. the number in the family;
2. whether large-scale freezing of meat and garden produce will be taking place: a separate freezing compartment is useful in this case, to ensure that food being frozen does not raise the temperature of stored frozen food;

3. the amount of floor space available;
4. the amount of money available.

Running costs

These depend on much the same factors as for a refrigerator: size, situation, amount of use, number of times opened, time of year (more electricity is used in summer). One extra factor is that a freezer kept reasonably full is more efficient than a half-empty one.

It is estimated that each 15 litres uses one unit of electricity per week, e.g. a 100-litre freezer will use about seven units in one week.

Freezing capacity

The daily freezing capacity is an indication of how much fresh food can be deep-frozen to —18°C in any twenty-four hour period. It is usually one tenth of the freezer capacity, and will be indicated in the instruction book and on the rating plate.

Situation
1. Freezers should be stored in a cool, dry, well-ventilated place: a cold corner of the kitchen, the utility room, the garage.
2. Do not place beside a boiler, cooker or heater. These would all raise the running costs, as the motor would have to work harder to keep the temperature down.
3. Dampness will cause rusting of cabinet and metal components.
4. Allow at least 3 cm ventilation space around the freezer.

Power cuts

The contents of a freezer will stay frozen during cuts of up to eight hours. A well-packed freezer could be unaffected for up to twelve hours. During a power cut or breakdown, *do not open the lid or door*. When power resumes, leave unopened for two hours, to allow freezer to return to its normal temperature. If there is a prolonged stoppage, check contents of freezer quickly. If food is soft, use at once: do not refreeze. Partially thawed food may be refrozen, although there may be deterioration of colour, texture, flavour and nutrients. Protein foods (meat and fish) may be dangerous if thawed and refrozen. It is possible to insure against freezer breakdown.

Defrosting

Defrosting should take place when there is little food in the freezer, e.g. after Christmas or before freezing summer fruits and vegetables.

The *frequency* of defrosting depends on:
1. the type of freezer — chest freezers produce less frost;
2. the amount of freezing which takes place;
3. the number of times the freezer is opened;
4. the temperature of the room in which the freezer is placed.

To defrost
1. Wrap frozen food in layers of newspaper and cover with an eiderdown, or place in refrigerator.
2. Disconnect electricity.
3. Place one or two bowls of very hot water inside for ten minutes and close door. This will loosen frost. Remove bowls.
4. Using a plastic or wooden spatula (never metal), scrape frost from sides. Collect from bottom of freezer.
5. Wash inside walls, baskets and shelves with warm water, containing one or two tablespoonfuls of bread soda.
6. Dry thoroughly.
7. Turn freezer to lowest temperature, turn on electricity, and after one hour return frozen food.
8. Wash outside of freezer with hot, soapy water. Rinse, dry and polish with silicone polish.

Economy in using a freezer
1. Keep it as full as possible.
2. Store it in an unheated room.
3. Open door only when necessary; make sure door has a good seal.
4. Chill food in refrigerator before freezing.
5. Defrost once or twice a year, as required.
6. Chest freezers are slightly cheaper to run.

DISHWASHERS

A dishwasher is a machine which is capable of washing a large number of dishes in an efficient, labour-saving and hygienic way. Modern dishwashers are fully automatic and easy to use. An electrically driven pump drives water through a spray or rotating arm, forcing the food particles from the dishes. This action is assisted by the use of very hot water, strong detergent, and rinse-aids.

Dishwashers may be top-loading or front-loading. Most dishwashers are front-loading: they are easier to load and fit under a worktop. Although some small, table-top models are available, most dishwashers are floor-standing, with a drop-down door. Some can be built-in at waist height. Capacity is measured by the

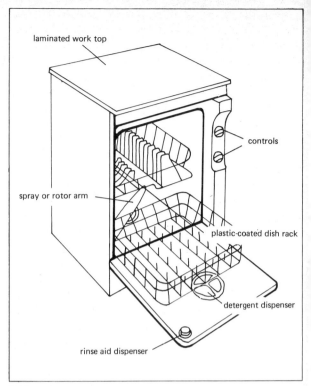

Dishwasher

number of place settings which can be washed at one time: this varies from six to twelve place settings. The standard machine holds ten to twelve place settings, i.e. a day's washing-up for a family of four.

Construction

Most dishwashers are made from enamelled steel, lined with stainless steel. This is hard wearing and rust resistant.

Dimensions: usually about the size of a floor-standing kitchen unit: approximately 60 cm wide; 60 cm deep and 90 to 115 cm high.

Controls usually consist of an on/off switch and a dial which can be set to a variety of cycles, according to the type of wash required.

The average dishwasher has the following components:
1. a *heating element* at the base and a thermostat;
2. *water softener,* which is filled at intervals with salt;
3. *motor* and *pump,* which forces water from the base of the machine into the spray arms or impeller;
4. central column and *spray arms,* rotated at great speed by the force of the water as it is pumped through the machine;
5. two plastic-coated *racks,* designed to hold specific utensils, with a basket to hold cutlery upright; these

should be angled to allow water to reach all utensils and to drain off after rinsing; should hold utensils securely, and be easy to load — most slide out on castors to facilitate loading;

6. *detergent dispenser;*
7. *rinse-aid dispenser;*
8. *filters,* to prevent large food particles blocking the jets or pump;
9. *drain pump.*

Installation

1. A dishwasher requires a 13 or 16 amp earthed socket.
2. Most dishwashers have a laminated worktop. If not they can be fitted under the existing worktop.
3. The dishwasher should be positioned either beside the sink near existing plumbing and drains, or near the dining area. Ideally it should be plumbed in. It can be connected either to the hot water supply or — if it has a built in heater — to the cold supply. Hot supply means shorter cycle, but hot water tank may be emptied. Cold supply means longer cycle, but is more efficient.
4. The dishwasher may be connected to taps by hose fittings, but this prevents use of taps and sink during the washing cycle, and is inconvenient.
5. Make sure there is sufficient space behind machine for plumbing, and in front for opening the door.
6. Incorrect plumbing may cause problems: be sure to employ a reputable plumber.

Loading

1. Scrape plates thoroughly and empty cups, etc.; there is no need to rinse delph.
2. Load dishwasher according to manufacturer's instructions. Cups and other containers should be placed facing downwards. Silver and stainless steel cutlery should be kept apart.
3. Dishes from two or three meals may be stored in the dishwasher until it is full, e.g. breakfast and lunch dishes can be loaded into the machine, which is switched on after dinner.
4. Never overload or dishes may not be properly washed.
5. Although many utensils are now made to withstand the heat of a dishwasher, the following items may be damaged or may not be cleaned successfully in a dishwasher:
   lead crystal glass;
   hand-painted or very fine china or glass;
   wooden or wooden-handled utensils;
   plastics which are not heat resistant;

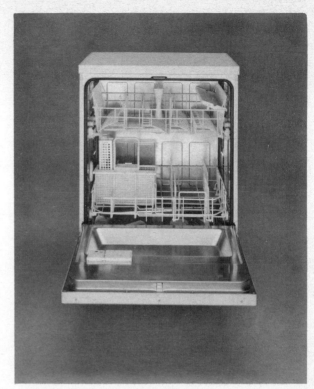

Dishwasher opened for loading (Prospect)

   saucepans with plastic-type handles;
   bone or plastic-handled cutlery;
   narrow necked utensils, e.g. vases;
   some non-stick finishes.
6. Casseroles or saucepans with baked-on food may require steeping first.

Programmes

Most dishwashers are fully automatic — this means that once the machine has been loaded and switched on, it will carry out the wash programme from beginning to end. The heavy duty or biological cycle includes the whole programme; the normal cycle leaves out the first stage.

Normal cycle

1. *Pre-rinse* removes loose food particles and softens dried on food. It is useful to use this cycle alone after each meal, to prevent food drying onto plates before the main evening wash. Some machines have a special rinse-and-hold cycle for just this.
2. *Heating:* the machine refills with clean water which is heated to 65°C, hotter than hands can bear. During heating, high pressure spraying removes the less difficult stains.
3. *Washing cycle:* water and detergent are sprayed under pressure by the rotating arms; the high

187

velocity of the spray removes the remaining food from the dishes.

4. *Rinsing cycle:* dishes are rinsed with warm, then hot water. Rinse-aid is added during the final rinsing.
5. *Drying cycle* may be carried out by residual heat from the final rinsing or by heating the washing chamber.

A complete cycle can take anything from thirty to ninety minutes.

Modern features
1. Water softener is essential in hard-water areas.
2. Biological cycle is a long programme, suitable for cleaning heavily soiled dishes, saucepans and oven-to-table wear. There is a long pre-wash using biological detergent, followed by the normal cycle.
3. Short cycle is for lightly soiled delph.
4. Rinse-and-hold cycle — see above.

Choosing a dishwasher
1. Choose a model to suit the size of family.
2. Consider the amount of kitchen space available.
3. Study the interior design: are racks easy to manipulate? Are they well-designed to hold each type of utensil?
4. A dishwasher should be well insulated, to reduce noise and prevent heat loss.
5. Is it fully automatic? — compare the number of programmes. Is there a biological cycle? a pre-wash cycle? a plate warming/drying cycle?
6. Does it include a water heater? water softener?
7. Has it basic safety features? Does it stop when door is opened? Is there a door lock — important if there are children in the house?
8. Some machines have a more vigorous high-pressure wash in the lower rack (for very dirty dishes and saucepans) with a gentler wash in the top rack for the slightly dirty dishes and glasses.

Advantages
1. A dishwasher saves the tedious, time-consuming job of washing-up at least three times a day.
2. It washes more efficiently, due to hotter water, stronger detergent, and automatic drying.
3. Dishes are sterilised by the hot water and chlorine in the detergent.
4. Use of tea towels — which often harbour germs — is eliminated.
5. If used correctly, it can be more economical than three or four washing-up sessions.
6. A dishwasher keeps kitchen tidier: dirty utensils can be stored in it until it is full, or clean dishes can be left in it until ready for use.

7. Fewer breakages occur than when handwashing dishes.

Disadvantages
1. There is quite a high initial expense.
2. Special detergents and rinse-aids are expensive.
3. It can scratch lead crystal, remove design from some china and damage such materials as wood, plastic and bone.
4. It is unsuitable for many saucepans and tins, which tend to rust in a dishwasher.
5. Saucepans take up a lot of valuable dishwashing space.
6. Extra delph and cutlery are required, if the machine is to be used economically.

DETERGENTS

Dishwashing detergents consist of a mixture of water softeners, detergent (grease solvent) and chlorine which destroys bacteria. Enzyme detergents are available for use with biological cycles.

Detergent may be added manually. In fully automatic machines, it is filled into a dispenser and added automatically at the correct point in the washing cycle. Always use the amount and brand recommended by the manufacturer. The brand recommended is specially formulated to suit the machine.

RINSE-AIDS

These are wetting agents which reduce the surface tension of the final rinsing water, so that the dishes dry without streaking. The dispenser releases the rinse-aid into the water at the final stage of the cycle. The rinse-aid dispenser is topped up at intervals.

WATER SOFTENERS

Water softeners prevent a build-up of hard-water chemicals, which may cause deposits on articles being washed and may damage machine.

Care and cleaning
1. Empty and clean filter if required. Failure to do this results in an inefficient wash and the risk of a blockage causing an overflow.
2. Fill water softener and rinse-aid dispenser when necessary.
3. Wash edges of door and other dirt traps at least once a week.

4. Wipe outside with damp cloth. Polish occasionally with silicone polish.

Economy
1. Read manufacturer's instructions thoroughly and follow them.
2. Never use machine when half full.
3. Use correct quantity of detergent and rinse-aid.
4. Use the shorter programme if dishes are not heavily soiled. This also has a lower temperature.

QUESTIONS/CHAPTER 18

1. Write an informative description on two of the following cookers:
   (a) micro-wave cookers;
   (b) solid-fuel cookers;
   (c) split-level cookers.
   In each case, refer to the advantages and disadvantages as well as general features.
2. Describe the working of a cooker auto-timer. Compare electric and gas cookers under the following headings:
   (a) structure;
   (b) cost;
   (c) care and ease of maintenance;
   (d) availability of modern features.
3. Explain the working principle of a refrigerator. Assuming you wish to buy a refrigerator and freezer, list the points you would consider when deciding between separate machines and a combined fridge/freezer. State the temperatures found in the food storage compartments with the following star-markings:
   (a) one star;
   (b) two stars;
   (c) three stars.
4. List five fuel-saving economy points to be followed when using each of the following:
   (a) a food freezer;
   (b) a solid-fuel cooker;
   (c) a dishwasher.
5. List some general points to consider when purchasing large items of electrical equipment.
   Name five modern features available in modern electric cookers which save time or labour. Discuss three in detail.
6. Describe the structure of a dishwasher and explain briefly how it works. Describe the average washing cycle and list the points to be remembered when
   (a) loading the machine;
   (b) using detergent and other products;
   (c) cleaning the machine.

19.
Small appliances

Directly plugged appliances include kettles, percolators, toasters, electric casseroles. They are more economical than alternative forms of cooking and heating, as no current is wasted, and heat is supplied exactly where it is needed. They are generally quick and efficient as they have been designed for a specific function. Many include convenient extras such as thermostats, automatic cut-out and so on. All work from a normal 13 amp socket.

ELECTRIC KETTLES

There are two types of electric kettle: the standard electric kettle and the automatic kettle. Both contain an element which must be covered with water before the kettle is switched on. Both kettles take about three minutes to boil one litre of water. Automatic kettles have a bi-metal thermostat which switches off the kettle when it boils. Modern kettles may be manufactured from one of the following materials: chrome-plated copper, stainless steel and enamelled steel. Coloured finishes are available in enamelled steel and heat-resistant plastic. Handles, knobs and feet of kettles are made from plastic or wood: as these are poor conductors of heat, they do not become too hot. The wattage of electric kettles is approximately 3 kW.

Points to look for
1. Handle should be securely fixed, easy to grip, and comfortable.
2. Spout should pour well.
3. Size: the average kettle holds 1.7. litres. Larger and smaller sizes are available.
4. Finish should be easily cleaned and stain resistant.

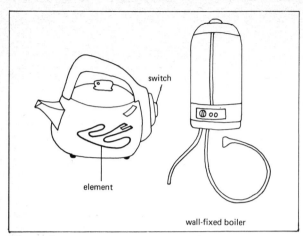

Electric kettle and water boiler

5. Lid should fit well and stay in place when pouring. The knob on the lid should be comfortable and large enough to lift without burning the fingers.
6. Base should be stable. Feet should be well secured, heat resistant, and should not scratch surfaces.
7. Element should be low in the kettle so that small amounts of water can be boiled. It should be easy to replace the element.
8. Safety features: steam vent should face away from handle; safety cut-out, in case kettle boils dry.

Advantages
1. boils water more quickly than using a hot plate;
2. more efficient and more economical on fuel.
   Note: A small, wall-fixed boiler is more expensive than a kettle, but is useful if large amounts of boiling water are required.

COFFEE PERCOLATORS

These are thermostatically controlled boiling jugs, which force the boiling water up through a central tube, to seep down through the coffee grounds, back into the main jug. The coffee is measured into a perforated metal container which sits at the top of the percolator, under the lid. Percolators can be made from various materials, the most popular being stainless steel, chrome-plated metals, and pottery — the latter is considered to make the best coffee. The machine can be adjusted to the strength of coffee required.

TOASTERS

Like most directly plugged utensils, after the initial outlay, toasters are much cheaper to run, using less than one third of the electricity consumed when toasting under a grill. Most have a chrome or brushed chrome finish. All modern toasters are automatic: either the toast pops up out of the toaster, or the toaster switches off. Most models toast two slices at a time; larger models can toast four. A hinged tray at the base is easily removed for cleaning. Some elaborate models can be adapted to grill food.

CONTACT GRILLS

These are useful for entertaining and for those with limited cooking facilities. Sizes vary between 18 x 20 cm and 30 x 30 cm. They consist of two heavy, ridged, aluminium heating plates, using one to two kilowatts, coated with non-stick PTFE. The food is sandwiched between them, so that it is in direct contact with the cooking plates. The food cooks rapidly and economically by conduction. Foods which can be cooked include grilled meat and fish; toasted sandwiches; reheating of frozen foods on shallow trays; and a limited amount of baking.

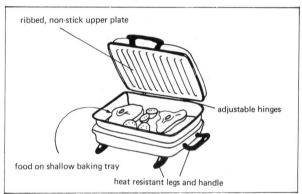

Contact grill

Points to look for
1. adjustable lid, so that thick foods or a shallow tin can fit under it;
2. detachable plates with alternative plates for waffles, etc;
3. heat-resistant handles and legs;
4. variable controls and thermostatically controlled indicator light.

Use
1. Preheat according to instructions, usually five to ten minutes.
2. Brush with oil before first use.
3. All food must be of similar thickness: bones may have to be removed.

4. Time accurately: overcooking is a common fault.
5. Drain off extra fat during prolonged cooking.
6. After use, unplug and cool with lid up.
7. Cleaning: wipe, while warm, with soft kitchen paper. Remove stubborn stains with a damp cloth or nylon brush. Wipe outside with damp cloth. Never use metal utensils or steel wool. Never immerse grill in water though the plates can be immersed if they are removable.

Advantages
1. quick and handy to use;
2. easy to clean;
3. can be used at table;
4. oil or fat is not required — useful for those on special diets.

SANDWICH TOASTERS

These work on a similar principle — with shaped plates which seal the edges of toasted sandwiches. Waffle attachments are also available.

Electric deep fat fryer (Krups)

DEEP FAT FRYER

Useful for families who like fried food, it can deal successfully with large amounts of food. Most have three heat settings and are thermostatically controlled. Reliable models have a safety cut-out which prevents overheating. Lid prevents fat splashing on hob, and reduces risk of fire. Filter on lid reduces smoke and odours. Most have a wire basket, raised by a lever while the lid is still closed: this reduces accidents. Although a large quantity of oil is required, it can be used several times. The fryer must be used on a heat-resistant surface. Before buying, check whether the particular model can be immersed in water for cleaning. Some models can be used as casseroles and for pot roasting.

ELECTRIC FRYING PAN OR MULTI-COOKER

This is a deep square pan, with a domed lid. It can be used for deep or shallow frying, making soups and stews, roasting, boiling, and even baking cakes. The element on the base is thermostatically controlled, with several heat settings. Controls are on the main handle which can be unplugged in order to wash the pan. A ventilating grille can be adjusted according to the type of cooking being carried out.

SLOW COOKERS

Most slow cookers consist of a removable stoneware casserole, (capacity 2.5. to 3.5 litres) set in an insulated outer casing. They are heated by an electric element fitted round the inside of the casing. The low wattage (170 watt: about the same as a light bulb) makes the slow cooker very economical, even though it is using electricity over a long period. Slow cookers are used for dishes which require long, slow cooking: soups and stews, especially those made from the cheap, tougher cuts of meat. The low temperature ensures little shrinkage or evaporation. Ingredients are placed in the casserole, cooked at the higher setting for one to two hours, depending on the recipe, and the temperature is then reduced to the lower setting for several hours; it can be safely left on all day so that a hot meal is ready in the evening.

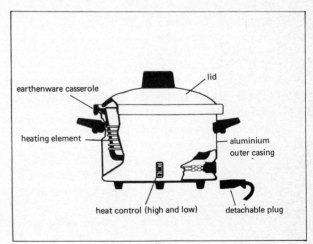

Slow cooker

Note: It is essential that the initial (higher) cooking temperature should be maintained for sufficiently long to kill any bacteria which might be present in meat or fish. Failure to do this might cause *food poisoning:* the lower temperature might act as an incubator for the multiplication of food poisoning bacteria.

Care

1. If there is a removable cooking pot it should be soaked in warm water and then washed in the usual way.
2. Wipe the outer casing with a soapy cloth. Never submerge or use abrasives.
3. If there is not a removable cooking pot, the cooker should be washed carefully without being submerged.

Multi-cooker: stews, simmers, roasts (Kenwood)

HEATED FOOD TRAYS AND TROLLEYS

These keep food hot and palatable for a considerable time.

Food trays may be made from stainless steel or heat resistant glass, heated by an electric element underneath. They are surrounded by a metal frame, which is fitted with heat resistant handles, and stands on four heat resistant legs.

Heated trolleys: most have a hot plate on top, with a cabinet underneath fitted with shelves. Some have a number of covered stainless steel dishes which fit over the element. They are capable of keeping complete meals warm. Trolleys are fitted with wheels or castors and are reasonably mobile.

Use

1. Most need to be warmed up for thirty minutes.
2. Some have both a hot and a warm area on the tray surface.
3. Most have variable heat controls and an indicator light.
4. Always cover dishes to prevent food drying out.
5. Avoid keeping food warm for longer than one hour if possible — see below.

Advantages of heated trays and trolleys

1. They are useful for keeping food hot.
2. They are economical on fuel.
3. They are ideal for those who entertain a lot: main course can be kept warm while first course is eaten.
4. They are handy for keeping plates and dishes warm.

Disadvantages

1. Initial cost — especially that of trolleys — is high.
2. Prolonged use may reduce vitamin content of food.
3. There is a danger of *food poisoning*. Foods which are contaminated by bacteria, if insufficiently cooked or subjected to low standards of hygiene after cooking, could become dangerous if stored for prolonged periods on a warm food trolley or tray.

ELECTRIC MIXERS

The electric mixer takes much of the hard work out of cooking. It saves time and labour, and, in the case of a mixer on a stand, it leaves the cook free to get on with the next stage of the meal. A food mixer is powered by an electric motor which drives the beaters, whisks or hooks. Small mixers have a light motor and often a limited range of speed and functions. The large household mixers have a more powerful motor, a wide range of speeds, and a large number of accessories. Their whisking and beating action is faster and more thorough than hand beating and obviously less tiring. The handheld mixers work by simple rotary action. Many of the larger models incorporate rotary and planetary action, i.e. the beaters revolve and also move around the bowl.

HANDHELD MIXERS

1. Cheaper, useful for cakes and small-scale cooking:
2. less powerful, not as strong or heavy;
3. can be used in saucepans and any suitable sized bowl;
4. only one to three speeds available;
5. unless a stand is supplied, cannot be left unattended;
6. many are noisy and vibrate in the hand;
7. some expensive models have stands and attachments, and are more versatile than standard models.

LARGE MIXERS OR FOOD PREPARATION MACHINES

1. powerful and heavily built; suitable for baking (including bread) and catering for large amounts;
2. housewife is free while machine is in operation;

3. mixes large amounts quickly and thoroughly; not as efficient for small amounts;
4. large range of speeds (three to fifteen) and attachments available;
5. expensive;
6. large and difficult to store; needs to be left on the worktop ready for use unless special cabinet is available.

Use

1. Read instructions carefully.
2. Normal recipes may be used, but some changes may be necessary. If in doubt, stick to recipes in the booklet.
3. Use correct beater and speed for the process (see below).
4. Avoid overrunning the machine: five minutes is the maximum for most mixers.
5. Start at a slow speed to avoid splashing liquids and flour.
6. Warm the bowl and beaters slightly before creaming mixtures.
7. Stop mixing now and then to scrape down mixture from the sides.
8. Do not overload the machine: light mixers can be strained by heavy fruit cake mixtures.
9. Avoid overbeating, especially when whipping cream or adding flour to a creamed or whisked mixture. It is preferable to fold in flour gently with a metal spoon.
10. Use a straight-sided bowl, if one is not supplied with the machine.
11. Handheld mixers are useful for creaming potatoes and sauces in the saucepan.
12. Most foods should be at room temperature before mixing: remove from refrigerator one hour before use. Cream should be chilled.
13. As a general rule, the hook is used at slow speeds, the beater at medium speed, and the whisk at high speeds.

Cleaning

1. Remove plug from socket.
2. Remove beater and bowl and wash in warm, soapy water.
3. Wipe over machine with cloth wrung out of hot soapy water. Do not use abrasives. Rinse and dry. Never immerse machine in water.
4. Cover when not in use or store in cupboard.

Liquidiser/Blender

This is probably the most useful of all food preparation machines. It cuts food preparation time to a minimum and eliminates many time-consuming operations in the kitchen. A liquidiser may be a free-standing machine with its own motor or work as an attachment from a large food mixer. Four to six stainless steel, rotating knives are powered by the motor. The blades revolve at high speeds grinding, pulverising or emulsifying the food. Most have suppressed motors to avoid interference with radio and television.

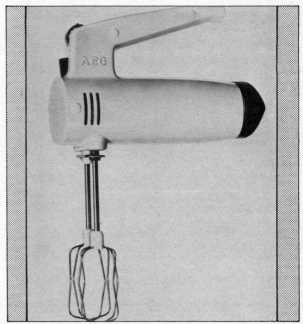

A simple but useful electric mixer

Which beater to use?		
Beater	Hook	Whisk
creaming fat and sugar	shortcrust pastry	meringues
mayonnaise	biscuit dough	whipped cream
icings and fillings	scone dough	batters
creaming potatoes	yeast dough	whisked sponges
rubbing in fat	mixing fruit into	sweets (marshmallows)
	heavy fruit cakes	icing (American frosting)
		soufflés and mousses

CHOOSING A BLENDER

1. Arrange a demonstration, if possible.
2. Check capacity: many small blenders hold very little food.
3. There should be a choice of speeds.
4. Goblet should be heat resistant with a handle and pouring lip.
5. If the liquidiser is to be used regularly for large amounts of food, check that it has a high wattage (400 — 450 watts: wattage is shown on the base of the machine). Machines with a low wattage are not very powerful.

A blender can be used for

1. blending: soups, raw or cooked; mousses; sauces — e.g. roux sauces; correcting curdled or lumpy sauces.
2. grinding: coffee (some models); granulated sugar into caster or icing sugar; nuts.
3. crushing: biscuits.
4. grating: cheese, breadcrumbs and stuffing.
5. chopping: ice; nuts; raw vegetables; herbs.
6. mixing: batters; mayonnaise and other dressings; drinks — e.g. milk shakes.
7. purée: raw and cooked fruits; fruit fools; baby foods; sorbets; dips; paté; sandwich spreads; soups.

Use

1. Follow manufacturer's instructions.
2. Never fill more than two-thirds full for liquid foods, half full for thick foods, to allow for the rise of liquid when it is turned on.
3. Blend large quantities a little at a time.
4. Chop solid foods and add liquid before blending.
5. Do not overload: this puts a strain on the motor.
6. Warm blender in hot water before adding very hot liquids. Cool boiling liquids before adding.
7. Make sure lid is securely in place. Hold lid down when switching on.

Food preparation machine can be a useful kitchen extra (Kenwood)

8. Use central hole in goblet lid for dripping oil into mayonnaise and dropping in cubes of food such as bread.
9. Stop machine to scrape down sides if necessary *Never* stir while machine is turned on.
10. Avoid overrunning the motor. Do not use at high speed for longer than 45 seconds. Two or three short bursts are better.
11. When blending small amounts make sure there is enough food to cover the blades.
12. Have liquidiser absolutely dry when chopping dry foods. Stop when food is sufficiently chopped or it will be ground to a powder.
13. Keep safely away from children at all times.

Advantages
1. saves time and labour.

Disadvantages
1. practice is required to attain a high degree of efficiency;
2. difficult to clean, especially under the blades.

Cleaning
1. Rinse out food.
2. Half fill with fairly hot water with a squeeze of washing-up liquid. Turn on for a few seconds.
3. Empty, fill with clean water and rinse.
4. If necessary, use a bottle brush to clean under the blades.
5. Sterilise goblet with Milton before using for baby foods.
6. Never immerse base of goblet in water. Avoid abrasives.

Other mixer attachments
Mincer: ideal for mincing raw or cooked meat, fish and vegetables. Food may be minced coarsely or finely as required.
Coffee grinder: for coarse or fine-ground coffee.
Juice extractor: useful for squeezing juice from fresh citrus fruits.
Slicer: for carrots, cucumber, cabbage, apples and other salad ingredients. This is also useful for preparing marmalade.
Potato peeler: this has an abrasive surface which peels large amounts of potatoes or root vegetables at one time.
Can opener.
Cream maker.
Wheat mill.
Food processors: these combine the functions of a mixer and blender in one piece of equipment.

THERMOSTATS
The word thermostat has been mentioned many times in this chapter. Almost all appliances which produce heat have a built-in thermostat: this reduces fuel consumption and makes the appliance safer and more efficient. A thermostat is a device which keeps a temperature constant. Most thermostats are based on the principle that different metals and liquids expand and contract at various temperatures.

How they work
Many electrical appliances have a simple thermostat based on a *bimetal strip:* two different metals (e.g. brass and Invar) are welded together. These form part of the electrical circuit. When heated, one metal expands more quickly than the other, causing the strip to bend slightly and break the circuit: this cuts off the supply of heat. The metals cool and the bimetal strip straightens and makes contact with the circuit again, switching on the current. Most thermostats can be set by a dial or knob, which moves the metal strip one way or another depending on the heat required.

QUESTIONS/CHAPTER 19
1. Significant savings of energy can be made in the home by careful planning and efficient use of household electrical equipment. Discuss this statement with reference to three of the following:
   (a) an electric kettle;
   (b) a toaster;
   (c) a slow cooker;
   (d) a deep-fat fryer.
   In the case of (c) and (d), explain how they work and list the rules to be followed when using them.
2. Mention two food preparation machines which you have used during your course. State which you think was the more useful and labour-saving, giving reasons why. In the case of the machine of your choice, give the rules for using it and list the food processes it can accomplish.
3. Find out all you can about food processors. Collect leaflets etc. from your local electrical shop/department store and write details into your Home Economics copy, using some of the headings supplied in this chapter.
4. Name three pieces of small electrical equipment which would be particularly suitable for entertaining. Explain the advantages of each to the hostess and in the case of one, describe how it should be cleaned after use.

20.
Home laundry

For hundreds of years, the methods by which people washed their clothes changed little. Today scientific advances have brought us easy-care fabrics, synthetic detergents and efficient machines, which have made the tedious job of washing for the family quicker, more simple and less physically exhausting.

THE PURPOSE OF WASHING

(i) to remove soil;
(ii) to remove unpleasant odours;
(iii) to give clothes a fresh, clean appearance;
(iv) to destroy harmful micro-organisms and parasites which infest dirty, unwashed garments and household linen.

SOILING

The dirt which must be removed during washing includes
- protein-based stains, e.g. blood and food stains;
- grease stains from fatty foods and oily substances;
- chemical stains such as paints and pigments;
- dirt and grit which damage cloth by friction.

Some forms of soil are water-soluble and are easily washed out of clothes; others, such as grease, are insoluble in cold water and require hot water and detergent to remove them. Certain stains, particularly protein stains, are easier to remove when cool water is used, as hot water sets the protein in the fabric.

In order to achieve the best possible results when laundering, some knowledge of the principles of washing action and washing products is required.

THE PRINCIPLES OF WASHING

Washing is based on three principles:
(i) the solvent power of water;
(ii) detergent action;
(iii) friction or agitation.

(i) Solvent power of water
Water has the power of softening soil and removing certain stains. Water does not mix readily with solids such as fabric and dirt. This is due to the *surface tension* of water which causes water molecules to be attracted to one another, but to repel other molecules such as grease and dirt. This is why, if water is dropped onto most surfaces, particularly grease, it tends to stick together in a bead. If soap or synthetic detergent is added, it will increase the 'wetting power' of water by reducing the surface tension. As a result, the water will soak into the fabric or stain more quickly (see below).

Hard water
The presence of lime in water interferes with the washing power of soap.

Disadvantages of hard water
1. It is difficult to make a lather; it wastes soap and detergent.
2. Scum clings to clothes, baths etc.
3. It 'furs' up kettles so that they take longer to heat up. This wastes fuel.
4. Central heating boilers and pipes fur up and become blocked.
5. It is not good for washing skin and hair — it leaves hair dull.
For water softeners see page 63.
For more on water see chapter 6, p. 60.

(ii) Detergent action
Each molecule of soap or synthetic detergent is made up of two parts — a water-loving head and a water-hating (hygrophobic) tail which is attracted to grease and other 'non watery' objects. The molecule, under a microscope, looks very similar to a tadpole.

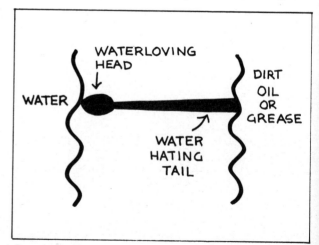

Soap molecule

When a detergent is added to water, the 'tails' try to escape by floating to the surface of the water or by burying themselves in any non-water substance e.g. fabric, soil. The water-loving ends, however, are happy in the water and attach themselves to the water molecules so that a bridge is formed between the water and the 'foreign' substance, which is called an emulsion (see diagrams).

Soon, detergent molecules completely surround each molecule of soil, lifting it out of the fabric and keeping it suspended in the water until it is rinsed away.

(iii) Agitation or friction

It would take a long time for clothes to clean themselves if we just allowed them to steep in detergent. Friction, such as rubbing and squeezing the clothes or agitating them in a washing machine, helps loosen dirt by forcing water through the fabric. The constant movement also prevents soil resettling on the fabric.

Temperature

Except in the case of protein stains (which should be soaked in cold water), heat speeds up the cleaning action of soaps and synthetic detergents by enabling them to dissolve more easily and by softening grease and other stains.

LAUNDRY PRODUCTS

DETERGENTS

A detergent may be defined as any substance which cleans and removes dirt. As most cleaning agents have a detergent effect, they are in fact detergents. In general use, the word detergent has now come to mean a synthetic detergent or washing powder, and though this may be regarded as not strictly correct, it is really only an example of how the meanings of words can change over time

A. SOAP

Soap is made by boiling animal fats or vegetable oils with strong alkalis such as caustic soda.

The following additives may be used in soap, depending on its intended purpose.

(i) Perfumes and dyes — added to toilet soap to improve scent and colour;

(ii) Antiseptics — added to some toilet and household soaps to enable them to reduce the spread of germs;

(iii) Oils e.g. lanolin — to counteract alkalinity and to reduce the drying effect on the skin;

(iv) Builders such as borax and phosphates are added to household soaps and soap powders to soften water, improve their cleaning power and to keep soil in suspension in the water. Soaps containing builders are strong and harsh and are not suitable for washing the skin or for washing delicate fabrics.

Soap powders are made from a mixture of liquid soap, alkalis and other builders (see above) which are spray-dried to a powder. Many contain sodium perborate (a bleach) to improve stain-removing qualities. Examples are Lux (soap flakes), Persil and Fairy Snow.

Soap and soap powders (a) reduce surface tension; (b) remove soil and hold it in suspension. But (i) they do not work well in hard water, causing scum, and (ii) they discolour whites, causing yellowing.

B. SYNTHETIC OR SOAPLESS DETERGENTS

These are generally made from mineral oils mixed with a powerful acid, and then neutralised by an alkali e.g. sodium hydroxide. The resulting mixture is spray dried to a powder.

Builders used in synthetic detergents include:
(i) water softeners e.g. phosphates to reduce scum;
(ii) bleach e.g. sodium perborate removes stains at high temperatures;
(iii) stabilisers which retain suds and keep soil suspended in the water;
(iv) sodium sulphate to prevent lumping;
(v) flourescers: these are optical brighteners which cause the invisible ultra-violet rays of the sun to reflect from the surface of the fabric as visible light. This has the effect of whitening and brightening the fabric but may fade colours after continual use;
(vi) enzymes (see below).

BIOLOGICAL DETERGENTS

These are synthetic detergents to which enzymes are added which 'digest' protein stains, i.e. break them down to their simpler components. Enzyme detergents are effective on protein stains such as blood, meat, egg, vomit and urine, which might otherwise be difficult to remove.

Points to remember when using enzyme detergents:
- The enzyme part of the powder works at low temperatures, therefore clothes should be steeped in cool or lukewarm water.
- As enzymes work slowly, the clothes should be soaked in the powder for some time, preferably overnight to enable enzymes to break down the stains.
- If the temperature of the water is higher than 65°C, the enzymes are inactivated, although the detergent part of the powder will work normally.
- Wool or silk which are largely composed of protein will be damaged by frequent washing in enzyme detergents.
- Always wear rubber gloves to protect skin from enzyme action.

Use
1. Steep clothes overnight in warm water (40°C).
2. Unless clothes are badly soiled, the same water can be used to wash the clothes.
3. Heat it up by pouring in some boiling water until the correct temperature is reached. A washing machine heats up the water at this stage.
4. The detergent part of the powder is now dissolved and activated, removing dirt and grease in the usual way.
5. Rinse two or three times in warm, then cool water.
6. Dry in the usual way.

LOW FOAMING POWDERS

These are manufactured without the addition of the lathering agents and stabilisers which are used in many detergents to create and maintain suds.

They are used in front-loading washing machines as large amounts of suds could damage the works of the machine and cause it to overflow.

LIQUID DETERGENTS

At present, the principal liquid detergents used in laundry are light-duty detergents such as Stergene which have been specially formulated for washing delicate fabrics and woollens. Research is currently taking place into the use of general purpose liquid laundry detergents, similar to washing-up liquids. Their main advantage is that they do not need to be dissolved, as do powdered detergents.

Advantages of detergents
1. They work well in hard and soft water.
2. They do not produce scum.

3. They lather easily and maintain the lather for some time.
4. Additives ensure that they work effectively and thoroughly.
5. Bleaches in the detergent whiten whites but tend to fade coloureds in time.

SPECIAL PURPOSE PRODUCTS

1. WATER SOFTENERS

These remove hardness, e.g. lime, from water; examples are Calgon and washing soda (see below).

Use according to directions, and according to the hardness of the water. Both can be used in hot or cold water and are added just before the detergent.

2. WASHING SODA (SODIUM CARBONATE) Na_2CO_3

This is a medium-strength alkali used in laundry work. With the develment of effective detergents, it is used less frequently now, although it is still used in the manufacture of some cleaning agents. It acts as a water softener and grease solvent, and is useful for cleaning badly-soiled clothes or utensils. It must never be used in aluminium containers as it reacts with and damages them. Do not use when washing woollens, as it is too alkaline.

3. BLEACHES

Most bleaches work by oxidation, i.e. they produce oxygen which reacts with the colour or stain in the fabric, lessening its intensity until it eventually disappears. Most bleaches work more effectively in hot water. Because most modern detergents contain bleach, the separate use of bleach is becoming less necessary and therefore less frequent.

NATURAL BLEACHING

Sunlight and moisture together have a bleaching effect so that clothes drying on a clothesline are slightly bleached by the sun; if coloured, they may fade. Green plants also have a bleaching action; the oxygen produced during photosynthesis (the chemical manufacture of starch in the leaves) reacts on fabrics placed over them, in effect bleaching them. The old tradition of laying sheets to bleach in the sun over the back garden bushes really works!

CHEMICAL BLEACHES

1. Sodium hypochlorite, a chlorine bleach, is the most commonly used bleach today (e.g. Parazone). It is used mainly to disinfect and remove stains from clothes, and is also used to clean and disinfect sinks and drains. It is suitable for use on cotton and linen but must not be used on woollens and synthetics. Dilute according to directions. Never use undiluted. Hot water increases the effectiveness of the bleach.

2. Sodium perborate is a bleach used in soap powders and synthetic detergents.

3. Hydrogen peroxide: this is available in different strengths. Use according to directions; its main use is the removal of stains from woollens and the other delicate fabrics.

POINTS ON USING BLEACH

1. Use the bleach most appropriate to the fabric.
2. Dilute bleach according to instructions. Too concentrated a solution will discolour or rot the fabric. On the other hand, too dilute a solution will have little effect.
3. Length of soaking will depend on concentration of bleach solution and the level of discoloration. Several short (e.g. 10 minute) treatments are safer than one concentrated soaking.
4. Many bleaches react with metal (except stainless steel) so use a plastic basin or bucket for soaking and avoid metal plug chains etc. which will cause iron mould stains. Metal zips and trimmings can have the same effect.
5. Avoid using bleach on
   - fabrics which are not colour-fast;
   - synthetic fabrics e.g. nylon;
   - regenerated fabrics e.g. rayon;
   - animal fibres, such as wool or silk;
   - elastic or elasticised fabrics e.g. Lycra;
   - fabrics treated in one of the following ways: drip-dry, mothproofed, waterproofed, permanently pleated.
6. A triangle on the care label indicates that chlorine bleach may be used. This symbol ⊠ indicates that bleach may not be used.
7. Rinse thoroughly after using bleach, and if possible boil to remove every trace of bleach.
8. Dry thoroughly. If left lying about damp, bleached clothes are prone to iron mould and mildew.
   Note: Avoid bleaching where possible. It is a particularly harsh treatment which shortens the life of a fabric considerably and, if carelessly used, may damage it beyond repair. As many modern detergents contain some bleach, further bleaching is usually unnecessary.

4. FABRIC CONDITIONERS

These are used in the last rinse, after washing clothes, to keep fabrics soft. They consist of chemicals which coat the surface of the fibres, acting as a lubricant, making them slide over each other instead of entangling in one another. They are ideal for towels, woollens and baby clothes which are inclined to felt and harden with wear.

Use
(a) Follow directions; usually one measure of conditioner to a sink or machineful of water is mixed into the final rinsing water.
(b) Make sure that every trace of detergent has been rinsed from fabrics otherwise the conditioner will not be effective.
(c) Agitate the water well to mix in conditioner before clothes are added and move the articles about in the water to ensure that they are evenly coated.
(d) Do not rinse afterwards.

Advantages of conditioners
1. they make fabrics, especially woollens, soft and fluffy;
2. reduce matting and felting;
3. reduce wrinkling, making clothes easier to iron;
4. reduce static electricity* on synthetics;
5. have a germicidal effect; useful for baby clothes and nappies.
   *Static electricity is caused by friction of the fabric against the body. It causes the garment to cling and attracts dirt.

Disadvantages of conditioners
Overuse of fabric conditioners reduces the absorbancy of the fabric.

5. NYLON WHITENERS

It has already been established that bleaches should not be used on synthetic fibres. Nylon whiteners may be used instead. They contain chemicals which reduce the yellow colour in old synthetic fabrics and they have fluorescers which appear to brighten by absorbing and reflecting ultra-violet light from the sun.

To use: the clean, wet fabric is immersed in a solution of the whitener for a short time and then rinsed thoroughly. Whiteners unfortunately have only a temporary effect on fabrics. They begin to yellow again after a time.

6. STARCH

Starch is used
(a) to give fabric, especially cotton and linen, a fresh, crisp appearance;
(b) if used in strength, it stiffens fabric considerably, e.g. table linen;
(c) it helps fabrics stay clean longer by putting a protective layer on clothes and linen.
Starch is used less frequently today. This is partly because man-made fabrics retain their crispness more successfully and also because many fabrics can be stiffened permanently through modern processes, such as 'trubenisation'.

How starch works

The fabric is impregnated with diluted starch grains. When ironed, the hot iron bursts the starch cells and the spaces between the fabric threads are filled with starch which stiffens the fabric.

Composition

Laundry starch is made from cheap local sources of starch such as rice and maize. It also contains borax, which gives flexibility to the fabric so that creases and cracks are avoided, and waxes which help produce a shine and make fabrics easier to iron.

Types

(i) boiling water starch — large grains (see below);
(ii) instant starch — precooked fine grains which are mixed with cold water;
(iii) liquid (plastic) starch — not really a starch; this consists of a type of resin (PVA) which crisps up fabrics without giving a stiff 'starched' appearance;
(iv) aerosol starch: this is the simplest, but also the most expensive method of starching clothes. It is ideal for stiffening small areas such as collars and cuffs. The aerosol consists of minute starch particles dissolved in a liquid. The can should always be held *upright* when using and the nozzle rinsed after use to prevent clogging. Note: Follow the instructions on the can, particularly those relating to dampness of articles and distance of can from fabric.

Using boiling water starch

1. Remove as much as possible of old starch by steeping in cold water and rubbing now and then. Rinse several times.

2. Blend 2 tablespoons starch with 6-8 tablespoons of cold water. Stir in 1 litre of boiling water to cook the starch. When clear, dilute with cold water according to the stiffness required. Stir well.
3. Immerse the article to be starched, squeezing and kneading it about in the water until well coated.
4. Wring out tightly or spin dry.
5. The article may be ironed while damp, or dried completely, then damped down before ironing with a hot iron.
Note: Do not store starched articles for a long time as
(a) stiffly starched articles may crack on crease lines, and
(b) starched articles are susceptible to mildew.

6. DISINFECTANTS

These are used to kill bacteria on bed linen and clothes and to give a fresh smell to laundered articles. Their main importance is in times of illness and infection — to prevent the spread of germs. For a disinfectant to be effective, it is essential to use the correct concentration, usually 20 ml to each litre of water (hot or cold). Sterilise for a minimum of 15 minutes.

Normal disinfectants such as pine disinfectants, and Dettol, do not clean clothes or remove stains.

Note: bleaches also have a disinfectant action, but their use is limited to certain fabrics.

QUESTIONS/CHAPTER 20

1. Give the composition and explain the cleansing action of (a) enzyme detergents, (b) soap powders. Explain the terms surface tension and hard water. What are the disadvantages of hard water?

2. Explain the action and use in laundry of:
   (a) bleach;
   (b) fabric conditioners;
   (c) nylon whiteners.

3. List the types of starch available for laundry. Explain the stiffening action of starch in clothes. Give directions for the laundering of a white linen table cloth, using starch to stiffen it. Explain how the starch is made up, ready for use.

4. Give the basic principles of washing. Name some forms of soil which occur in garments, and, in each case, the type of cleaning agent necessary to remove it. Write a note on the importance of temperature in laundry.

21.
The family wash

WASH-CARE LABELS

Because of the wide variety of fabrics and finishes available today, it has become more and more difficult (a) to identify the type of fabric, and (b) to know how to launder it correctly. A set of wash-care labels is now in use which describes how to wash, rinse and finish most fabric groups.

Care labels are sewn into most readymade garments, are printed on detergent packets and correspond with the programmes on most washing machines. International symbols are also used (see below).

Note: a cross through a symbol indicates that the process should not be used.

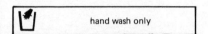
hand wash only

PREPARING CLOTHES FOR WASHING

1. Empty pockets, brush out any areas which may contain dust and fluff, e.g. pockets, trouser turn-ups; close zips and buttons.
2. Mend any tears; darn holes; sew on loose buttons or trimmings. Washing will be likely to worsen them.
3. Check stains; those which are likely to come out in a normal wash, e.g. grease stains, can be left alone. Treat others according to type (page 206).
4. Sort the washing into groups according to wash-care labels. Separate delicates and articles which are likely to run, for hand washing.
5. Steep clothes which are badly soiled, to soften the dirt.
6. Apply soap/detergent/commercial soil remover, if necessary, to badly soiled areas, e.g. collars, cuffs, trouser hems, to loosen stains.

symbol	washing temperature		agitation	rinse	spin/wring	fabric	benefits
	machine	hand					
1 95	very hot (95°C) to boil	hand hot 50°C or boil	maximum	normal	normal	white cotton and linen articles without special finishes	ensures whiteness and stain removal
2 60	hot 60°C	hand hot 50°C	maximum	normal	normal	cotton, linen or rayon articles without special finishes where colours are fast at 60°C	maintains colours
3 60	hot 60°C	hand hot 50°C	medium	cold	short spin or drip dry	white nylon; white polyester/cotton mixtures	prolongs whiteness — minimises creasing
4 60	hand hot 50°C	hand hot 50°C	medium	cold	short spin or drip dry	coloured nylon; polyester; cotton and rayon articles with special finishes; acrylic/cotton mixtures; coloured polyester/cotton mixtures	safeguards colour and finish — minimises creasing
5 40	warm 40°C	warm 40°C	medium	normal	normal	cotton, linen or rayon articles where colours are fast at 40°C, but not at 60°C	safeguards the colour fastness
6 40	warm 40°C	warm 40°C	minimum	cold	short spin	acrylics; acetate and triacetate, including mixtures with wool; polyester/wool blends	preserves colour and shape — minimises creasing
7 40	warm 40°C	warm 40°C	minimum do not rub	normal	normal spin do not hand wring	wool, including blankets, and wool mixtures with cotton or rayon; silk	keeps colour, size and handle
8 30	cool 30°C	cool 30°C	minimum	cold	short spin do not hand wring	silk and printed acetate fabrics with colours not fast at 40°C	prevents colour loss
9 95	very hot (95°C) to boil	hand hot 50°C or boil	maximum	cold	drip dry	cotton articles with special finishes capable of being boiled but requiring drip drying	prolongs whiteness, retains special crease resistant finish

Washing symbols

grade		3	2	1	0
treatment	symbol	no special caution	caution prescribed	special care	treatment prohibited
washing	wash-tub	95°	60°	30° or 40° according to articles	⊠
chlorine bleaching	triangle	Cl			⊠
ironing	iron	•••	••	•	⊠
dry-cleaning	dry-cleaning cylinder	Ⓐ	Ⓟ	Ⓕ	⊗
	colour	green	green orange	orange	red
drying	dry flat	line dry	tumble dry	drip dry	⊠

WASHING IN AN AUTOMATIC MACHINE

1. Wait until there is a full load of a particular type; it is extravagant to wash a few items unless the machine has an economy (half load) programme.
2. Follow directions supplied with the machine, particularly those relating to the wash load (weight of clothes), amount of detergent, temperature, length of wash and spin cycles.
3. Put detergent and conditioner into dispensers. For very soiled fabrics, a pre-wash may be necessary, using a biological detergent.
4. Put the washing into the machine, taking care not to overload it (it should be possible to turn your hand freely between the clothes and the top of the drum).
5. Set the programme controls for (a) temperature, (b) washing programme and (c) long/short spin.
6. Attach hoses to tap and sink, if machine is not plumbed in; plug in and switch on.
7. The wash should proceed without further attention. The average machine goes through the following programme:
   (a) pre-wash, using biological detergent;
   (b) main wash, during which water is heated to correct temperature;
   (c) spinning and rinsing (conditioner, if used, will enter the final rinsing water);
   (d) final long or short spin.
   Note: Programmes for synthetics may have a 'rinse and hold' setting in which clothes are left floating in final rinsing water to reduce creasing, until the short-spin switch is manually operated.
   NB. Make sure you do not open the door during this time or water will spill out.

Washing machine

HAND WASHING

1. Prepare clothes as above, sorting them into groups.
2. Dissolve detergent completely in very hot water; add sufficient cold water to bring it to the required temperature.

3. Start with cleanest items requiring hottest temperature:
   (a) white cotton/linen;
   (b) pale, fast coloureds;
   (c) white nylon/polyester and mixtures;
   (d) coloured synthetics;
   (e) darker coloureds.
4. Change water and proceed with a cooler wash for acrylics, wool mixtures, wool and silk, again washing the palest or cleanest things first.
5. Squeeze lather gently through fabrics and rub stains gently, paying particular attention to soiled areas, e.g. shirt collars.
6. Wring cottons and linens tightly; squeeze silks, wools and certain synthetics gently. Many synthetics should be drip-dried.
7. Rinse thoroughly in warm water, followed by cold. Squeeze or wring; spin if required.
8. Hang to dry, or tumble dry.

Special treatments

(a) *Underwear:* wash frequently. Because many items of underwear, e.g. foundation garments, contain elastic which is damaged by high temperature, take care to wash in hand-hot water and rinse in cold, to restore elasticity.

(b) *Synthetics:* do not allow them become too soiled. Wash frequently, using fabric conditioner in the final rinse to reduce static electricity.

(c) *Flame-resistant finishes, e.g. children's nightwear:* wash in a synthetic detergent to protect finish. Such finishes should not be washed using biological detergents.

(d) *Sportswear:* allow all mud to dry completely, then brush off. Soak in a mild solution of vinegar to remove perspiration. Then wash according to type in hot soapy water. If garment contains elastic, use a lower temperature.

(e) *Woollens*

(i) Use a gentle soap powder. Dissolve washing powder completely in hot water before adding cold to bring it to the cooler temperature necessary for washing woollens. High temperatures cause wool to shrink, felt and pill (form into fluffy beads).

(ii) Wash by squeezing gently in warm soapy water. Avoid rough handling, e.g. rubbing or wringing.

(iii) Rinse three or four times in warm water, squeezing out excess water each time.

(iv) Arrange garment on a towel, pulling carefully into shape. Roll up to remove surplus water.

(v) Dry flat, away from sunlight or direct heat. Press on wrong side using a cool iron and pressing cloth. Avoid pressing ribbed sweaters.

Note: Hand-knitteds need particularly delicate handling expecially when wet to avoid pulling them out of shape.

(f) *Coloureds:* Most modern coloured fabrics are colour fast and can be washed in hot (60°C) soapy water (wash care label 2 or 4). It is a good idea to wash each coloured garment by hand for the first time, to check whether the dye runs. Synthetics are generally less likely to run. A cold rinse followed by another containing vinegar helps reduce dye loss. Wash care labels 5 and 8 are used on garments which are less colour-fast. Garments which are likely to lose a lot of dye should be washed separately in warm, not hot, water.

To test whether a fabric is colour-fast: Wash an inconspicuous part of the garment, rinse and iron while damp between two pieces of white fabric. If any colour appears, take care to wash separately, as above.

(g) *Steeping:* Steeping clothes helps to soften soil so that a less harsh treatment can be used when washing. Steep heavily soiled clothes overnight in warm soapy water, making sure to dissolve detergent beforehand. Never steep in hot water as this will set rather than loosen the stain. Use a plastic bucket or basin for soaking clothes. Many metals may cause iron mould stains. Protein stains should be steeped in biological detergent. Never steep woollens.

(h) *Boiling:* This helps to keep white fabrics white and removes certain stains. It also has the power of destroying germs, thus sterilising the fabric. This is useful for babies' nappies, for example, or during an infectious outbreak in the house.

Clothes can be boiled in a large saucepan, in a boiler — a large vessel specially made for boiling clothes, or in a washing machine. Only boil white cottons and linens; coloureds will fade and synthetics are usually damaged by the high temperature.

Boil articles for 15-20 minutes in water containing a little detergent. Rinse thoroughly and dry.

DRYING CLOTHES

Excess water may be removed from rinsed fabrics by
(a) wringing;
(b) rolling in a towel;
(c) spin drying;
(d) drip drying.

Wringing may be done by hand, by hand wringer or by a wringer (mangle) on a washing machine. Wringers can be adjusted to suit thickness and type of garment. They are ideal for cottons and linen, e.g. towels and bed linen, although they can cause creasing. They should not be used for synthetics.

Woollens and delicate garments such as hand-knitteds which might stretch should be rolled in a towel and pressed well to remove excess water, before drying flat. *Spin drying* is suitable for most fabrics. Take care to follow directions regarding maximum load and length of spin for each fabric (see page 000).

Drip drying: most synthetics e.g. nylon, polyester and many natural fibres when specially treated can be drip dried so that little or no ironing is necessary. When laundering drip-dry articles, it is essential to follow the washing instructions exactly, otherwise the drip-dry effect will be lost.

- Never use water hotter than hands can bear (48°C), (exception is articles with No. 9 wash-care label).
- Never rub or wring tightly.
- Do not allow drip-dry articles to become too soiled, or rubbing will be necessary to remove stains.
- Rinse two or three times; final rinse in cold water.
- If line drying, do not wring. Place on a plastic hanger (avoid wood and metal hangers which might stain the article), pull into position and hang to dry.
- Spin drying: only spin for 10-20 seconds.
- Tumble drying: avoid packing drum tightly. Tumble for about 10 minutes, giving a final cold tumble.
- Ironing should not be necessary if instructions have been followed. Just touch up, if necessary, using a cool iron.

To completely dry the garment you may
(a) line dry
(b) dry flat
(c) drip dry
(d) tumble dry.

The familiar garden clothes line

(a) *Line drying:* fresh outdoor smell in good weather; sunlight helps to bleach and disinfect garments and, of course, it's free! It may cause yellowing of woollens.

(b) *Drying flat:* used for woollens, knitteds etc. Must be rolled in towel first. Very slow to dry.

(c) *Drip dry:* simple and quick. Indoor drying may cause puddles, therefore hang. Little or no ironing necessary.

(d) *Tumble drying:* a very expensive form of drying. It may cause condensation unless the drier is vented to extract air. Very useful when weather is bad. (More on tumble drying on page 215).

A space-saver for drying clothes

SPONGING AND PRESSING

Now and then between washing or dry-cleaning, a garment although not soiled may look less than fresh, or may show slight staining e.g. around collars. When this occurs it can be given a new lease of life quickly and easily by 'sponging and pressing'.

SPONGING

1. Use warm water containing a little mild detergent.
2. Shake garment well and brush down with clothes brush.

3. Lie garment flat on table and wipe down from top to hem using a sponge or soft cloth, wrung out of the soapy water.
4. Pay particular attention to neck area, cuffs and any stains which may be present. Rub gently with cloth if necessary, or use suitable stain remover.
5. Rinse sponge/cloth and lightly wipe over again.
6. Repeat on back. Hang up and allow to dry slightly.

PRESSING

1. Press with a hot iron, using a pressing cloth if necessary.
2. Press on wrong side as far as possible.
3. Arrange pleats and creases carefully before pressing.
4. Use a lifting and heavy downward pressing movement rather than ironing the garment.
5. Avoid pressing in unwanted creases by arranging each section carefully before pressing.
6. Air garment well before wearing.

IRONING

1. Use a medium-weight steam or dry iron and make sure the sole plate is clean.
2. Most fabrics iron best when slightly damp. Any garments which need to be damped, e.g. starched articles, should be sprinkled with water, rolled up tightly in a towel and left for 30-60 minutes before ironing.
3. Use iron at the correct temperature for the fabric. Check care label; if in doubt, start with a cool iron.
4. Sort ironing into fabrics which need cool, medium and hot temperatures.
5. Switch on iron; allow a few minutes for it to heat, then begin with fabrics requiring a cool iron. Increase heat for fabrics in the medium range, then finish with those needing a hot iron, e.g. cottons and linens. Test doubtful fabrics on an inconspicuous part first.
6. Most garments iron best on the reverse or wrong side unless a shiny finish is wanted, e.g. on table linen.

   Ironing on the wrong side
   (a) prevents shining, especially on dark fabrics;
   (b) prevents flattening the pile of corduroy, velvet etc.;
   (c) prevents melting iron-on decorations, plastics etc.
   (d) prevents marking and soiling raised seams and welts, e.g. on denim jeans;

(e) shows off quilting, embroidery, crochet and lace to advantage. These finishes should always be ironed on the reverse side over a folded towel or flannel pad. Use a steam iron or damp cloth over fabric.
7. Iron double parts on the inside first, e.g. hems, seams; then main garment on the right side. Iron all garments until completely dry.
8. Take care to avoid creasing by arranging fabric carefully and squaring up the corners before you place the iron down. Iron with smooth movements.
9. Pleats, trouser creases etc. need special care; line up crease carefully, then press heavily with a hot iron using a damp cloth over fabric (or use a steam iron)
10. Gathers should be lifted slightly with left hand while ironing carefully into the gathers with the toe of the iron. Never press iron on top of gathers.
11. Garments such as shirts should be ironed methodically, e.g. yoke first, then one side of front, the back, other front, collar, sleeves and cuffs.
12. Allow clothes to air on hangers or a clothes horse, then fold as follows: fasten buttons, zips etc.; lay garment face down on ironing board, fold each side of the back towards the centre, fold in sleeves, then fold from bottom in two or three folds.
13. Place folded ironing in hot press to air.

Note:
• Many modern fabrics do not need to be ironed, e.g. towels, nappies, sweaters, underwear, sheets and other drip-dry fabrics, particularly if they have been correctly washed and tumble-dried.
• Have a needle and thread on hand while ironing, to do instant repairs e.g. sewing on shirt buttons.

IRONING TEMPERATURES

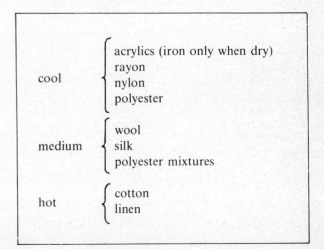

cool	acrylics (iron only when dry) rayon nylon polyester
medium	wool silk polyester mixtures
hot	cotton linen

STAIN REMOVAL

Stains may be removed by (a) washing, (b) bleaching, (c) use of solvents, absorbents and other stain-removing agents.

(a) Washing: if the fabric is washable, normal washing will remove most stains.

(b) Bleaching: used for stubborn stains on white cottons and linens.

(c) Stains on non-washable fabrics and certain difficult stains must be removed by solvents and absorbents.

REMOVING STAINS

Stain	Treatment	Precautions
1. Grease e.g. oil, fat, make-up	Scrape off solids with blunt knife. Wash in hot soapy water, rinse, dry. Non-washables: press between two sheets blotting paper using hot iron, or dab with a solvent e.g. benzine, carbon tetrachloride or commercial drycleaning agent e.g. Dab-it-off, Dry-clean.	Use solvents in well ventilated room. Air well after use. Fumes may be toxic.
2. Protein stains e.g. blood, egg, meat, chocolate, gum	Soak in warm water using biological detergent per 500 ml). Wash as usual. Rinse. Non-washables: use commercial drycleaner.	(1 teasp. Do not use hot water; it will set stain and inactivate enzymes.
3. Beverages e.g. tea, coffee, alcohol, fruit juices	Place stained fabric over a bowl, rub borax into stain and pour boiling water over. Many such stains will come out during normal washing. Stubborn stains may need bleaching.	
4. Ballpoint, grass, hair lacquer	Dab gently with cloth dipped in methylated spirits. Rinse and wash as usual.	Methylated spirit is inflammable.
5. Perspiration, urine	Steep in biological detergent. Then wash as normal using biological detergent. Rinse thoroughly.	Avoid using biological detergent on babies' nappies. Use commercial steriliser for napkins e.g. Napisan.
6. Chewing gum	Use ice-cube to harden, then pull off. Soften remainder with butter. Remove grease stain with solvet.	
7. Tar	Scrape off excess with blunt stick. Soften with butter, wipe off, then wash to remove grease stain or dry clean.	
8. Beer	Cold water — at once. If dried in, normal washing should remove. Otherwise use surgical spirit.	
9. Paint (oil based) (emulsion)	Rub with turpentine or white spirit. Wash according to fabric. Wash at once in cold water.	Remove at once.
10. Nail polish	Rub with nail polish remover (amyl acetate).	This solvent is inflammable. Never use on acetate fabrics.
11. Mildew and difficult fruit stains	Use bleach solution on white cotton and linen. Wash and rinse. Coloureds: hydrogen peroxide.	See directions for bleaching.
12. Iron mould/rust	Small stains: lemon juice. Large, dark stains: use iron mould remover e.g. salts of lemon or Move-ol. Wash thoroughly.	Commercial iron mould removers are poisonous.
13. Ink	Rinse at once in cold water.	Avoid spreading stain.
14. Shoe polish	Sponge with carbon tetrachloride. Rinse well.	
15. Scorches	Rub with glycerine, then wash normally. More serious scorches in cotton and linen may need bleaching.	

Solvents break down the stain, usually by chemical reaction. They are rubbed in with a clean white cloth and a pad of cloth should also be placed beneath the stain to soak up any residue. Examples: benzine, Dab-it-off.

Absorbents remove grease and some other stains by soaking them up, i.e. absorbing them. The product is shaken on, or pressed firmly into the stain, allowed time to absorb the stain and then brushed off. Commercial aerosol absorbents e.g. Dry-clean, consist of an absorbent dissolved in a liquid which evaporates quickly, once sprayed on the stain. Traditional absorbents are Fuller's earth, French chalk and talcum powder. These are used on items such as hats, fur etc. which cannot be washed.

Most stain-removing chemicals are available in a chemist's shop.

STAIN-REMOVING AGENTS

1. Soap and synthetic detergents (page 197): these remove grease and general soil, e.g. tea, coffee, fruit juice, alcohol.
2. Enzyme detergents (page 197-8): these are useful for removing protein-based stains e.g. blood, gravy. Avoid using very hot water when soaking stains or the enzymes will not work.
3. Acids e.g. lemon juice, salts of lemon: remove iron mould. Vinegar helps remove perspiration stains.
4. Alkalis, e.g. washing soda, remove grease stains, e.g. oil and also have a softening effect on the water.
5. Bleaches: most of the stronger bleaches are only suitable for removing stains from cotton or linen. Always follow instructions. Never use undiluted.
6. Solvents such as turpentine, carbon tetrachloride, benzine are usually used on non-washable fabrics, particularly for removing grease.
7. Absorbents are also used on non-washable fabrics; they include French chalk, Fuller's earth, talcum powder and spray-on dry-cleaning agents e.g. Dry-clean.
8. Other agents, e.g. acetone, remove specific stains.

POINTS ON REMOVING STAINS

1. Stains and dirt damage fibres. They should be removed as soon as possible before they get hard and dry into the fabric. Blot off any excess first.
2. Remove stains before washing.
3. Use the gentlest method first, i.e. steep in cold water.
4. Test the stain remover on a hem or other unseen part of the garment before using.

5. Always start on outer edge of stain and work inwards. Do not rub; dab gently.
6. Use a clean pad of white cloth under the stain. Rub on remover with another clean cloth, e.g. old sheet.

Safety

1. Many stain removers are poisonous. Store in a safe place away from children, in a clearly marked bottle.
2. Use in a well ventilated room. The fumes of many solvents are toxic if inhaled.
3. Air garment thoroughly after using a solvent. If washable rinse well.
4. Never use near a naked flame.
5. Acetate fibres are damaged by acetone, carbon tetrachloride, trichlorethylene and strong acids and alkalis.

DRY CLEANING

Dry cleaning is generally carried out on fibres which cannot be washed: clothes, upholstery, soft furnishings and carpets. Fabrics are dry-cleaned by using solvents and absorbents to remove the stains, instead of immersing them in water. Dry-cleaning at home is usually limited to 'spotting', i.e. removing small stains from fabrics. Commercial dry-cleaning involves immersing the articles in solvents such as perchloroethylene in a large dry-cleaning machine. This is similar to an automatic washing machine. It revolves the clothes in a drum containing the solvent, then tumble dries them before they are finally pressed.

Before sending articles to dry cleaners
1. empty and brush out pockets;
2. carry out repairs;
3. check whether fabric and trimmings are dry cleanable.
   Some types of button must be removed.

The international dry-cleaning symbol is a circle. A letter inside the circle indicates which cleaning fluid should be used.

Ⓐ   All solvents.

Ⓕ   White spirit and solvent 113.

Ⓟ   Perchloroethylene, white spirit, solvent 113, solvent 11.

⊗   Do not dry clean.

Note: After dry-cleaning, whether it is done at the cleaners or at home, clothes must be well aired. The fumes from many dry-cleaning solvents are dangerous.

HOME CLEANING

1. Shake garment well.
2. Remove stains with appropriate stain remover.
3. Using clean cloth, lightly rub the article all over with a mild grease solvent. Rub soiled areas such as collars and cuffs particularly well.
4. Change cloths as they become dirty.
5. Air well out of doors.
6. Press.
7. An aerosol dry cleaner may be used if wished. When dry, brush well using a clean clothes brush.

COIN-OP CLEANERS

These are more economical than normal dry cleaners. A 'load' of clothes may be dry-cleaned at one time. They are not pressed, just hung straight after drying. This method of cleaning may be sufficient for dresses and woollens, but garments which require a good pressing, such as tailored suits and coats, should be professionally dry-cleaned.

DYES AND DYING

Dyes are strong pigments used to revive faded colours or produce a new colour. They can also be used to create patterns and designs in a fabric, for example tie-dye and batik work.

TYPES

1. Water dyes: these are dissolved in boiling water. Salt is added to fix colour. Wet garments are immersed, then simmered in a solution of the dye until the colour has taken (approximately 20 minutes). They may be used on cotton, linen, silk, some nylon and woollens. They should not be used on many synthetics, e.g. acrylics. A wide range of colours is available.

2. Cold water dyes: they must first be dissolved in hot water, then diluted with cold water. A fixer and salt are also added. They are suitable for dying large articles which could not be boiled in the conventional way. Use on cotton, linen, wool, silk and viscose. The colour range of cold water dyes is more limited than hot water dyes.

3. Liquid (instant) dye: can be used to dye in the usual way, or for painting fabrics. Fabric is simply immersed according to instructions.

4. Washing machine dye: this is a hot water dye together with a detergent which is prepared, then added to the filled washing machine. The wet fabric is then put into the machine and the controls set for the longest and hottest programme. To obtain a good colour, never dye more than one-third of the capacity of the machine at one time. One large drum of dye dyes 1 kilo of fabric in a machine. It is not necessary to wash the article beforehand.

Note: After dying, run the machine through a complete cycle with a cup of bleach in the water, then run it through once again to remove all traces of bleach.

STRIPPING

If the article to be dyed is patterned, patchy or darker than the colour required, it is necessary to remove the colour from the fabric. Commercial strippers are available to suit each manufactured dye, e.g. Dygon. Follow directions carefully. Strippers, like bleaches, have a degenerative effect on the fabric.

RULES FOR DYING

1. Find out the type of fabric and check whether it can be dyed.
2. Fabric to be dyed must be spotlessly clean, well rinsed and wet. Strip out colour beforehand if necessary.
3. Wear rubber gloves and an overall in case of splashes.
4. Read instructions carefully through, then follow them to the letter, especially regarding the amount of dye for the weight of fabric.
5. Dissolve powder completely in boiling water; mix in enough water to cover article.
6. Add dye-fix, e.g. salt or commercial fixing agent.
7. Shake damp article loose, then gently lower into dye vessel.
8. Boil or simmer for required length of time (hot water dyes).
9. Stir continuously. The container should be large enough to allow the article to move about freely while stirring.
10. Time accurately, then remove and rinse several times in cold water until water runs clear.
11. Dry away from direct heat; line dry or use tumble drier on a low-heat setting.

Note: Avoid being skimpy with the dye, e.g. trying to dye too many articles. The results will be uneven and the colour unsatisfactory.

TIE-DYING

Article is knotted tightly or pleated and held in place with clothes pegs, in a random pattern or in a regular design. Inserting coins, pebbles into the knots will give interesting variations.

BATIK

This originated in the East. Ornate designs are painted onto the fabric with melted wax and allowed to dry. The article is immersed in cold dye (hot water would melt the wax). When dry, the wax is removed by ironing with a hot iron and absorbent paper.

QUESTIONS/CHAPTER 21

1. What is the purpose of wash-care labels? Describe the basic information found on a typical care label. Sketch the appropriate international symbol for the following:
   (a) iron with a cool iron;
   (b) may be bleached;
   (c) tumble dry;
   (d) do not dry clean.
2. Describe the procedure for preparing and washing clothes in an automatic washing machine. List the stages of a typical full cycle of an automatic machine wash.
3. Classify the stain-removing agents used for dry-cleaning in the home and give two examples of each type. List the precautions which should be taken when using cleaning agents. Describe how to remove grease stains from a wool skirt.
4. Give instructions for the correct method of laundering the following:
   (a) white cotton sheets or towels;
   (b) a hand-knitted woollen sweater.
   Explain the importance of steeping in laundrywork.
5. Describe how the following should be dried and ironed:
   (a) a silk blouse;
   (b) a pleated wool/terylene skirt;
   (c) a cotton shirt;
   (d) denim jeans.
6. List the general rules for removing stains from garments. Using modern stain-removing agents, describe how to remove the following:
   (a) lipstick on a shirt;
   (b) ball-point on a white cotton dress;
   (c) tar on a man's suit.
   What precautions should be taken when using dry-cleaning solvents in the home?
7. List the types of dye available for home dying and write a note on the use of each. Describe in detail how to prepare and dye a household article or a garment.

22.
Washing equipment

The family wash can be done
(a) at the laundry;
(b) at the laundrette;
(c) by hand;
(d) by machine.

THE LAUNDRY

Advantages
1. No work at all involved; ideal for very busy people.
2. Washing can be collected and delivered.
3. Produces a very good finish on certain items e.g. table linen.
4. No major outlay on equipment.
5. Some laundries do repairs.
6. Useful for rainy spells or when home machines break down.

Disadvantages
1. Very expensive.
2. Constant heavy laundering tends to wear out articles.
3. Items often lost at laundry.
4. Linen is out of use for longer than when home laundering; you may need extra clothes and linen.

THE LAUNDRETTE

Advantages
1. No expensive outlay on equipment.
2. Handy in emergencies, or for those living in cramped accommodation.
3. Can be cheaper than laundering at home.
4. Drying facilities are also available; clothes may be fully dried or damp dried.

5. Machines are often larger and are capable of dealing with large items e.g. blankets, or a bigger wash.
6. It is possible to have the supervisor deal with your wash (a service wash), leaving you free to shop or work.

Launderette ready for action

Disadvantages
1. Unless a car is available, it is difficult to transport large bundles of washing.
2. Inconvenient and time-wasting to have to leave the house in order to wash your clothes.
3. There may be queues on rainy days.

HANDWASHING

Advantages
1. Good for non-fast coloured articles.
2. Necessary for delicate fabrics which might be damaged by machine washing.
3. Handy for small amounts of washing; it would be wasteful to turn on a machine for a few items. (Usually it is necessary to wait until you have enough for a full load in order to get best value from a washing machine.)

Disadvantages
1. A large family wash can be very tiring.
2. Very time consuming.
3. Harsh on hands; use rubber gloves.
4. Handwashing rarely leaves clothes, especially whites, as clean as when they are machine washed, when higher temperatures and stronger detergents can be used.

MACHINE WASHING

Advantages
1. Automatic machines take all the work out of washing.
2. Clothes are washed more thoroughly, although a gentle (wool) programme may also be used.
3. Large amounts can be washed together.
4. Washing machines have programmes to suit most fabrics, and most include spin drying.
5. Much cheaper than using a laundry, and when the machine has been paid for, cheaper than the laundrette.

Disadvantages
1. Machines are expensive to buy and service.
2. They are expensive to run, when you add the cost of detergent, water-heating etc.
3. Failure to sort washing can lead to many articles being damaged or discoloured.

THE LAUNDRY AREA

Laundering in most houses takes place in the kitchen; this is unsatisfactory for several reasons.
1. It is rarely large enough.
2. It is inconvenient to have the same sink used for cooking and laundry, e.g. if one wants to steep clothes.
3. There is a greater concentration of steam.

The ideal alternative which is included in many new houses is the utility room, fitted with a sink and a plumbing connection for a washing machine. A tumbler drier, deep freeze and even ironing equipment may also be housed in the utility room. There must be a convenient drain outlet and sufficient electric sockets to power each piece of equipment which is used in the room.

WASHING MACHINES

Most housewives would now regard a washing machine as an essential piece of household equipment. It is labour- and time-saving, and leaves the housewife more freedom to get on with other tasks. It is particularly useful if there are babies or toddlers in the house.

PRINCIPLE

A washing machine cleans clothes by agitating them in hot water and detergent. Automatic machines rinse and spin, and some even tumble clothes dry. There are three methods of agitation, all brought about by an electrically driven motor:

1. by tumbling: clothes are rotated first one way, then the other in a horizontal drum;
2. by impeller: a wheel-like implement situated at the back or base of the tub revolves at speed, producing sufficient turbulence to move the clothes about in the water;
3. by agitator: a rotating paddle situated in the centre of the base of the machine gives half-turns first in one direction, then the other, moving the clothes about in the water.

Washing machines may be single tub, twin tub or automatic.

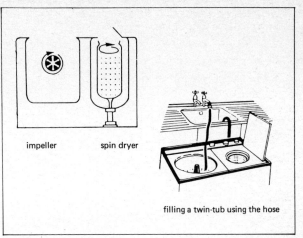

impeller   spin dryer

filling a twin-tub using the hose

Twin-tub washing machine

SINGLE TUB WASHING MACHINES

Most have

1. a thermostatically-controlled water heater,
2. a top-opening lid,
3. impeller or agitator action,
4. adjustable electric or hand wringers.

Advantages

1. Single tub machines are cheap to buy and run.
2. Cleaner articles can be washed first, then removed, and dirtier articles added next and so on. This saves water and electricity.
3. Clothes can be boiled in the machine.

Disadvantages

1. This method involves more manual work.
2. It saves less time and labour than automatic machines.

TWIN TUBS

These consist of a single tub as above and a spinner, fitted side by side in one cabinet. The capacity ranges from 1.8 to 3.2 kg dry clothes. Most are semi-automatic.

1. Heating and wash cycles are automatic.
2. Spinning and rinsing are usually automatic.
3. Filling and emptying are carried out manually by hoses fitted to the sink.

Advantages

1. Twin tubs are cheaper than automatics.
2. The same soapy water can be used first for whites, then coloureds; one tub washing, while the other is spinning.

3. Spinner leaves clothes damp dry.
4. Twin tubs cost less to run than automatics.
5. Spinner can be used for handwashed clothes.
6. Any detergent may be used.

Disadvantages

1. Some manual operations are required, e.g. transferring clothes from washer to spinner.
2. Many only take fairly small loads.
3. Clothes are inclined to crease.

AUTOMATIC WASHING MACHINES

These carry out a preselected programme of washing, rinsing and spin drying. Programmes vary according to requirements of different fabrics. They include:

1. soaking;
2. biological wash;
3. rinse, spin and hold;
4. main wash;
5. several rinses and spins;
6. final long spin.

This complete programme would be used for heavily soiled cottons and linens. More delicate fabrics (synthetics) would start at 4, i.e. have a shorter, cooler main wash, fewer rinses, and shorter spins, with either a very short final spin or clothes left floating in water until a manually operated short spin is switched on. This latter prevents delicates becoming creased and is called a **spin delay**.

Up to fifteen programmes are available on many machines. Most programmes on modern automatics correspond to the wash-care labels on clothes and detergent packets.

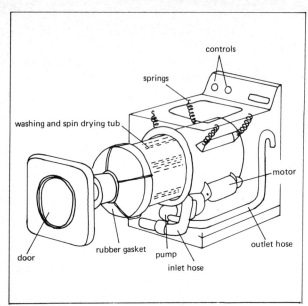

Front-loading washing machine

During washing, the drum rotates gently one way then another. After washing and rinsing, the drum rotates at high speed and throws the clothes against sides by centrifugal force. This forces the water out through the holes in the drum.

Combined washing and drying machine (Candy)

Automatic machines may be front-loading or top-loading.

1. Front-loading machines have a horizontal drum and usually wash by tumbling action. These use less water than top-loaders and spin-dry by centrifugal force, i.e. the water is forced out of the clothes through tiny holes in the drum.
2. Most top-loading machines have an agitator in a vertical perforated drum. These use more water and also spin by centrifugal force.
3. Both types may be fully automatic or semi-automatic. Fully automatic machines complete the entire programme without attention. Semi-automatic machines require some manual dial changes.
4. Hot water may come from the hot water supply or a built-in heater. The latter is preferable, as pre-wash and rinse cycles will use cold water. This helps to remove certain stains, e.g. blood, and prevents emptying the household hot water supply.
5. Capacity is 3 to 4 kg dry clothes.
6. Some very expensive automatic machines tumble dry the wash after the final spin.

Advantages

1. Automatics are more convenient and labour-saving — no supervision is required.
2. They have a large capacity.
3. Front loaders can be placed under a worktop.
4. Cycle can be stopped at any stage, and changes made in the programme.

Disadvantages

1. Spinning action is less efficient than that of separate spin-dryers.
2. Low foam powders must be used on front-loading automatics. They are very expensive.
3. Some programmes are lengthy, up to two hours.

Construction

Washing machines are usually made from enamelled pressed steel. A perforated, stainless steel *drum* is fitted within an outer container, which collects the water for removal. Doors on front loaders are sealed with a rubber gasket. Legs are usually adjustable so that they can be levelled on the floor.

Detergent dispenser may consist of a filter tray which fits on the agitator; a pull-out drawer at the front of the machine; or a lift-up flap on top. If machine is to be fitted under a worktop, the dispenser must not be on the top of the machine. Most dispensers have three compartments: for pre-wash detergent, main wash detergent, and fabric conditioner.

An electric *motor* (300 watts) drives the pump which fills and empties the machine. A 2,500 watt *heater* is fitted in the base of the machine.

Dimensions of automatics are similar to base kitchen units, approximately 800 to 915 mm high; 550 to 650 mm deep and 550 to 650 mm wide. Twin tubs: 750 to 810 mm high; 420 to 520 mm deep; and 760 to 860 mm wide.

Controls usually consist of an on/off button, programme selector dial, and heater dial. Some models use a selection of key plates which are slotted in position to produce each programme. Temperatures used range from cold to boiling and depend on the fabrics being washed. Programmes may be interrupted and sections left out in certain models.

Installation

1. All washing machines require an earthed 13 or 16 amp socket.
2. The machine must be level — otherwise drum will rotate unevenly and noisily.
3. Automatics should be plumbed in as near to sink and/or plumbing fitments as possible. Hose fitments may be used, but they are awkward and inconvenient.
4. Good ventilation is required to remove steam.
5. The washing machine may be installed in the kitchen if there is room. Alternatives include utility room, back porch, garage, downstairs bathroom.
6. Top-loading machines and front-loaders with detergent dispensers on top cannot be fitted under a worktop, unless it has a hinged flap, or the machine is on castors to move it out for use.
7. Check that water pressure is sufficiently high.
8. Use a reliable plumber to plumb in the machine. It may be connected to hot or cold supply or both.
9. Before use, be sure to remove transit brackets.

CHOOSING AN AUTOMATIC WASHING MACHINE

Consider the following

1. size of family;
2. amount of money available;
3. space available in kitchen or utility room;
4. type and size of washes: i.e. two or three large washes a week or more frequent small washes;
5. time available — automatics are more convenient for the working wife;
6. drying facilities available.

Check machine

1. Is it a reliable make, electrically approved, etc?
2. Read instruction book and brochures.
3. Are controls easy to use and understand, and relatively child-proof?
4. Check whether the following points suit your requirements.
   (a) number and type of programmes;
   (b) do programmes include biological wash for very soiled clothes?
   (c) a slow reverse spin after the main spin keeps creasing to the minimum;
   (d) some models have a programme for small washes with a low intake of water — this is economical and saves water;
   (e) safety features: child-proof locks; it should not be possible to open door during spin; controls out of children's reach.

Use

1. Read and follow manufacturer's instructions.
2. Use recommended detergent — usually a low-foam powder. Amount depends on size and type of wash load, degree of soiling, softness of water, and type of detergent.
3. Check wash-care labels, and sort accordingly.
4. Make sure colours are fast.
5. Load machine; do not exceed recommended load. Synthetics need lots of room to avoid creasing.
6. Select suitable programme and heat setting. Make sure heat setting and spin are low and short respectively for synthetics.
7. Add fabric conditioner to final rinse, if required.
8. Remove clothes and line dry or tumble dry.

Care and cleaning

1. Leave door open after removing clothes to dry out machine.
2. Clean filter occasionally if required.
3. Rinse thoroughly after using bleach or dye.
4. Never overload machine: this strains the fan belt and motor and gives poor washing results.
5. Wipe outside after use. Use a silicone polish now and then to prevent rusting.

Washing economy

1. Always wash a full load unless the machine has an economy wash programme.
2. Soak clothes to soften soiling. A shorter, cooler programme will then suffice.
3. Do not use very hot temperature settings unless they are required, e.g. for white sheets, babies' napkins.

4. When using a twin tub, re-use water from the first wash to do another, more heavily soiled wash.
5. Follow manufacturer's instructions to make the most of the machine and to avoid unnecessary repair bills.

DRIERS

These include simple drying cabinets with rails, spin driers, and tumble driers. They are very useful in our damp climate and are particularly useful if babies and toddlers form part of the household. Some form of drier is essential in a flat, where outdoor drying may not be possible.

Drying cabinets

Most of these consist of a gas or electric convector heater, enclosed in a metal box with a perforated or grill top. Over this is fitted a series of wooden or plastic-covered wire rails on which are hung the clothes to be dried or aired. An enamelled cabinet surrounds the whole fitment in many models.

The hot air rising from the heaters causes convection currents which dry the clothes. In some models a fan speeds up drying.

Advantages
1. cheap to buy;
2. variable heat control;
3. noiseless.

Disadvantages
1. expensive to run;
2. clothes dry unevenly;
3. danger of scorching and fire;
4. cause condensation.

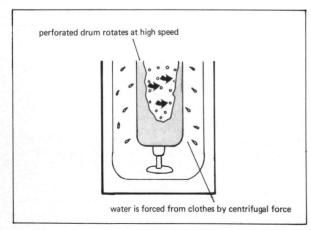

Spin driers action

Spin Drier (Hoover)

Spin driers

Spin driers remove excess water from clothes by centrifugal force. The drier rotates at such a high speed that the clothes are thrown against the sides of the drum and the water forced out of them. Water is drained away by gravity or by a pump.

There are three types:
1. an individual spin drier:
2. a spin-rinse drier: this has a pump and is usually part of a twin tub machine;
3. the spin cycle of an automatic machine.

When buying, check the following points:
1. Is hose long enough to reach comfortably into sink?
2. Is flex long enough to plug into socket, while hose is fitted to sink?
3. In order to prevent accidents, the motor of an approved spin drier should only work when the door is closed.
4. Has model a manual rinse or automatic rinse?

214

Advantages
1. cheap to buy and run;
2. soaking wet clothes are spun until they are damp dry, so they dry more quickly on the line and do not drip;
3. most models rinse as well.

Disadvantages
1. noisy;
2. does not dry clothes completely.

Tumble driers

Clothes are dried by rotating them gently in warm air. Air is warmed around heating elements and is blown into the drier by a fan. Here it becomes saturated with moisture from the drying clothes. The moisture laden air is filtered and leaves the machine through a ventilating duct. All tumble driers are front-loading. loading.

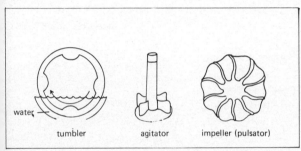

Essential parts of a washing machine

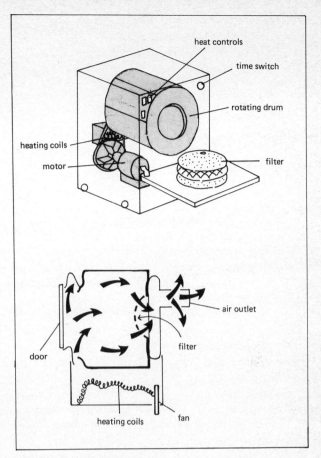

How a tumble drier works

The exterior has an enamelled finish. The clothes drum may have a stainless steel or enamelled finish. The drum usually has three or four baffles or ridges to assist the rotation of the clothes. The door at the front may be perforated to assist removal of moist air. Most models have an air venting hose to take the damp air out of a window. Like spin driers, tumbler driers should stop when the door is opened, and start again when it closes.

Controls are a timer, and a heat selection switch, with choice of two or more temperatures. Most machines cut off the heater for the final 10 minutes to reduce creasing.

Capacity is between 2.5 and 5 kg dry clothes.

Use
1. Sort clothes according to fabric and degree of dryness required. Do not overload.
2. Select correct heat and time setting for fabrics.
3. Clothes must be spun dry before putting into tumbler.
4. Clean filter after each drying session.

Advantages
1. Tumble driers are not too expensive to buy.
2. Clothes can be tumbled to any degree of dryness: damp-dry for ironing or bone dry.
3. Tumble drying is an ideal alternative to line drying when weather is bad.
4. Drying in a tumble drier reduces creasing.
5. Fewer clothes are required, as they can be washed and tumble dried quickly when necessary.

Disadvantages
1. The machine is very expensive to run.
2. Room needs to be well-ventilated. If drier is not vented, it may cause condensation.
3. Many people prefer the freshness of outdoor drying.
4. Machine drying can cause build-up of static in synthetic fabrics.

If kitchen is small, consider stacking machines. A tumble drier can be stacked on certain washing machines, using a special kit.

Economy

1. Line dry whenever weather permits.
2. Spin-dry clothes before drying in a tumbler — the spin dryer uses very little electricity.

IRONS

Irons may press clothes by dry heat or with the addition of steam. They have a wattage of between 750 and 1200 watts.

Dry iron

This is a thermostatically controlled iron, which presses and removes creases by dry heat.

The shiny underside of the iron, called the **sole plate,** is usually made from polished aluminium, chrome or PTFE-coated metal. Directly over it, with the same shape as the sole plate, is the element. An adjustable thermostat, controlled manually by the **heat control dial,** turns the current off when the sole plate reaches the correct temperature. When it cools the current is switched on again. A **pilot light** indicates whether the current is flowing or not.

The top and handle of the iron are usually made from a plastic such as bakelite, which resists heat. Insulating material over the element directs heat downwards. The modern dry iron is lightweight, with a pointed sole plate and a low, open handle, which enable sleeves and other awkward parts to be ironed easily. Some models have button slots near the point of the iron, which makes it easier to iron around buttons.

Steam iron

The steam iron is constructed in a similar way to the dry iron, but the body of the steam iron also contains a small **water tank,** filled through a hole in the handle. This drips water onto the hot sole plate. The heat of the sole plate converts the water into steam, which is released through steam holes in the sole plate. When steaming is required, the heat control dial is set to 'steam' and a button is depressed. This opens a valve which releases water from the storage tank. Steam irons only produce steam in a horizontal position. Once the iron is resting upright, the steaming ceases. Steam irons may be converted to dry irons instantly by releasing the steam button, and switching thermostat dial to temperature required. Some steam irons have an extra steam booster, which forces extra steam from the sole plate; it is useful if a lot of pressing is done. Others have a spray which dampens clothes while ironing.

Using a steam iron

1. Always unplug when filling. Do not overfill.
2. Use either distilled water or defrosted ice to fill.
3. Allow time for water to heat up before using.
4. Never rest the iron in a horizontal position.
5. Empty tank after use. This is done by carefully turning the iron upside down until all the water drains out.
6. Some manufacturers supply cleaning fluids to remove hard-water deposits from inside the water tank and demineralisers, which are used with normal tap water.

Care and use of irons

1. Use a 13 amp earthed plug. Never connect to a light socket.
2. Allow time for iron to heat up before use.
3. Always rest on heel-rest or iron stand.
4. Take care of flex and check regularly for wear. Replace flex when it becomes worn.
5. To remove scorch marks from sole plate, rub with methylated spirits or use a proprietary iron cleaner

Choosing an iron

1. Consider type required: dry, steam, or spray and steam.
   This is a matter of personal preference.
2. Modern irons work efficiently without weight; therefore choose a light-weight iron which is comfortable to hold.
3. Iron should be well-balanced in horizontal and vertical positions.
4. Iron should be thermostatically controlled, with a long (at least 2.3 m), durable flex.
5. Controls should be accurate and easy to use without burning fingers. Test the iron in the hand before buying.

Standard international heat settings

Hot   (210°C)*** cotton, linen, rayon
Warm (160°C)**   polyester, wool
Cool   (120°C)*   acrylic, nylon, acetate, polyester

Always check wash-care label before ironing. If there is none, test cool iron on an unseen part of the garment.

IRONING MACHINES

There are two types of ironing machine: rotary ironers and flat press ironers. Ironing machines are about ten times more expensive than hand irons, and use about three times more electricity.

Rotary ironers

These consist of a padded roller, which rotates against a heated, curved metal plate. A small motor revolves the roller; it is controlled by a foot pedal, like that on a sewing machine, which leaves the hands free to feed the clothes onto the ironer. The ironer is placed on a table and flat garments are carefully fed into the roller which presses them against the ironing plate.

This is quick and convenient for flat items, such as sheets. The machine is expensive, and considerable practice is required to master this ironing technique.

Flat press ironers

These are smaller versions of the large ironing machines used in dry-cleaners. They have a flat, padded area with curved edges, and a lever-operated sole plate. This is lowered onto the pad, held for sufficient time to smooth the fabric and then raised. The lever and sole plate exert pressure on the clothes and remove creases.

QUESTIONS/CHAPTER 22

1. Compare washing the family wash at the launderette and at home, using an automatic washing machine.

2. Describe the principle and washing action of washing machines. Describe the structure of an automatic machine and list the points to be remembered when using it.

3. Describe the type of electric iron which you would choose for your home, giving reasons for your choice. Write an informative note on the chosen appliance, referring to:
   (a) cost;
   (b) use;
   (c) care;
   (d) working principle.
   What features of the appliance do you consider should be covered by guarantee? Give reasons for your answer.

4. Assess the advantages of each of the following for use in the average home:
   (a) spin drier;
   (b) drying cabinet;
   (c) tumble drier.
   Which do you consider the most appropriate for the mother of a large family; give reasons for your choice. State the capacity and cost of the selected drier and explain the principle on which it works.

23.
Hygiene in the home

Many of the diseases which attack man are caused by tiny organisms so small that they can only be seen by using a powerful microscope. Micro-organisms, as they are called, include moulds, yeasts and viruses, but the chief cause of food poisoning is bacteria — often called 'germs'.

Food poisoning is a collective name for the many food-borne diseases caused by bacteria. It usually occurs when we eat or drink food which is contaminated with pathogenic (disease-bearing) bacteria. It is almost always caused by lack of hygiene, either by a person handling food or by careless hygiene in the home, shop or factory.

BACTERIA

These are minute one-celled creatures which are found almost everywhere: in the soil, water, animals and in man. Not all bacteria are harmful (some, for example those used in making yoghurt and cheese are actually beneficial), but those which are can cause serious disease and even death.

CONDITIONS REQUIRED BY BACTERIA

In order to survive and multiply, bacteria need
   1. food;   3. moisture;
   2. warmth;   4. air.

Bacteria also need *time* to multiply. If we get into the habit of using up food quickly, there is less chance of food poisoning.

1. Food

Bacteria, like us, need food to survive. They are attracted to
(a) moist foods such as soups, stock, stews, milk, egg custards;
(b) protein foods e.g. meat, fish and particularly poultry;

(c) left-overs such as cooked meats which have been allowed to stand for some time before being used up.

Chicken, shellfish and minced meat are common causes of food poisoning — make sure to cook them thoroughly.

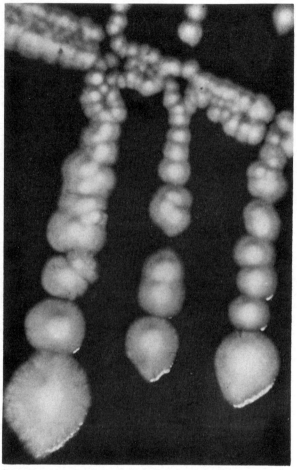

Colonies of typhoid bacteria (C. James Webb)

2. Warmth

Normal room conditions are ideal for bacterial growth. They multiply at a fantastic rate. If one was present in food left in a warm kitchen, overnight it could become several thousand, given ideal conditions.

Cold temperatures slow down growth, which is why perishable food should be stored in a refrigerator. Very low temperatures (below zero) e.g. deep freezing, stop bacterial growth but *do not kill* bacteria. When frozen food is thawed out, any bacteria present will start to multiply again.

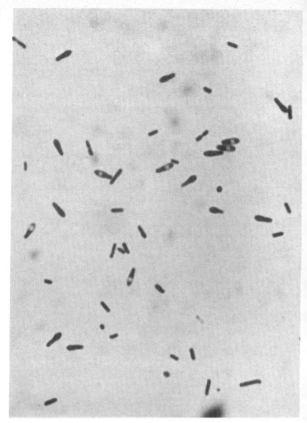

Bacteria of botulism (C. James Webb)

3. Moisture

Bacteria need moisture in order to survive. For this reason they are less likely to attack dry food such as cereals or dehydrated foods. As a steamy atmosphere will increase the chance of bacterial growth, it is essential to ventilate kitchens and bathrooms well.

4. Air

Most bacteria need oxygen to survive. Some of the most deadly forms of food-poisoning bacteria can multiply equally well without oxygen, e.g. in the soil or in canned foods. For this reason vegetables must be well washed and cans of food should be examined for flaws or bulges in the can.

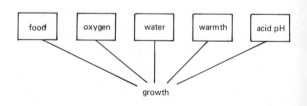

Conditions for the growth of fungi

218

LACK OF HYGIENE

Bacteria thrive in dirty dark conditions. If we do not keep our homes clean and disinfected, bacteria will flourish and infect our food either directly or indirectly.

Bacteria can be destroyed by (a) high temperatures e.g. 100°C; (b) soap and hot water; (c) disinfectants and other chemicals.

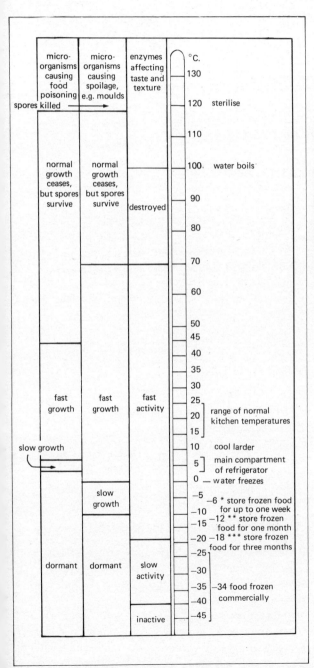

Relation of temperature to growth of bacteria

SPREADING DISEASE

Bacteria are spread in the following ways:
1. By people, through lack of personal hygiene and careless unhygienic habits such as spitting.
2. By animals and insects; flies are one of the greatest hazards. They breed on excreta and transfer bacteria back onto the food we eat. Rats, mice and fleas also carry bacteria and are always a danger to health. Pets carry fleas and bacteria which they carry into the home, particularly if allowed in the kitchen.

A rat (Rentokil Ltd.)

3. Dirty utensils and equipment: these should be washed in hot, soapy water and disinfected where necessary. Particular attention should be paid to kitchen sinks, cloths etc.
4. Lavatories: many food-poisoning bacteria live in the bowel and are easily passed on to the hands when using the lavatory.

PERSONAL HYGIENE

Everyone has the responsibility to prevent spread of disease by following the basic rules of hygiene. Those working with food must be particularly vigilant in order to avoid food poisoning.
1. Always wash hands thoroughly before handling food, after handling raw meat (particularly poultry) and after handling pets or using the lavatory.
2. Avoid coughing and sneezing over food.
3. Do not handle face or hair unnecessarily; tie long hair back when handling food.
4. Cover cuts with a clean waterproof dressing and change it when it becomes soiled.
5. Have a regular bath or shower.

Sources of bacterial infection

FOOD HYGIENE

1. Buy food only from clean shops.
2. Keep food cool and covered (see food storage).
3. Wash fruit and vegetables thoroughly before use.
4. Keep raw and cooked food separate at all times.
5. Handle foods as little as possible.
6. Cook suspect food e.g. meat and poultry thoroughly to destroy any bacteria present.
7. **Left-overs** are a likely source of contamination; cool quickly and store in the refrigerator. Use up as soon as possible. When reheating, bring food to a high temperature to destroy any bacteria present.
8. **Frozen foods:** bacteria survive freezing. Thawed food must never be refrozen. Defrost poultry and joints before cooking; then cook thoroughly.

FOOD STORAGE

1. Store perishables, particularly milk, meat, fish and poultry, in the refrigerator.
2. Store dry foods in vermin-proof containers in clean, dry presses.
3. Fruit and vegetables should be stored in a cool, dry, dark place, e.g. ventilated cupboard, refrigerator or garage. Avoid storing in the kitchen.
4. Clean storage cupboards regularly — food presses once a week.

KITCHEN HYGIENE

A dirty, badly ventilated kitchen provides an ideal environment in which bacteria can flourish.
1. Ventilate well to remove moisture-laden air.
2. Clean kitchen surfaces, utensils and equipment thoroughly straight after use, using hot, soapy water.
3. Disinfect sinks and drains regularly.
4. Kitchen cloths must be kept scrupulously clean. Bleach or boil regularly to kill germs.
5. Keep kitchen bin covered and empty daily. Wash and disinfect weekly.
6. Sweep floor daily. Wash and disinfect at least once a week.
7. Keep pets out of the kitchen.

HOME HYGIENE

1. Keep the lavatory scrupulously clean. Wash and disinfect regularly, keeping a cloth and brush solely for this purpose.
2. Cover when flushing.
3. Keep home free from dust. Wash all surfaces regularly.
4. Cover the dustbin; clean and disinfect weekly.

DISPOSAL OF REFUSE

Most household refuse contains large numbers of bacteria. It must therefore be disposed of regularly and hygienically otherwise it will attract flies and other vermin.

Refuse may be organic, i.e. it will rot down and return to natural sources, e.g. food, plants, peelings; or it may be inorganic — more solid waste which will not break down in time, e.g. cans, polythene and other plastics, delph, glass, certain fibres and metal.

METHODS OF DISPOSING OF WASTE

Much of our household waste can be recycled, that is, used again in one of the following ways:

1. Compost heap: as well as garden refuse, fruit and vegetable peelings, tea leaves etc. can be rotted down to provide valuable compost — free!
2. Paper: many charities collect waste paper to raise funds for worthy causes. This is recycled to produce more paper.
3. Glass bottles: some charities collect bottles for recycling.
4. Dumps: in country areas refuse is often emptied into pits; when full, the pit is covered with soil, allowing much of the waste to rot down. Make sure these dumps are as far as possible from the house as they can attract flies and vermin.
5. Burning: this is a more hygienic way of disposing of refuse if you do not have a bin collection.
6. Most householders dispose of their waste in dustbins which are then collected by local authority trucks. The waste is used to reclaim land, e.g. swamps, which is otherwise of little use.
7. Waste disposal units: these are electric grinding machines which grind waste food into pulp which is then flushed down the drain.

KITCHEN BINS

These should be situated near the food preparation area. They are usually made of plastic, often with a removable inside which makes it easier to empty. Pedal or swing-top bins are available. Pedal bins are more hygienic as they need not be handled when using.

Dustbins should be made of hard-wearing zinc, galvanised iron or strong plastic. They should have a lid which fits tightly. to keep out animals and vermin. Empty, clean and disinfect weekly. Keep bins at a convenient distance from the house but not too near, as they attract flies.

Avoid using polythene bags alone to dispose of refuse as animals are likely to tear holes in them, causing litter and attracting flies.

For sewage disposal see page 67-8.

QUESTIONS/CHAPTER 23

1. List the conditions which favour the multiplication of bacteria in the home. How may these be eliminated? How is disease spread? List five rules of personal hygiene which help prevent the spread of disease.

2. What general rules should be observed if a kitchen is to be kept hygienic and free from bacteria. List the commonest causes of food poisoning in the average kitchen.

3. Name four methods of disposing of household waste. List the qualities you would look for when buying a large dustbin. How should this be kept clean and hygienic?

24.
Running a home

Many people consider cleaning to be the least enjoyable part of running a home, yet it is an essential job and must be done. Those who organise their housework properly get the work done more quickly and efficiently — and find they have more time to spend on the more enjoyable aspects of running a home. The disorganised or lazy person who lets the work pile up, or does it in a slapdash way, will find that the housework gets too much and will feel resentful and frustrated by their own inefficiency.

CLEANING EQUIPMENT

A basic set of cleaning equipment is necessary if one is to do the job well. Keep all the cleaning equipment, if possible, in one cupboard (under the stairs is often a good place). Brushes, dustpans etc. can be hung up and cleaning agents and small equipment should be stored neatly on shelves. It is a good idea to keep a set of basic cleaning requirements (e.g. dusters, cloth, polish, cream cleanser etc.) in a bucket or basket, which can be carried around with you while you work, to save repeated journeys to the cleaning cupboard.

BASIC EQUIPMENT

Brushes
Most consist of a handle, base (stock) and bristles which are glued or heat-set into holes in the base. Brush handles and bases are usually made from wood or

plastic. Bristles can consist of bristle (hog, pig, boar), hair (horse, badger, camel) or plastic — fine and soft or stiff and tough.

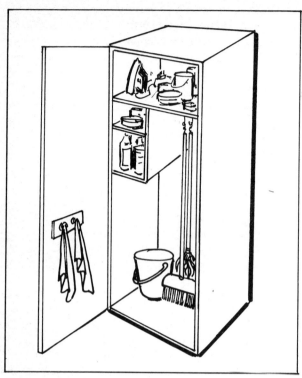

Broom cupboard

Household brushes include
  sweeping brush
  hand brush
  bristle brush (for carpets)
  long-handled high dusting brush
  lavatory brush
  scrubbing brush
  vegetable brush
  dish brush (or mop)
  shoe-polishing brushes

Care

1. Hang up if possible after use.
2. Comb hair, fluff etc. from bristles regularly.
3. Wash as necessary in warm, soapy water, rinse in warm then cold water and hang to dry.
4. Avoid allowing water into base of bristles; this will loosen them. Never leave brushes soaking in water (e.g. scrubbing brushes).
5. Brushes without handles should be laid on their side to dry, never on their backs or bristles.
6. Disinfect brushes periodically, lavatory brushes more frequently.

Floor mop

Floor mops may consist of the traditional type consisting of cotton 'threads' securely attached to a broom handle. These may be used dry, for dusting over floors, or wet, for washing floors, using a specially designed bucket for squeezing out the water.

They should be washed as necessary; a little paraffin in the water will help to dissolve polish.

The more modern floor mop is the squeegee type, consisting of a replaceable sponge head which is fitted into a hinged holder. These are very quick to use and a lever enables water to be squeezed out very efficiently.

- Never try to squeeze mop when dry.
- Wash after use in hot, soapy water.
- Rinse well and hang to dry.
- Disinfect periodically.
- Store with head upright or by hanging.

OTHER CLEANING EQUIPMENT

vacuum cleaner (page 97-8)
carpet sweeper (page 99)
floor polisher (page 99)
dustpan
dusters
washing cloths
chamois or synthetic cleaning cloths e.g. Vileda
buckets.

CLEANING AGENTS

Modern cleaning agents simplify housework. Cleaners are available to suit every type of household material. Many can be used for several jobs. Several cleaners are poisonous and should be used with care. Many have an irritant effect on the skin. Wear protective rubber gloves. Always store dangerous substances in a locked press, out of the reach of children. Many fatal accidents occur because of children ingesting poisonous household chemicals.

A wide range of cleaners is available in aerosol form.

1. Abrasive cleaners clean by grinding the stain or tarnish from surfaces. Many commercial abrasives are combined with a bleach and a detergent.
   Examples: sand, salt, steel wool, scouring powders, paste cleaners.
2. Absorbent cleaners are used on items which are unsuitable for washing or dry-cleaning, such as wallpaper, upholstery, hats, furs. They absorb grease. The absorbent is sprinkled over or pressed into the surface, left for some time, then removed by brushing or vacuuming.
   Examples: talc, bran, French chalk, Fuller's earth.

222

3. Acids remove tarnish from metal and dissolve stains on substances such as brick and marble. It is essential to rinse the surface thoroughly after using an acid.
Examples: lemon juice (for brass), vinegar (for window cleaning).

4. Alkalis are used to soften water and are excellent grease solvents. Never use them on aluminium; they react with it, causing blackening and pitting.
Examples: bicarbonate of soda, ammonia, washing soda, caustic soda in cooker and drain cleaners.

5. Bleaches are discussed fully in Chapter 5, under the heading, Drains. They are used to remove stains from fabrics, to whiten yellowed cotton and linen, and for their disinfectant power on lavatories and sinks. Do not use them on baths, as they react with the surface. Never use bleaches and lavatory powders together, as they produce a dangerous chlorine gas.
Examples: chlorine bleach (for laundry), hydrogen peroxide (for disinfection), sodium perborate (contained in many synthetic detergents).

6. Carpets: the shampooing of carpets is discussed in Chapter 11.

7. Disinfectants; see Chapter 5.

8. Lavatory cleaners, see page 156.

9. Dry cleaners contain a grease solvent mixed with an absorbent powder, and usually come in aerosol form. When sprayed on, the solvent evaporates, leaving the powder behind which is brushed off with the dirt. This is suitable for removing small spots from clothes or upholstery. Before use, test on a concealed area, as the solvent may also remove colour. Do not use on animal skins, rubber or plastic.
Example: Goddard's Dry Clean.

10. Floor polishes: see page 100.

11. Furniture polishes: see page 110.

12. General purpose cleaners are suitable for several types of surfaces; chiefly those that are enamelled, walls, paintwork and floors. They usually consist of a detergent combined with a bleach or ammonia. They should be rinsed after use, despite claims that this is unnecessary. Most are in liquid or paste form; others, in powder form, must be dissolved in warm water.
Examples: Ajax liquid, Jif, Flash, Vigor.

13. Grease solvents are volatile substances which dissolve grease and then evaporate quickly. Many are highly inflammable and toxic if inhaled or swallowed. Some may leave a stain which then must be washed off. Use in a well ventilated place and, after cleaning, air the garment out of doors. Example: Dab-it-off.

14. Metal cleaners and polishes vary considerably, although most consist basically of a fine abrasive, mixed with alkaline or other grease solvents. The appropriate cleaner should be used for each metal: brass cleaner for copper and brass, silver cleaner for silver, and so on. There are some all-purpose metal cleaners, but they may be too harsh for soft metals. After using metal cleaners, food containers and cutlery should be thoroughly washed, rinsed and dried before being used. Metal cleaners are available in liquid form or as wadding impregnated with the cleaner.
Examples: Brasso, Silvo, Duraglit.

Metal dips contain an acid and a detergent. They are handy for cleaning cutlery, especially forks, and for ornate silver which is difficult to clean. The silver is left soaking in the solution for a short time, washed, rinsed, and buffed to a shine. These dips are not suitable for silver plate.

15. Oven cleaners take several forms — stick, jelly or spray. As they are usually based on strong alkalis, such as caustic soda or sodium triphosphate, rubber gloves should be worn when applying.
Examples: Kleen off, Shift, Easy-off.

16. Scourers clean by friction. They are made from plastic or wire mesh, sometimes impregnated with soap. Others have a sponge base with a scouring top of synthetic fibre.
Examples: steel wool, Brillo, Golden Fleece.

17. Window cleaners consist of detergent dissolved in liquid, and often contain an acid or alkali (ammonia). Some more viscous cleaners contain a fine abrasive powder.
Examples: Ajax window cleaner. Windolene.

18. Drain cleaners: many consist of strong alkalis, e.g. sodium hydroxide, which melt away grease in the drain (page 68).

CLEANING ROUTINES

If a room is used daily, it needs to be cleaned and tidied daily. Rooms are usually cleaned in the following order: air, tidy, sweep, dust, vacuum, wash, polish. Some rooms require no sweeping, only the vacuuming of the carpet.

Other rooms such as bedrooms need little washing, except a weekly wipe over the paintwork.

Clean methodically and thoroughly

Collect all the cleaning agents and equipment you

will need together in the room before you start. Remember:

Bed making raises dust, so it should be done first, once the bed has been aired.

Cleaning a fire is a dirty job, which should be done before the general cleaning of the room.

Sweeping raises dust, so dust after sweeping.

Dusting: don't flick a duster about aimlessly. Using a slightly damp soft cloth, carefully wipe over all surfaces. This will pick up dust, not spread it around.

Vacuuming picks up all dust, so vacuum after dusting.

Kitchen and bathrooms need to be scrupulously clean.

Disinfect sinks, lavatories and drains weekly.

Most cleaning is done from the top of the room downwards. The ceiling should be cleaned first, then furniture; otherwise cobwebs will fall on the clean surfaces. Plan work so that each room is cleaned in turn, down through the house. Start upstairs each day: bedrooms and bathroom, then the stairs, hall, living rooms, bringing rubbish and washing from each room as it is cleaned, until the kitchen is reached. There the washing can be dealt with and the rubbish disposed of.

CLEANING A LIVING ROOM

Daily clean

1. Open windows.
2. Put away newspapers, toys, hobbies.
3. Empty ashtrays, collect rubbish, empty wastebasket.
4. Clean out and reset fire.
5. Vacuum carpet.
6. Dust furniture, water flowers and plants if necessary.
7. Wash over paintwork, sills and fire surround.
8. Polish woodwork if necessary.

Weekly/periodic clean

1. Same as above, giving a thorough clean. Dust ceiling, walls, high light fittings.

2. Tidy shelves and drawers.
3. Vacuum curtains and furniture.
4. Polish furniture, windows, mirrors, metals, lamps.
5. Thoroughly vacuum room, moving all furniture.

For cleaning a bedroom see p. 148-9.
For cleaning a bathroom see p. 156.

SEASONAL CLEANING OR SPRING CLEANING

1. Tidy all cupboards, drawers, wardrobes, discarding unwanted items and storing seasonal clothes and bedding not required.
2. Dry-clean or wash curtains, loose covers, bedding.
3. Clean ceilings, walls, furniture thoroughly.
4. Clean all small items thoroughly: ornaments, lamps, books, picture frames.
5. Clean floors, removing old polish, shampooing carpets. Do remember to spread out the weekly or seasonal cleaning so that you never have to spend too long on strenuous jobs. The old idea of an annual turnout and spring clean is no longer necessary with smaller rooms and houses, easily cleaned surfaces, and lots of mechanical aids.

QUESTIONS/CHAPTER 24

1. Make a list of basic cleaning materials necessary in order to keep a home clean. Find out the cost of each item.
   Explain the working principle of a vacuum cleaner.

2. Classify household cleaning agents. In the case of three groups, explain:
   (a) their purpose;
   (b) how to use them;
   (c) precautions.

3. Study the daily and weekly routine for cleaning a living-room. Adapt these routines to suit a dining-room. List also what you would use in order to spring-clean the room.

25.
Household work routines

Today, the person who runs a home (whether it is a husband of wife) has an easier task than in the past. Machines such as vacuum cleaners, dishwashers and washing machines and modern surfaces and cleaning agents make the work load easier, so that, if properly organised, housework should be completed quickly, leaving lots more time for hobbies, part-time work or relaxation.

It must not be forgotten that housework takes second place to the needs of the family, especially the children. It would be more beneficial to yourself and the children on a sunny summer's day to be on the beach having a picnic than indoors shampooing carpets or cleaning the silver!

A well thought-out weekly plan of work should ensure that the house is clean and well organised. Where there are no children, it is easy to keep to a work plan and easy to keep a home clean. It goes without saying that children, especially small children, make it impossible to adhere rigidly to a timetable. One must always be prepared to down tools to comfort a fretful child or help them with their problems.

Encourage children to help about the house: small children have a natural urge to learn and imitate household tasks. Many mothers dismiss offers of help from youngsters and later complain that their teenagers are slow to help. Boys and girls alike should be made to share many of the household chores. As members of the family, they have duties as well as rights. It is unfair to allow a mother to become a slave to her family. Unfortunately, in many cases it is the fault of the mother herself, who fails to train each child to do his share of the household chores and who, for the sake of peace, takes on an unequal part of the daily workload instead of spreading it around.

MAKING A WORK PLAN

Here are some sample work plans. As no two families lead exactly the same kind of life, adapt these work plans to suit your family circumstances. Make sure essential jobs get done first. Each week morning, a couple of hours are set aside for special jobs, and in the afternoons some time is allocated for hobbies and 'outside' jobs like shopping, gardening etc. Remember, both full-time housewife and dual-career wife should allocate certain jobs to each member of the family.

This is good training and will allow the housewife (or husband) more time to her/himself.

Weekly work plan (full-time housewife with four young children).

7.00	Get up, wash, dress. Get children up, dress if necessary
7.30	Prepare breakfast, set table, pack lunches
8.00	Breakfast
8.20	Husband and children leave for work and school
8.30	Make beds, tidy bedrooms and bathroom
9.00	Wash dishes, clean up kitchen, tidy sitting-room
9.30	Daily washing
10.00	Coffee
10.10	Weekly jobs:

Monday: change bed linen, weekly wash
Tuesday: clean bedrooms, bathroom
Wednesday: clean hall, stairs, landing; clean a window or two; do some polishing
Thursday: clean kitchen, cooker, defrost and clean fridge
Friday: clean sitting-room and dining-room
Saturday: baking and cook-ahead meals
Sunday: church, longer lunch preparation

12.00	Prepare lunch
12.45	Lunch. Children back to school or rest
1.45	Preparation for dinner, tidy kitchen and wash up
2.00	Relax, personal grooming
2.30	Recreation and/or other jobs, for example:

Monday: sewing/mending
Tuesday: food shopping
Wednesday: ironing, airing, tidy hot-press
Thursday: visit friend, library. Alternate baby-sitting with another mother, leaving one of you free for sport or relaxation
Friday: household and personal shopping
Saturday: food shopping, gardening
Sunday: relax with family, plan week's menu, budgeting

5.00	Prepare dinner
6.00	Dinner
6.45	Husband/older children wash up, tidy kitchen
6.45	Mother washes children and puts younger ones to bed
7.30	Relaxation, recreation, entertainment

Organisation for a wife who works outside the home

Many of these tips apply also to the full-time house-wife.

1. A working wife must accept that her home will never be as spick and span as that of a woman who is at home all day, but neither should it be allowed to get into a mess. Good organisation helps.

2. Learn to think ahead, plan work, and make lists of shopping, cleaning and chores. Avoid wasting time: in a working wife's day, it is scarce.

3. Buy as many labour-saving devices as necessary: a good automatic washing machine, a cooker with an auto-timer and an easily cleaned oven surface, a pressure cooker, and perhaps a dishwasher and tumble drier, if finance permits. Some people find a freezer useful: others consider it makes as much work as it saves. If there is time to bake, an electric mixer is useful. A liquidiser speeds up many cooking processes.

4. Use paper towels for spills; oven-to-table ware saves washing up; use non-stick saucepans and tins.

5. The house should be easily cleaned and drip-dry, so to speak. Walls should be covered in washable vinyl paper or paint. Avoid floors that need constant care: a carpet with an oll-over design is good. Have laminated surfaces in the kitchen. Use the latest polishes and cleaning agents to take the hard work out of cleaning. All clothes should be easy care or drip-dry, especially those of the children. Bed linen in drip-dry terylene will be more expensive initially, but will last longer and saves hours of ironing.

6. Train the family from the beginning to make their own beds (duvets make this very easy), keep their rooms tidy, and put their things away. Regular jobs should be shared out regardless of sex. To avoid monotony, the jobs can be changed now and then. Many jobs can be done before work, by getting up half an hour earlier. There is nothing worse than coming home to a sink full of breakfast dishes.

Weekly work plan (career wife with three older children)

7.15 Get up, dress, prepare breakfast
7.40 Breakfast
8.00 Father and children make beds and tidy bedrooms. Girl packs lunches. Boy washes and dries dishes. Girl 2 tidies kitchen. Mother cleans bathroom, tidies living-room
8.30 All leave for work or school. Mother shops at lunchtime. Children stay in school for study.
6.00 Parents return from work, children from school

6.15 Prepare dinner. Girls help and set table. Boy sets fire or helps with cooking
6.45 Dinner
7.30 All family tidy up, wash and dry dishes in turn
7.30 Mother and/or father:
Monday: advance cooking for 2–3 days' meals
Tuesday: family wash
Wednesday: ironing
Thursday: weekly clean of kitchen, cooker, fridge
Friday: weekly clean of bathroom and other bedrooms
7.50 Children: more study, help mother, hobbies, TV
Father: hobbies, household repairs, helps mother
9.00 Relax. Before bed, tidy living-room

Saturday
9.00 Sleep in. Breakfast
9.30 Weekly clean of living-room, hall, stairs, bedrooms in rotation
11.00 Coffee, make shopping list
11.15 Do weekly shopping. Family tidies rest of house
12.30 Prepare lunch with help from family
1.30 Lunch
Afternoon: any jobs which did not fit into time-table e.g. tidying cupboards, polishing, cleaning paintwork, baking. Keep some Saturdays free for hobbies, relaxing, or gardening. Father cleans windows, gardening, repairs
5.15 Prepare tea
6.00 Tea. Parents have a night out

Sunday
11.00 While preparing lunch, advance cooking for the early part of the week, as well as bulk cooking for the freezer, may be done.

Employment of a cleaning woman once or twice a week would do much to reduce the amount of housework done by the working wife.

For work plan for two flat mates, see page 53.

ENERGY AND FATIQUE

Many housewives suffer from fatigue due to sheer hard work. This can be advoided by spreading the work load more evenly, taking a breather now and then for a cup of coffee, allocating more work to the rest of the family, and getting the husband to do the physically strenuous jobs: cleaning windows, polishing floors, washing walls. Mental fatigue is another hazard encountered by the housewife. The sheer repetitiveness of some jobs can be boring and frustrating. Beds which are made every day get tossed each night, only to be made again the next day. Meals which are prepared with much thought and trouble disappear quickly into hungry tummies. Housework gets undone so quickly, especially where there are children, that there is rarely time to stand back and feel proud of a job before it needs to be done again.

Unfortunately, this is what housework is all about. It is better for a mother to accept this, and to organise her work better than to mope and moan. Do the jobs you dislike first, as quickly as possible. You can then look forward to more rewarding activities, such as dressmaking, gardening and other more lasting jobs. Do the hardest jobs in the morning, as energy output is higher then. Try timing unpleasant jobs, aiming to beat the previous time each day.

The way in which one works is important. Stand in a comfortable position and sit where possible, as when ironing. Simplify work by arranging equipment and furniture in a logical order where possible. This applies especially to the kitchen. Make sure that working heights are comfortable. Think ahead and save time and energy: when bringing the ironing to the hot-press, collect baby's fresh nappy; when setting a table in another room, use a trolley.

Note: Ergonomics is the study of work routines in relation to surroundings. Its aim is the saving of energy.

QUESTIONS/CHAPTER 25

1. Plan a daily work plan for a housewife who works from 8.30 a.m. to 1.30 p.m. each day.
2. Write an essay on the importance of cooperation in running a home.
3. 'A woman's work is never done.' Discuss. Mention some points which would help a working wife cope more ably with her work load.
4. 'You are only young once.' Discuss in relation to whether you consider it fair that children have to help in the home.

PART II

26.
The World of Fibres and Fabrics

Learn to distinguish fabric by understanding its (a) fibre content (b) production or manufacture (c) structure (d) properties (e) finishes (f) colour treatments. All these influence its quality and durability. Most rolls of fabrics now have a content label attached to them. Because of the advance in the mixing of fibres and the development of new ones it is now difficult to recognise fibre content immediately. A fabric's origin is its fibre. Few fibres have all the characteristics required to make a good quality fabric.

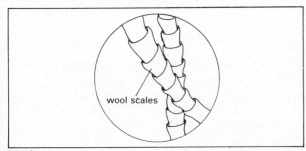

Wool

Wool – black-faced hill sheep (J. Allan Cash Ltd)

TYPES OF FIBRE

The many fibres available are divided into two groups each with further sub-divisions:

CLASSIFICATION OF FIBRES

Natural Fibres	Man-Made Fibres

a. *Animal*
  (i) Animal hair — Wool
  (ii) Silk — Mulberry Silk
 	
b. *Vegetable*
  (i) Seed — Cotton
  (ii) Bast — Flax (linen)
    Jute
  (iii) Leaf — Sisal
  (iv) Fruit — Coir
 	
c. *Inorganic Mineral*
  Asbestos
  Silver and gold
  Glass — Fibreglass
	a. *Regenerated*
	  Viscose rayon, Acetate,
	  Triacetate (Tricel),
	  Fibrolane (Protein fibre)
	
	b. *Synthetic*
	  (i) Polyamide — Nylon
	  (ii) Polyester — Terylene
	  (iii) Acrylics — Courtelle;
	    Modacrylic — Elura, Verel
	  (iv) Polyurethane — Elastomeric
	  (v) Polyvinyl Chloride — PVC
	  (vi) Polyolefin — Courlene

The manufacture of yarn from wool is divided into two areas:
a. woollen yarns,
b. worsted yarns.

MANUFACTURE OF WOOLLENS AND WORSTEDS

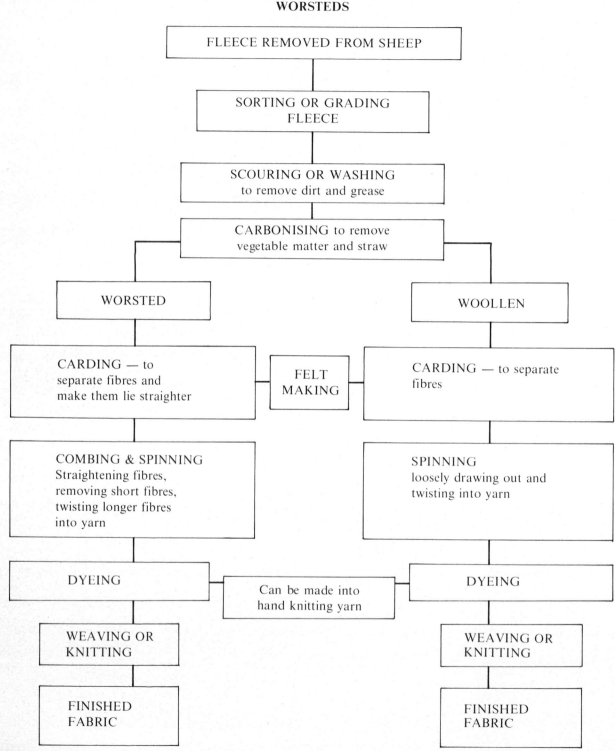

FLEECE REMOVED FROM SHEEP

SORTING OR GRADING FLEECE

SCOURING OR WASHING
to remove dirt and grease

CARBONISING to remove
vegetable matter and straw

WORSTED

WOOLLEN

CARDING — to
separate fibres and
make them lie straighter

FELT MAKING

CARDING — to separate
fibres

COMBING & SPINNING
Straightening fibres,
removing short fibres,
twisting longer fibres
into yarn

SPINNING
loosely drawing out and
twisting into yarn

DYEING

Can be made into
hand knitting yarn

DYEING

WEAVING OR KNITTING

WEAVING OR KNITTING

FINISHED FABRIC

FINISHED FABRIC

NATURAL FIBRES

WOOL

SOURCE	PRODUCERS	COMPOSITION
Mainly sheep, e.g. Merino, Suffolk, Lincoln, Cheviot, Corriedale (crossbred)	Australia Argentina New Zealand USSR	Keratin, a protein which contains carbon, hydrogen, oxygen, nitrogen and sulphur

PROPERTIES OF WOOL

Advantages	Disadvantages
1. Warm and comfortable to wear.	1. Tends to be expensive.
2. It has natural absorbency properties.	2. Weaker wet than dry.
3. Acts as an insulating barrier.	3. Damaged by (a) careless washing — shrinks and felts, (b) chlorine bleach — yellows and weakens, (c) prolonged sunlight, (d) moths.
4. Does not crease easily — it has a natural tendency to spring back.	4. Scorches and chars easily.
5. Wears and drapes well.	5. Its hairy surface may irritate very sensitive skin.
6. Resists static electricity.	
7. Resists flames — does not melt, it smoulders.	
8. Mixes successfully with other fibres.	
9. May be made moth, shrink and rain proof.	

The Wool Mark

Pure new wool products all carry the international Woolmark symbol of quality. The Woolblend mark indicates garments rich in wool which have been quality-tested. There are certain items excluded from this symbol group.

SILK

USES OF WOOL

All garments, furnishing fabrics, upholstery, carpets.

Wool fabrics

Flannel, tweed, gaberdine, crepe, velour, serge, boucle, jersey, cashmere, angora, alpaca, barathea, cheviot, Harris tweed, Donegal, Connemara and Blarney tweeds.

Silk spinning in India (J. Allan Cash Ltd)

SOURCE	PRODUCERS	COMPOSITION
The cocoon of the silkworm	China, Japan, India, Italy, South Korea	It is a continuous filament of the proteins Sericin and Fibroin.

PRODUCTION OF SILK

COCOONS

The Bombyx Mori moth lays eggs on leaves of the mulberry tree. The hatched worms feed on the leaves growing to 2-3½ inches long. After thirty days the worm develops two silk-producing glands. It begins to secrete silk fluid through these glands forming two silk filaments held together by a gummy substance, sericin. The worm spins a cocoon around itself in 24-72 hours.

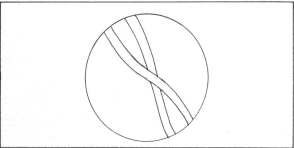

Silk

SORTING

The cocoons are sorted out. Sufficent moths are allowed to hatch out to produce the next batch of eggs. The remainder of the cocoons are placed in hot water to soften the sericin.

SOFTENING GUM

After boiling the cocoons to soften the gum, the loose filament ends are picked up and wound on to skeins. It is then baled and sent to the factory.

THROWING THE YARN

The raw silk is twisted and doubled and then wound on bobbins. By regulating the twist various yarns are produced.

DEGUMMING

A soap solution is used when removing the gum. It is then rinsed thoroughly.

DYEING, PRINTING, FINISHING.

The fabric is dyed, printed and wound into fabric bales.

USES OF SILK

Lingerie, blouses, jackets, skirts, dresses, upholstery fabrics.

Silk fabrics

Brocade, chiffon, crepe de chine, damask, satin, georgette, velvet, pongee, shantung, taffeta.

PROPERTIES OF SILK

Advantages	Disadvantages
1. Lightweight, thin, soft, warm and comfortable to wear. 2. Wears and drapes well. 3. Does not crease easily. 4. Resists flames. 5. Beautiful lusterous smooth surface. 6. Absorbent. 7. Dyes easily and does not shrink.	1. Tends to be expensive. 2. Silk is damaged by *a.* careless laundering — dry clean or wash gently, *b.* perspiration, *c.* some strong detergents, *d.* prolonged strong sunlight, *e.* chemicals, *f.* moths.

Cotton growing in California (Barnaby's Picture Library)

SOURCE	PRODUCERS	COMPOSITION
Fibres from the cotton boll (i.e. ripened seed pod)	America, Egypt, West Indies	Almost pure cellulose

PICKING
The cotton balls are harvested.

GINNING
(a) Leaves, sticks and other matter are removed by the ginning machine.
(b) The cotton lint is then separated from the seeds.

BALING
The cotton lint is compressed and packed into 500-pound bales.

CLASSING AND GRADING
Samples are taken from each bale to determine its quality.

PICKING
The bales are loosened and broken up. Further impurities are removed, e.g. remaining seeds. A roll or web of cotton fibre called a LAP is then produced.

CARDING
The lap is passed through a machine which removes shorter fibres. A roll (about $\frac{1}{2}''$ thick) of disentangled fibres remains. This is called a *sliver*.

COMBING
Short fibres are removed and the rest of the fibres are straightened to form yet another sliver.

DRAWING AND ROVING
More slivers are formed. They are of a finer quality.

PROPERTIES OF COTTON

Advantages	Disadvantages
1. Very easy to sew. 2. Wears well. 3. Fairly inexpensive. 4. Dyes and prints readily. 5. Mothproof. 6. Absorbent. 7. Smooth and soft to touch. 8. Cool to wear during summer weather. 9. Easy to launder. 10. Can be treated with special finishes.	1. Can be damaged by mildew. 2. Creases quickly unless treated. Requires frequent ironing. 3. Shrinks easily if laundered carelessly. 4. Burns quickly unless treated. 5. Very little elasticity. 6. Very cheap cottons when laundered lose their stiff quality and become limp. 7. Soils easily.

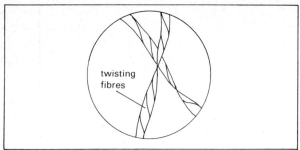
Cotton

SPINNING
Fibres are twisted and wound on to bobbins.

WEAVING OR KNITTING
After weaving or knitting the fabric is dyed and printed.

DYEING, PRINTING AND FINISHING
Fabric is completed.

USES OF COTTONS
Underwear, jackets, blouses, skirts, dresses, furnishing and household fabrics, industrial fabrics.

Cotton fabrics
Made into light, medium and heavyweight fabrics, broderie anglaise, canvas, calico, chintz, corduroy, cretonne, denim, drill, gauze, gingham, flannelette, lawn, muslin, organdie, poplin.

LINEN

SOURCE	PRODUCERS	COMPOSITION
Inner fibres of the flax plant	USSR, Europe USA, New Zealand	Cellulose

PRODUCTION OF LINEN

Bales of Flax (J. Allan Cash Ltd)

236

A. HARVESTING
The flax stalks are pulled. They are then dried and the seeds are removed.

B. RETTING OR ROTTING
The flax stalks are soaked so that the gums and woody core will ferment. At this stage the flax fibres will separate from the rest of the stalk. This is done by (a) chemical treatment in tanks, or (b) the traditional retting method in ponds, lakes and rivers.

C. SCUTCHING
The fibre is separated from the rest by rollers and steel pins on a hackling machine.

D. COMBING
The long fibres are separated.

E. CARDING, DRAWING AND SPINNING.

F. BLEACHING.

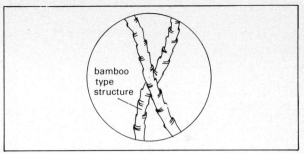

Linen

USES OF LINEN
Blouses, skirts, dresses, jackets, household and furnishing fabrics, bed linen, industrial fabrics.

Linen fabrics
Canvas, cambric, crash, damask, holland.

PROPERTIES OF LINEN

Advantages	Disadvantages
1. Durable — wears and launders well. 2. Absorbent. 3. Cool to wear in hot summer weather. 4. Good conductor of heat. 5. Absorbent and dries quickly. 6. Resists dust and grime fairly well. 7. Acids and alkalis have little effect on linen. 8. Mothproof.	1. Creases easily — requires frequent ironing. 2. Needs frequent attention to keep it looking fresh. 3. Quite expensive. 4. Easily damaged by mildew. 5. Shrinks. 6. Burns readily. 7. Linen tends to wear along creases and edges. 8. Does not dye easily.

MAN-MADE FIBRES

Man-made fibres consist of two main groups:
(a) Regenerated natural fibre-forming materials e.g. wood pulp, cotton linters. These form natural polymers:
(b) Synthetic chemical fibre-forming substances e.g. coal, oil. These form synthetic polymers.

REGENERATED FIBRES

TYPE	RAW MATERIAL
Viscose rayon	Wood pulp
Acetate	Cotton linters
Triacetate	Wood pulp
Fibrolane (a protein fibre)	Protein — Casein

Viscose rayon

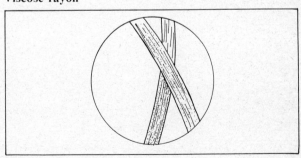

Viscose rayon

Examples: Durafil, Evlan, Vincel, Enka.

PRODUCTION

1. A series of chemical processes removes the cellulose from good quality trees.
2. The resulting thick syrupy solution is forced through

2. The resulting thick syrupy solution is forced through spinnerets (similar to spin dryers with holes only at their base).
3. As it passes from the spinnerets it begins to form filaments. They are passed through a bath of acid to solidify or harden.

4. The filaments are stretched and twisted to form yarn for knitting or weaving.

USES

Satin, brocade, taffeta, furnishing fabrics, lingerie, evening wear.

PROPERTIES OF VISCOSE RAYON

Advantages	Disadvantages
1. Drapes well. 2. Attractive and comfortable. 3. Mothproof. 4. Reasonable resistance to mildew. 5. Absorbent.	1. Fibres are weaker when wet; therefore requires careful laundering. 2. Creases easily. 3. Must not be wrung out. 4. Flames quickly if it catches fire.

Acetate

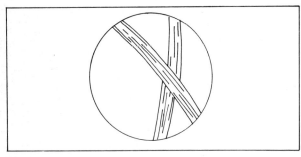

Acetate

Examples: dicel, Celanese.

PRODUCTION OF ACETATE

1. The cellulose from the cotton linters is treated with acetic acid, sulphuric acid and acetic anhydride. A complicated chemical process produces a syrupy cellulose base liquid.
2. This treated spinning solution is filtered and de-aerated.
3. It is filtered again and then forced through spinnerets.
4. From the spinnerets it passes through an enclosed warm air chamber where the filaments solidify or harden.
5. The filaments, still warm, are stretched and twisted to form filament yarn, tow or staple fibre.

PROPERTIES OF ACETATE

Advantages	Disadvantages
1. Drapes well. 2. Attractive appearance. 3. Absorbent. 4. Elastic properties. 5. Mothproof. 6. Reasonable resistance to mildew.	1. Weakened and damaged by a. sunlight, b. alkalis, c. acids, d. boiling water, 2. Weak when wet. 3. Burns readily.

USES

Rainwear, swimwear, umbrellas, underwear, furnishing fabrics.

Triacetate

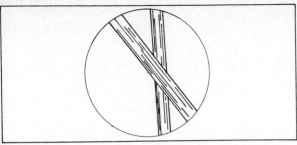

Triacetate

Examples: Tricel, Arnel.

Production is similar to Acetate:

1. Wood pulp is treated with acetic anhydride and acetic acid in the presence of sulphuric acid.
2. When the chemical process is completed the triacetate is washed and dried. This produces triacetate flakes.
3. These flakes are dissolved in chemicals to produce a spinning solution.
4. Production is completed as for Acetate.

USES

Woven and knitted fabrics, dress fabrics, ties, ribbons, evening wear.

PROPERTIES OF TRIACETATE

Advantages	Disadvantages
1. Can be permanently pleated. 2. Silky warm feel. 3. good crease resistance. 4. Does not shrink or stretch. 5. Launders well.	1. Burns rapidly. 2. Not as hard wearing as other fabrics. 3. Attracts dirt easily. 4. Develops static electricity. 5. Not safe for children's clothing.

Protein fibres

Example: Fibrolane (from Casein).

PRODUCTION OF PROTEIN FIBRES

1. Skimmed milk is treated with acid until it coagulates. A curd is formed.
2. The curd is washed, dried and ground finely.
3. This fine powder is dissolved in caustic soda, allowed to ripen, filtered and de-aerated.
4. The spinning solution is forced through spinnerets into an acid coagulating bath.
5. The filaments are drawn off, hardened, stretched, washed and dried.
6. They are then prepared as staple yarn.

USES

Blended with other fibres for suitings, furnishing fabrics.

PROPERTIES OF PROTEIN FIBRES

Advantages	Disadvantages
1. Blends well with other fibres. 2. Creases resistance is good. 3. Dyes readily. 4. Warm, resilient, and soft. 5. Absorbent.	1. Uses are restricted due to its sensitivity to water. 2. On its own it has a low strength quality.

SYNTHETIC FIBRES

Complex organic chemicals, e.g. polyamides, polyesters, form synthetic fibres.

SYNTHETIC	EXAMPLE	RAW MATERIAL
Polyamide	Nylon	Carbon, Petroleum, Oxygen and Nitrogen.
Polyester	Terylene	Petrochemicals.
Acrylics	Courtelle	Polyacrylonitrile
Modacrylic	Elura, Verel	Similar to Acrylic
Polyurethane	Elastomeric	Organic polymers formed by a chemical process
Polyvinyl Chloride	Plastic	Basic chemicals found in saltwater and petroleum
Polyolefin	Courlene	By-products of petroleum.

PRODUCTION OF SYNTHETIC FIBRES

The raw materials used and the spinning method vary in each group. The basic principles of production are the same for all synthetics.

GENERAL METHOD OF PRODUCTION

1. The basic raw materials are chemically and/or physically converted into fibre-forming units called molecules.
2. These units are formed into chains called "polymers" by the process "polymerisation", i.e. by heat to give (a) thick liquid or (b) molten liquid.

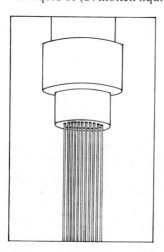

Spinneret

3. The spinning process may be done in one of three ways:
(a) forcing molten liquid through spinneret into the air where it solidifies (melt spinning);

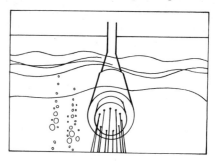

Melt spinning

(b) the thick liquid from the spinneret goes into chemical baths which cause filaments to solidify (wet spinning);

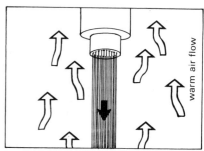

Wet spinning

(c) the fibre-forming thick liquid is dissolved in a solvent which evaporates in warm air as soon as the filaments leave the spinneret.

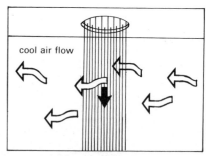

Dry spinning

4. The filaments are stretched and drawn. Heat is used to set filaments, thus preventing stretching when used.
5. Filaments may be cut into staple fibre or 'spun' as for natural yarn.

240

Polyamides

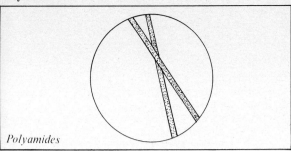

Polyamides

Examples: Bri-Nylon, Enkalon, Celon, Nylon.

USES

Drip-dry garments, underwear, hosiery, children's garments, water proof fabrics, sails, parachutes, ropes.

Polyester

Examples: Terylene, Trevira, Dacron.

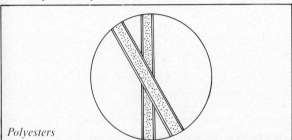

Polyesters

USES

Wadding for duvets, pillows and sleeping bags, blouses, skirts, dresses, most outer garments, underwear, household items e.g. curtains.

Acrylics

Examples: Courtelle, Acrilan, Orlon.

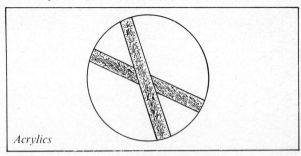

Acrylics

USES

Knitted and woven garments e.g. nightwear, fake furs, jersey fabrics for dresses.

Modacrylics

Examples: Verel, Taklan.

Modacrylics are modified forms of the acrylic fibre. They have a slightly different chemical composition.

USES

Curtains, fire-fighting clothing, nightwear.

PROPERTIES OF POLYAMIDES

Advantages	Disadvantages
1. Durable, strong and wears well. 2. Easy to launder. 3. Does not stretch or shrink. 4. Resists creases. 5. Good resilience and elasticity. 6. Not destroyed by most household chemicals.	1. Nylon pills. 2. Feels sticky in warm atmosphere. 3. Weakened by strong sunlight and air. 4. Develops static electricity. 5. Melts and can stick to skin. 6. Damaged by chlorine bleach and washing at high temperatures.

PROPERTIES OF POLYESTER

Advantages	Disadvantages
1. Warm, soft to handle. 2. Mothproof. 3. Resistant to mildew and sunlight. 4. Strong and durable. 5. Crease resistant. 6. Wears well. 7. Launders easily.	1. Non-absorbent. 2. Melts quickly. 3. Attracts dirt quickly. 4. Develops static electricity. 5. Wringing may damage fibres. 6. Damaged by boiling water.

PROPERTIES OF ACRYLICS

Advantages	Disadvantages
1. Light, warm and soft to touch.	1. Poor absorbency.
2. Strong and durable.	2. Attracts dirt.
3. Resistant to creases, moths and mildew.	3. Develops static electricity.
4. Wears well.	4. Burns and melts easily.
5. Easy to launder.	5. May stretch when wet.
6. Resistant to many chemicals.	6. Tends to pull out of shape.

PROPERTIES OF MODACRYLICS

Advantages	Disadvantages
Flame retardant because of its vinyl units.	1. Poor absorbency.
2. Soft, warm and light to handle.	2. Tends to pill.
3. Strong and hardwearing.	3. Attracts dust.
4. Drapes well.	4. Melts quickly so do not use too hot an iron.
5. Easy to launder.	
6. Resistant to moths, mildew and creases.	

Polyurethane
Examples: Elastomeric fibres — (Rubber, Spandix) Lycra, Spanzelle.

USES
Swimwear, girdles, support hosiery, belts.

PROPERTIES OF POLYURETHANE

Advantages	Disadvantages
1. Can be moulded easily.	1. Damaged by chlorine bleach.
2. Good elasticity and resilience.	2. Rubber may be harmed by light and perspiration.
3. Provides excellent support in garments.	3. Weakened by detergents, heat and alkalis.

Plastic
Examples: PVC

USES
Shower curtains, upholstery, rainwear.

PROPERTIES OF PLASTIC

Advantages	Disadvantages
1. Versatile in industry.	1. Poor absorbency — not suitable for clothing.
2. Blends with other fibres.	2. Low resistance to heat.
3. Stain resistant.	
4. Resistant to sunlight and insects.	

Polyolefine
Examples: Ulstron, Courlene.

USES
Ropes, nets, rainwear, shower and bathroom curtains.

PROPERTIES OF POLYOLEFINE

Advantages	Disadvantages
1. Reasonably durable. 2. Resists acids, alkalis, moths, mildew. 3. Light and flexible.	1. Non-absorbent — not suitable to be worn for hours at a time. 2. Melts quickly. 3. "Tires" with time.

FIBRES TO YARN

Silk and all man-made fibres are continuous filaments. They may be cut into shorter lengths to form staple fibres. Most natural fibres are in a staple form. Fibres or filaments are drawn out and twisted to form a yarn. Staple yarn is made up of short staple fibres. Filament yarn is made up of continuous mono-filaments.

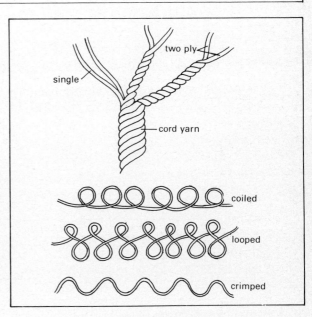

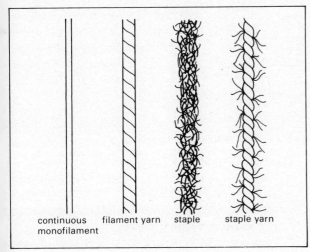

continuous filament yarn staple staple yarn
monofilament

Yarns

TYPES OF YARN

(a) Single or one-ply — single strands or filaments twisted together.

(b) Ply yarns — yarns are made up of two or more yarns twisted together.

(c) Cord yarns — ply yarns twisted together.

(d) Novelty yarns — composed of different fibre types, colours, thicknesses and twist e.g. bouclé, knot yarns.

(e) Textured yarns — crimped, coiled or looped to improve texture and appearance of yarns.

YARN TO FABRIC

Yarns may be woven, knitted, felted or knotted to produce a fabric.

Woven fabric is composed of two sets of yarn forming lengthwise (warp) and crosswise (weft) threads. The lengthwise threads are stronger than crosswire threads. Formed along the edges of the warp is the selvidge edge.

BASIC WEAVES
(a) *Plain weave:*

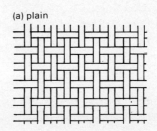

(a) plain

1st row

Weft over one warp, weft under one warp, weft over one warp, to end of row.

2nd row

Weft under one warp, weft over one warp, weft under one warp, to end of row.

(b) *Basket weave:*

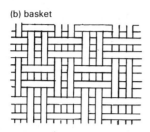

Pass weft yarn under two warp threads, then over two warp threads, to end of row. Reverse these for rows 3 and 4.

(c) *Twill weave:*

A diagonal ridge or pattern forms across the fabric. Pass weft yarn under two warp yarns and then over two warp yarns.

(d) *Satin weave:*

This has a very shiny surface.

Knitted fabrics are worked by hand or machine to form continuous interlocking loops. A variety of knits exist e.g. single knits, rib knits, jersey, tricots, raschel knits.

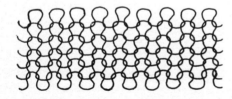

Knitted Structure

Felting is short lengths of wool fibres pressed and bonded together with heat and moisture. Not durable for garments. used mainly for hats, soft toys, decorations.

Knotting is crocheting, lace, netting. Worked by hand or machine.

Fusing: an outer fabric bonded or fused to a backing fabric. Fused fabrics may be woven or knitted.

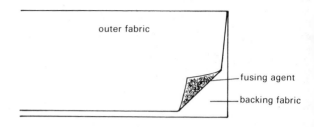

FABRIC MIXTURES AND BLENDS

Fibres are mixed or blended together to produce fabrics which are easy to wash and comfortable to wear e.g. polyester/cotton; cotton/wool. When natural and man-made fibres are combined, the fabric produced has the advantages of both fibres e.g. durable, strong when wet and dry, absorbent, crease-resistant, resilient. Launder mixed fibres following the method recommended for the most delicate of the fibres e.g. cotton/silk, launder as for silk.

TEXTURE AND PATTERN

Texture is introduced by

(a) *Napping:* revolving wire brushes lifting up short fibre ends to produce fleece.

(b) *Glazing:* a resin applied by smooth metal rollers at a fast speed e.g. glazed cotton.

(c) *Brushing:* lifting up the long fibre ends of spun yarn.

(d) *Plissé:* shrinking fabric in different areas to produce a puckered or wrinkled effect, e.g. seersucker.

(e) *Knitting:* stretchy fabric e.g. jersey.

(f) *Weaving:* plain, knitted or patterned (using a Jacquard loom). Plain or coloured fibres may be used to produce pattern.

(g) *Embossing:* raising a design on the surface of the fabric.

(h) *Embroidery:* traditional and modern stitches worked in cotton, linen, silk and wool on a ground fabric.

(i) *Flocking:* applying short fibres to the adhesive surface of a printed design.

Pattern is applied to the fabric surface by

(i) *Tie dying:* Folding, tying or wrapping fabric, immersing it in a dye bath and drying. It may then be dyed using another colour. The dye or dyes used may be absorbed unevenly by the fabric.

(ii) *Batik:* areas not to be dyed are waxed. The fabric is dyed and the wax removed. This process may be repeated to introduce a few colours.

(iii) *Screen Printing:* a stencil is made from a thin film which is attached to a screen or frame. The screen is placed over the fabric to be printed and the dye forced onto the fabric at the selected areas.

(iv) *Embroidery:* worked by machine onto a base fabric.

(v) *Machine Printing:*

(a) *Direct or Roller Printing:* the fabric is passed between an engraved roller with the dye and a drum.

(b) *Resist Printing:* A dye-resistant paste is used. The fabric is later dyed and then the paste is removed.

(c) *Discharge Printing:* The chosen design is bleached out of a dyed fabric by a paste which contains a bleaching agent.

FINISHES WHICH IMPROVE FABRIC PERFORMANCES

Fabrics are often improved by certain treatments. Many of their disadvantages may be counteracted.

1. *Easy care, Minimum care, Drip-dry and Crease resistant*

Fabrics carrying these labels may have been treated with a resin or heat-setting finish. They are easy to launder and require little or no ironing (The word *Calpreta* in the label indicates this type of finish).

2. *Colourfast*

Fabrics thus labelled will not fade when laundered following recommended instructions. Often used on cotton.

3. *Shrink resistant*

Fabrics have undergone a shrinking process so that they will not shrink when laundered. *(Sanforized, Rigmel* or *Tebilised* on the label).

4. *Flame-retardant*

Fabrics have undergone a treatment which will give them a permanent non-flammable finish. It is used on children's nightwear and clothes for the elderly. This finish is destroyed by bleaching or boiling. The fabric will not burn if flame-proofing has been used. A flame-resistant finish means that the fabric burns so slowly that the flame goes out. *(Timorax).*

5. *Mothproof finish*

Fabrics are treated with chemicals so that they repel moths. Fabrics affected include silk and wool. *(Mitin* and *Eulan).*

6. *Mercerised*

Caustic soda is applied to fabrics to give them a shiny surface. Fibre strength and absorbency are improved.

7. *Water repellent*

Fabrics have been coated with chemicals to reduce their absorption of water. Yet they remain porous.

8. *Waterproof*

The fabric is treated with rubber in one of three ways
(a) outside surface,
(b) inside only OR
(c) between two layers of fabric.
The fabric remains non-porous and water will not penetrate the fibres.

9. *Showerproof*

A silicone layer is applied to the fabric to give a shower-proofing effect.

10. *Anti-static*

A chemical finish applied to reduce static electricity and clinging of fabric.

11. *Mildew resistant*

Reduces growth of mildew on garment.

12. *Permanent press*

Fabrics will launder easily, resist creases and hold their shape.

13. *Permanent pleating*

Garment will hold its pleats easily.

14. *Stain and Spot resistant*

A special finish is applied which will help fabric repel oil and water-based stains.

27.
Simple Tests to Identify Fibres

DANGER!
1. Handle all chemicals with care.
2. Precautions should be taken when doing the burning test.
3. Write down all test results.

BURNING TEST
Take a small sample of fibre and burn it slowly. Does it burn continuously of melt? Note any change. remove from flame. Does it (a) continue to burn or (b) extinguish itself. Note changes in colour, odour and residue.

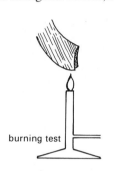

burning test

MICROSCOPIC TEST
Use a single fibre and examine its longitudinal and cross-sectional views. Use diagrams under each fibre section for reference.

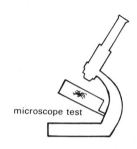

microscope test

SOLVENT TEST
Chemicals are used to distinguish animal, cellulosic and synthetic fibres from each other. Place small fibre samples in a test tube. Pour the recommended amount of solvent into the test tube carefully. Observe and record the changes which occur.

A. NATURAL FIBRES

	BURNING TEST	SOLVENT TEST	STAINING TEST	SULPHUR TEST	PROTEIN TEST	ACETONE TEST	CELLULOSE TEST
			Shirlastin A				
WOOL	Burns in flame; odour of burning feathers or hair; residue of soft inflated ash	wool dissolves	Bright golden yellow	Dark brown to black	Positive; protein present. Colour, orange	Negative	Negative
SILK	Burns slowly; odour as for wool; residue of crushable grey ash bead	Silk dissolves	Orange brown	No colour change	Orange	Negative	Silk dissolves
COTTON	Burns quickly with bright yellow flame; odour of burning paper; residue of grey ash	Cotton absorbs solvent and swells	Lavender	No colour change	Negative	Negative	Cotton disolves
LINEN	Burns in a yellow flame; odour as for cotton; residue of pale grey ash	Linen swells	Violet blue	No colour change	Negative	Negative	Negative

B. REGENERATED FIBRES

	BURNING TEST	SOLVENT TEST	STAINING TEST	SULPHUR TEST	PROTEIN TEST	ACETONE TEST	CELLULOSE TEST
			Shirlastin A				
VISCOSE RAYON	Burns with a yellow flame, odour of burning paper, residue white afterglow, grey/black ash	Swells	Pink	No colour change	Negative	Fibre weakened	Disintegrates slowly
ACETATE	Burns with a bright flame, odour of boiling vinegar, residue brittle black bead	Swells	Green-yellow	No colour change	Negative	Dissolves slowly	Dissolves
TRI-ACETATE	As for Acetate	Swells	*Shirlastin A* unstained *Shirlastin E* Yellow	No Colour change	Negative	Weakens disintegrates and gels	Fibre weakens

C. SYNTHETIC FIBRES

	BURNING TEST	SOLVENT TEST	STAINING TEST	SULPHUR TEST	PROTEIN TEST	ACETONE TEST	CELLULOSE TEST
			Shirlastin A				
POLYESTER (TERYLENE)	Melts with a black sooty smoked flame, odour sooty, residue — smooth hard brown bead	Negative	*Shirlastin A* Unstained *Shirlastin E* Cream	No colour change	Negative	Negative	Negative
POLYAMIDE (NYLON)	Melts, burns with an erratic flame, odour of celery, residue- hard grey bead	Negative	Yellow	No colour change	Negative	Polyamide dissolves	Polyamide dissolves
ACRYLIC	Burns quickly with a dark smoky flame, odour, unpleasant acrid smell, residue — uneven hard bead	Negative	Pinkish grey	No colour change	Negative	Negative	Negative

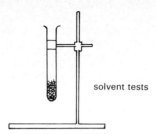
solvent tests

(c) Acetates from rayon, natural and synthetic fibres using the Acetone test.

(d) Wool from silk using the sulphur test.

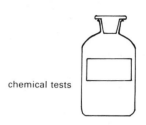
chemical tests

STAINING TEST

Shirlastin A is used to identify non-thermoplastic fibres, Shirlastin E to identify synthetic fibres. Follow instructions carefully.

CHEMICAL TESTS

These are used to distinguish:

(a) Animal fibres from all others using Alkali test and Protein test.

(b) Cotton, linen and rayon with their cellulose content from wool, using the cellulose test.

Use only small amounts of chemicals i.e. 3-4 ml. The following show the results of tests to identify.

A. natural fibres
B. regenerated fibres
C. synthetic fibres

28.
Before You Sew

WARDROBE PLANNING

To get the most out of your sewing it is essential to plan ahead so that your wardrobe contains garments which

(a) provide the kind of looks that create your individual style.

(b) are wearable and practical for your lifestyle.

(c) are so well balanced that they are part of a well planned colour-coordinated wardrobe.

(d) fit within your budget range.

(e) are fashionable but do not belong to the extremes of fashion.

Remember the best of fashion classics survive. Good fashion style is based on the careful selection and adaptation of the designs which suit you best. Your personality and confidence will help you select garments which will be comfortable to wear.

GUIDELINES

1. Study fashion magazines, pattern books and visit a few stores.
2. Take a look at the new proportions and lengths.
3. Notice the fabrics in use e.g. textures, prints, fibre content and colours.
4. Do any of these suit you or will you have to adapt them?
5. Decide on a small wardrobe of versatile garments which may be interchangeable to provide outfits for different occasions.
6. Before planning a new wardrobe look through what you have already. Make a list of basic colours and styles.
7. Visit fashion stores and try on the styles that appeal to you. Only then can you decide if these styles suit you.
8. Choose garment styles and fabrics which are seasonless and timeless for maximum value.
9. Choose clothes to suit each occasion e.g. school or work, seasonal wear e.g. summer, sports, parties etc.

A BASIC WARDROBE

Selecting a versatile wardrobe on a limited budget is a special task for each individual. Here is a simple breakdown of the essential elements of a basic wardrobe.

Underwear

Badly fitting underwear can destroy the outward appearance of any outer garment. Underwear often forms ridges which are very noticeable. It is worthwhile investigating the many styles available. Today's foundation garments come in fine lightweight and comfortable-to-wear fabrics. You should be correctly measured and fitted when buying bras.

Tights, Socks

Choose colours which compliment your complete garment colour range. Consider denier (sheerness) and texture. The finer the denier the more expensive the tights.

Separates

Select top quality separates as they prove to be the most vital part of any wardrobe. Because of the endless combinations, you will have something to wear for all occasions. Examples of good separates: trousers, skirts, shirts, jackets and sweaters.

Jacket or Blazer

Its colour, fabric and style should link up with other garments to give a complete look. A simple style with no specific fashion extremes is best. Jackets or blazers are ideal for in between seasons when the weather is good.

Coat

You can expect to pay more for a coat that is designed to last a few seasons. Quality is very important. It must be classic in design and colour if it is to work with all your clothes. An extreme design looks silly once that fashion season is over.

Shirts, Blouses, Sweaters

Simple shirts and blouses in well-tailored designs are suitable for day wear. Frilly designs are ideal for special occasions. A white tee shirt is invaluable for summer and winter.

Carefully chosen sweaters may be teamed with any skirt or trousers. Different thicknesses influence when they will be worn. As most good quality sweaters are expensive they may be worn over trousers or skirts for casual or more formal occasions.

Skirts, Trousers

Select skirts and trousers which are cut correctly. Badly tailored skirts and trousers never look well. Fit is also important. Skirts and trousers should match the coat or jacket which you have chosen.

Accessories

These are an important part of a wardrobe. They add the finishing touches to every outfit. Colour, design and quality are essential points to remember when buying accessories. You should be able to switch accessories when creating casual or formal moods. Leather accessories are a better investment than cheap imitations. With proper care they last longer and look smart at all times. Basic accessories include boots, shoes for everyday, sandals for evening wear, belts and one or two bags. Necklaces, earrings and bracelets dress up or dress down an outfit. These must be chosen with care.

COLOUR WISE

1. Select colour schemes which go with your skin tone, eyes and hair colour. Avoid colours which overpower your own colouring.
2. Experiment with fabrics in the store by holding them to your face. Check in a mirror to see if they emphasise your colouring or do they look insipid and cold.
3. Use colour to create illusions of figure size. e.g. to make your figure appear smaller use cool colours. To make it appear slightly larger use warm colours.
4. Brightly coloured accessories will liven up any outfit.

FASHION LINE

The visual element of style line is related closely to detail lines, body lines and silhouette lines. Our eyes will follow the natural line of the garment. Lines are used to flatter our figures and hide our faults e.g. too short, too small, too fat etc.

Vertical lines are used to make the figure taller and thinner.

Horizontal lines emphasising width and shortening the figure are stronger than any other line.

Diagonal lines lead the eye away from particular figure faults e.g. short waist. Diagonal lines should move from left to right.

Soft Curves visually flatter the figure by softening garment lines.

Fashion lines may be introduced as part of the garment, e.g. seams, frills, belts, or they may be part of the fabric, e.g. prints, stripes, plaids or fabrics with different textures.

CARING FOR YOUR CLOTHES

Always make sure that your clothes are clean. If they are cared for properly you will be well groomed. A high

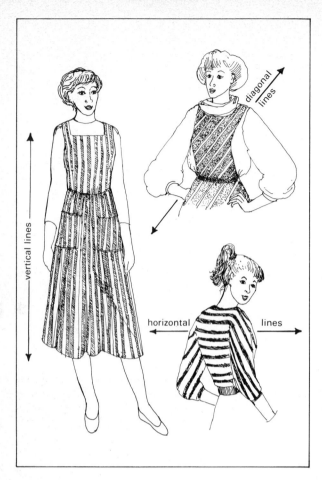

CARE LABELLING

Most garments carry care labels indicating how best they should be washed or dry cleaned. The instructions may be written or in the form of symbols or both. Always follow the manufacturers' instructions accurately. Garments carelessly cared for may shrink or even lose their shape. Labels may give six or seven points of information. The HLCC code has divided all washing processes into nine or ten groups. The tenth group deals with non-machine washable garments.

WASHING SYMBOLS

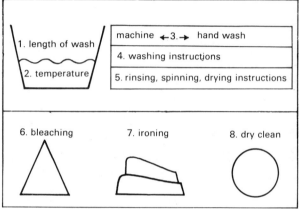

standard of personal hygiene is essential if garments are to be fresh.

GUIDELINES

1. Hang up or fold away freshly laundered garments or garments not in use.
2. Change and wash tights and underwear every day.
3. Repair garments as soon as possible e.g. sew in buttons, resew hems, repair holes and tears.
4. Remove stains and spots immediately.
5. Launder summer or winter clothes before storing them away until the next year.
6. Store clothes in well ventilated drawers and wardrobes.
7. Close zips, hooks and eyes when hanging up clothes.
8. Get coats and jackets dry cleaned regularly.
9. Launder or dry clean each garment according to its care label and teltag instructions regularly.
10. Use a moth repellent which has no obvious odour.

WASHING & DRYING INSTRUCTIONS

WASHING TEMPERATURES	LENGTH OF WASH	DRYING INSTRUCTIONS	
30°C Cool	Maximum	dry flat	—
40°C Warm			
50°C Hand hot	Medium	line dry	|||
60°C Medium hot			
95°C Very hot to boiling	Minimum	drip dry	
100°C Boiling (Linen & cotton).		tumble dry	◯

BLEACH, DRY CLEANING AND IRONING INSTRUCTIONS

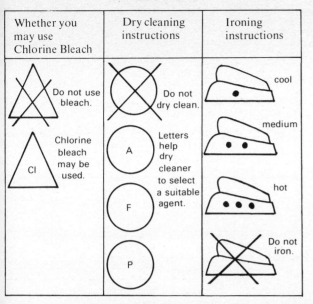

Whether you may use Chlorine Bleach	Dry cleaning instructions	Ironing instructions
Do not use bleach.	Do not dry clean.	cool
Chlorine bleach may be used. (Cl)	Letters help dry cleaner to select a suitable agent. (A) (F) (P)	medium / hot / Do not iron.

The garment care label instructions will correspond to the HLCC code printed on all detergent packets and washing machine programmes. It is up to you to check labels etc. correctly.

STAIN REMOVAL

IMPORTANT POINTS TO REMEMBER

A. Label all stain removing agents "POISONOUS".

B. Store with care.

C. Work in a well ventilated room.

D. Do not use near a naked flame.

E. Test on an inside seam allowance.

F. Use dilute solutions at first. Increase their strength where necessary.

G. Remove stain immediately and always before washing.

CHART FROM DETERGENT PACKET

FABRIC CARE GUIDE...For superb results...on all temperatures...and on all fabrics.

CODE	1 95	2 60	3 60	4 50	5 40	6 40	7 40	8 30	9 95	HAND WASH ONLY	DO NOT WASH
MACHINE*	Very hot to boil Maximum wash	Hot Maximum wash	Hot Medium wash	Hand-hot Medium wash	Warm Maximum wash	Warm Minimum wash	Warm Minimum wash	Cool Minimum wash	Very hot to boil Medium wash		*The terms 'Minimum, Medium and Maximum Wash' refer to the washing time and agitation required. Follow the manufacturer's instructions.
HAND WASH	Hand hot (50°C) or boil	Hand hot (50°C)	Hand hot (50°C)	Hand hot	Warm	Warm	Warm Do not rub	Cool	Hand hot (50°C) or boil		
SPIN	Spin or wring	Spin or wring	Cold rinse Short spin or drip-dry	Cold rinse Short spin or drip-dry	Spin or wring	Cold rinse Short spin Do not wring	Spin Do not hand wring	Cold rinse Short spin Do not wring	Cold rinse Drip-dry		
FABRICS	White cotton and linen fabrics without special finishes.	Cotton, linen or viscose fabrics without special finishes and colour-fast at 60°C.	White nylon; white polyester/ cotton fabrics.	Coloured nylon, polyester: cotton and viscose fabrics with special finishes; acrylic cotton fabrics; coloured polyester/cotton fabrics.	Cotton, linen or viscose fabrics with colour fast at 40°C, but not at 60°C.	Acrylics: acetate and triacetate, including mixtures with wool: polyester/ wool blends.	Wool, including blankets and wool mixtures with cotton or viscose; silk. †Machine washable wool, eg Superwash.	Silk and printed acetate fabrics with colours not fast at 40°C.	Cotton articles with special finishes capable of being boiled but requiring drip-drying.		

STAIN REMOVING AGENTS

	Agents	Suitable uses	Example of stain
1.	Enzyme detergents	Protein stains	Blood, egg, gravy. Use warm water
2.	Synthetic detergents	Grease and general stains	Beer, fruit juice, beverages e.g. tea, coffee
3.	Solvents e.g. turpentine, carbon tetra- chloride, Benzine	Non-washable fabrics	Normal stains

STAIN REMOVING AGENTS

	Agents	Suitable uses	Example of stain
4.	Alkalis e.g. washing soda	Grease stains	Oils, butter
5.	Acids e.g. a. Salts of lemon or lemon juice b. Vinegar solution	specific stains only	a. Iron mould b. Perspiration
6.	Other agents e.g. Acetone	Specific stains only	Nail varnish
7.	Bleaches e.g. hydrogen peroxide carefully.	Always follow instructions carefully Use diluted form only	Stains on cotton, linen.

STAIN REMOVAL CHART

Stain	Treatment	Dangers
1. unidentified stains	Sponge with cold water. Steep in an enzyme detergent. Bleach linens and cottons. If unsuccessful get it dry cleaned	Stain may be fixed permanently
2. chewing gum	Allow to harden. Scrape or ease off gently. Treat grease stain with grease solvent, benzine or carbon tetrachloride	If chewing gum is removed roughly the fabric may be damaged
3. perspiration	Soak in cold water. Wash in an enzyme detergent solution. Rinse thoroughly	If washed in too hot water stain may be fixed
4. nail varnish	Dab with nail varnish remover or acetone. Wash and rinse thoroughly to remove chemical	Acetone is inflammable Do not use it on acetate or tricel fabrics
5. grease make-up eye make-up lipstick Butter	Steep in hot soapy solution of synthetic detergent. Wash and rinse thoroughly OR treat with a grease solvent especially fabrics which are not washable	Air out of doors after cleaning. Use solvent in a well ventilated room

STAIN REMOVAL CHART

Stain	Treatment	Dangers
6. Ink (a) Ballpoint pen (b) felt tipped pen	Treat with methylated spirits. Rinse well and wash as for fabric. Soak in warm enzyme detergent solution. Wash and rinse well	Hot water will fix stain. Use warm only Hot water will fit stain
7. blood and protein stain	Soak in cold water and then in a warm enzyme detergent solution. Rinse thoroughly. Wash and rinse again	See 6 above. Enzyme detergents do not work in very cold or very hot water
8. tea, coffee etc.	Soak in a hot synthetic detergent solution. Wash and rinse thoroughly. Soak in a warm enzyme detergent. See 7	See 6 & 7
9. shoe polish	Treat with carbon tetrachloride. Wash following garment instructions	Work in a well ventilated room. Air out of doors
10. grass	Sponge with methylated spirits. Rinse well. Wash following garment instructions or soak in an enzyme detergent solution	See 9. Methylated spirits is inflammable
11. tar	Gently scrape off with back of a knife. Treat with a grease solvent or wash in hot detergent solution. Rinse thoroughly	Do not damage fabric when scraping off tar
12. beer	Wash in warm soapy water. Treat with a solution of vinegar or surgical spirit if necessary. Rinse well	Treat cotton and linen separately from wool and silk. Use dilute solutions of vinegar
13. paint	Treat emulsions with methylated spirits or wash immediately with cold water Use turpentine or white spirit for oil-based paint. Rinse thoroughly and wash following garment instructions	Work near an open window. Air well Remove paint immediately

Stain	Treatment	Dangers
14. iron mould	Soak the stain in a solution of lemon juice. Repeat if necessary. Rinse thoroughly. OR Treat with a commercial iron mould remover	Commercial iron mould remover is poisonous
15. mildew	Treat coloured fabrics with hydrogen peroxide. Rinse well. Wash according to fabric. Treat white fabrics with a dilute solution of hypochlorite bleach e.g. Parazone	Do not use hypochlorite bleach on silks and wool. It yellows and weakens their fibres

Final Note

Look after footwear, bags and other accessories carefully. Clean according to composition, whether this is leather, suede, patent leather or any of the other materials used in making these items.

29.
Basic Sewing Equipment

Good basic sewing equipment is an essential part of home sewing. Organise all your sewing equipment in one press. Keep threads, needles, measuring, marking and cutting equipment together in a sewing box or a biscuit tin.

MEASURING EQUIPMENT

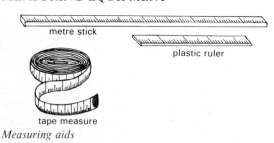

Measuring aids

1. Tape Measure
Choose one 152cm long, made of non-stretch fibre glass with metal tips at each end. It should be clearly marked in centimetres and inches.

2. See-through Plastic Ruler
30.5 cm — 46 cm long, clearly marked and with a metal edge if possible.

3. Metre Stick
Made of metal or wood. It is suitable for marking hem lengths.

4. Sewing Gauge
15 cm long with a sliding arrow indicator.

5. Hem Gauge
Used to mark hem depths.

MARKING EQUIPMENT

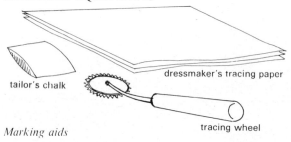

Marking aids

1. Tailor's Chalk
Available in a variety of colours. Use chalk for synthetic fabrics. Wax is usually extremely difficult to

remove from synthetic fabrics. Tailor's chalk also comes in a pencil form.

2. Dressmaker's Tracing Paper
This is a type of carbon paper and it is available in different colours. Use the colour nearest to that of the garment fabric. To transfer pattern markings use a tracing wheel with the dressmaker's tracing paper.

3. Tracing Wheels
The wheel edge is serrated and marks through the dressmaker's tracing paper on to the garment fabric.

CUTTING EQUIPMENT
The scissors selected for cutting fabric should never be used on paper. Keep a separate scissors for cutting paper.

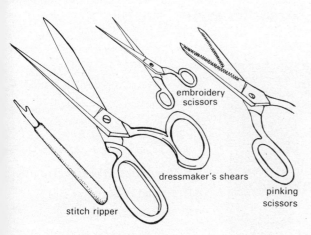

Cutting aids

1. Dressmaker's Shears
Should be sharp right to the point, well balanced and have bent-handles for good control.

2. Embroidery Scissors
Small scissors (7-10 cm) with sharp points for cutting buttonholes, corners and other details.

3. Pinking Shears
Suitable for neatening raw edges, have serrated zig-zag blades.

4. Stitch Ripper
This is used for unpicking a row of stitching along a seam.

STITCHING EQUIPMENT

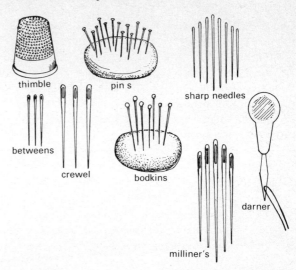

1. Thimble
It is placed on the middle finger and used to push the needle through fabrics, especially thick or heavy fabrics e.g. tweeds, corduroy or even wools.

2. Pins
Choose fine rustproof stainless steel pins. Pins are available in a variety of sizes and thicknesses.

3. Needles
Sharps — all purpose needles suitable for most fabrics as they are available in many sizes.

Betweens — short, round-eye needles. Suitable for fine hand sewing on all fabrics.

Crewel — also known as embroidery needles. They

NEEDLES	SUITABLE FOR
9-12 Sharps, betweens	Very light fabrics e.g. tulle, organdie, chiffon
8-10 Sharps, betweens, embroidery, milliners	Light and medium light fabrics e.g. cotton lawn, silk, single knits, gingham, taffeta
5-8 Sharps, betweens, embroidery, milliners	Medium and medium heavy fabrics e.g. corduroy, poplin, tweed, denim, wool
1-5 Sharps, betweens, embroidery, milliners	Heavy and very heavy fabrics e.g. suiting, wool, tweeds
Darners	Embroidery woollen thread. Repairing knitted and heavy woven fabrics

have a long large eye for holding several strands of embroidery thread.

Bodkins — are used for threading elastic, cord or ribbon through a casing.

Milliners — suitable for tacking and millinery as they have a long fine shape.

Darners — large long needles with a very large eye which will hold woollen thread.

Needles range from 1-12 in size. The lower the number the thicker the needle.

4. Threads

Select a thread which suits the garment fabric in colour, weight and fibre content.

(a) Cotton thread: suitable for natural fabrics e.g. cotton organdie. Size 60 for fine light fabrics; Size 50 for medium weight fabrics; Sizes 30 and 40 for heavy and very heavy fabrics.

(b) Polyester thread: suitable for man-made and jersey fabrics, e.g. trevira, terylene, rayon.

(c) Silk thread: suitable for silk and very fine natural fabrics. It is available only in one size i.e. size A.

Note: special threads are available for tacking, sewing buttonholes and buttons, fasteners, top-stitching and embroidery.

Use up odd spools for temporary sewing e.g. tacking.

5. Pincushions

Two types are suggested (a) wrist type, (b) large type to hold all pins and needles.

THE SEWING MACHINE

Learning to use and control a sewing machine takes lots of practice. Learn to control the sewing machine before attempting to sew a garment together. Practise sewing straight lines, curves, corners, stopping and reversing very slowly.

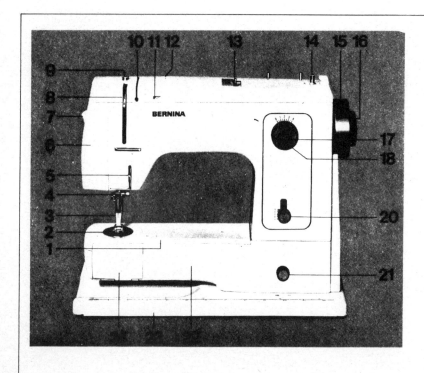

9 Winder pre-tensioning
10 Thread tension and guide
11 Tension indicator window
12 Thread tension regulator disk
13 Selector lever for plain and utility stitching
14 Winder spindle
15 Handwheel
16 Handwheel release
17 Left—Center—Right adjusting knob (needle position)
18 Zig-zag setting knob (stitch width)
20 Stitch length adjustment
21 Drop feed control
22 Free-arm
23 Baseplate
24 Hinged cover (shuttle)

1 Free-arm cover
2 Needle plate
3 Presser foot
4 Needle holder
5 Thread regulator
6 Face plate
7 Light switch
8 Take-up lever

Bernina sewing machine

TYPES OF MACHINES

(a) foot pedal machine
(b) hand worked machine
(c) electric straight stitch machine
(d) electric zig-zag machine with its embroidery, buttonhole, overlocking, stretch and blind hem stitchings.

MACHINE NEEDLES

Machine needles varying in size e.g. 80 (11), 90 (14), 100 (16), should be sharp for even stitching. Blunt needles damage the fabric. Change needles frequently.

THREADING

Thread the machine following the instructions given in the manual. Raise the presser foot, place spool and bobbin in position. Bring thread from spool across machine, pass through all thread guides, around tension discs and tension spring. Pass thread through further thread guide and finally into needle. Check that thread on bobbin is even and place bobbin in position, passing thread through bobbin tension. Turn the machine wheel towards you and holding needle thread

NEEDLE	USES
Sharp point	Woven fabrics e.g. wool
Ball point	Jersey knits
Wedge point	Leathers and synthetic leathers (vinyls)
Double and triple points	Machine embroidery and decorative edges

Inserting bobbin case

in left hand raise bobbin thread. Pull both threads between presser foot to back of machine.

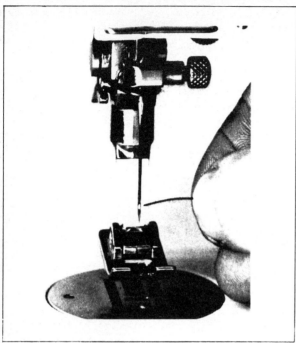
Threading machine needle

STITCH LENGTH

Select a suitable stitch length by adjusting a knob or a lever (following the instructions of the manual).

TENSION

When machining, the upper spool thread and the lower bobbin thread interlock to form stitches. Both threads must be even.

Some machines have a self-adjusting tension which means that the tension never has to be adjusted when changing from fine to heavy fabrics.

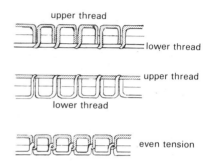

Tension Faults
(a) *Tension too loose* — i.e. top thread too loose.
(b) *Tension too light* — i.e. top thread too tight.

Correct Tension
Normal interlocking stitching looks like diagram.

RULES FOR GOOD MACHINING

1. Using instruction book, set machine at correct stitch, insert bobbin and thread needle with upper thread.

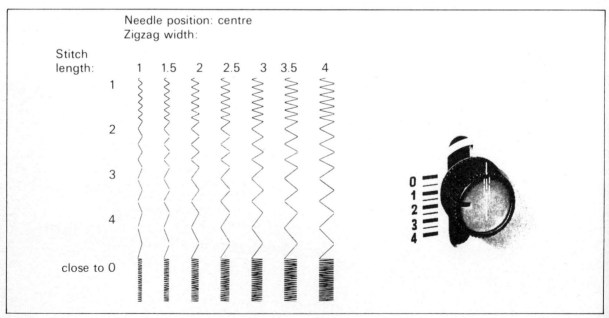
Results of varying stitch length and width

MACHINE FAULTS	POSSIBLE CAUSES
a. Needle thread breaking	1. Threaded incorrectly. 2. Needle inserted incorrectly. 3. Blunt or bent needle. 4. Upper thread tension too tight. 5. Poor quality thread.
b. Needle breaking	1. Needle unsuitable for thread and fabric. 2. Upper thread tension too tight. 3. Needle inserted incorrectly. 4. Pulling or pushing fabric through machine. 5. Needle too low when removing stitched fabric. 6. Presser foot incorrectly positioned.
c. Lower bobbin thread breaking	1. Poor quality thread. 2. Bobbin thread tension too tight. 3. Dirt in bobbin case. 4. Bobbin too full or unevenly threaded. 5. Bobbin placed in bobbin case incorrectly. 6. Bobbin is jammed in bobbin case.
d. Puckered seams	1. Blunt or damaged needle. 2. Upper or lower thread tension too tight. 3. Different upper and lower threads. 4. Other thread ends caught up in bobbin case. 5. Stitch too long for fine lightweight fabrics.
e. Jammed machine	1. Thread caught around spool pin and/or bobbin case. 2. Handwheel still in a released position after bobbin has been threaded. 3. Presser foot not functioning correctly.
f. Noisy machine	1. Thread and fluff caught up inside bobbin case and under needle plate. 2. Machine needs oiling and cleaning. 3. Damaged bobbin case and holder.

STITCH FAULTS	POSSIBLE CAUSES
Looped stitches	1. Incorrect size of needle. 2. Damaged or incorrectly inserted needle. 3. Machine not threaded properly. 4. Upper thread tension too loose.
Skipped stitches	1. Different quality upper and lower threads. 2. Needle inserted incorrectly. 3. Machine incorrectly threaded. 4. Damaged or blunt needle. 5. Incorrect size of needle. 6. Pulling fabric from machine.
Uneven stitches	1. Pushing or pulling fabric during machining. 2. Stitch adjuster not set correctly. 3. Needle inserted incorrectly. 4. Needle and/or thread unsuited to fabric. 5. Presser foot not lowered fully. 6. Worn, faulty or dirty feed-dog.

2. Insert new needle if necessary.
3. Test stitch and adjust as required.
4. Tack garment pieces together and remove pins before machining.
5. Place fabric under presser foot from front. Turn machine wheel towards you to insert needle in fabric.
6. Lower presser foot and begin stitching. Guide fabric carefully. Do not push or pull it.
7. When row of machining is completed, raise needle and presser foot to their highest point.
8. Pull threads and fabric toward the back of the machine for 10 cm. Cut threads.
9. Check row of machining.

Note:
Use the same colour and type of thread for both bobbin and upper thread. Use a slight zig-zag stitch for jersey fabrics.

IF FAULTS DO OCCUR CHECK WHETHER

1. the correct needle and thread are being used;
2. the needle is inserted correctly;
3. the feed-dog is clean;
4. the machine is threaded properly;
5. the bobbin is threaded properly;
6. there are threads caught in bobbin case;
7. the handwheel has been turned to the correct position;
8. the tension is set correctly.

MACHINE ATTACHMENTS

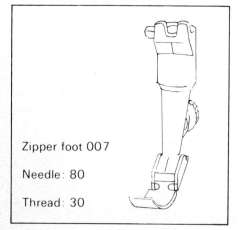

Zipper foot 007

Needle: 80

Thread: 30

Stitch width: 0
Stitch length: 1.5—2
Automatic: (0)   straight stitch -----
Needle position: according to side set left or right
Drop feed control: sewing

(a) Zipper foot —
allows stitching to be placed very close to zip raised edge. Adjustable for use on right or left of needle.

(b) Hemming foot —
turns in a narrow hem and machines it as it folds in the fabric.

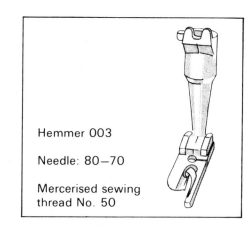

Hemmer 003

Needle: 80—70

Mercerised sewing thread No. 50

(c) Seam or hem guide —
attached to machine. Allows for accurate stitching of all edges, curved or straight.

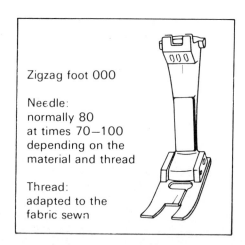

Zigzag foot 000

Needle:
normally 80
at times 70—100
depending on the
material and thread

Thread:
adapted to the
fabric sewn

(d) Zig-zag foot —
allows needle to swing back and forth through the fabric. This foot is often used for machine embroidery stitches, turning hems on jersey fabric, inserting elastic and shell edgings.

Other Attachments
Blindstitch foot, Embroidery foot, Buttonhole foot,

Small darning foot and wool darning foot, Button presser foot, Tailor tacking foot, Shell hemmer, Pintuck foot.

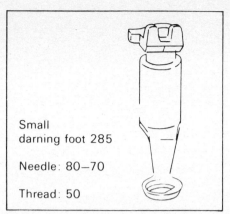

Small
darning foot 285

Needle: 80—70

Thread: 50

Darning foot

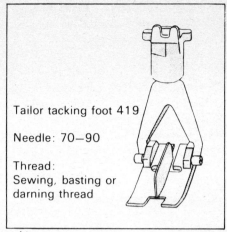

Tailor tacking foot 419

Needle: 70—90

Thread:
Sewing, basting or darning thread

Tailor tacking

Note: not every sewing machine will have all the above attachments.

30.
Choosing and Using Paper Patterns

To select the correct pattern size, follow four basic rules:
1. Measure accurately.
2. Know your correct figure type.
3. Compare your measurements with those of the pattern.
4. Never buy a pattern a size larger as each pattern is designed with additional fullness for comfort and movement.

TAKING BODY MEASUREMENTS

Accurate measurements are vital when determining correct pattern size.
1. Get a friend to take your measurements.
2. Always wear well-fitting underclothes and your everyday shoes. Do not take measurements over blouses, dresses, skirts or trousers.
3. Stand up straight with both feet firmly on the ground. Hold your shoulders back properly.
4. Hold tape measure straight. Measure snugly against the body, never loosely or tightly.
5. Double check measurements. If you check bust, waist and hip measurements occasionally, changes can be recorded. You may have to change to a different figure type or pattern size.

FEMALES

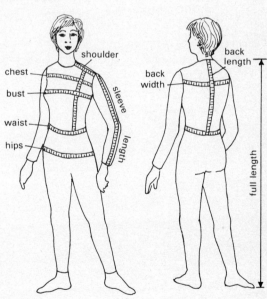

Bust
Standing behind your friend, place measuring tape over fullest part of bust and bring straight under arms across the back, raising tape slightly higher at centre back.

Waist

Measure comfortably around the thinnest part of natural waistline.

Hips

Measure around fullest part of hips i.e. 18 cm - 23 cm below waistline.

Back waist length

From neckbone in a straight line to waist.

Height

Take off your shoes. Measure from "top to toe".

Full length

From neckbone to desired length e.g. hem of blouse, dress, jacket.

Chest width

Above bust from armhole to armhole, 10 cm below neck base.

Back waist

Across from armhole to armhole 10 cm below neckbone.

Shoulder length

From neck to shoulder edge.

Sleeve length

Measure from shoulder to elbow (elbow slightly bent) and from elbow to wrist.

MALES

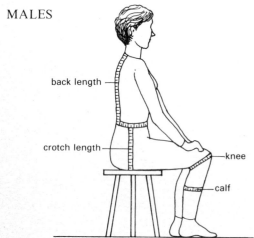

Trouser measurements

Chest

Place measuring tape around fullest part of chest.

Waist

Measure around thinnest part of waistline.

Hips

Measure around fullest part of hips 17 cm - 20 cm below waist.

Neck

Measure around neck and add 12 mm to neck measurements.

Back waist length

From base of neck to waistline at back.

Shoulder length

Base of neck to edge of shoulder.

Inside leg

From crotch to required hem length.

Outside leg

From waist along outside leg side seam to required hem length.

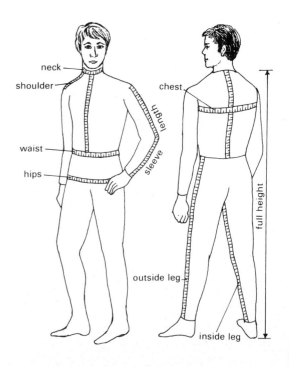

YOUR FIGURE TYPE

Everyone around us varies in shape and size. Because of the varying heights and body proportions, patterns have been divided into figure type groups.

PERSONAL MEASUREMENT CHART

	Pattern measurements	Your own measurements	Adjustments
Bust/chest			
Waist			
Hip			
Back length			
Back width			
Chest width			
Full length			
Shoulder			
Sleeve length			
Outside leg			
Inside leg			
Crotch depth			
Knee			
Neck (for shirt)			

Note: Pattern sizes are determined by body measurements e.g. bust, waist and hip measurements.

Study your figure and compare your measurements with each figure type. The following will help you find out to which figure type group you belong. Consider
(a) length of your body — (long or short);
(b) difference between bust, waist and hip measurements;
(c) location of hips and bust in relation to your waist. These are all related to your body proportions.

FEMALE FIGURE TYPES

A. *Young Junior Teen*
  Developing pre-teen and teen figures. Trendy teenage fashions. Height: 1.55-1.60 m.

B. *Junior*
  Young developing figure with shorter waist. Pre-teenager and teenager fashions. Height: 1.63-1.65 m. Slightly taller than Young Junior Teen.

C. *Miss Petite*
  For the shorter Miss figure. It is between Junior Petite and Miss figure types. Height: 1.57-1.63 m.

D. *Junior Petite*
  A well-proportioned developing figure with small waist. Height: 1.52-1.55 m.

E. *Miss*
  Well proportioned developed figure with longer waist to hip measurement. Height: 1.65-1.68 m.

F. *Half sizes*

Shorter fully developed figure with larger waist and hips. Height: 1.57-1.60 m.

G. *Women's*

Larger fully developed figure with longer back waist length. Height: 1.65-1.68 m.

MALE FIGURE TYPES

A. *Boys and Teen-boys*

For growing and maturing boys and young men who have not quite reached adulthood.
Height: varies.

B. *Men*

Fully matured men of an average build.
Height: 1.78 m.

CHOOSING AND BUYING A PATTERN

1. Take accurate measurements and know your figure type.
2. Compare these with pattern. Select (a) blouse, jacket, dress patterns by bust measurements, (b) skirt, trousers patterns by waist and hip measurements.
3. Buy a pattern that is the correct size.
4. Choose a simple design with few pattern pieces if you find sewing difficult e.g. Easy to Sew, Extra Sure.
5. Select patterns of a reliable make which are known for their high quality design and clear accurate instructions.

CHOOSING AND BUYING FABRIC

1. Choose a fabric from pattern's suggested fabric list. It will suit the garment style.
2. Check envelope back for amount of fabric required.
3. Pattern may advise you not to choose specific fabrics e.g. one-way designs, or they may emphasise that

Envelope front

only one type of fabric is suitable e.g. jersey, knits.

4. One-way designs or nap fabrics require extra fabric.

5. Fabrics are sold in many widths, 90 cm, 115 cm, 140 cm and 150 cm.

6. Suitable fabric will be washable, shrink resistant, firmly woven and easy to use.

7. Choose fabric which has an attractive colour and design.

PATTERN INFORMATION

A. *ENVELOPE FRONT*

A wide selection of styles of views, in sketch or photographic form, illustrate the total design with fashion details e.g. tucks, belt, on the envelope front. Fabrics and accessories are carefully chosen to illustrate the designer's concept of his creations.

B. *ENVELOPE BACK*
1. Style number.
2. The back view of the garment.

3878
6 PIECES

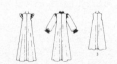

MISSES' NIGHTDRESS IN TWO LENGTHS. — No allowance made for matching plaids, checks, stripes or large patterned fabrics. For fabric with nap, pile, shading or one-way design: use nap requirements and nap layouts. **Suggested fabrics** — Cotton lawn, batiste, soft shirtings, pongee, crepe de chine, combed cotton, wool/cotton blends. **To complete garment** — Thread, 1,2 cm wide bias binding. Model 1: 6 mm wide elastic to fit wrists.

Size / Taille	Small Petite 10-12	Medium Moyenne 14-16	Large Grande 18-20	
	83-87	92-97	102-107	cm
	64-67	71-76	81-87	,,
	88-92	97-102	107-112	,,
	40,5-41,5	42-42,5	43-44	,,
Mod. 1 **Nightdress** Even lengthwise striped or plain fabric				
Chemise de nuit Tissu uni ou à rayures longitudinales régulières				
90 cm*	4,60	5,20	5,80	m
115 cm*	3,70	3,80	3,90	,,
Mod. 1 **Nightdress** Even or uneven lengthwise striped or plain fabric				
Chemise de nuit Tissu uni ou à rayures longitudinales régulières ou irrégulières				
115 cm**	4,60	4,90	5,30	,,
Mod. 2 **Nightdress** Chemise de nuit				
90 cm*	4,10	4,20	4,70	m
90 cm**	5,60	5,70	5,80	,,
115 cm*	3,00	3,00	3,50	,,
Mod. 3 **Nightdress** Chemise de nuit				
90 cm*	2,20	2,50	2,80	m
115 cm*	2,20	2,30	2,30	,,
Broderie trim Garniture de broderie anglaise				
2 cm	4,00	4,20	4,40	,,
Nightdress length: Model 1 or 2	135	136	138	cm
Model 3	99	100,5	102	,,
Nightdress width: Model 1 or 2	249	258	268	,,
Model 3	206	215	225	,,

★ fabric without nap.	★★ with nap.	★★★ with or without nap
★ tissu sans sens.	★★ avec sens.	★★★ avec ou sans sens

Envelope back

3. Describes the garment — gives details of fashion, details visible and not visible for each view.

4. Gives standard body measurements.

5. Informs you if extra fabric is required for plains, stripes and one-way designs.

6. Charts view of garment, size and amount of fabric, interfacing and lining required.

7. Gives details of finished back length and width at lower edge for each view.

8. Sewing notions, type and amount recommended for each view.

9. Suggested fabrics suitable for design chosen.

Note: Mark size, view, width and amount of fabric.

C. *INSTRUCTION SHEET*
This is divided into two areas of information.
(a) Layout and Cutting Out Guide,
(b) Sewing Guide.

(a) *Layout and Cutting Out Guide*
1. Identifies each pattern piece,
2. Explains how to prepare and arrange the fabric.
3. Identifies and explains pattern markings.
4. Layout guide for fabrics of various widths.
5. Gives special guidelines for nap or one-way designs, bias layouts etc.
Note: Mark the layout you wish to use.

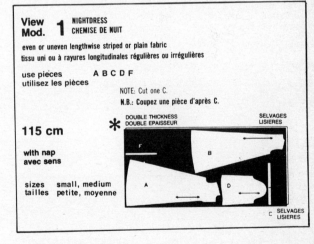

(b) Sewing Guide
1. Sewing directions in a step-by-step form.
2. Sketches to explain what each sewing technique outlines that you should do.
3. Helpful guidelines are given on stitching, trimming, construction techniques and alterations.
4. Each stage of construction is outlined in bold print.

PATTERN MARKINGS

Pattern construction symbols or markings guide you to accurate sewing. Follow them carefully when making every garment.

1. *Straight grain:* This arrow must be placed directly on top of the selvedge thread or lengthwise grain.
2. *Place to fold:* Bracketed grainline on centre front or centre back of a pattern indicates that the pattern piece should be placed to the fabric fold (parallel with the straight grain) before cutting.
3. *Cutting line:* This heavy outer line of the pattern is marked with a scissors.
4. *Seamline or stitching line:* This is indicated by a long thin broken line 15 mm inside cutting line.
5. *Notches:* Single or double notches act as a guide for accurate joining of garment pieces.
6. *Fold line:* A solid bold line indicating where the garment is to be folded when being made. It may be at front edges of a garment e.g. coat, blouse.
7. *Balance marks* (large and small dots). These act as a guide for accurate joining of garment seams. Triangles and squares are also balance marks which help during construction.
8. *Dart:* Broken lines with corresponding construction symbols are matched to make a dart.

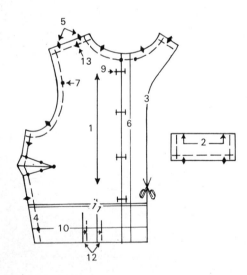

9. *Buttonholes and Button:* Indicates location and length of button-hole and recommended button size.
10. *Hemline:* Depth of hem suitable for garment being made.
11. *Adjustment lines:* Double lines where lengthening or shortening is done on the pattern before placing it on fabric and cutting it out.

12. *Construction symbols:* e.g. tucks, gathers, openings, pleats are clearly indicated by broken and/or solid lines.
13. *Direction of sewing:* This is shown by little arrows which are on the seamline.

PREPARING YOUR PATTERN

1. Select pieces required for view chosen.
2. Check layout for view, size and suggested fabric.
3. Cut just outside bold line of pattern piece.
4. Check your measurements again with pattern measurements. Adjust at this stage if necessary.
5. Using a cool iron, press pattern pieces if they are creased.

PATTERN ADJUSTMENTS

1. Use lengthening and shortening lines to alter pattern length.
2. Vertical lines are used to insert or remove width.
3. By adding to or taking away a small amount from seams, very small adjustments may be made.

Beware: Do not over fit.

Make adjustments on corresponding or adjoining pieces, also when making all alterations e.g. seams, hems.

To shorten: Fold pattern along alteration line with pleat half the depth required. Pin carefully.

To lengthen: Cut pattern on alteration line. Separate pieces the amount required and insert a heavy backing paper. Pin or sellotape in position.

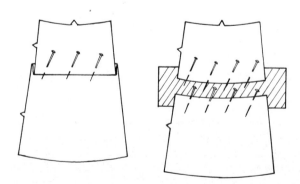

Shortening and lengthening

To add extra width: Cut a vertical line from shoulder to hem. Insert backing paper.

266

To reduce width: Make a vertical pleat from shoulder to hem. Pin or sellotape in position.

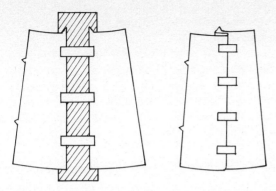

Widening and reducing

Check
1. Re-draw straight or curved edges after adjustments.
2. The seam lengths must match adjoining seam lengths.
3. Is the grain line still straight?
4. Adjust dart lines if they are altered by the pattern adjustments.

PREPARING YOUR FABRIC
1. If fabric is creased, press using a warm iron.
2. Identify right side of fabric.
3. Straighten fabric ends by pulling a crosswise thread (i.e. weft thread). Cut on this line across width of fabric.
4. If fabric is off grain, straighten it by pulling on the bias and then pin selvedges together and steam press.
5. Pre-shrink fabric if necessary.
6. Following pattern instructions, place pattern on fabric.

Layout of Pattern
1. Mark selected layout. Follow it carefully, folding fabric correct way i.e. lengthwise or crosswise, right sides together.
2. Pin selvedges together placing pins 1-1.5 cm apart.
3. Place pattern pieces on fabric keeping grainline of pattern parallel to that of fabric. Check using tape measure.
4. Do not cut until all pattern pieces have been placed on fabric.
5. Check that layout instructions have been followed e.g. place on fold, cut two, lay out pattern piece twice etc.

6. For nap and one-way designs, place pattern pieces in one direction.
7. If the fabric design has to be matched, match at seamlines, and not on cutting lines.
8. Cut out each pattern piece the correct number of times.

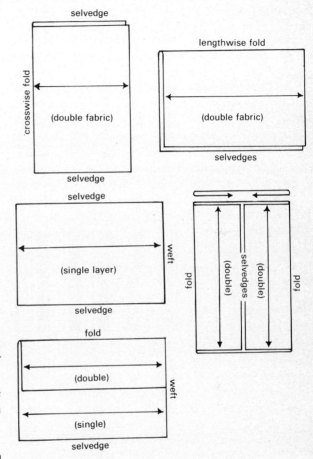

Folding fabrics – five ways

Cutting Out
1. Using a bent-handled scissors cut out with long even strokes.
2. Do not cut out pattern with pinking shears.
3. Keep left hand flat over pattern piece and never lift fabric while cutting.
4. Be sure to cut notches outwards.
5. Fold fabric pieces when finished cutting out. Scrap fabric can be used for testing machine stitch.
   Note If pattern has no seam allowance mark 1.5 cm seam allowance with pins and then tailor's chalk. Cut on chalked line.

Fabrics with pile, nap, shading, one-way designs, diagonal designs, plaids, stripes and prints require special attention when laying out the pattern. More fabric is needed so that pieces can be matched.

Directional Fabrics

1. *Napped and pile fabrics* seem to be lighter in colour and texture in one direction and darker when placed the other way. Special instructions are always given for cutting these fabrics. If you rub your hand against the direction of the nap, the fabric will feel rough. Do it the other way and the fabric is quite smooth. All pattern pieces must be placed in the same direction.

2. *Stripes:* Certain patterns recommend that you do not use striped fabric. In these cases stripes cannot be correctly matched. Stripes should follow the same direction, vertical or horizontal in the garment. There are two types of stripes — (a) balanced, (b) unbalanced.

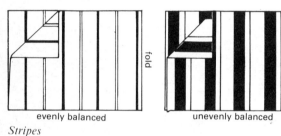

evenly balanced   unevenly balanced

Stripes

3. *Plaids and checks:* Allow extra fabric when using plaids and checks. They may be even or uneven. In even designs, stripes are the same in both selvedge and weft directions. In uneven designs, the spacing and design are different in one or both directions. The most dominent line of these fabrics should be placed on the centre front and centre back lines. At skirt seams match plaids and checks horizontally.

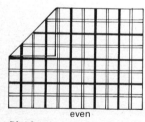 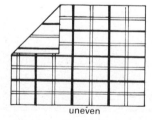

even   uneven

Plaids

Transfer pattern markings by
(a) tailor's tacks
(b) tailor's chalk
(c) carbon paper and tracing wheel.

HOW TO SEW KNITS

Knits are very popular for casual wear because of their comfortable, easy care and practical qualities. It is recommended to use a pattern marked "Sized for Stretch Knits Only".

Patterns for knits are sized to suit the stretch of the fabric recommended on the back of the pattern. Every envelope carries a diagram "Pick-a-Knit-Rule" (Simplicity patterns). This helps you decide how stretchy the knit fabric really is e.g. Very, Moderate or Limited.

Limited Stretch

FOR THIS PATTERN — 10cm OF KNIT FABRIC MUST STRETCH CROSSWISE FROM HERE → AT LEAST TO HERE →

Moderate Stretch

FOR THIS PATTERN — 10cm OF KNIT FABRIC MUST STRETCH CROSSWISE FROM HERE → AT LEAST TO HERE →

Very Stretchy

FOR THIS PATTERN — 10cm OF KNIT FABRIC MUST STRETCH CROSSWISE FROM HERE → AT LEAST TO HERE →

SEWING GUIDELINES

1. Choose the correct pattern.
2. Select a recommended fabric.
3. Use a "with nap" layout. Shading may occur.
4. Use stretch linings and underlinings with knits.
5. Select a slight zig-zag stitch for seams to allow some ease.

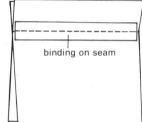

binding on seam

6. Do not use blunt needles. Select one suitable for knits.
7. Binding may be used e.g. along shoulder seams, to prevent unnecessary stretching.
8. Use zig-zag seams for neatness.

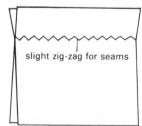

slight zig-zag for seams

9. Press from wrong side using a pressing cloth.
10. Allow garment to hang for 48 hours before turning up hem.
11. For hems, use the "lettucing" method of hemming.
12. Topstitch for a professional finish.
13. Follow the usual guidelines for fitting garments.
14. Note whether your knit is washable or dry-cleanable.

31.
Pattern Layouts

1. *Night dress*

3. Remove pattern, cut tailor tacks and separate garment pieces.
4. Tack and machine shoulder and side seams.
5. Remove tacking, press open and neaten seams.
6. Make up ruffle for neck edge. Apply ruffle and press.
7. Neaten armhole edges with bias binding.
8. Turn up hem and apply ruffle. Slipstitch. Press. Attach ribbon to centre front of neckline.

2. *Trousers/shorts/pyjamas*

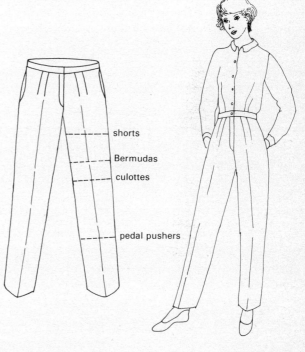

Measurements required	Fabric required				Suitable fabrics
Bust, length to hem	Size	10	12	14	Cotton, lawn, brushed cotton, seersucker, silk, polyester cotton
	90 cm	2.80	2.90	3.00 m	
	115 cm	1.90	2.00	2.10 m	

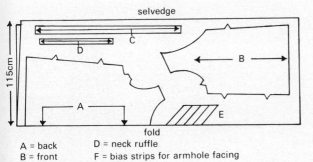

selvedge

115cm

fold

A = back
B = front
C = hem ruffle
D = neck ruffle
F = bias strips for armhole facing

ORDER OF WORK

1. Prepare pattern and fabric. Check measurements. Alter if necessary on pattern piece before cutting out fabric.
2. Lay out pattern on fabric as shown in pattern delta. Pin, cut and tailor tack.

Measurements required	Fabric required				Suitable fabrics
Trousers: Waist, hips, crotch length, length to hem	Size	10	12	14	Denim, poplin, linen, gaberdine, corduroy, fine wool
	90 cm	2.40	2.40	2.60 m	
	115 cm	2.20	2.30	2.40 m	
Shorts: As for trousers	90 cm	1.60	1.60	1.60 m	Soft or crisp fabrics, cottons, linen blends
	115 cm	1.40	1.40	1.60 m	

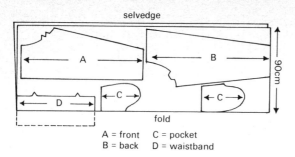

selvedge

A = front   C = pocket
B = back   D = waistband

90cm

fold

Pyjamas

Use layout and order of work for trousers. Omit zip and side pockets in pyjamas. For pyjamas top or jacket, use layout and order of work for (a) man's shirt or (b) lady's shirt blouse. Suitable fabrics include fine cottons, blends, brushed cotton and brushed nylon.

Note: From basic trouser designs, you can develop pyjamas, shortie pyjamas, jeans, shorts, sportswear, jumpsuits and add to them attractive casual tops and shirts.

ORDER OF WORK

1. Prepare pattern and fabric. Check measurements. Alter if necessary on pattern piece before cutting out fabric.
2. Lay out pattern on fabric as shown in pattern delta. Pin, cut and tailor tack.
3. Remove pattern, cut tailor tacks and separate garment pieces.
4. Tack darts, pleats, side pockets and all seams (side and crotch seams). Fit and alter if necessary.
5. Machine darts, inner and outer leg seams and

pleats. Finish off threads. Remove tacking, press darts and neaten seams.

6. Tack and machine crotch seam i.e. front to back at inner leg edge. Press seam open and neaten.
7. Insert zip. (Lap right front opening edge over left for girls; and left front opening edge over right for boys.).
8. Prepare, assemble and attach waistband. Press. Attach hook and eye closure or button and button-hole.
9. Measure length of trousers, turn up hem and stitch in position.
10. Bring leg seams together and press creases down along centre leg of trousers.

3. *Simple culottes*

Measurements required	Fabric required				Suitable fabrics
Waist, hip, length to hem	Size	10	12	14	Corduroy, denim, fine wool, linen, gabardine
	90 cm	2.70	2.70	2.80 m	
	115 cm	1.80	1.90	1.90 m	

Culottes may be A-line with darts or fuller with gathers caught into the waistband.

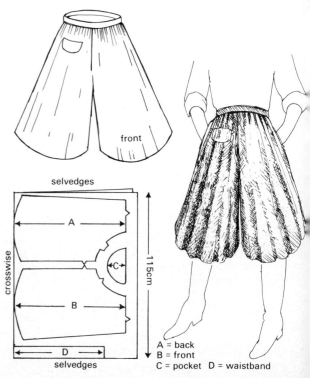

front

selvedges

crosswise

115cm

A = back
B = front
C = pocket D = waistband

selvedges

270

ORDER OF WORK

1. Prepare pattern and fabric. Check measurements. Alter if necessary on pattern piece before cutting out fabric.
2. Lay out pattern on fabric as shown in pattern delta. Pin, cut and tailor tack.
3. Remove pattern, cut tailor tacks and separate garment pieces.
4. Gather waist, tack seams, fit and alter if necessary.
5. Prepare and attach pocket. Machine back to front at inner leg edge. Press and neaten seams.
6. Machine crotch seam from front to end of zip opening. Press open and neaten seam.
7. Insert zip at centre back. Stitch back to front at side seams. Press. Neaten seams.
8. Prepare and attach waistband to gathered edge.
9. Attach hook and eye at waistband edges.
10. Turn up hems. Press carefully.

4. *Unlined housecoat or dressing-gown*

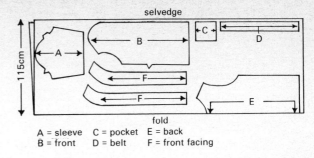

A = sleeve   C = pocket   E = back
B = front   D = belt   F = front facing

ORDER OF WORK

1. Prepare pattern and fabric. Check measurements. Alter if necessary on pattern piece before cutting out fabric.
2. Lay out pattern on fabric as shown in pattern delta. Pin, cut and tailor tack.
3. Remove pattern, cut tailor tacks and separate garment pieces.
4. Tack together for first fitting. Try on and make any necessary alterations.
5. Prepare, assemble and attach pockets to garment.
6. Machine side, shoulder and underarm seams. Press open and neaten.
7. Attach upper collar and facings to garment. (Interface if required).
8. Press carefully.
9. Insert sleeves, neaten armhole seams and press.
10. Neaten hem edges of sleeves and garment. Remove all tacking. Attach belt loops. Complete belt and give a final press to the completed garment.

5. *Jumpsuit*

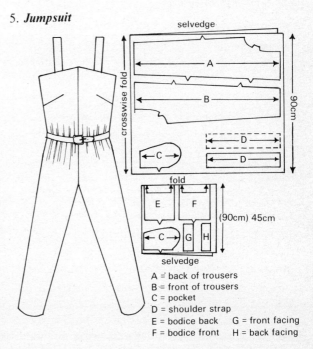

A = back of trousers
B = front of trousers
C = pocket
D = shoulder strap
E = bodice back   G = front facing
F = bodice front   H = back facing

Measurements required	Fabric required (short dressing gown)			Suitable fabrics
Across back, shoulder, bust/ chest, sleeve length, dressing-gown length	Width	8-10	12-14	14-16	Cotton, silk, satin, seersucker, terry towelling, brushed cotton, velour, lightweight wools
	90 cm	3.90	4.40	5.00 m	
	115 cm	3.00	3.20	3.30 m	
	140 cm	2.50	2.60	2.70 m	

Measurements required	Fabric required				Suitable fabrics
Bust, neck to waist, Hips, waist to ankle	Size	10	12	14	All cottons, linen — some blends
	90 cm	3.20	3.20	3.30 m	
	115 cm	2.80	2.90	2.90 m	

A jumpsuit consists of a trousers part with a camisole top added.

ORDER OF WORK

1. Prepare pattern. Cut out and tailor tack. Remove pattern and separate garment pieces.
2. Assemble for first fitting. Make alterations if necessary.
3. **Bodice:** Machine and press darts. Prepare and attach shoulder straps and facings. Machine side seams and facings in a continuous row of stitching. Neaten seams and free facing edges. Press.
4. **Bottom:** Machine, press and neaten inner leg and centre crotch seam. Apply pockets to side edges at back and front. Press seam into pocket. Tack, machine, press and neaten side seams.
5. Tack and machine bodice to bottom at waistline seam.
6. Attach waistline casing and insert elastic.
7. Complete hems and give a final press.

6. *A-line skirt with gathers*

Measurements required	Fabric required				Suitable fabrics
Waist, hips, length	Size	10	12	14	Cottons, Viyella, fine gaberdine, wool, light wool, crepe, silk, rayon
	90 cm	2.00	2.00	2.10 m	
	115 cm	1.60	1.60	1.70 m	
	150 cm	1.20	1.20	1.30 m	

ORDER OF WORK

1. Prepare pattern and fabric. Check measurements. Alter if necessary on pattern piece before cutting out fabric.
2. Lay out pattern on fabric as shown in pattern delta. Pin, cut and tailor tack.
3. Remove pattern, cut tailor tacks and separate garment pieces. Tack seams, gather waistline and fit.

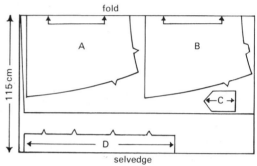

A = front   C = pockets
B = back   D = waistband

Alter if necessary. Make and attach pockets. Press.
4. Tack up side seams leaving space for zip opening. Machine, press and neaten seams.
5. Insert zip. Press carefully.
6. Adjust gathers to fit waistband. Prepare and attach waistband to skirt. Add hook and eye to waistband edges. Press.
7. Measure and turn up hem.
8. Give completed skirt a final pressing.

7. *Pleated skirt*

Measurements required	Fabric required				Suitable fabrics
Waist, hip, length from waist	Size	10	12	14	Cotton, Fine wools and tweeds, Corduroy, wool, double knits
	115 cm	1.90	1.90	1.90 m	
	150 cm	1.60	1.60	1.60 m	

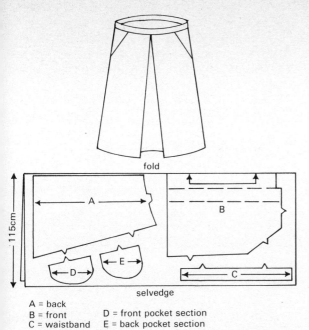

fold

115cm

A

B

E

D

C

selvedge

A = back
B = front   D = front pocket section
C = waistband   E = back pocket section

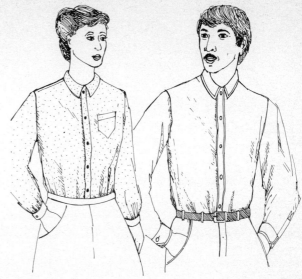

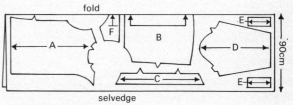

fold

F

A

B

E

D

C

E

90cm

selvedge

A = front   D = sleeves
B = back   E = cuffs
C = collar   F = yoke

ORDER OF WORK

1. Prepare pattern and fabric. Check measurements. Alter if necessary on pattern piece before cutting out fabric.
2. Lay out pattern on fabric as shown in pattern delta. Pin, cut and tailor tack.
3. Remove pattern, cut tailor tacks and separate garment pieces. Tack pockets, seams, darts and fit on garment. Adjust if necessary.
   FRONT: Form and tack front pleat, Machine and press as instructed by the pattern.
4. BACK: Tack, machine and press darts. Machine centre back seam leaving an opening for zip. Press open and neaten. Attach pocket sections to side seams.
5. Machine side seams. Press and neaten.
6. Insert zip. Attach waistband. Sew hook and eye to waistband as a fastening.
7. Mark and turn up hem.
8. Press completed pleated skirt.

8. *Shirt blouse or man's shirt*

Measurements required	Fabric required			Suitable fabrics
Bust (or chest), length to waist, length of sleeve, waist, hips	Size	10	12	14	Poplin, silk, cotton and cotton/wool blends, lawn, polyester
	90 cm	2.50	2.60	2.60 m	
	115 cm	2.20	2.20	2.20 m	

ORDER OF WORK

1. Prepare pattern and fabric. Check measurements. Alter if necessary on pattern piece before cutting out fabric.
2. Lay out pattern on fabric as shown in pattern delta. Pin, cut and tailor tack.
3. Remove pattern, cut tailor tacks and separate garment pieces. tack and fit. Make adjustments if necessary.
4. Machine darts, yoke and seams in place. Press. Neaten seams. Edge machine facings.
5. Prepare collar and attach it to neck edge of shirt.
6. Prepare and machine sleeve seams. Press open and neaten.
7. Insert sleeve and neaten armhole seam allowance. Make and attach cuff.
8. Work buttonholes and sew in buttons on cuff and front opening of shirt.
9. Mark and turn up hem.
10. Give shirt a final press.

9. *Classic blouse*

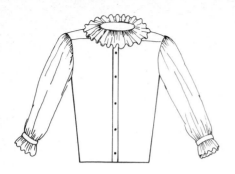

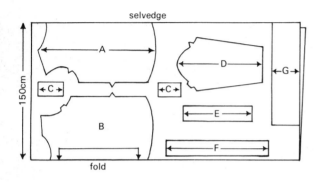

selvedge

150cm

fold

A = front   D = sleeve   G = neck ruffle
B = back   E = cuff ruffle
C = cuff   F = front facing

Measurements required	Fabric required				Suitable fabrics
Bust, waist, hip, wrist, back to waist length, sleeve length, across back.	Size	10	12	14	Silk, fine cottons, blends, lace
	90 cm	2.00	2.70	3.20 m	
	115 cm	2.50	2.50	2.50 m	

ORDER OF WORK

1. Prepare pattern and fabric. Check measurements. Alter if necessary on pattern piece before cutting out fabric.
2. Lay out pattern on fabric as shown in pattern delta. Pin, cut and tailor tack.
3. Remove pattern, cut tailor tacks and separate garment pieces.
4. Tack garment together, fit and adjust if necessary.
5. Interface front edges and attach facing. Neaten free edge of facing. Complete front edges.
6. Machine, press and neaten shoulder and side seams.

7. Prepare and attach ruffle to neck edge. Press.
8. Make and insert sleeves. Neaten armhole edges. Press.
9. Make and attach ruffle to cuff. Complete cuff and attach to sleeves.
10. Turn up and hem lower edge. Press completed garment.

10. *Casual unlined jacket (loose fitting)*

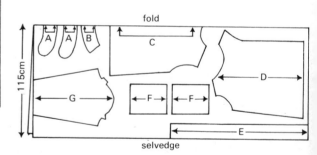

fold

115cm

selvedge

A = collar   E = belt
B = back facing   F = pocket
C = back   G = sleeve
D = front

Measurements required	Fabric required				Suitable fabrics
Bust (chest), waist, hips, length, sleeve length, across back	Size	10	12	14	Wools, tweeds, heavyweight silks
	115 cm	2.40	2.50	2.50 m	
	140 cm	2.00	2.00	2.10 m	

ORDER OF WORK

1. Prepare pattern and fabric. Check measurements. Alter if necessary on pattern piece before cutting out fabric.
2. Lay out pattern on fabric as shown in pattern delta. Pin, cut and tailor tack.
3. Remove pattern, cut tailor tacks and separate garment pieces.
4. Tack for first fitting. Fit and alter if necessary.
5. Make and attach pockets.
6. Attach interfacing to wrong side of garment at front foldline edges and back neck edge.
7. Machine, press and neaten shoulder and side seams.
8. Work bound buttonholes.
9. Make collar and tack in position.
10. Join front and neck facings. Tack in position to neck edge over collar.
11. Machine, trim and layer turnings. Press facing to wrong side.
12. Complete bound buttonhole facing.
13. Prepare and attach sleeves. Neaten armhole turnings. Press.
14. Complete hems of cuffs and lower hem of jacket. Sew on buttons.
15. Press again.

11. *Dress*

Measurements required	Fabric required				Suitable fabrics
Bust, waist, hip, length from neck to waist and from waist to hem, length of sleeve.	Size 90 cm 115 cm	10 4.00 3.50	12 4.20 3.30	14 4.20 m 3.30 m	Soft fabrics, cottons, wool, (crepe/jersey) linen, rayon

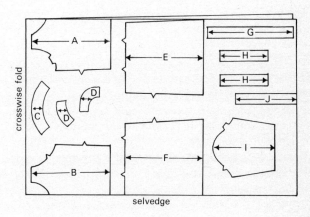

A = bodice back
B = bodice front
C = back neck band
D = front neck band
E = skirt front
F = skirt back
G = belt
H = cuff
I = sleeve
J = front bodice band

ORDER OF WORK

1. Prepare pattern and fabric. Check measurements. Alter if necessary on pattern piece before cutting out fabric.
2. Lay out pattern on fabric as shown in pattern delta. Pin, cut and tailor tack.
3. Remove pattern, cut tailor tacks and separate garment pieces.
4. Tack together for first fitting. Alter if necessary.
5. BODICE: Front shirt opening. Machine, press open and neaten shoulder seams. Make up and attach neck band. Machine, press open and neaten side seams.
6. SKIRT. Machine, press open and neaten seams of skirt. Gather waist edge.
7. Attach skirt to bodice. Attach casing waist and insert elastic. Insert sleeves and attach cuffs.
8. Turn up hem and press.
9. Work buttonholes on shirt opening and cuffs. Sew on buttons.
10. Make a belt of self fabric or contrasting fabric.

32.
Stitches

INTRODUCTION

Sewing machines have made needlework much easier for us. However, fine hand-sewing is necessary for many parts of a garment e.g. hemming waistband to row of maching, top-sewing ends of waistband, slip-hemming hems of garments etc. Stitches may be divided into three groups

    (a) temporary stitches
    (b) permanent stitches
    (c) hand embroidery stitches.

GUIDELINES FOR NEAT STITCHING

1. Sew only where there is a source of good light.
2. Work with the garment resting on a table.
3. Select the right type of needle and thread. The colour and fibre in the thread should match those of the garment fabric.
4. Use a single thread of a suitable length; not too long and not too short. Knots tend to form if the thread is too long.
5. Place a thimble on the middle finger of the right hand. It should be used when hand sewing. The blunt end of the thimble helps when pushing the needle through the fabric. Some people find it easier to sew from left to right especially people who are left-handed.
6. Always pin before tacking garment pieces, hems etc. together.
7. Begin temporary stitches with a knot to secure the thread end.
8. Begin permanent stitches with one or two back-stitches concealing the thread end between fabric fold.
9. Temporary stitches should hold the garment pieces securely together. When the permanent stitches have been completed, temporary stitches should be easy to remove.
10. Work stitches evenly and accurately. Do not pull stitches too tightly. If you begin a row of stitching, complete it to keep the tension even.
11. Finish off each row of stitching correctly. Work backstitching to fasten off thread securely and conceal thread end in fabric fold (Check instructions on stitches for exceptions).
12. Remove tacking and press completed permanent stitches.

TEMPORARY STITCHES
TACKING (OR BASTING)

This is used during the early stages of garment construction
  (i) To hold matching stripes, plaids, balance marks, notches etc. of two garment pieces together for first fitting and machine or hand stitching.
 (ii) To attach interfacing to garment piece and hold it in position during machining.
(iii) Used near fitting line, it is a good guide when stitching.

Note: Before tacking, pin garment pieces together matching notches, fitting line etc. Use a thread of contrasting colour, making sure that it will not mark the fabric, e.g. never use black on white.

Straight Tacking

Types	Uses
(a) Even	Marking centrefront and centreback lines of garment. Holding darts, seams and hems in position during fitting and machining.
(b) Uneven	Attaching interfacings and linings. Keeping lower edge of hem in position until completed.

Method
1. Match notches and edges of garment. Place pins at right angles to fabric edges.
2. Begin by using a knot or a double backstitch.
3. Always work from right to left. Make stitches and spaces equal in size, (10 mm to 12 mm approx.) for even tacking. For uneven tacking work long stitches (15 mm approx.) with small spaces between them (10 mm approx.) on side facing you. For extra firm tacking work a backstitch every 3 cm.
4. Fasten off thread securely with a double backstitch.

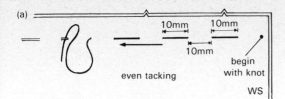

(a) even tacking

10mm 10mm
10mm
begin with knot
WS

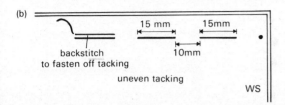

(b) uneven tacking

15 mm 15mm
10mm
backstitch to fasten off tacking
WS

Diagonal Tacking

This type of tacking is suitable for keeping a few layers of fabric in position until fitting and machining have been completed. e.g. on collars, facings, interfacings, linings and fine fabrics.

Method
1. Start with a knot and insert the needle into the fabric vertically making a diagonal stitch as you work.
2. Always work from right to left.
3. Fasten off thread securely with a double backstitch.

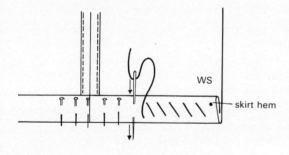

WS
skirt hem

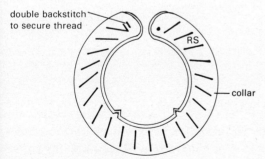

double backstitch to secure thread
RS
collar

Slip-tacking or Basting

Slip-basting is a temporary stitch used (i) to hold matching stripes and plaids of seams in position, (ii) on complicated curved seam sections of garments, (iii) when fitting and altering garments on the right side.

Method
1. Mark seam allowance on garment pieces.
2. On upper layer of garment fabric turn seam allowance to wrong side.
3. Place fitting line of upper layer to fitting line of matching garment piece. Pin to hold in position.
4. With right sides facing, working from right to left, slip the needle between folds of fabric to conceal thread and bring out at upper folded edge.
5. Slip needle through the lower single layer making a stitch 3 mm in length. Bring out the needle 10 mm further on through upper layers of fabric at folded edge.
6. Repeat this process. Fasten off threads with a backstitch.

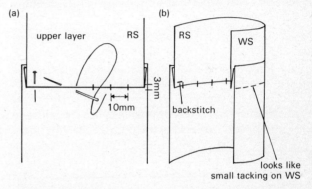

(a) upper layer RS 3mm 10mm
(b) RS WS backstitch looks like small tacking on WS

Machine Tacking

This is suitable for firm, closely woven fabrics that will not gather or mark. Fine fabrics tend to form gathers when machine tacked.

Method
1. Pin seams together matching notches, fitting lines and placing pins at right angles to raw edge of seam.
2. Set machine at its longest straight stitch. The upper tension may be loosened slightly to ensure that the machining is easy to remove.
3. Using a contrasting colour of thread, machine along the seam 1 mm inside the seamline.

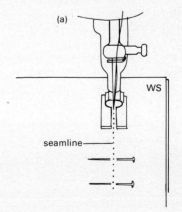

(a)
WS
seamline

4. When permanent stitching has been completed unpick the machine tacking.

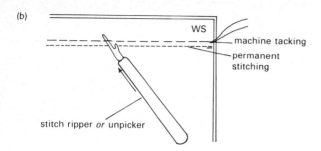

stitch ripper *or* unpicker

Cut thread end 30 mm away from loop. The thread ends should always be longer than loop.
Repeat this process at all balance marks. Remove pins.

5. Remove each pattern piece by pulling uncut loops through, leaving a small tear in the pattern, or cutting the loops, removing pattern and leaving pattern without any tears. Roll the fabric away from the pattern gently.
6. Separate fabric layers by pulling apart carefully and cutting the threads between the layers. Each garment piece is marked with tufts of thread on balance marks.

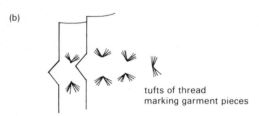

tufts of thread
marking garment pieces

7. Fold each garment piece to prevent tailor tacking coming out.

Tailor Tacking (also called Tailor's tacks)

This is the most accurate way of transferring pattern markings e.g. balance marks, hem turnings, darts and pleats from the pattern to both layers of garment fabric. Tailor tacking is done after cutting out and before the pattern is removed from the fabric. It may also be used to mark a single layer of fabric under the pattern piece.

Method
1. Cut out garment but do not remove pattern.
2. Using a long unknotted double thread, make a small stitch through pattern marking and both layers of garment fabric. Pull thread through leaving a thread end 30 mm in length.

3. Work a second stitch over the first in exactly the same spot forming a 25 mm loop.

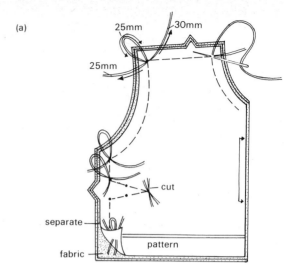

PERMANENT STITCHES

RUNNING

Running is like minature tacking stitches, small straight stitches about 1-2 mm in length. Used for seams, tucks, gathering, easing and repairing garments. It is worked from right to left.

Method
1. Using an unknotted single thread begin with a back-stitch.
2. Work stitches along fitting line keeping stitches and spaces equal in size; stitch 2 mm, space 2 mm, stitch 2 mm etc.
3. Fasten off thread with a backstitch.

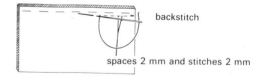

backstitch

spaces 2 mm and stitches 2 mm

GATHERING

Gathering is used (i) to control fullness at shoulder, yoke, cuff and waist edges, (ii) to ease in material at armhole. Gathers are a fashion feature which add softness to garment lines. Gathering can be worked by hand or machine.

Method
1. Work by hand two rows of running stitches parallel

to each other within seam allowance and about 1 mm and 3 mm from fitting line.

2. Begin with a double backstitch and leave threads loose at the end of each row. This will be used for pulling up gathers.
3. Pull both threads and push the fabric gently along them until gathers of the required size form.
4. Secure gathering threads by winding threads in a figure of eight around a pin.
   Size of gathering stitch = 2 mm.
   Size of easing stitch = 2-3 mm.

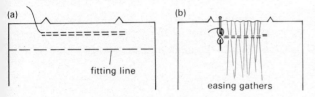

(a) fitting line

(b) easing gathers

Threadmarking

This is used to mark (i) the position of the centre-front and centreback of garment, (ii) the position of buttonholes, pockets, curved seams and fitting line, (iii) position of hem lines e.g. cuffs and hem edge of garment.

Method
1. Use a long unknotted double thread of a colour that contrasts with the fabric.
2. Work a line of tacking loops (25 mm loops) on fitting line of pattern from right to left.
3. Clip the loops and roll pattern away from fabric.
4. Pull the upper fabric away and clip the threads between the layers, leaving tufts on both garment pieces.

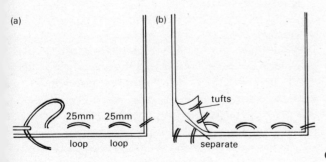

(a) 25mm 25mm loop loop

(b) tufts separate

Machine Gathering

Work two rows of machining using a long straight stitch. Loosen the tension slightly. Complete as for hand-gathering.

BACKSTITCHING

Backstitching is used (i) to secure thread ends at the beginning and end of a row of stitching, (ii) to join seams instead of machining, (iii) to repair short, sections of seams that have ripped. Strong and secure, the backstitch gives extra strength to areas where there is extra strain.

Method
1. Pin and tack garment pieces together, right sides facing.
2. Working from right to left, make a double backstitch and bring needle 2 mm to left of first stitch. Keep stitches 2 mm in size.

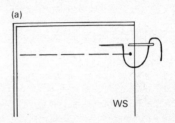

(a)

WS

3. Take a stitch backwards 2 mm into end of first stitch and bring needle 2 mm to left of second stitch. On side facing you, backstitching looks like machining. Underneath it overlaps and looks like stem stitch.

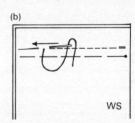

(b)

WS

4. Repeat this process leaving no spaces between stitches. Fasten off thread with a double backstitch.

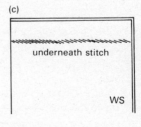

(c)

underneath stitch

WS

OVERCASTING

Overcasting is worked on raw edges on the wrong side of a garment as a method of neatening them. It prevents ravelling and fraying occurring during wear and laundering.

Method

1. Working from right or left insert the needle through back of fabric at right angles to raw edge bringing it through to side facing you.
2. Pull thread through leaving 1 cm of thread end along raw edge. This will be enclosed by stitches.
3. Insert needle again at right angles to raw edge. Bring it through to right side forming a diagonal stitch 5 mm deep as you work.

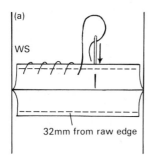

4. Hold edge flat and enclose 1 cm of thread end with diagonal stitches.
5. Space stitches evenly, keeping them equal in length and depth.
6. Fasten off threads by taking three stitches backwards to form three crosses or a double back-stitch.

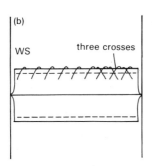

Note: If the fabric frays easily work a row of machining 2 mm from raw edge before overcasting.

TOP-SEWING OR OVERSEWING

Top-sewing is a small strong slanted stitch used to join two folded or selvedge edges together e.g. tapes and ribbons, straps, lace and ends of waistband.

Method

1. Hold folded edges between thumb and first finger of left hand.

2. Working from right to left, insert needle with unknotted thread through the single fold nearest to you, leaving single thread end between folds.

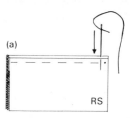

3. Draw needle through fold nearest to you. With needle at right angles to fold, insert it through both folds forming a slanted stitch as you work.
4. Work along edge of folds keeping stitches small, slanted, near the edge and evenly spaced.

5. Fasten off threads by forming three crosses, to the right over last three stitches.

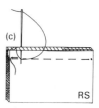

HEMMING

Hemming is a strong small slanted stitch used to finish the hem edge of cuffs, collars, bindings, tapes, facings and waistbands. Hem stitches, no matter how small they are, tend to be visible on the right side of garments. Hemming is usually not used on hems of dresses and skirts.

Method

1. Tack hem in position. Place the folded edge over index and second finger with thumb and third finger holding it in place. Work from right to left.

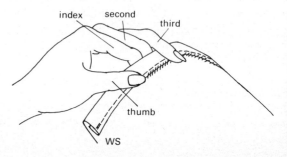

2. Insert needle under and through fold of fabric from left to right leaving thread end tucked under fold.

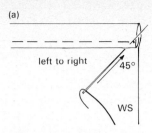

(a)

left to right
45°

WS

3. Insert the needle into two threads of single fabric and pick up two threads of folded edge as the needle points to the left.
Note: The needle points to the left at an angle of 45° also.

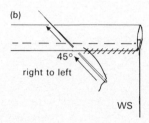

(b)

45°
right to left

WS

4. Pull thread through and work a row of small and even stitches. Stitches should be firm, not too loose nor too tight.
5. Finish off thread by forming a V-stitch, working to the right over last stitch. Slip needle through folded edge and cut thread.

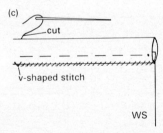

(c)

cut

v-shaped stitch

WS

Slip-hemming

It is used to secure a folded hem edge on trousers, skirts, dresses and blouses for an almost invisible finish on right and wrong sides. Also suitable for attaching lining to garment.

Method
1. Tack hem in place.
2. Hold hem between thumb and first finger with the hem fold away from you or facing you. Always work from right to left.

3. Slip needle through fold of fabric and make a small backstitch to secure thread end.
4. Insert needle into single fabric and pick up one or two threads.

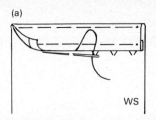

(a)

WS

5. Pass needle along fold for 5 mm-7mm. Bring needle and thread through firmly but not too tightly.

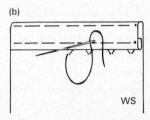

(b)

WS

6. Work until the hem fold is attached to single fabric. Fasten off thread on folded edge with a backstitch. Run thread end through fold and cut.

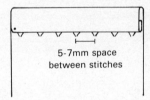

5-7mm space
between stitches

Blind Hemming

This method of attaching a hem is suitable where the edge has been neatened by zig-zag machining, binding, overlocking and overcasting.

Method
1. Neaten raw edge of hem using zig-zag machining.
2. Tack hem in place 10 mm below raw edge.
3. Secure thread, fold back edge of hem.
4. Pick up two or three threads of the garment fabric and then pull thread through.
5. Insert needle into hem and make a small stitch (two or three threads.)

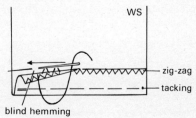

WS

zig-zag
tacking

blind hemming

6. Pull thread through but do not gather the fabric.
7. Fasten off thread with a backstitch.

HERRINGBONE STITCH

Herringbone stitch is used:
(i) over raw edges of stretchy and heavy fabrics which do not ravel easily (hems, seams etc);
(ii) as a decorative stitch e.g. worked with embroidery thread;
(iii) for holding pleats in position until garment is completed. In this case it is a temporary stitch.
(iv) to neaten and hem raw edges with one sewing process.

Method
1. Working from left to right make a double backstitch 4 mm from edge of fold.
2. Insert needle into single fabric 2 mm from raw edge to right of backstitch. Draw thread through.

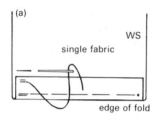

3. Pick up a stitch on fold a little to the right of last stitch. All crossed stitches are opposite a space on the other side.

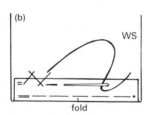

4. Do not pull the thread tightly or a ridge will form.
5. Fasten off thread by making a backstitch and slipping the thread through fold.

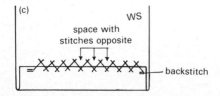

BLANKET STITCH

Blanket stitch, sometimes called loop stitch is used:
(1) for neatening raw edges where a flat finish is needed e.g. seams, (2) as a decorative finish when worked in embroidery thread e.g. scalloping, appliqué, embroidery, (3) for covering over thread loops to form carriers for belts and buttons.

Blanket stitches may be placed close together for decorative finishes and over thread loops. When neatening raw edges space them 3-5 mm apart depending on the thickness of the fabric. Turning a corner in blanket stitch can be done, as is shown here, very effectively.

Method
1. Hold raw edge of fabric towards you. Blanket stitch is worked from left to right with a single thread.
2. Make a backstitch 2 mm in from raw edge on the left hand side or work a few running stitches the depth of the blanket stitch to raw edge.
3. Hold thread under left thumb, place needle in single fabric at right angles to raw edge and bring it over the thread.
4. Draw through to form loop.

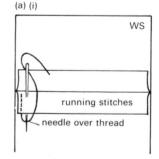
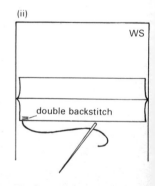

5. Continue to form loops keeping thread of each stitch under your thumb until needle is passed over it to form the next stitch. Draw thread out firmly but not tightly.
6. Blanket stitches should be evenly spaced, straight and of the same size.
7. Finish off thread with a backstitch or by running it into the fabric for a few stitches.

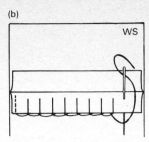

TOPSTITCHING

This outlines or emphasises the cut of a garment along its structural lines. It may be worked by hand or machine. Topstitch each area as the garment is being made. Used for collars, cuffs, pockets etc. When working topstitching you must be careful to keep it the same distance from the edge at corners, curves and other difficult areas.

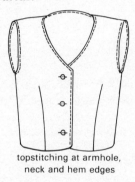

topstitching at armhole,
neck and hem edges

SADDLE STITCH

This is a decorative stitch worked by hand to give each garment a professional touch. A slightly darker or lighter colour thread than that of the fabric may be used. Saddle stitch is a row of small running stitches.

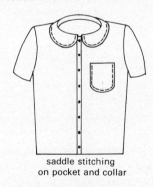

saddle stitching
on pocket and collar

EMBROIDERY STITCHES

Embroidery stitches are an attractive way to decorate garments and give them an individual personal finish. Embroidery will add a delightful finish to aprons, tray cloths, pillow cases and other household articles.

(1) Embroidery threads: Many different threads are used in embroidery. Embroidery threads or skeins are made up of six strands which may be divided up into two or more strands. The number of strands to use will be influenced by the fabric weight, thin, thick.

(2) Frames: A frame may be used to keep the fabric smooth and taut. Some embroidery can be done in the hand.

(3) Needles: Sharp, long, slim-eye crewel needles are the most suitable. The thread passes easily through the large eye.

(4) Designs: Designs can be bought or drawn by hand using a suitable chalk pencil.

(5) Scissors: A small scissors with long fine points for cutting and trimming is desirable.

Note: Embroidery can now be done with a swing needle machine or by hand in the traditional way.

GENERAL RULES

1. Secure thread ends with a backstitch or a few running stitches along the design and cover with embroidery stitches.
2. Stitches should be firm but not too tight, even, smooth and neat.
3. Complete by bringing the needle to the wrong side and running the thread end under stitches worked. Never use knots to secure embroidery threads. They ruin the appearance of the finished work.
4. All embroidery should be pressed on a well padded surface. If the surface is too hard use a cotton sheet folded several times to give a well padded surface.

FLAT STITCHES

(a) Stem stitch

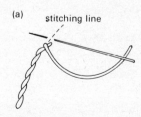

1. Work from left to right along the design line.
2. Start with a few running stitches along stitch line or a backstitch.

3. Make small even slanting stitches. Place the needle through fabric at right side of last stitch and bring it out on the left, half way back beside first stitch.
4. Place needle forward again and make another stitch. Repeat until design is covered.

   Uses: stems, outlines, motifs.

(b) Satin stitch

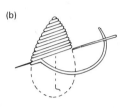

1. Begin with a few running stitches.
2. Pass needle across the area to be filled in and through design line to back. Bring it out through design line at the beginning of first stitch.
3. Stitches are worked closely together, straight or slanted across design shape to form a smooth band of stitches with straight outside edges.
4. Do not pull stitches too tightly.
   Uses: Leaves, petals, motifs, monograms.

(c) Long and short stitch

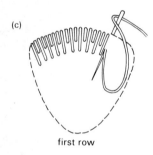

first row   second row

1. Work first row in alternate long and short satin stitches. Follow design outline carefully.
2. Work second row so that long and short satin stitches lie close to the first row.
3. Finish off threads securely.
   Uses: Flowers, motifs.

CROSSED STITCHES

(a) "Assisi" cross stitch

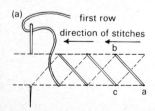

first row
direction of stitches
b
second row
c   a

First row
1. Working from right to left begin with a backstitch.
2. Bring needle out at 'a'. Crossing over, insert needle at 'b' and bring it out at 'c'.
3. Work a row of diagonal stitches.

Second row
4. Working from left to right insert needle crossing over stitches to make cross.
5. Bring needle to wrong side and fasten off thread with a backstitch.

   Uses: Borders on tray cloths, pockets.

(b) "St George" cross stitch

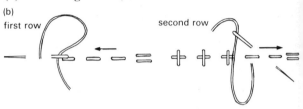

first row   second row

1. Working from right to left begin with a backstitch.
2. Work a row of large running stitches (evenly spaced).
3. From left to right cross each stitch.

   Uses: Garments, household items.

CHAIN STITCHES

(a) Lazy daisy stitch

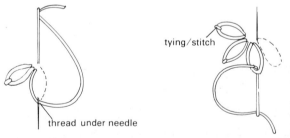

tying/stitch

thread under needle

1. Begin by working a few running stitches along design line.
2. Hold thread down with left thumb. Insert needle at starting point.
3. Bring needle out at lower edge a small distance away over thread.
4. Insert needle under loop to form a tying stitch.
5. Bring needle to wrong side and pass thread through stitches. Cut thread.

   Uses: Daisy design, petals.

(b) Chain stitch

1. Begin with a backstitch.
2. Hold thread under left thumb as in lazy daisy stitch.
3. Insert needle at starting point and bring it out at lower edge over thread to form loop.
4. Pull thread through gently.
5. Insert needle into first chain stitch beside the thread.
6. To fasten off bring needle to wrong side and tuck thread through stitches.

Uses: To outline or fill in designs.

Other loop stitches
Buttonhole stitch
Zig-zag chain stitch
Fly stitch
Feather stitch.

(c) Fly Stitch

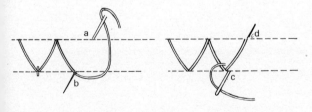

1. Begin with a backstitch and bring needle up on the left.
2. Holding thread under left thumb insert needle at 'a'. bring needle out at 'b', making a diagonal stitch.
3. Make a tying stitch at 'c', and bring needle out at 'd' to start next stitch.
4. Finish off thread neatly.

Uses: Form of daisy stitch for a repeat pattern as a decorative edging.

(d) Double feather stitch
1. Start with a backstitch to secure thread.
2. Bring needle out at 'a'. Hold thread under left thumb.

3. Insert needle at 'b' and bring out at 'c' on stitching line.
4. Make a similar stitch to left of stitching line.
5. Continue working right and left stitches alternately.
6. Fasten off threads securely on wrong side.

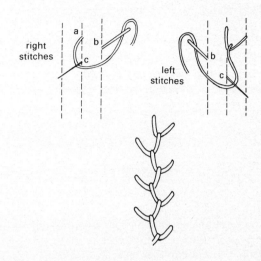

Uses: Cuffs, collars, inset panels on children's clothes.

KNOTTED STITCHES

French knot

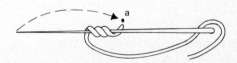

1. Bring thread to right side and hold with left thumb.
2. Wind or encircle thread three times with needle.
3. Twist needle back to point 'a', and insert it near starting point.
4. Push needle and thread through to back of fabric. Make other knots if close together. Fasten off with a backstitch.

Uses: Centre of flowers i.e. single dots, spotted or shaded clusters.

Other decorative stitches
Whipped running Stitch
Blanket stitch
Herringbone stitch
Smocking.

33.
Seams

INTRODUCTION

Garment pieces are held together by seams. A seam must never be uneven, puckered or pulled. Raw edges of the seam allowances are finished so that it does not ravel. The direction of sewing for each seam is clearly indicated on the pattern piece. Seams are machine stitched in the direction of the grain to prevent stretching.

GENERAL RULES

1. Choose a suitable needle and thread for fabric being used.
2. Test on a double layer of the fabric before starting to sew the garment.
3. If using a knitted or jersey fabric consult the sewing machine instruction book for details of type of stitch to use.
4. Fasten off threads securely.
5. Press each line of stitching before neatening the seam allowance.

PLAIN OR FLAT SEAM

1. Pin the two pieces of garment fabric together, right sides facing. Match all balance marks e.g. tailor tacks and notches.
2. Tack just outside the 1.5 cm fitting line.
3. Machine along fitting line from one edge of the fabric to the other edge. Bring machining out to edge of garment seam.

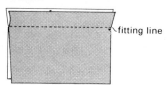

fitting line

4. Remove tacking and press seam open along line of machine stitching.

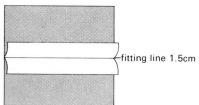

fitting line 1.5cm

SEAMS

Types	Suitable uses
1. Plain or flat seam	Medium or heavy-weight fabrics. Jackets, coats, skirts.
	Suitable also for knitted or jersey fabrics using a slight zig-zag stitch.
2. French seam	Fine or light-weight fabrics e.g. cotton lawn, silk, muslin. Blouses, lingerie, underwear, children's clothes.
3. Felled seams/ Self-finished seams (a) run and fell seam (b) machine fell seam	Medium weight fabrics e.g. cotton, poplin, denim. Shirts, sportswear, jeans, pyjamas and beachwraps.
4. Decorative seams (a) lapped seam (b) slot or Chanel seam (c) welt seam	Yokes and seams for a decorative finish on blouses, dresses and jeans. Skirts and on the centre back line of dresses and jackets. Medium or heavy weight fabric. Casual shirts, jackets, suits, coats, shirt-dresses and jeans.

METHODS OF NEATENING SEAM ALLOWANCE

TYPES	DIAGRAM	METHOD
1. Edge-machining		Suitable for light and medium weight cottons, silk and light weight fine wool. On raw edges of seam allowance turn under a small fold. Tack and machine along the folded edges.
2. Zig-zag machining		Used on all fabrics except very fine ones e.g. organdie. Consult machine instruction handbook. Test the selected zig-zag stitch on a piece of garment fabric. Machine seam allowance 2 mm from edge. Trim edges evenly. Zig-zag along the raw edge.
3. Pinking		Suitable for non-fraying fabrics e.g. flannel. Using a pinking shears, trim all seam allowances evenly.
4. Overcasting		Worked on fabrics that do not fray easily. Prepare seam allowance by trimming them to a suitable width. Work a row of machine stitching 3 mm in from raw edge to strengthen seam allowance. Overcast edges separately, working from left to right. Fasten off thread securely.
5. Blanket stitching		Suitable for heavyweight fabrics that fray easily e.g. tweed, wool. Also worked on armhold and pocket seams. Work blanket-stitching from left to right. Fasten off threads securely.

6. Binding
  (i) Bias
  (ii) Paris
		Binding is used on fabrics that fray easily.
		<center>BIAS</center>(a) Press open one fold of bias binding.
		(b) Pin and tack right sides of bias binding to right side of seam allowance, raw edges together.
		(c) Machine along crease line.
		(d) Remove tacking and turn bias binding to wrong side of seam.
		(e) Pin, tack and hem to row of machining.
		(f) Remove tacking and press.
		
		<center>PARIS</center>(a) Press the binding lengthwise in two, having upper side 3 mm wider than lower side.
		(b) Place wider side of binding underneath the seam allowance with narrow side on top. The raw edge is now encased by binding.
		(c) Pin and tack binding to seam allowance.
		(d) Machine near edge of binding through to binding on underside of seam allowance.

5. Use a suitable method of neatening the seam allowance for fabric being used.

LAYER, SNIP AND NOTCH

Unusual seams must be trimmed after machining to remove excess seam allowance, so that when pressed they lie flat. Examples of special seam situations include:
- (a) crossed seams,
- (b) curved seams,
- (c) corners and points.

(a) *Crossed Seams*

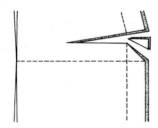

Crossing seams

1. Pin, tack and machine two seams. Remove tacking and press open.
2. With right sides together pin seams, matching intersecting point of seams carefully.
3. Tack and machine. Remove tacking, trim corners diagonally. Press seams open.

(b) *Curved seams*

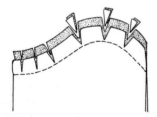

Layering seams

1. Layer turnings of seam by 5 mm and 10 mm. This prevents ridges.
2. On outward curves cut V-shaped notches from the seam allowance at 13 mm intervals.
3. On inward curves snip into the seam allowance at 5 mm intervals.
   Note: Do not cut past the row of machining.

(c) *Corners and points*
1. Grade or layer seam allowance.
2. On inward corners secure corner with a second row of machining 1 mm inside seam line. Snip into stitching.
3. On outward corner trim point to within 1.5 mm of corner.

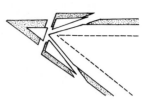

Corners and points

FRENCH SEAM

1. With wrong sides facing, notches and balance marks matching, pin garment pieces together along seam fitting line.
2. Tack along seam fitting line. Remove all pins.

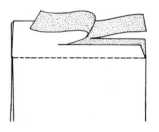

3. Depending on desired width of finished seam, machine 5 mm outside fitting line in seam allowance.

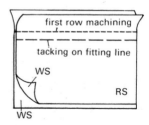

4. Fasten off threads securely. Remove tacking and trim to within 3 mm of machining. Press seam allowance open.

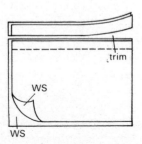

288

5. With right sides facing crease along first row of machining. Press.

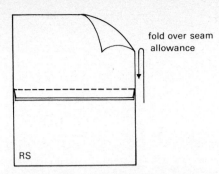

fold over seam allowance

RS

6. Pin and tack along fitting line enclosing raw edges of seam allowance.
7. Machine on fitting line. Remove tacking. Press seam towards back of garment.

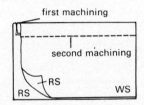

first machining

second machining

RS

RS   WS

FELLED OR SELF-FINISHED SEAMS

RUN AND FELL SEAM

1. Pin both pieces of garment fabric along fitting line with right sides facing. Match balance marks and notches.
2. Tack near fitting line and remove pins.
3. Work a row of running stitch on fitting line. Remove tacking.

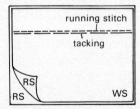

(a)

running stitch

tacking

RS

RS   WS

4. Trim lower seam allowance to 5 mm and upper seam allowance to 10 mm.

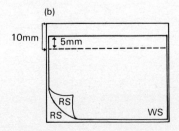

(b)

10mm   5mm

RS

RS   WS

5. Press seam open.
6. Turn under 4 mm on edge of upper seam allowance and place over lower seam allowance.
7. Pin and tack folded edge to garment.
8. Hem folded edge to running stitches.

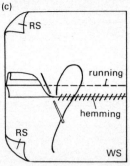

(c)

RS

running

hemming

RS

WS

9. Fasten off threads securely. Remove tacking. Press seam.

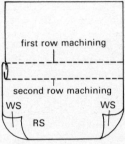

first row machining

second row machining

WS   WS

RS

MACHINE FELLED SEAM

This seam is prepared, worked and finished in the same way as the Run and Fell seam. Instead two rows of machining replace the rows of running and hemming. Work from right side of garment.

DECORATIVE SEAMS

LAPPED SEAM

1. Work out which garment piece is to be the underlay and which the overlay. Overlay pieces are usually flat. Underlay pieces are often fuller e.g. gathered.
2. Turn under the seam allowance of overlay along the fitting line, to wrong side.
3. Press folded edge.

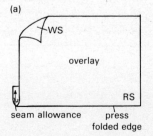

(a)

WS

overlay

RS

seam allowance   press folded edge

4. Working from right side of garment, pin folded edge of overlay on fitting line of underlay.
5. Tack close to folded edge. Remove pins.
6. Machine through all layers of fabric, 2 mm from folded edge.

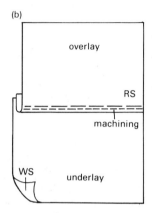
(b)

7. Remove tacking and press. Trim and neaten raw edges of seam allowance using a suitable seam finish.

SLOT OR CHANEL SEAM

1. Tack a plain or flat seam along fitting line.

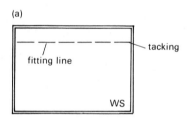
(a)

2. Press seam open.

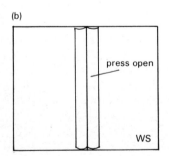
(b)

3. Cut a strip of fabric the length of the seam and 3 cm wide i.e. slightly wider than seam allowance.
4. Mark centre line of underlay fabric with a row of tacking.

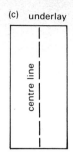
(c) underlay

5. Place centre line of underlay on seamline of garment from wrong side. Tack in position.

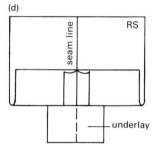
(d)

6. From right side of garment, machine 4 mm on each side of seamline, Remove all tacking and neaten raw edges.

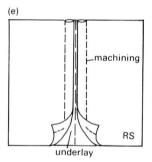
(e)

7. Press seams from wrong side of garment.

WELT SEAM

1. Tack and machine a plain seam on fitting line. Remove tacking.

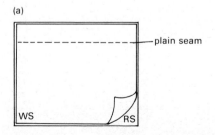
(a)

2. Press seam allowances towards one side.
3. Trim lower seam allowance i.e. the underseam, to 6 mm.

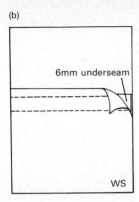

6mm underseam

WS

4. From right side of garment work a row of machining 6 mm from seamline enclosing the trimmed seam allowance.

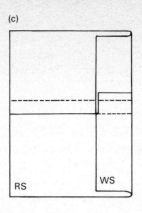

(c)

RS   WS

DOUBLE WELT SEAM

Complete 1-4 as for welt seam.
5. Machine on right side of garment 2 mm from seam-line. Two rows of machining are visible from right and wrong sides of garment.

34.
Fitting and Shaping Garments

Garments should be fitted several times while they are being made. Major alterations or adjustments are always made on the paper pattern before laying them out on the fabric. Fitting allows minor alterations to be made during assembly of each garment piece. Three fittings are necessary: (a) First (b) Second (c) Final.

Fitting garments

FIRST FITTING

Tack darts, shoulder, side and waist seams along fitting lines. Try on right side out over undergarments you intend wearing with the garment. Pin openings e.g. zip, front, cuff. Stand correctly and take a look in a mirror. Walk around, sit down, move your arms and bend. The garment should allow comfortable movement and adequate ease. Check that the garment looks in proportion. Are all closures and darts in their correct position? Distribute all alterations evenly. Alterations may be done from wrong side. Remove garment and tack along new fitting lines. Try on again and check the alterations.

SECOND FITTING

Machine and press darts and seams. Attach collar and facing. Tack sleeves into armholes. Try on the garment again. Check that seams are straight, sleeves and closings are in their correct position. Make any necessary alterations. Take off the garment, tack and check new alterations.

FINAL FITTING

When garment is completed except for hem, try it on to mark hem length. Follow instructions given on marking of hem on page 372. Pin up hem. Stand straight on a stool. Get a friend to check that the hem edge is even i.e. the hem edge should be parallel to the floor. Remove garment, complete hem and give a final pressing.

INTRODUCTION TO SHAPING GARMENTS

Unnecessary fullness in garments is avoided by the use of (a) darts, (b) gathers, (c) tucks and (d) pleats. The amount of fullness depends on the style of the garment and on the figure. By controlling fullness, the garment will fit and shape the figure, allowing sufficient room for movement. Areas of the garment requiring shaping include bust, sleeves, shoulders, waist, neckline and wrist.

DARTS

Darts are used to arrange the fullness of garments at bust, shoulder, elbow and waist. They fit the curving shape of your body. Darts give a smooth and well-fitted appearance to garments. They form an important part of sewing basics as they are usually the first sewing detail of most garments.

Special Points

1. Darts point or taper to the fullest part of the figure e.g. bust.
2. Mark darts carefully before tacking.
3. Adjust length and position of darts before machining.
4. Match darts on right and left sides of garments e.g. on bodice, skirt and trousers. They should be exactly of the same length and in the same position.

TYPES OF DARTS

1. Standard single pointed dart.
   Used at shoulder, waist and bust lines.

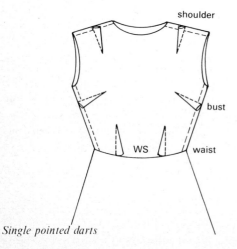

Single pointed darts

2. Double pointed darts.
   Used on jackets, dresses, blouses and shirts.

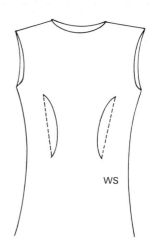

Double pointed darts

3. Curved or french dart.
   Used on jackets and A-line dresses to shape the waistline.

Curved or French dart

CONSTRUCTION OF DARTS

STANDARD SINGLE POINTED DART

Preparation
1. Mark position of dart with tailor tacking or tailor's chalk.
2. Matching tailor tacking fold the fabric right sides together on a straight line.
3. Insert pins at matching tailor's tacks to hold in position. The dart is wide at one end and tapers to a point.
4. Tack from point to wide end at edge of fabric.
5. Fit on garment. Adjust length and position of darts if necessary.
6. Remove tailor tacking.

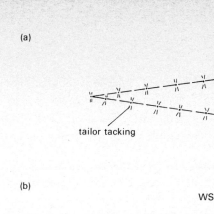

(a)

tailor tacking

(b)

RS
WS

tacking

Preparation of dart

Machining

1. Beginning at wide end of dart near edge, machine from edge to point. The last few stitches taper to nothing along folded edge.

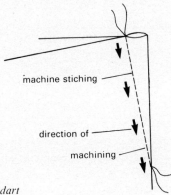

machine stiching

direction of

machining

Machining dart

Finishing

1. Fasten threads of darts securely with a square knot and a double backstitch.

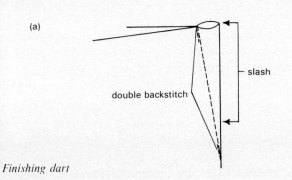

(a)

double backstitch

slash

Finishing dart

2. Remove tacking.
3. For deep darts and darts on heavy fabric slash centre fold of dart to within a few threads of the point.
4. Press open. Neaten raw edges using zig-zag, blanket stitching or overcasting.

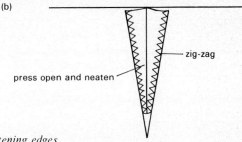

(b)

zig-zag

press open and neaten

Neatening edges

5. Place a pressing cloth or brown paper between garment and dart to prevent marks on right side of garment.
6. (a) Slashed darts are pressed flat.
   (b) Vertical darts e.g. shoulder, waistline are pressed towards centre back or front.
   (c) Horizontal darts e.g. bust are pressed downwards towards waist.

(b) DOUBLE POINTED DART

Marking

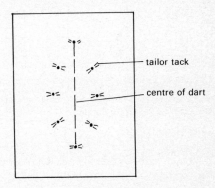

(a)

tailor tack

centre of dart

Marking dart

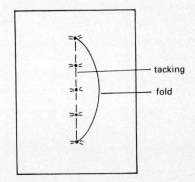

(b)

tacking

fold

Tacking dart

1. Mark the position of dart with tailor tacking.
2. With right sides together fold the dart matching tailor tacking.
3. Pin and tack in position. This tapers to a point at both ends. Remove tailor tacking.

Machining
1. Using tacking as a guide, machine from one point to the other taking care to keep the dart flat.

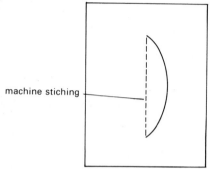

Machining dart

Finishing
1. Clip fold of dart at centre point on either sides of centre so that dart will lie flat.

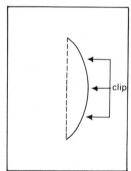

Clipping curved edge

2. Neaten raw edges using overcasting or blanket stitching.

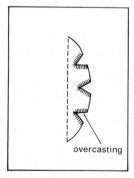

Neatening raw edges

3. Press towards centre front or back.

(c) CURVED OR FRENCH DART

Marking
1. Mark position of dart seam line using small tacking.
2. Reinforce dart with a line of machining just inside seam line.
   Note: This dart is slashed down its centre and has two curved edges. Because of this it cannot be folded in the same way as other darts.

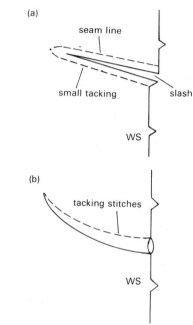

Preparing curved dart

3. With right sides and edges together pin dart along its seam line.
4. Tack and remove pins.

Machining
1. Machine from wide end to point following curved line of tacking carefully. Finish off threads securely.

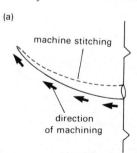

Machining dart

294

Finishing
1. Remove tacking. Press down.
2. If the dart does not curve easily and smoothly clip allowance.
3. Neaten raw edges using overcasting.

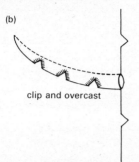

clip and overcast

Finishing dart

4. Press.

DART TUCK

A dart tuck is an inverted dart with the fullness inside the garment and the narrowest point at the edge. It is the combination of a dart and a tuck to give a released fullness for a soft appearance.

Method
1. Mark position carefully.

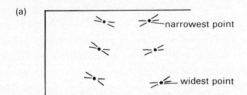

narrowest point

widest point

Marking dart tuck

2. Pin and tack.

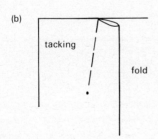

tacking

fold

Tacking dart tuck

3. Machine using line of tacking as a guide. Finish threads securely.
4. Remove tacking. Press fold line of dart. Never press the released fullness below machining.

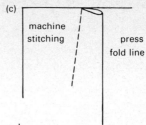

machine stitching

press fold line

Finishing dart tuck

GATHERS

Gathers are usually used to add softness and fullness to garments. The gathered fullness is eased into a narrow part of a garment.

gathers

ruffle

gathers

gathers

flounce/frill

Position of gathers on garments

1. across the shoulders on yokes of shirts, dresses, smocks and blouses,
2. cuffs of dresses and blouses,
3. around the waist of trousers, skirts and culottes,
4. necklines of dresses, blouses and shirts,
5. sleeves at sleeve head and cuff edge,
6. flounces, frills and ruffles at neck, hem edge and sleeve edges.

Gathering can be worked by hand or machine. Gathers are made by pulling a line of stitching so that the fabric is drawn up forming small folds. It is used on single soft fabric using two rows of gathering stitches.

295

GATHERING

Preparation

1. Follow pattern instructions on position of gathers.
2. Mark the beginning and end of two rows of stitching on fabric.

(a)

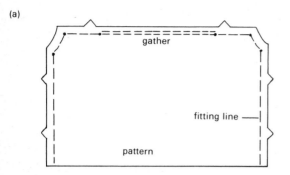

Example of pattern instructions

3. *Hand*
   Beginning with a double backstitch work a row of small running stitches 2 mm inside fitting line. A second row can then be worked nearer raw edge. Leave ends of thread free.
   Machine
   Lengthen machine stitch and loosen upper tension for a loose bobbin thread. Test stitch on a piece of garment fabric. Adjust according to thickness of fabric. Work two rows of machine gathering 2 mm and 4 mm from fitting line. Leave long threads for drawing up gathers from one or both ends.

(b)

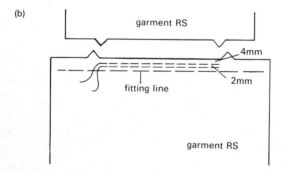

Gathering by hand or machine

4. Pull up gathering threads or bobbin threads, easing the gathers until they fit the flat piece to be joined to them right sides together.
5. Secure thread ends by winding them around a pin in a figure of eight.

(c)

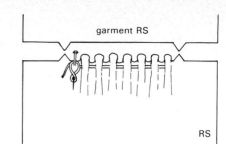

Drawing up gathers

6. Adjust and distribute gathers evenly. Pin each section carefully dividing gathers equally.
7. Tack on fitting line and remove pins.

(d)

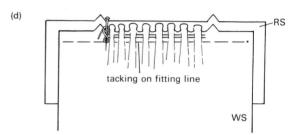

Easing gathers into position

SHIRRING

Shirring is several rows of gathering worked accurately for an exciting finish to garments. It is used at cuffs, neck and waist of garments and can be embroidered or smocked.

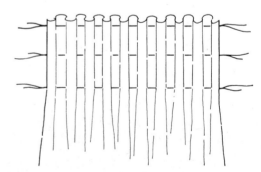

Shirring

ATTACHING GATHERS TO A YOKE

Preparation

1. Using pattern instructions work two rows of gathering between notches. Leave thread ends loose for drawing up fabric.

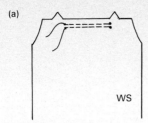

Working rows of gathering

2. Draw up gathering threads until this section fits the yoke.
3. With right sides and raw edges together place the gathered fabric over yoke. Match notches, fitting line and balance marks carefully.

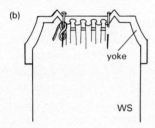

Easing gathers into position

4. Pin and tack in position.

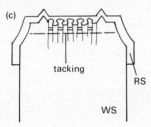

Tacking gathered fabric to yoke

Finishing
1. Machine along fitting line. Remove tacking.
2. Press the seam allowance towards the yoke.

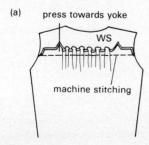

Machining and pressing seams

3. Neaten raw edges using bias binding or blanket stitching. Sometimes a facing is used to cover seam allowances e.g. in a shirt.

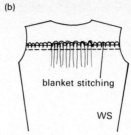

Neatening raw edges

TUCKS

Tucks are both functional and decorative. They resemble pleats and consist of fabric (on the straight grain) on the right side of a garment. Machining is worked along some or all of their length. Tuck widths vary depending on their function and style. Pin tucks are very narrow tucks frequently used on children's or babies' clothes and lingerie. Accuracy is important for an even finish. If they are not uniform the appearance of a garment is unattractive.

TYPES OF TUCKS

1. pin tucks
2. spaced tucks
3. blind tucks
4. dart tucks (see Darts)
5. corded tucks
6. crossed tucks.

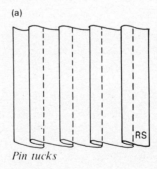

Pin tucks

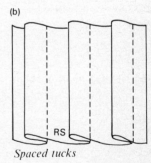

Spaced tucks

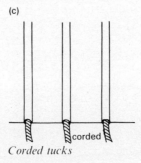

Corded tucks

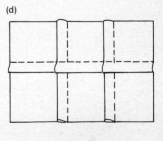

Crossed tucks

297

MAKING TUCKS

1. Each tuck will be of a stated width, e.g. ¼". Allow 2-3 times this width of fabric in order to make the tuck. Follow the pattern instructions carefully; patterns will include any allowance needed for tucks.
2. Mark tuck stitching and fold lines on fabric. This must be marked very accurately.

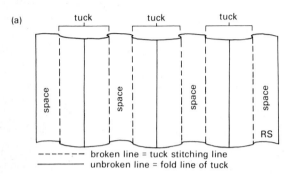

(a)

tuck   tuck   tuck

space   space   space   space

RS

-------- broken line = tuck stitching line
———— unbroken line = fold line of tuck

3. Working from left to right pin and tack tuck along its full length. Do not tack tuck to garment, tack through folded fabric.
4. Continue this for each tuck until all have been tacked.

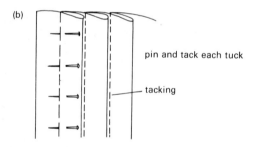

(b)

pin and tack each tuck

tacking

Machining and Finishing
1. Machine each tuck carefully along the side that will be visible.

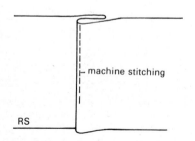

machine stitching

RS

2. Remove tacking.
3. Press each tuck fold separately. Press back and front of tucks using a damp pressing cloth.

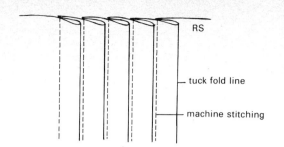

RS

tuck fold line

machine stitching

PLEATS

Pleats are decorative folds of fabric providing fullness and extra width in skirts, shirts, back of bodice and jackets. They are also used as a fashion feature on pockets. For a tailored finish, pleats are pressed firmly until the edge is crisp and sharp. Unpressed pleats provide a softer style.

Fabrics used must drape well, e.g. wool, wool blends, silks, cotton blends and most synthetics. Light synthetic jersey does not pleat successfully.

TYPES OF PLEATS

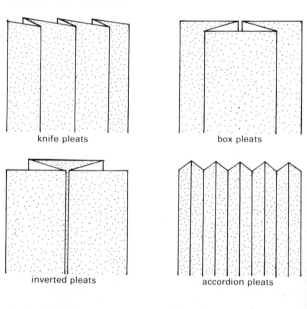

knife pleats   box pleats

inverted pleats   accordion pleats

1. Knife pleats
2. Inverted pleats
3. Box pleats
4. Accordion or sunray pleats
5. Kick pleats.

Knife pleats and accordian pleats can be pleated professionally for a permanent pleat finish. All pleats must be marked accurately for machining if an even finish is to be achieved. Pleats are often edge-stitched or top-stitched along fold-line on outside or inside to reduce strain on point of release. They also add a decorative touch to the garment. The width of pleats depends on the type and number of pleats. When calculating the amount of fabric required for each pleat, a good guideline is three times the finished pleat width.

General Guidelines
1. Always work on a large flat surface.
2. Consider turning up and tacking hem in position if skirt has a lot of pleats.

Marking All Pleat Lines
1. Carefully mark position of pleat lines on fabric. Different colours of thread may be used to show fold line and pleat stitching lines.
2. Markings can be transferred to right or wrong sides. Follow pattern instructions.
3. Bring fold line to broken lines in the direction of pattern arrows.
4. Pin and tack each pleat along fold line from hem edge upwards.

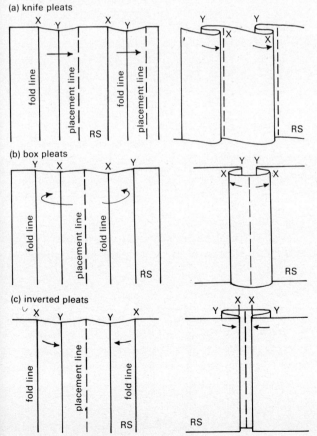

Marking and folding pleats

5. Tack zip and waistband or bodice of dress to pleats.
6. Fit on garment. Make any necessary alterations.

Machining
1. Follow pattern instructions for machining of all pleats.
2. Machine and remove tacking.

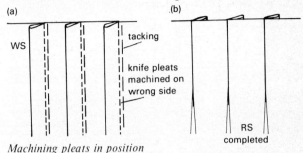

Machining pleats in position

3. Press carefully on right and wrong side.
4. Complete garment.

Hem Finish
1. Mark position of hem with tailor tacking. On pleats mark through all layers. Tailor tacking can be separated later.

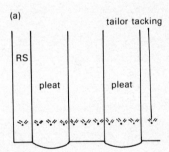

Marking hemline

2. Snip some machine stitching holding pleat together.
3. Trim away all seam allowance to depth of finished hem. Press seams open.

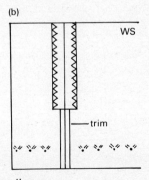

Trimming seam allowance

4. Keep hem as deep as possible for added weight.
5. Turn up a hem suited to fabric being used. Finish carefully.

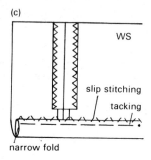

Completing hem

6. Refold and tack pleats into their original place.

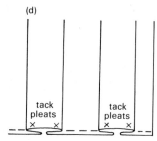

Refolding pleats

7. Press and remove tacking.

Pleat Finishes

Arrowheads or decorative stitching can be used to finish pleats at points of strain. Edge machining or top stitching are usually added to fold on the right sides of pleats when they have been stitched and pressed. It must be worked before a waistband or bodice is attached.

Arrowhead

1. Mark position of arrowhead triangle on right side of garment.

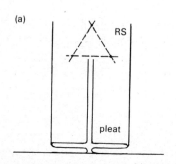

2. Secure buttonhole twist with a small backstitch at point X.
3. Insert needle at point Y and bring out at point Z.
4. Insert needle at point X and repeat the process until the triangle is filled. Keep stitches straight and close together but not overlapping.

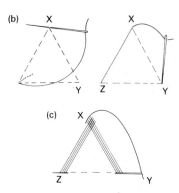

5. Bring thread to wrong side of garment and fasten off with a double backstitch.

Topstitching

On right side of garment machine from waist to release point; slope the stitching towards folded edge near pleat release point.

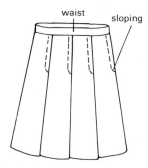

Edge-stitching

Edge-stitch pleat on right side of garment just on fold line of pleat to release point and from release point to hem.

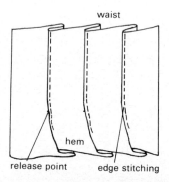

35.
Pressing

To achieve a professional finish when making garments, careful pressing is necessary. Press each seam or dart before it is joined to another garment piece. A garment insufficiently pressed while it is being made will not be saved by a final pressing when completed.

Pressing is not ironing. Ironing refers to the long sweeping movements back and forth over a garment. Pressing is the application of pressure in short sharp movements. The iron is placed on the fabric for a few seconds, lifted and replaced again.

PRESSING EQUIPMENT

1. *Iron* — An iron with combination characteristics of a dry and steam iron is useful. A dry iron with a damp cloth is quite adequate for most pressing situations.

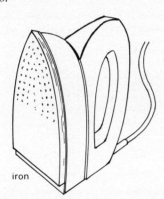

iron

2. *Ironing Board* — The ironing board should be level and adjustable to different heights. A well-padded surface with removable easy care cover is desirable. Silicone-treated covers to prevent scorching are available. A removable padded surface e.g. white under-blanket and loose cotton cover, can be used in place of an ironing board.

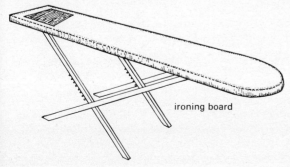

ironing board

3. *Sleeve board* — A sleeve board is like a miniature ironing board. It is useful for pressing small areas that will not fit over the end of an ironing board. e.g. sleeves, cuffs and necklines.

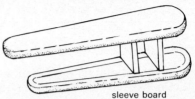

sleeve board

4. *Seam roll* — Designed for pressing seams. It is a long rounded and firmly packed cushion. Because of its rounded shape, only the seam is pressed. No ridges or creases form on the right side of the garment. A substitute for a seam roll is a rolled up towel.

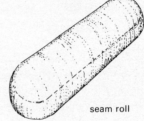

seam roll

5. *Tailor's ham* — This is a tightly stuffed cushion oblong and rounded in shape. It is useful for pressing shaped areas of a garment e.g. darts, tucks, sleeve heads.

tailor's ham

6. *Pressing pad* — it consists of five or six layers of fabric joined together to form an ideal soft surface for pressing embroidery, buttonholes etc.

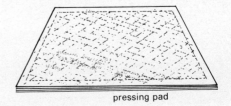

pressing pad

7. *Needleboard* — Suitable for pressing pile fabrics e.g. velvet. It is made of a bed of fine wires attached to a flat canvas surface and prevents the pile being flattened during pressing.

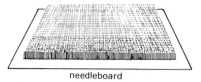
needleboard

8. *Clothes brush* — Useful for brushing away tailor's chalk before pressing and bringing up the surface after pressing.

clothes brush

9. *Pressing cloths* — Muslin and thinker cottons are suitable as pressing cloths. Use muslin for fine fabrics and thicker cottons for heavier fabrics. A woollen press cloth should be used on woollen fabrics.

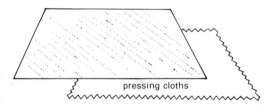
pressing cloths

10. *Coat hangers* — Wooden hangers with bars should be used for hanging pressed pieces while they cool.

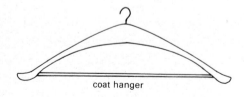
coat hanger

11. *Brown paper* — To avoid ridges appearing on the right side of garment place strips of brown paper under darts, seams, pleats and upper hem edges.

GENERAL RULES FOR PRESSING

1. Remove pins, tailor tacks and tacking stitches from garment. Press lightly if some tacking has to remain in garment, remove tacking and press again.
2. Test a spare piece of the garment fabric to determine the most suitable heat setting or temperature to use. Adjust the temperature as required.
3. Press from the wrong side of the garment. If you must press on the right side, use a pressing cloth between the fabric and the iron.
4. Press with the grain of fabric. Do not stretch garment edges or curves. Use the pointed front of the iron.
5. Wring out the pressing cloth fully until only a little moisture remains in it. Never use a wet pressing cloth.
6. Arrange the section to be pressed. Apply the iron to that section. Remove it and press again.
7. Press each stage after it has been machined e.g.

CHART FOR PRESSING

FABRIC	IRON SETTING
1. *Linen:* (a) lightweight (b) heavyweight	Medium to hot
2. *Cotton:* (a) lightweight (b) heavyweight	Warm to medium
3. *Wool:* (a) lightweight ((b) heavyweight	Warm
4. *Rayon:*	Cool to warm
5. *Man-made fabrics:*	Cool
6. *Silk:*	Cool to low
7. *Velvet and pile fabrics:*	Steam rather than press
8. *Stretch fabrics:*	Cool to warm
9. *Knitted fabrics:*	Cool
10. *Lace:*	Depends on fabric type
11. *Elastomeric* e.g. lycra	No pressing
12. *Fur fabrics:*	Never press natural fur Low to warm heat for synthetic fur

dart, seam, before attaching it to another garment piece. *Example:* Always press seams before they are crossed with other seams.

8. Do not leave an imprint of the iron on the fabric. Re-press any creases or marks while the fabric is damp and warm.

9. To prevent seam allowances, darts, pleats or tucks "marking" the right side of the garment use brown paper under their folds.

10. Allow the garment to dry fully after pressing.

11. Use the correct pressing equipment for the area being pressed e.g. seam roll for seam: tailor's ham for darts and curved seams.

12. Know the fabric you are pressing i.e. fibre content, texture, thickness and weight.

13. Do not over-press. When the garment is completed give a final pressing.

PRESSING SEQUENCE

(a) Darts

Use a tailor's ham with its rounded or curved surface when pressing darts. Press darts to one side. Do not allow the top of the iron to go beyond the point of dart. Press from the wider end to the point. Vertical darts are pressed towards the centre of the garment: horizontal darts downwards: slashed darts are pressed open and neatened.

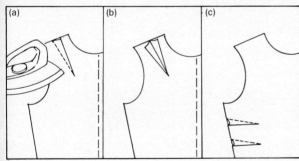

Darts

(b) Seams

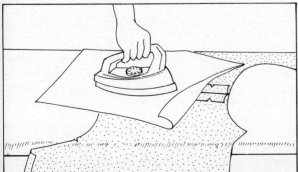

Straight seams

As soon as seams are stitched they should be pressed along the stitching line. Press in the same direction as the seam was sewn. Place strips of brown paper between the seam allowance and garment to prevent ridges forming on the right side. A seam roll will help to give a good finish to flat seams. A tailor's ham is a useful item if seams are curved. Clip curved seam allowances and press again.

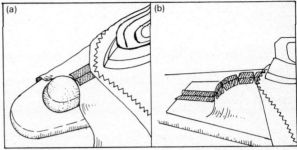

Curved seams

(c) Tucks

Press tucks to the stitching line. Use strips of brown paper under folds to prevent marking the right side. Press tucks from underneath side of folded edge.

(d) Pleats

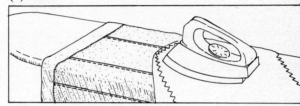

Pleats

Remove pins. Tack. Do not remove tacking. Arrange the pleats carefully on ironing board. Place strips of brown paper under the folds.

Press lightly at first, using a damp pressing cloth between the pleats and the iron. Check that the pleats are hanging correctly. Set the creases of the pleats fully. Do not press tacking stitches. Remove tacking carefully. Remove the garment from the ironing board. Place wrong side down. Press lightly from right side of garment. Do not remove the garment from the ironing board until the fabric is completely dry.

(e) Gathers

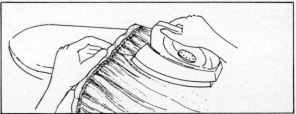

Gathers

Hold gathers with your left hand. Press from the ungathered part of garment into gathers using the front of the iron. Work from the wrong side of the garment. Gathered seam allowance e.g. gathers into a yoke, should be pressed flat before attaching to another garment piece.

(f) Sleeves

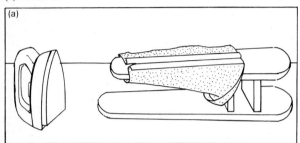

Underarm seam

(a) *Underarm seam*

Place the sleeve over a sleeve board with wrong side out. Press underarm seam flat using strips of brown paper under seam allowances and a pressing cloth over them. Turn right side out and press again.

(b) *Sleeve head seam*

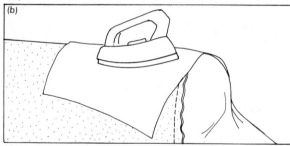

Sleeve head seam

Press the sleeve head seam towards the armhole. Do not press over the row of machining or flatten the sleeve head. Move the sleeve around the sleeve board until the pressing has been completed.

(g) Hems

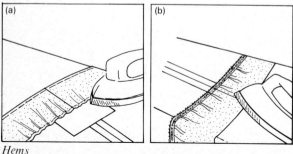

Hems

Place a wide strip of brown paper between the garment and hem turnings. Do not press over the tacking stitches that hold folded edge of hem in position.

Press upper hem edge gently or ridges will appear on the right side. Remove the strip of brown paper. When the hem has been stitched remove tacking and press again. For a well defined hem edge press firmly.

(h) Zips, hooks and eyes

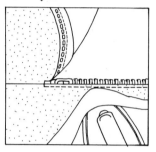

Zips

Open zip and lay garment flat, right side facing the ironing board. Using a pressing cloth work the iron from garment towards stitching of zip. Avoid placing the iron over the zipper teeth or hooks and eyes. Many fastenings are made of a plastic type material which would melt under the iron. If pressing from the right side of the garment place brown paper between fabric and zip edges.

(i) Seams at finished edges

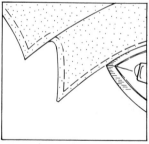

Seam edge of collar

Examples of these include collars, cuffs and facings etc. On these parts of the garment, the seam line is pushed 1 mm towards the wrong side of the garment with the tip of the iron. Press from the seam line towards the garment on the wrong side. If pressed from the right side ridges will result.

FINAL PRESSING FOR THAT PROFESSIONAL FINISH

A final pressing of the finished garment will touch

up all areas of the garment which have been pressed at each stage of construction. This will not make up for careless pressing done during construction. Press from the wrong side of the garment
(a) collar, sleeves and cuffs
(b) bodice, waist seam
(c) skirt, hem
(d) belts, trims, decorative edges.

Shrinking Fullness

Woollen fabrics tend to be bulky at hems and sleeve heads. They can be pressed to shrink excess fullness. Work from wrong side of garment. Cover the excess fullness with a damp pressing cloth. Press lightly with a warm iron for a few seconds. Lift the iron and re-press until shrinkage is completed. Finally press using a dry pressing cloth.

Over-pressing

Over-pressing often results in shine marks, ridges or lines. To remove shine marks cover the area with a damp pressing cloth. Hold a hot iron 1.5 cm away from cloth until it begins to steam. Never allow the iron to touch the steaming pressing cloth. Remove the pressing cloth. Brush the area with a clothes brush. In the case of ridges or lines, re-press the area while the fabric is damp from the steaming pressing cloth. Dry thoroughly.

36.
Underlining and Lining

Underlining is a layer of fabric attached to the garment fabric before the seams are machined. Place between the garment fabric and the lining. It
(a) adds body to garment,
(b) helps support garment pieces and so keeps their shape,
(c) lessens creasing and clinging,
(d) reduces seating and static electricity,
(e) makes machining and pressing easier, especially if using a very fine fabric,
(f) provides a base to which hems etc. may be sewn.

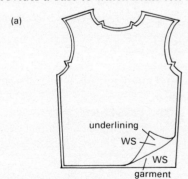

(a)

underlining
WS
WS
garment

CHOOSING UNDERLINING

1. Check that underlining and garment fabric will drape well together.
2. Interfacing should never be crisper than the garment fabric.
3. Use different weight underlining to achieve different effects e.g. soft, crisp, firm.

4. Choose an underlining which corresponds to cleaning qualities of garment fabric e.g. washable, dry cleanable.

SUITABLE UNDERLINING

Organdie, organza, taffeta, jap silk, rayon, non-woven polyester, fine cotton, tricel.

USING UNDERLINING

(sometimes referred to as "mounting" underlining).
1. Cut out underlining using garment pattern pieces. Do not include collar, cuff, pocket, double yoke or belts.
2. Transfer pattern markings e.g. darts, tailor tacks, to underlining only. Remove pattern pieces.
3. Pin wrong side of underlining to wrong side of garment fabric.
4. Tack pieces together on foldline of darts, centre front, centre back and outside fitting line.

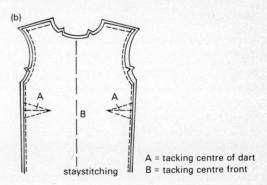

(b)

A
A
B

staystitching

A = tacking centre of dart
B = tacking centre front

5. Staystitch underlining and garment fabric together 10-13 mm from edge.
6. Make up garment in the usual way taking extra care trimming, layering, neatening and pressing.
7. Remove tacking and press as you complete each stage of construction.

LINING

Lining is the last step in the making of a well-finished garment. A lining is an exact replica of the garment which is attached to it at various places e.g. skirt at waist, jacket at edges.

ADVANTAGES OF LINING GARMENTS

1. Gives body and helps them drape or hang well. Prevents garment stretching.
2. Conceals all raw edges and so prevents fraying.
3. Reduces static electricity and creasing.

CHOOSING LINING

1. Choose lining fabric after purchasing garment fabric.
2. A lining should not be heavier than the garment fabric.
3. Choose lining fabrics which complement the weight, texture and style of garment.

DIFFERENT LININGS AND THEIR USES

Lining fabric	Weight	Uses
cotton lawn	light	lining for light weight cottons, blends, wools, tweeds and viscose
taffeta	medium	medium to heavy weight wools
silk — all forms e.g. china silk, crepe and satin	light to heavy	fine fabrics e.g. silk to heavy weight fabrics in coats, jackets
polyester, acetate, rayon	light to medium to heavy	silk, man-made fibres
nylon jersey	light	jersey fabrics and most fabrics

4. Lining fabrics should match washing and dry cleaning qualities of garment.
5. Choose a colour which matches colour of garment.

CUTTING OUT LININGS

1. Make up garment following instructions given with pattern to lining stage.
2. Place pattern lining pieces on folded lining fabric. Cut out and tailor tack. Separate garment lining pieces.
3. Check pattern lining pieces against garment.
4. When lining a coat or jacket allow at least 1 cm pleat at centre back i.e. place centre back 1-3 cm away from fold.

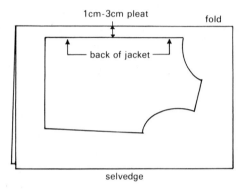

5. When back piece is cut out, tack along centre fold to keep pleat in position.
6. Remove pattern from lining fabric. Press back pleat to one side.
7. Make up as for garment.

LINING A SKIRT

1. Follow instructions given for cutting out lining.
2. Make skirt and insert zip. Do not attach waistband or turn up hem.
3. Make up lining. Press seams open.
4. With wrong sides facing place lining over skirt.

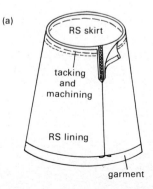

Match seams, notches, centre back, centre front and darts. Tack together at waist edge.

5. At zip, turn seam allowance of lining to wrong side. Slip-stitch to zip tape.
6. Machine along fitting line at waist.
7. Pin, tack and machine waistband to skirt. Complete by slip-stitching free-folded edge of waistband to stitching.
8. Mark up and complete skirt hem.
9. Turn under hem on lining to wrong side. Slip-stitch hem. Garment hemline should be 1.5-3 cm below lining hemline.
10. Work 1 cm bar tacks to attach lining hem to skirt seams.

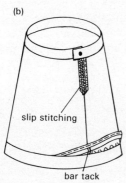

(b)

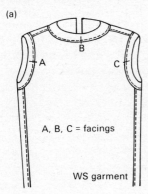

slip stitching

bar tack

Note: A separate full lining (as above) or a half lining may be used for a skirt.

LINING A DRESS

1. Follow instructions given for cutting out lining.
2. Tack together and machine seams. Press.
3. Make up garment to lining stage.

(a)

B

A   C

A, B, C = facings

WS garment

Garment completed to lining stage

4. If sleeves are not to be lined, neaten armholes carefully.
5. With wrong sides together, pin lining to garment at shoulder and side seams, centre front and centre back.
6. Diagonally tack round armholes, neck and shoulder seams.
7. Turn in neck edge and armhole of lining to facings. Snip curved edges. Tack to garment facings.
8. Roll back lining. Join garment seams to lining seams with running stitches (4 cm below armhole to 6-8 cm above hemline).

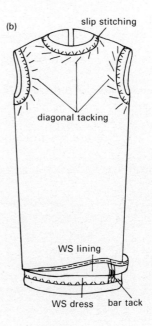

(b)   slip stitching

diagonal tacking

WS lining

WS dress   bar tack

Attaching lining to garment

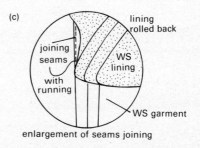

(c)   lining rolled back

joining seams

WS lining

with running

WS garment

enlargement of seams joining

Attaching lining to garment

9. Slip-stitch lining to garment facings at neck edge and armholes. Remove diagonal tacking.
10. Turn up garment hem and lining hem. Attach lining hem to garment at seams with bar tacks.
11. Remove all tacking and press.

LINING A SLEEVE

1. Finish lining main part of garment.

2. Make up sleeve and lining separately. Press seams open.
3. Slip linings over sleeves, wrong sides together.

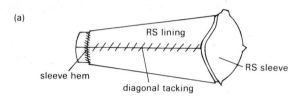

(a)

RS lining

RS sleeve

sleeve hem

diagonal tacking

4. Pin at underarm seams and around armhole. Tack diagonally along seams and armhole, shaping lining as you work.
5. Fit on garment to check that there are no wrinkles. Both sleeve and lining must hang correctly. Attach sleeve to garment.
6. Slip-stitch or hem sleeve lining to bodice lining at armhole.
7. Turn up lining at hem and slip-stitch to sleeve hem.

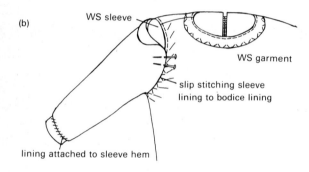

(b)

WS sleeve

WS garment

slip stitching sleeve
lining to bodice lining

lining attached to sleeve hem

Inserting sleeve into garment

LINING AND ZIPS

1. Cut lining to end of zip opening.

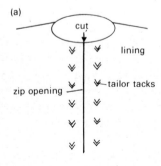

(a)

cut

lining

zip opening

tailor tacks

Marking zip opening

2. Snip out into corners of seam allowance.

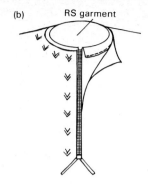

(b)

RS garment

3. Fold under turnings of lining, down sides and across end of zip.
4. Tack in position to zip tape.
5. Hem or slip-stitch lining to zip tape.
6. Remove tacking and press carefully.

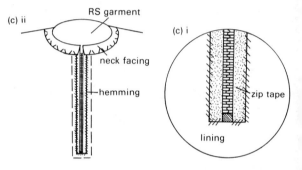

(c) ii

RS garment

neck facing

hemming

(c) i

zip tape

lining

LINING A JACKET

1. Cut out lining following pattern instructions carefully. Allow an extra 1–3 cm at centre back for pleat.
2. Tack darts and seams. Adjust if necessary following garment adjustments. Machine and press seams open.
3. Stitch pleat on wrong side of lining for 5-6 cm.
4. Snip sleeve armhole seam at notches. Do not cut machining. Press seam open between notches.
5. Fold under seam allowance on front, neck and hem

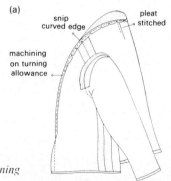

(a)

snip
curved edge

pleat
stitched

machining
on turning
allowance

Preparing lining

edges, (lower hem and seam hem), to wrong side. Notch or clip turnings to make them lie flat.

(b)

Attaching lining to jacket

6. Pin lining to garment working from centre back. Sew seam allowances together using running stitches, 5 cm below armhole to 15 cm above lower edge.
7. Slip garment sleeves into lining sleeves. Pin at shoulder seams and underarm seams. Turn up lining sleeve hem and tack in place.
8. Tack turned-in edge of lining to jacket facings at front and neck edges. Fit on to check there are no wrinkles in garment or lining.
9. Turn up lining hem. Pin lining to garment, 10-15 cm above hem edge. Keep pins 5 cm apart.
10. Just below pin line, make a 5-10 mm tuck across garment lining.
11. Fold under 5 mm on raw edge and pin to garment hem. Tack lining hem to garment hem.

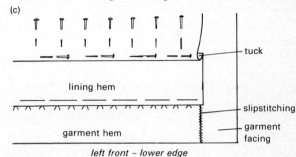

(c)

tuck

lining hem

slipstitching

garment hem

garment facing

left front – lower edge

Neatening lining hem

12. Slip-stitch hem in place. Remove pins. Lining folds gently over slip-stitched hem and allows for ease of movement during wear.
13. Slip-stitch lining to sleeve hem and to front and neck facings.

37.
Interfacing

INTRODUCTION

Interfacing is applied to the wrong side of the fabric and is then covered by a facing or it may be applied to the wrong side of the facing. It strengthens and rein-forces shaped areas of garments e.g. collars, cuffs, necklines, belts, pockets and waistbands. Interfacing prevents a garment stretching and helps to maintain its shape. A crispness is added to cuffs, collars and all interfaced areas.

TYPES OF INTERFACING

1. *Non-woven*

This is a combination of synthetic fibres bonded or fused together. As there is no selvedge, pattern pieces may be laid and cut in any direction. Non-woven inter-facings are available in three forms; lightweight, medium and heavyweight. These are washable and dry-cleanable. (*Examples:* Vilene, Lantor). They do not shrink or fray.

2. *Woven*

This type of interfacing, made up of cotton, synthetic or a blend of fibres, is woven with warp and weft threads. Like any woven fabric it has a selvedge or straight grain. These interfacings must be cut on the straight grain to correspond with the straight grain of

Interface – shaded areas, i.e. collar, cuffs and centre front opening

the garment. Choose a woven interfacing which suits the weight of fabric being used. It may be necessary to pre-shrink the interfacing before attaching it to the garment.

(Examples: canvas, muslin, calico, lawn, organdie, organza). Woven interfacings may be lightweight, medium and heavyweight.

Note: Woven and non-woven may be fusible or sew-in.

Fusible or iron-on interfacings

Non-woven and woven interfacings are available in this quick-to-use form. There is resin coating on the back of the interfacing and when pressure and heat are applied to the right side of the interfacing it fuses to the wrong side of the garment fabric. Sometimes steam or moisture are required when using fusible interfacings. Always follow manufacturers' instructions. Test first on a piece of the garment fabric.

Fusible webs

(a) Narrow fusible non-woven interfacing is available for use on hems of garments, curtains etc. (*Example:* Wundaweb).

(b) A band has been specially developed for use on waistbands, cuffs, pockets and pleats of all light and medium-weight garments. This band has slits on the centre line which allow a fold to be permanently ironed in. It gives a crisp edge and holds the garment's shape. (*Example:* Fold-a-Band).

Note: Sew-in and fusible knitted interfacings are available for use with soft knit fabrics.

SELECTING INTERFACING

1. Follow instructions given on pattern envelope.
2. Select an interfacing which suits the weight of fabric. An interfacing should not be heavier than garment fabric. For stretch fabrics choose a knitted or stretch interfacing. (*Example:* Supershade by Vilene).
3. Check that interfacing can be washed and/or dry-cleaned as for fabric.
4. Pre-shrink interfacing if necessary.
5. Make a list of interfacings you have found suitable as you learn to sew.

USING INTERFACING

1. Use pattern pieces as instructed to cut interfacing pieces.
2. (a) On non-woven interfacings — cut pattern pieces in any direction as there is no selvedge on interfacing.

INTERFACINGS TO SUIT DIFFERENT FABRICS

FABRICS	WEIGHT	INTERFACINGS
georgette	fine	very light iron-on, woven or self fabric
polyester/cotton	light	very light iron-on or sew-in woven
cotton, very fine wool, denim, jersey, fine tweeds and wools	a. medium b. medium stretch	a. light sew-in or iron-on (i) woven or (ii) non-woven b. medium sew-in non woven.
tweeds, wools, (suiting and coating)	heavy	heavy iron-on or sew-in canvas or non-woven

(b) On woven interfacing — place selvedge of pattern with selvedge of interfacing.

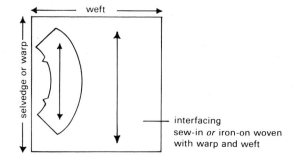

interfacing
sew-in *or* iron-on woven
with warp and weft

Cutting out woven interfacing

3. When joining interfacing do not form seams. Overlap seam allowances and herringbone or zig-zag stitch together.
4. Place wrong side of interfacing to wrong side of garment.
5. Iron-on or herringbone stitch in place. Machine fabric pieces together, catching interfacing along seamline. Trim and grade seam allowance. Trim interfacing to within 1 mm of stitching.

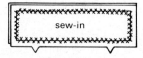

sew-in

Attaching sew-in interfacing

6. Apply interfacing to underside of collars and cuffs on wrong side of fabric.

See chapters on collars, cuffs, waistbands etc. for more specific information on attaching interfacings.

38.

Openings

INTRODUCTION

Garments need to have openings so that they can pass over the larger parts of the body e.g. head, bust, hands or hips. When closed they fit snugly around the neck, waist and wrist. Openings can be functional and decorative. There are several methods for finishing an opening. The type of fabric and the position of the opening will influence the method used. Consider the following chart before making a final choice.

OPENINGS AND SOME OF THEIR USES

OPENING	FABRIC	SUITABLE USES
A. continuous wrap or bound opening	fine, lightweight, medium-weight	(a) wrist openings — blouses, shirts, dresses (b) neck openings — children's clothes, lingerie (c) side openings — shorts, pyjamas, skirts
B. faced slit opening or slash opening	fine, lightweight, medium or heavy-weight	(a) neck openings — blouses, dresses, casual outfits (b) Cuff openings — shirts, blouses, dresses
C. shirt sleeve opening or placket opening	medium-weight	shirts, jackets, casual clothes — shorts, trousers, skirts

SPECIAL POINTS

1. Openings should always run in the same direction as the selvedge.
2. All openings must be strong and hardwearing.
3. Alterations to opening length are made before the opening is cut.
4. When making openings on sleeves, cut and work the openings at the same time.

CONTINUOUS WRAP OPENING OR BOUND OPENING

Preparation

1. Mark correct position and length of opening on garment.

2. Slash required length on straight grain of fabric, i.e. in the same direction as selvedge.

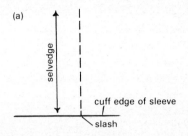

Preparing garment

Note: Openings are often part of a seam. Press seam open and snip turnings.

3. Cut a selvedge strip of garment fabric, twice the length of opening and 5 cm wide.

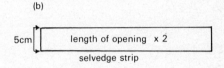

Cutting out binding strip

Application of binding

1. Open out slashed part of garment. Place binding strip to edge of opening with right sides together.
2. Pin and tack in position. The garment edge will drop below centre edge of binding strip.
3. Machine 8 mm from edges of opening. For extra strength at base of opening reinforce by machining again on top of first row nearer raw edge for 2.5 cm across the centre.

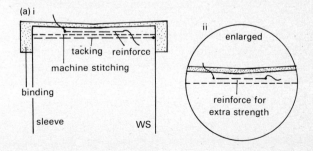

Applying binding strip

4. Remove tacking, press turnings and binding strip away from garment.

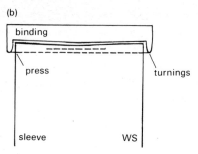

(b)

binding

press

turnings

sleeve   WS

Pressing turnings

Finishing

1. On outer edge of binding strip turn in 8 mm. Place folded edge on line of machining on wrong side of garment. Tack.

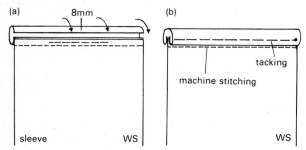

(a)   8mm   (b)

tacking

machine stitching

sleeve   WS   WS

Turning binding strip to WS

2. Hem folded edge to line of machining taking care that no stitches are visible on right side of garment.

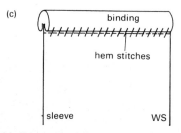

(c)   binding

hem stitches

sleeve   WS

Hemming binding strip in place

3. Remove tacking. Press opening so that binding strip is folded to the wrong side of garment.

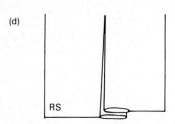

(d)

RS

Pressing opening

4. Strengthen base of opening with a row of machining or backstitch.

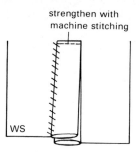

strengthen with machine stitching

WS

Final machining

FACED SLIT OPENING OR SLASH OPENING

Preparation

1. Mark position and length of opening on right side of garment with tailor's chalk or small tacking stitches, following the straight grain of fabric.

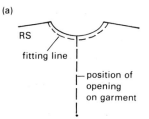

(a)

RS

fitting line

position of opening on garment

Preparation of garment

2. Following pattern instructions cut facing to required shape (e.g. for cuff or neckline) on the straight grain of fabric.
3. Mark position of opening on facing.
4. Turn under a narrow fold to wrong sides on outer edges of facing. Press.
5. Machine near folded edge.

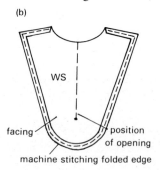

(b)

WS

facing

position of opening

machine stitching folded edge

Preparation of facing

Application of facing

1. Pin and tack centre of facing to centre of opening on garment with right sides facing.
2. Work a row of small tacking 7 mm on each side of

312

tacked centre line, decreasing to a point at bottom of opening. This forms a V shape.

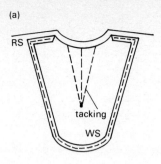

(a)

RS

tacking

WS

Tacking facing to garment

3. Machine just beside tacking line, turning at lower point and then continuing up the other side.
4. A second row of machining can be worked to reinforce narrow point of opening.
5. Remove tacking.

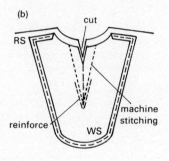

(b)

cut

RS

reinforce

machine stitching

WS

Machining facing to garment

6. Cut carefully down tacked centre line between rows of machining to within a few threads of stitching at base.

Finishing

1. Fold facing to wrong side. Tack around opening and press in position.
2. Machine close to open edges.
3. Remove tacking and press.

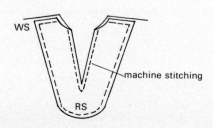

WS

machine stitching

RS

Facing turned to WS of garment

SHIRT SLEEVE OPENING OR PLACKET OPENING

Preparation

1. Measure and mark position of opening on garment with a row of machining. Secure any seamlines of opening with a row of machine stitching. Mark centre of opening.
2. Cut along this line and snip into corners. Do not cut beyond row of machining.

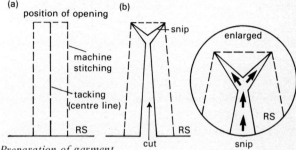

(a)
position of opening

(b)

snip

enlarged

machine stitching

tacking (centre line)

RS

RS

cut

RS

snip

Preparation of garment

3. Cut out underlap and overlap on straight grain of fabric. These form a binding for the raw edges. Follow pattern instructions for size of binding pieces.

Application of binding

1. On wrong side of opening nearer underarm seam, pin and tack right side of underlap binding fabric.
2. Machine along seamline. Remove tacking, trim and press seam.

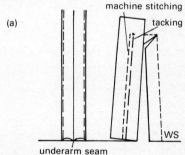

machine stitching

tacking

(a)

WS

underarm seam

Attaching underlap

3. Turn in 6 mm along free edge of underlap. Press.
4. Fold underlap over raw edge to row of machining. Pin and tack.

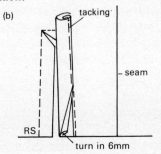

(b)

tacking

seam

RS

turn in 6mm

5. From right side of garment, machine stitch underlap into position. This row of machining is visible on right and wrong sides of garment.

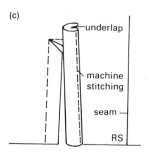

6. On wrong side of other edge of opening, pin, tack and machine overlap to garment.
7. Trim and press seam.
8. Turn in 6 mm on triangular end and remaining free edges of overlap.

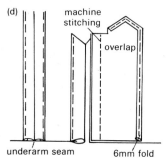

Attaching overlap

9. Pin and tack folded edge to row of machining.

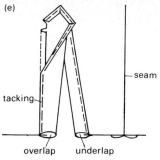

Finishing
1. Machine through all thicknesses, stitching the upper triangle of placket in position, then machine down both sides of overlap from right side.

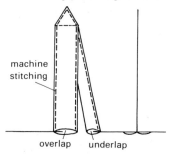

2. Finish off threads securely.
3. Remove tacking and press.

39.

Facings

Facings are applied to garments to neaten and strengthen their shaped raw edges; armhole, neckline, waistline and front edges of blouses, skirts, jackets etc. One edge of the facing has the same shape as the shaped garment edge. Facings, usually cut from the garment fabric, are often in two pieces. Functional and invisible facings are on the inside of garments; functional and decoratives are visible from the right side. Interfacing is used to strengthen some facings, (turn to Chapter 37 on interfacings for further details).

TYPES OF FACINGS

(a) *Shaped facing* e.g. armholes, necklines;
(b) *Bias facing* e.g. used on garments to reduce bulk when fabric is thick and heavy;
(c) *Straight facings,* see chapter 47 on hems;
(d) *Extended front edge facing* on part of garment e.g. front of blouse, jacket, coat.

SHAPED FACINGS

(a) NECK FACING

It may be a round, square or V-shape neckline. A neck facing may be used on garments with or without a collar.

Preparation
1. Pin, tack and machine shoulder seams of garment.

Remove tacking, press seams open and neaten edges.

2. Along neck edge of garment machine a row of stay-stitching 1.5 cm from raw edge.

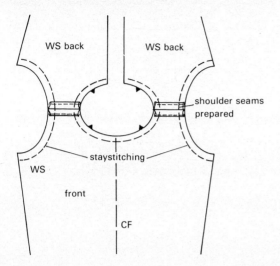

Preparing garment

3. Tack, machine and press facing seams. On outer edge of facing turn in 5 mm to wrong side. Tack and edge machine-folded edge. Remove all tacking stitches and press.

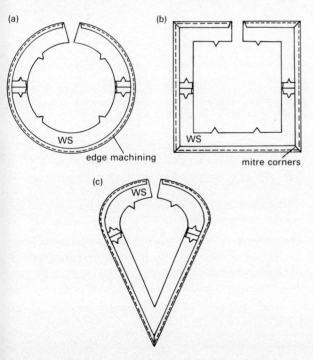

Preparing facings

Application

1. Pin facing to garment right sides together, matching shoulder seams, notches, centre fronts and opening edges.

2. Tack facing to garment.

3. With facing side up, machine facing to garment on fitting line. Remove tacking.

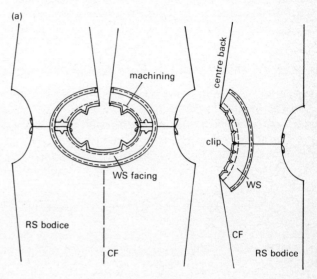

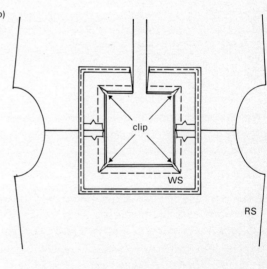

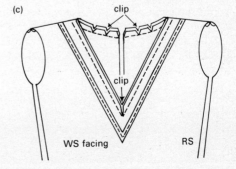

315

4. Trim and layer
   seam turnings.

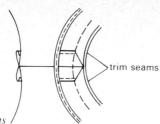

Trimming overlapping seams

5. On square shaped facing clip into corners; on V-shaped facing clip into V at bottom of facing; notch curved edge of round facing allowance.

Finishing

1. Remove tacking and press seam allowance away from garment towards facing.
2. Tack and understitch facing to seam allowance 2 mm from neck edge. Remove tacking.
3. Turn facing to inside of garment, pin at seams and centre front. Fold under opening edges of facing and pin to zip tape.

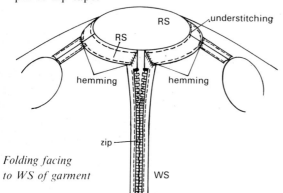

*Folding facing
to WS of garment*

4. Hem facing to zip tape and shoulder seams to prevent it rolling to right side.
5. Fasten off all machine threads.

(b) ARMHOLE FACING

Suitable for garments without sleeves e.g. dresses, blouses, waistcoats and pinafores.

Preparation

1. Prepare the garment by tacking, machining and neatening shoulder and side seams. Press open.
2. Tack, machine and press open facing seam. Remove all tacking.

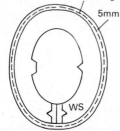

Preparing facing

3. Neaten outer edge of facing by turning 5 mm to wrong side and edge machining it just along fold.

Application

1. Pin and tack facing to garment armhole right sides together and notches, seams etc matching.
2. With facing side up, machine on fitting line. Remove tacking.

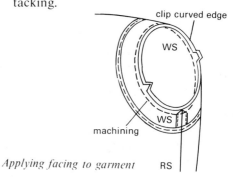

Applying facing to garment

3. Trim and layer turnings. Clip curved edge.

Finishing

1. Press seam allowance towards facing. Understitch facing as before.
2. Turn facing to inside and tack in position. Press.

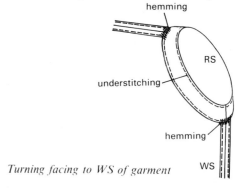

Turning facing to WS of garment

3. Hem facing to garment at shoulder and side seams. Remove all tacking. Press if necessary.

BIAS FACING

Bias binding is often used to neaten a curved edge e.g. armhole, neckline.

Preparation

1. Cut out bias binding of a suitable length and width in garment fabric. Width at least 4 cm i.e. 2 by 1 cm turnings + 2 cm finished facing.
2. Lengthwise, along the binding fold under 1 cm turnings on both sides. Press.

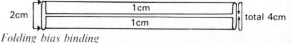

Folding bias binding

Application

1. Place fitting line of bias binding to fitting line of curve, right sides together. Tack and machine along fitting line.
2. Remove tacking, trim and layer turnings to 8-10 mm.

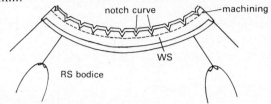

Attaching bias binding to garment

Finishing

1. Notch curved edge and press bias binding to wrong side. Pin and tack folded free edge of bias binding in position.
2. Slip-stitch or hem to garment, taking care not to pull stitches too tightly.

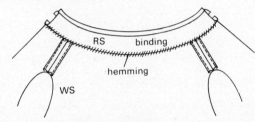

Hemming bias binding to machining

FRONT EDGE EXTENDED FACING

This facing is usually part of the garment e.g. blouse. If it is a separate piece just attach it at front edge seam.

Preparation

1. Mark position of front and centre lines, buttons and buttonholes on extended facing.
2. Cut a piece of interfacing to match shape of facing.
3. Tack in position along front edge foldline with small tacking stitches. Work a row of running stitches beside tacking. If sew-on interfacing use herringbone stitch to attach it to garment. Iron on fusible interfacing.
4. Join back neck facings to front facings at shoulder line. Machine and press open.

Application

1. Tack garment and facing along neck fitting line, right sides together.
2. Machine on fitting line, trim, layer and notch seam allowance.
3. Turn facing to wrong side and press. Understitch facing to seam allowance.

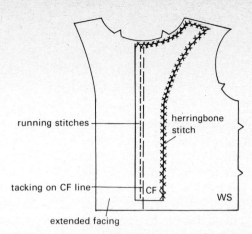

Attaching sew-on interfacing

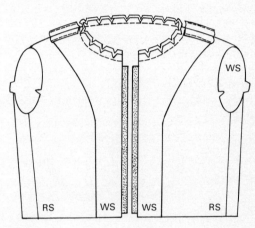

Finishing

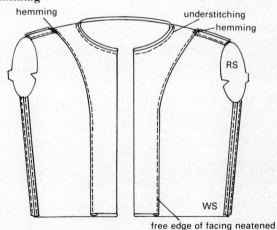

Facing turned to WS of garment

1. Neaten outer free edge of facing with edge machining.
2. Hem facing edge to shoulder seams to hold it in place.
3. Press.

40.
Collars

INTRODUCTION

Collars must be prepared and attached to garments following the exact directions given in the pattern instructions. This is not always an easy sewing process and practice makes perfect. A collar neatens the raw edge of a neckline. It is a decorative feature which is often used as the focal point of a dress, blouse etc. A variety of collars may be seen in any pattern catalogue. The curve of the neck edge of the garment corresponds to that of the collar. The shape of the neck edge will determine whether the collar rolls over, lies flat or stands up. Outer edges of collars vary in shape e.g. straight, curved or scalloped.

Collar shapes

Collars with all their variations fall into three shapes
(a) flat

Flat collar with lace edging

(b) rolled

Rolled collar

(c) standing.

Standing collar

CHARACTERISTICS OF A WELL-MADE COLLAR

1. The neck edge of collar should fit the neck edge of garment without gathers or puckers forming.

2. All curves, corners and points should match each other identically.
3. The seam edge and the underside of collar should not be visible.
4. The cut and stitching of the collar should be perfect.

Preparation of garment
1. Attach collar to garment before sleeves. Fit the garment to check. neckline fitting lines. Alter if necessary.
2. Staystitch neck edge of garment if not already done.

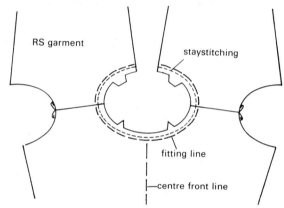

Preparing neck edge of garment

3. Pin collar to neck edge of garment to check that it lies correctly.

MAKING THE COLLAR

1. Cut out collar following pattern instructions (straight collars have grain running vertically or horizontally; on shaped collars the grain runs top to bottom i.e. parallel to centre back).
2. Tailor tack pattern markings, e.g. Shoulder lines, centre front, centre back, curves and points. Transfer all markings that will help to make accurate outlines.
3. Decide which piece will be the upper and lower collar.

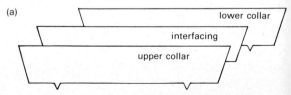

4. Cut out interfacing using collar pattern. The type (i.e. iron-on or sew-in) and weight (heavy, soft or light) of interfacing will be influenced by collar shape and fabric.
5. Pin and tack or iron on interfacing to wrong side of collar.
6. Pin and tack collar pieces together, right sides facing, notches and tailor tacks matching. Do not tack notched edge of neck.
7. Beginning at the centre of the outside edge, machine on fitting line. Repeat and complete the other half. Fasten off threads and remove tacking. Press gently. Do not machine neck edge.
8. Layer seam allowance

(a) interfacing to 1 mm of machining. Herringbone stitch to seam allowance if necessary.

(b) upper collar to 5 mm.

(c) under collar to 3 mm.

Trim corners of straight collars and notched curved outer edge of shaped collars.

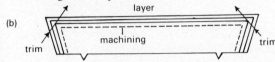

9. Turning collar to right side, push out seam curves and points carefully to get a crisp edge.
10. Rolling seamline of upper collar to the underside, tack 2 mm in from outer edge. Press from under collar.

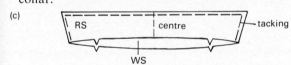

ATTACHING COLLARS

A. FLAT COLLAR OR PETER PAN COLLAR WITH SHAPED FACING

Preparation
1. Prepare garment and staystitch neckline edge.
2. Cut out, tailor tack, machine, trim and press collar.

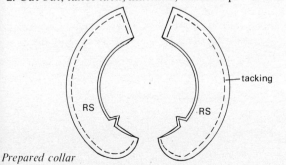

Prepared collar

Application
3. Place under collar to neckline on right side of garment, matching centre front, centre back, balance marks and tailor tacks. Pin and tack in position. Remove pins.

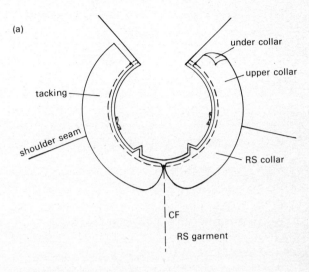

Tacking collar to garment

4. Fit the garment. The collar should lie flat around garment neck edge.
5. Prepare facings; tack and machine seams, press open and remove tacking. Turn in 5 mm around unnotched outer edge of facing and machine stitch 3 mm from folded edge. Press.

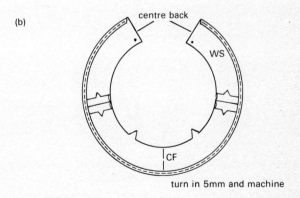

Prepared facing

6. Place right side of facing over collar matching notches, tailor tacks, shoulder seams etc. Pin and tack in position.
7. Machine facing over collar through all layers of

fabric. Remove tacking, trim, grade and clip curved seam edge.

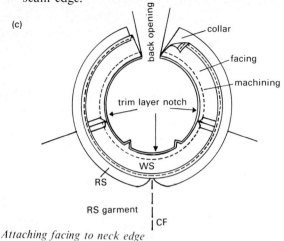

(c)

Attaching facing to neck edge

8. Press facings away from neck edge. Understitch facing to seam allowance 1 mm from seamline. This prevents facing and collar rolling outwards.

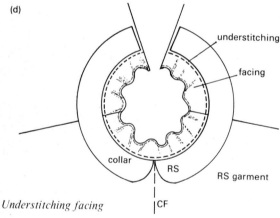

(d)

Understitching facing

9. Turn facing to wrong side. Press.
10. Anchor facing to centre back opening and shoulder seams using hemming or slipstitching.

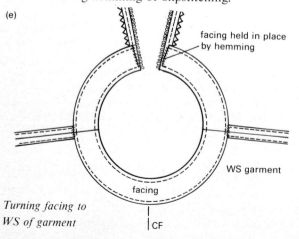

(e)

Turning facing to WS of garment

B. PETER PAN COLLAR WITH A BIAS STRIP FACING

1. Follow steps 1-4 as for Peter Pan collar with shaped facing.
2. Measure neck edge of collar and cut a strip of bias binding the same length.
3. With right sides facing, pin and tack bias binding over collar at neck edge.

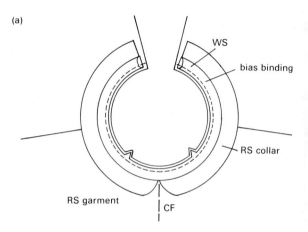

(a)

Machining bias strip in place

4. Machine along fitting line through all layers of fabric, from centre back edge to centre back edge on the other side. Remove tacking. Trim, layer and notch neck edge.
5. Press seam allowance and bias strip away from collar.
6. Turn in raw edge of bias binding and fold to wrong side of garment. Tack.
7. Slipstitch bias binding to garment at folded edge and ends of strip. Remove tacking and press.

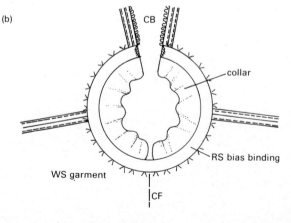

(b)

Completed bias strip facing

320

C. STRAIGHT COLLAR OR SIMPLE SHIRT COLLAR

A straight collar is a type of rolled collar. This collar may be cut in one piece or two pieces. Prepare the collar and garment as instructed. Straight collars may be applied with a
(i) Shaped facing;
(ii) Bias strip facing;
(iii) Self facing.
for (i) and (ii) use methods given for flat collar or Peter Pan collar.

Application of straight collar with a self-facing
1. Prepare garment and collar.
2. Pin and tack under collar to garment; from centre back to shoulder seams, and from shoulder seams to centre front, matching notches and tailor tacks as you work.

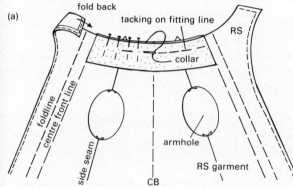

Tacking collar to garment

3. With right sides together fold front facing over collar. Matching notches and tailor tacks, tack in position along fitting lines to shoulder seams.
4. Machine from centre front A to shoulder seam B. Lift back upper collar and machine under collar from B to C. Machine from C along facing to centre front D. Machine on fitting line through all layers of fabric.

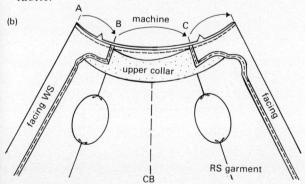

Machining facing and collar

5. Trim, layer and notch neck edge. Trim across corners of front facings.
6. Fold facings to wrong side of garment pushing out corners of front facings. Press neck edge seam of under collar into collar.
7. Fold in 1.5 cm along free raw edge of upper collar. Press.
8. Pin, tack and hem folded edge to machining. Fasten off all loose threads. Remove tacking and press.

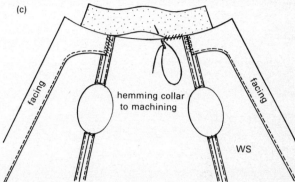

Hemming folded edge to machining

D. COLLAR WITH STAND

This collar folds down at the top of the stand, over the stand. The stand is a narrow band joining the collar to the neck edge of the garment.

Preparation
1. Cut out and make up collar as on page . . . .
2. Using pattern cut out band and interfacing. Attach interfacing to wrong side of under band.
3. Pin the interfaced under band to undercollar right sides together. Pin the second band piece to upper collar right sides together. Tack in position.

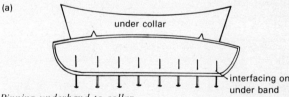

Pinning underband to collar

4. Machine on fitting line from end A along edge B to end C. Do not machine notched edge.
5. Remove tacking, trim, layer and notch seam allowance. Press band away from collar.

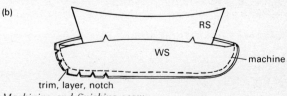

Machining and finishing seam

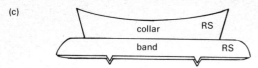

(c)

collar RS

band RS

Collar and band turned to RS

Application

1. Complete garment front facing.
2. With right sides together, pin and tack interfaced under band to garment neck edge.
3. Machine along fitting line from A to B. Remove tacking, trim, layer and notch turnings. Press seam allowance towards band.

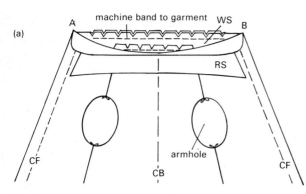

(a)

Machining collar band to neck edge

4. Fold in 1.5 cm along remaining free raw edge of band. Tack folded edge to within one thread of machining. Slipstitch to machining.

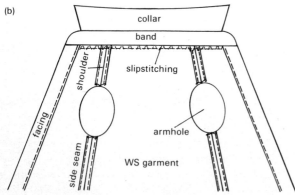

(b)

Slip-stitching folded edge to machining

5. Remove tacking and press.

E. STANDING COLLAR OR MANDARIN COLLAR

A mandarin collar consists of a band cut in one or two pieces. The collar may be wide or narrow, straight or curved. It follows the natural curve of the neckline.

Preparation

1. Cut out collar and a strip of interfacing for one half of collar. Attach interfacing to collar.
2. Pin, tack and machine three sides of collar if cut in two pieces. Do not machine notched edge. Remove tacking.

   If collar is cut in one piece, fold and machine both ends to within 15 mm of neckline edge.

Collar cut in one piece

Collar cut in two pieces

3. Trim and layer seam allowances and corners. Turn right side out and press.

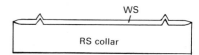

RS of completed collar

Application

1. Place interfaced collar to neck edge of garment, right sides together, notches, centre fronts and centre backs matching.
2. Pin and tack in position.
3. Machine along fitting line from A to B. Remove tacking.
4. Trim, layer and notch seam allowance. Press seam into collar.

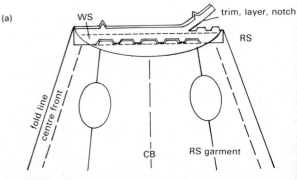

(a)

Machining collar to garment

5. Fold under 1.5 cm along free edge of collar. Tack in place.

(b)

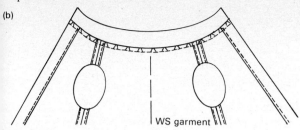

Slipstitching folded edge to machining

6. Slipstitch to row of machining to complete collar.

(c)

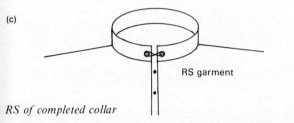

RS garment

RS of completed collar

F. TIE COLLAR

This is an extended version of a foldover or standing collar. The extension forms an attractive tie at the front neck edge.

Preparation

1. Cut out and attach interfacing to collar part of tie. Do not interface ties.
2. Prepare garment, seams, facings etc.
3. Fold tie in half lengthways.
4. Tack and machine from A to B and C to D along seamline. Do not machine collar opening.
5. Turn ties right side out. Press along seamline.

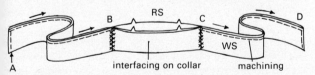

RS
B   C   D
WS
A   interfacing on collar   machining

Preparing tie collar

Application

1. Clip garment where collar part of tie ends.
2. Tack under collar to neck edge of garment.
3. Machine from E to F. Snip under collar at E and F. Trim, layer and notch seam allowance. Press seam allowance into collar.

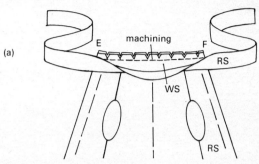

(a)   machining
E   F
RS
WS
RS
RS

Machining tie collar to garment

4. Turn in seam allowance of remaining free edge of collar.
5. Tack and slipstitch to line of machining.
6. Press.

(b)

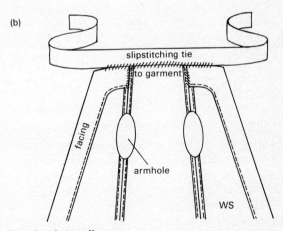

slipstitching tie
to garment
facing
armhole
WS

Completed tie collar

41.
Sleeves

INTRODUCTION

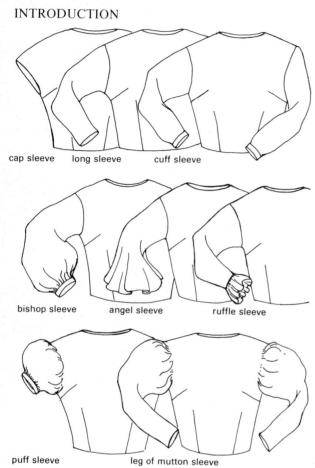

cap sleeve   long sleeve   cuff sleeve

bishop sleeve   angel sleeve   ruffle sleeve

puff sleeve   leg of mutton sleeve

Variations on sleeve shapes

There are many styles of sleeves varying in length and shape. Fashion and fabric influence each style or shape. All sleeves have been developed from one of three basic sleeve shapes.

BASIC SLEEVE SHAPES

A. SET-IN

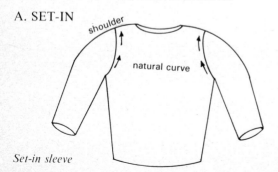

Set-in sleeve

This sleeve is inserted into the garment armhole with a seam that follows the natural curve of the arm and shoulder meeting point.

B. RAGLAN

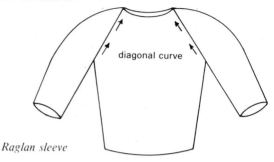

Raglan sleeve

A **raglan sleeve** crosses diagonally into the bodice of a garment. It replaces part of the front and back of the garment. A diagonal seam from the underarm of the sleeve to the neckline joins the raglan sleeve to the garment.

C. KIMONO

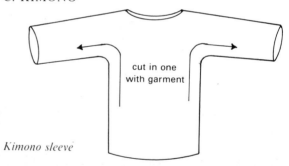

Kimono sleeve

The **kimono sleeve** is cut in one piece with the garment. It is an extension of the garment. A kimono sleeve does not fit or shape the figure. It drapes the body and tends to be bulky when sewing.

MATCHING SLEEVES

(How to tell the back of the sleeve pattern from the front.)

Double notches usually indicate the back of the sleeve head. Single notches mark the sleeve front. The front of the sleeve head is smaller and lower than the back of the sleeve head. Always check the sleeves before insertion. Sleeve notches must match the notches on the bodice. Mark all tailor tacks carefully.

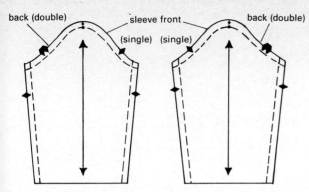

back (double)   sleeve front   back (double)

(single)   (single)

Right and left sleeve

A. SET-IN SLEEVE

Preparation of sleeve and garment

1. Clearly mark the **head** or **crown** of each sleeve in a contrasting thread. Tailor tack.

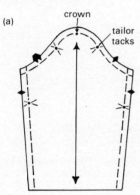

(a)   crown   tailor tacks

Marking sleeve head

2. Separate sleeves from pattern pieces. Check that you have each sleeve turned in the correct direction (a right sleeve and a left sleeve).

3. Run a row of gathering stitches between the notches 2 mm from the fitting line. A second row of stitching can be worked 4 mm from the same fitting line. Leave the thread ends loose to draw up the fullness of the sleeve head.

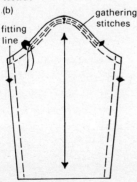

(b)   gathering stitches

fitting line

Working two rows of gathering

4. With right sides together and notches matching, pin and tack the sleeve seam. Machine, remove tacking and press open.

5. Neaten the seam allowance and press again.

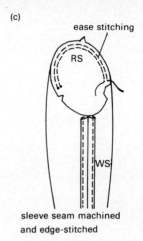

(c)   ease stitching

RS

WS

sleeve seam machined and edge-stitched

Working underarm seam

6. Pin, tack, machine and neaten shoulder and side seams of garment. Try on garment for fitting. Alter the position and size of armhole if necessary.

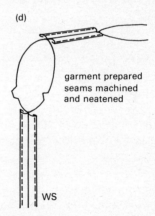

(d)

garment prepared seams machined and neatened

WS

Preparing garment

Note: The sleeve must never be made smaller than the armhole of the garment during easing.

Insertion

1. Turn sleeve right side out and garment inside out.

2. With right sides together place sleeve in armhole of garment.

3. Pin into position. First pin underarm seam to side seam, then shoulder seam to sleeve head, matching all tailor tacks and notch points.

4. Pull easing threads to fit sleeve into armhole of garment. Ease and distribute sleeve fullness evenly

325

between all matched points. Fasten easing threads around pins to hold them in position.

5. Continue to pin sleeve to garment on fitting line from sleeve side. Insert all pins across seam line at right angles to seam allowance edge.

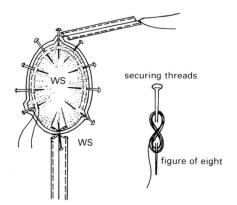

Pinning sleeve to garment

6. From sleeve side, tack sleeve to garment using small stitches.
7. Remove each pin as you tack. If gathers or pleats form, take smaller tacking stitches to distribute fullness evenly.
8. Turn right side out and try on garment. Fit the sleeve. Check that it hangs correctly and is of the correct length. Bend your arm and move your shoulder to check for ease of movement. Make any necessary alterations.
9. Machine very slowly from underarm seams on sleeve side on fitting line. Overlap a few stitches at the end to strengthen the seam. Remove tacking.

Finishing

1. Remove tacking and ease stitching.
2. Press seam allowance into sleeve from the wrong side using a sleeve board. Press lightly on right side. The seam allowance helps to support the sleeve head.
3. Trim and notch seam allowances.
4. Select a suitable armhole seam finish if garment is not to be lined e.g. overcasting.

ALTERNATIVE METHOD FOR SET-IN SLEEVE

Preparation

1. Pin, tack and machine shoulder seam of garment. Remove tacking and neaten seam edges. Press seam open.

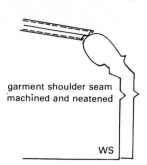
(a)

Preparing garment

2. Run two rows of gathering stitches around sleeve head between the notches, 2 mm and 4 mm from fitting line as before.

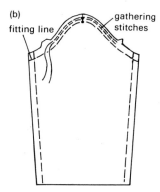
(b)

Preparing sleeve

Insertion and finishing

1. Pin sleeve to garment matching all notches, tailor tacks and balance marks.
2. Ease and distribute the fullness evenly between the notches.

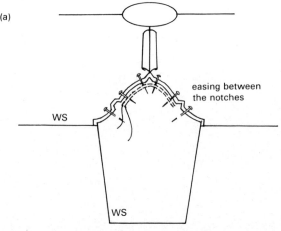
(a)

Pinning sleeve to garment

3. Tack carefully using small stitches just outside fitting line.
4. Machine on fitting line. Remove tacking and ease stitching. Trim and neaten raw edges.
5. Lightly press sleeve seam into the sleeve from wrong side and right side.
6. Pin and tack the underarm seam.
7. Machine in one seam from hem end of sleeve to garment hem. Clip curve.

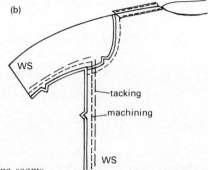

Machining seams

8. Remove tacking. Press seams. Neaten raw edges using a suitable seam finish e.g. zig-zag.

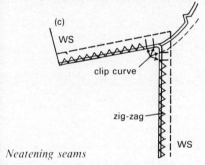

Neatening seams

B. RAGLAN SLEEVES

Preparation

Sleeve with dart at shoulder

1. Pin, tack and machine shoulder dart into position.

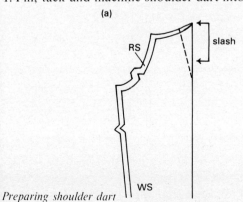

Preparing shoulder dart

2. Remove tacking thread and press dart open.
3. In some cases the dart may have to be slashed open and then pressed. Neaten raw edges with zig-zag machining.

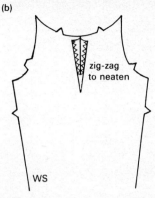

Neatening shoulder dart

Two-piece sleeve

1. Pin, tack and machine shoulder seam.

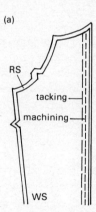

Machining seam

2. Remove tacking and press seam open. Neaten raw edges.

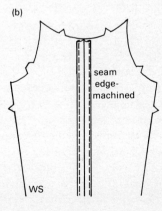

Neatening seam

327

Insertion and finishing

1. With right sides facing match notches of sleeve to those of garment.
2. Pin and tack into position. Machine along the fitting line. Remove tacking stitches.

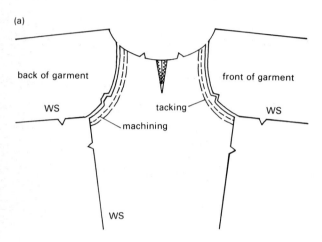

(a)

back of garment

front of garment

WS

tacking

machining

WS

WS

Inserting sleeve into garment

3. Below the notches machine 6 mm in from edge. This strengthens the seam.
4. Slash or snip allowances at notches.
5. Trim close to second row of stitching. Neaten raw edges with zig-zag, blanket stitch or overcasting.

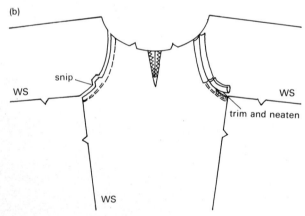

(b)

snip

WS

WS

trim and neaten

WS

Trimming and neatening seams

6. Press open remainder of seam allowance from notches to neckline edge.
7. To ensure that this seam lies flat slash or notch the seam allowance at intervals.
8. With right sides facing, pin and tack underarm seam of sleeve and side seam of garment, matching all notches and intersecting armhole seams. This forms one continuous seam.

9. Machine the seam. Remove tacking and press seam open.
10. Clip the curve under the arm. Use a suitable finish to neaten seam allowance.

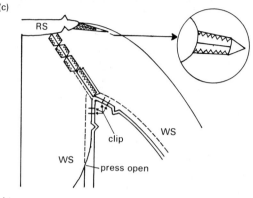

(c)

RS

WS

clip

WS

WS

press open

Finishing seams

Note: A raglan sleeve may also be inserted after the dart or shoulder seam and sleeve seam have been machined.

C. SIMPLE KIMONO SLEEVE

Kimono sleeves are usually cut as part of the garment. However, they may be cut with a shoulder seam.

Preparation

1. With right sides together pin and tack shoulder seams (if any), side and underarm seams together.
2. When the kimono sleeve has no gusset, cut a 13 cm length of bias binding to help reinforce underarm section of sleeve.
3. Press bias binding open. Fold in two and place along the underarm section of garment, centring the fold line over the fitting line. Tack into position.

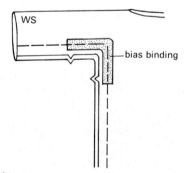

WS

bias binding

Preparing kimono seam

Finishing

1. Machine the seam from sleeve edge to hem edge of garment. When machinining over bias binding, use a

328

small zig-zag stitch. This allows some give in the seam.

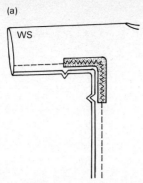

(a)

WS

Machining seam

2. Remove tacking and snip the curved underarm seam, but not the bias binding reinforcement.
3. Press seam open. Neaten raw edges of seam allowance with a suitable seam finish.

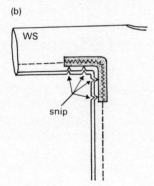

(b)

WS

snip

Snipping curved seam

POINTS TO REMEMBER IN FITTING A SLEEVE

1. Always tack darts and seams. Even if they are pinned carefully the fabric might slip under the machine foot.

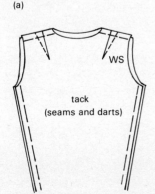

(a)

WS

tack
(seams and darts)

2. Tack the sleeve into the armhole for first fitting.
3. Try on the garment. It should feel comfortable when you stretch or raise your arm and bend your elbow.
4. The shoulder seam should be exactly on top of the shoulder. Adjust to your own shoulder curve if necessary.
5. There should be no wrinkles or signs of pulling on the sleeve. (See chapter on alterations.)
6. The sleeve seam should not be too loose or too tight.
7. A sleeve must hang evenly and straight.

(b)

8. It is very important to distribute gathers evenly at sleeve head, cuffs and even elbows whenever used.

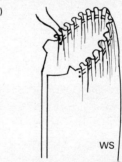

(c)

WS

9. Check that the length does not spoil the appearance of the sleeve e.g. a three-quarter sleeve should be half way between wrist and elbow.

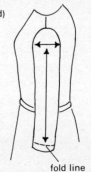

(d)

fold line

NEATENING ARMHOLE SEAMS

A. BIAS BINDING

*Where it is used: **fine woollen fabrics, tweeds, unlined jackets, coats.***

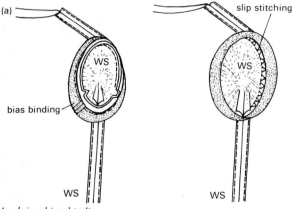

Applying bias binding

Method

1. Remove all tacking and easing stitches from the sleeve.
2. Trim the seam allowance to 12 mm. Layer it to avoid any bulk.
3. Place right side of bias binding to seam allowance on the garment side with edges together.
4. Pin and tack bias binding to garment 5 mm from raw edges.
5. Machine bias binding to seam from garment side. Remove tacking stitches.
6. Turn in raw edge of bias binding and pin just above row of machining.
7. Tack and slip stitch to row of machining. Remove tacking and press.

B. TOP SEWING OR OVERCASTING

*Where it is used: **cottons, fine fabrics.***

Method

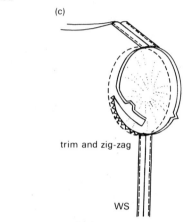

Top sewing raw edges of seams

1. Remove gathering and tacking stitches.
2. Trim the armhole seam allowance to 15 mm.
3. Turn 5 mm of raw edges in, facing each other, and tack carefully.
4. Using overcasting or top sewing, neaten the edges.

C. ZIG-ZAG

*Where it is used: **cottons, wool, jersey, double knits.***

Method

Working zig-zag machining

1. Having removed tacking and gathering threads, trim the armhole seam allowance to 15 mm.
2. Keeping edges even, zig-zag together.
3. Finish off threads with a backstitch.

D. BLANKET-STITCHING

*Where it is used: **wool, tweeds.***

Method

Working blanket stitching

1. 10 mm outside fitting line, work a second row of machining.
2. Trim seam allowance to 12 mm.
3. Work a row of blanket stitching along raw edges keeping them together.

SPECIAL FINISH FOR DELICATE FABRICS

FRENCH SEAM

This is an ideal finish for sleeves in fine materials e.g. silk, lawn. These materials are too delicate for bias binding as they fray very easily. If the sleeve head has gathers the french seam is not suitable. For instructions on working a french seam, turn to Chapter 33 on seams.

Neatening sleeve edges

When choosing a sleeve edge finish, consider the style of the sleeve e.g. long or short sleeve. Is the garment casual or dressy? By using different sleeve finishes you can achieve a variety of images. For a very sharp well-made finish interfacings should be used.

FINISHES

1. Straight hem;
2. Casing;
3. Facing (a) shaped, (b) binding;
4. Scalloping or scalloped hem.

STRAIGHT HEM

Preparation

1. Fit on garment and check sleeve length.
2. Mark the position of hemline.

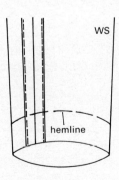

Marking hemline

3. Cut out the interfacing equal to the circumference of the sleeve plus 13 mm for joining interfacing with an overlap. The interfacing depth should be equal to that of sleeve hem.

Application and Finishing

1. Position interfacing 1.5 cm over hemline marking. Allow ends of interfacing to overlap. Sew together using running stitches.
2. Pin and tack interfacing along the hemline.

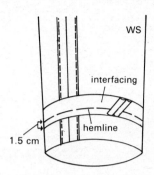

Applying interfacing to hemline

3. On the hemline secure interfacing to garment with a row of running stitches.
4. Using herringbone stitches attach interfacing to garment along its upper and lower edges.

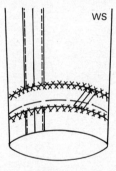

Working herringbone stitches

5. Turn in a fold on raw edge of sleeve. Cover the interfacing with hem.
6. Tack hem near folded edge.
7. Slip-stitch hem to garment. Remove tacking and press carefully.

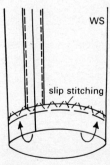

Finishing sleeve edge

CASING

Preparation

1. Try on garment and check the position of casing. Alter if necessary.
2. Mark foldline of casing.

(a)

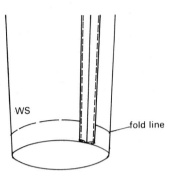

Marking fold line

3. On wrong side turn up the fabric along the marked foldline. Tack carefully making sure edges are even.
4. Fold in raw edge 6 mm. Press lightly and tack to sleeve. Leave an opening near sleeve seam so that the elastic can be inserted easily.

(b)

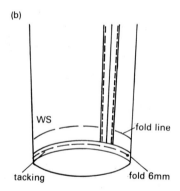

Folding raw edge

(c)

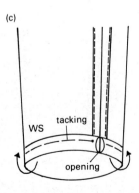

Turning up edge to form casing

Finishing

1. Machine upper and lower folded edges of casing to sleeve.

(a)

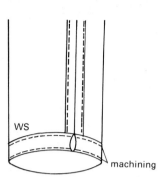

Machining casing

2. Neaten all threads with a backstitch.
3. Insert the elastic and overlap ends 13 mm. Join together with a row of machine stitching.

(b)

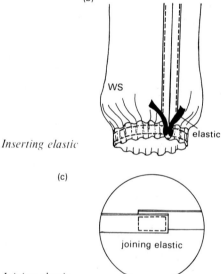

Inserting elastic

(c)

Joining elastic

4. Complete upper row of edge machining.
5. Press and finish off any remaining loose threads.

(d)

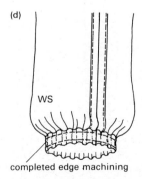

Finished casing

332

FACINGS: A. SHAPED

Method

1. Join the facing ends together. Trim seam allowance and press open.

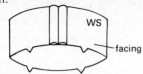

(a)

Joining facing ends

2. Pin facing to sleeve with right sides together. Raw edges should be level or meeting.
3. Tack 6 mm from edge. Machine and remove tacking.

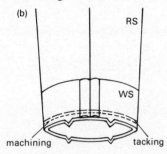

(b)

Attaching facing to sleeve edge

4. Fold facing along line of machining to wrong side of sleeve. Tack along folded edge.
5. Turn under 6 mm on raw edge of facing to form a narrow hem.

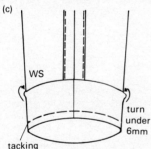

(c)

Folding facing to WS of sleeve

6. Pin and tack hem to sleeve.
7. Attach hem to sleeve using hemming or slip-

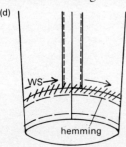

(d)

Hemming facing to sleeve

stitching. This stitching must not be seen on the right side of sleeve.
8. Remove all tacking and press.

FACINGS: B. BINDING

Types used are (a) commercial bias binding and (b) self binding.

Preparation

1. Cut a strip of bias binding 4 cm wide and equal in length to the sleeve circumference plus $2\frac{1}{2}$ cm for a join.
2. Pin bias binding to sleeve, right sides together with raw edges meeting. Mark position of bias binding join on straight grain.

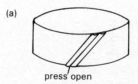

(a)

press open

Joining bias binding

3. Remove bias binding from sleeve. Join ends together. The seam will be in a diagonal direction. Press seam open.

Application and finishing

1. With raw edges and right sides together, pin and tack bias binding to sleeve. Machine.
2. On free edge of bias binding turn in a narrow fold.

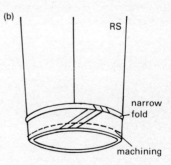

(b)

Attaching bias binding to sleeve edge

3. Turn bias binding to the wrong side of sleeve making sure that it is not visible from the right side. Press carefully.
4. Tack and slip-stitch folded edge of bias binding to wrong side of sleeve.

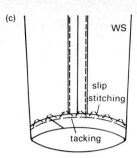

Hemming facing to sleeve

5. Remove all tacking.

SCALLOPED HEM

Preparation
1. Mark the position of scallops on wrong side of sleeve and facing fabric. This can be done by using coins, patterns, transfers or even a compass. Scallops point out from the sleeve edge.
2. With right sides together pin and tack facing to sleeve.
3. Carefully mark the outline of scallop shape with small tacking stitches.

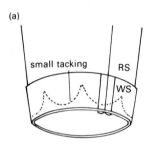

Marking position of scallops

Finishing
1. Machine beside tacking stitches marking the outline of scallops.
2. Remove tacking and trim turnings around; scallop shape to 6 mm deep.

3. Notch or clip scallop edges and into the point between each scallop.

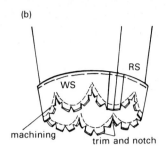

Machining and trimming scallops

4. Using your first finger and thumb fold along line of machining. Turn facing to wrong side of sleeve.
5. Tack near folded edge. Lightly press.
6. Turn in 6 mm on raw edge of facing. Tack and slip-stitch to sleeve.
7. Remove tacking and press.

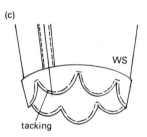

Turning facing to WS of sleeve

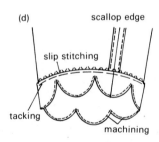

Finishing scalloped hem

42.
Cuffs

INTRODUCTION

Cuffs are applied to sleeves to neaten their hem edges before the sleeves are set into the armhole. Cuffs may be straight or shaped bands.

TYPES OF CUFFS

extended cuff
turnback cuff.

Remember

1. Pin and tack sleeve into garment and try on garment to check length of sleeve.
2. Pin cuff to sleeve to check (a) length of sleeve plus cuff, (b) width of cuff around arm or wrist for comfort and ease. Without an opening a cuff must be large enough for the hand to pass through easily.
3. If cuff is to be lapped over, complete opening before applying cuff. If opening does not occur on seam, work opening before joining underarm seam.
4. Interface all cuffs.
5. For a good finish trim, layer, notch and press all cuffs.
6. Choose fastenings which suit the fabric and design of cuff.

INTERFACING CUFFS

Interfacing gives extra strength and support to cuffs. Choose the interfacing according to the fabric being used e.g. (a) cotton lawn — lightweight, (b) fine wool — medium weight and (c) tweeds — heavyweight. Iron-on or sewn interfacing may be used.

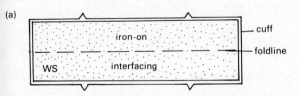

(a) *Lightweight interfacing:* This very fine interfacing may be applied covering the whole cuff on the wrong side. Its edges are held in place by machining during cuff construction and application to sleeve.

(b) *Medium weight interfacing:* Cut this interfacing to fit one half of the cuff. It extends 15 mm beyond foldline into the other side. This helps to give a good rolled

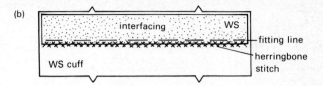

edge at foldline. Attach it by ironing it on or tacking and herringbone stitching it at foldline side. The other sides will be caught in during machining.

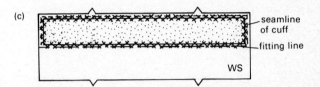

(c) *Heavyweight interfacing:* Attach interfacing to one half of the cuff. Iron-on or herringbone stitch on all sides to cuff. This interfacing is cut out so that it fits just to the foldline and seamlines. It does not extend into the seam allowances as it would be too bulky.

EXTENDED CUFFS — BANDCUFF

Preparation

1. Prepare sleeve edge by working two rows of machine gathering around sleeve, both inside seam allowance 1 mm and 6 mm from fitting line.
2. Pull machining to form gathers. Arrange fullness around wrist so that the cuff will slip over the hand comfortably.

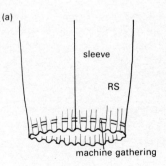

Preparing sleeve

3. Cut out and tailor tack cuff band using pattern. Apply iron-on or sew-in interfacing following the instructions already given.

4. With right sides together, tack and machine cuff ends. Press seam open.

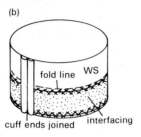

(b)

fold line WS

cuff ends joined interfacing

Preparing cuff band

Application

1. Tack interfaced half of cuff band to gathered sleeve right sides together, matching tailor tacks and notches.
2. Machine along fitting line. Trim and layer seam allowance. Remove tacking and press seam allowance towards cuff band.

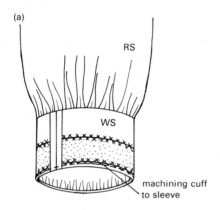

(a)

RS

WS

machining cuff to sleeve

Machining cuff to sleeve

3. Fold cuff to inside of sleeve along foldline, wrong sides facing and tack 2 mm from folded edge.
4. Fold in remaining free edge of cuff on fitting line. Tack and slipstitch or hem to machining.

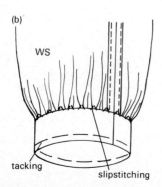

(b)

WS

tacking

slipstitching

(c)

RS

RS

Finishing cuff edge

5. Remove tacking and press.

EXTENDED CUFFS — LAPPED CUFF WITH OPENING

Preparation

1. Prepare sleeve by working sleeve opening and underarm seam. Remove tacking and press.
2. On cuff edge of sleeve work two rows of machine gathering (1 mm and 6 mm from fitting line inside seam allowance).
3. Interface cuff using iron-on or sew-in interfacing. With right sides together fold cuff along foldline lengthwise.

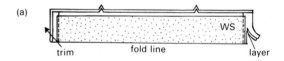

(a)

WS

trim fold line layer

Preparing cuff band

4. Machine, trim and layer cuff ends. Turn right sides out, pushing out corners gently. Tack 2 mm along foldline edge.

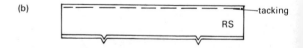

(b)

RS tacking

Application of Cuff

1. Pin interfaced half of cuff to sleeve edge right sides together at notches, front and back edges of opening etc.
2. Pull machine gathering until sleeve fits cuff. Do not make sleeve smaller than cuff.
3. From gathered side tack and machine cuff to sleeve on fitting line.
4. Trim, layer and press seam allowance into cuff.

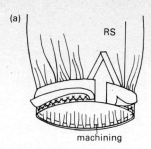

(a)
RS
machining

Machining cuff band to sleeve

5. Turn cuff right side out and tack close to foldline edge. Turn in free raw edge of cuff and tack in place.
6. Slipstitch or hem to machining.

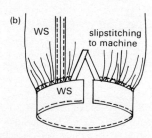

(b)
WS
slipstitching to machine
WS

Slip-stitching lopped cuff

7. Complete cuff with button and buttonhole.

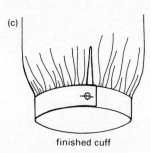

(c)
finished cuff

Completing cuff fastening

SHIRT-SLEEVE CUFF

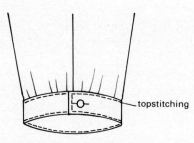

topstitching

Shirtsleeve cuff

This is attached to a sleeve which has a shirt-sleeve placket opening and edges of cuff are topstitched.

TURNBACK CUFFS — STRAIGHT TURNBACK CUFF

Preparation

1. Cut out cuff band in one or two sections. Tailor tack. Interface one half of cuff, extending it beyond fold-line. Iron-on or herringbone stitch interfacing to cuff band.
2. Join cuff ends together. Press seam open.

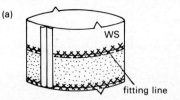

(a)
WS
fitting line

Preparing cuff band

3. With wrong sides facing, fold cuff band in two lengthways. Tack along fold line and seamline.

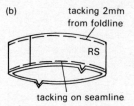

(b)
tacking 2mm from foldline
RS
tacking on seamline

Application

1. With wrong side of sleeve facing upper cuff, pin and tack raw edges together along fitting line. Match cuff seam with underarm seam.
2. Machine on fitting line. On seam allowance, work a second row of stitching 3 mm from first row. This strengthens cuff turnback.

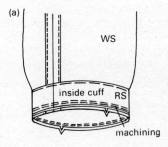

(a)
WS
inside cuff RS
machining

Attaching cuff to sleeve

3. Remove tacking. Neaten raw edge of seam allowance with zig-zag machining or overcast stitching.
4. Roll cuff to right side of sleeve and press seam to wrong side of sleeve.

5. Neaten seam allowance with bias binding. Slipstitch bias binding to machining and sleeve.

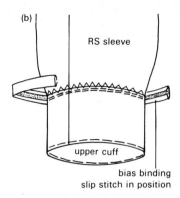

Using bias binding

6. Remove all tacking and press.

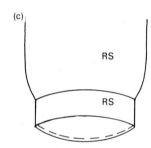

Finished cuff

TURNBACK CUFFS — SHAPED TURNBACK CUFF

Preparation

1. Cut out cuff pieces and tailor tack. Interface one cuff piece. (Use iron-on or sew-in interfacing).
2. With right sides together tack and machine cuff pieces on fitting line. Do not stitch notched end.

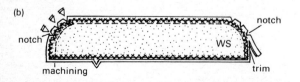

Preparing shaped turnback cuff

3. Trim, layer and notch seam allowances.
4. Turn cuff right side out and press along seamline. Tack 2 mm in from seamline edge.

Application

1. With right side of cuff to wrong side of sleeve tack notched edges together.
2. Machine along fitting line. Work a second row of stitching 3 mm from fitting line in seam allowance.

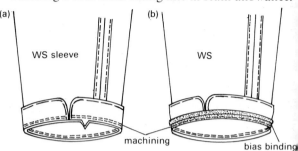

Applying bias binding

3. Remove tacking and zig-zag raw edges.
4. Neaten raw edges with bias binding. Machine right side of bias binding to top of cuff and sleeve edge. Trim seam allowance. Remove tacking and press cuff away from sleeve.
5. Fold in raw edge of bias binding. Turn to right side of sleeve, tack and slip hem in place. remove all tacking.

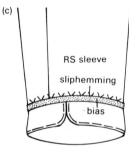

Slip hemming bias to sleeve

6. Roll cuff to right side of sleeve keeping seamline on the wrong side of sleeve.

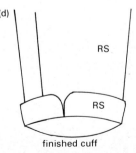

Finished cuff

338

43.

Fastenings

Fastenings are needed in most garments to keep garment openings closed and in position while they are being worn. There is a wide variety of fastenings from which to choose, each with its own particular use. Fastenings can be *functional* or *decorative* or both. Fastenings can be divided into three categories, (a) Visible fastenings, (b) Concealed fastenings, (c) Decorative fastenings.

GENERAL RULES

1. Choose fastenings which suit the fabric and their position on that fabric e.g.
   (a) strong fastenings on closing points if there is extra strain,
   (b) strong sturdy fastenings for heavy fabrics,
   (c) small light fastenings for fine fabrics.
2. Consider the position of the fastening. Will it be easily accessible to the wearer e.g. rouleau loops are difficult for young children to fasten. Fastenings should be easy to use.

3. Sew fastenings on doubled fabric for extra strength. Stitches should not be visible from the right side of the closed garment.
4. Complete the opening (except rouleau loops, bound buttonholes and zips) before attaching fastenings.
5. Select fastenings that suit the method of cleaning the fabric e.g. laundering or dry cleaning.
6. Girls' and women's garments fasten right-over-left and boys' and men's left-over-right. Remember cuffs and sleeves fasten front-over-back.
7. Avoid mixing different types of decorative fastenings on one outfit.
8. Fastenings not part of a fashion detail should be concealed.

BUTTONS AND BUTTONHOLES

Buttons and buttonholes are both decorative and functional. Buttons should pass through the buttonholes easily. If the buttonhole is too large it will spoil

TYPES OF BUTTONHOLES	USES
1. hand-worked buttonhole	On fine or delicate fabrics for blouses, dresses, children's clothes.
2. Machine-worked buttonhole	Medium weight fabrics for shirts, dresses, children's clothes and casual outfits.
3. Bound buttonhole	On all garments for a professional finish made from silk, linen, wool and cotton.
4. Tailored buttonhole	Tailored garments. Garments made of closely woven fabric e.g. worsted wool for men's suits.

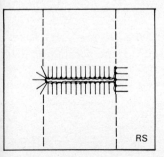

Hand-worked buttonhole

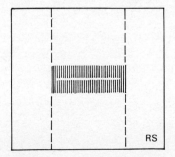

Machine-worked buttonhole

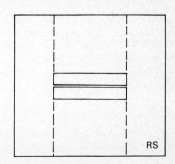

Bound buttonhole

the finished appearance of the garment. There are four types of buttonholes:

Remember:
1. Buttonholes are worked when the garment is completed and just before sewing on the buttons (except for bound buttonhole).
2. Use proper thread e.g. for hand-worked buttonhole twist.
3. A lightweight interfacing strengthens buttonholes on fabrics that fray easily.
4. Work buttonholes on double fabric.
5. Buy the size and number of buttons recommended by the pattern. The size of the buttonhole will be influenced by the size of the button. A good guideline is that the buttonhole length should equal the diameter of the button plus its thickness. If the buttonhole is too big the garment will open. if it's too small it will pull and fray easily.
6. The outer edge of the buttonhole should never be placed too close to the closing edge of the garment. The distance should be about half the width of the button but not closer than 13 mm.
7. The first button is positioned about half the button width plus 5 mm, below the neck edge. Never position the last buttonhole through the hem. It should be placed at least 8 cm away from the hem edge.
8. Work at least two practice buttonholes on a spare piece of the garment fabric. This tests the suitability of the stitch and thread on the fabric.
9. To get perfect buttonholes work all of them during the same period of sewing.

POSITION OF BUTTONHOLES

All patterns include markings for the exact position of buttonholes. The finished buttonholes should follow the grainline of the fabric. Buttonholes may be placed in a vertical or horizontal direction.

Vertical — are suitable for loose fitting clothes where there is little pull or strain. For vertical button-

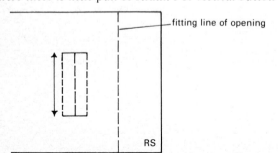

holes the 'pull' is downwards. The ends may be round or barred.

Horizontal — are used most frequently on cuffs, fitted dresses, blouses and waistbands, where there is a lot of strain. The pull is away from the closing. Horizontal buttonholes have a barred end and a round end nearest the opening edge of garment. never allow the button to extend over the edge of the garment when using this type of buttonhole.

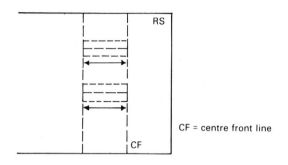

WORKED BUTTONHOLES

Marking buttonholes

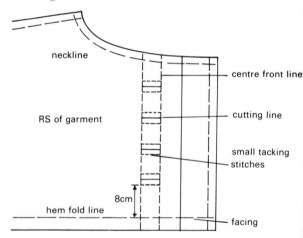

Marking position of buttonholes

1. Carefully mark the cutting line of buttonholes on fabric using tailor's chalk and small tacking stitches to mark the outline.
2. Mark centre front lines of garment.
3. Space buttonholes evenly from neckline to hem edge.
4. On fabrics that fray easily use interfacing between garment and facing.

Working
1. At either end of buttonhole place a pin.
2. Position the buttonhole area of garment over a

metal surface e.g. lid of metal box and slit the opening with a sharp blade. The classroom tables would be damaged if you slit the buttonhole opening with a razor on their surface. if no metal surface is available, cut opening with a sharp scissors.

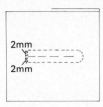

Marking outline of buttonhole

3. Remove pins and overcast raw edges if inclined to fray. Machine 1 mm away from raw edges on finer fabric.
4. With right side of garment facing, work from left to right.

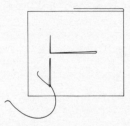

Beginning buttonhole

5. Bring the needle through to the left hand corner by inserting it between the two layers of fabric. Pull it through so that the thread end remains between the folds.

Working lower edge

6. *Lower edge:* Take double thread coming from eye of needle in your right hand and wind it around the point of the needle, from left to right (anti-clockwise). Draw out the needle upwards to form a knot at the buttonhole edge.

   Continue working in buttonhole stitch across the lower edge, keeping stitches equal in size and neatly spaced. Pull thread out firmly each time but not too tightly.

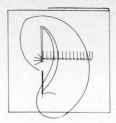
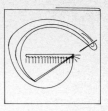

Working round edge

7. *Round end:* Work five or seven overcasting stitches in a semicircle or fan shape around the outer edge of opening i.e. edge of buttonhole nearest garment edge. The centre stitch should fall in line with the buttonhole opening.

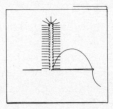

Working upper edge

8. *Upper edge:* Work buttonhole stitch along the second side in the same way as lower edge. Bring needle over the buttonhole through the knot of first stitch on lower edge.

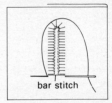

Begining bar end

9. *Barred end:* Work two bar stitches across end of buttonhole, across the depth of both rows of buttonhole stitches. From left to right across barred end, work five or seven buttonhole stitches catching the garment fabric underneath. these stitches lie at right angles to the buttonhole opening.

Finishing

Completed buttonhole

1. Bring needle to wrong side near knot of last stitch. Fasten off by passing the thread under stitches at the back and then through fold of fabric. Cut off thread ends once thread has been secured.
2. Press on the wrong side.

Note: A buttonhole may have two square or barred ends. It is worked in the same way as above except replace round end with square end.

MACHINE-WORKED BUTTONHOLES

Buttonholes can be made using a special buttonhole attachment or a very close zig-zag stitch on sewing machine.
1. Follow sewing machine manual instructions for preparing, marking and sewing buttonholes. Information is given on stitch length and width.
2. Usually one side of the buttonhole is machined forward and the other side backward with bar stitches at both ends.
3. Machine-worked buttonholes are cut when the buttonhole stitches have been completed.

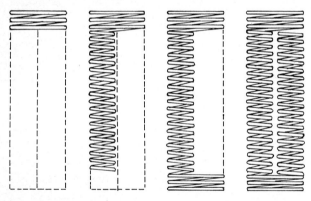

Machine worked buttonhole

BOUND BUTTONHOLE

Preparation
1. On right side of garment mark position of buttonhole openings.

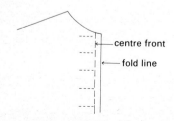

centre front

fold line

Marking position of buttonholes

2. Cut binding strip on straight grain or true cross of garment fabric, 5 cm wide and 3 cm longer than buttonhole. The binding strip could also be cut from a contrasting fabric as a decorative feature.
3. Mark centre of binding strip with tailor's chalk.
4. With right sides together place the centre line of binding strip along centre of buttonhole.

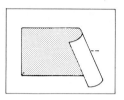

Positioning binding strip

Working
1. On wrong side of garment, machine 5 mm from centre line of tacking along the two sides and across each end to form a continuous rectangle i.e. from A to B to C to D to E and finishing at A.

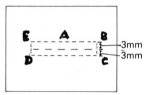

Machining rectangle

2. Slash through the centre tacking line to within 5 mm of each end. From this point snip diagonally into each corner. Do not cut the stitches.
3. Secure machine threads. Remove tacking.

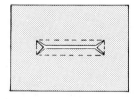

Cutting buttonhole opening

4. Pull binding strip through to wrong side of buttonhole.

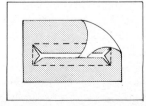

Pulling binding strip to WS

5. On wrong side arrange binding to form an inverted pleat on each side of slit. The binding edges meet at centre of buttonhole opening.

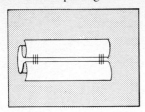

Making pleats on WS

6. To hold binding in position, work a row of diagonal tacking stitches across buttonhole binding from right side of garment.

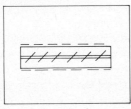

Working diagonal tacking

Finishing
1. On wrong side of buttonhole stitch triangular pieces at each end of opening to pleated binding strip.
2. To mark position of buttonhole on facing put pins through each end of buttonhole from right side.

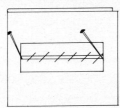

Marking facing

3. Slash facing between pins to within 5 mm of each pin. As before, cut diagonally into the corners.
4. Fold and tack under raw edges of facing to binding on wrong side of buttonhole. Slip-stitch facing to buttonhole binding on wrong side of buttonhole.

Attaching facing to buttonhole binding

5. Secure all threads. Remove tacking. Press from wrong side.

BUTTON LOOPS

For an edge-to-edge opening, thread or rouleau loops may replace buttonholes as a method of fastening the garment. They add a professional touch which complements all styles. Thread loops are suitable for a single fastening and can be worked on a folded edge. Use thread loops at a neck opening to fasten a small button or metal hook. Rouleau loops are worked along the seam edge of the opening. They are suitable for fastening a continuous row of buttons. Rouleau loops are stronger than thread loops and should be used on firmly woven fabric.

Thread Loop or Bar
1. Mark the position of the button. On loop edge using the centre and ends of button as a guide, mark position of loop with pins.

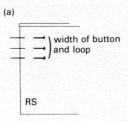

2. The length of the loop should be equal to the diameter of the button plus its thickness.
3. Place a narrow piece of card to wrong side of loop edge. It helps to keep the fabric firm while the loop is being made.

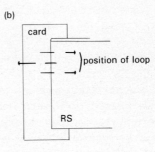

4. Using buttonhole twist or any strong thread, work a back stitch on wrong side of edge.
5. Bring needle between fabric folds to left hand pin on garment edge.

343

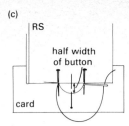

(c)

RS

half width
of button

card

6. Insert needle into folded edge at right hand pin keeping the thread loop under head of centre pin. Work four more stitches in the same way. Remove card and pins.
7. Work buttonhole or blanket stitch over extending strands.

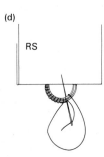

(d)

RS

8. Keep stitches close together. Fasten off threads on wrong side of edge with double backstitch.

ROULEAU LOOPS

Rouleau loops can be made from individual lops or a continuous row of loops. This depends on space required and fabric being used.

Making rouleau loops

1. Cut pieces for rouleau to correct length on bias of fabric. The bias strip for rouleau loops should be equal to twice the finished width plus seam allowances.
2. With right sides together, fold bias strip in half lengthwise. Tack and machine seamline of bias strip just stretching the bias as you sew. A slight zig-zag stitch can be used on the machine.
3. Remove tacking and trim seam allowance until slightly narrower than the rouleau itself. If too much is cut away, the rouleau loop will be very weak. Fasten machine threads securely at each end of fabric tube.

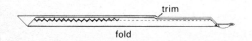

trim

fold

4. Slip a tapestry needle into the fabric tube. Secure eye of needle to one end of rouleau fold with overcasting stitch.
5. Ease tapestry needle down fabric tube. Pull gently and it will come through to the other end.

6. Remove tapestry needle. Roll rouleau loop between your fingers and press with seamline along one edge.

Note: If making a continuous rouleau loop do not cut but wind it like serpent curves to form loops. Keep loops close together.

Attaching rouleau loops

1. On garment mark position, i.e. width and depth, of rouleau loops along fitting or seam line of right-hand side of opening.
2. *Single loops:* Cut each loop the required length. *Continuous Loops:* Do not cut.

   Place each rouleau loop with seamed side up on right side of garment, edges together. Point the loop away from edge of opening. The loop should be equal to the button diameter plus twice the loop thickness.

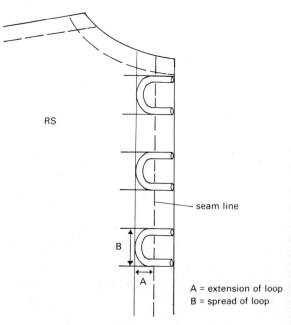

RS

seam line

B

A

A = extension of loop
B = spread of loop

Attaching loops to garment

3. Tack along seamline keeping loops evenly spaced and of the correct size. Machine rouleau loops to garment seam line.

344

4. Trim excess bulk in seam allowance before attaching facing or other edge finish.

Attaching facing
1. Place facing over rouleau loops on garment, right sides together.
2. Tack and machine in place through loop ends and garment working from garment side. Use first row of machining, holding rouleau loops in place, as a guide.

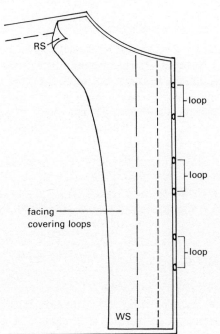

Machining facing to garment over loops

3. Remove tacking and trim turnings.
4. Turn facing to wrong side of garment, allowing the rouleau loops to extend beyond opening edge.

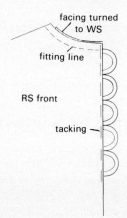

5. Tack close to opening edge. Neaten raw edge of facing. Press from wrong side. Remove tacking.

BUTTONS

Select buttons which match, contrast or complement the garment fabric and style. Buttons are made from a variety of materials — plastic, wood, ivory, bone, steel, brass, ceramics, porcelain, glass etc. Most buttons are mass-produced from the practical and adaptable material called *plastic* (i.e. cellulose, polystyrene and polyvinyl resins). Buttons are both functional and decorative.

Selecting buttons
1. When purchasing garment fabric choose buttons to suit the garment style and the fabric, e.g. small buttons on fine fabrics, in blouses etc., heavier buttons for coats and jackets.
2. Use a pattern as a guide for size and number of buttons. Do not alter the size recommended as the manufacturers have calculated the fastening overlap required by the garment.
3. Button moulds covered in the garment fabric can be used if no suitable button is available.

Types of buttons
A. Sew-through or flat buttons have a thread shank.
B. Buttons with a metal or plastic shank — shank buttons.
C. Re-inforcing buttons — a small flat button placed on the wrong side of garment behind a larger button on the front of the garment, e.g. coats and jackets.
D. Link buttons — threads are run between two buttons and then buttonhole or blanket stitch is worked over the threads linking the two buttons together. Used most often with cuffs and capes.
E. Covered buttons — button moulds covered with the garment fabric.

General Guidelines
1. Complete the buttonholes at one sewing session beforesewing on buttons.
2. Try on garment. Matching centre front lines mark the position of buttons through the centre of each buttonhole with crossed pins.
3. Use a buttonhole twist, polyester thread or a heavy duty cotton thread. Choose the thread that is most suitable for the fabric. Double the thread to reinforce the button if necessary.

4. Buttons should be spaced evenly to prevent the opening gaping when fastened.

6. Sew buttons on securely, but not too tightly, to avoid unnecessary pulling or strain on the fabric.

7. A thread shank may be formed behind flat buttons if necessary.

How to sew on a button

1. On right side of garment make two backstitches over pins to secure thread firmly to fabric.

2. Place button in position over crossed pins. If necessary lay a matchstick or pin across button between holes to allow shank to be worked later.

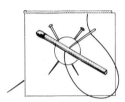

3. Bring needle up and down through holes of button to form stitches. Sew securely but not tightly.

4. Continue until the button is firmly in position. Remove crossed pins and matchstick.

5. Bring needle to right side between button and fabric. Wind thread around stitches behind button to form thread shank.

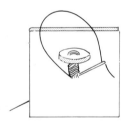

6. Bring needle to wrong side and fasten off thread by working three blanket stitches or buttonhole stitches over threads.

Attaching different buttons

A. *Flat buttons* with four holes may be stitched in four ways
   1. Cross 2. Square 3. Parallel 4. Decorative.

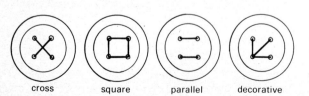

cross   square   parallel   decorative

B. *Shank buttons:* Attach with small stitches passed through the shank, into the fabric and repeat until button is quite secure.

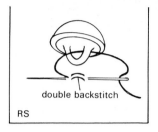

double backstitch

RS

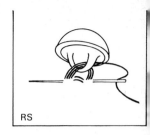

RS

C. *Reinforced buttons:* Place a small flat button on the wrong side of garment behind the outer button. Sew directly from one button to the other. Allow a shank to form between the fabric and outer button. Finish the shank in the usual way.

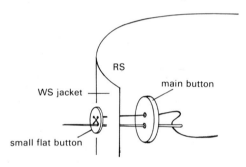

RS

WS jacket

main button

small flat button

D. *Link buttons:* Run four threads between two buttons. Leave threads the required length; this depends on the fabric thickness. Work a row of blanket stitches or buttonhole stitches close together until the threads between the buttons are covered.

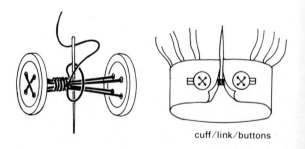

cuff/link/buttons

PRESS STUDS OR SNAP FASTENERS

Press studs, usually available in black and silver metal, come in many sizes and shapes. Smaller sizes 6-11 mm are suitable for fine and medium weight fabrics; large sizes 12-17 mm suit heavy fabrics. Press studs are used on overlapping garment edges where there is little or no strain. Use a thread that will match the colour of the press studs being used.

(a)

knob or ball section

socket or well section

A press stud is made up of two sections (a) ball or knob section, usually sewn to wrong side of overlap, (b) socket or well section sewn to right side of underlap.

Sewing on press studs

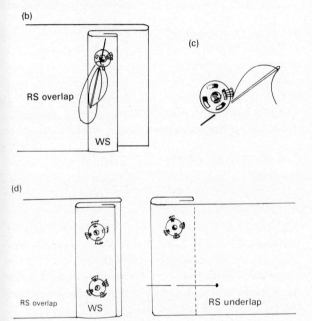

(b)

RS overlap

WS

(c)

(d)

RS overlap   WS

RS underlap

1. Mark position of knob 3 mm in from overlap edge on wrong side of overlap.
2. Sew on double fabric using a strong thread. Stitches should not be visible on right side of garment. Using buttonhole or blanket stitch sew knob section in position on overlap. Work three or four stitches in each hole.
3. Finish off threads using a double backstitch on wrong side. Pass thread between folds.
4. Slip a pin through centre of knob section. Close garment opening and let the pin touch underlap.
5. Work a backstitch where pin touches underlap. remove pin and place socket section over backstitch.
6. Attach it as for first half to right side of underlay.
7. Fasten off thread securely.

HOOKS, EYES AND BARS

Hooks, eyes and bars, available in a variety of sizes, are strong and firm. Select the size according to its position and use.

Example: (a) Hooks and eyes: where edges meet e.g. waistbands of skirts, neck edges, (b) hooks and bars: where there is an underlap and an overlap e.g. waistbands.

How to attach hooks and eyes
1. Mark the position of hook and eye with pins as in diagram.
2. The hook is in line with the edge of overlap. The eye is opposite hook on wrong side of underlap. It projects slightly beyond underlap edge.

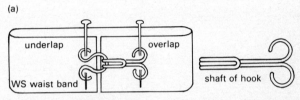

(a)

underlap   overlap

WS waist band   shaft of hook

Positioning hook and eye

3. *Sewing on hook:* Begin with a double backstitch. Working from just under hook sew five overcasting stitches along the shaft to hold hook in place. Slip needle between folds of fabric and bring to right-hand loop. Use blanket stitch, overcasting or buttonhole stitch around the two loops of hook. The stitches should not be visible on right side of garment. Secure threads with a backstitch and then slip thread through fold.

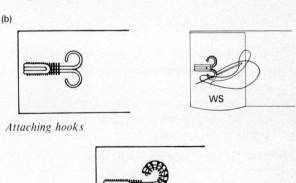

(b)

WS

Attaching hooks

4. *Sewing on eye or bar*
   (a) Attach eye, opposite hook, to wrong side of underlap; attach bar to right side of underlap. (b)

Begin with a backstitch. Fix the eye or bar in position with two stitches over each side near edge of opening. (c) Buttonhole stitch, blanket stitch or overcast loops of eye or bar in position, (d) Fasten off threads with a backstitch and pass needle through fold.

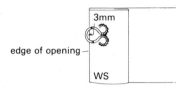

Attaching eye

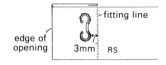

Attaching bar

EYELET HOLES

Eyelet holes, decorative as well as functional, are used for fastenings when threaded with tape, ribbon or cord.

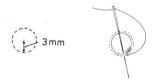

1. Using tailor's chalk mark the position of each eyelet keeping them evenly spaced.
2. Mark a circle 3 mm outside this mark. Work a row of small running stitches on this line to strengthen opening.
3. Cut centre of circle with a scissors. Stitch around the hole using buttonhole stitch or overcasting to cover running stitches.
4. Secure thread with backstitch on wrong side and then run thread at back of stitches or through fold.

NYLON FASTENING TAPE (HOOK AND LOOP VELCRO)

This is a two part nylon tape used similarly to hooks and eyes. One surface is covered with small rigid plastic hooks, the other with a softer loopy pile surface. When pressed together they stick firmly to each other. A variety of colours and widths is available. It is used on waistbands, belts, cuffs and fronts of jackets, of loose

fitting garments. Velcro can irritate the skin if used on tight-fitting garments. It should not be used on fine fabrics where extra bulk must be avoided. Keep Velcro closed when laundering the garment

How to apply

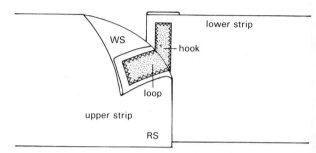

1. Cut to required shape and size.
2. Pin and tack in position. Machine lower strip 2 — 3 mm in from edge of Velcro using a small zig-zag stitch.
3. Hem upper strip in place so that stitches are not visible from right side. Machine stitch if desired.
4. Fasten off threads with a double backstitch.

Note: May be used for an overlap or edge-to-edge opening.

ZIPS

Zips are a fast and secure way of opening and closing garments. Zips, now available for an amazing range of fastening tasks, come in many colours and lengths, (from 10 cm to 86.5 cm). To get correct length, measure from top to end of teeth only. Never include the tapes when measuring a zip.

IDENTIFY YOUR ZIP PARTS

The top and end stops prevent the *slider* slipping off the teeth. The guideline is the stitching line of zip. See diagram.

Buying Zips
1. The pattern will give instructions on type and length of zip to use. Buy the correct zip. Do not make any adjustments. Too short a zip causes strain at the opening end and in time the zip will break.
2. Select a zip that will complement garment style and fabric weight. Special zips have been developed for specific fastening tasks e.g. open-end zips for jackets.
3. Zip colour should match type of fabric.

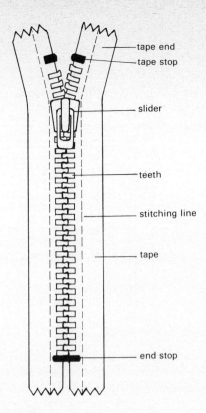

tape end
tape stop
slider
teeth
stitching line
tape
end stop

TYPES OF ZIP

A. Conventional
1. *Metal:* coloured or plain metal teeth attached to a cotton tape. Tend to be stronger than synthetic zips. They are available in a variety of weights e.g. light, medium, heavy.
2. *Synthetic:* Nylon or polyester teeth or coils, attached to a cotton or cotton-blend tape. Synthetic zips are suited to dry-cleaning and home laundering. They do not shrink.

B. Special purpose
1. *Open-end or separating:* This opens at both ends. The teeth separate completely as there is no button or end stop. This zip is available in a reversible form. Quite suitable for jackets, coats, anoraks etc.
2. *Invisible:* When the zip is closed the teeth or coil is hidden behind the tape. It looks just like a seam. Used for skirts and dresses.
3. *Two-way:* This zip has sliders on both top and bottom of zip. It can be opened from either the top or bottom. Suitable for casual garments.
4. *Separating or open-end:* Both sides separate completely as there is no bottom stop. Most often used for jackets and coats with detachable hoods etc.

General guidelines on sewing in zips
1. If zip is creased, press out flat before insertion.
2. Zips are inserted before the garment is made up by hand or by machine.
3. Replace normal sewing-foot of machine with a zipper-foot.
4. Leave correct size of opening to fit zip length.
5. Always close zip during insertion and machining.
6. Pin zip from the top downward.
7. Machine at least 2–3 mm from teeth along stitching line.
8. Seams etc should be matched at zip opening.
9. Do not stretch zip or seam as you sew.
10. Remember to use a medium iron when pressing synthetic zips. Hot irons may melt them.
11. Avoid strain at top of zip by using a hook and eye.

INSERTING LAPPED OR CONCEALED ZIPS

Preparation
1. Machine seam right up to end of zip opening. Fasten off threads with a double backstitch at end to strengthen base of opening.
2. Tack opening along fitting line and press seam open. Neaten raw edges of the entire seam allowance with edge-machining.

Insertion
1. Close zip. With right sides together place zip on the underside of garment opening, matching the fitting line of zip with fitting line of garment.

(a)

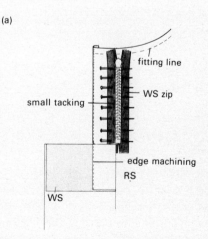

fitting line
WS zip
small tacking
edge machining
RS
WS

2. Pin and tack securely 1 mm inside fitting line. Machine in position 3 mm from zip.
3. Remove tacking stitches.

4. Turn zip facing right side up. Press and tack near seamline.

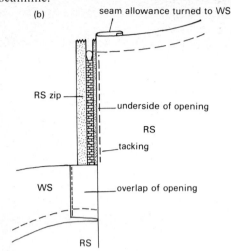

(b)

seam allowance turned to WS

RS zip

underside of opening

RS

tacking

WS

overlap of opening

RS

5. Place overlap of opening over zip so that its edges hide the zip completely. It overlaps the underfold by 1-2 mm.
6. Pin in position. Overcast edges of opening to prevent them slipping during stitching.

Finishing
1. Work a row of small tacking stitches from top of zip through all layers of fabric to base of opening. The row of tacking should be 8-13 mm from edge of opening.
2. Machine overlap in position; stitch across the bottom of zip, turning at corner, and continuing up the side to top of opening.

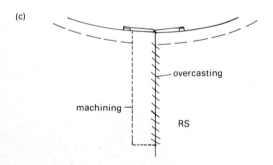

(c)

overcasting

machining

RS

3. Finish off machine threads securely and remove tacking. Neaten ends of zip tape with buttonhole stitch or bias binding.
4. Press zip opening from wrong side of garment, using a dry pressing cloth.

Used for
Front, back and side openings on dresses, skirts and trousers.

INSERTING EDGE-TO-EDGE OR SEMI-CONCEALED ZIPS

Preparation
1. Machine seam along fitting line up to end of zip opening, backstitching loose machine threads at end to strengthen base of opening.

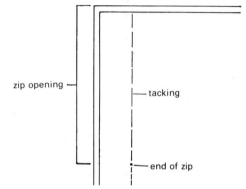

zip opening

tacking

end of zip

Preparing zip opening

2. Tack opening closed on fitting line. Press seam opening. Neaten raw edges of seam allowance with edge-machining or zig-zag stitching.

Insertion
1. Close zip fully.
2. With wrong side facing, place right side of zip onto wrong side of zip opening, centring teeth on top seam.
3. Place pins as in diagram i.e. at right angles to zip, to hold it firmly in place.
4. Working from right side of garment, tack zip to garment on both sides of zip teeth along zip tape. Check that teeth, tacking and seam line are parallel to each other.

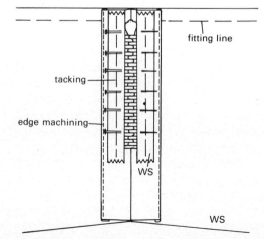

fitting line

tacking

edge machining

WS

WS

Tacking zip to garment

Finishing

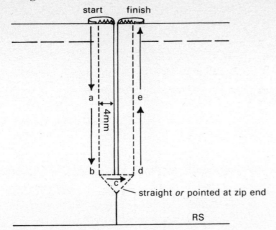

Machining zip in position

1. Machine zip to garment from right side: (a) Beginning at the top, stitching down one side, (b) pivoting at corner, (c) across the end of zip opening, square or pointed, (d) pivoting at corner and (d) up the other side to top edge again. Keep row of machining 4–10 mm from centre.
2. Remove tacking, secure loose machine threads and press from wrong side.
3. Using overcasting, binding or blanket-stitching neaten edges of zip tape ends. Secure edges of zip tape to seam allowance using overcasting.

Used for

Centre front and back seams.

INSERTING INVISIBLE ZIPS

The invisible zip is inserted to the opening edges before the seam is machined. A special invisible zipper-foot must be used and none of the machining is visible on the right side of garment.

Preparation

1. Tack full length of seam and press open. Neaten seam allowance.

Insertion

1. Place right side of closed zip down on wrong side of garment, centring zip teeth on seamline. Pin at right angles to zip.
2. Tack zip to seam allowance only. Remove seam tacking and pins.

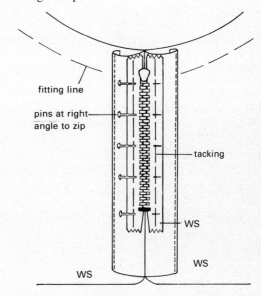

Tacking zip to seam allowance

3. Open zip.

Finishing

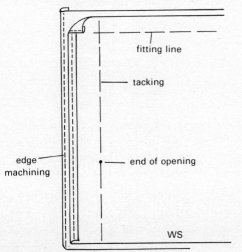

Preparing seam

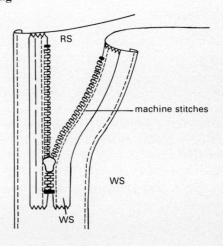

Machining zip to seam allowance

351

1. Machine zip tape to seam allowance. Keep stitches as close as possible to teeth. Avoid stitching the garment fabric.
2. Close zip and machine opposite zip tape to seam allowance.
3. Remove tacking. Fasten off loose machine threads with a backstitch.
4. Press.

Used for

skirts and dresses.

INSERTING TROUSER ZIPS

Two types of zips are used at the centre front of men's women's and children's trousers (a) straight zip, (b) curved zip.

(a) STRAIGHT TROUSER ZIP

Preparation

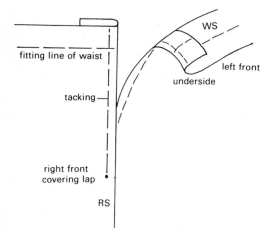

Preparing zip opening

1. Tack and machine crotch seam to base of zip opening.
2. Fold under turnings of facing on seamline of right front covering lap, to wrong side. Tack close to folded edge.
3. On underside fold back left front facing to wrong side along seamline. Tack in position and press.

Insertion

1. Place folded edge of underside to right side of zip near zip teeth.
2. Tack underside to zip tape. Machine from top to end of tape 1 mm from folded edge of underside. Fasten threads securely.

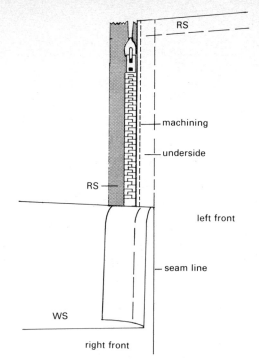

Machining zip to underside

3. Remove tacking and press.
4. Bring right front covering lap over zip and left front, overlapping the left front underside.
5. Tack diagonally to hold firmly in position for stitching.

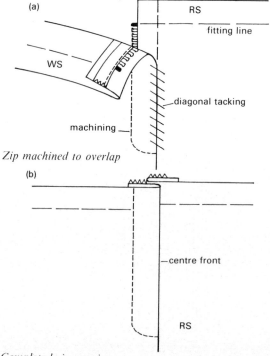

Zip machined to overlap

Completed zip opening

Finishing
1. Tack right front covering lap to zip tape close to teeth. On right side mark in stitching line with tailor's chalk.
2. Using tailor's chalk as a guide machine along this marked line.
3. Fasten off threads, remove tacking and press.

(b) CURVED ZIP

Preparation of right front of trousers
1. Mark the position of zip on fly opening.
2. Place zip on trousers front, right sides together.
3. Pin and tack right fly piece over zip, keeping edges even with garment edges.
4. Machine 3 mm from edges from top to end of zip through all layers.
5. Fasten off loose threads and remove tacking stitches.
6. Turn right side of zip and fly outwards. Press along row of machining.
7. Stitch 3 mm from zip teeth along folded edge.

1. Attach fly facing to left front of trousers opening.
2. Turn fly facing to wrong side. Press.
3. Machine stitch outline of fly from right side.

Finishing
1. On right front mark a line 11 mm from machining at finished edge, curving it to 3 mm at end of zip to meet seam. Use tailor's chalk.
2. Place edge of left fly on tailor's chalk line. Tack in position close to folded edge of fly.
3. With wrong side facing, pin and tack left fly facing to right side of zip tape.
4. Stitch zip tape to left fly facing with two rows of handstitching; one row 2-3 mm from teeth, the other 2 mm from tape edge.
5. From right side of trousers machine the fork-tack-triangle.
6. Remove all tacking, fasten off threads and press.

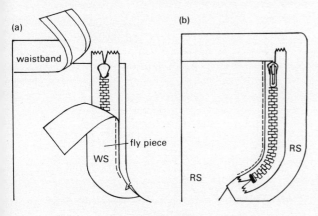

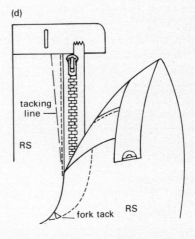

Preparation of left front of trousers

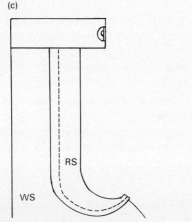

Completed fly opening

SLIDER ZIP

Slider zips allow adjustments to the waistband without altering the garment. Adjustable slider zips have two sections: (a) slider, (b) track.

Attaching slider

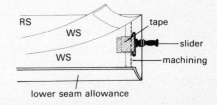

1. Turn seam allowance at end of waistband to wrong side. Press and tack.

2. Cut a short length of tape and slip it through slot of slider.
3. With groove part projecting, pin and tack slider to wrong side of waistband.
4. Machine using a cording-foot across width of waistband over tape and close to slot of slider.
5. Remove tacking. Top stitch waistband ends.

Attaching track

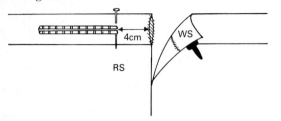

1. Measure 4 cm from edge of outer part of waistband along centre line.
2. From this point, mark the position of track with tailor's chalk.
3. With track grooves facing upwards, stop end of zip away from opening, tack and machine track to waistband.
4. Slip machine threads between the fold. Remove tacking.

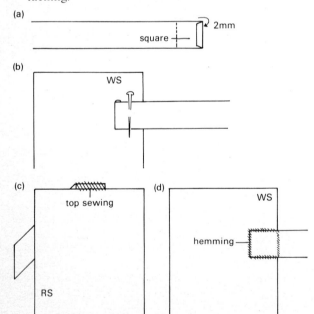

TIE STRINGS

Tie strings, made from tape or ribbon, are frequently used to fasten pillowslips, aprons, children's clothes and dressing gowns. Tie strings can be placed on edge-to-edge openings or overlapping openings.

EDGE-TO-EDGE — tie strings stitched to opening edge
1. Fold 2 mm to wrong side of tape.
2. Place it onto wrong side of opening, until it forms a square of its own width. Pin and tack to opening.
3. Turn back tape until its edge is level with opening edge.
4. Top-sew edges together from right side. Hem three remaining edges to wrong side.

OVERLAPPING — one tie string is stitched to opening edge and the other moved beyond fitting line

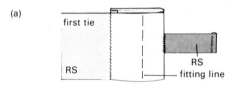

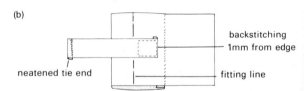

1. Attach edge-to-edge tie string as above.
2. Fold 2 mm to wrong side of second tape.
3. Place tape square in position so that the square lies 2 mm outside fitting line.
4. Backstitch 1 mm in from edge on sides of square.

Finishing
To neaten raw edges of the strings, turn in a narrow hem 2 mm wide. Fasten threads securely.

44.
Finishing Touches

There are many ways of finishing raw edges and attaching trims to garments. Trims add interesting decorative details to garments, often concealing raw edges.

A. BIAS BINDING

Bias binding is usually used to neaten raw edges. It may be of a contrasting fabric or made from the garment fabric or a commercial bias binding. For a decorative finish bias binding should be visible on the right side of the garment. As a functional binding it is turned and concealed on the wrong side. Commercial bias binding comes in a variety of colours and widths. The fibre content of the binding should match that of the garment fabric e.g. natural with natural.

Marking bias strips

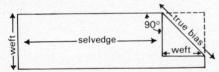

1. Press fabric to remove creases.
2. Fold fabric diagonally from one corner so that the weft edge lies along selvedge (form 90° angle at beginning of fold). The sloping fold is the true bias.
3. Press true bias fold. Cut along bias fold to remove triangular end.

Cutting bias strips

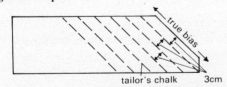

1. Using pins or tailor's chalk, mark cutting lines of bias strips 3–4 cm apart parallel with true bias edge. Strips are four times the finished binding width.
2. Cut along marked sloping lines for individual bias strips. Do not cut for continuous bias binding.

Joining individual strips
1. Cut short ends of bias strips along selvedge thread. When bias strips are joined the seam slopes in the direction of the selvedge.

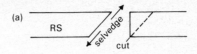

2. Mark seamline on each end using tailor's chalk.
3. With right sides of bias strips together, lap short ends over each other. Pin at seamline (corners project over the seam edges).

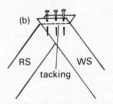

4. Tack and machine bias strips on seamline.
5. Trim extending corners, remove tacking and press seam open. Finish off threads.

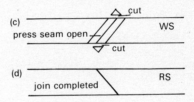

Joining continuous bias binding

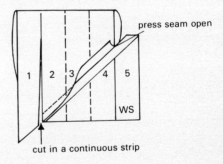

1. Fold marked continuous bias strip right sides together and short ends meeting. Corner points project beyond seamline.
2. Tack and machine seam.
3. Remove tacking, secure machine threads and press seam open.
4. Cut continuous bias binding of the required length.

Note: When joining bias binding while attaching it to garment, tack and machine bias ends on straight grain.

355

Remove tacking, press seam open and attach to garment.

Applying bias binding

Binding a straight edge
1. Trim seam allowance or edge to be bound. Remove tacking and press.
2. Cut a length of bias binding four times the finished width plus extra for neatening raw ends.

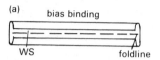

3. Open out one side of binding. With right sides together and edges even, tack binding to garment on inside seamline of binding.

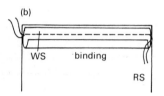

4. Machine along seamline. Remove tacking. Press binding away from garment.
5. Fold bias binding over seam allowance, to wrong side. Tack in position and hem to machining.

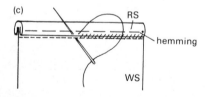

Binding curved edges
1. Trim seam allowance to 6 mm and stay-stitch edges that stretch.
2. Cut, join, stretch and fold suitable length of bias binding.
3. As before open out stretched side of bias binding, tack and machine it to garment, right sides together and edges even.
4. Remove tacking and fold bias binding over seam to wrong side.
5. Tack and hem bias binding to machining already worked.
6. Remove tacking and press from wrong side.

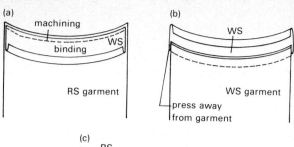

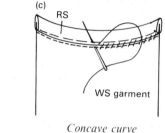

Concave curve

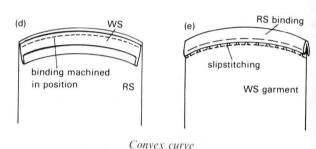

Convex curve

Uses of bias binding
  (a) casing
  (b) piping
  (c) facing
  (d) binding
  (e) neatening raw edges.

B. ATTRACTIVE LACE FINISHES

Lace, attached to hems, cuffs, collars and neck edges may be used as a decorative finish on lingerie, dresses, nightwear.

Methods of attaching lace

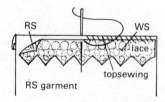

Top-Sewing lace
1. Turn up a narrow hem, tack and hem or machine in position. Remove tacking and press lightly.

2. With right sides together and edges even, tack lace to hem.
3. Top-sew lace to hem working right to left.
4. Remove tacking. From wrong side of garment press lace away from hem.

Machining lace using straight stitch

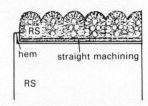

1. Fold and tack in place a narrow hem to right side of garment.
2. With wrong side of lace facing right side of garment, tack lace edge to fold edge of hem.
3. Machine 1 mm from lace edge through all thicknesses. Remove tacking.
4. Press from wrong side of garment.

Machining lace using zig-zag stitch

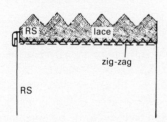

1. Fold and tack hem to wrong side of garment.
2. Pin lace to tacking stitches on right side of garment. Tack in position.
3. Set machine at zig-zag stitch following instructions in machine manual.
4. Zig-zag through all layers attaching lace to hem.

Whipping lace

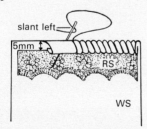

1. Trim 2 mm from edge of garment.
2. With right sides together, tack lace to garment 5 mm from raw edge.

3. Working from right side of garment begin with a backstitch.
4. Roll a narrow hem over lace edge and whip-stitch from right to left.
5. Slant needle to left, inserting it from wrong side bring needle out to right side just below rolled hem.
6. Space stitches evenly. Secure thread as for hemming. Remove tacking and press lace gently.

Faggoting lace

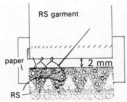

1. Turn under hem, tack and stitch in place.
2. Pin and tack lace and finished hem 2-4 mm apart on a piece of light card.
3. Working from left to right, make a backstitch on hem and take a small stitch on lace to right of backstitch. Bring needle over thread.
4. Work another stitch on hem to right of last stitch on lace, bringing needle over thread in each case.
5. Complete row of stitching with a backstitch, and run thread through hem fold.
6. Remove tacking and supporting card. Press gently.

Frilled lace with bias binding

(a)

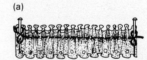

Gathering lace

1. Work a row of gathering 5 mm from edge of lace.
2. Pull up until it is of the required size.
3. With right sides together, tack lace to garment, edges even.
4. Place right side of bias binding over wrong side of lace. Tack and machine 5 mm from edge along crease line of binding.

(b)

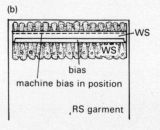

Machining bias binding

357

5. Remove tacking and press binding over raw edges to wrong side of garment.
6. Tack and hem folded edge of hem in position. Remove tacking and press.

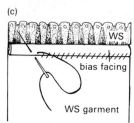

Hemming bias binding to machining

C. SCALLOPING

1. Using tailor's chalk or tailor's tacking, mark position of scallops on garment. Use chain stitch to pad scallops.
2. Holding edge of garment in left hand secure thread with a backstitch.
3. With thread under left thumb insert needle on outline marking of scallop. Bring out beside thread of backstitch, over thread held by thumb.
4. Pull thread gently towards you to produce a knot at scallop edge.

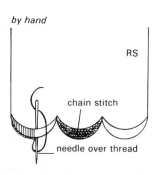

5. Keep stitches close together as you sew. Neaten edge if necessary when stitching is completed e.g. loose fraying threads.

Note: The scalloped shaped edge may also be machined using a very close zig-zag stitch.

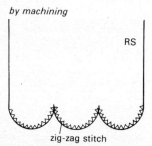

D. SHELL HEMMING

Suitable for lingerie made from delicate fabrics e.g. silk.

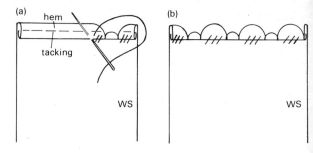

1. Turn under a very narrow hem to wrong side. Press and tack close to folded edge.
2. Begin by running thread between hem fold. Work three hemming stitches.
3. With wrong side facing you, insert needle through back of hem and bring out through single fabric just below hem. Pull thread out tightly.
4. Repeat. Make another loop. Work three hemming stitches and make a loop. Continue until shell hemming is completed.
5. Keep spaces even. Finish off thread as for hemming.

E. APPLIQUÉ

Small pieces of *leather fabric* may be cut into a variety of shapes and attached to garments as decorative trims. Ideal for children's clothes and casual clothes, these pieces of fabric may be applied by hand (using blanket stitch) or by machine (using zig-zag). Fabrics suitable for appliqué include *pretty prints, stripes* and *textured fabrics*. Do not use fabrics that fray easily. Use fusible interfacing on wrong side to prevent fraying.

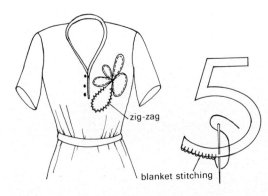

1. Draw your design and transfer it to fabric. Cut out.
2. Tack to right side of garment, or turn in 2 mm around motif and then tack in position.

3. Work a row of running 2 mm from edge. Attach to garment using blanket stitch in a contrasting or matching thread. If you use machining use a close zig-zag stitch.
4. Remove tacking and press.

F. BRAIDS

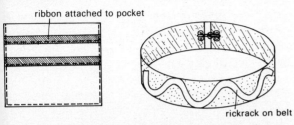

ribbon attached to pocket

rickrack on belt

A large assortment of braids, including ribbons, laces, rickrack, embroidered bands, provide a range of creative finishes for garments. Always mark the position of the braids carefully and accurately. Measure the length correctly. Apply by hand or machine, depending on the type being used.

Uses

On pockets, cuffs, panels, collars, borders, edges, ruffles.

G. RUFFLES

The inner edge of a ruffle is shorter than that of the outer edge. The outer edge will be fuller and fluted when set in position.

Types of Ruffle
1. Straight — inner curve gathered.
2. Circular — inner curve straightened.

Straight ruffles on cuffs
1. Cut ruffle from a continuous piece of fabric or join pieces together. Remove tacking and press seam open.
2. Neaten seam allowance using zig-zag machining.
3. Turn under small hem on outer edge of ruffle. Tack and machine or slip-stitch hem fold.
4. Work two rows of gathering at inner edge and pull threads to distribute fullness evenly.

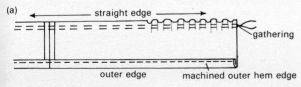

(a)

straight edge

gathering

outer edge   machined outer hem edge

Preparing ruffle

5. With right sides together tack and machine ruffle to garment edge.

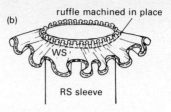

(b)

ruffle machined in place

WS

RS sleeve

Machining ruffle to garment

6. Trim and neaten raw edge (using zig-zag machining or bias binding).
7. Press seam allowances away from ruffle towards garment.

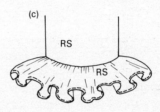

(c)

RS

RS

Completed ruffle

Uses

Hems, cuffs.

Circular ruffle on neck edge
1. Prepare as for straight ruffle but do not gather inner edge.
2. Place circular ruffle along edge of garment, wrong side of ruffle to right side of garment.
3. Tack in position. Place right side of facing over right side of ruffle. Tack and machine through all layers. Trim, layer and notch seam allowance.

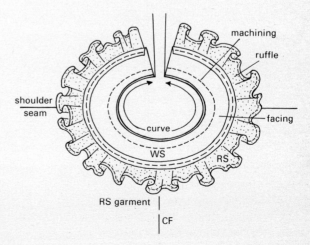

machining

ruffle

shoulder seam

curve

facing

WS

RS

RS garment

CF

359

4. Neaten outer edge of facing. Fold facing to wrong side, understitch facing to seam allowance, slip-stitch to shoulder seam.
5. Remove tacking and press.

Uses

Ruffles may be used at cuffs, necklines and hem edges.

H. FRILLS

Both inner and outer edges are of the same length. For a very gathered effect use twice the length of fabric; for a little fullness use half as much as the garment length. Frills may be made from the garment fabric or chosen from a variety of commercial frilled trimmings. Frills may be used at cuff edges, necklines, etc.

Making a frill

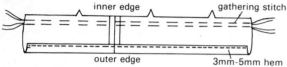

Preparing frill

1. Cut out frill with the selvedge running across width of frill using pattern *or* (a) cut length to equal twice finished length for lots of fullness, and (b) cut width to equal finished width plus turnings.
2. Using a narrow flat seam or run and fell seam, join frill pieces together. Press seam open.
3. Turn under a narrow hem 2–5mm on outer edge of frill. Machine or slip-hem in position.
4. Work two rows of gathers on inner edge of frill. Draw up gathers until they are of the required fullness.

Attaching frill to single edge

There are three ways of doing this:

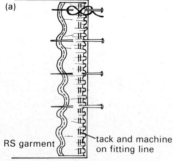

Pinning frill to garment

1. (a) Pin and tack frill to garment edge, right sides together, edges even.
   (b) Machine frill along fitting line.
   (c) Remove tacking and neaten seam allowance with zig-zag machining or blanket-stitch.

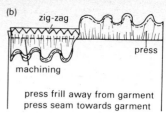

Machining frill to garment

(d) Press frill away from garment and press seam in towards garment.
2. Bind raw edge of frill with bias binding before attaching to garment.
3. Turn in garment seam allowance to wrong side, covering raw edge of frill. Tack and stitch in position. Remove tacking and press gently. Do not flatten gathers of frill.

Attaching frill to collar or cuff

1. Prepare frill; gather and hem.
2. With right side facing place frill to upper cuff or collar, edges together.

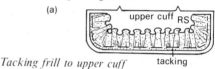

Tacking frill to upper cuff

3. Place right side of under cuff to right side of upper cuff, matching notches.

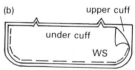

Tacking undercuff to upper cuff

4. Tack and machine on fitting line through all layers. Remove tacking, trim, layer and turn right side out.
5. Press gently and tack outer edge of cuff.

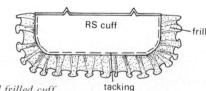

Completed frilled cuff

OTHER DECORATIVE FINISHES

(a) hand embroidery
(b) mock-hemming
(c) hem-stitching
(d) quilting
(e) smocking
(f) patchwork
(g) beading
(h) fringes
(i) topstitching
(j) saddle stitch
(k) fur
(l) sequins
(m) machine embroidery.

45.

Waist Finishes

Waist edges of skirts, trousers and shorts are neatened when they have been completed except for the hem. Waistbands should feel comfortable around the body. They should not feel tight and restricting. The method of neatening the waist will be influenced by:
- (a) garment style and type of fabric,
- (b) figure shape,
- (c) strength required, firm or soft.

TYPES OF WAISTBANDS

1. Waistband of self-fabric
   - (a) Unstiffened
   - (b) Stiffened: iron-on, interfacing, petersham, canvas.
2. Petersham waistband (faced waistline).

Note: Most waistbands are stiffened with interfacing to prevent stretching and folding of fabric.

General Rules

1. Measure your waist before cutting out waistband fabric.
2. When fitting skirt, trousers or shorts, tack waistband in position.
3. Fit the band to your waist; fit garment to the band.
4. Complete garment except for hem. Attach waistband and then turn up hem.
5. Cut out waistbands with their length running with the straight grain of fabric.

Preparation of garment

1. Stitch darts at waist of garment.
2. Pin, tack, machine and neaten seams.
3. Press darts and seams.
4. Insert zip at waist opening before applying waistband.

Preparation of waistband

A. Unstiffened

1. Measure waist and cut out waistband.
2. Tailor tack waistband along fitting lines and foldline.

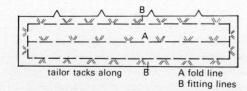

(a)

tailor tacks along   B   A fold line
B fitting lines

3. With right sides together, fold waistband in two along foldline. Tack and machine both short ends 15 mm from edge.

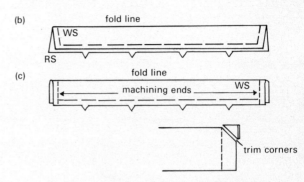

4. Layer turnings and trim corners. Turn right side out. Press along foldline and both ends, pushing out corners to get true outline. Remove tailor tacks from foldline.
5. To hold foldline in place, work a row of tacking 2 mm from edge.

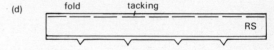

(d)

B. Stiffened

1. Cut out waistband. Tailor tack fitting lines and foldline.
2. Cut interfacing for waistband.
   - (a) Sew-on; length of waistband and half its width.
   - (b) Iron-on; 1 cm less than length and width of waistband.
3. (a) Sew-on; place interfacing to foldline on unnotched half of wrong side. Tack in position.

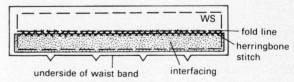

Attaching interfacing to waistband

Attach to foldline using a herringbone stitch. Remove tailor tacks at foldline.

(b) Iron-on; place fusible side to wrong side of waistband 1 cm in from edges. Apply heat to interfacing until it fuses to the fabric. Remove tailor tacks at foldline.

4. Complete the waistband by folding in two along foldline, right sides together, machining and trimming ends. Turn right side out, press and tack close to foldline.

Attaching the waistband

1. Pin and tack waistband to waist edge of garment along fitting line, right sides together matching notches, tailor tacks, centre fronts and centre backs.
2. Try on garment and check fitting of waistband. Does the skirt hang properly? Adjust during fitting if necessary.
3. Machine waistband to waist of garment on fitting line, working from waistband side.

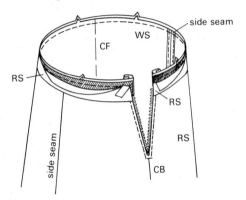

Machining waistband to garment

4. Layer interfacing and seam allowance slightly. Do not remove too much as seam allowance helps to support waistband during wear. Remove tacking and press seam allowance into waistband.

Finishing

1. Fold under remaining raw edge of waistband and pin to row of machining.
2. Tack and hem to machine stitches. The hemming should not be visible on right side of garment.

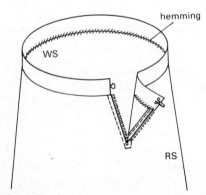

Completed waistband

3. Press. Select a suitable fastening for ends of waistband e.g. hooks and eyes: button and buttonhole; Velcro.

MACHINED BAND — suitable for casual clothes

1. Prepare waistband using stiffened waistband method.
2. Pin and tack stiffened edge of right side of band to wrong side of garment.
3. Machine on fitting line from waistband side. Press seam upwards.

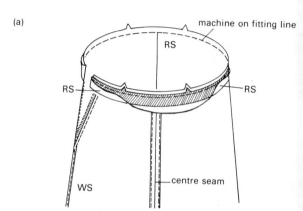

4. On free edge of waistband fold under seam allowance and tack to machining on right side of garment.
5. Machine around band on right side 5 mm in from edge. Remove tacking and press.

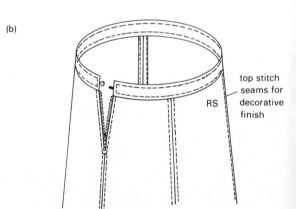

PETERSHAM WAISTBAND, FACED WAISTLINE

Preparation

1. Take waist measurement.
2. Measure length of shaped petersham 3-4 mm longer than waist to allow for turnings at ends. Alter-

natively, stretch a length of straight petersham by steaming it into shape.

3. Neaten ends of petersham. Turn in 2 mm at ends of petersham to wrong side. Fold under 5 mm on raw edges. Hem both ends.

(a)

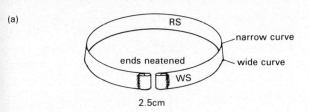

4. Attach a hook and eye or Velcro or a flat metal clip to petersham so that it fits the waist when closed.

(b)

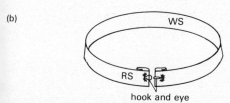

Application

1. Turn garment right side out having completed it except for waist and hem.
2. At waist, trim garment seam allowance to 10 mm. Zig-zag or overcast raw edge.
3. Place petersham on right side of garment over raw edge of garment with shorter unstretched edge to fitting line.
4. Pin and tack the petersham carefully. Ease waist of garment to fit petersham.

Finishing

1. Try on garment to check that the waist is comfortable and the garment hangs correctly.
2. Machine close to edge of petersham on fitting line. Work a second row of stitching 2 mm outside this row if desired. Press.

(a)

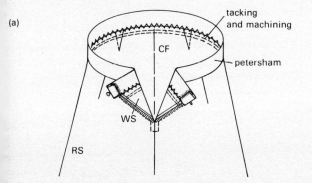

3. Turn petersham to wrong side and pin in position. Slip-stitch to zip tape and seams. This prevents the petersham waistband rolling to right side of garment.

(b)

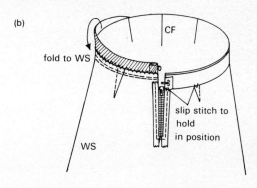

WAIST FASTENINGS OR CLOSURES

These include:
hook and eye
Velcro
metal clip
button and buttonhole
press fasteners.

MAKING A WAIST JOIN BETWEEN BODICE AND SKIRT

1. Tack and machine bodice darts, shoulder seams and underarm seams. Neaten all seams and press flat.
2. Complete skirt except for waist opening, waist and hem. Press.
3. With right sides together pin bodice to skirt, matching centre fronts, side seams, notches, balance marks, centre backs and edges of opening.
4. Tack on fitting line and try on garment.

(a)

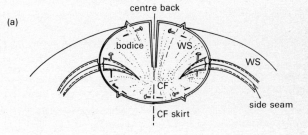

Pinning bodice to skirt

5. Machine bodice to skirt along fitting line. Remove tacking, trim and press seam upwards towards bodice.

363

6. Neaten raw edges with zig-zag stitch. Trim bulky seam allowance where seams cross. Attach waist seam to underarm seam at waistline with slip-stitching or herringbone stitch to hold seam in place.

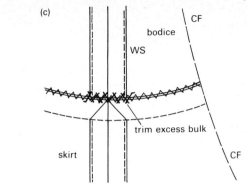

Machining waist seam

Attaching waist seam to side seam

46.

Pockets

Pockets can be functional or decorative or both. There are two basic types of pocket from which all pockets were developed.

TYPES OF POCKETS

1. Patch pocket

This is sometimes referred to as a visible pocket because it is applied to the right side of the garment. It is usually made from the same fabric as the garment. Patch pockets can be square, pointed or rounded at the lower edge or rectangular in shape.

Variations
  (a) unlined   (b) self-lined and lined
        (c) patch pocket with flap.

2. Invisible or bag pocket

Pockets in this group consist of a lining which has been pushed to the wrong side of the garment through a slash or seam. A binding, flap or welt marks the opening to the hidden linings.

Variations
  (a) pocket in side seam   (c) flap
  (b) bound   (d) welt.

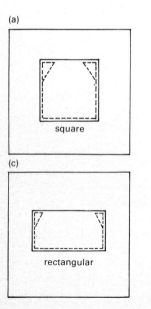

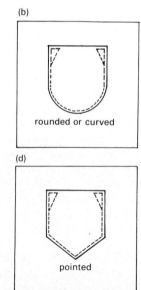

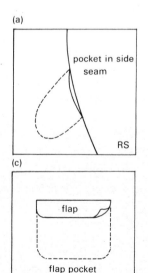

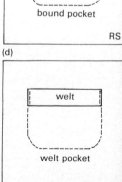

Special points

1. Mark the position of the pocket to the right side of garment using tailor tacks.
2. Mark the turnings on the pocket and linings.
3. Tack the pocket to the garment and fit. Pockets must be at a level where your hands can slip into them easily. If positioned too low on the garment they will look uncomfortable. Adjust pockets if necessary and mark their correct position with pins.
4. If pockets are made from loosely woven material e.g. wool, their openings should be reinforced with interfacing. This strengthens and holds the pocket opening. Reinforce corners of patch pockets with machined triangles.
5. Always keep the correct shape to the pocket i.e. square, curved or pointed.
6. When making invisible or bag pockets pull the lining through the slash to the wrong side very carefully.
7. Assemble pockets and attach to garments before the seams are machined.
8. Match the selvedge line of the pocket with the selvedge line of the garment.
9. Pockets on both right and left sides of garment should be matched in size and position.

Marking all pockets

When the paper pattern is pinned to the fabric, mark in the shape and position of each pocket using tailor tacks. Remove pattern and snip tailor tacks to separate garment pieces. It is important to tailor-tack so that pockets of matching position have the same shape, length and position on garment.

PATCH POCKETS

Preparation

A. Unlined patch pocket

1. Mark turnings of pocket with a row of tailor tacking. Remove pattern from fabric. Separate pocket pieces by snipping the tailor tacking.

(a)

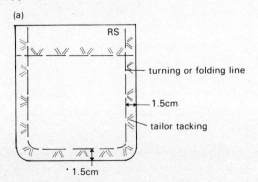

2. On top edge of pocket turn under 6 mm to wrong side. Tack and machine 2 mm in from folded edge.

(b)

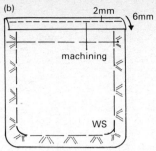

3. Fold top edge of pocket to right side along the marked foldline. Tack in position. Machine round the fitting line of pocket working from one end of hem fold, along curved edge to hem fold on the other side.

(c)

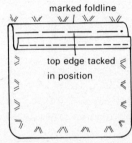

4. Trim corners and turnings of hem facing. Layer turnings if fabric is bulky. Turn hem to wrong side of pocket. Press.
5. Fold turnings along the fitting line to wrong side. Roll machine stitching to underside so that it is not visible from right side. Tack in position. remove all tailor tacking.

(d)

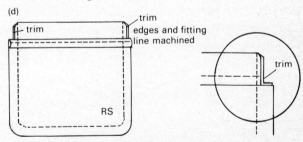

6. On a rounded pocket clip curved edge, on a square pocket mitre corners. Slip-stitch mitre in place.
7. Slip-stitch hem to pocket.

(e)

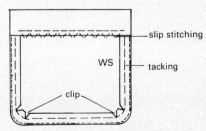

365

B. (i) Self-lined patch pocket

1. Using tailor tacking, mark the seam lines of pocket. A self-lined patch pocket is twice the length of the finished pocket plus turnings of 1.5 cm.

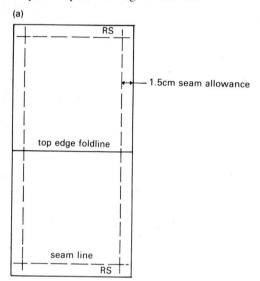

(a)

2. With right sides together fold the pocket along top edge foldline.
3. Tack three sides along the seam line. On the bottom edge leave an opening to turn pocket right side out.
4. Machine each side and part of the bottom edge. Secure threads.

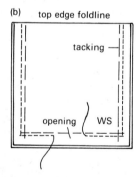

(b)

5. Trim and layer seam allowances. Trim corners carefully. Remove tacking.

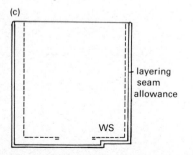

(c)

6. Turn the pocket right side out and press.
7. Slip-stitch the opening and press the pocket again.

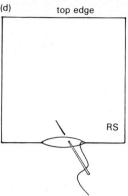

(d)

Note: For a *double pocket,* instead of one continuous pocket piece, two pocket pieces are used. With right sides together, tack and machine four sides of the pocket pieces on seam line, leaving an opening on one side. Trim and layer turnings. Turn right side out. Press and slip-stitch opening shut.

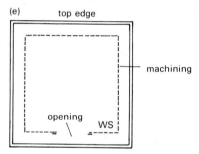

(e)

Double pocket

B. (ii) Lined patch pocket

1. Cut out the pocket lining following the pattern instructions. It should fit the pocket between the foldline of pocket hem to lower edge of pocket.

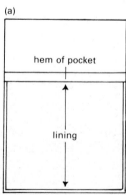

(a)

Position of lining on pocket

2. On upper edge of lining turn under 1.5 cm to wrong side.

366

3. With right sides of lining and pocket together, pin the lower and side edges of lining to pocket edges.
4. Tack just inside seam line.

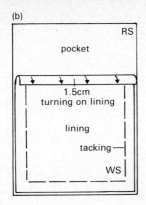

(b)
RS
pocket
1.5cm
turning on lining
lining
tacking
WS

5. Fold hem facing of pocket along foldline. With right sides of fabric together, bring it over the lining and tack.

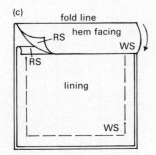

(c)
fold line
hem facing
RS
WS
RS
lining
WS

6. Machine along seamline on three sides of pocket.
7. Trim and layer seam allowances. Clip curved edges and step corners.

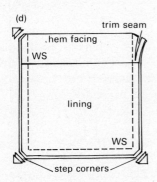

(d)
trim seam
hem facing
WS
lining
WS
step corners

8. Turn pocket and lining right side out. Press carefully, pushing out the corners to get the correct shape on pocket edges. Roll outer seam to underside. Sew pocket hem facing to lining using a row of hemming.

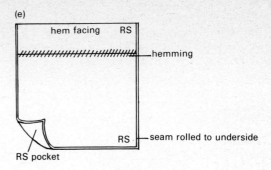

(e)
hem facing   RS
hemming
RS   seam rolled to underside
RS pocket

C. Patch pocket with flap or facing
1. Using pattern, cut out a facing of the correct shape and size.
2. Work a row of tailor tacking to mark seam lines.

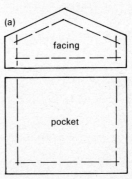

(a)
facing
pocket

3. Place the right side of facing to wrong side of pocket, upper edges together.
4. Pin, tack and machine pocket to facing along the upper edge seamline. Press facing away from pocket.

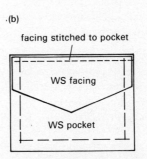

(b)
facing stitched to pocket
WS facing
WS pocket

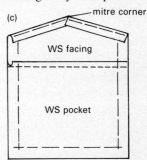

mitre corner
(c)
WS facing
WS pocket

5. Turn under 1.5 cm to wrong side on lower edge of facing. Tack and mitre corner, at pointed edge.
6. Fold facing to right side of pocket along seam line. Pin, tack and machine facing to pocket.

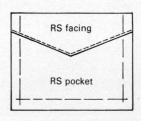

(d)
RS facing
RS pocket

7. Remove tacking and press.
8. Fold and press turnings to wrong side of pocket. Again mitre corners or clip curves.

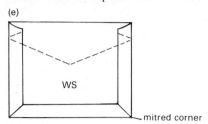

Attaching patch pockets to garments
1. Remove all tacking and give the pockets a final pressing.
2. Place wrong side of pocket to right side of garment.
3. Check the position of the pockets by fitting on garment. Match pocket edges to tailor tacks on garment.
4. Work a row of diagonal tacking along the sides, top edge and centre of pocket. This helps to keep the pocket in position when machining. Remove tailor tacking.

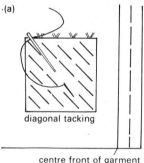

Tacking pocket in position

Finishing
1. Machine 3 mm in from edge of pocket. Reinforce upper corners with triangles of machining. Alternatively, attach the pocket with slip-stitching from right side.
2. Finish off threads. Remove all tacking.

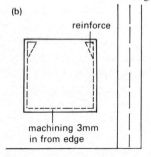

Machining pocket to garment

3. Press carefully.

INVISIBLE OR BAG POCKETS

Pocket in side seam — cut as part of the garment or attached to the side seam allowances.

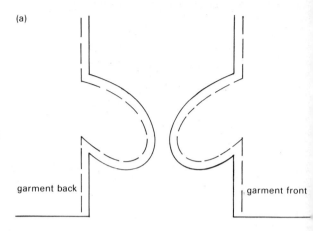

Pockets part of garment

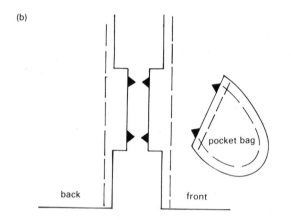

Preparation
1. Cut out two pocket pieces for each pocket using the garment fabric or lining if the fabric is bulky.
2. Reinforce the seam in garment with iron-on interfacing if the fabric is heavy. Place over both seam fitting lines if necessary.

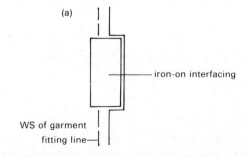

Reinforcing seam

3. Pin and tack each pocket piece to extending seam edge of garment with right sides facing. Match all notches and tailor tacks.

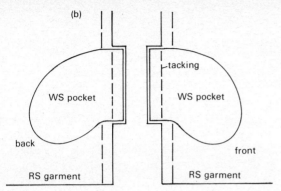

Tacking pockets to garment

Working

1. Machine pocket pieces to side seam edges on front and back of garment pieces.

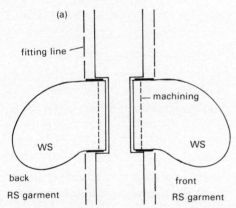

Machining pockets to garment

2. Remove tacking. Neaten the seams' edges with zig-zag stitch. Press seams open.

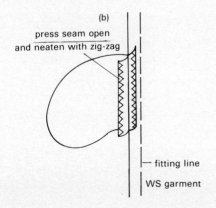

Neatening seams

3. Pin and tack side seams of garment and bag pieces of pockets together with right sides facing. Match all notches and tailor-tacks.

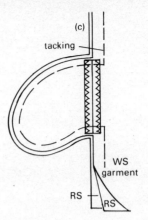

Tacking garment side seam

Finishing

1. Machine along fitting line of side seam from top of seam, around pocket bag, pivoting at corners A and B, down to hem.
2. The corners of pocket at A and B should be reinforced with a second row of machining for 3 cm on each side of corner.

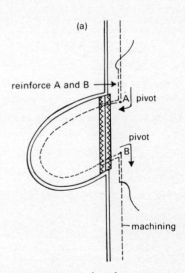

Machining seam of garment and pocket

3. Snip seam allowance on back piece at points A and B if necessary. Press pocket in towards front of garment.
4. Neaten side seams and pocket seams with zig-zag machining or blanket stitching. Overcast clipped edges.

369

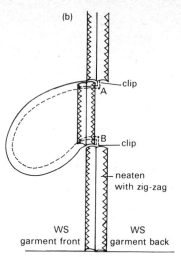

Completing pocket

5. Press seams.

BOUND POCKET

Preparation

1. Mark position of pocket opening on garment with a row of tacking.

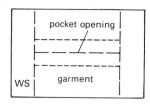

Preparing garment

2. Cut binding strip on straight grain of garment fabric.
   Width = width of pocket opening plus 5 cm
   Length = 10 cm approx.
3. Mark centre of binding strip with tailor's chalk or fold in half and crease along fold.

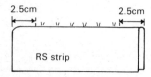

Preparing binding strip

4. With right sides together place foldline of binding strip along tacked pocket opening.
5. Open out binding strip and tack in position along opening line.

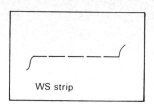

Tacking binding strip in position

Working

(a) Binding the pocket opening

1. Bind the pocket opening following the method for a bound buttonhole — see chapter 43, fastenings. Machine 6 mm on each side of tacking and across ends. Corners made must be right-angled corners.

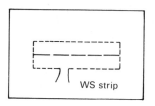

Machining pocket rectangle

2. On wrong side slash the centre line of opening to within 10 mm from ends. Clip diagonally into each corner. Do not cut the machine stitches.

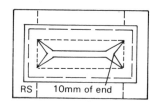

Cutting pocket opening

3. Fasten off machine threads securely. Remove all tacking. Gently pull binding strip to wrong side.

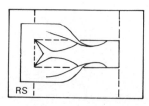

Pulling binding strip to WS

4. Press binding away from pocket opening along short sides only. On wrong side make an inverted pleat with edges meeting at centre of pocket opening. Press.

370

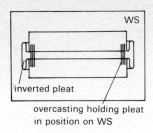

Forming inverted pleat

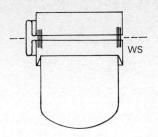

Pressing underpocket downwards

5. Hold folded edges together at centre of pocket opening with overcasting or diagonal tacking. Work from right sides of garment.

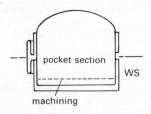

Working diagonal tacking

6. Stitch triangular pieces at each end of opening to pleated binding strip on wrong side of garment.
7. Press on wrong side.

(b) Attaching the pocket pieces
1. Cut two pocket pieces of self-fabric or lining. The choice will be influenced by the weight of fabric being used.
2. On wrong side of garment, place straight edge of under-pocket piece to lower edge of binding strip. With right sides together tack in position.
3. From right side of pocket opening, machine through all layers on lower seam line binding strip. This attaches under pocket piece to both binding strip and garment.

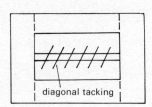

Machining underpocket

4. Remove tacking and press under pocket piece down wards over binding.

5. On wrong side of garment place upper pocket piece over lower pocket piece with right sides together. Tack upper edge to binding strip.
6. From right side of pocket opening, machine through all thicknesses to complete the rectangular line of binding. The upper pocket piece is now attached to binding strip.

Finishing
1. Matching pocket edges tack side and lower edges of pocket pieces together.
2. Starting at the top, machine pocket pieces together along sides and curved edge. Catch base of triangular ends in seam of pocket. Work two rows of machining.
3. Finish off threads securely. Remove tacking.

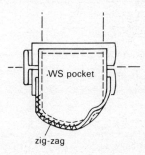

Neatening raw edges

4. Neaten raw edges with zig-zag machining or blanket stitching.

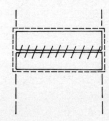

Completed bound pocket from RS

371

47.

Hems

Hems are used to finish the lower edge of garments. They give weight to the edge so that garments hang well. The final sewing process of assembling a garment is usually turning up the hem. A well-finished hem should not be visible on the right side of the garment, unless, it is used as a decorative feature.

Points to consider

1. The hem depth is influenced by (a) weight of fabric, (b) garment style.

   Deep wide hems are needed for heavy fabrics e.g. tweeds.

   Narrow hems are best for fine and delicate fabrics e.g. cotton, cotton blends, silks.

   For a circular skirt in lightweight wool use a narrow hem with excess fullness removed.

HEM DEPTHS

Type of fabric or garment	Depth of hem
a. Sheer e.g. organdie, voile, chiffon, georgette	3–5 mm
b. Fine e.g. silk, cottons	2–3 cm
c. Heavy e.g. tweed, wool	2.5–4 cm
d. Dresses	2–3.5 cm
e. Skirts (i) flared (ii) straight	1.5–2 cm 2–3.5 cm
f. Shirts, blouses	1.5 cm
g. Trousers, jeans, shorts	2.5–4 cm
h. Nightwear, frills, Sleeves, fuffles.	1.5–2 cm

2. Hem lengths are determined by
   (a) garment style,
   (b) fashion at the time,
   (c) type of fabric e.g. stiff, soft,
   (d) height of the person who will wear the garment.
3. The overall proportion of the garment suggests a particular length and depth of hem. Hem lengths: mini, short, knee length, just below the knee, mid calf, midi, maxi, ballet length and evening.

Preparing the hem

1. Hang garment for 24 hours before marking the hem. This allows fabric time to drop, especially in the case of bias-cut garments.
2. Mark the hemline length using a chalk hem marker or pins. The wearer should get another person to mark the hem length for them.

3. Put on garment, wearing the appropriate under-clothes and shoes. A change in either will alter fit, posture and hem length. The wearer should stand still and not look down. The fitter should work so that the hem is at their eye level. While marking hem length, the fitter moves around; the wearer never moves.
4. Select length most suited to the wearer, marking it with chalk or pins.

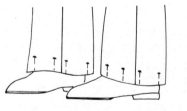

5. Help the wearer down from table or stool. Take off garment, turn it wrong side out and place it flat on a table.

6. Crease hem fitting line. turn in hem to wrong side of garment.
7. Press edge of hem lightly. Do not iron. Work a row of tacking 1 cm from fold edge of hem.
8. Mark depth of hem and trim excess fabric.
9. Fold in free upper hem edge. Neaten edge with one of the hem finishes suggested in this chapter.
10. Tack upper hem edge to garment and stitch in position. Remove tacking and press lightly from hem fold upwards, using a dry pressing cloth. Do not press stitches or upper hem edge.

What to do with seams within hems

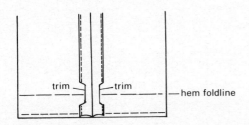

1. Mark hem depth.
2. Trim seam allowance of flat seam within hem depth from 3–5 mm.
3. Be careful not to clip seam stitching.

What to do with corners in hems

Corners in hems require careful treatment to remove excess bulk, so that they lie flat when completed.
1. At corner, fold fabric to wrong side, allowing a 3 mm turning beyond fold.
2. Crease along fold. Cut triangle of corner on creased foldline.

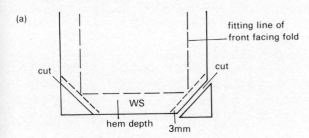

3. Turn and tack 3 mm to wrong side at a, b and c.

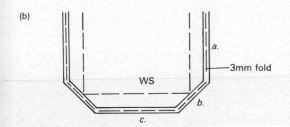

4. Form mitre join as you turn hem to wrong side. Topsew mitre edges together.

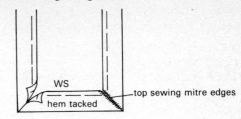

What to do with hem fullness
A. *Pleats or darts* (for fine, lightweight fabric)
1. Turn under fold at upper hem edge to wrong side. Edge machine 1 mm in from fold.
2. Make and pin small darts or narrow pleats around the garment hem, keeping them in the same direction. Do not force them into position.

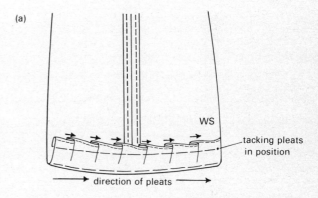

3. Taper darts and pleats to a point. If they are too bulky, trim away excess fabric on wrong side of hem. Neaten raw edges with overcasting stitch before completing the hem.

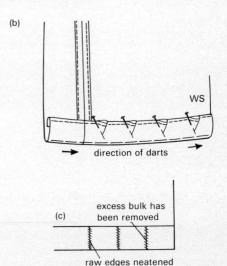

B. Gathers
1. Using a gathering stitch, work a row of gathering 5 mm below raw edge of hem on single fabric.
2. To adjust excess fullness, draw up thread until hem is of the required size.

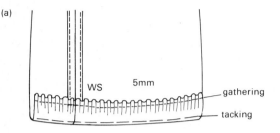

3. Press lightly using a dry pressing cloth under hem-turning on wrong side of garment.
4. Neaten raw edges with bias binding.

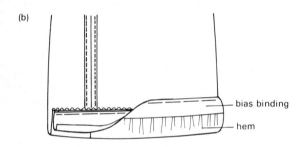

C. Shrinking excess fullness

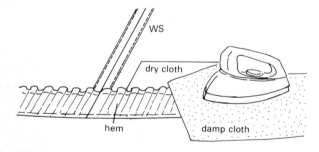

1. Follow points 1 and 2 as above in Gathers.
2. Between garment and gathers of hem, place a dry pressing cloth. Place a damp pressing cloth over hem gathers.
3. Use a hot iron to shrink excess fullness. Press until hem is dry and flat. Hang up garment until completely dry.
4. Neaten raw edges of hem with a suitable finish e.g. bias binding.

TYPES OF HEMS
  (a) plain
  (b) eased
  (c) narrow
  (d) circular or flared hem
  (e) machined
  (f) jersey
  (g) bias faced.

Hem finishes
Raw edges of hems are neatened using the method most suited to the fabric; this can be selected from those listed below.

A. Fine and lightweight fabrics
1. *Turned under* to wrong side; fold under 6 mm of hem, turning at raw edges. Slip-stitch hem fold to garment.

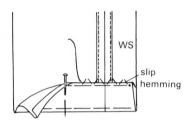

2. *Zig-zag* raw edge of hem. Tack hem 10 mm away from zig-zag machining. Pull back edge. Use catch-stitch or tailor's hemming between hem and garment, slightly below zig-zag machining.

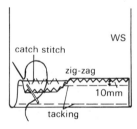

3. *Machine-stitched narrow hem:* fold under narrow hem turnings. Tack and machine close to upper hem edge i.e. 2 mm from fold.

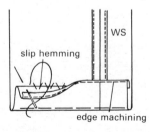

4. *Edge machining:* fold under 6 mm of hem turnings to wrong side. Tack and edge machine near fold. Remove tacking and slip hem into position.

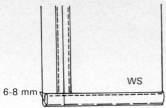

5. *Blind stitching:* work blind hem using the machine. Follow the instructions given in the machine manual.

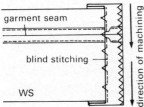

6. *Stitched and pinked:* this is a quick neatening process, for all hems. Machine 6 mm from raw edge. Pink and slip-stitch to garment.

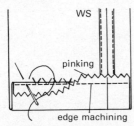

B. Medium and heavyweight fabrics

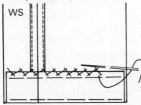

1. *Herringbone* for very thick fabrics. Prepare hem. Tack 5 mm from upper edge. Working from left to right use herringbone stitch to hold hem in place.

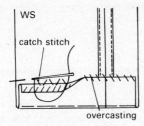

2. *Overcast and catch-stitch* Neaten raw edge of hem with vercast stitches. Tack hem to garment 10 mm below overcast edge. Turn back neatened edge. Attach hem to garment, using catch-stitch slightly below overcast edge.

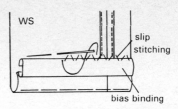

3. *Bias binding and slip-hemming* With right sides together, tack binding to hem along crease of binding. Keep raw edges even. Machine on crease line, remove tacking and press binding up over seam allowance. Slip-stitch upper edge of binding in place.

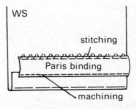

4 *Paris binding and Slip hemming* Tack lower edge of binding 6 mm on upper edge of hem. Allow 6 mm of an overlap. Machine 3 mm in from upper edge of hem. Remove tacking. Slip-stitch binding to garment.

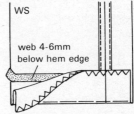

5. *Bonded or fused hem* Place fusible web tape 4-6 mm below upper edge of hem on wrong side. The web tape will not touch the iron. Follow manufacturer's instructions when using fusible web tape to get good results.

C. Jersey hems

Raw edges of jersey hems are neatened with zig-zag stitch. As you machine, pull the fabric to stretch it. This is called "fluting" or "lettucing". For a flat finish, zig-zag edge without pulling the fabric. Turn up narrow hem and slip-stitch to garment.

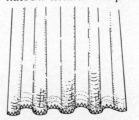

Fluting or lettucing

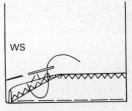

Flat finish

48.

Belts

Belts are used as part of a complete outfit to emphasise the waistline. If you wish to add a belt it must be planned carefully so as not to appear as an extra idea. A belt should be chosen with three points in mind: (a) belt width, (b) fabric used, (c) position on garment. Belts may be very narrow or wide, depending on the type of waistline (long or short) and design of garment.

General guidelines
1. Calculate belt length accurately and add extra for tie, overlaps, buckles, etc.
2. Use an interfacing suited to belt fabric to strengthen belt.
3. Buckle size should complement belt width.
4. If making a join, place seam on the cross i.e. diagonally, for a flatter less visible finish.

SASH OR TIE BELT
1. Cut out belt the desired length and twice the finished width plus 2.5 cm turnings all around.
2. Join if necessary, using a diagonal seam. Machine and press open.

(a)

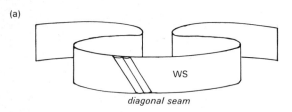

diagonal seam

3. With right sides facing, fold belt in half lengthways.
4. Tack and machine along fitting line, leaving a gap of 8 cm on one side. Trim and layer turnings at side and ends. Step ends if pointed. Remove tacking.

(b)

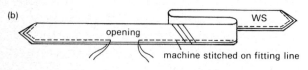

opening

machine stitched on fitting line

(c)

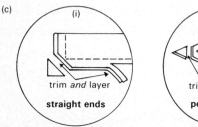

(i) trim *and* layer
straight ends

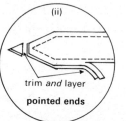

(ii) trim *and* layer
pointed ends

5. Turn belt right side out, roll edges of seamline and tack 2 mm from edge.
6. Slip-stitch opening. Remove tacking and press again using a dry pressing cloth under iron.

(d)

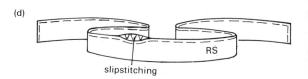

RS

slipstitching

STRAIGHT STIFFENED BELT

Stiffening may be iron-on or sew-in interfacing, canvas, petersham or even organdie. Select one which suits fabric of belt.
1. Cut out fabric for belt the desired length and width plus 15 mm turnings along straight grain. Allow for overlap.

(a)

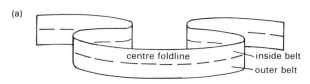

centre foldline — inside belt
— outer belt

2. Cut out suitable interfacing or stiffening to correct length. Allow for overlap.
3. Mark centre of fabric lengthways on wrong side with tailor's chalk. Place interfacing to foldline and attach to belt fabric (iron on or sew-in using herringbone stitch).

(b)

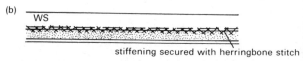

WS

stiffening secured with herringbone stitch

4. Turn in seam allowance to wrong side over interfacing on long and short sides. Tack and herringbone in place.

(c)

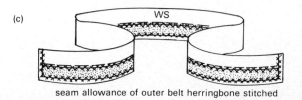

WS

seam allowance of outer belt herringbone stitched

5. Remove tacking. Turn in edges on inside belt fabric and fold over interfacing. Tack to outside of belt 2 mm in from edges.

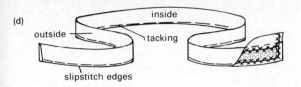

6. Slip stitch folded edges together. Remove tacking and press.

Attaching buckles

1. Machine end of belt 1.5 cm from raw edge. Trim to 5 mm. Overcast edges to neaten them and prevent fraying.

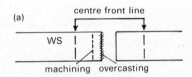

2. Mark position of prong of buckle at centre front line near overcast edge.
3. Neaten raw edges of hole with buttonhole stitch or overcasting.

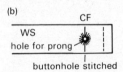

4. Slip hole over prong and fold in overcast edge. Tack, hem and topsew in place. (hem along end line, topsew side edges).

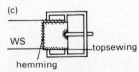

5. Mark position of eyelets on other end of belt (two or three to allow adjustments, 2-3 cm apart).
6. Pierce holes and use buttonhole stitch to neaten raw edges. Commercial eyelets may be used instead of hand-worked eyelets.

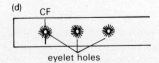

BELT CARRIERS AND LOOPS

Belt carriers and loops, made from fabric or thread, hold the belt in a comfortable position when fastened. Belt carriers also allow for movement, bending, reaching etc. Use belt carriers which suit the garment fabric. *Before attaching belt carriers:* Fit on garment and fasten belt. Mark position of carriers with pins. Allow 3-5 mm for ease.

FABRIC CARRIERS

1. Cut out carriers along selvedge of fabric (twice finished width plus turnings, length equals width of belt plus 2 cm for ease).
2. With right sides facing, fold lengthways. Machine along fitting line. Do not stitch ends.

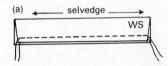

3. Turn right side out and press seamline to centre, lengthways on inside of carrier.
4. At each end turn in 5 mm.

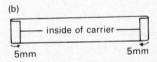

5. Tack to right side of garment at marked position. Hem three outer edges or machine-stitch around ends to form a square. Press carefully.

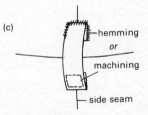

THREAD CARRIERS

See page

FABRIC LOOP

1. Work 1-4 inclusive, from fabric carriers.
2. Join ends together using topsewing.
3. Place over belt to hold overlapping belt end in place.

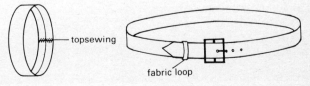

49.
Simple Tailoring

A. Preparing jacket

1. Cut out jacket. Tailor tack darts, turnings, crease roll of lapel and position of pocket. Separate garment pieces.
2. Tack together for first fitting. Try on and alter if necessary. When jacket fits correctly remove sleeves. Machine bust darts, shoulder and side seams.
3. Remove tacking and press seams open. Cut open darts and press flat.

Note: Press at each stage of construction for a professional finish.

B. Attaching interfacing to lapels

An interfacing of canvas is suitable for tailored jackets and coats.

1. Cut out canvas for (a) collar, (b) lapels and front of jacket, (c) back section of jacket.
2. Pin and tack canvas to jacket along crease roll of lapels, smoothing it into position as you sew.
3. Holding jacket with left hand and rolling lapel back, pad-stitch canvas to jacket. Work towards the lapel edge with needle pointing to that same edge.
4. Pad-stitch up and down until lapel section is completed.
5. Tack a strip of pre-shrunk tailor's linen to neck and opening edges of jacket along seamline. This may be caught in by machining.

Pad stitching canvas to collar

C. Attaching interfacing to under-collar

1. Tack canvas to under-collar along roll line.
2. Pad-stitch collar, shaping and rolling both collar and canvas as you work.
3. From neck edge to roll, work several rows of running stitches 5 mm apart.
4. Join under collar to coat. Notch curved edge. Snip where lapel meets collar. Press seam open. Herringbone-stitch upper seam allowance to collar and lower seam allowance to jacket.

D. Work bound buttonholes and pockets next.

(See Chapters 43 and 46).

E. Attaching front facings and upper collar

1. Join front facings to upper collar. Tack, machine, remove tacking and press seams open.

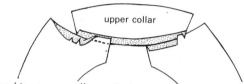

Attaching upper collar to facings

2. Snip where lapel meets collar. Notch curved edge if necessary.
3. With right sides facing, pin and tack outer collar and facings to jacket.
4. Machine along seamline.
5. Trim and layer seam allowances.

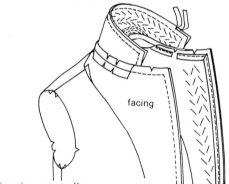

Trimming seam allowances

6. Fold one seam allowance over canvas and herringbone in place. Press.

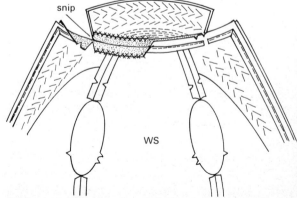

Folding seam allowance over canvas

378

7. Fold facing to wrong side of jacket and tack 2 mm from front edge to neck edge around collar and down the other side.

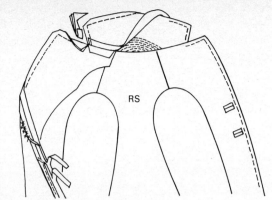

Turning facing to WS of jacket

8. Pin and tack free edge of upper collar to neck edge of jacket.
9. Herringbone front facings to canvas. Complete facing opening for bound buttonholes.
10. Press jacket.

F. Finally
1. Insert sleeves and turn up their lower hem.
2. Sew in shoulder pads.
3. Turn up and complete lower hem of jacket. Press.
4. Make up and attach lining.

Fitting a jacket
1. Always fit on over clothing you intend wearing under jacket.
2. Check that (a) jacket hangs straight, (b) shoulder lines lie smooth over shoulder, (c) centre front and centre back are in correct position.
3. Try on jacket after each of the following: (a) tacking seams and inserting sleeves, (b) adjusting any part of jacket, (c) turning up hem.
4. After each adjustment has been completed check that (a) collar sits smoothly (b) no wrinkles have formed (c) hems are even.

SHOULDER PADS

Shoulder pads smooth the shoulder seam edge from which the sleeve hangs. They also help to hide sloping or round shoulders. Shoulder pads are available in various thicknesses and shapes depending on their use e.g. blouse, dress, suit, jacket. For a quality finish cover shoulder pads with lining fabric before attaching them to the garment. They are made from foam rubber or polyester fleece.

Attaching shoulder pads

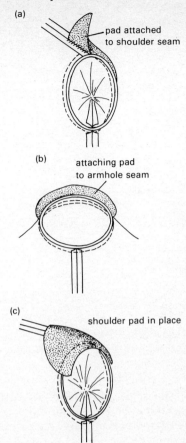

(a) pad attached to shoulder seam

(b) attaching pad to armhole seam

(c) shoulder pad in place

1. Place pad with its pointed end in centre of shoulder seam and its thick curved edge extending 5 – 10 mm into sleeve head.
2. Fit on garment and check position of shoulder pad.
3. Attach shoulder pad to armhole and shoulder seam allowance. Leave 2 cm at ends of shoulder pad free.

GODETS

This is a triangular shaped piece of fabric inserted at a seam or slash to give fullness at the hemline.
1. Cut out godet with straight grain down centre of godet fabric. (edges at side are on the bias).

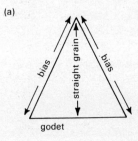

(a)

bias — straight grain — bias

godet

2. Mark position of slash with tailor's chalk. Machine 4 mm each side of this line, stitching to a point at top of slash line.
3. Slash along tailor's chalk line between rows of machining, to within 1 mm of top.

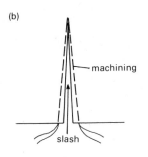

(b)

machining

slash

4. With right sides facing, pin and tack godet to garmentgarment, tapering garment and keeping godet straight.
5. Machine along seamline. Remove tacking and press open.
6. Neaten seam using overcasting or blanket stitching.

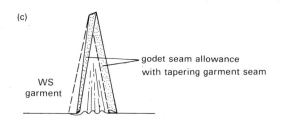

(c)

WS garment

godet seam allowance with tapering garment seam

50.
Repairing Garments

INTRODUCTION

Garments should be repaired, i.e. darned or patched, as soon as possible. Check garments before washing. Keep garments to be repaired separate from the other clothes after washing. Fabrics give way at elbows, knees, collars, cuffs and pockets because of constant washing, wear and accidental damage. If a garment seems to be weakening at a certain point reinforce it before the fabric gives way. On outer garments, repairs should be as invisible as possible. Always work in good light.

DARNING

Darning by hand is suitable for knitted garments and knitted fabrics e.g. jumpers, knitted skirts, dresses and socks. Darning by machine is most often used on woven household items e.g. sheets, table linen.

General Guidelines
1. Work preventive darns on thin vulnerable areas.
2. All darning should be worked on the wrong side of garment except swiss-darning (work a line of upward and downward loops from the right side).
3. Try to copy the texture of the original garment fabric.
4. Select darning thread that is close to those of the garment. It must be similar in fibre content, colour and thickness.
5. To allow for shrinkage leave loops at end of each row.

6. Use a suitable fine darning needle with a long eye.
7. The outline of the darn should be worked in round, diamond or even octagonal shapes to prevent strain on the threads. Do not work a darn in a square shape.
8. Extend darn outside the weakened area, to strengthen repair.
9. Free loops around edge of hole should be picked up to form part of darn. This prevents loops laddering.
10. Secure threads very carefully at beginning and end of darn.
11. When stitching has been completed press garment from wrong side using a damp cloth.

DARNING BY HAND

Use a long darning needle with a large eye. If possible select the same thread as garment *or* buy darning wool which is available on cards and in a few colours. Place the area to be darned over a darning mushroom or over your fingers.

Prevention Darn
Uses: Vunerable areas worn thin and weakened before holes have formed in garment.

(a) Woven fabrics
1. Mark area to be darned with a circle in tailor's chalk or a row of running stitches.

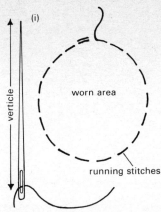

(i)

verticle

worn area

running stitches

2. Beginning outside weakened area, from wrong side of fabric secure thread at lower left hand corner.

3. In vertical lines, pass needle over one thread, pick up the next and pass needle over the next thread. Continue until row is finished.

4. Work rows of running type stitches, weaving them in and out of fabric evenly and loosely.

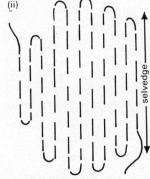

(ii)

selvedge

5. Keep spaces between vertical rows even. Leave a small loop at ends of each row of stitching as you work backwards and forwards.

6. Fasten off thread securely. Press from wrong side of garment.

(b) Knitted garments

Swiss darning is a suitable method of invisibly strengthening a weakened area on knitted garments.

1. Using a suitable needle and thread, from right side of garment work from right to left.

2. Pick up loops following and covering original knitting.

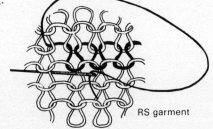

Swiss darn

RS garment

3. Turn fabric upside down and work second row as first, linking first row to second row.

4. Continue until area is covered and run thread up along the side of darn. Cut thread and press from wrong side.

Darning a hole

1. Mark area to be darned with tailor's chalk on wrong side of garment.

2. Begin at lower left-hand corner on wrong side of garment outside of hole.

3. Decide on shape of darn.

4. Working with selvedge threads pick up and pass over threads the length of the hole and leave loop at end of row.

weaving needle under and over

5. Alternate picking up and passing over threads in each row, increasing the number of stitches until centre of hole is reached. Decrease number of stitches in remaining rows to match first half of darn.

6. Leave a small loop at end of each row. Work stitches firmly but loosely.

first stage

7. Work across darn, weaving under and over vertical

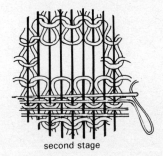

second stage

381

darning threads. Keep threads close together. Pick up all free loops to avoid laddering at darn edge.
8. Continue until hole is covered. Fasten thread securely. Press from wrong side of garment.

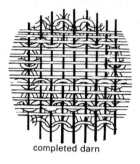

completed darn

Hedge-tear darn or three-cornered tear

This L-shaped jagged tear occurs when warp and weft threads split. The fabric may be torn by nails, hooks, wood etc. Use a suitable needle and matching thread.
1. From wrong side draw edges of tear together using overcasting, herringbone or fishbone stitch. Do not pull too tightly.

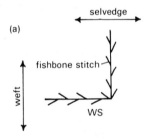

2. Beginning 1 cm below and 1 cm to left of tear, darn with the weft to 1 cm above tear. Work from AB to CD leaving loops.

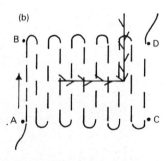

3. Darn with the selvedge from ED to FG i.e. to 1 cm outside tear. Extra strength is given at the right-angled corner by overlapped stitches or double darn.

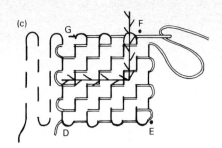

4. Press from wrong side.

Jersey ladders

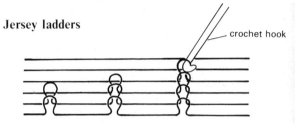

crochet hook

On right side of garment use a very fine crochet hook to pick up loop at bottom of ladder. Pass this loop over thread above it and continue until end is reached. Secure with a backstitch.

MACHINE DARNING

Follow the instructions given in the sewing machine booklet. Use machine darning foot, embroidery hoop, fine machine needle and suitable thread.

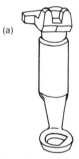

(a)

1. Mark area to be darned with tailor's chalk and stretch fabric over embroidery hoop.

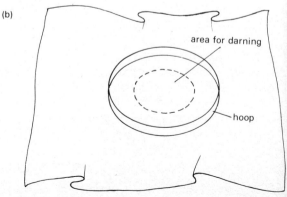

(b)

area for darning

hoop

2. An extra piece of fine fabric may be tacked to back of area to be darned. Match selvedge with selvedge.
3. Lower drop-feed control.
4. Adjust stitch width and length according to booklet.
5. Place fabric on machine and lower darning foot.
6. Holding hoop correctly work from right to left on right side of fabric. Machine in the same direction as fabric weave.
7. Work evenly as irregular movements may cause thread to break and loops to form.
8. Work in three directions:
   (a) with weft,
   (b) with selvedge,
   (c) with selvedge over hole.

(i) with weft   (ii) with selvedge

9. Outline of darn should be round or diamond shape, with stitching extending into strong part of fabric.
10. Fasten off threads, trim backing fabric and press from wrong side.

Remember: Always move fabric back and forth for selvedge and weft, never sideways.

Note: Darning with wool by machine is suitable for socks. Select a fine woollen thread. Machine first rows of stitching as above. Set machine to zig-zag and work second rows of stitching close together. A third row of stitching is not needed. Secure threads and press.

PATCHING

Small areas are darned, larger areas are patched. Patching is suitable for garments and household items.

General guidelines
1. A patch should cover hole and extend beyond weakened area around hole.
2. Select fabric and thread to match garment fabric. New fabric must be washed and pressed before it is used.
3. Cut patch to the straight thread.
4. Always match warp and weft of patch to warp and weft of garment.

5. Open out garment seams if necessary.
6. Using small stitches attach patch neatly on right and wrong sides of garment.
7. Plain cotton patches are attached on wrong side of garment, print patches on right side.

Plain cotton patch
1. Cut patch on straight thread to required size i.e. large enough to cover hole and worn area plus 6 cm on all sides.
2. Fold in 6 mm turnings to right side and tack 5 mm from edge.

Wrong side
1. Pin and tack right sides of patch to wrong side of garment matching threads i.e. selvedge with selvedge, weft with weft.

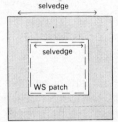

Wrong side

2. Hem, topsew, or machine, starting in middle of one side (machining may be a straight or small zig-zag stitch).
3. Remove tacking and crease patch diagonally.

Right side
1. Mark 12 mm in from stitching at corners. Snip from hole diagonally into new corner points and trim surplus fabric on all sides.
2. Snip in corners for a further 3 mm. Fold in raw edges. Pin in position.

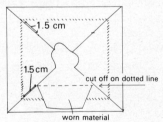

Right side

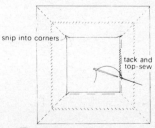

Topsew or machine-stitch the sides

3. Tack, remove pins and machine-stitch sides 1 mm from fold.
4. Remove tacking and press carefully.

Print patch
1. Using a matching fabric cut patch the required size, plus 10 mm turnings, straight to a thread.
2. Fold in 10 mm turnings, straight to a thread, to wrong side of fabric. Tack 5 mm from edge.

Right side

Patch on RS

1. Tack wrong side of patch to right side of garment with selvedge and pattern matching.
2. Machine (straight stitch) or topsew along edges.
3. Remove tacking and press.

Wrong side

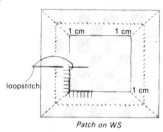

Patch on WS

1. Crease patch diagonally.
2. Cut from centre hole to 10 mm from each corner. Mark between these corner points and trim surplus fabric.
3. Using blanket or loop-stitch neaten raw edges together. Do not stitch through right side of garment.

Note for dress patch

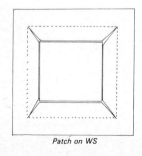

Patch on WS

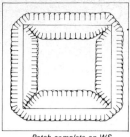

Patch complete on WS

1. Work right side of print patch and wrong side (see 1 and 2 above).
2. Snip to within 1 mm of corner.
3. Press turnings open.
4. Blanket-stitch each raw edge separately.

Decorative patches

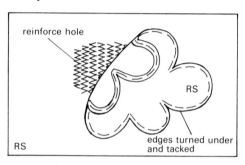

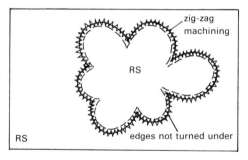

Contrasting patches for reinforcing or repairing knees, elbows and accidental tears of childrens clothes are frequently used. These attractive patches may be applied using zig-zag machining for an applique effect.
1. Cut out required shape and colour of patch.
2. Reinforce hole or worn area with a few rows of zig-zag machining following the direction of the selvedge.
3. Tack wrong side of patch to right side of garment matching selvedge.
4. Zig-zag by machine or blanket-stitch outer edge of patch to garment.
Instead of 3 and 4 above you may wish to turn in 3

mm to wrong side around patch. Machine or topsew in place. Neaten back of patch.

Fusible patches

Patches may be bought with an adhesive backing. Using a warm iron, press patch with wrong side (adhesive side) facing right side of fabric. Zig-zag around edge.

Fusible web, e.g. Bonding or Bondaweb, is a sticky web on a paper backing. Both sides of web have adhesive qualities. Cut out patch of a suitable size. Cut out web of the same size. Place web to right side of patch with paper side facing worker. Using a warm iron press web to patch. Allow to cool and remove paper backing. Place right side of patch with its web backing to wrong side of tear. Again match selvedges. Press patch to garment using a warm iron. Allow to cool.

(a)

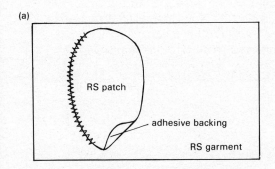

(b)

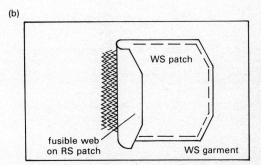

Acknowledgments

The publishers are grateful to the Electricity Supply Board (ESB) for their courtesy and help in providing photographs of electrical appliances. Thanks are also due to Fritz Gegauf Ltd, Bernina Sewing Machine Manufacturers, Switzerland, for supplying the illustrations of a Bernina sewing machine in Chapter 29.